DECISION IN THE WEST

The Atlanta Campaign of 1864

MODERN WAR STUDIES

Theodore A. Wilson
General Editor

Raymond A. Callahan
J. Garry Clifford
Jacob W. Kipp
Jay Luvaas
Allan R. Millett
Series Editors

DECISION IN THE WEST

The Atlanta Campaign of 1864

Albert Castel

Maps by Laura Kriegstrom Poracsky

University Press of Kansas

Published by the University Press of Kansas
(Lawrence, Kansas), which was organized by the
Kansas Board of Regents and is operated and funded by
Emporia State University, Fort Hays State University,
Kansas State University, Pittsburg State University, the
University of Kansas, and Wichita State University

Library of Congress Cataloging-in-Publication Data

Castel, Albert E.
Decision in the West : the Atlanta Campaign of 1864 / Albert
Castel ; maps by Laura Kriegstrom Poracsky.
    p. cm. — (Modern war studies)
Includes bibliographical references and index.
ISBN 0-7006-0562-2 (cloth)   ISBN 0-7006-0748-X (pbk.)
I. Atlanta Campaign, 1864. I. Title. II. Series
E476.7.C28   1992
973.7'37—dc20   92-10882

British Library Cataloguing in Publication Data is available.

Printed in the United States of America

10 9

The paper used in this publication meets the minimum requirements
of the American National Standard for Permanence of Paper for
Printed Library Materials Z39.48-1984.

THIS BOOK IS DEDICATED
TO THOSE VISIONS OF THE PAST
WHICH ALWAYS ARE PRESENT
AND WHICH WILL REMAIN SO
IN THE FUTURE

CONTENTS

Contents

MAPS

ILLUSTRATIONS

PREFACE

IN A SENSE the writing of this book began on a Friday afternoon in October 1942 in Wichita, Kansas. I then was thirteen, almost fourteen, and I went after school to the Wichita Theater for the four o'clock showing of *Gone with the Wind*. I had seen it once before, to be precise on the afternoon of February 17, 1940, when I went with my parents to the Wichita premiere of the movie at the Orpheum Theater (all seats were reserved, and tickets cost an extraordinary $1.12, tax included). Yet, while impressed by the film's magnitude and stirred by some of the scenes, there was much that I had been unable to follow or fully comprehend. Now not only was I two-and-a-half years older and relatively more sophisticated, in the meantime I had been reading enormous quantities of Alexander Dumas, Victor Hugo, Kenneth Roberts, Conan Doyle, and Henryk Sienkiewicz, both acquiring and developing a taste for dramatic, romantic history. Hence I was ripe for what happened on viewing the movie the second time. When I left the theater four hours later and walked through the October evening to my home seven blocks away, I was in love with *Gone with the Wind*.

Saturday morning I began to read the novel in the form of a soft-cover Motion Picture Edition that I had inherited from my father's father in January 1942 but which had not interested me until now. By Friday I had finished, whereupon I saw the movie again at the same theater and at the same time. In the ensuing two weeks I saw it two more times and reread the novel twice.

Love is a glutton that craves whatever will feed it. Since the central, pivotal historical event of *Gone with the Wind* is the Atlanta Campaign, I next went to the public library and checked out the fourth volume of *Battles and Leaders of the Civil War*, that late-nineteenth-century classic of Civil War literature consisting of articles written by the men who fought the war.

After reading everything it contained on the campaign and literally memorizing the accompanying illustrations, I perused most of the rest of the volume and the preceding three. I had been interested in the Civil War before, but no more so than in several other historical eras. Now it became a passion inseparable from what had inspired it—*Gone with the Wind*. For my fourteenth birthday I asked my parents to give me, and I got, the recently published first volume of Douglas Southall Freeman's *Lee's Lieutenants*. After reading this book and

Freeman's four-volume *R. E. Lee,* I devoured everything else that I could get hold of pertaining to the Civil War. Also, I started drawing pictures of the war, concentrating on the Atlanta Campaign. Eventually, when I accumulated a large number of those drawings, I assembled them in a folder to which I added an introduction—an account of the Atlanta Campaign. This was my first venture into historical writing.

In college it was inevitable that I would major in history and specialize in the Civil War: why not take advantage of the knowledge so plesasantly acquired? After obtaining a Ph.D., I wrote several books and a fair number of articles about the Civil War. None of them, however, dealt with the Atlanta Campaign. I often thought of writing a book about it, but just as often backed off from the task. It daunted me. But then I began to approach fifty. If I was going to write the book at all, the time had come to start. And so I did.

Thus my motivation—or if you will, inspiration—for this book. Admittedly it is sentimental in origin. But as the reader will find, the outcome is quite the reverse. That is because I also have a justification. The Atlanta Campaign was one of the most dramatic and decisive episodes of the Civil War, comprising military operations carried out on a grand scale across a spectacular landscape, pitting some of the war's best (and worst) generals against one another, involving multitudes of civilians as well as soldiers, and producing results that if they did not constitute a turning point in the struggle between the North and the South, definitely assured that this struggle would turn out as it did. Yet in spite of this or—who knows?—perhaps because of it, there existed and continued to exist only one legitimate historical work that dealt with the campaign as such and as a whole. This was Jacob D. Cox's *Atlanta,* published in 1882 as part of Charles Scribner's Sons Campaigns of the Civil War series and written by a Northern general who had taken part in the campaign. Inevitably this book, while broadly accurate and containing much of value, had with the passage of time become inadequate in its coverage and obsolete in its analyses. What was needed was a new study that would draw on the enormous quantity and variety of sources that had become available since Cox's time, would incorporate the findings and insights of subsequent historians, notably Thomas L. Connelly and Richard M. McMurry in their writings about the Confederate side of the campaign, and above all, would view the subject with the cold, clinical eye of scholarly objectivity. This book, *Decision in the West,* represents an attempt to produce such a study.

Before the reader proceeds to judge how well it succeeds or how badly it fails in that attempt, however, let me comment on certain aspects of the book which may seem strange and surprising. The first has to do with its literary style. Apart from some analytical, introductory, and transitional passages, I have written it in the present tense instead of the conventional past tense of historical works. I did not do this just to be different or out of mere affectation. On the contrary, I had two serious and so, I think, worthwhile purposes. One was to give the reader a sense of immediacy, a feeling that he is a witness of, even a participant in, the events being narrated, and thus enhance the drama of the story that is being related. The other purpose, closely allied, was to take maximum advantage of what is known as the "fog of war" technique of writing military history. Most famously used by Freeman in his magnificent *R. E. Lee,* this approach consists of describing battles and campaigns on the basis of how a commander perceived them at the time they took place, rather than from the standpoint of historical hindsight. Not only does this make for greater realism, it also permits the reader, as it were, to enter a commander's mind and view events as he sees them and to follow his thought processes as he makes his decisions and issues his orders. On the whole I believe I have achieved both of these objectives, and I hope that the reader will agree. If not, then at least let him credit me with good intentions.

The second aspect of the book that requires explanation is its accounts of battles, of the actual fighting. Sometimes these differ markedly, even drastically, from the standard versions. I did not expect such an outcome. Indeed, I assumed that because so much had been written about them in biographies and autobiographies and in general histories and specialized studies, the basic facts about the major engagements of the Atlanta Campaign were firmly established and that all I would need do is try to present them in an interesting fashion, perhaps here and there adding some new information or making minor modifications in old interpretations. Therefore I was first astonished, then exasperated, when, upon delving into the sources, I discovered that all of the existing descriptions of these battles, in particular those that occurred around Atlanta during the last six weeks of the campaign, were to a greater or lesser degree filled with mistakes, misconceptions, and myths. The reason for these defects was obvious: superficial and uncritical research, an inadequate understanding of the nature of the Civil War and of war in general, and bias-inspired distortions and prevarications. Likewise the remedy for them was obvious, as it also was necessary: to start my own accounts of these battles from scratch and base them on a thorough and systematic examination of all known pertinent sources, Union and Confederate. I am confident that the result of this arduous and time-consuming labor is a much closer approximation of the truth of what happened—and did not happen—on the battlefields of Georgia during the spring and summer of 1864 than has hitherto been available. Whether or not this confidence is warranted, time and other historians will tell.

Finally, I wish to say something about the book's depiction of Sherman as a commander. By and large, it is a harsh one. I did not intend it to be. When I started this book, I shared the prevailing view that Sherman was second in ability only to Grant among Union commanders, and I considered his conduct of the Atlanta Campaign to be his main and rightful claim to that status. As in the case of the battles, not until my own researches made me better acquainted with what Sherman actually had done and, more to the point, failed to do during the campaign did I begin to change my opinion. Ultimately, although acknowledging his strengths and giving him credit when credit was due, I had to conclude that he suffered from serious flaws as a commander and that these flaws manifested themselves frequently on the way to Atlanta. The evidence on which this verdict is based will be found in the pages that follow.

Such, then, are the motivation, the justification, and some explanations for this book. It is not the book I dreamed of writing; that dream quickly shattered against the adamantine rocks of literary and scholarly reality that all historians encounter. It merely is the best that I was able to write with what knowledge and talent I possess. Would that I possessed more.

One thing, though, I have had in bountiful supply. That is the aid and encouragement of others. First among them, for she was there at the beginning, is my daughter Ann, who accompanied me on my initial, longest, and most rewarding research trip through the South in the late spring of 1976 and then again in the summer of 1977 when I visited certain depositories of source materials in Pennsylvania, New York, Washington, D.C., and Virginia. She gave me extra pairs of eyes, hands, and feet, thereby enabling me to accomplish much more in the way of research, and to do it faster, than I could have on my own. Her payment, apart from seeing some interesting places and beautiful country, was a number of marvelous suppers at the best available local restaurants. Her punishment, totally unintended, consisted of too many cinnamon roll breakfasts. I hope she remembers the former and forgives the latter. In any case, she has my gratitude.

Accompanying me on most of my subsequent research expeditions was Larry Massie of the Allegan Forest. No one could be a more intelligent and enterprising co-worker when in a library or archive; it would be impossible for anyone to show greater physical stamina and steadier nerves during our long, tiring, and sometimes frenetic journeys; and when we were not engaged in research or travel he was at all times a most congenial and considerate companion. My debt to Larry cannot be paid, only acknowledged.

I also owe much, as in fact do all Civil War historians, to Dr. Richard M. McMurry of Georgia. At one level the extent of my obligations to him is recorded, adequately I hope, in this book's many citations of his writings on the Atlanta Campaign, writings which, along with the late Thomas L. Connelley's *Autumn of Glory: The Army of Tennessee, 1862–1865,* have moved the study of that subject out of the nineteenth century, in the process transforming it. On another level, he kindly consented to read and evaluate a large portion of this book while it was in its formative stages, with the result that he saved me from many errors and oversights (for those that no doubt remain, I alone am responsible). Richard McMurry has been as good a friend as he is a scholar, and I know of no better scholar in the field of Civil War history.

Next come two Davises: William C. "Jack" Davis of (most of the time) Mechanicsburg, Pennsylvania, and Dr. Stephen A. Davis of Atlanta, Georgia. The first gave me courage and confidence when it was badly needed and has graciously done me many favors, both professional and personal. The second gave me the benefit of his superb knowledge of the battles around Atlanta and provided me with valuable materials and information that otherwise I would not have had. To both I say thank you, thank you very much.

Before I submitted the manuscript of this book to the publisher, I asked my fellow native of Kansas, Thomas Goodrich of Topeka, to read it, with the proviso that he be as tough in his criticisms of it as I had been when I critiqued one of his writings. He said he would be and he was—and I was delighted. Viewing what I had done through the eyes of a reader who knows how to write, he pointed out many things that should be removed and many other things that could be improved. Thanks to him this is a shorter book (readers might want to thank him, too) and, I hope, a better one.

Finally, I wish to express my gratitude to another Massie. This one is Priscilla, Larry's wife. Through her efforts and skill, what would have been impossible became possible at a critical moment in the preparation of the book for publication. I am fortunate to have a friend with such a wife—although not nearly as fortunate as he is to be her husband.

Many more people deserve a paragraph of thanks for their contributions. But due to lack of space the best I can do is name them and briefly, yet gratefully, refer to what they did to help. They are Alan S. Brown of Kalamazoo, Michigan, true scholar and true friend, for being both; Fred M. Woodward, director of the University Press of Kansas, for his faith (greater than mine) in this book; my son Charles and Roger L. Rosentreter, a former student, now editor of *Michigan History,* for also providing good company on research expeditions; the members of the Burnham-Macmillan Fund Committee of the Department of History, Western Michigan University, for their generous support of my research; Dr. Stephen Mitchell, former vice president for academic affairs at Western Michigan University, for his prompt action in the spring of 1976 in making right what would have been a wrong; Opal Ellis, secretary of the Western Michigan University history department, for typing most of the manuscript; David Roth, editor and publisher of *Blue & Gray Magazine,* for his friendship and advice; Bob Younger of the Morningside Bookshop, Larry Daniel of Memphis, Thomas G. Dyer of the University of Georgia, Christopher Losson of (presently) the University of Mississippi, and the Ladies Library Association of Kalamazoo, all for helping me obtain otherwise unobtainable source materials; Art Miller of Kalamazoo and Fred Soflin, Sr., of Platte City, Missouri, for expressing an interest in my work that helped keep me working; the staffs of all the historical societies, archives, libraries, and museums referred to in the Bibliography, for their indispensable assistance and for in so many cases going beyond the requirements of duty; Susan McRory, Susan Schott, and above all the copyeditors, Virginia Seaver and Martha Thorp, of the University Press of Kansas, for transforming my disreputable-looking manuscript into a publishable book; Laura Kriegstrom Poracsky, for her maps; and, last but, as it should be, nevertheless most, my wife, for her logistical (or, to be more precise, quartermaster) support and for her love.

In a previous book, *The Presidency of Andrew Johnson,* published in 1979 also by the University Press of Kansas, I acknowledged in the preface "Max and Hilde, my almost constant but not always silent companions while I wrote." Max and Hilde were not, as some people assumed, two children; rather they were two dachshunds to whom my wife and I belonged. They continued to be almost always present but not always silent while I wrote this book. Now, after long and good lives, they are no more. But they left behind two friends: Calico Kate and Clarence the Tom, both of whom also have often been present as I wrote—and much more silent.

Albert Castel

Hillsdale, Michigan

DECISION IN THE WEST

The Atlanta Campaign of 1864

CHAPTER ONE

JANUARY

Part One: The North

ON NEW YEAR'S DAY 1864 a fierce, frigid wind sweeps down from the Great Lakes, across the Ohio River, and on toward the Gulf of Mexico. In Louisville and Cincinnati, thermometers plunge far below zero. Outside of Nashville, where the snow is ten inches deep, four soldiers of the 39th Ohio freeze to death in a boxcar. Near Chattanooga, men of the 37th Indiana dig tree roots from the icy ground in quest of wood to keep their bonfires going. At the village of Dalton, Georgia, quartermaster clerk Robert Patrick of the 4th Louisiana cannot write because the ink freezes on the tip of his pen. In Atlanta, Mary Mallard, wife of a Presbyterian minister, prepares a "delightful ice cream" merely by placing a bowl of custard on the porch. Even in palm-treed Savannah, people huddle by their fireplaces and stoves, for the northern wind reaches there too.[1]

It also is cold in Washington, D.C., but bright sunshine warms the air. At the White House the customary New Year's Day reception takes place. President Abraham Lincoln stands in the East Room shaking hands with the visitors filing by. He is, an English observer notes, "the Tallest Man of All," his grip like "cast-iron." He looks somewhat haggard, having just recovered from a mild form of smallpox contracted late in November while traveling to Gettysburg, Pennsylvania, to deliver a speech; but a newspaper reporter thinks he appears "to retain all the vivacity of his earlier Presidential days" as he greets everyone with "a Western geniality."[2]

Lincoln has good reason to feel happy. The year just ended was one of triumph for the Union cause. At Gettysburg, Lee's hitherto invincible legions were thrown back with heavy loss; at Vicksburg, over 30,000 rebel troops were forced to surrender along with the last major Confederate stronghold on the Mississippi; and at Missionary Ridge, outside of Chattanooga, the main Southern army in the West was routed and driven into Georgia. Most of Tennessee, Arkansas, and Louisiana, plus large portions of Virginia, Alabama, and Mississippi now lie under Union control, and everywhere the vastly outnumbered rebel armies stand on the defensive while the Northern hosts marshal in seemingly irresistible might to crush them. Furthermore, in the words of the *Indi-*

anapolis *Journal,* "The nation"—meaning the North—"wages war and pros-
pers." The average profit of business firms is between twelve and eighteen
percent, employment and wages never have been higher, and the total value of
crops produced in 1863 is double that of 1861. Little wonder, then, that wealthy
and well-informed George Templeton Strong of New York writes in his diary at
the end of 1863 that "there is almost universal feeling that rebellion has received
its death blow" and that most Northern newspapers predict in their New Year's
editorials that 1864 will bring victory and peace.³

The price of success, however, has not been cheap; on the contrary, the North
has paid a huge human toll for its victories. Out of the approximately 2,000,000
men so far mustered into the Union army, at least 250,000 are dead—one-third
from battle, the rest from disease, exposure, and overstrain. Many of the
survivors lie in hospitals or have returned home with missing arms, legs, and
eyes, or with their health shattered by typhoid, malaria, or dysentery, or with
their faces disfigured and forever hideous. All over the North there are human
wrecks, almost all young men, waiting and sometimes wanting to die. And
down South, tens of thousands of Northern soldiers cram makeshift prisons
where hunger and sickness kill them faster than battle would.

But soldiers are not the only ones suffering and dying. In the frontier village of
Toledo, Iowa, the physician's wife, Marjorie Ann Rogers, receives a telegram
stating that the husband of "a dear, sweet, patient, frail little mother of three" has
been killed on the battlefield. Procuring with difficulty a buggy—practically all
of the horses have gone to the army—Mrs. Rogers drives out into the country
where the young woman lives to break the news. The first thing the young
woman says on seeing Mrs. Rogers is, "Oh, I had such a lovely letter from my
husband; he said our army had had another victory and he hoped the war
would soon end and the 'boys would come marching home.'" Then, noticing
the expression on Mrs. Roger's face, she asks, "Has there come any news for me
since the last mail?"

"Yes, here is a telegram."

"Have you read it? Oh, read it to me."

Mrs. Rogers reads it. The young woman does not speak or shed a tear, just
stares at Mrs. Rogers as if she were not telling the truth. Then she faints. Mrs.
Rogers calls neighbors to help. After a while the young woman becomes
conscious but says only, "I want to see my mother and then die." The mother
comes in response to a telegram and remains with her until she dies. Years later
Mrs. Rogers writes, "Nothing could keep her, she wanted to die and God let her
die, and I was glad she could."⁴

This Iowa wife and mother lost her will to continue living. Many more
Northerners have lost their will to continue fighting. Five thousand men a

month are deserting from the army. Thousands of other soldiers fail to report back from leave, skulk in rear areas claiming to be on "detached service," or lounge around hospitals pretending to be sick or otherwise incapacitated. According to surgeon William Fuller of the 1st Michigan Infantry, "there is not a village in the land" which does not contain ex-soldiers who have obtained discharges by faking illness and who "make no attempt to conceal their trickery." When in the summer of 1863 the government, seeking to replenish the army's dwindling ranks, had resorted for the first time to conscription, riots broke out in Chicago, Milwaukee, New York and, Portsmouth, New Hampshire. The worst was in New York, where mobs of Irish slumdwellers roamed the streets for three days, looting, burning, and killing blacks because they resented them as job competitors. It had taken regular troops, rushed from the battlefront, to restore order, by which time 120 people were dead, and the governor of New York was demanding that the draft be suspended in his state. Some men refused to register for the draft, others did not report when called, and large numbers have gone to Canada or to the Far West. In the coal fields of eastern Pennsylvania and the back country of southern Ohio, Indiana, and Illinois, draft resisters threaten, beat up, even occasionally shoot enrollment officers.

Actually, as such, conscription produces few troops. What it does do is cause men to enlist in order to avoid what in most localities is the social disgrace of being drafted or else to hire substitutes to serve in their place. The newspapers are filled with advertisements from "substitute brokers" who promise for a fee to provide a military alter ego for citizens who do not fancy a soldier's life (and death). Since the draft operates only in states that have not provided their stipulated number of troops, some of the Northeastern states, notably Massachusetts, fill their quotas by recruiting Irish and German immigrants or by sending agents to occupied areas of the South to enlist blacks. And even many of the more-or-less willing volunteers, who remain the principal source of recruits, are attracted by the government's offer of a $302 bounty to every man who signs up for three years, a sum that is commonly supplemented by financial inducements from states, counties, and communities. Thus the enlistment bonus in the small town of Niles, Michigan, totals $600, enough for a "prudent poor man [to] purchase a snug little home for his family and leave them perhaps more comfortable than they were before." Because of the large amounts of money being given volunteers, a new criminal profession flourishes—"bounty jumper." Men join up, collect the bounty, then desert at the first opportunity in order to repeat the process. Soldiers of this type add nothing to the real strength of any army. By the same token, recruits who in effect have been bribed into joining are not likely to fight with the same determination displayed by the patriotic, enthusiastic "boys" of '61 and '62.[5]

Yet desertion, demoralization, and disaffection are, to varying degrees, the inevitable by-product of any long, arduous, and costly war. Much more serious and ominous than these things is the attitude of the Democratic party. The vast majority of Northern Democrats desire to preserve the Union; but they also believe that it was the antislavery fanaticism of the Republicans that had provoked the South into secession, thereby bringing on the war. Likewise, most Northern Democrats support the war effort—indeed, some of the Union's best generals and hardest fighting troops are Democrats—but dislike the way it is being conducted. They fear and charge that conscription, the suspension of the writ of habeas corpus in the Border States, and the arrest of alleged disloyalists by military authorities represent attempts by the Republicans to use the war to destroy civil liberties and states' rights and to entrench themselves permanently in power. They also believe and declare that Lincoln's Emancipation Proclamation is an unconstitutional and revolutionary act that fosters "nigger equality" and stiffens Southern resistance, thereby prolonging the conflict. For these reasons they have, as a party, become more interested in ending the war than in winning it, at least under Republican auspices and on Republican terms. The Democrats' basic view, proclaimed repeatedly by their leaders and newspapers, is that the effort to subdue the rebellion by force has failed and, in spite of the victories of 1863, will continue to fail and that the best, indeed only, way to reunite the nation is to offer the Confederates peace on the basis of "the Union as it was and the Constitution as it is": that is, the South would be allowed to come back into the Union as if it never left it, and slavery would remain in existence (or be reestablished) as if Lincoln had never issued his proclamation and as if thousands of blacks had never enlisted in the Union army to fight for freedom.

The Republicans respond by calling the Democrats pro-Southern and pro-slavery traitors, labeling them "copperheads," and deriding them as "butternuts," a midwestern term signifying back-country bumpkins. But except for a few who are driven literally wild by hatred of Republicans and abolitionism, the Democrats are not traitors. Instead they are a party composed of politicians who are bitter over the loss of long-accustomed power to the upstart Republicans and who crave to get it back, of whites who are disgusted and frightened by the very idea of free blacks, of conservatives who are alarmed by the revolutionary changes brought by the war and who are afraid that there will be more, and of people who simply find it intolerable that fellow Americans should be slaughtering one another for, as they see it, no valid or necessary cause. Hence the Democrats are unable to see two great, fundamental facts. The first is that any attempt to repudiate the Emancipation Proclamation would so outrage numerous Northerners that it probably would touch off another civil war, this one in the North. The second is that the majority of Southerners have no desire to return to the Union under any terms but are determined to secure what they have fought and bled for three years to secure—Northern recognition of their national independence.

Most Northerners realize this. They also support emancipation for practical as well as moral reasons: it is a means of both putting down and punishing the rebels. And after the great military victories of 1863 they reject and resent the assertion that the effort—to which so many of them have sacrificed so much— to restore the Union by force is hopeless. Consequently the Democrats' denunciation of the war, their opposition to emancipation, and their agitation for peace have cost them heavily. At the beginning of 1864 they hold only two governorships—of New York and New Jersey—and during the recent fall elections they have failed to carry a single state. Moreover thousands of lifelong Democrats, especially those serving in the army, no longer support the party. Either they vote for Republican candidates or join the Republican party, which has changed its official name to the Union party in order to attract such "War Democrats." As the Boston poet and pundit James Russell Lowell points out in the January *North American Review,* the Democratic party is out of step with Northern public opinion, which "is overwhelmingly resolved that the war shall be prosecuted."

Nevertheless the Democrats remain formidable. They control most of the big cities, where large populations of German and Irish immigrants resent what they deem, not without cause, the antiforeign and anti-Catholic prejudice that characterizes many of the mainly native-born Protestant Republicans. Democrats are powerful, almost predominant, in the Border States, in the lower Midwest, and in New York and New Jersey; nowhere, except for a few states in New England and on the Great Plains, are they hopelessly outmatched by the Republicans, whose majorities in some instances are paper-thin. The Democrats' propaganda is spread by hundreds of newspapers, ranging from four-page rural weeklies to such mass-circulation journals as the *New York World,* the *Chicago Times,* the *Detroit Free Press,* the *Cincinnati Enquirer,* the *Boston Courier,* and (notwithstanding its name) the *St. Louis Republican.* The arrest and imprisonment of hundreds of civilians on untried and unproved charges of treason enables them to pose as the champions of civil liberties against Republican military tyranny. By advocating states' rights the Democrats strike a responsive chord among the large numbers of people who venerate the principles of Jefferson. Their opposition to emancipation, which they accompany with inflammatory appeals to racial prejudice, has enormous appeal, particularly to workingmen who fear that they will be forced to compete for jobs with liberated blacks flooding up from the South.[6]

And above all, the Democrats' assertion that the war is a failure and that only peace can restore the Union, although a losing card now, is potentially a winning one.

This had been demonstrated in 1862. The North began that year confident of crushing the rebellion by the end of the summer at the latest. Its optimism increased as Admiral David G. Farragut took New Orleans, Ulysses S. ("Unconditional Surrender") Grant sliced through Tennessee into Mississippi, and General George B. McClellan's huge army advanced to the gates of Richmond, Virginia. Then things began to go wrong. Confederate General Robert E. Lee drove McClellan back, routed General John Pope's Federal army at Second Bull Run, and invaded Maryland. At practically the same time, other Confederate forces swept across Tennessee and Kentucky toward the Ohio River. To be sure, Lee retreated back into Virginia after having been checked at Antietam on September 17, and in October the Confederates evacuated Kentucky. Even so, the North's expectation of victory in 1862 had been blasted; no end to the fighting and dying seemed in sight. Disappointment and discouragement gripped many Northerners. In the fall elections the Democrats, who blamed Lincoln for the military setbacks, scored spectacular gains. They carried fourteen out of nineteen congressional seats in Ohio and did nearly as well in New York, Indiana, Illinois, Pennsylvania, and New Jersey. Overall they halved the Republican majority in the House of Representatives from seventy to thirty-five. Also they took away from the Republicans the governorship of New York and the legislature of Indiana. In effect the North repudiated Lincoln's leadership; had he been running for reelection, he would probably have been defeated.

During the remainder of 1862 and the first half of 1863 the war continued to go badly for the North: a futile bloodbath at Fredericksburg, Virginia, humiliation at nearby Chancellorsville, stalemate in Tennessee and along the Mississippi, all climaxed—like the onset of doom itself—by Lee's invasion of Pennsylvania. Had not Lee, after a desperate and almost losing struggle by the Union army, been turned back at Gettysburg on July 3 and had not Grant, overcoming awesome obstacles with brilliant strategy, captured Vicksburg, Mississippi, the following day, the Democrats that autumn almost surely would have won control of Ohio and other key states, making it practically impossible for the government to go on with the war. As it was, these victories revived Northern morale, turned the political tide, and enabled the Republicans to carry every state that held elections except New Jersey.

The lesson of 1862 and 1863 is clear: the course of the war determines the course of politics. Its meaning for 1864 also is clear. Should the Federal armies move forward decisively to victory, Lincoln and the Republicans will remain in power. But if these armies bog down or seem to do so and if the casualty lists lengthen without any sign of ever ending, then there will be a very good chance that the majority of Northerners will give up on the war and turn to the Democrats with their false, yet seductive, promise that the restoration of peace will bring the restoration of the Union.[7]

Clement Laird Vallandigham of Dayton, Ohio, is confident that this will happen. Moreover he is doing everything he can to make it happen. He is not the most powerful Democratic leader in the North, but undoubtedly he is the most famous—some would say notorious. Unlike the vast majority of his fellow Democrats, who rallied around the flag when the rebels fired on Fort Sumter, he opposed the war from the outset. As a member of the House of Representatives he refused to vote for appropriations to wage it. In speeches both in Congress and out, he called for an immediate cessation of hostilities. Even many Democrats considered him too extreme, and the Republicans denounced him as a traitor. In the 1862 election they used huge sums of money, gerrymander, and a prominent War Democrat to take away his congressional seat. Undaunted, he stepped up his campaign against the war. In a speech at Mount Vernon, Ohio, on May 1, 1863, he attacked and defied a decree issued by Major General Ambrose E. Burnside, commander of the Department of the Ohio, prohibiting declarations of "sympathy for the enemy." Burnside thereupon ordered Vallandigham arrested. At 2 o'clock on the night of May 4 a squad of soldiers broke down the front door of Vallandigham's house with crowbars, smashed open his bedroom door with musket butts, and hauled him off to Cincinnati, where two days later a military court found him guilty of sedition and sentenced him to prison. Lincoln, perceiving that to incarcerate Vallandigham would make him an even greater martyr and hero to Democrats than he already had become thanks to Burnside's high-handedness, directed that Vallandigham be escorted to the rebel lines in Tennessee. After a brief sojourn in the Confederacy, he made his way by blockade runner to Bermuda, thence to Canada. From there he campaigned *in absentia* for the governorship of Ohio, for which the state's Democrats had nominated him in angry reaction to his arrest. Gettysburg, Vicksburg, and an extraordinary Republican effort caused him to go down to defeat. "Glory to God in the highest; Ohio has saved the Union!" exclaimed Lincoln. Nonetheless Vallandigham received nearly 200,000 votes—more than any previous unsuccessful gubernatorial candidate in Ohio history. This meant that there were that many men in the third most populous state of the North who supported a man who advocated stopping the war at once.

Vallandigham is sympathetic to the South, where he has friends and family (a nephew wears Confederate gray). And he hates the Republicans, whom he regards as fanatic revolutionaries. But like most of his fellow Copperheads, he is loyal—in his fashion—to the Union. As he has told Confederate leaders during his enforced exile in the South, he desires above all else to reunite the nation. He simply believes that this should and can be done by peace and compromise. Neither is he a demagogue. Instead he is the reverse of that—a dogmatic conservative who is utterly sincere when he declares that it would be better for the North to lose the war than to win it at the expense of states' rights, civil liberty, and political freedom, all of which he feels Lincoln is destroying. It is his sincerity—or if you will, his obstinacy—that makes him formidable. Nothing discourages him; nothing deters him; nothing changes his mind. When Southerners say that they want independence, not reunion, he ignores them. Despite losing his seat in Congress, despite being defeated for governor, despite being criticized for his extremism by many leaders of his own party, he is absolutely sure that the future will vindicate him. In June 1863 he had predicted, while being interviewed by a Confederate official, that if the war were to last fifteen more months—that is, until September 1864—the people of the North would reject the Republicans and elect a Democratic president who would make peace with the South. Now it is January 1864; Vallandigham, who is residing at the Hirons House in Windsor, Ontario, across the river from Detroit, looks forward eagerly to September and vindication.[8]

Oliver Perry Morton agrees with Vallandigham that if the war is not over by autumn, the Republicans will be in serious trouble. Unlike Vallandigham, however, Morton, is not pleased by the prospect. Morton, a Republican, is the governor of Indiana and is dedicated to putting down the rebellion by force. Even before the war began he declared that "if it was worth a bloody struggle [the reference is to the Revolutionary War] to establish this nation, it is worth one to preserve it." He has sent from Indiana to the Union army 125,000 troops, well in excess of the state's quota. Although Indiana had only 5,000 serviceable muskets in its arsenal in April 1861, he has seen to it that its soldiers are among the best equipped and supplied of those from all the Northern states. When in the spring of 1863 the Democratic-controlled legislature, seeking to curtail his power, had adjourned without appropriating any money, he kept the state government and its war effort going by obtaining money from wealthy men, Republican officeholders, and the War Department. Hoosier Democrats call him a dictator, and they are not altogether wrong. They would like to impeach him, but since that is impractical, they have resolved to make a supreme effort to turn him out of office on election day, October 11.

Morton, a burly black-bearded man who ordinarily "does not scare worth a damn," is afraid they might just do that. Indiana long has been a Democratic state. He himself belonged to that party until he joined the Republicans in opposing the Kansas-Nebraska Act of 1854. Not until 1860, thanks largely to dissension among the Democrats, had the Republicans won an election in the state. Then in 1862 the Democrats regained control of the legislature (fortunately for Morton, Indiana governors served four-year terms). In addition, Indiana has no law authorizing its troops in the field to cast absentee ballots, a situation that favors the Democrats, for the soldier vote is overwhelmingly Republican. Thus, as far as Morton is concerned, Northern victory by fall is a political necessity. With that in mind, on January 18 he writes a letter to Lincoln. "Considerations of the most vital character," he warns, "demand that the war shall be substantially ended within the present year." Therefore he "respectfully but earnestly" urges Lincoln to call for "all the men that may be required to bring the war to a safe and speedy termination. If doubts are entertained that a sufficient number of men will be procured under the last call, let another be made immediately. . . . It is much better to make the estimate too large than too small."[9]

Lincoln agrees. He, too, knows that the North can still lose the war—lose it by failing to win it before the fall elections—and he is just as determined as Morton to do everything to win it before then. At the end of the month, Lincoln prepares a proclamation, to be issued on Feburary 1, summoning the loyal states to furnish 200,000 men in addition to the 300,000 called for on October 17, or else be subjected to the draft. In sum, Lincoln proposes to increase the Union army, which already has 700,000 troops on its muster rolls, by 500,000. That is twice as many men as the Confederates have present for duty altogether.

However, as Lincoln also knows, all of those new soldiers will make little difference unless enough of the old soldiers make a certain decision. As 1864 gets under way, the North faces a situation that would be ludicrous were it not potentially disastrous. Of the 956 infantry regiments in the Union army, 455 are scheduled to disband during the spring and summer. So are 81 of the 158 volunteer artillery batteries and approximately one-half of the cavalry regiments. The reason for this is that most of the men in these units had enlisted in 1861 for three years or until the war ended, whichever came first. Barring a Confederate collapse early in 1864—something that would be foolish to count on—it now appears that the three years will end before the war does. If that happens, or even if it is about to happen, it will be extremely difficult, probably impossible, for the North to wage successful war. The "boys of '61" are the hard core of the Union army, hardened at Shiloh and in the Seven Days, at Antietam and Stones River, at Champion's Hill and Gettysburg. Without them the North would retain superiority in quantity but lack the quality needed to overcome the tough men in gray, most of whom have been fighting for over two years and have become experts at it. In a regular battle and if properly led, a veteran regiment can whip three or four times its number of neophytes; and experienced artillery and cavalry units are quite literally irreplaceable.[10]

The obvious solution would be for the government simply to require all troops to serve until the war is finished, which is what the Confederates are doing. But Lincoln and his fellow Republicans fear the reaction of the veterans and voters (often one and the same) should such a step be taken. Hence the War Department has adopted a plan suggested, appropriately enough, by Governor Morton: if a veteran reenlists for three years or the duration, he will be awarded $402 bounty, the title of Veteran Volunteer, a red-and-blue chevron to wear diagonally on the lower part of each sleeve of his uniform, and a thirty-day furlough. Furthermore, if three-fourth of the men in a regiment or battery sign up for another hitch, those who do so will receive a thirty-day leave as a group and a promise that their organization will retain its separate identity and not be merged with another newer and less distinguished outfit.

Response of the veterans to this offer at first is uncertain, even ominous. When they "joined the colors" in '61, with bands playing and crowds cheering, "not one man in a hundred believed that there would be any war or fighting," later writes one of them.

> All were unanimous in the conviction that the South would not fight, and that if the North put armies in the field, the terrified secessionists would hasten to seek shelter from the storm they had invoked. It was a picnic, a pleasure-trip, a triumphant jaunt through Dixie, with flying banners and beating drums, with all the pleasure of a free excursion, sight-seeing, new faces and places, and pay, food, and clothing during the absence. Some there were who saw loot as they contemplated the wealth of the Southern plantations; there were romantic dreamers who caught glimpses in the distance of dark-eyed women with raven hair; and others, idlers by nature, who enjoyed in anticipation the languid delights of the orange groves, the flowering hedges, the beauty of the magnolia blossoms, and the genial air of the sunny South.

But there had been war and there had been fighting—lots of it. And campaigning through Dixie was no pleasure trip. It was long marches in the mud or under a torrid sun, bivouacs among frigid mountains or dank swamps, and grinding fatigue and boredom. As for plantations and dark-eyed women with raven hair, far more common were shabby cabins inhabited by gaunt women whose teeth were black from dipping snuff. Above all there was the terrible fear-frenzy of battle, agony and death, and corpses—hundreds, thousands of corpses, swollen, stinking, covered with flies. Now most of the boys who had joined up with the bands playing and the crowds cheering in '61 are gone; gone, too, are romantic illusions about war.

Little wonder the veterans—rather, the survivors—hesitate to reenlist, that many declare in bitter voices that they have done their part and intend to get out of the army before their luck runs out, that there are plenty of able-bodied men back home who can take their places and be welcome to them. Yet in the end the vast majority decide to stay on. Their reasons are mixed: the $402 bonus, their officers' persuasive appeals to patriotism and pride, the bonds of friendship and esprit de corps, a determination to finish the job of putting down the rebellion, and the prospect of a thirty-day furlough. For a great many the last reason is the clincher. Few of them have had a leave since enlisting. They are eager to see family, friends, wives, sweethearts. Only those who "veteranize" qualify for furloughs; otherwise you remain behind in camp. To escape from camp is a big inducement in itself. This is especially true for the veterans of the Army of the Cumberland and the Army of the Tennessee in and around Chattanooga. They have been campaigning all summer and fall. Their uniforms are threadbare, rations are scanty, shelters are flimsy, and the awful cold that came on New Year's Day persists. Mike O'Brien of the 10th Illinois announces that he will enlist for three more years just to "get out of this damned place." Mike doesn't "mean quite so bad" as he expresses it, explains a comrade. He does want "to see that good old mother of his away up there in his native home on the wide prairie"; however the 10th Illinois is "nearly frozen out"; consequently it is "easily frozen in for another three years, or to the end of the war."

As soon as the stipulated three-fourths of the men of a regiment agree to reenlist, a mustering officer discharges them from their original service, then swears them in as Veteran Volunteers. Next they march to the nearest railroad or steamboat station, leaving those who have not veteranized (if there are such) to take care of the camp and gear. Stay-behinds are dubbed "stoten-bottles," but the expression is not contemptuous; any man still around after two-plus years of war is not likely to be a coward or a "dead-head"; most of the soldiers who refuse to reenlist are in poor health or have bad family situations.

Typically the veterans spend their leaves at home with parents or wives, visiting and being visited, telling about their adventures, eating their fill of favorite foods, helping out on the farm, and (if single) "sparking" old and new sweethearts. Many get married—or, if already married, catch up on lost time; there will be a sharp rise in the number of babies born come autumn. For some the furlough is a "sweet dream—thirty days of unalloyed enjoyment" which pass all too quickly. Others, especially the single men, soon experience an "uneasiness at home, a feeling of being in 'hot water,'" as one of them puts it. They find that they have little in common with old friends, that they miss their army comrades, that they even have an "eager longing for the hardtack and army ration of the front."

All winter long the veteran regiments journey home and then back to the front. Most return greatly strengthened by men recruited during the furlough. Thus the 50th Illinois adds 200 recruits, the 12th Michigan comes close to regaining its original 1,000, and the 7th Pennsylvania Dragoons double their size to an amazing 1,300. Until recently the government, instead of maintaining the existing regiments with replacements, has followed the policy of constantly creating new regiments, thereby providing the Republicans with useful political patronage in the form of officers commissions. As a consequence, many old regiments have dwindled to fewer than three hundred men, in some cases less than two hundred. By veteranizing, such outfits are able to restore their battle-worthiness.[11]

Because of Lincoln's call for 500,000 new troops and because the majority of the veterans reenlist, the North will have armies sufficiently strong and experienced to defeat the Confederacy before the leaves begin falling and the voters go to the polls in autumn. Provided, that is, those armies are competently commanded. The North always has had the raw power needed to win the war. Its problem has been in finding generals capable of using that power effectively. This has been notably, tragically, yet almost absurdly, the case in the East.

In effect, if not by design, the North has invested the greatest single share of its physical and emotional resources in trying to win the war quickly with an "On to Richmond!" strategy. Lured by the tempting target of the Confederate capital only one hundred miles from Washington and believing that its capture would cause the rebellion to collapse, Lincoln's government has assembled its largest and best-equipped army, the Army of the Potomac, near Washington and has launched offensive after offensive into Virginia. Each time, despite enormous numerical superiority, the Army of the Potomac has suffered defeat or has retreated in order to avoid defeat. Its only accomplishment has been to turn back Confederate counteroffensives into Maryland and Pennsylvania; in January 1864 it is no closer to taking Richmond than it had been in January 1863 or January 1862. The reasons for its failure are many, but the basic, the decisive, one is that it never has had a commander—George B. McClellan, Ambrose E. Burnside, Joseph Hooker, George G. Meade—capable of waging a successful offensive campaign against Lee. Quite simply, all of them were overawed by Lee, an attitude that affects the rank and file of the Army of the Potomac, causing them to feel that no matter how well they fight, the Gray Fox will find a way to beat or baffle them.

Meanwhile in the West—as the region between the Appalachians and the Mississippi is called—the North has been winning the war, and the South has

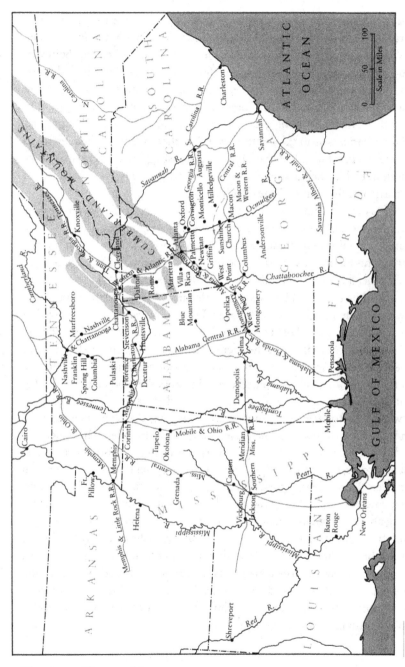

The Western Theater, 1864

been losing it, although many people on both sides still do not fully realize this fact. Fort Donelson, New Orleans, Island Number Ten, Shiloh, Corinth, Stone's River, Vicksburg—all have marked Northern penetrations of the Southern heartland. To be sure, on September 20, 1863, the Confederates had checked the Union advance at Chickamauga, near Chattanooga, bringing troops from Virginia to do it. But two months later the Federals, heavily reinforced, had sallied forth from Chattanooga, broken through at Missionary Ridge, and planted their banners atop the mountains of Northern Georgia. In contrast to the Army of the Potomac, the Union forces in the West have a record of victory and conquest. Unlike that ill-starred army, they have generals who know how to win. In particular they have Ulysses S. Grant.

No need to describe him. That has been done often and well enough. Besides there are the photographs—especially the one of him standing atop Lookout Mountain, overlooking Chattanooga, after his troops have taken it: the inevitable cigar is in his mouth, his uniform and beard are scruffy, and he looks as hard as nails. No need either to describe his pre-1861 career; without the post-1861 career it would be utterly and deservedly buried in oblivion. What is important to know is that he has the knack for war. He is aggressive, as he showed at Belmont, Fort Henry, and Fort Donelson. He remains cool and clearheaded in times of crisis, as at Shiloh where the enemy surprised and nearly defeated him. He is tirelessly determined, as he demonstrated during the long months when he tried to find a way through or around the wilderness that encompassed Vicksburg, failing again and again until he finally succeeded. He is bold and clever, as proved when he outsmarted the Confederates defending Vicksburg in what is the war's most brilliant campaign of maneuver. Last, but far from least, he is lucky, as was made manifest at Missionary Ridge, where his troops, against his intent and without his orders, drove the Confederates from a position that should have been impregnable. "We all regard Gen'l Grant as fate," wrote one of his generals, Manning Force of Ohio, during the siege of Vicksburg; "we feel that he knows everything about the situation and everything that is to happen about it."[12]

Grant's triumphs at Vicksburg and Missionary Ridge have established him as the North's best military leader. Accordingly, Republican congressman Elihu Washburn, with Lincoln's concurrence, has introduced a bill reviving the rank of lieutenant general, last held by George Washington. Lincoln intends to promote Grant to that rank and give him the mission of winning the war by autumn. If Grant can't do it, who can?

Grant would like to begin moving into Georgia and Alabama immediately, or at any rate sometime during the winter: don't give the enemy a chance to catch his

Grant at Lookout Mountain (Francis Trevelyan Miller, ed. *The Photographic History of the Civil War.* 10 vols. [New York: the Review of Reviews, 1911; henceforth cited as *Photographic History*], 10:30)

breath, to rally, to rebuild. But it simply is not practicable. The weather continues to be numbingly cold, the roads are either ice-covered or muddy, too many crack combat units are leaving on veteran furlough, and the troops are weary in body and spirit after the terrible strains of the 1863 campaigns; they need time to recuperate.[13] Moreover, before any large-scale offensive can be undertaken, something has to be done about the supply situation.

The soldiers of the Army of the Cumberland at Chattanooga and of the Army of the Ohio at Knoxville are on half rations. Some days they have nothing to eat except what they scrounge from the scantily populated countryside. Most of them still are attired in ragged summer-issue uniforms, many are barefoot or wear moccasins made of rawhide, and some are even pantless and have tied blankets around their waists like kilts! Thousands of horses and mules have died from hunger and overwork; their stinking carcasses line the roadsides, and the surviving ones look like four-legged scarecrows. In sum, the Union forces along the Tennessee River would have trouble advancing even if no enemy opposed them.

At Louisville, Nashville, and Memphis the quartermaster warehouses bulge with all kinds of supplies. The problem lies in transporting them to where they are needed. The Army of the Cumberland, camped in and around Chattanooga, receives the bulk of its supplies via the Nashville and Chattanooga Railroad. Because of the mountains, this line does not run directly to Chattanooga. Instead, it joins the Memphis and Charleston Railroad at Stevenson, Alabama, from where it proceeds eastward across the Tennessee River and into Chattanooga. After their victory at Chickamauga in September the Confederates have attempted to starve the Army of the Cumberland out of Chattanooga by destroying large sections of that line, including the bridge over the Tennessee at Bridgeport. Consequently everything going to Chattanooga must be transferred there from the railroad by means of wagons traveling a single, wretched, twisting road or else by steamboats that are inadequate both in number and in cargo capacity.

As for the Army of the Ohio at Knoxville further up the Tennessee, if anything it is worse off than the Army of the Cumberland. Although there are road and river routes from Nashville and Kentucky to Knoxville, they are so poor that only a trickle of supplies passess over them. Of necessity, therefore, the Army of the Ohio draws most of its supplies via Chattanooga, which means that it gets only the little that the Army of the Cumberland can spare. Furthermore this little must come by already overtaxed steamboats up the Tennessee: Confederate cavalry had torn up long stretches of the Tennessee and Georgia Railroad between Chattanooga and Knoxville.[14]

In December the War Department had sent Colonel Daniel McCallum to

Daniel McCallum, railroad man (*Photographic History,* 5:289)

Tennessee to reopen the Memphis and Charleston to Chattanooga. A powerfully built and autocratic Scotsman in his early forties, McCallum is a railroad genius who before the war had been superintendent of the New York and Erie. In February 1862 he had become military director and general manager of all army railroading and had taken personal charge of rail transport for the Army of the Potomac, which he had helped make the most lavishly supplied army hitherto known to history. With a construction crew of 285 men brought from the East, he has gone to work with furious efficiency on the Memphis and Charleston, rebuilding it from Bridgeport to Chattanooga, a distance of twenty-nine miles. At exactly 2 P.M. on January 14, his laborers hammer the last spikes into place. A few hours later troops of the Army of the Cumberland cheer the arrival of the first "cracker train" from Nashville.

So far, so good. But if the Union forces in Tennessee are going to carry out a major offensive southward, they need more than just enough to eat on a day-by-day basis. They have to accumulate huge stockpiles of everything needed for war, and they have to be assured of regular deliveries. Given the present condition and operation of the various rail lines in Tennessee, neither is possible. There are only 39 locomotives and 400 freight cars in service on the 292 miles of track that connect Nashville with Chattanooga, Knoxville, and the other points in Tennessee and Alabama where Union troops are posted. In comparison, 40 engines and 800 cars are assigned to the mere 70 miles of railroad supplying the Army of the Potomac in Virginia. In addition the most important of the Tennessee lines, the Nashville and Chattanooga, is in such bad shape that trains have to creep along it at eight miles per hour; even then, accidents are frequent. Finally, numerous locomotives and long stretches of track on all the lines are unusable because of lack of maintenance.

McCallum has reported these deficiencies to Major General George H. Thomas, commander of the Army of the Cumberland. He also has told Thomas that John B. Anderson, superintendent of military railroads in the Division of the Mississippi, does not "comprehend the magnitude" of supplying a large army "over a long line of railroad, through the enemy's country." Early in January, Thomas transmits McCallum's findings to Grant with a recommendation that McCallum be given charge of the Tennessee railroads. Grant in turn asks the War Department for authority to place McCallum in control of all railroads in his Military Division. On January 28, Grant gets it, and shortly thereafter McCallum sets out to achieve the self-assigned objective of putting into operation in Tennessee two hundred locomotives and three thousand cars, the quantities he estimates as being "necessary for the business anticipated."[15]

Another obstacle to an early advance southward from Chattanooga is Lieutenant General James Longstreet. Back in September the Confederate government had sent Longstreet and two elite infantry divisions from Lee's army to northern Georgia where they had helped win the Battle of Chickamauga. Subsequently Longstreet with 20,000 troops had moved north against Knoxville. On November 29 he had assaulted it and suffered a stinging repulse (he is a good general as long as he has Lee to tell him what to do and he does what he is told). This defeat and the approach of a Federal relief column had caused Longstreet to swing off toward the Virginia border. By January he no longer is a serious threat, for his army has dwindled to 12,000 or so hungry, shivering, discontented men.

Grant, however, does not know this. Lacking reliable intelligence, he believes that Longstreet has a large army which can quickly be made larger by reinforcements from Virginia. He also fears that Longstreet will attack Knoxville again or else will slice westward into the rear of the Army of the Cumberland, cutting its communications to Nashville. Hence upon visiting Knoxville in person early in January, Grant orders Major General John G. Foster, commander of the Army of the Ohio, to push Longstreet completely out of Tennessee. Foster, with about 20,000 troops, advances to the French Broad River but soon is compelled to return to Knoxville by a combination of too much cold and snow and too little food and forage. On January 23 he telegraphs Grant, now back in Nashville, that it is "absolutely necessary" for his soldiers to go into winter quarters. Grant, alarmed by a false report that two divisions from Lee's army are on the way to Longstreet, promptly vetoes that idea and insists on offensive operations. To that end, Grant decides to replace Foster, who is suffering from a severe leg injury and has asked to be relieved, with Major General John M. Schofield, a younger, more vigorous man. Meanwhile, Longstreet remains in eastern Tennessee, a potential if not potent threat to Grant's left flank.[16]

Grant also wants to secure his right flank before advancing. That flank rests on the Mississippi River, where Federal forces hold Memphis, Vicksburg, Natchez, Yazoo City, and other key points. The Confederates, however, still more or less control the interior of the state of Mississippi. Should Grant remove most of his troops from Mississippi in order to use them for the Georgia-Alabama campaign (which is exactly what he plans to do), then the rebels could harass Northern shipping on the Mississippi or, far worse, penetrate West Tennessee and attack the vital railroad supply lines out of Nashville. Therefore, to forestall these dangers, he has authorized an expedition eastward from Vicksburg through the center of Mississippi to Meridian, near the Alabama border. Its purpose is to damage Mississippi's rail system so badly that the Confederates will not be able to assemble a large force in the state. Commanding the expedition will be the general who conceived it. He is a general who has come to believe that the war should be waged against the South's people as well as its army. On January 31, three days before setting out from Vicksburg, he instructs his adjutant, Major Roswell Sawyer, to notify all Southerners in the country about to be invaded that the United States government has "any and all rights" that it chooses to enforce against rebels—the right "to take their lives, their horses, their lands, their everything." By telling them this, Sawyer will "prepare them for my coming."[17]

The name of this general is William Tecumseh Sherman.

Part Two: The South

The cold wind from the North also blows through the streets of Richmond, Virginia, on New Year's Day. That afternoon, like Lincoln in Washington, President Jefferson Davis of the Confederate States of America is holding a reception. He stands in the drawing room of the White House of the Confederacy, a three-story mansion on the corner of Twelfth and Clay streets, shaking hands with callers; three days later his right hand still will be sore (he lacks Lincoln's cast-iron grip). Five foot ten, thin, and with the erect carriage of a West Pointer (class of 1828), his high-cheekbone face is "decidedly handsome," his hair is "slightly sprinkled with gray," and the goatee that grows below his pointed chin is totally gray. Although this is not apparent, his left eye is sightless, the consequence of herpes contracted several years before the war while he was serving in Washington as a senator from Mississippi, and he suffers from chronic neuralgia and dyspepsia. Normally he dislikes formal social functions and shows it, for he is a serious-minded man who regards them as a waste of time and energy. Today, however, he is smiling and radiates cordiality; when a special friend approaches, he is "as warm and free as a boy" in his greeting. Beside him is his tall, buxom wife, Varina, who likewise welcomes the visitors with a smile and sometimes a witty remark that draws laughter. Indeed, laughter is heard throughout the room, which is packed with Richmond's haute-monde. The women wear their finest diamonds and best remaining prewar dresses (or new gowns acquired from blockade runners), most of the men are attired in dashing gray uniforms with silk sashes and gold-hilted swords, and everyone acts as happy, as merry, as he or she could possibly be.[18]

But that is all it is—acting. Underneath the gaiety are worry and even fear. A year ago in the same place and for the same occasion these people had high hopes of victory: a few weeks before, Lee had slaughtered the Yankees on the banks of the Rappahannock at Fredericksburg, and word (false, but believed to be true at the time) had just arrived from Braxton Bragg that he had defeated the main Federal army in Tennessee near Murfreesboro. Their hopes had grown still higher, approaching certainty, with Lee's glorious triumph against two-to-one odds at Chancellorsville in May and when his invincible army had marched north into Pennsylvania the following month. Then came the twin disasters of Gettysburg and Vicksburg in July. Briefly, in September, Chickamauga had brought a resurgence of hope, but in the end this made the debacle at Missionary Ridge in November all the more devastating. On December 31 the *Richmond Examiner* accurately summed up 1863: "Today closes the gloomiest year of our struggle. . . . The Confederacy has been cut in twain along the line of the

Mississippi, and our enemies are steadily pushing forward their plans by bisecting the eastern moiety." What once had seemed to most Southerners impossible now is more than possible—defeat at the hands of the Yankees. The first words that Mary Chesnut of South Carolina, presently residing in Richmond, writes in her diary for January 1, 1864, are: "God help my country."

Along with the lost battles and lost territory are the lost men. At least 150,000 Southern soldiers have died, tens of thousands more have been incapacitated by wounds or illness, or are languishing and frequently dying in Northern prison camps. These losses come from a white population of only 5 million and from an army that never has exceeded 400,000 troops in actual service. Furthermore, desertion is great and growing greater. Many of the deserters, to be sure, are conscripts; but many, too, are volunteers who hitherto have served faithfully and fought well until discouraged by defeats, demoralized by seeing their comrades mowed down in futile assaults, physically depleted by long marches and short rations, and often rendered desperate by letters from their wives saying, "The children are crying for food—can't you come home?" Altogether, at the beginning of 1864, 60,000 Confederate troops are absent from their units without leave, enough to make a good-sized army.[19]

Rare is the Southern woman who does not have a husband, a son, a brother, or all three in the army. Almost as rare is the woman who has not had a family member or a sweetheart killed, wounded, crippled, or captured. In Newnan, Georgia, seven-year-old Myrtie Long cannot "bear to see my mother and aunts and so many of their friends looking like somber shadows when they had looked like flowers before." Now most of them wear "rusty black," no jewelry, no laces. Gone, too, is their "gay conversation": it has given way to "grim silence." No, she cannot bear it, and so seeks consolation outside among the fruit trees, the horses, and the slaves, things she believes will never change.

"Look at this war," a South Carolina officer writes his wife, "it has come to everybody. States, towns, villages, families—all feel it and share in it." If the war has brought prosperity to the North, for the South it is just the opposite. Numerous ships are still getting through the Yankee blockade, but they carry mostly military needs. Civilians are able to obtain only a trickle of the many things imported before the war, such things as woolens, silks, medicine, and—most missed of all—coffee. Union conquests have cut off beef from Texas, pork and wheat from Tennessee, and sugar from Louisiana. Northern invaders have laid waste hundreds of plantations and farms, destroyed scores of villages and towns, and left thousands of people homeless and destitute. Refugees from enemy-occupied areas have swarmed into the lower South, where many of them are living wretchedly in shacks, tents, and even caves. Much of the rail system has been seized or wrecked by the Federals, and what remains is so dilapidated that trains crawl along at an average "speed" of fifteen miles per hour and even then suffer frequent derailments. The only things in abundant supply are tobacco and paper money. The Confederate government has printed $1.2 billion of the latter. Since it cannot back the dollars with gold and silver, it can only promise to redeem them when the war and independence are won. In January 1863 a gold dollar had equaled three Confederate paper dollars; now, after a year of defeats, it is worth twenty of them. Soaring prices are the inevitable consequence. Residents of Richmond pay $200 for a barrel of flour, $20 for a bushel of corn, and three dollars for a pound of bacon—that is, if they can afford it. "How the poor live," muses a government official, "is inconceivable."[20]

At the start of the war—in fact, even before it had begun—Southern leaders had counted on having Great Britain recognize Confederate independence. They believed that "Cotton Is King," that Britain needed the South's cotton in order to keep its textile mills running and to prevent mass unemployment and possible revolution, that the English nobility would sympathize with their fellow aristocrats of the South, and that the British government would welcome the division of the United States, thereby enabling it to counterbalance the arrogant Yankees with a friendly Confederacy. They were mistaken. Britain remained coldly neutral; it found other sources of cotton in Egypt and India; British public opinion strongly opposed aid to the slaveholding American rebels whose representative in London showed his aristocratic breeding by spitting tobacco juice on ladies' skirts; and English statesmen realized that recognition of the Confederacy automatically meant war with the North—this Lincoln had made bluntly clear. Such a conflict would deprive Britain of much-needed Northern grain, expose its merchant fleet to the powerful Federal navy, and bring a Yankee invasion of Canada. London is unwilling to face such consequences unless convinced that the Confederates are going to win. After Gettysburg and Vicksburg it doubts that very much.

The failure to secure British recognition is a greater setback for the Confederacy than any military defeat, for with recognition, victory and independence would be practically assured: recognition would pit the North against the world's strongest naval power; it would lead to the Royal Navy's breaking the blockade of the South; it would open the way for loans from the Bank of England; and it would bring aid from France, whose emperor, Napoleon III, desires an independent Confederacy in order to complete his takeover of Mexico but who fears to fight the United States alone. When Southerners finally realized that Britain was not going to side with them, they had reacted like a lover spurned. Their newspapers denounced "perfidious Albion" for truckling to Lincoln out of greed for Yankee gold; their government ordered James S. Mason, its tobacco-spitting diplomatic agent in London, to leave England; and on December 7, 1863, Jefferson Davis informed the Confederate Congress that "the only reliable hope for peace is in the vigor of our own resistance." In other words, the South must fight for and win independence on its own—neither the British nor any other foreigners are going to help.[21]

Not all Southerners, however, want independence. They are the Unionists, people who have remained loyal to the "old flag" and who oppose secession. These "tories" not only pervade the mountains of East Tennessee but are numerous in the back country of the Carolinas, in the piny hills of Alabama and Mississippi, in the Ozarks of Arkansas, and in the interiors of Florida and Texas. Most of them are non-slave-owning farmers who regard the rebellion as a conspiracy by and for the big planters. They have formed armed bands, some quite large, who defy Confederate authority and terrorize Confederate adherents. Also they have organized the Heroes of America and other secret societies that supply information to the Federal forces, aid Northern prisoners of war to escape, and induce Confederate soldiers to desert. Thousands of these "tories," mainly from East Tennessee, serve in the Union army.

Other Southerners simply have lost the will to go on with the war. Either they consider it lost, or else they think it is not worth the cost—the dead, the wounded, the depredations, the privations, the sheer misery. They are found everywhere, more or less, but are most numerous in the same regions where Unionists abound. Generally they had had little or no enthusiasm for secession back in 1861; now they favor peace through a "reconstruction" of the Union. Their most prominent and influential spokesman is William W. Holden, editor of the *Raleigh* (N.C.) *Standard*. As 1864 begins, he plans to run for governor on a platform calling for a "convention of the people," which, although he denies it, can have no other purpose than to take North Carolina out of the Confederacy and back into the Union. Should he be elected—and he is confident he will be—the Confederate government would be faced with a disastrous prospect: despite its numerous Unionists and defeatists, North Carolina provides more troops and supplies than does any other Southern state, its seaport at Wilmington is the main haven of blockade runners, and its secession—a right implicitly recognized by the Confederate constitution—from the Confederacy would force Lee's army to abandon Virginia, if not to surrender, and would probably cause other Southern states to defect also. When on January 4 Mary Chesnut hears in Richmond of a rumor (which turns out to be false) that North Carolina's present governor already has offered the Federals "terms of peace," she shivers, "as one does when the first handful of earth comes rattling down on the coffin in the grave of the one you cared for more than all."[22]

This, then, is the South at the outset of 1864: armies battered, driven back, and riddled with desertion; vital territory and communication lines lost; diplomatic fiasco and economic shambles; thousands of ragged, hungry, homeless people; discouragement, dissension, and disaffection; a hideous, ever-mounting toll of dead young soldiers, the flower of its manhood; and facing an implacable enemy far superior in numbers and resources. Is the South, therefore, doomed to defeat?

No. The Confederacy still has strengths; it still has assets; it still has reason to hope for victory. Thus its huge territorial losses, in particular along the Mississippi, are in one way actually advantageous: no longer having such large areas to defend, the Confederate armies need not spread themselves so thin but instead can concentrate on holding a few vital points. On the other hand, not even counting the economically and strategically isolated Trans-Mississippi, the Confederacy retains control of an immense domain, far greater in size than any European nation other than semi-Asiatic Russia: the better parts of Virginia, the Carolinas, and Florida, nearly all of Georgia and Alabama, and the interior of Mississippi. As the Northern armies seek to penetrate this Southern heartland, their already long and exposed supply lines will become even longer and more exposed. It is a significant fact that throughout the entire war the Federals have secured deep lodgments in the South only where their navy has been able to provide logistical support on such rivers as the Mississippi, the Cumberland, and the Tennessee. Whenever a Union army has attempted to move a long distance inland away from a major navigable river, it has encountered serious difficulties, as witness the Army of the Cumberland, which in 1863 spent six months at Murfreesboro, Tennessee, before accumulating enough supplies and transport to advance one hundred miles to Chattanooga, where it then was partially trapped, nearly starved, and had to be rescued! There is no reason to think that the Federals will not continue to find it hard to mount and sustain large-scale overland campaigns, especially in the West, where they now are almost totally dependent on a few ramshackle and vulnerable railroads.

Furthermore, in spite of their terrible defeats and heavy casualties, the Confederate armies remain very formidable. They consist mainly of battle-hardened veterans who are not about to quit fighting (numerous as they are, deserters still constitute a small minority). In fact, reversing the customary situation, Southern front-line soldiers frequently write letters urging the folks back home to stand firm and not become discouraged! To be sure, they are short of food, clothing, shoes, and many other things; but they have plenty of rifles, cannons, and ammunition. Much of their equipment, it should be added, comes from the Confederacy's own factories. When the war had begun, the South had had only the Federal arsenal at Harpers Ferry, Virginia, for making rifles in quantity, and its only large foundry had been the Tredegar Iron Works at Richmond. It had had not a single powder mill or chemical plant and no machinery for the mass production of artillery, cartridges, pistols, swords, uniforms, and shoes. Now, thanks to the endeavors of Pennsylvania-born Josiah Gorgas, head of the Ordinance Bureau, and the "Yankee ingenuity" of a lot of Southern natives, the Confederacy is self-sufficient in all basic military matériel. So long as its supply line stays open and operates with reasonable efficiency, no Confederate army is in danger of losing a battle because of insufficient guns and bullets.[23]

The Confederacy also has Lee. For two years he and his hard-hitting Army of Northern Virginia, although usually outnumbered two to one, have kept at bay the North's biggest and best-supplied army. Even after suffering the awful losses of Gettysburg and sending two of his best divisions under Longstreet to the West, Lee has been able to turn back the half-hearted offensives of the Army of the Potomac. He intimidates the enemy forces, who almost expect to be defeated by him whenever they venture too far into Virginia, and he inspires courage in his own people, who regard him as a veritable demigod. Twice—in the Antietam Campaign and in the Gettysburg Campaign—he has brought the South to the verge of winning the war with his boldness and skill, only to be frustrated by bad luck. It is possible he can do it again—and have better luck.

Last but most important, the vast majority of Southerners—Unionists and Holdenites notwithstanding—still are willing to go on sacrificing, suffering, and struggling for The Cause. They are a proud, some say arrogant, people to whom the idea of losing to the Yankees, whom they consider an inferior breed, simply is intolerable. They are deeply religious and cannot believe that a just God will let them go down to defeat at the hands of the Northern hypocrites and freethinkers. Southerners are bitter over the death and maiming of so many of their young men and over the devastation and grief that the blue-clad invaders have inflicted. Southerners want revenge and are resolved to make the enemy pay a stiff price. And they are afraid of what will happen if Lincoln's legions prevail. A Rebel soldier in a letter published in the *Atlanta Intelligencer* on January 1, 1864, writes:

From the North and West a cloud is slowly gathering, and although it now seems a mere speck in the horizon . . . it shows signs of increasing proportions. A few short months and the whole South will be enveloped with a black cloud of war, whose darkness will eclipse the gloom which has hitherto covered our country. Five hundred thousand armed men, filled with a desire to achieve our subjugation, will be hurled upon the gallant men who are now struggling for independence.—Should we not be prepared to meet this gathering storm, God help us and our country! Slavery, degradation, beggary, and lost honor will be our lot!

What this soldier means by "subjugation," "degradation," and "beggary" is defined by another Confederate, Lieutenant William L. Nugent of Mississippi, who shortly after the fall of Vicksburg writes his wife Nellie: "What good will it do us if we submit? Our land will be a howling waste, wherever it has been invaded & we shall be forced to abandon it to the *freed negroes* & the wild beasts. . . . I am willing to continue to fight to the last."[24]

But in the final analysis, the Confederacy's best chance of survival lies outside of itself: it is the psychological and political vulnerability of the North. If between January and November of 1864 the Confederate armies can inflict intolerably heavy casualties on the Yankees and not suffer too many themselves, if they can successfully defend the South's essential production areas and communication lines by driving back or stalemating the invaders, if they can, in sum, manage to hold out long enough and well enough, then, as we have seen, there is a good possibility that the majority of Northerners will decide that going on with the war is not worth the financial and human cost and so will replace Lincoln and the Republicans with a Democratic president and Congress committed to stopping hostilities and instituting peace negotiations, an outcome that almost surely would lead to Confederate independence.

Southerners are aware of this possibility. It gives them hope—their greatest, sometimes their only, hope. Writing to his wife Sarah on January 9, Private Edwin H. Fay, serving with Confederate forces in Mississippi, states: "We may be able to hold out Twelve months longer but I don't think the Yanks can with the pressure on them. The Presidential campaign is already beginning to open in them."[25] Likewise the editor of the *Augusta* (Ga.) *Constitutionalist* declares on January 22:

> Every bullet we can send against the Yankees is the best ballot that can be deposited against Lincoln's election. The battlefields of 1864 will hold the polls of this momentous decision. If the tyrant at Washington be defeated, his infamous policy will be defeated with him, and when his party sinks no other war party will rise in the United States.

And also on January 22 a resolution of the Confederate Congress itself urges the people to make a supreme effort in the coming year, because

> A large number [of Northerners] revolt from the unjust war waged upon the South and would gladly bring it to an end. . . . Brave and learned men in the North have spoken out against the usurpations and cruelties daily practiced [by Lincoln's administration]. The success of these men over the radical and despotic faction which now rules the North may open the way to peaceful negotiations and a cessation of this bloody and unnecessary war.[26]

In plain words, Southerners are counting on the Northern Democrats to bring about peace and Confederate independence. And Southerners believe that they can make this happen by denying military victory to the North in 1864. Whether or not they are right is what this year will decide.

No one is more determined to outlast the North than is Jefferson Davis. Whatever else he is or is not, he is a fighter. When commanding the First Mississippi Rifles during the Mexican War, he had offered to take an enemy stronghold with fifty men armed only with knives. The same pugnacious spirit animates him now. He knows the terrible odds against the South. He has known them from the first and so, unlike too many other Southern politicians, has expected a long, hard, and costly struggle. But he has never doubted, and he does not doubt now, that the South can win the war so long as it does not lose its will to win. For this reason he is prepared to keep on fighting until the Confederacy is either victorious or totally crushed. As far as he is concerned, there are no other choices.

To enable the South to withstand the North in 1864, Davis already has done three things of major importance. The first is to attempt to curtail the rampant monetary inflation that is both the consequence and a cause of declining confidence in the Confederacy by having the Congress enact laws to restructure the currency and impose taxes on all types of property at rates ranging from five to twenty-five percent. The South, where most people before the war had paid no taxes of any kind, soon will experience the most drastic fiscal measures of any civilized country during the nineteenth century.

The second step that Davis has taken to prepare for the showdown in 1864 is to increase the size of the army. In the spring of 1863 it numbered 360,000 men available for combat. After Gettysburg, Vicksburg, Chickamauga, Missionary Ridge, and scores of lesser engagements, it assembled fewer than 250,000 effectives. Therefore, at Davis's behest, Congress is in the process of passing legislation that retains in the army for the duration of the war all soldiers presently serving; makes, with few exceptions, all males between eighteen and forty-five eligible for the draft; and assigns youths of seventeen and elders between forty-five and fifty to local defense reserves. By these measures the Confederacy will achieve, at least on paper, a degree of manpower mobilization that also is unequaled in the nineteenth century by any nonprimitive nation. John B. Jones, chief clerk of the War Department in Richmond, hopes that these new laws will enable the South to "put 400,000 effective men in the field; and these, well handled, might resist a million of assailants from without."[27]

The third thing that Davis has done to make ready for 1864 is to appoint a new commander for the Army of Tennessee. It is his most important act of all. The Army of Tennessee is the Confederacy's main military force in the West, and its chronic lack of success is the main reason why the South is in such a desperate plight. Its defeats at Fort Donelson and Shiloh in early 1862 opened up the interior to Northern invasion. The failure of its counteroffensive into Kentucky in the fall of 1862 and of its attempt to smash the Union Army of the Cumberland at Murfreesboro at the close of that year had enabled the Federals to secure their hold on Tennessee. Its passiveness throughout the first half of 1863 had contributed greatly to the loss of Vicksburg. And its barren, blood-drenched "victory" at Chickamauga and its humiliating debacle on Missionary Ridge had left the enemy forces poised on the boundaries of Georgia and Alabama. In short, the Army of Tennessee is to the South what the Army of the Potomac is to the North, except that the former has no Antietam or Gettysburg to its credit and the South can less afford its failures than the North can afford the Army of the Potomac's recurrent frustrations.

It is not that the Army of Tennessee does not fight hard: it has some of the toughest, bravest, best-drilled troops in the Confederacy, troops whose ferocity and determination in battle are unsurpassed. Rather, this army has never had outstanding leadership at the top. As a Virginian who has served with both armies observes, it "differs from the Army of Virginia, in that the one has Gen'l Lee and the other—hasn't."[28] Its first commander, Albert Sidney Johnston, had been noble and gallant but indecisive and (the worse defect in any general according to Napoleon) unlucky; at Shiloh he had bled to death from a minor wound. Pierre Gustave Toutant Beauregard, the dashing Creole from Louisiana, then had taken over and had done well, saving the army from destruction at Corinth, Mississippi, by making a clever retreat. However he could not get along with Davis, who for his part preferred to get along without him. When Beauregard, for reasons of health, had absented himself from the army without prior permission, Davis had gladly seized the occasion to supersede him with Braxton Bragg, with whom he had served in the Mexican War. Bragg had proved good at making plans but bad at executing them. As a result he had lost battles and the confidence of most of his generals, who after both Murfreesboro and Chickamauga had pleaded for his removal. Davis had listened to them and sympathized, yet had kept Bragg because he knew of no replacement whom he trusted to do better. The disgrace of Missionary Ridge left Bragg no choice except to resign, which he did on November 29, 1863. Lieutenant General William J. Hardee, the senior corps commander, had become the army's acting commander.

Davis had offered to retain Hardee on a regular basis. A West Pointer, veteran of the Mexican War, author of *Hardee's Tactics* (the standard drill book for both North and South), and a corps commander in all of the Army of Tennessee's major battles except Chickamauga, the tall sinewy forty-eight-year-old Georgian seemed a most appropriate choice. However, to Davis's surprise and dismay, Hardee had declined the offer on the grounds that he felt "unable to serve the country successfully in this new sphere of activity"—ambiguous words but implying that he preferred to avoid such a great responsibility.[29]

Not only had Hardee's refusal surprised and dismayed Davis; it had also annoyed him. It meant that he had to select a commander from among the only other three generals who were qualified by rank and experience for so crucial a post: Lee, Beauregard, and Joseph E. Johnston. Lee, obviously, would be ideal; however, just as obviously, no one could take his place as head of the Army of Northern Virginia. As for Beauregard, to appoint him would be the same as admitting that it had been a mistake to remove him in 1862; Davis refused to make such an admission, especially since he did not think that it was a mistake.

That left Johnston.

Davis despises Johnston; Johnston loathes Davis. Johnston believes that Davis has denied him due rank and command; Davis considers Johnston vain and selfish. Davis regards Johnston as lacking in offensive spirit and as overwilling to retreat; Johnston thinks Davis is unrealistic in his military expectations. Johnston is reluctant to commit himself to a specific plan or to communicate his intentions to the government; Davis resents what he deems to be Johnston's excessive secretiveness and insufficient deference. Davis blames Johnston for the loss of Vicksburg, contending that Johnston had made no serious effort to relieve its beleaguered garrison; Johnston holds that Davis himself is responsible for that disaster and accuses Davis of trying to make him the scapegoat. Davis is aware that Johnston and his wife are close friends of Senator Louis T. Wigfall of Texas, a bellicose alcoholic who is one of Davis's loudest-mouthed critics; the Johnstons look down their aristocratic noses at the "western" Davises from Mississippi. Johnston had not adhered to the Confederacy until his native Virginia had seceded following Fort Sumter, and he had resigned his United States army commission with tears in his eyes, declaring that he hoped that he never would have to draw his sword against the old flag; Davis feels that the establishment of Southern independence is a sacred cause for which he willingly would lay down his life. Johnston privately doubts that the Confederacy can win the war; Davis permits no such doubts to enter his mind, and he has nothing but contempt for those whom he suspects of harboring them. Finally, both the president and the general are proud, touchy men, utterly convinced of their own righteousness and rightness.[30]

Joseph E. Johnston (*Photographic History,* 10:241)

Naming Johnston commander of the Army of Tennessee was wormwood and gall to Davis. If he could have avoided doing it, he would have. But, as we have seen, he found himself with no other choice. In addition, numerous newspapers and congressmen clamored for Johnston's appointment, Secretary of War James A. Seddon urged it, and, most influential of all, so did Lee, who either ignored, or was ignorant of, the fact that Johnston, a West Point classmate, was jealous of Lee's success and fame. Therefore, on December 16, 1863, Davis had telegraphed Johnston to turn over the Army of Mississippi, which he has headed since spring, to Lieutenant General Leonidas Polk and proceed to Dalton, Georgia, to assume command of the Army of Tennessee.

One week later, Davis had written Johnston a letter stating what he wanted him to do with the Army of Tennessee: attack and defeat the Union forces at Chattanooga. "Vigorous action" was necessary to regain Tennessee, a region vital to the war effort. Happily it also appeared to be practicable. According to reports received in Richmond, the Army of Tennessee's loss at Missionary Ridge was "not great." With the addition of a couple of brigades from Mississippi, stragglers and convalescents, and the cavalry sent with Longstreet to East Tennessee, it "would furnish a force perhaps exceeding in numbers" that engaged in that battle. Moreover the same reports state that the army had adequate artillery and ample ammunition, enough wagons and horses, was "tolerably provided" with clothing, shoes, and blankets, and had thirty days' rations on hand. Just as importantly, its morale was high: Hardee had telegraphed on December 11 that "the army is in good spirits . . . and we are ready to fight." Hence Davis hoped that Johnston would "soon be able to commence active operations against the enemy."[31]

Johnston, who had arrived at Dalton on December 27 and assumed his new command the next day, finds little resemblance between the Army of Tennessee described in Davis's letter and the Army of Tennessee he sees camped nearby. It has few more than 40,000 soldiers "present for duty," of which only about two-thirds are "effectives" capable of combat. Many of these men are without overcoats, blankets, or shoes; in one division, two entire brigades are barefoot and cannot march at all. Thousands of the troops spend the entire day clustered around bonfires trying to keep warm. Rations are scanty, irregular, and poor; scurvy is common. Hungry soldiers steal food from the local farmers and plunder supply trains and quartermaster depots; officers and sentinels make no attempt to stop them for fear of being killed. There are not enough horses to pull all the cannons or enough mules to haul the wagons. The cavalry units that are not in Tennessee with Longstreet likewise are short of horses and woefully understrength. With few exceptions the infantry's discipline is bad. Some regiments do not even conduct roll calls, drills, or inspections; and their men come and go as they please. Although casualties at Missionary Ridge indeed had been light (a mere 2,500 killed, wounded, and missing), this merely makes that defeat all the more humiliating and demoralizing. Moreover it occurred after the loss of 18,000 men in the wasted, useless "victory" at Chickamauga. Little wonder, then, that there is much despondency, even despair, in the ranks. "Our army up here," writes Benjamin Glover of Finley's Florida Brigade to his wife, "is very tired of the war, the fact is they will never fight as they have done. They now think we are whipped and they are running away as fast as they can." On average, thirty men a day are deserting to the Federals, men who, in the words of an Alabama soldier, feel that "there is no use to fite them anymore."[32]

Is Davis simply ill informed about the condition of the Army of Tennessee? Or—a dark thought crosses Johnston's mind—was his friend Senator Wigfall right when he warned him in a recent letter that "every effort would be made [by Davis] to produce your defeat"? Certainly attempting a winter invasion of Tennessee with his present force could have no other outcome. In any case, all he can do is set the president straight about the Army of Tennessee and its capabilities. Writing to Davis on January 2, Johnston states that he agrees that it is important to recover the territory lost in Tennessee; but "difficulties are in the way." The Army of Tennessee is outnumbered two to one by the enemy at Chattanooga and in northern Alabama, its artillery is wretched, and its cavalry is weak and inefficient. The Army of Tennessee does not have enough supplies for a long campaign, and even if it did have, there are insufficient wagons and horses to carry them. In sum, the army lacks the strength and the means to invade Tennessee with reasonable prospects of success. Hence, "I can see no other mode of taking the offensive here than to beat the enemy when he advances, and then to move forward."

Johnston's reply perplexes Davis. When he had written to Johnston urging an early offensive, Davis had had before him a dispatch from Bragg (his resignation, to be precise) declaring that in spite of the defeat at Missionary Ridge, the Army of Tennessee was "still full of zeal and burning to redeem its lost character"; a report from Colonel Joseph C. Ives, a presidential aide who had visited Dalton, stating that the forces there were battleworthy and well supplied; and Hardee's December 11 telegram, which Davis had quoted to Johnston, asserting that "the Army of Tennessee is in good spirits" and "ready to fight." Now here is Johnston with a completely different picture of that army. Also, to make the matter more puzzling still, Hardee has sent the War Department a letter dated December 17 which in effect contradicts his December 11 telegram: "To enable this army to take the field, re-enforcements are necessary," and "in our present condition it is necessary to avoid a general action; and should the enemy . . . advance, a retrograde movement becomes inevitable." What, wonders Davis, is the truth about the Army of Tennessee?

In an attempt to find out, he directs Secretary of War Seddon to obtain from Johnston a more detailed account of its condition, which Johnston provides. It merely repeats in essence what he already has said. Davis remains unconvinced. Eager, almost desperate, to drive back the Federals in the West, he finds it difficult to accept the harsh facts about the Army of Tennessee. Also he suspects Johnston of doing what he has done so frequently throughout the war—inventing excuses for not attacking, for holding back, for falling back. Yet Davis knows from past experience that endeavoring to change Johnston's mind with arguments will merely lead to another quarrel and that a peremptory order to launch an offensive regardless of his objections would cause the general to submit his resignation, thereby creating a military-political crisis. So Davis decides not to write Johnston at all and in effect to let him have his way—for the time being.[33]

"Boys, this is Old Joe!" That is how hard-fighting and hard-drinking Major General Benjamin Franklin Cheatham introduces Johnston to the Tennesseans of his division at Dalton. They see a short, trim man of fifty-seven with gray sideburns, mustache, and imperial. His uniform is impeccable, he wears all the regalia of his high rank, his hat is decorated with a star and feather, and he has a jaunty air which one observer likens to that of a gamecock. As befits a professional soldier, his gray eyes are sharp, and the expression on his ruddy face is stern. All in all he is impressive—"the very picture of a general," in the eyes of one private. Most of the troops welcome Johnston, some with "unbridled enthusiasm," for they think him a great commander who will lead them to victories that will wipe away the stigma of Missionary Ridge. Others, however, are indifferent, even sullen. When Johnston reviews Hindman's Division, which contains large numbers of Alabama conscripts, he does not elicit, according to Captain James A. Hall of the 25th Alabama, "a single cheer in any Brigade except Vaughan's Tennessee Brigade and that a faint one." Hall decides that he will have to teach his men to "love & respect" their new commander.[34]

Johnston spends January inspecting the Army of Tennessee, getting acquainted with its generals, observing its rank and file, learning its strengths and weaknesses, and taking steps to improve its condition. Its greatest immediate need, he quickly perceives, is more and better rations. Most of its food, along with all other supplies, comes by way of the Western and Atlantic Railroad, a single track line that runs north from Atlanta to Dalton, a distance of precisely ninety-six miles. This road, which is owned and operated by the state of Georgia, is not carrying enough provisions to meet even the army's daily requirements, much less to enable it to accumulate a reserve. So on January 12 Johnston telegraphs both Davis and Governor Joseph Brown of Georgia, warning them that unless the operation of the Western and Atlantic improves, he will have to retreat. Davis, knowing that this is no idle threat coming from Johnston, passes the warning on to the War Department with instructions to act quickly, which it does: within a week, additional rolling stock has been assigned to the Western and Atlantic. By January 25 Johnston is able to report that the "daily receipts of provisions and forage from Atlanta are now fully equal to the consumption" and that it will be possible to stockpile a food reserve.

Johnston also moves to restore the Army of Tennessee's badly dilapidated discipline. On January 8 his adjutant general issues a forty-four-paragraph "General Orders, No. 5," which is to be "read at the head of each company at least once a week." Among other things, it stipulates the time for reveille, sick call, meals, drills, dress parade, and taps; it also contains detailed instructions for calling rolls, conducting inspections, mounting guard, and even digging latrines. Although most of its troops have served more than two years, in effect the Army of Tennessee is being given basic training.[35]

Improved rations and tighter discipline do much to raise the army's spirit. But the biggest morale booster is a system of furloughs which Hardee has instituted and Johnston implements. Under it, one out of every thirty enlisted men and one company officer out of every three (if there are that many) are allowed a thirty-day leave of absence, with the "lucky ones" to be chosen by lot. For the first time in the war, sizable numbers of the soldiers of the Army of Tennessee are able to visit their families and friends back home. That is, if they have a home they can go to. All of the Kentuckians and Missourians and many of the Tennesseans and Arkansans come from regions under Union control, as do some of the Alabamans and Mississippians. In addition the Arkansans, Texans, Louisianans, and Missourians have vast distances and the Mississippi River to cross. Nevertheless a few men from such areas manage to visit their families; one of them is Captain Thomas Key, an artillery officer and prewar newspaper editor from Helena, Arkansas, whose journey, vividly described in his journal, is filled with more hardships, perils, and narrow escapes than most soldiers experience during a campaign. Others, instead of trying to make it home through enemy-held country, do like Lieutenant Edwin H. Rennolds of the 5th Tennessee, who visits relatives elsewhere in the South, in his case Virginia. Wherever they go, the vast majority of the furloughed troops return in due course to their units, bringing with them food and news from home to share with less-fortunate comrades, fresh clothing, and revived spirits. Some, needless to say, leave behind future mementos of their furlough. Two months after being with his wife, Julia, in Atlanta, where she is living as a refugee, Lieutenant John W. Davidson of the 29th North Carolina receives a letter from her: "You know Johnny I was expecting a *friend* of mine when you left. *She did not come* as I hoped she would, & oh how I grieved to think she had disappointed me. . . . I thought to myself that I had paid dear for the pleasure of your society for a few weeks."[36]

Feeding, clothing, disciplining, and improving morale, even trying to persuade an obstinate president of the folly of attempting an offensive with inadequate means, are the sort of problems a military commander can expect. However, Johnston also finds himself confronted with a situation that definitely is out of the ordinary as well as quite dangerous in its potentialities. On January 2, exactly one week after he has taken command, he meets with most of his top generals in the parlor of the William C. Huff house, his headquarters in Dalton. Hardee, who has requested the meeting, announces that Major General Patrick Cleburne wishes to present a proposal of great interest both to the army and to the Confederacy. Cleburne—thirty-five, close to six feet tall, lean of build, with

Patrick Cleburne (John Berrien Lindsley, ed., *The Military Annals of Tennessee* [Nashville:1886], 153)

prematurely gray hair, cold gray eyes, and the face of a hungry cat—reads from a twenty-five-page memorandum. The government's plan, he states, to raise additional troops by broadening age limits and narrowing exemptions will not suffice. The only way the South can obtain the manpower needed to achieve victory is to take hundreds of thousands of slaves into the army. If promised freedom for themselves and their families, blacks will make good soldiers. To be sure, arming and freeing them will be a revolutionary step. Yet unless it is done, in all likelihood the Confederacy will be defeated and subjugated. "As between the loss of independence and the loss of slavery, we assume that every patriot will freely give up the latter—give up the Negro slave rather than be a slave himself."

Cleburne's words carry weight. He is not an ordinary man or a run-of-the-mill general. Born in County Cork, Ireland, he had served three years as a common soldier in the British army. In 1849 he had migrated to America, bringing with him an ancestor's Damascus sword and a pair of boxing gloves. Settling in the Mississippi River town of Helena, Arkansas, he had first worked as a pharmacist, then had become a well-to-do lawyer and land speculator. But war is his true calling. After it broke out in 1861, he had risen rapidly from captain of a Helena volunteer company to major general in command of an infantry division. In the words of his friend and patron, Hardee, "he unites the rare qualities of a strict disciplinarian, a brave and skillful leader and popular commander." His division, which consists mostly of Arkansas and Texas troops, is the best one in the Army of Tennessee and the only Confederate division whose regiments are authorized to carry their own unique battle flags—blue banners with a white circle or "moon" in the center. Just recently the Confederate Congress has passed a special resolution commending the division for having covered the retreat of the rest of the Army of Tennessee from Missionary Ridge.

When he finishes reading the memorandum, Cleburne names fourteen generals and colonels who have endorsed it, among them Major General Benjamin F. Cheatham of Tennessee. Hardee declares that he also supports Cleburne's proposal, as does Major General Thomas C. Hindman, an acting corps commander and, like Cleburne, a prewar lawyer in Helena, where they had adjoining offices and were close friends. On the other hand, Generals W. H. T. Walker, Patton Anderson, and William Bate—all division commanders—denounce it; they consider it, in Anderson's words, "revolting to Southern sentiment, Southern pride, and Southern honor." Johnston likewise disapproves, although he does not say so. Instead, to Cleburne's disappointment, he refuses to put it to a vote or to transmit the memorandum to the War Department. It relates, he warns, more to political than to military issues, and he advises everyone present to keep quiet about it. They agree to do so.

But Major General W. H. T. (William Henry Talbot) Walker will not let the matter drop. A hot-tempered Georgia aristocrat and West Pointer whose multiple wounds in the Seminole and Mexican wars gained him the nickname of "Shot-Pouch," he deems Cleburne's proposal almost treasonable (he also resents the fact that Cleburne, the Irish immigrant and backwoods lawyer, is senior to him in rank and far superior in reputation). After the meeting, Walker asks Cleburne for a copy of the memorandum. Cleburne, figuring that this might be a way to get his views before the government after all, gives him one. On January 12, Walker mails it directly to President Davis, since Johnston has refused him permission to send it to the War Department. In an accompanying letter, Walker charges that Cleburne's "propositions would ruin the efficacy of our army and involve our cause in ruin and disgrace."

Davis reads the memorandum. As such it does not perturb him. For a long time he has believed—very much in private—that slavery is destined to disappear, and he is quite willing to end it if that would help save the Confederacy. But he realizes that a great many Southerners, perhaps the majority, share Walker's attitude and that the revelation of Cleburne's proposal would touch off a furor that would be damaging to the war effort. Hence, via Secretary of War Seddon, Davis instructs Johnston to order his generals not to publicize the memorandum or to discuss it further: under the "present circumstances of the Confederacy" this would be "productive only of discouragement, distraction, and dissension." On January 31 Johnston sends a circular to his generals so instructing them. Cleburne promptly destroys all but one copy of his memorandum and promises that he will "cease to advocate the measures mentioned."[37]

As January draws to a close, the Army of the Tennessee is on the mend; Johnston informs Davis on the twenty-third that he has never seen "as healthy a body of troops" and that "their officers think them in excellent temper for battle." Nevertheless it still is far from being ready for any extended offensive operation. The shoes of the infantry are wearing out faster than they can be replaced, with the result that whole brigades are incapable of marching; the artillery horses remain so feeble from insufficient forage that it would be impossible to maneuver the cannons in case of battle; and most of the cavalry lingers with Longstreet in Tennessee. Moreover, Johnston has come to the conclusion that once he is able to take the offensive, he should do so by way of West Tennessee rather than Chattanooga. In a January 15 letter to Davis he declares that the enemy forces around Chattanooga are too strong to be assailed with a reasonable prospect of success and that therefore it would be better to shift his army, when it is in condition to move, to northern Mississippi from where, after being reinforced by Polk's Army of Mississippi, he could invade West Tennessee, an area that offers easier marching and more plentiful supplies than does rugged, barren East Tennessee. Should the Federals presently concentrated around Chattanooga try to take advantage of his departure from North Georgia by advancing on Atlanta, a force of 3,000 cavalry could delay them until they were obliged to retreat in order to safeguard their communication lines and Nashville against his army. [38]

Davis's response to this new plan has been the same as it was to Johnston's defensive-offensive proposal of January 2: silence. He will not, in view of what Johnston reports about the deficiencies of the Army of Tennessee and despite the fact that he continues to doubt the truth of those reports, order an immediate offensive against the enemy at Chattanooga. On the other hand, he will neither concede that such an offensive is impracticable nor agree to either of the plans that Johnston has presented as an alternative—the main Union army in the West is at Chattanooga, and it is *that* army and *there* that Johnston must strike if the South is to hold on and hold out in 1864. Thus January ends with Davis and Johnston locked in disagreement over strategy, the inevitable consequence of which is that the Confederacy's de facto strategy in the West will be one of merely reacting as best it can to Federal moves.

And in Mississippi, the Federals are about to move.

CHAPTER TWO

FEBRUARY

Part One: Sherman

ON FEBRUARY 3, Major General William Tecumseh Sherman rides out from Vicksburg. Accompanying him are four divisions of infantry, a brigade of cavalry, and nine batteries of artillery—altogether 26,000 soldiers. They march in two columns by parallel roads, cavalry to the fore. Their objective is Meridian, Mississippi, 150 miles to the east. Once there, they might go farther; it all depends.

"Have you seen Sherman?" asks Walt Whitman after the war. "Try to picture Sherman—seamy, sinewy, in style—a bit of stern open air made up in the image of a man."[1] That is what the poet sees when Sherman has become a Great Man. But he is not that yet, not in February 1864, and the officers who ride beside him and the soldiers who glance up at him as they tramp along the Mississippi roads merely see a thin man about six feet tall wearing a black slouch hat and a shabby blue uniform coat and puffing a cigar. His cheeks and brow are furrowed with wrinkles, making him look older than the forty-four which he will be in a few more days; he has a long narrow nose, his mouth is wide, and his reddish beard is short, being scarcely more than a stubble. The eyes are blue (some say gray), and although they are "kindly as a rule," they also can be "cold and hard as steel sometimes." He speaks rapidly and almost incessantly, in a sharp, rather sarcastic tone, emphasizing his words with quick flicks of the hands. He possesses, and in a sense is possessed by, immense nervous energy. It feeds his body and a mind that never ceases churning away, except possibly when he sleeps, which is not much—a few hours at night, supplemented by an occasional quick nap in the afternoon. He is a man who must keep moving, like wind in the stern open air which Whitman says is his essence. All of his life and all through the war, Sherman has been on the move; he is on the move now; and during the next eleven months he will do a great deal more moving.

Sherman commands, as he has since October, the Army of the Tennessee, which should not be confused with the Confederate Army *of* Tennessee: the Southerners, as a rule, name their armies after states or parts thereof; the Northerners prefer rivers. The Army of the Tennessee was Grant's army; its

William Tecumseh Sherman (*Photographic History,* 10:79)

regimental banners are inscribed with Fort Donelson, Pittsburg Landing, Corinth, Champion's Hill, and Vicksburg. Undisputably it is the most successful Union army, and its men also think it undisputably the best, at least when it comes to what counts most—fighting. For Sherman to command it is an honor and a distinction, particularly if one considers that a scant two years ago he was a general in disgrace, his military career a shambles.

Early in the autumn of 1861, Sherman, freshly promoted to brigadier general after a fine performance (one of few on the Northern side) at Bull Run, found himself in charge of Union forces in Kentucky. At that time Kentucky was second only to Virginia in political-strategic importance; as Lincoln observed, losing Kentucky would mean losing the war. Sherman had not wanted such a tremendous responsibility and had tried hard to avoid it. When, nevertheless, he got it, he had cracked under the strain. He imagined that he was about to be crushed by an overwhelmingly superior Confederate army, whereas in fact he heavily outnumbered the enemy, who had not the slightest intention of attacking. His frantic pleas for impossible numbers of reinforcements and his dire predictions of total disaster if he did not get them caused the War Department in November 1861 to replace him with Don Carlos Buell. Transferred to Missouri to serve under General Henry Wager Halleck, then head of Union forces west of the Mississippi, Sherman promptly panicked again, urging retreat even though the Confederates were not advancing. Halleck had to relieve him, informing Washington that "I am satisfied that General Sherman's physical and mental system is so completely broken by labor and care as to render him for the present entirely unfit for duty." Sherman's wife, Ellen, hastened to St. Louis and took him back to their home in Lancaster, Ohio, to rest. The *Cincinnati Commercial* published a story, copied widely by other newspapers, under the headline "General William T. Sherman Insane." Aware that he had disgraced himself, Sherman contemplated suicide and refrained from committing it only out of consideration for his children. When Sherman returned to St. Louis at the beginning of 1862, Halleck assigned him to drilling recruits—a sort of sergeant with a star. "I do not think," he wrote his brother, Senator John Sherman, "I can again be entrusted with a command."

Sherman, when the war began, had lacked war experience. Unlike most of the other top Northern and Southern generals, he had not served in Mexico and had not so much as seen a battle until Bull Run. He also lacked self-confidence; indeed, he was in 1861 a man oppressed by a sense of failure and inadequacy. Thirteen years after graduating from West Point in 1840, he was still only a captain in the commissary department, with no foreseeable prospect of promotion. Resigning from the army, he had tried his hand at banking in California and speculation in Kansas, but had failed at both. "I look upon myself," he wrote his wife from Kansas, "as a dead cock in the pit." For awhile it seemed as if he might have to take a job running the Ohio salt mill of his foster father and father-in-law, former Senator Thomas Ewing, Sr. (which would have put him in a situation similar to that of Grant, who after leaving the army, ended up working in a store owned by his father). However, thanks to several army friends (among them Bragg and Beauregard), in 1859 Sherman had become superintendent of a newly established military academy in Louisiana. At this he was successful—until Louisiana seceded, whereupon he resigned and returned North, again a failure and, in his own words, a vagabond. On April 12, 1861, as the Confederates bombarded Fort Sumter, he was a $40-a-month president of a streetcar company in St. Louis. Meanwhile his younger brother John, considered by everyone in the Sherman-Ewing clan definitely as William's inferior in intellect and personality, had become a nationally famous politician and a powerful Republican senator. It was due as much to John's Washington contacts as to anything else that Sherman, after the war got under way, secured a colonel's commission, then promotion to brigadier general in the Union army.

Along with his lack of war experience and self-confidence, Sherman in 1861 suffered from an excess: too much imagination, the concomitant of his brilliant but erratic intellect, which reminded a fellow general of "a splendid piece of machinery with all of the screws a little loose." In Kentucky and Missouri those screws nearly popped out altogether. Unable to secure reliable information about the Confederates' strength and intentions, he imagined them to be far stronger and more aggressive than they possibly could be, with the result that he became a prey to fear, in complete contrast to how he had acted when in the physical presence of the enemy on the battlefield at Bull Run.

What Sherman needed was someone to guide and steady him, to bear the burden of command responsibility while he learned about war, learned to trust himself, and learned to control his mind. Fortunately for him and fortunately for the North, he got what he needed. Late in Feburary 1862, Halleck, who in spite of everything retained faith in Sherman's competence, assigned him to lead a division in the army of a general who right from the start realized that the enemy is as scared of you as you are of him and that the secret of success in war is to go ahead with your plans without worrying overmuch about what the other side might do. This general, of course, was Grant, who had just won the North's first major victory by capturing Fort Donelson and the Confederate army defending it.

During the next twenty-two months, Sherman served, except for a few brief intervals, under Grant. On the surface, Sherman's performance was not spectacular; in fact, on some counts it could be called poor. At Pittsburg Landing he was surprised by the Confederate onslaught, and his division was practically destroyed. His attempt, on Grant's orders, to seize the outer defenses of Vicksburg at Chickasaw Bluffs on December 26, 1862, ended in a bloody repulse. He participated in none of the major battles that led to Grant's investment of Vicksburg in May 1863, and Sherman's corps suffered heavy losses in a vain attempt to storm the fortress city. And at Missionary Ridge his assault on the Confederate right wing, which Grant intended to be the decisive stroke, was stopped cold by Cleburne's Division.

But if Sherman did not win, as such, any battles, he won the confidence and friendship of Grant. The quiet, inward-looking Grant was impressed by Sherman's quick, kaleidoscopic mind and effervescent personality, so unlike Grant's own. Grant appreciated Sherman's unhesitating and unquestioning execution of orders; and above all he was grateful to Sherman for standing by him during his own periods of tribulation, in particular after Pittsburg Landing when, despondent over being relegated by Halleck to a meaningless second-in-command, Grant decided to resign from the army only to be talked out of it by Sherman. In sum, Sherman became Grant's first lieutenant, his right-hand man, and apart from his chief of staff, John A. Rawlins, his closest confidant. Sherman does not exaggerate at all when he writes brother John that with Grant "I am as a second self."[2]

Thus the Sherman who rides forth from Vicksburg on February 3 has proved himself to be a good and loyal lieutenant. But is he more than that? Is he now capable of successfully planning and directing a large-scale military operation on his own and of bearing the strain of independent command? In particular, has he learned to control that ever-active brain and its vivid imagination, so that he no longer will worry excessively about what the enemy might be doing on "the other side of the hill"? Concerning the last question, we know this—that Sherman himself is aware of the problem: "I am," he remarked to a staff officer during the siege of Vicksburg, "a much brighter man than Grant, I can see things quicker than he can, and know more about books than he does, but I'll tell you where he beats me, and where he beats the world: he don't care a cent for what he can't see the enemy doing, but it scares me like hell!"[3]

Becoming aware of a defect is the first step towards curing it. Sherman has taken that step. Whether he has taken or is capable of taking the necessary additional steps remains to be seen.

Part Two: Meridian, Okolona, and Dug Gap

Meridian, Mississippi, is a village with a prewar population of only eight hundred.[4] It contains, however, warehouses crammed with Confederate supplies, repair shops, barracks, an arsenal, and a hospital. Sherman wants to burn these things. Also the two railroads that bisect Meridian connect it with Mobile to the south and Selma to the east, both major Confederate supply bases. Sherman intends to tear up as many miles of their tracks as possible. Then, if all goes well and it appears feasible, he might go on to Demopolis, Alabama, another Rebel supply center, or even to Selma, where there are ironworks and munition factories to be destroyed. In any case, once Meridian and its railroads are obliterated, it will be a long time before the Confederates can send large forces either into West Tennessee or to the Mississippi River, and thus a few garrisons will suffice to guard these areas, freeing the bulk of his army for the upcoming offensive southward from Chattanooga. Moreover, as soon as the Meridian operation is completed, he proposes to turn west and move up the Red River to Shreveport, the capture of which will paralyze the enemy in Louisiana. His goal, in short, is to create a strategic cordon sanitaire in the heart of the lower Mississippi Valley.[5]

Sherman also has another purpose in mind when it comes to Meridian. He believes that defeating the Southern armies is not the only or even the best way to win the war. The Southern people also must be defeated; their will and ability to continue fighting must be crushed. "The war which now prevails in our land," Sherman wrote Halleck in September 1863, "is essentially a war of races. . . . The South, though numerically inferior, contend that they are not bound to submit. This issue is the only real one." So Sherman plans to make the expedition to Meridian an experiment in terror. His troops will devastate fields, slaughter livestock, wreck railroads, and demonstrate to the inhabitants of central Mississippi and Alabama that the Richmond government is helpless to protect them and that only by submitting to Federal authority can they have peace, security, and an end to misery. To be sure, such methods are harsh, even cruel. But as he has told a Tennessee woman who complained about the depredations of his troops on the march to Knoxville: "War is cruelty. There is no use trying to reform it, the crueller it is, the sooner it will be over."[6]

Sherman is not the first or the only Northerner to advocate terror. More than a year earlier the soldiers of the Army of the Tennessee had decided, in the words of one of them, that the "kid glove policy" of dealing with the Rebels had failed, but that the Southerners "would not endure to see their property destroyed and their families brought to distress. Desertion would soon disorganize their armies, and leave no more fighting to do." Accordingly, while operating in northern Mississippi during the winter of 1862–63 they had set fire to fences and buildings "all along the line of march, and in some instances almost under the eye of General Grant"; in addition they had deliberately burned down the entire village of Holly Springs because they had heard that its inhabitants, mainly women, had thrown bricks and even fired pistols at Northern prisoners of war. Later, during the Vicksburg campaign, they had burned grist mills, cotton gins, and corn cribs; killed cattle, sheep, hogs, and chickens; pillaged mansions and log cabins alike; and taken food from women and children. Similar scenes marked their trail through East Tennessee to Knoxville, despite the fact that many people in that region were Unionists and had little worth plundering or destroying.[7]

The Northern generals deplored and denounced the depredations of their soldiers; none more so than Sherman, who declared that the Army of the Tennessee "brought shame to itself" and who wrote to Ellen from Mississippi: "I doubt if history affords a parallel to the deep and bitter animosity of the women of the South. Not a man is seen; nothing but women with houses plundered, fields open to cattle and horses, [Union] pickets lounging on every porch, and desolation sown broadcast." Yet orders from Grant and other commanders against pillaging, backed by threats of punishment, proved utterly futile. The troops ignored them, their field officers either were unable or unwilling to enforce them, and the depredations continued. The Union army, like all American armies, is democracy under arms. If the great majority of the soldiers believe something is right and necessary, they will do it, regardless of all the generals and all their orders. Sherman, by advocating what he calls "war, pure and simple: to be applied directly to the civilians of the South," is belatedly recognizing that fact; and by planning a march of devastation to Meridian, he is merely going along with what would happen in any event.[8]

Essentially the Meridian expedition is a raid, to be made mainly with infantry rather than cavalry, but nevertheless a raid. Sheman has a decided penchant for such operations. After Pittsburg Landing he led a task force deep into Mississippi to burn a railroad bridge; while on the way to Chickasaw Bluffs he detached a division to wreck a rail line in Arkansas; and both before and after the capture of Vicksburg he devoted considerable time to tearing up tracks around Jackson, Mississippi. Such sweeps obviously appeal to his restless nature, his need to be constantly, windlike, on the move.

Lieutenant General Leonidas Polk, commanding Rebel forces in Mississippi, Alabama, and East Louisiana, is called the bishop for an excellent reason: he is one. Upon graduating in 1827 from West Point (where he was a friend of Jefferson Davis), he resigned his army commission to enter the Episcopal ministry and in time became bishop of the Diocese of Louisiana. Shortly after the war began in 1861, Davis appointed him a major general. It was a mistake. Although Polk grew a beard that made him look like a general rather than a priest,

Leonidas Polk—bishop and general (*Military Annals of Tennessee,* 92)

he proved at best mediocre, at worst execrable, as a military leader. Put in charge of the defense of the Mississippi, his blunders allowed both it and Kentucky to be opened up to decisive Federal advances. Then, as a corps commander, he mishandled his troops at Shiloh and Murfreesboro, and at Chickamauga his failure to attack on schedule was a major reason why that hard-won Southern victory proved barren. Polk, however, has a talent for posing as a military elder statesman and for shifting the blame for his mistakes to others; his unflinching courage in battle, his imposing presence, and his fatherly solicitude make him popular with the rank and file; his clerical status gives him great prestige with the pious Southern public; and he retains the confidence of Davis, who feels that his old schoolmate's personal qualities more than compensate for any professional deficiencies. Therefore when Bragg demanded that Polk be court-martialed for insubordination during the battle of

Chickamauga, Davis instead transferred him to Joseph Johnston's Army of Mississippi, the command of which Polk inherited when Johnston was assigned to the Army of Tennessee.[9]

Polk has in Mississippi 10,000 infantry stationed at Canton and Brandon, about 6,000 cavalry dispersed in a semicircle east of Vicksburg, and another 4,000 cavalry in the northern part of the state. Obviously the only way he can parry Sherman's 26,000-man thrust toward Meridian is to concentrate his troops rapidly while receiving reinforcements from Johnston and the Confederate garrison at Mobile. Sherman, who is well posted on Polk's strength and dispositions through scouts and a "special private spy," understands this and has planned accordingly. He will march with utmost speed to Meridian, taking along only a minimum wagon train and having his soldiers live as much as possible "off the country," a modus operandi pioneered by Grant during the Vicksburg Campaign. At the same time a joint army-navy force will move up the Yazoo River to threaten the railroad center at Grenada; Rear Admiral David G. Farragut's Gulf Squadron will menace Mobile; Grant will have Thomas demonstrate against Johnston at Dalton; and Brigadier General William Sooy Smith, head of the Federal cavalry in the Military Division of the Mississippi, will march rapidly down from Memphis with 7,000 horsemen and link up with Sherman at Meridian, thereby providing him with the additional strength and mobility needed to go into Alabama, where the people have been duly warned of his "coming."

Sherman's scheme succeeds admirably as regards Polk. Athough the bishop has realized since late Janaury that the Federals were preparing "to move on the western front of his department," he is uncertain about their exact objective or objectives. Consequently his forces, which he considers "inadequate to the emergency" in any case, remain scattered. This in turn enables Sherman's twin columns to step along at a fast pace. On February 5 they enter Jackson, quickly repair a partially destroyed pontoon bridge over the Pearl River, and three days later reach Morton, a station on the Southern Railroad. Polk had planned to concentrate his infantry here for a stand but did not have time to do so. Now he decides that Sherman indeed is heading for Mobile: a road branches off from Morton in that direction, and ominously, Farragut's fleet is reported to be hovering outside Mobile Bay. So Polk orders Sears's Brigade,* just arrived at Meridian by train from Mobile, to return there.[10]

The men of Sears's Brigade are Mississippians. Among them is Captain Wil-

---

*In the Confederate army, brigades, divisions, and corps are officially designated by the name of their commander, whereas in the Union army they bear numerical designations (e.g., 3rd Brigade, 1st Division, XV Corps). That is why in referring to Confederate brigades, divisions, and corps, these words as a rule are capitalized, but not so in the case of the same type of Federal units when, for purposes of convenience, they are referred to by the name of their commanders.

liam Pitt Chambers of the 46th Mississippi, who before the war had taught school at Enterprise, a village five miles south of Meridian. He is deeply religious; every evening he holds a prayer meeting for his company. And he is passionately devoted to the Confederacy, in whose service a brother has died. Yet when he learns on the morning of February 9 that his brigade is to turn round and go back to Mobile, he is tempted to desert. Many of his fellow Mississippians do desert. Three days later he writes in his journal: "We had come home as it were to check the progress of the invader who was marching through the center of the State. With indignant hearts, we learned of his advance, and the wholesale destruction that attended it. We knew that our forces in his front were steadily falling back; but *now* the whole State was to be abandoned without a single blow."[11]

From Morton the Northern invaders proceed on February 10 to Hillsburgh, which is "mostly destroyed by fire," then on the following day to Lake Station. Here, according to Captain Lucius M. Rose, chief acting signal officer, "the Signal Corps went through the town like a dose of salts, and just as we were leaving I noticed a man hunting around to get someone to make an affidavit that there had been a town there."[12]

Continuation of the Union march eastward causes Polk to change his mind: Meridian, not Mobile, must be Sherman's objective, at least for the time being. Therefore on February 11, Polk orders Major General Samuel French and his two infantry brigades, which have been brought to Meridian with the intention of sending them to Mobile, to remain there and help evacuate all military supplies to Demopolis. Fortunately, Major George Whitfield of the Confederate Railroad Bureau already has assembled most of the region's available locomotives and freight cars at Meridian. Working frantically around the clock, the Confederates place everything movable aboard the cars. Early on the afternoon of February 14 the last trainload departs, following French's infantry and being followed by a rear guard of cavalry. A few minutes later, Federal troopers gallop into the village, and at exactly 3:30 P.M., Sherman himself arrives.

He finds nothing of military value—no trains (apart from a disabled locomotive) on the tracks, no rifles or cannons or machinery in the arsenal, no provisions or munitions or uniforms in the warehouses, not even any beds in the hospitals. Neither—and from his standpoint this is most frustrating of all—does he find Major General William Sooy Smith and his 7,000 horsemen from Memphis. According to Sherman's calculations, they should have gotten to Meridian before he did. Had they done so, the Rebels would not have slipped away with all their trains and supplies. Moreover, without Smith's men it will be too risky to go on to Demopolis and Selma.[13]

Sherman is not the only general to be concerned about the nonarrival of reinforcements. Another is Polk, now at Demopolis. Repeatedly he has telegraphed Johnston for help. Each time, Johnston has answered that he can send none: "The enemy, much more than double my number, is in motion on my front." This is not true. The Union forces at Chattanooga are neither moving nor showing any signs of moving, and with so many men on leave, they have far less than a two-to-one superiority over the Confederates at Dalton. Johnston simply does not want to reduce his own army out of fear that the Federals might indeed advance against him.[14]

Such, then, is Polk's situation on February 14: he is unable to stop Sherman without sizable reinforcements; but the only general who can provide those reinforcements is unwilling to do so. The bishop, however, has a valuable asset: President Davis is his friend but Johnston's enemy. More importantly, Davis feels that it will be a military and morale disaster for the Confederacy if Sherman is allowed to parade through Mississippi and Alabama to the Gulf. Therefore on February 17 he peremptorily orders Johnston to send three divisions of Hardee's Corps—Cheatham, Cleburne, and Walker—to Polk with all possible speed and secrecy, starting immediately. That same day, Secretary of War Seddon telegraphs Polk: "You will be re-enforced." Davis hopes that Polk, bolstered by Hardee, will be able to "destroy" Sherman before he can either invade Alabama or return to Vicksburg.

Davis's order leaves Johnston with no choice except to obey or resign. He obeys. Only yesterday he has notified the president that if a large force were transferred from the Army of Tennessee to Polk, the enemy at Chattanooga surely would advance and seize Atlanta. But if Davis chooses as usual to disregard Johnston's advice, so be it. He will not argue further, he has done his duty, and if need be, he can prove it. So, on February 18, Johnston instructs Hardee (whom Davis, wishing to forestall more foot-dragging by Johnston, already has notified) that he is to leave at once for Alabama and report to Polk. The three designated divisions of his corps will follow as rapidly as they can be loaded aboard trains and carried from Dalton to Montgomery.[15]

Departing first is Cheatham's Division. In the Army of Tennessee it is second only to Cleburne's in fame; its men consider themselves second to none as fighters—and with good reason, for they have taken part in all of the army's major battles and have never failed to reach their objective when attacking or to hold their position when defending. Most of them come from upper- and middle-class families in West and Middle Tennessee. They are stalwart, intelligent, high-spirited youths in their late teens and early twenties; and they are devoted to the Confederacy and their commander—stout, black-mustachioed, forty-three-year-old Major General Benjamin Franklin Cheatham, likewise a Tennessean (his mother's grandfather founded Nashville). No West Pointer, Cheatham was colonel of a volunteer regiment during the Mexican War and, in the words of one of his men, was "born to command." He leads charges in person, shouting "Come on, boys, and follow me." In combat he finds a stimulation that off the battlefield he seeks in whiskey. Bragg considered him "dangerous" because of his heavy drinking and because he joined with most of the army's other generals in calling for Bragg's replacement. After Chickamauga, Bragg tried to diminish Cheatham's influence by assigning three of his brigades to other divisions. By restoring these brigades to Cheatham's command, Johnston delighted the Tennesseans and gained their gratitude; they, at least, cheer whenever he rides by.[16]

Cheatham's Division, about 6,000 men on two trains, leaves Dalton during the morning of February 20 and begins arriving in Atlanta that evening. The next morning, even though it is Sunday, Cheatham and about one-third of Strahl's Brigade "take on a high tight." Running after him, the men call on "Mars Frank" to make a speech, something he notoriously is incapable of doing, although he does possess a remarkable talent for cussing when angry. He tries to get away from them, but they keep heading him off and insisting on a speech. Finally he says, "Come along boys, you are all my boys," and they relent. "If there ever was a General and his men," recalls a member of the 19th Tennessee, "of whom it could be said, the men belong to the General, and the General belongs to the men, it was Gen. Cheatham and his division."[17]

Later in the day the division rides the rails to West Point (where many of the soldiers attend church services), then on February 22 it goes on to Montgomery. It is a "very lively trip," Lieutenant Rennolds of the 5th Tennessee notes in his diary, with "the boys enjoying themselves writing and throwing notes to the girls who lined the way."

This same day a second division, Cleburne's, begins boarding the trains at Dalton. Scheduled to follow it is Walker's Division. Soon Polk will have available approximately 16,000 of Johnston's best troops. Added to the 15,000 infantry and cavalry he already has on hand, he will be in position to defeat or even smash Sherman.[18]

This should not be. Grant has promised Sherman to threaten Johnston at Dalton, thereby preventing Johnston from aiding Polk. Why has Grant not done so?

The answer is Longstreet—or, rather, incompetent spies who informed Grant that Longstreet had received two divisions from Johnston, that he was being

Benjamin F. Cheatham (*Military Annals of Tennessee,* 127)

heavily reinforced from Virginia, and that he soon would strike again at Knoxville. Not until February 12, when Grant realized that none of this was true, did he direct Thomas to conduct a "reconnaissance in force" against Dalton. Heavy rains then obliged Thomas, whom Grant earlier had ordered to send 14,000 men to Knoxville, to take more than week to get the movement under way. Moreover, because Thomas was suffering from an attack of neuralgia, "from which I suffer intensely," he was unable to take personal charge of it. Consequently, not he, but his senior corps commander, Major General John M. Palmer, heads the 25,000 Union troops who on the morning of February 22 finally set out from the Chattanooga area for Dalton.[19]

As they do so, Sherman and his men are marching back to Vicksburg. They spent five days in and around Meridian. There, to quote Sherman's official report, "10,000 men worked hard and with a will," employing axes, crowbars, sledges, claw bars, and fire. When they finished, "Meridian, with its depots, store-houses, arsenal, hospital, offices, hotels and contonments" no longer existed. He might have added, but refrained, that his troops also burned a newspaper office, all the shops, and a number of private dwellings. Outside of Meridian the rest of Sherman's army have wrecked railroad tracks to the north and south and to the east and west. Hundreds of soldiers have ripped up rails with crowbars, then tossed them on bonfires made from ties piled four feet high. The heat of the fires, notes Captain Andrew Hickenlooper, Sherman's chief of engineers, in his diary, has caused the rails to "invariably bend from 30 to 40 degrees," making it impossible to relay them unless they are first straightened out. Altogether, according to Sherman, 115 miles of track, 61 bridges and culverts, and 6,075 feet of trestlework have been obliterated.

But this is not all. Fanning out through the countryside, the invaders have plundered farms, plantations, and villages, burned thousands of cotton bales and hundreds of thousands of bushels of corn, killed and eaten poultry and livestock in uncountable numbers, torched houses, shops, and farm buildings, and made off with hundreds of horses and mules. Also they have taken thousands of slaves—or, rather, the slaves have gone with them.[20] To the blacks the blue-clad soldiers are liberators whom they are eager to follow into the promised land of freedom. Many of the soldiers, on the other hand, frankly regard the "niggers" as barely human. "You have no idea," an Illinois enlisted man writes home after his first contact with slaves, "what a miserable, horrible-looking, degraded set of brutes these plantation hands are." If the Northern troops support emancipation, as most of them do, it is rarely out of idealistic humanitarianism. Instead they favor it for the same pragmatic reasons that they justify terror against Southern civilians. "Slavery," to quote the letter of an Indiana soldier to his wife, "was the cause of the war, and unless it is abolished our free institutions will again be endangered by a 2nd rebellion." Or as a chaplain in the XVII Corps puts it, "We do not fight to free the slaves, but free the slaves in order to stop the fight."[21]

Sooy Smith's cavalry also are on the march on February 22. They are not, however, heading toward Meridian or any other destination in Mississippi. Instead they are fleeing in utter rout back to Memphis.

Why is this? Why has Sooy Smith worse than failed to carry out his part in Sherman's plan to eliminate the Confederate forces in Mississippi as a factor in upcoming military operations in the West? The answer is threefold.

First, Sherman has badly underestimated the amount of time it would take Smith to reach Meridian. According to his orders, Smith was to leave Memphis no later than February 1 and proceed rapidly to Meridian, where, as we have seen, Sherman expected to meet him. But because Smith believed, with good cause, that he dare not undertake the expedition until reinforced by a mounted division from northern Tennessee and because heavy rains and overflowing rivers seriously delayed this division in its march to join him, he was unable to set out for Meridian before February 11, ten days behind schedule.[22]

Second, once he did get under way, Smith averaged a mere fifteen miles a day as his troops concentrated on plundering houses, burning cotton, and liberating slaves, 3,000 of whom joined them, constituting (to quote Smith's report) "incumbrances" that further slowed his march. Not until February 20—the same day that Sherman began returning to Vicksburg—did Smith reach West Point, Mississippi, still 150 miles from Meridian.

Third, last, and worst of all from a Union standpoint, opposing Smith was Major General Nathan Bedford Forrest. Semiliterate and devoid of formal military training, Forrest has a genius for warfare that already has made him legendary and that will cause him to be considered by many historians to be the greatest cavalry commander of the Civil War. With only 2,500 men to Smith's 7,000, Forrest fell back before the slow Union advance, waiting for a chance to strike. It came on February 21, when Smith, realizing that it now was pointless to go on to Meridian, began to retreat. Declaring that the Yankees "are scared," Forrest pursued. On the morning of February 22 near Okolona he caught up with Smith's rear guard and attacked—he always attacks if possible, for he believes that getting the "bulge" on an enemy is more important than numbers. Assailed on front and flank—another standard Forrest tactic—the rear guard broke in panic and the rest of Smith's column began to run. That is what it still is doing on the night of February 22, even though Forrest, with his men, horses, and ammunition all exhausted, no longer is pursuing.

On February 26 the survivors of Smith's expedition begin straggling into Memphis, bedraggled, demoralized, and so weary that they barely can stay on their horses—those who retain them. In four days they have covered more distance retreating than they did in twice that time advancing. Their sole accomplishment has been to provide a vivid demonstration of the perils of tangling with Forrest and his "critter company." It will not be the last one.[23]

While Smith's men stagger back into Memphis, Thomas's troops head back toward Chattanooga (at Grant's insistence, Thomas took personal charge of the operation). For the past three days (February 24–26) they have been skirmishing with the Confederates along Rocky Face Ridge, an almost solid range of steep, craggy hills to the north, west and south of Dalton. In the process they have discovered two things. One of them is that the ridge—in particular Buzzard Roost Gap, through which the railroad runs—is virtually impregnable to an attack from the north: the 10th Michigan, which was due to go on veteran furlough in a few days, lost sixty men in a matter of minutes while "feeling" the Rebel defenses. The other is that, potentially at least, Johnston is vulnerable to a flanking move. On the afternoon of February 25, Colonel Thomas J. Harrison's 39th Indiana Mounted Infantry, having been ordered by Palmer to explore the western approaches to Rocky Face, entered Dug Gap, a man-made pass five miles south of Buzzard's Roost Gap, drove away the infantry company stationed there, and then repulsed an attack by a small Confederate cavalry regiment. Nothing except inadequate strength prevented it from pushing on to the railroad south of Dalton, cutting Johnston off from Atlanta. Moreover, not until the following morning was it compelled to retreat when assailed by Granbury's Brigade of Cleburne's Division, just arrived back from Alabama in response to frantic dispatches by Johnston to Richmond declaring, in effect, that Grant's entire army had beset him.

Thomas is most impressed on learning of what Harrison's Hoosier troopers have done—and might have done. To be sure, one could not expect Johnston to be caught off guard again at Dug Gap. But are there not other passes through the southward extension of Rocky Face which can be penetrated with more than a mere mounted regiment? Thomas begins to study his maps and scouting reports. Soon he pays special attention to a pass about twelve miles south of Dalton. It leads to a village called Resaca on the north bank of the Oostanaula River and, much more important, to the Western and Atlantic Railroad. Its name—a sinister-sounding one—is Snake Creek Gap.[24]

On the morning of February 28, Sherman rides into Vicksburg, sends a brief dispatch to Grant—his first since setting forth on the Meridian expedition— and then boards the steamboat *Diana* to go to New Orleans for a conference with Major General Nathaniel P. Banks, Union commander in Louisiana, about preparations for the campaign up the Red River against Shreveport. "I know," he assures Grant in the dispatch, "if we wipe out Shreveport as I have done Meridian you can safely call for 20,000 men from here and Arkansas in all April." Likewise, in a report to Halleck, written while aboard the *Diana,* he declares that as a result of breaking the railroads at and around Meridian, "no car can pass through that place this campaign" and that his forces "made a swath of desolation 50 miles broad across the State of Mississippi, which the present generation will not forget."[25]

Sherman's claim about the amount of destruction he has done is valid enough. The same holds true for what he says about the impact of the raid on Mississippians. "The people," Major General Stephen Dill Lee, overall commander of Confederate cavalry in Mississippi and Alabama, notifies Polk on March 13, "are badly whipped and much depressed"; and the spectacle of Yankees marching unopposed through the heart of their state has caused many men in Captain Chambers's regiment to desert, and those who remain "are dispirited, and can not fight." On the other hand, Sherman greatly overestimates the seriousness and duration of the damage inflicted on the railroads. Thanks to the enterprise of Major Whitfield, the officer whose foresight made possible the evacuation of supplies, machinery, and rolling stock from Meridian before Sherman got there, the lines bisecting that town will be back in full service by April, because the task of repairing them is being facilitated by the fact that the rails bent on the bonfires of ties can be straightened out quickly by running them through machines designed for that purpose. (The Federals, it would seem, will have to develop another, a more effective, way to wreck railroads.)[26]

But most important of all, Sherman has failed in his strategic objective of neutralizing the Confederate forces in Mississippi and thereby freeing Union troops in that region for the upcoming spring offensive. Forrest, his already enormous prestige enhanced by his spectacular victory at Okolona, remains able and, no doubt, more than willing to strike at the long lines of railroad that sustain the Yankee legions poised along the borders of Georgia and Alabama. This is a menace that will have to be dealt with. If it is not, the consequences may be disastrous.

Sherman also does not know (and would be incredulous if told) that most people in the North and the South alike think that he has suffered a defeat. He has himself to blame for this erroneous impression. Because he has done such a good job of concealing the true purpose of the Meridian expedition, the prevailing assumption in both sections is that he was endeavoring to take Mobile or at least Montgomery. Hence his turning back after having reached Meridian is being deplored by many Northern newspapers, especially Democratic ones, as a Union failure and is being hailed by all Southern newspapers as a Confederate success, the consequence of Forrest's brilliant victory at Okolona. Indeed, the illusion of having foiled Sherman's designs, along with a report from Johnston that he has repelled a full-fledged attack on Dalton and the news of triumphs in Florida and at Charleston, bolsters morale in the South and strengthens the belief that the strategy of outlasting the North not only can work but is working. Thus, when word of Okolona reaches Richmond, War Department clerk Jones writes in his diary: "We shall probably end the war this year—and independence will compensate for all. The whole male population, pretty much, will be in the field this year, and our armies will be strong. So far we have the prestige of success, and our men are resolved to keep it, if the dissensions of the leaders do not interfere with the general purpose."[27]

Quite likely, Jones's cautionary comment about "dissensions of the leaders" is inspired by an announcement made that very day by the War Department, to wit that "General Braxton Bragg is assigned to duty at the seat of government, and, under the direction of the President, is charged with the conduct of military operations in the armies of the Confederacy."

Davis no doubt sincerely believes that it will benefit the war effort to thus utilize the services, otherwise lost, of a man who, in spite of his defeats, is a professional soldier who possesses a high order of strategic and administrative ability. Nevertheless Davis's appointment of Bragg to be, in effect, the army's chief of staff is a blunder. It is utterly inexplicable to the vast majority of Southern soldiers and civilians, and it lends credibility to the accusation of Davis's critics that he is contemptuous of public opinion and is controlled by personal bias in military affairs. The *Richmond Examiner* is justified in sarcastically commenting that "this happy announcement should enliven the fires of confidence and enthusiasm . . . among the people like a bucket of water on a newly kindled grate."[28]

There are, however, a few people who welcome Bragg's unexpected resuscitation. One of them is Johnston. On learning of it, he telegraphs Bragg: "I have had the pleasure to see the announcement of your position." Probably he hopes that Bragg, as its erstwhile commander, will provide Davis with a better understanding of the needs and problems of the Army of Tennessee. If so, then Johnston does not realize that anything that Bragg tells the president will be colored by an intense personal resentment against certain of its top generals, notably Hardee, Cheatham, and Cleburne, all of whom had tried to have him deposed as its commander prior to the debacle at Missionary Ridge, which he attributes in large measure to their intrigues. Even more to the point, Johnston also fails to take into account the fact that Bragg owes everything he has had, does have, and can have by way of military status to Davis's friendship. For that reason alone, any enemy of Davis's is likely to be Bragg's enemy too.[29]

On February 29, Lincoln also makes a change in the command structure of his army. Unlike the one made by Davis, it is neither unexpected nor unwelcomed. What he does is to affix "A. Lincoln" on the bill, just passed by Congress, creating the grade of lieutenant general, to which Grant is to be appointed so that he can head the whole Union army.[30] It is the most important document he has signed since the Emancipation Proclamation. The latter transformed the purpose of the war. This one transforms the way in which the war will be waged. For the first time the North's military might will be directed by a man who is capable of using it with maximum effectiveness.

CHAPTER THREE

MARCH

Part One: Hood Comes to Dalton

ON MARCH 2, Captain George C. Binford, 18th Tennessee, writes his Cousin Bob in Virginia from a camp near Dalton: "Gen. Hood has taken command of a corps in our army. My Division is in his corps. I have not seen him yet. One of his aides, an old schoolmate of mine, came round to see me this evening.—Says the Gen. is fine, healthy and will visit the different Regts. to form their acquaintances in a day or two. I expect we will like him very much."[1]

John Bell Hood is thirty-two and a lieutenant general. He has gained this high rank at such a low age on the battlefield. At Gaines's Mill on June 27, 1862, his Texas Brigade broke the Union line, winning the battle and the reputation as the best fighters in Lee's army. Given command of a division, he delivered the final, crushing charge that turned Second Manassas into a second Yankee rout. His counterattack, ordered by Lee, hurled back the first Federal assault at Antietam and saved both the Army of Northern Virginia and the Confederacy from disaster. On the second day of Gettysburg, Hood's attack against the Army of the Potomac's left nearly won the battle for Lee, failing in large part because his corps commander, Longstreet, refused to allow him to make it in the way he wanted. Last—and the climax—it was the ad hoc corps he headed at Chickamauga which smashed the Army of the Cumberland's right wing and forced it to seek refuge behind the fortifications of Chattanooga. No wonder, then, that President Davis recommended, and on February 11, 1864, the Confederate Congress unanimously approved, his promotion to lieutenant general, with rank to date from September 20, the day of his triumph at Chickamauga.

In all of these battles, Hood attacked. In all of these attacks the troops under him suffered tremendous losses. At Gaines's Mill, 572 out of about 2,000; at Second Manassas, 1,000 out of 3,000; at Antietam, on being asked by Lee, "Great God, General Hood, where is the splendid division you had this morning," he truthfully answered: "They are lying on the field where you sent them, sir. . . . My division has been wiped out"; at Gettysburg, 2,300 out of 6,000; and at Chickamauga, probably no more than two-thirds of the three divisions he led into battle still stood when the fighting ended. To be sure, such casualty

John Bell Hood (*Photographic History*, 3:123)

rates are not peculiar to Hood; numerous other brigade and division commanders in both the Army of Northern Virginia and the Army of Tennessee possess
equivalent records. They result from the way in which Civil War battles are
fought, particularly by Southerners. What distinguishes Hood is that he has been
more successful than any other Confederate battlefield leader in transmuting the
blood so lavishly shed by his soldiers into dramatic victories. Furthermore, he
does not ask of his men anything he is not willing to give himself. One need only
look at him to know that. His left arm hangs limp, almost useless, by his side, the
consequence of having been mangled by shrapnel at Gettysburg. And his right leg
consists of a 4½" stump; the rest of it was sawed off by a surgeon on the field of
Chickamauga after a .58-caliber lead Minie ball shattered the thigh bone. That
he is alive at all comes close to being miraculous. That he is back, ready to go into
battle again, goes beyond ordinary courage. If ordered by this general to expose
oneself to death for his country, can any true soldier refuse?

Before his body was wrecked at Gettysburg and Chickamauga, there were
few Confederate generals as physically impressive as Hood. He stood six feet
two in his cavalry boots, was lean and well proportioned, and his long blonde
hair and even longer and blonder beard gave him the look of a reincarnated
Viking warrior. He possessed, too, a "swinging dash" and an almost boyish
enthusiasm, which, along with his bravery, made him enormously popular with
his troops. Yet he was no mere "Come on, let's charge 'em!" cavalier. As a West
Pointer and regular army officer, he believed in discipline, drill, and training;
and he practiced what he believed with the soldiers under his command. This,
as much as anything else, explained his battlefield exploits. At Gaines's Mill,
for example, on his orders, the Texas Brigade advanced at a steady walk,
maintaining formation and not firing until it reached point-blank range,
whereupon it fired a volley and rushed forward; the Northern troops—tough
ones who all afternoon had thrown back other Confederate assaults—turned
and fled.

There is no disputing that Hood is a superb combat leader; in the entire
Confederate army only Cleburne matches him, and Cleburne has not had the
chance to participate in the glorious victories that Hood has with the Army of
Northern Virginia. But is Hood more than a thunderbolt to be cast into the
storm of battle? He is often referred to as gallant, but no one calls him brilliant.
He nearly flunked out at West Point, where he graduated in 1853 forty-fifth in a
class of fifty-five, and his ignorance and naiveté about anything other than
military affairs and horses is a source of both amusement and embarrassment to
his friends, as when attending a performance in Richmond of Sheridan's *The
Rivals,* he commented about one of this famous play's characters, "By Jove, I
believe that fellow Acres is a coward"! Furthermore, although his troops are as

well-drilled and disciplined as can be hoped for of any Southerners, he takes little interest in such mundane matters as provisions, clothing, shelter, and sanitary conditions. And potentially most serious of all, it is possible that he is running out of luck.

Without luck and lots of it, Hood would not have been so spectacularly successful; in fact, he probably would not even be alive. Early in the Peninsular Campaign he escaped being shot by a Yankee soldier only because one of his Texans disobeyed his order to advance with rifles unloaded and so could shoot the Yankee first. The great breakthrough assault at Gaines's Mill, bravely and skillfully conducted as it was, might have failed had not a regiment of Union cavalry blundered into the defenders' reserve artillery, preventing it from blasting Hood's troops as they reached their objective. As for smashing the Federal right at Chickamauga, this occurred mainly because a mix-up in orders resulted in a Union division's pulling out of line just before the Confederate onslaught. And of course this stroke of good fortune was canceled, as far as Hood personally was concerned, by the Minie ball that tore into his right leg.²

So—what next? Can a man this badly mangled, who cannot walk except on crutches, and who requires the help of a body servant to dress, undress, and tend to his intimate personal needs—can such a man, even one as young, vital, and resolute as Hood, again be an effective battlefield leader?

Obviously Jefferson Davis thinks he can be; otherwise he would not have promoted him to lieutenant general, the second highest grade in the Confederate army, and assigned him to command a corps in the Army of Tennessee. So, too, do Lee and Longstreet, both of whom strongly endorsed the promotion. Likewise Johnston, who as soon as he learned about Hood's promotion, telegraphed the War Department: "Lieutenant General Hood is much wanted here."³ And Hood himself has no qualms or doubts. He believes that he has earned his lieutenant generalcy by his achievements, which surpass those of any of his brighter classmates at West Point (such as John M. Schofield and James Birdseye McPherson over in the Yankee army). Also his self-confidence is boosted by the knowledge that on two major occasions he had been right and his superiors had been wrong with regard to the conduct of a battle. The first was at Fredericksburg where, contrary to the opinion of Lee and most of the other generals, he had asserted that the Federals would not again attack after their bloody repulse. The second was at Gettysburg, where three times he had asked Longstreet to allow him to strike the enemy's exposed left flank rather than attack frontally, only to be refused because Longstreet, not wanting to fight at Gettysburg at all, insisted on carrying out Lee's battle plan literally, even though it was obvious that Lee had misconceived the Union deployment.⁴ Hood cannot help but reflect that if he had been listened to, Fredericksburg could have been turned into more than a strategically barren defensive victory and that Gettysburg would have had an altogether different outcome.

As for the amputated leg—he is tired of hearing people talk about it. He now has an artificial leg made of cork, plus a couple of spares, paid for with donations from the men who still proudly call themselves Hood's Texas Brigade; these were brought through the blockade from Europe. To be sure, crutches remain necessary for walking, but he can ride a horse, which he mounts with the help of orderlies who boost him into the saddle and place his wooden foot into the stirrup, after which they strap both him and the crutches to the horse. Thus secured, he can trot for long distances, all really that is necessary for a corps commander—or, for that matter, an army commander. Those who question his physical ability to serve in the field, he declares, are nothing but "old women in trousers" who soon will see how wrong they are.

Neither is he worried about his luck running out. Has he not survived an amputation that would kill most men? Is he not by far the youngest lieutenant general in the entire Confederate army, he who less than two years ago had been just another colonel? Has he not, in recent weeks, been the lion of Richmond society and become a personal friend of the president himself, dining often at the Executive Mansion and accompanying Davis on horseback rides? And to top it all, has he not persuaded the beautiful, the accomplished, the exquisitely charming Sally Buchanan Preston to marry him, something that has required great persistence, for her aristocratic South Carolina parents object to him because they think he lacks the proper social and cultural background; it was also good luck, since Buck, as she is called, has many admirers—handsome, wealthy, polished men with both their legs. In sum, Hood has everything a soldier traditionally craves: rank, glory, and love. During the months ahead he hopes to win more of the second as he helps lead the Confederacy to victory, and while doing so (who knows?), perhaps he will even gain more of the first. In any event, when this year's campaign ends—and if all goes well, the war too— he will return to Richmond and marry Buck, for which occasion he has instructed a Richmond tailor to hold for him a bolt of the finest Confederate gray cloth and the best golden general's stars.[5]

Part Two: Grant Goes to Washington

The expected telegram arrives on the afternoon of March 3:

Major-General Grant
Nashville, Tenn.:
   The Secretary of War directs that you will report in person to the War Department as early as practicable, considering the condition of your

command. If necessary you will keep in telegraphic communication with your command while en route to Washington.

H. W. Halleck
General-in-Chief[6]

Grant knows that in Washington he will be presented with the commission of lieutenant general and placed in command of the United States Army. He spends March 4 preparing for the trip and sending messages to Schofield, Thomas, and Sherman, advising them of his forthcoming departure and instructing them as to what to do during his absence. In addition he writes Sherman, from whom he has just learned of the successful outcome of the Meridian expedition, a letter marked "Private":

Dear Sherman:

The bill reviving the grade of lieutenant-general in the army has become law, and my name has been sent to the Senate for the place. I now receive orders to report to Washington immediately in person. . . .

I start in the morning to comply with the order, but I shall say very distinctly on my arrival there that I accept no appointment which will require me to make that city my headquarters. This however, is not what I started out to write about.

Whilst I have been eminently successful in this war in at least gaining the confidence of the public, no one feels more than me how much of this success is due to the energy, skill, and harmonious putting forth of that energy and skill, of those who it has been my good fortune to have occupying a subordinate position under me.

There are many officers to whom these remarks are applicable to a greater or less degree, proportionate to their ability as soldiers, but what I want is to express my thanks to you and McPherson as the men to whom, above all others, I feel indebted for whatever I have had of success. How far your advice and suggestions have been of assistance, you know. How far your execution of whatever has been given you to do entitles you to the reward I am receiving, you cannot know as well as me. I feel all the gratitude that this letter would express, giving it the most flattering construction.

The word *"you"* I use in the plural, intending it for McPherson also. I should write to him, and will some day, but starting in the morning I do not know that I will find time just now.

Your friend,

U. S. Grant,
Major-General[7]

The next day, accompanied by his thirteen-year-old son, Frederick, and his chief of staff, Brigadier General James A. Rawlins, Grant takes the train to

Cincinnati, where he arrives that night. On the morning of the sixth, a Sunday, he and Frederick cross the Ohio River to Covington, Kentucky, and briefly visit his father, mother, and three sisters. The last time he saw them was three years ago. Then he was a nobody, a failure who would be poverty-stricken had not his father provided him with a storekeeping job in Galena, Illinois. Now he is the most important man in the nation save Lincoln, and some newspapers are urging that he be elected in place of Lincoln. One of the reporters who are hanging around asks him about that. He answers curtly, "I know nothing about it, and shall have nothing to do with it."[8]

Early in the afternoon he returns to Cincinnnati and boards the first of several trains that will take him to Washington. He reaches the capital two days later and walks to the Willard Hotel to seek a room for Frederick and himself. The desk clerk does not recognize the "short, round-shouldered man in a very tarnished major general's uniform" and is about to assign him a small chamber on the top floor. Then the clerk looks at the registration book and sees "U. S. Grant & Son—Galena, Illinois." At once he puts the two down for parlor 6, "the best in the house." Soon word circulates through the lobby that this scruffy-looking officer with the boy is Grant—"Unconditional Surrender" Grant, the victor of Vicksburg and Chattanooga, the new commander of the North's army, who will lead it to final victory. A cheering crowd gathers, and Grant, blushing with embarrassment, scurries up the stairs with Frederick to parlor 6. Even had he planned it that way, Grant could not have arrived on the Washington scene in a more ostentatiously unostentatious fashion.

In the evening he goes to call on Lincoln at the White House. Grant is unaware that this is the time for the weekly presidential reception. Hence he finds himself in the middle of another excited, clamorous crowd. For a while he has to stand on a sofa so everybody can see him, "a little scared-looking man." Finally he gets away from the mob and talks briefly with Lincoln and Secretary of War Edwin M. Stanton. They tell him to come back tomorrow, when he will be given his lieutenant general's commission. At midnight he returns to the Willard House and climbs into his bed in parlor 6. Probably he sleeps quite soundly; he never does otherwise, except when lonely for his wife.

At 1 P.M., on March 9, Grant stands facing Lincoln, who makes Grant seem shorter than ever. Members of the cabinet, as well as Halleck, Rawlins, and Frederick, look on. Lincoln hands Grant the commission and reads a brief statement, thanking him for past services and promising to sustain him in the future. Grant in turn reads a briefer statement, expressing gratitude and promising to do his best to merit the great responsibility now placed upon him. He then asks the president what special service is required of him. Take Richmond, Lincoln answers, adding that "our generals have not been fortunate in that direction" and asking if the lieutenant general thinks he can do it. Yes, Grant responds, provided he has enough troops. He will have, Lincoln assures him.

This is all. Lincoln does not ask Grant how he plans to go about taking Richmond, and if he had, Grant could not have told him. He needs first to visit the Army of the Potomac and its commander, Major General George Gordon Meade, something Grant intends to do right away. After leaving the White House and after, on Stanton's insistence, having his photo taken at Matthew Brady's studio, he boards a train and travels to Brandy Station, Meade's headquarters in Virginia. During the evening he talks to Meade, his staff, and his generals. In the morning, Grant heads back to Washington, having made two decisions. The first is to establish his headquarters in the East and not, contrary to his original intention, to return to the West. It simply will be impossible, he now realizes, to direct all of the Union armies without being in a position to resist personally the pressures that inevitably will come from the Washington authorities to abandon his own plans and pursue those of others. The second is to keep Meade at the head of the Army of the Potomac. The only man he can trust as a replacement is Sherman; but Sherman, as Grant already has told Meade, who bluntly asked him if such a change was going to be made, is needed in the West. Also Grant knows that supplanting Meade with a western general would create resentment in the Army of the Potomac, which is very sensitive about its comparative lack of success. Besides, Meade is honest, unselfish, and a skillful commander, as he has demonstrated at Gettysburg and during subsequent campaigning in northern Virginia. What he lacks—what the entire army of the Potomac lacks—is aggressiveness. Grant plans to change this. He will join the Army of the Potomac in the field; Meade will conduct its tactical operations; but Grant will supply the strategy and the iron determination to carry it out.

Back in Washington and back at the White House, Grant for the first time talks to Lincoln alone. He informs him of his decisions; Lincoln approves and in turn shows Grant a plan he has prepared for taking Richmond. It calls for transporting troops down the Potomac and landing them at a place where, Lincoln points out, their flanks will be protected by rivers. That is true, comments Grant; but the same rivers will also protect the Confederate flanks. Lincoln thereupon withdraws his plan, which probably is not so much a plan as it is a test: he wants to find out if Grant is a defensive-minded general like so many of his predecessors who have taken on the job of capturing Richmond, or whether he thinks in terms of offense. Quite clearly the latter is the case, and Grant passes the test.

By evening Grant is on the way back to Nashville, having begged off from a White House banquet in his honor. He has had enough of being gawked at in

Washington. Much needs to be done, and done speedily, to prepare the upcoming spring campaign, the master plan for which is forming in his mind. In particular he wants to talk to Sherman.[9]

Sherman, as Grant sits aboard a train chugging westward, sits aboard the steamer *Westmoreland,* churning up the Mississippi to Memphis. A week ago he was in New Orleans, conferring with Banks about the Red River expedition. Banks is to command the expedition; a flotilla of gunboats and transports under Rear Admiral David D. Porter will accompany it; and Sherman will add 10,000 of his own troops under Major General A. J. Smith. Banks, Sherman has emphasized before leaving New Orleans, is to keep Smith's force no more than thirty days and to send it back to the Army of the Tennessee as early in April as possible so that it can participate in the advance southward from Chattanooga. Sherman knows that Grant considers the Red River foray a waste of time and manpower and that the only reason it is taking place at all is that Lincoln has sanctioned it in hopes of countering the French intervention in Mexico by putting United States forces in Texas. Obsessed as he is with securing the lower Mississippi Valley, Sherman personally thinks that the expedition can serve a useful military purpose provided it is made quickly and successfully. This is why he is sending Smith along with Banks; Smith is a tough, experienced, and capable professional, whereas Banks is the quintessential political general, his main claim to military fame being the spectacular manner in which he was pummeled and chased by Thomas J. ("Stonewall") Jackson in the Shenandoah Valley in 1862. Surely, Sherman reasons, even Banks can go up the Red River and seize Shreveport, the main Confederate base in the Trans-Mississippi, if aided by Smith's battle-hardened veterans and Porter's gunboats.[10]

Sherman returned to Vicksburg on March 7, then two days later started up the river for Memphis. En route he received Grant's letter expressing gratitude to him and McPherson for their contributions to his military success. Now, on March 10, from "near Memphis," Sherman answers his friend's "more than characteristic" letter. Grant, he declares, does both him and McPherson "too much honor." After all, Grant won his first battles without their aid. These, like his subsequent victories, derived basically from the

> simple faith in success you have always manifested, which I can liken to
> nothing less than the faith a Christian has in a Savior. . . . Also, when
> you have completed your last preparations you go into battle without
> hesitation, as at Chattanooga, no doubts, no reserves; and I tell you it was
> this that made me act with confidence. . . .

My only points of doubt were in your knowledge of grand strategy, and of books of science and history, but I confess your common sense seems to have supplied all these.

Now as to the future. Don't stay in Washington. Halleck is better qualified than you to stand the buffets of intrigue and policy. Come West; take to yourself the whole Mississippi Valley. . . . Here lies the seat of the coming empire, and from the West, when our task is done, we will make short work of Charleston and Richmond and the impoverished coast of the Atlantic.[11]

These words testify to the depth of the friendship between Grant and Sherman, they are perceptive about the qualities that make Grant a great military leader, and in the last sentence they are even prophetic. But soon Sherman learns that his plea to Grant to remain in the West is wasted ink. On March 12 the War Department announces that henceforth, by order of the president, army headquarters will be in Washington "and also with Lieutenant-General Grant in the field," that Halleck will be chief of staff under Stanton and Grant, that Sherman is to be the new commander of the Military Division of the Mississippi, and that McPherson will succeed Sherman as head of the Army of the Tennessee. Next, on March 14, Grant summons Sherman to meet him in Nashville. Sherman takes a steamer from Memphis to Cairo, then trains to Louisville and Nashville, where he arrives on the evening of March 17 and finds that Grant has just published an order assuming "command of the armies of the United States, headquarters in the field, and until further orders will be with the Army of the Potomac."[12] So, Grant will go to the East while he, Sherman, will stay behind to complete the conquest of the Confederacy in the West. Although disappointed and also amazed that Grant has decided "to go East, a stranger among strangers," Sherman calmly accepts his new assignment, second in importance and responsibility only to that of Grant himself. He believes in Grant, he believes in Northern victory, he believes in himself, and he believes he will succeed. He will, he resolves, succeed by doing everything possible to make failure impossible.

On March 18, Sherman takes command of the Military Division of the Mississippi and confers with Grant about the future grand strategy of the war and how to implement it. They hold a "full conversation," but at the end of the day much remains unsettled. Hence on the following day, Sherman takes a seat beside Grant on the train that is carrying Grant, his wife, Julia, and his staff to Cincinnati and then to Washington. Serious talk, however, proves impossible: there is too much noise and not enough privacy. Instead of discussing military matters, Sherman ends up answering Julia Grant's questions about social etiquette in Washington. In Cincinnati, which they reach at night, Sherman meets his own wife, Ellen, who happens to be staying at the Burnet House, where the Grants also take a room. In the morning, Sheman and Ellen, who is six months pregnant, drive out in a buggy to the nearby village of Reading and visit their daughter Minnie at the Mount Notre Dame convent school (Ellen is a fanatically devout Catholic—"More Catholic than the Pope," in the words of her husband, who, much to her despair, refuses to join her church but at least refrains from subscribing to any other brand of Christianity). Back in Cincinnati at the Burnet House after lunch, Ellen and Julia chat in one room while Grant and Sherman talk in another.

When, some hours later, the men emerge, the North for the first time has a master plan for winning the war: Grant, directing the Army of the Potomac, will endeavor to destroy Lee's army while trying to take Richmond; Sherman will seek to do the same to Johnston's army while aiming at Atlanta. They will advance simultaneously, as will all the other Union field forces, and they will not cease attacking until they achieve their objectives. Hitherto, Federal armies have operated independently, with little or no reference to the military situation as a whole. Because of their lack of common purpose and coordination, they have failed to take full advantage of their numerical superiority; so the Confederates, utilizing their interior lines, have been able to maximize their inferior strength by shifting forces from one front to another, as most notably when they transferred Longstreet's corps from Virginia to Georgia for the Battle of Chickamauga. Grant and Sherman intend to prevent this from happening again. They will keep the pressure on in both East and West until somewhere the Rebels crack under the strain. Moreover—and this is the devastating beauty of this simple, indeed obvious, plan—it does not make much difference if the crack occurs in Virginia or in Georgia. Either way the Confederacy will be as good as doomed. The only thing that might frustrate the plan is if no crack occurs before the autumn elections. In that case it might be the North rather than the South which calls it quits.

That night, Grant's party takes an express train for Washington; a year and a week will pass before Sherman and he will meet again. Sherman remains in Cincinnati with Ellen another day, pestered by "sight-seekers," then leaves by mailboat for Louisville, whence he proceeds by train to Nashville, arriving there on March 23. At once he gets busy preparing for his part in the forthcoming campaign, a campaign that will have such consequences and reverberations that a quarter of a century hence Sherman, his hair and beard white, will stand in a hallway of the Burnet House in Cincinnati surrounded by old soldiers and young reporters and, pointing to the room where Grant and he had talked, say: "Yonder began the campaign . . . we finally settled on a plan. He was to go for Lee and I was to go for Joe Johnston. That was his plan. No routes prescribed. . . . It was the beginning of the end as Grant and I foresaw right here."[13]

Part Three: Atlanta

Back in January, when Halleck had solicited his views on the North's proper strategy for 1864, Grant had written of an advance from Chattanooga to Mobile, with Atlanta and Montgomery to be the "important intermediate points." Now, two months later, the objective point has become simply Atlanta. The maps explain why. They show four rail lines radiating from the Atlanta area. Almost due eastward is the Georgia Railroad, which runs to Augusta, where it joins a line that connects it with Charleston, Raleigh, and Richmond. In a generally southern direction is the Macon and Western, which at Macon connects with the Central of Georgia, which goes to Savannah and the sea. Branching off from the Macon and Western a short distance southwest of Atlanta at East Point is the Atlanta and West Point Railroad, which proceeds westward to the Alabama border, where it links up with lines leading directly to Montgomery and indirectly (via the Alabama River steamboats) to Selma and Mobile. Finally, heading northwest is the Western and Atlantic, the railroad that supplies Johnston's army at Dalton, where it intersects with a line to Knoxville while itself running to Chattanooga. In sum, Atlanta is the center of a rail network that binds together practically all that remains of the Confederacy east of the Mississippi.

But that is not all. Because of these railroads the Confederate government has made Atlanta its main industrial, logistical, and administrative base in what is geographically the lower South and militarily the West. Located in the city are an arsenal that produces cartridges, shells, friction primers, gun carriages, knapsacks, and saddles; a five-story former gristmill, which now is a pistol factory with three hundred workers, many of them women; two foundries and a rolling mill for turning out cannons, armor plate, and rails; numerous smaller plants that make everything from rifles to belt buckles; and flour mills, packing plants, and a half-dozen military hospitals. All of the rail lines meet in the center of the city, where they are served by the long red-brick colonnaded depot called the Car Shed, roundhouses, marshaling yards, and all of the other facilities needed for the operation and maintenance of locomotives and rolling stock. Lining their tracks are warehouses filled with the fruits of Atlanta's industry and with military matériel brought by the trains from Rome, Athens, Augusta, Macon, Columbus, Selma, and other towns in Georgia and Alabama. Nearby, in the "Five Points," Atlanta's business district, are the headquarters of the Confederate quartermaster, commissary, ordnance, engineer, payroll, provost marshall, conscript, medical, transportation, niter and mining, and naval departments for Georgia and adjacent states.

Atlanta itself is a product of the railroad. It had begun in 1837 as Terminus, the site of milepost zero on the 138 miles of track being laid by the state-owned Western and Atlantic northward to what was to become Chattanooga. By 1843 enough people had settled at Terminus to warrant incorporation of a town called Marthasville in honor of the daughter of Georgia's governor. Soon, however, the inhabitants had become dissatisfied with this awkward, backwoodsy name and so had changed it to Atlanta, a name suggested by the chief engineer of the Western and Atlantic, who claimed that it was the Latin feminine for Atlantic. As other rail lines linked up with the Western and Atlantic, the town had grown rapidly. By 1850 it had 2,500 residents; in 1860, nearly 8,000. Many of them, particularly the businessmen, were Northerners, attracted by the present prosperity and future prospects of this bustling little city, which already was becoming famous as the "Gate City." The war brought an influx of new people: laborers, machinists, artisans, military and civilian officials, refugees, soldiers' wives, and a motley assortment of speculators, adventures, criminals, and blacks without masters (or at least none they acknowledged). At the outset of 1864, Atlanta has upwards of 20,000 inhabitants, making it second in population among Confederate-held cities only to Richmond, likewise swollen vastly by the war.

Serving the people of Atlanta and the swarms of visitors, travelers, and soldiers-on-leave who flock into the city are a dozen or so hotels, scores of boardinghouses, several banks, many shops and stores, a concert hall, a theater entitled the Athenaeum, and numerous saloons and brothels, the latter no doubt providing customers for such physicians as Dr. I. A. Clopton, who specializes in "Syphilitic Affections" and claims to have cured "more than 500 men now in the army," among them "one Major General and several Colonels." Seven newspapers appear daily: the *Intelligencer,* the *Southern Confederacy,* the *Reveille,* the *Commonwealth,* the *Appeal,* the *Register,* and the *Rebel,* with the last three being journalistic refugees from, respectively, Memphis, Knoxville, and Chattanooga. In addition the Confederate Press Association, which sends telegraphic reports to newspapers throughout the South, has its headquarters in the city. For those who want them—and some still do—slaves can be purchased from several auctioneers, the most prominent of whom is Robert A. Crawford, no. 10 Peachtree Street, who advertises: "I am paying good prices for sound and healthy Negroes—BOYS and GIRLS, YOUNG FELLOWS, YOUNG WOMEN, CARPENTERS, BLACKSMITHS, SHOE MAKERS, HOUSE SERVANTS, WAITERS, and DRIVERS." A few blocks from the Five Points is the tree-covered State Square, where stands the combination city hall and country courthouse, a two-story brick building topped by a white cupola in standard Southern style. Adjoining the square are most of the main churches, notably the high-spired Second Baptist and the Central Presbyterian. Beyond the business district, many handsome houses, some of them veritable mansions, line Whitehall, Mitchell, Peachtree, and other thoroughfares, all of which are illuminated by gas lamps. However, the areas between the streets, which tend to follow ridge lines, are thinly built; and about a half-mile from the Five Points, dwellings become few and scattered. The surrounding countryside is hilly, pine-covered, and dominated by the 1,700-foot-high granite monolith of Stone Mountain, fifteen miles east of the city. Atop Stone Mountain is an observatory; from it a person gazing to the west and north has a panoramic view of Atlanta, the Chattahoochee River, and Kennesaw Mountain. He can also see, amidst the green pine forests near the city, lines of trenches and redoubts, their red dirt making them look like giant, jagged scars. Construction of these fortifications had begun in July 1863, after the loss of Vicksburg, and still is under way. Captain Lemuel P. Grant, a citizen of Atlanta and an engineer officer in the Confederate army, directs the work, the physical part of which is being performed by hundreds of slaves drafted from plantations throughout Georgia. Like his fellow Atlantans, Captain Grant hopes these defenses will never need to be used; but the Yankees are only a little more than one hundred miles to the north.

Having to girdle itself with fortifications is far from the only price Atlanta pays for being so vital to the Confederacy's war effort. Night as well as day, trains chug and rattle through the heart of the city, the locomotives blowing their whistles and spewing forth billows of smoke and ashes. Processions of army wagons churn up clouds of red dust on the unpaved streets during dry weather and create quagmires when it rains. A "disagreeable manure sink" exists around the government stables near the corner of Alabama and Whitehall streets; the area around the Macon and Western freight depot, next to the Car Shed, reminds one observer of a "barnyard where cattle congregate"; the slaughter pens on the west side have such "vast accumulations of filth" as to threaten "pestilence at no distant period"; and the thousands of new residents so overtax the sewerless city's sanitary facilities that many backyards "are perfect seeth pools of filth and nastiness." Everywhere, complains the irate editor of the *Daily Intelligencer,* the air is permeated with "the triple distilled extract of the quintessence of stink," an odor so horrible that even the noses of "the most hardened wagon yard men curl" in disgust. Just as bad—in fact worse from the standpoint of all respectable citizens—vice, crime, and disorder run rampant. The saloons, gambling dens, and brothels that infest the Five Points attract, as they are designed to do, hordes of patrons, mostly soldiers, who usually get drunk, often engage in fights, and sometimes kill or maim each other. What a grand jury terms "idle and vicious boys" hang around the "places of vice," littering the sidewalks with goober shells, playing seven-up, insulting passersby, and committing all sorts of mischief. Blacks, many of them runaway slaves, congregate on the streets or in houses, where they drink, hold cockfights, and defy the curfew laws to engage in "nocturnal revelry"; their conduct is so "insolent" that some whites wonder if slavery can survive the war even if the South wins. Robberies and burglaries occur so frequently that the *Intelligencer's* editor sarcastically comments that "we have neither seen nor heard of anything of importance in the city beyond a few store breakings, but as these appear to be a legitimate calling in Atlanta, we have ceased to take any note of them." One victim is the wife of the pastor of the Central Presbyterian Church, Mary Mallard, she who on frigid January 1 made ice cream by placing a custard on her porch. During the night of March 22, while a storm rages, thieves break into her chicken coop and take nearly all of the poultry, sparing only a few hens and some ducks. "It is supposed," she writes her mother in Liberty County, Georgia, that "this kind of rascality is carried on by Negroes hiring their own time and those working upon the fortifications. They are aided, it is supposed, by low white men."

Efforts by the city and military authorities to curtail crime and rowdiness achieve scant success. The courts are overwhelmed with cases, the vast majority of arrested persons never come to trial, and of those who do, only a small percentage are convicted. Old laws are inadequate, and new ones prove futile, for both the city police and the provost marshal's troops are too few, feeble, and incompetent to cope with the criminal element or to control combat veterans on leave who are determined to have a good time. (The police, about thirty in number, consist of greybeards, cripples, and riffraff; with a couple of exceptions, the one hundred provost-marshal guards are boys under eighteen!) The breakdown of law, order, and common decency in the city is so bad that most Atlantans would welcome restoration of the martial law that Bragg imposed back in 1862 but that was quickly revoked by President Davis as a result of protests from Governor Brown and Georgia's congressman.[14]

Atlantans blame much of the crime and violence in their city on the soldiers who come there on leave. In turn, men of the Army of Tennessee resent what they deem to be the exorbitant prices they have to pay in "this swindling hole of the South," and they resent the contemptuous attitude of its people. Indeed, some of them, reflecting rural backgrounds and puritanical religious attitudes, loathe Atlanta. To Captain Sebron G. Sneed of the 6th Texas, Granbury's Brigade, it is the "modern Sodom in whose streets vice and immorality seek not the cover of night or secrecy, but in open day unblushingly and unrestrained stalk with open front," and where the "'strange woman' sits to lure the unwary."[15]

Regardless of how Johnston's soldiers feel about Atlanta, they must be ready to fight hard and die hard for it, as even Captain Sneed acknowledges. Should Atlanta fall, the Confederacy again will be cut in two, for then the sole remaining rail connection between the Carolinas and Virginia in the east and Alabama and Mississippi in the west will be a single and vulnerable line running from Montgomery via a roundabout route to Macon, itself a mere eighty miles further south in Georgia. Should Atlanta fall, the ability of the Confederate armies, especially the Army of Tennessee, to wage war effectively will suffer a crippling blow, for although it might be possible to transfer many of the city's factories elsewhere before the Yankees marched in, that could not be done with the rolling mill, the foundries, the meat-packing plants, and other such installations. Should Atlanta fall, Lee's army in Virginia will go hungrier than it already is, for it draws much of its food from Georgia's farms and plantations via Atlanta's railroads or lines connected with them. Should Atlanta fall, it will mean that the Northern legions have penetrated to the very heartland of the South and are in position to cut deeper into it still. Above all, should Atlanta fall, the North will gain a victory that the South cannot permit if its strategy of winning by not losing is to succeed.

Part Four: Richmond and Dalton

Jefferson Davis is determined that Atlanta shall not fall; no one could be more determined. That is why, after reluctantly appointing Johnston commander of the Army of Tennessee in December, he had called on that general to launch an offensive as quickly as possible into Tennessee: what better way to safeguard Atlanta than to drive the Federals out of Georgia, out of Tennessee, perhaps even back to the Ohio River? But Johnston had replied that he could not advance quickly or at any time in the foreseeable future, that his army lacked too much of everything, and that in any case it would be better to let the Yankees attack first, defeat them, and then go over to the offensive.

Davis did not like this answer, so typical of Johnston, but he let it pass for the time being. After all, perhaps the Army of Tennessee did need time to repair and prepare itself, especially after such a debacle as Missionary Ridge. But now two months have gone by; the winter is ending and spring is beginning; and if the Confederacy is going to strike first in the West, it must do so soon. Therefore Davis scarcely can believe his one good eye when, on March 4, he reads a newly arrived letter from Johnston, addressed to Bragg, in which the commander of the Army of Tennessee states: "Letters received from the President and Secretary of War soon after my assignment to this command gave the impression that a forward movement of this army was intended to be made in the spring." If this is so, Johnston continues, "and the President's intentions are unchanged, I respectfully suggest that much preparation is necessary": specifically, many reinforcements (Longstreet's army, Polk's infantry, troops from

Beauregard in South Carolina), more food and transport, more horses and mules, and better-organized and -led artillery. Doesn't Johnston, an exasperated Davis asks himself, understand that a "forward movement" of the Army of Tennessee is not only intended but expected and that it should take place as soon as possible and not sometime in the "spring"? And what, in God's name, has Johnston being doing all of these weeks at Dalton if his army is still not ready to advance? Davis at once instructs Bragg to correct any misunderstanding (if such it is) that Johnston has about the nature of his assignment and to let him know that the government—meaning Davis—doubts (to put it mildly) that Johnston's forces are in such bad shape as he claims.

Bragg does this with as much tact as an untactful man can muster. He informs Johnston that his "inference from the letter of the President and Secretary of War is correct" and that it is desired that he have "all things in readiness at the earliest practicable moment for the movement indicated," as the "season is at hand and the time seems propitious." As for the Army of Tennessee's deficiencies, particularly artillery and transport, these seem "so different from the account given by General Hardee on turning over the command that hopes are entertained there must be some error on your part."

A week later, as he peruses Bragg's letter, it is Johnston's turn to be exasperated—and also disappointed, for he had hoped that Bragg would give Davis a more realistic appraisal of the Army of Tennessee's situation. The ever-so-polite words of his reply to Bragg on March 12 convey, rather than mask, these feelings:

> General: I have had the honor to receive your letter of the 4th instant in which I am desired to "have all things in readiness, at the earliest practicable moment, for the movement indicated."
>
> The last two words quoted give me the impression that some particular plan of operations is referred to; if so, it has not been communicated to me.

Johnston's impression is correct: A "particular plan of operations" is being referred to; it has been conceived by Davis and Bragg, and although it has not been communicated to Johnston, it is about to be. Even as Johnston pens his sarcastic response to Bragg's March 4 letter, Bragg is writing him another letter, marked "Confidential," outlining this "particular plan" and the rationale behind it. As soon as Johnston has the "means and force," he is to advance into Tennessee east of Chattanooga, cross the Tennessee River at Kingston, and meet Longstreet's army, which meanwhile will have marched to that area. This move, by cutting off Knoxville from Chattanooga, should force the Federals into the "open field," where they can be defeated. However if the Federals do not offer battle, Johnston and Longstreet are to march rapidly over the mountains towards Nashville, a maneuver that will compel the enemy to abandon Chattanooga and fall back to the Cumberland River, perhaps will even lead to the capture of Nashville. In any event, once the Union forces have retreated to the Cumberland, Johnston then can cross that river and push on into Kentucky. Besides Longstreet's 16,000 men, 3,000 cavalry under Major General William T. Martin, 5,000 infantry from Polk, and 10,000 troops from Beauregard will join Johnston, along with his own army of 41,000, giving him a total strength of 75,000. Furthermore, Bragg continues, "it is proposed to throw a heavy column of cavalry as a diversion into West Tennessee." Additional horses and transportation "will be furnished as soon as practicable," ammunition is abundant, and "it is believed the means of subsistence are ample." Once Johnston reaches Middle Tennessee, his army will be in a "country full of resources" and hence "entirely self-sustaining." The grand object of the offensive will be to take advantage of the "scattered forces of the enemy" and reclaim "the provision country of Tennessee and Kentucky."

Bragg entrusts this letter to his military secretary, Colonel John B. Sale, who travels to Dalton and delivers it on March 18 to Johnston, along with verbal elaborations. Johnston reads the letter and listens to Sale, then on the following day he transmits a long telegraphic message to Bragg, presenting reasons why the plan won't work: The Army of Tennessee does not have, nor is it likely to have in the near future, the wagons and animals needed to haul sufficient supplies into East Tennessee in order to occupy the railroad between Chattanooga and Knoxville long enough to "incommode the enemy forces" in the latter city. Moreover, because of their interior position, the Federals could easily prevent him and Longstreet from joining around Kingston "by attacking one of our armies with [their] united forces." Last but not least, "Grant's return to Tennessee indicates that he will retain that command for the present at least," in which case "he will advance as soon as he can with the greatest force he can raise." Therefore the only prudent, indeed the only feasible, thing to do is to await Grant's attack, repulse it, and "then make our own"; or "should the enemy not take the initiative, do it ourselves" by invading Middle Tennessee via northern Alabama. In any event, all of the troops—Longstreet's, Polk's, and Beauregard's—slated to join him for the advance into Tennessee, as proposed by Davis and Bragg, should instead be sent at once to Dalton.[16]

Once again Johnston had rejected Davis's proposal for an immediate thrust into Tennessee, on the grounds that his army is incapable of offensive action. Accordingly, the key question that Davis asks himself upon reading Johnston's message likewise remains the same: Is Johnston telling the truth about the condition of the Army of Tennessee, or is he just playing his old game of inventing excuses for doing nothing? On Davis's desk is another communication from Dalton which suggests that the latter is in fact the case. Dated March 7, it comes from Lieutenant General Hood:

His Excellency President Jefferson Davis:

My Dear Sir: I have delayed writing to you so as to allow myself time to see the condition of this army. . . . I am exceedingly anxious, as I expressed to you before leaving Richmond, to have this army strengthened so as to enable us to move to the rear of the enemy and with a certainty of success. An addition of 10,000 or 15,000 men will allow us to advance. We can do so, anyhow, by uniting with Longstreet. . . . We should march to the front as soon as possible, so as not to allow the enemy to concentrate and advance upon us. The addition of a few horses for our artillery will place this army in fine condition. It is well clothed, well fed, and the transportation is excellent. . . . the troops under General Polk and Loring united with the forces here, and a junction being made with General Longstreet, will give us an army of 60,000 or 70,000 men, which I think, should be sufficient to defeat and destroy all the Federals on this side of the Ohio River. . . . I never before felt that we had it so thoroughly in our power. . . .

You find, Mr. President, that I speak with my whole heart, as I do upon all things in which I am so deeply interested. God knows I have the interest of my country at heart, and I feel in speaking to you that I am so doing to one who thoroughly appreciates and understands my feelings. . . .

My prayer is that you may be spared to our country, and we may be successful in the coming campaign.[17]

By writing this letter, which is accompanied by letters to Secretary of War Seddon and to Bragg saying essentially the same things, Hood breaches military protocol, which holds that no subordinate general shall, except out of sheer necessity, communicate directly with the president or the War Department without the knowledge and permission of his commander. Obviously, however, Hood has no fear of being reprimanded by Davis, for it is also obvious that Davis had asked him, before Hood left Richmond, to report on the condition of the Army of Tennessee, particularly with respect to supplies and transport. More than that, Hood is well aware of Davis's eagerness for an early offensive in the West and so makes quite sure that the president will perceive that he fully shares that eagerness. One day in February, while still in Richmond, Hood told Mrs. Chesnut that "the President was finding fault with some of his officers in command," whereupon Hood had declared: "Mr. President, why don't you come and lead us yourself? I would follow you to the death." Mary Chesnut's response to this revelation was to say to Hood: "Actually—if you stay here in

Richmond much longer, you will grow to be a courtier. You came a rough Texian!"[18]

The effect of Hood's sub rosa communication, of course, is to gainsay everything that Johnston asserts about the offensive capabilities of the Army of Tennessee and to deepen Davis's suspicion—now approaching conviction— that Johnston lacks, not the means, but the will to strike at the enemy. Per Davis's instruction, Bragg on March 21 answers Johnston with a telegram, the curtness of which conveys the displeasure of the president and his chief of staff: "Your dispatch of the 19th does not indicate an acceptance of the plan proposed. The troops can only be drawn from other points for advance. Upon your decision of that point further action must depend."

In other words, only if Johnston actually begins an offensive will he get reinforcements; otherwise, not a single regiment.

Johnston quickly protests, declaring: "In my dispatch of 19th I expressly accept taking offensive, only differ with you as to details." But this avails him nothing. Davis and Bragg remain resolved to deny Johnston troops until he not only agrees to their plan but also begins executing it. They doubt that he will do either. [19]

Davis and Bragg has good cause to so doubt. As far back as January 21, Johnston wrote Jeb Stuart, the dashing head of the cavalry of the Army of Northern Virginia, that he regretted having been assigned to the command of the Army of Tennessee, adding "I have never believed . . . that we had the means of invading the enemy's country."[20] Nothing that has happened since has lessened his regret; in fact, quite the contrary. Davis has rejected nearly everything Johnston has proposed or requested: expansion of the Army of Tennessee's food-supply base; greater control by his headquarters over the quartermaster and commissary officers in Georgia; permission to reorganize his forces into three corps rather than two; the assignment to the Army of Tennessee of Major General Mansfield Lovell as a corps commander and of Colonel E. Porter Alexander as chief of artillery; and the transfer to Dalton of Polk's infantry. At the same time, Davis has persisted in urging Johnston to advance into Tennessee despite the latter's repeated declarations that this is utterly impracticable; Davis has stripped him of his best troops and sent them on a wild goose chase into Alabama while his army was being menaced by a far superior enemy force; and Davis has accused him, in effect, of lying about the weaknesses of the Army of Tennessee.[21] Only in two instances of consequence have Johnston's wishes been respected: allowing him to employ as his chief of staff

Brigadier General William W. Mackall, an experienced administrative officer and close friend; and posting Hood to the Army of Tennessee.

Johnston considers the latter "my greatest comfort since getting here—indeed the only one in a military way." He believes Hood is exactly what the Army of Tennessee needs: a great battlefield leader untarnished by that army's bitter heritage of defeat and internal dissension; a young general who can impart to the soldiers of the West the same spirit that characterizes Lee's troops in the East; and a corps commander who will be a more reliable and competent lieutenant than Hardee, whose ability Johnston deems mediocre and whom he suspects of having deliberately given Richmond a false impression of the battleworthiness of the forces at Dalton. So he happily welcomes Hood, whom he had "wanted very much." He invites Hood to dine with him, he takes long rides with him, and he discusses the army's condition and prospects with him—something he never does with Hardee.[22] Since Johnston surely knows, through Senator Wigfall and other Richmond sources, of Hood's friendship with Davis, perhaps he hopes to win the young general over to his side or at least to enlist his support in persuading the president that the Army of Tennessee is incapable of carrying out a successful offensive. If such is the case, then how chagrined and angry he would be if he could read the letter that Hood already has written to Davis.

Sitting in his log-and-canvas headquarters in Lookout Valley near Chattanooga, Major General Oliver Otis Howard, commander of the XI Corps, Army of the Cumberland, writes in his diary under the date March 28: "I am rather anticipating Johnston's undertaking some game before long. If he takes the initiative he may bother us considerably."

Other high-ranking Union officers in Tennessee express a similar concern. Their forces are scattered throughout the state and into Alabama; also many soldiers and units are absent on veteran furlough, thus greatly reducing the combat effectiveness of entire brigades and divisions. Should the Rebels perchance strike now and in strength, they indeed could cause trouble.[23]

Does this then mean that the Confederacy, by failing to launch an offensive in the West in the late winter or early spring, is letting a golden strategic opportunity slip by? Theoretically, yes; in actuality, no. Although some of his motives for saying so are suspect, Johnston is correct in maintaining that the Davis-Bragg plan is impractical and probably would lead to disaster. In spite of the veteran furloughs, the Union forces around Chattanooga and in northern Alabama number, according to their March returns, more than 82,000 infantry, cavalry, artillerymen, and engineers "present for duty," supported by close to 273 field pieces. By comparison, the Army of Tennessee totals only 55,000 troops of all arms and a mere 111 cannons, of which 42 are so small as to be of little value in battle. Furthermore, as Johnston has pointed out, the Federals can easily transfer forces from Chattanooga to the Nashville or the Knoxville areas should either be threatened; in fact, by using railroads, they can get to these places much faster than could the Confederates marching on foot. Finally, Johnston is also right in stating that even if, by some miracle, he could manage to bypass the enemy at Chattanooga and link up with Longstreet north of the Tennessee River, he would be unable to take along enough provisions or obtain a sufficient amount from the countryside to sustain his army for any length of time, much less push across the mountains westward to Nashville. The Army of Tennessee in truth does suffer from a serious shortage of wagons and draft animals; and in asserting that it could make its way through East Tennessee without major difficulty, both Davis and Bragg are ignoring the fact that during 1863 Bragg himself had rejected a move through that region (which he described as "destitute even of vegetation") as being logistically impossible—an opinion, incidentally, shared by Sherman, who in December 1863 told Grant "that any military man should send a force into East Tennessee puzzles me."[24]

The plans proposed by Davis and Bragg are the products of wishful thinking, as is a crackpot scheme of Longstreet's to mount his forces on mules and invade Kentucky. The simple, cruel truth is that the Confederates lack the means to take the offensive in the West with any reasonable prospect of success. Although it is doubtful that Johnston would adopt a different attitude under any probable circumstance, he again is right in arguing that the best thing for his army to do is to await the Union onslaught, defeat it, and then counterattack. Of course this strategy, too, might not work, but at least it gives the Army of Tennessee a fighting chance to foil the offensive now being prepared by Sherman.[25]

Part Five: Sherman Takes a Trip

Sherman leaves Nashville on the morning of March 25, traveling aboard a private car attached to the regular train to Decatur, Alabama. He wishes to talk to the generals of the various armies he now commands and to make arrangements for the campaign into Georgia. Accompanying him is Major General James Birdseye McPherson, his successor as commander of the Army of the Tennessee. McPherson is to Sherman what Sherman is to Grant—close friend and trusted lieutenant. Like Grant and Sherman, McPherson is a native of Ohio, where he spent a boyhood of dire poverty. Luckily a storekeeper had befriended him, sent him to a private academy, and helped him obtain an appointment to

James Birdseye McPherson (*Photographic History*, 10:129)

West Point. A brilliant student, he graduated in 1853 first in a class that contained, among others, John Bell Hood, to whom McPherson sometimes gave
much-needed tutoring in mathematics. During the Forts Henry and Donelson
campaign he served as chief engineer to Grant, who was highly impressed by his
diligence, skill, and intellect: "I should feel [McPherson's] loss," wrote Grant to
Halleck, "more than taking a division from me." At Grant's behest the War
Department promoted McPherson from colonel to brigadier general, then to
major general. In January 1863, Grant put him in charge of the XVII Corps, in
which capacity he played a major role in the Vicksburg campaign, notably at
the Battle of Champion's Hill, where his troops delivered the attack that drove
the Confederates back into their doomed fortress. As we have read, Grant
considers him, along with Sherman, to be a main contributor to his own

success. Sherman, for his part, believes that if the war lasts long enough and if McPherson lives, "he'll outdistance Grant and myself," for he "is a noble, gallant gentleman and the best hope for a great soldier." Physically, McPherson is about five feet ten, slender, "and a very handsome, gallant-looking man with rather a dark complexion, dark eyes," and a short brown beard already sprinkled with gray in spite of his being only thirty-five. Individuals find him pleasant, modest, and congenial; however the mass of his soldiers, while respecting his bravery and ability, dislike him because of his efforts (largely futile) to prevent and punish plundering. For some time he has been engaged to Miss Mary Hoffman of Baltimore, and prior to the Meridian Expedition he told Sherman he hoped to marry her before the spring campaign began. On March 14, Sherman, while on the way to confer with Grant, advised McPherson to "steal a furlough and run to Baltimore *in cog,* but get back and take part in the next move." But as soon as he returned to Nashville from Cincinnati, Sherman telegraphed the young general, who had gone to Cairo, Illinois, to join him at once. When McPherson arrived, Sherman said to him, "Mac, it wrings my heart but you can't go now." [26]

The train hauling the private car in which the two general are riding rattles south along the tracks of the Tennessee and Alabama Railroad. It passes through Franklin, Columbia, and Pulaski, crosses into Alabama, and stops for the evening at Athens. Here Sherman and McPherson visit Brigadier General Grenville M. Dodge, commander of what is called the Left Wing of the XVI Corps, Army of the Tennessee. Dodge, a handsome, middle-sized man not quite thirty-three, has another name—"Level Eye"—given to him by Indians in Iowa, where before the war he had worked as a railroad surveyor and engineer. Because of his knowledge of railroads he has been, since late 1862, in charge of rebuilding and protecting the Tennessee and Alabama, an assignment he has performed with notable efficiency. His combat experience is slight: the Battle of Pea Ridge in northwestern Arkansas early in 1862, where he commanded a brigade and was badly wounded with the result that he is a "a little hump-backed." But both Grant and Sherman have a high opinion of his military talents, far higher than they do of those of the head of the XVI Corps, Major General Stephen Hurlbut, a Republican politician from Illinois who dislikes serving in the field, perhaps because it interferes with his favorite activities—drinking and engaging in shady financial operations.

Sherman and McPherson spend only a brief time with Dodge, who is ailing. The main question they ask him is, "Are there practicable routes by which a large force can march through northeastern Alabama into the Coosa River Valley of Georgia near Rome?" Dodge answers yes, and two days later he sends McPherson a detailed report on the various roads, river crossings, and availability of forage. [27]

Grenville M. Dodge (*Photographic History*, 10:21)

On March 26, Sherman and McPherson travel to Huntsville, their train switching onto the Memphis and Charleston tracks at Decatur. Huntsville is the headquarters of the Army of the Tennessee, of which McPherson now formally assumes command. It also is the headquarters of the XV Corps, Sherman's old corps, now headed by Major General John A. Logan. He is "rather a visish [vicious] looking man" in the opinion of one of his soldiers; he has a stocky, barrel-chested body, a thick mane of black hair hanging about his neck, an enormous black mustache, a swarthy complexion, and black eyes that glow in battle with a warrior's light. For, like Cleburne, Forrest, and a goodly number of other civilians-turned-soldiers in both armies, the war has revealed in him a natural talent for fighting. When it began, he was a Democratic congressman from southern Illinois, where he was born in 1826. Known as Egypt, this region was settled mainly by Southerners; and because he himself was from a Southern family and vehemently antiabolitionist, some people thought he might not support the Union cause or might even join the rebels. All doubts about his loyalty, however, ended at First Bull Run, where, not content merely to watch the fighting like other congressional sightseers, he picked up a musket and, attired in frock coat and plug hat, took some potshots at the Confederates! Soon after, he resigned from Congress, raised a volunteer regiment, became its colonel, and went off to fight on a full-time basis. This he did quite well, first at Belmont, next at Fort Donelson, and above all during the Vicksburg Campaign, in which the division he then headed delivered the deciding blows at the battles of Raymond and Champion's Hill. By the time Vicksburg fell, Grant deemed Logan qualified to lead an independent army, and at the end of 1863 Logan became commander of the XV Corps. His men call him Black Jack and think he is "a very jolly sort of general" because of his free and easy ways off the battlefield and his flamboyant manner on it. Back home in Illinois he has an accomplished and attractive wife, Mary, who worships him and believes that someday he will make her First Lady. He himself has high hopes of someday residing in the White House, which is one reason he has switched his allegiance to the Republican party.[28]

On the twenty-seventh, Sherman and McPherson inspect bridges over the Tennessee and visit other facilities in northern Alabama, ending up at Scottsboro. In addition, Sherman telegraphs a series of dispatches to sundry generals in West Tennessee and Kentucky, instructing them on how to deal with Forrest, who suddenly has dashed into that area with a force reported to be anywhere from 3,000 to 8,000 strong (actually he has only about 2,000 and no artillery). Sherman assumes that Forrest merely is after recruits, and he is confident that if his orders are promptly executed, Forrest will be trapped and destroyed. Nevertheless, he is becoming annoyed by this Confederate raider who never seems to rest and whom the Northern cavalry never seems to be able to defeat.[29]

George H. Thomas (Robert Tomes, *War with the South* [New York: Virtue & Yorston, 1867], vol. 3)

From Scottsboro a night train takes Sherman and McPherson to Chattanooga and Thomas's headquarters. As his private car rattles along, Sherman cannot help but wonder what sort of reception he will get from Thomas. He and Tom were roommates at West Point and remained good friends afterwards; early in the war, while Sherman unhappily commanded in Kentucky, Thomas served under him. But he is several years older than Sherman, senior in rank, became commander of the Army of the Cumberland while Sherman still headed only a corps, and is famous as the "Rock of Chickamauga." Should Thomas resent Sherman's being placed over him, it would be quite human and very understandable. It also would be potentially disastrous, for the Army of the Cumberland is by far the largest and best-equipped component of the forces that Sherman plans to lead into Georgia, and without the full and willing support of Thomas and his generals, it will be difficult if not impossible for Sherman to succeed.

On the morning of March 28, Sherman and McPherson meet with Thomas. He is a large man, nearly six feet tall and weighing 220 pounds. His hair is light brown, and his short, thick, square beard is rapidly turning white. The eyes are blue and keen; the face is phlegmatic and stern; he moves slowly, almost ponderously; and he speaks in a deliberate manner with a soft voice which reveals that he is a Southerner—to be exact, a native of Southampton County, Virginia. In Southampton he has three sisters who no longer consider him their brother, and in the South as a whole he is regarded as a renegade. Why he remained loyal to the Union he never has explained and never will. Some say it is because of long absences from home during his regular army career, others allege the influence of his New Yorker wife. But perhaps the best clue to why he wears a blue rather than a gray uniform is in what he said following Missionary Ridge to a chaplain who asked him if the Union dead should be buried by states: "No, mix them up. I've had enough of state's rights."[30]

Thomas greets his old friend Billy Sherman warmly and is cordial to McPherson, who studied artillery and cavalry tactics under Thomas at West Point (another student was Hood). Nothing in his manner suggests resentment or constraint, and he is thoroughly professional as he describes the situation of his army and what he knows about Johnston's. Sherman expected Tom to act this way, but it is good to have that expectation confirmed. Sometime later, when one of Sherman's staff officers asks him if there is any truth to rumors that Thomas is disgruntled over not having received the top command in the West, Sherman replies: "Not a bit of it. It don't make any difference which of us commands the army. I would obey Tom's orders tomorrow as readily and cheerfully as he does mine today. But I think I can give the army a little more impetus than Tom can." If Thomas in fact does consider it unfair to be subordinated to

Sherman, he does not show it; perhaps, conceivably, he does not even allow himself to feel it. As he once said to an officer who told him that he felt wronged at being passed over for promotion, "Colonel, I have taken a great deal of pains to educate myself not to feel."[31]

Thomas's personal and historical admirers will not be so stoical. They shall argue that he deserved to be made overall Union commander in the West because his military experience and accomplishments were superior to Sherman's. As a young artillery officer his gallantry at Buena Vista gained him promotion to brevet major, whereas Lieutenant Sherman saw no combat at all in the Mexican War. During the 1850's, while Sherman was failing as a banker and speculator, Thomas was a West Point instructor and a major in the famous Second Cavalry Regiment, which had Albert Sidney Johnston as its colonel and Lee as its lieutenant colonel. When serving in Kentucky in 1861, Thomas, unlike Sherman, took a realistic view of the enemy's capabilities and tried to persuade Sherman to do the same. In January 1862, while Sherman was relegated to drilling recruits at St. Louis, Thomas won the first important Northern victory of the war at Mill Springs, crumpling the right flank of the Confederate front in Kentucky. During the siege of Corinth, Mississippi, during the late spring of 1862, he headed a corps; Sherman, only a division. Thomas could have superseded Buell as commander of what became the Army of the Cumberland in September 1862, but Thomas's sense of honor and duty caused him to decline the post when Lincoln offered it to him. His calm declaration that "This army can't retreat," along with his skillful tactics, prevented a disaster at Stone's River and helped make that vicious battle a strategic victory, even as Sherman was limping away from his bloody repulse at Chickasaw Bluffs. At Chickamauga, Thomas again saved the Army of the Cumberland from destruction with his rocklike stand against the otherwise triumphant Confederates. And at Missionary Ridge, when Sherman's attack on Bragg's right bogged down, it was Thomas's Cumberlanders who broke the enemy center in the most spectacular assault of the war. In sum, troops directly under Thomas never have experienced defeat; those under Sherman have known it more often than not. Consequently, Thomas, not Sherman, should have been placed in command of the West.[32]

This constitutes a powerful case. Yet it is irrelevant. Grant's choice of Sherman to be supreme commander in the West was inevitable. Grant and Sherman are bound together by shared tribulations, shared triumphs, and the ties of friendship and reciprocal gratitude; accordingly Grant can rely upon Sherman to carry out his plans with the utmost vigor and dedication. No such relationship exists between Grant and Thomas, nor can it exist. Grant's associations with Thomas during the war have all been brief and formal; Grant considers the big Virginian to be slow and unaggressive; and for reasons that are obscure, each man dislikes and distrusts the other. Hence it is best, as well as inevitable, that Grant has placed Sherman in charge of the West: Thomas could not possibly receive from Grant the confidence and freedom of action that Sherman enjoys, with the result that Thomas's conduct of operations almost surely would be hamstrung by a worried and suspicious Grant viewing events from afar in Virginia.[33]

March 29 finds Sherman aboard his private car on the way to Knoxville. This time McPherson is not with him, having returned to Huntsville. In Knoxville, Sherman confers with Major General John M. Schofield. Of all the Union commanders in the West, Schofield is the youngest, the least impressive in appearance, and the most lacking in combat experience. He is thirty-two (which does not prevent him from being almost bald), wears glasses, and has a frizzy beard which covers his chest like a black bib; and although of medium height, he gives the impression of being short because he is so plump. During three years of war he has been in only one battle—Wilson's Creek, August 10, 1861, a Union defeat in Missouri. Most of the time he has been commander of the Department of the Missouri, engaged in the frustrating tasks of trying to suppress Confederate guerrillas and of dealing with the rival Unionist political factions. However, this son of an Illinois Baptist preacher possesses a well-deserved reputation for keen intelligence. He finished first in mathematics in his class at West Point (that of 1853, the same that included McPherson and Hood), he returned to the academy as an instructor in that subject, and when the war began, he was on leave from the army, serving as a professor of physics at Washington University in St. Louis. Also he enjoys Halleck's friendship, Lincoln's confidence, and the gratitude of Grant for the prompt fashion in which he dispatched troops from Missouri to help out in the siege of Vicksburg. It was for these reasons that Schofield received command of the Army of the Ohio back in January, an assignment that delighted him, since it enabled him at long last to escape the military backwater and political jungle of Missouri and to serve in a major theater of operations. Intensely ambitious, cool and calculating, and bitter because political enemies are blocking his confirmation by the Senate as a major general, he intends to make the most of his opportunity by performing whatever is asked of him with utmost zeal, hoping thereby to enhance Grant's favorable opinion of him and to win Sherman's. Obviously these two generals will dominate the regular army after the war.[34]

Sherman learns two things of import from Schofield. One is that the Army of the Ohio is much smaller than he had thought—so small in fact that it does not deserve to be called an army. Two weeks ago, Grant had ordered the IX Corps transferred from East Tennessee to Virginia, with the result that Schofield was

John M. Schofield (*Photographic History,* 10:173)

left with only the XXIII Corps—two infantry divisions presently totaling less than 7,000 effectives—and about 2,000 functionable cavalry. The other item of information is that all signs indicate that Longstreet is pulling back toward Virginia, possibly with a view to reinforcing Johnston but probably to rejoin Lee. Sherman decides forthwith to add 5,000 Indiana recruits, recently arrived in Nashville, to the XXIII Corps, thereby giving it three divisions and something approaching respectable strength. He also tells Schofield that the Army of the Ohio will constitute the left wing of the Union forces invading Georgia and that he is to begin preparing to move down to the Chattanooga area within a month. As for Longstreet, should he indeed withdraw into Virginia, Schofield is to let him go and is to station enough troops near Morristown, Tennessee, to deter any future enemy sally toward Knoxville. Sherman leaves the conference favorably impressed with Schofield. "He has," Sherman soon writes brother John, "a good reputation for steadiness, courage & soldierly qualities and it is only a pity he got mixed up with politics."[35]

The next day, March 31, Sherman heads back to Chattanooga, stopping along the way to telegraph fresh instructions for apprehending Forrest, who five days ago had raided Paducah, Kentucky. A little before 9 P.M., Sherman arrives in Chattanooga and goes to Thomas's headquarters.[36] He wants to talk some more to Tom, mainly about supplies and organization but also about possible ways of defeating Johnston and taking Atlanta. Much remains to be done if, as he has promised Grant, his forces are to be ready by the end of April to launch an offensive into Georgia at the same time the Army of the Potomac moves against Lee in Virginia.

Some twenty-five miles to the southeast of Chattanooga, in the camp of Cleburne's Division near Dalton, Captain Key writes in his diary, describing a "sham battle" that was held during the day by Hardee's Corps: "The dark lines of men made a grand display as they moved in battle array, their guns glistening in the sunlight. There were many ladies on a distant hill to witness our fight. One line representing the Southerners threw out their skirmishers and drove back the Yankee line, and in turn the Yankees brought up their skirmishers and drove the Southerners skedaddle." After the "battle" ended, he adds: "We returned to camp expecting to have it renewed the following day with bloody carnage." Yesterday "distant cannonading was heard in the direction of the enemy."[37]

CHAPTER FOUR

APRIL

Part One: Sherman at Nashville

ON APRIL 1, Sherman confers some more with Thomas at Chattanooga, then proceeds to Nashville where he arrives the next morning. His tour of inspection is completed. He has talked to his top generals, found out what they have and need, and assigned them their roles in the forthcoming campaign. As outlined in a letter to Grant on April 10, Thomas's Army of the Cumberland, seconded by Schofield's Army of the Ohio, will advance against Johnston from the north and northeast. At the same time, McPherson's Army of the Tennessee will move through Alabama toward Rome, Georgia, thereby threatening to sever Johnston's communication line to Atlanta. Should Johnston, whom Sherman does not expect to make a stand at Dalton because of this threat, fall back behind either the Coosa or the Etowah River, McPherson will push on to Rome. Should Johnston retreat south of the Chattahoochee, which Sherman considers more likely, then McPherson will join Thomas in pursuing him to Atlanta.

In assigning McPherson what is obviously the key role, Sherman assumes that when the campaign gets under way, the Army of the Tennessee will have back in its ranks both of A. J. Smith's divisions in Louisiana and the two divisions of the XVII Corps presently on furlough, giving it "full thirty thousand of the best men in America." He also hopes that while he is invading Georgia, Banks will "carry Mobile and open up the Alabama River," which "will in a measure solve the most difficult part of my problem, viz., 'provisions.'" But if Banks cannot do that, Sherman will go ahead regardless: "Georgia has a million inhabitants. If they can live, we should not starve."[1]

In the April 10 letter to Grant, Sherman defines his mission as being "to knock Jos. Johnston, and to do as much damage to the resources of the enemy as possible." On the surface this seems to be in accordance with instructions Grant sent him on April 4 "to move against Johnston's army, to break it up, and to get into the interior of the enemy's country as far as you can, inflicting all the damage you can against their war resources." But if we examine the specifics of what Sherman proposes to do, we find that he actually violates the spirit, if not the letter, of Grant's instructions. Thus he intends to do first what Grant has directed him to do second—"get into the interior of the enemy's country." Furthermore, instead of endeavoring to "knock" Johnston and break up his army, Sherman merely will seek to maneuver him into retreating south of the Chattahoochee, whereupon he will, as he also informs Grant in his April 10 letter, send cavalry to cut the railroad between Atlanta and Montgomery and then "feign to the right, but pass to the left and act against Atlanta or its eastern communications, according to developed facts."[2] In other words his prime objective is, contrary to the clear implication of Grant's instructions, not Johnston's army, but Atlanta.

This shift in priorities in part reflects Sherman's dislike of battles, which he regards as dangerously unpredictable in outcome. In part, too, it stems from his penchant for Meridian-style raids, with their minimum of fighting and maximum of marching. But the fundamental reason for it is his belief, stated in an April 24 letter to McPherson, that Grant's offensive in Virginia will be the "principal" one and that his own in Georgia is "secondary."[3] Consequently he does not consider his main task to be defeating Johnston but rather preventing him from reinforcing Lee. "I will," he promises Grant in the April 10 letter, "ever bear in mind that Johnston is at all times to be kept so busy that he cannot in any event send any part of his command against you." Furthermore, Grant himself takes the same view of the matter. When he responds to the letter on April 19, he says nothing whatsoever about Sherman's plan as such, despite its de facto evasion of Grant's instructions. Instead, like Sherman, Grant emphasizes the need to forestall Lee and Johnston from reinforcing each other: "If the enemy in your front shows signs of joining Lee, follow him up to the full extent of your ability. I will prevent the concentration of Lee upon your front, if it is in the power of this army to do it."[4]

Before Sherman can move against Johnston, he must first solve what he defines as the "most difficult of my problems, viz., 'provisions.'" Although the railroads now supply amply the "daily wants of the army" collected around Chattanooga, "they do not," he informs Grant on April 2, "accumulate a surplus." What Sherman wants at Chattanooga is enough food, forage, ammunition, and other necessities to maintain 100,000 soldiers and 35,000 horses and mules for seventy days. This achieved, a break in the supply line from Nashville to Chattanooga, or from Louisville to Nashville, would not be calamitous: his forces still could keep pushing southward, or at least not have to retreat, while their supply line was being restored.

The key to obtaining the needed surplus is to increase greatly the flow of supplies from Nashville to Chattanooga. Nashville itself is, in the words of one quartermaster officer, "the biggest army depot today on the face of the earth"; its warehouses, many of which cover whole blocks and one of which is a half-mile long, actually are overstocked with provisions and forage, there being enough of the former to feed 200,000 troops three meals a day for four months! However, an average of only sixty-five to eighty freight cars a day are arriving in Chattanooga from Nashville. Making matters worse, the trains contain numerous passenger cars filled with soldiers returning from furlough; parents seeking the body of a slain boy; wives on the way to visit husbands; preachers and politicians; refugees returning home; and mere sightseers. Indeed, even the freight cars often are taken up by troops, horses, cattle, and all sorts of nonmilitary items being sent from the North by the Christian and Sanitary commissions. As a consequence, no more than six hundred tons, and usually less, of supplies reach Chattanooga a day, and arms and munitions sometimes lie as long as two weeks in depots before being delivered.

On April 2, in quick response to Sherman's telegram to Grant about the supply situation, Stanton authorizes him to "take possession of railroads within your command." At once Sherman instructs Lieutenant Colonel Adna Anderson, McCallum's appointee as general superintendent of railroad transportation in the Military Division of the Mississippi, to seize all trains that come to Nashville from Louisville, even though they belong to the privately owned Louisville and Nashville Railroad Company. In addition, on April 6 he issues an order that places tight restrictions on the transportation of passengers and private freight, practically prohibits the hauling of livestock, declares that units moving to the front will march whenever possible, and states that all military posts near a major depot must obtain their supplies by wagon. As he anticipated, this decree produces an outcry from "all the Christian charities who are perambulating our camps, more to satisfy their curiosity than to minister to the wants of the poor soldiers." It leaves him unmoved. To pleas for exemptions and passes, he makes a standard answer: "Show me that your presence at the front is more valuable than two hundred pounds of powder, bread, or oats." Few try and fewer succeed.

Something else Sherman noticed during his inspection tour was that the army is feeding thousands of people in East Tennessee and northern Georgia. So, on April 19, he publishes another order, one that bans the issuance of rations to civilians living south of Nashville. The largest group affected are East Tennessee Unionists. Their spokesmen so loudly protest that Lincoln eventually telegraphs Sherman asking him if he could repeal or modify the ban. Sherman replies in characteristic style: "We have worked hard with the best talent of the country, and it is demonstrated that the railroad cannot supply the army and the people too. One or the other must quit, and the army don't intend to, unless Joe

Johnston makes us." Lincoln acquiesces, and the ban remains in force. The result, records a *New York Herald* correspondent, is a "hegira of poor, forlorn refugees" into Nashville and Kentucky and "human sufferings that might appall the angels." Sherman regrets this but feels it cannot be helped. "In peace," he writes to Assistant Secretary of War Charles Dana on April 21, "there is beautiful harmony in all the departments of life—they all fit together like the Chinese puzzle; but in war all is ajar. Nothing fits, and it is the struggle between the stronger and the weaker; and the latter, however it may appeal to the better feelings of our nature, must kick the beam. To make war we must and will harden our hearts."

Sherman's order to Anderson to bolster rolling stock by impressment from the Louisville and Nashville produces 15 locomotives and 120 cars. These, along with 4 engines and 75 cars taken from two other Kentucky lines, brings the total of locomotives and cars serving Chattanooga to about 140 and 1,500, respectively. As a consequence, and owing to the other measures Sherman has taken, the delivery of supplies rapidly accelerates. By the last week of April it averages 135 cars a day and soon will be 145. This is more than the 130 minimum that Anderson has told Sherman would be necessary for the accumulation of a vast reserve. When Lieutenant Colonel James C. Donaldson, chief quartermaster at Nashville, informs him of these figures, Sherman comments: "That's good, that's good, Donaldson. We'll be ready for the start."[5]

The chief threat to the continuation of the flow of supplies to Chattanooga comes from the Confederates cavalry, in particular Forrest. This fact is underlined in blood when on April 12, the third anniversary of the war, Forrest's troopers attack and capture Fort Pillow on the Mississippi River forty miles north of Memphis. In the process they massacre a large portion of the black and white soldiers constituting the garrison when, instead of surrendering, they attempt to escape by running down to the river bank in the vain hope of being rescued by a gunboat. "The slaughter was awful," writes Confederate Sergeant Achilles V. Clark to his "Dear Sisters" two days afterward. "The poor deluded negroes would run up to our men [and] fall upon their knees and with uplifted hands scream for mercy but they were ordered to their feet and then shot down. The white men fared but little better."[6]

News of the "butchery" at Fort Pillow outrages the North and causes Grant to conclude that Major General Stephen Hurlbut must go as commander of the District of Memphis. On Grant's instructions, Sherman replaces Hurlbut with Major General Cadwallader C. Washburn and sends Brigadier General Samuel D. Sturgis to "assume command of all cavalry at or near Memphis." Sherman's orders to Washburn and Sturgis are short and to the point: "Sally out and attack Forrest wherever he may be." As bad as it is to have Forrest "cavorting" through western Kentucky and Tennessee with brazen impunity, it would be infinitely worse should he break into Middle Tennessee and start wrecking the railroads between Nashville and Chattanooga. That must be prevented at all cost, and Sherman is determined to do it.

Sherman has good cause to be worried about Forrest. At Johnston's headquarters in Dalton is a letter from Forrest, dated April 6, which contains this passage: "I am of the opinion that everything available is being concentrated against General [Robert E.] Lee and yourself. Am also of opinion that if all the cavalry of this and your department could be moved against Nashville that the enemy's communications could be utterly broken up."[7]

Second only to supplies, Sherman's main concern during April is organizing and assembling the forces with which he plans to invade Georgia. Thus, shortly after telegraphing Grant on April 2 that rail traffic to Chattanooga must be increased, he wires him another dispatch requesting approval for the following: forming Schofield's Army of the Ohio into three infantry divisions and one cavalry division, the latter to be commanded by Major General George Stoneman; restructuring the Army of the Cumberland, which now consists of four corps, into three corps by consolidating tne XI and XII corps under Major General Joseph Hooker; assigning Major General Oliver Otis Howard to command the IV Corps in the Army of the Cumberland; and replacing Palmer as head of the XIV Corps with Major General Don Carlos Buell "or any tried officer." "With these changes," Sherman believes, "this army will be a unit in all respects, and I can suggest no better." As he explains in a follow-up letter to Halleck, he wants to "make this grand army a unit in action and feeling" and so avoid "the dissensions which have so marred the usefulness" of the Army of the Potomac.[8]

The most important of the changes proposed by Sherman revolves around Hooker, popularly known (to his annoyance) as "Fighting Joe." One year ago Hooker had occupied, in essence, the same position now held by Grant: Lincoln had entrusted Hooker with the tasks of winning the war by leading the Army of the Potomac to Richmond. Success in that mission would have meant his becoming the hero of the North and, quite likely, the next president of the United States. It was all his for the taking—if he could have taken Richmond. But he failed. After a brilliant beginning, in which he used his more-than-two-to-one superiority to outmaneuver Lee, Hooker suddenly faltered, then halted. This gave Lee a chance to launch a counteroffensive. Using only a fraction of

Joseph Hooker; General Dan Butterfield stands to his left. (*Photographic History,* 10:160)

his army to pin Hooker in front, Lee sent the rest of it, under Stonewall Jackson, to strike the Federal right flank at Chancellorsville. The result was the greatest—and last—victory won by the team of Lee and Jackson, as once again the Army of the Potomac fell back from Richmond. Yet it was Hooker, not his army, who was defeated. Despite the mauling his army received from Jackson, it not only was capable of holding out; it retained sufficient strength to counterattack and force Lee, whose losses were heavy, either to give way or else to engage in a bloodletting contest that he could not win. Hooker, however, ordered retreat. Some said he was suffering from shock, for he had been knocked unconscious when a cannonball hit a stone pillar against which he was leaning. Others claimed that he had been "shot in the neck" by too much whiskey, still others suggested that maybe the trouble was that he had not drunk his customary quota, which by common repute was large. But the best explanation of his failure came from Hooker himself: "For once I lost confidence in Joe Hooker."

So did Lincoln and Halleck. When Lee followed up Chancellorsville with his second invasion of the North, they removed Hooker from command of the Army of the Potomac and put Meade in his place, just in time for Gettysburg. It seemed that Fighting Joe might fight no more. However, there could be no doubt that he had a knack for combat, at least as long as he did not have the ultimate responsibility and could lead in person. No general is braver under fire, none is more popular with his troops, than this tall, handsome, dashing forty-nine-year-old West Pointer from California by way of Massachusetts. More to the point, perhaps, he has influential advocates among the Radical Republicans. Hence, after William S. Rosecrans was defeated at Chickamauga, Lincoln placed Hooker in command of the XI and XII corps, sending him from the Army of the Potomac to rescue the Army of the Cumberland.

Hooker hoped to regain in the West the prestige he had lost in the East. At Chattanooga he took a long stride in that direction. His troops captured Lookout Mountain in a so-called Battle above the Clouds, thereby contributing considerably to the Confederate collapse on Missionary Ridge. Had he quietly let this performance speak for itself, it would have been both to his credit and to his advantage. Instead, in his official report and through friendly journalists, he exaggerated his accomplishments, wrote Stanton that Grant was simple-minded, and pulled Washington wires with the object of getting back the command of the Army of the Potomac.

Hooker may be, as a friend describes him as being, "a general fitted by education, experience, and by the highest qualities of mind and heart, to command men in the great game of war." But unfortunately for him, he also is afflicted with vanity, self-seeking ambition, and an astonishing lack of discretion. These defects have garnered him the enmity of many of his fellow generals, notably that of the two he can least afford to offend—Grant and Sherman. Grant had resented Hooker's arrogant and uncooperative attitude during the Chattanooga operations and had come close to removing him from command then. Sherman, who had known and disliked Hooker in California, shares Grant's resentment and would like to get rid of him now. Since, however, this is inexpedient, given Lincoln's tolerant view of Fighting Joe, the best thing Sherman can think of is to do what he proposes: make Hooker head of a corps formed by combining the XI and XII corps. In this way three benefits can be realized: Hooker's awkward status as a quasi-independent commander will be eliminated, he will be reduced to a definitely subordinate status in the Army of the Cumberland, and the otherwise insoluble problem posed by his malignant personal relationships with the commanders of the XI and XII corps will be solved.

These commanders are, respectively, Major Generals Oliver Otis Howard and Henry B. Slocum. Both of them despise Hooker, who in turn hates them. Howard's XI Corps held the extreme Union right at Chancellorsville; it was this corps that Jackson surprised and routed in his great flank attack, in spite of the fact that Hooker had cautioned Howard to be alert for precisely such an attack. Naturally Hooker blames Howard for having lost the battle, naturally, too, Howard resents being so blamed. As for Slocum, he was so disgusted by what he considered Hooker's craven failure to counterattck at Chancellorsville after his XII Corps had stemmed Jackson's onslaught that when ordered west under Hooker's command, Slocum had submitted a letter to Lincoln resigning his commission; only after matters had been so arranged that he would be in charge of guarding the Nashville and Chattanooga Railroad and thus would not serve directly under Hooker did he withdraw his resignation.

Grant and Lincoln approve Sherman's request concerning Hooker and the XI and XII corps, which now become the XX Corps. Likewise they authorize him to appoint Howard commander of the IV Corps, replacing Major General Gordon Granger, who has asked to go on leave, and to put Slocum in charge of the District of Vicksburg, thereby eliminating any possibility of contact and conflict between him and Hooker. Although technically a step downward for him, Hooker is pleased by the new arrangement (or so Thomas reports to Sherman). The new XX Corps consists, at least nominally, of 25,000 veteran troops—the largest in Sherman's entire army. With it, Hooker doubts not, he can play a spectacular role in the forthcoming campaign, if given the chance. He writes a friend:

> You must know that I am regarded with more jealousy in this my new sphere of operation than I ever was in the East. It is not without reason for it is as certain as any future event can be that I shall be regarded as the best soldier in this Army if I am not now, provided we have a few opportunities to establish our relative merits. An effort of course will be made to prevent this but the result will likely to be as futile as the last one. I have never yet seen the time that there was no place for a man willing to fight.[9]

Howard likewise is happy with his new assignment. Writing his wife on April 25, he declares:

> I feel in a measure emancipated now that the 11th Corps is no more. . . . After the reverse at Chancellorsville, it was hard for me to cherish a feeling of confidence in the old Corps. . . . I like the 4th Corps. It is much larger than any command I have ever had except during the first day of

the battle of Gettysburg [where by virtue of seniority he briefly headed all the Union troops present].

Actually, however, Howard should consider himself lucky to hold any command at all, much less that of a corps. Not only had he allowed his troops to be surprised at Chancellorsville; his performances at Gettysburg and Chattanooga had at best been mediocre. He is a poor tactician, unenterprising, and so ostentatiously pious that the troops call him Old Prayer Book. In fact, he had seriously contemplated entering the ministry after graduation from West Point in 1850, had become a Methodist lay preacher, is a strict teetotaler, and blushes whenever anyone curses or takes the Lord's name in vain, a trait that causes some of his fellow generals to employ such language as frequently and as extravagantly as possible whenever he is around. Yet this slender, brown-bearded, thirty-three-year-old native of Maine is intelligent (he taught mathematics at West Point), brave (an empty right sleeve, the result of a wound at Seven Pines, testifies to that), and totally dedicated to duty. Since Sherman and Grant consider this last quality to be as important, if not more important, than military talent per se, it is the principal reason that they have picked him to command the IV Corps, thereby supplanting Major General Gordon Granger, whose battlefield record is much superior but who, like Hooker, is disliked and distrusted by Sherman and Grant. Howard, for his part, knows to whom he owes his rescue from Hooker's command and his assignment to the IV Corps; furthermore—this is another important consideration with Sherman and Grant, who also place great value on personal loyalty—he is not likely to forget it.[10]

The only change proposed by Sherman that he is unable to make is replacing Palmer as head of the XIV Corps with Buell or some other "tried soldier." Sherman wants to do this because he deems Palmer "not equal to such a command" and because he wants to utilize the abilities of Buell, whom he feels was wrongly deposed as commander of the Army of the Cumberland in 1862. But Buell, who took over from Sherman in Kentucky in 1861 and then (as he sees it) saved Grant from disaster at Pittsburg Landing, does not care to serve under either of those generals and so, on being offered the XIV Corps, rejects it and resigns his commission. With no time to look for someone else, Sherman perforce keeps Palmer. Ironically, Palmer, as he informs Thomas, would be glad to turn over the corps to Buell or any qualified general. Described by one soldier as "the most common man, of his rank, that there is in the army," Palmer is fed up with what he regards as the arrogant clannishness of West Pointers; he wants to return home to his wife and children, so much so, in fact, that in December he submitted his resignation, only to have his friend Lincoln reject it.[11]

Sherman's plan of campaign assumes, as has been noted, that the two divisions that are with A. J. Smith on Banks's Red River expedition will be able to rejoin the Army of the Tennessee before Sherman launches his invasion of Georgia. This proves to be an unrealistic assumption. On April 20 "a rumor of a check" to Banks's army reaches Nashville, and the following day it is confirmed by a dispatch from Brigadier General John M. Corse, whom Sherman has sent to Louisiana to hasten Smith's return: "Banks was attacked . . . near Mansfield, La., on the 8th instant, and retreated to Grand Ecore a la Bull Run. He refused to let Smith go, for obvious reasons." Sherman promptly relays this discouraging news to Grant. The next day, Grant instructs Sherman to leave Smith out of his calculations: "I always believed that forces sent to Banks would be lost for our spring campaign." Sherman, who had believed otherwise, replies that he will.[12]

And Sherman does. On April 24 he notifies Grant that instead of McPherson's heading through Alabama directly toward Rome, Georgia, he will march from Decatur and Larkin's Ferry on the Tennessee River across the northeast corner of Alabama to Lafayette, Georgia, "where he will act against Johnston, if he accepts battle at Dalton; or move in the direction of Rome, if the enemy give up Dalton, and fall behind the Oostenaula or Etowah." There is, Sherman continues, "some risk" in having McPherson operate so far from the rest of the army; but "should Johnston turn his whole force" against him, McPherson will have several avenues of escape available; and if Johnston retreats southward, then "Thomas will have force enough to push on through" to Kingston, thereby preventing Johnston from falling on McPherson at Rome.

This new plan is less ambitious than Sherman's original one, in that the thrust to Rome has merely become an option and McPherson initially will move toward, rather than away from, the rest of the army. Even so, it also assumes that the XVII Corps's two furloughed divisions will be on hand for the beginning of the campaign; indeed, Sherman thinks that "some of them should now be in motion for Clifton [Tennessee], whence they will march to Decatur, to join General Dodge."[13] Obviously he does not know that all of the troops of both divisions presently are at Cairo, Illinois, and that it will be some time yet before any of them set out for Clifton or any other place south of there.

Part Two: Johnston at Dalton

Schofield's report to Sherman late in March that Longstreet appeared to be pulling out of East Tennessee is correct, although slightly premature. Not until April 7 does Jefferson Davis direct Longstreet to bring his corps to Charlottesville, Virginia, where it again will be part of Lee's army. Longstreet gladly and quickly complies, for there is nothing he can accomplish by remaining in Tennessee, where, as he telegraphs the War Department, "our animals are dying for want of forage." Hundreds of mostly destitute pro-Confederate civilians accompany his troops into Virginia, fearful of Unionist persecution if they stay behind. With Longstreet gone, as Sherman notes in an April 24 letter to Schofield, "there remains now in East Tennessee no rebel force that can come down on our flank that could seriously endanger us moving forward from Chattanooga."[14]

At Dalton, Johnston is unaware that Longstreet has been ordered back to Virginia. Johnston does sense, however, that Davis and Bragg are displeased by his rejection of their "particular plan of operations" whereby he was to link up with Longstreet for an advance into Middle Tennessee and Kentucky. Hence on April 8 he sends his assistant adjutant general, Colonel Benjamin Ewell, to Richmond to confer with the president. Ewell is to explain that Johnston is not opposed to an offensive as such but merely to the one specified, and it is his purpose to advance against the enemy as soon as practicable; that to this end Johnston has been "actively engaged in making preparations" but through no fault of his own was short at least one thousand wagons and needs artillery horses; that "the surest means of securing a forward movement" by Johnston is to provide him "at once" with enough reinforcements so that if the Federals attack first, he will be able to defeat them south of the Tennessee River, where the "results of a victory will be so much more favorable and those of a defeat so much less disastrous than if the battle were fought north of the river"; that the strength of the enemy around Chattanooga is at least 80,000 with another 15,000 from "McPherson's corps" on the way; and finally, that the Army of Tennessee's cavalry is "much weaker and more inefficient than was represented."

Ewell arrives in Richmond on April 13 and goes to see Bragg, who he understands is "the proper medium of communication with the President." Bragg arranges an interview with Davis for tomorrow; then he and Ewell have (in Ewell's words) a "full and free conversation." Bragg states that he wants Johnston "properly re-enforced" but fears that as a consequence of Longstreet's evacuation of Tennessee and the reported concentration of enemy forces in Virginia and North Carolina, "little could be done." However he is "desirous to have the matter settled," so he asks Ewell to have Johnston give a "categorical answer" by tomorrow as to whether he will assume the offensive if strengthened by 15,000 infantry from Beauregard's and Polk's departments.

Ewell at once telegraphs Johnston: "Longstreet has been ordered to Virginia. He cannot join you. Can I tell the President you will assume offensive with 15,000 additional troops? It is important that I receive your reply immediately."

For some reason Johnston does not answer until the next day. Then he does so in his characteristic equivocal style: "Assuming offensive must depend on relative forces. I shall be ready to do it whenever they warrant it." Meanwhile, that morning, Ewell meets with Davis and Bragg. Not having heard from Johnston, he takes it on himself to state that Johnston will advance if given 15,000 more men. He also presents Johnston's explanations as to why he objects to an offensive along the lines proposed by the president and Bragg. Davis listens "with apparent interest," then expresses regret that Johnston had not undertaken an offensive in time to prevent the enemy's present assemblage of forces against Lee. Yet, Davis adds, it still is "very important that offensive operations be assumed" by Johnston and that "all possible re-enforcements be at once sent" to Dalton. As regards future movements by Johnston's army, Davis comments that it is "not thought expedient to force a plan of campaign on any general commanding an army, as without the hearty co-operation of the general its successful execution would be almost impossible"; Ewell responds by saying that this is true, but that it also is "eminently proper for a general to state his objections whenever a plan is proposed to him, that these might be met or overruled, if the authorities so decide"—an observation to which Davis expresses assent. The conference ends with Davis's stating that it would be several days before he could give a "definite answer" to Johnston's request for more troops, but that "every effort" would be made to bolster his army.

Five days later, Ewell returns to the War Office, where Bragg tells him that "the pressure at Richmond" as a result of Grant's buildup "was too great to effectively aid" Johnston now but that "when circumstances warranted," substantial reinforcements would be ordered to him. Meanwhile a brigade would be transferred from Mobile to Georgia, and five large regiments presently with Beauregard would be sent to the Army of Tennessee in exchange for five small ones, thus giving Johnston "an immediate accession of about 4,000 men." On April 20, Ewell heads back to Dalton after handing Bragg a memorandum putting on record the verbal explanations of Johnston's views which he had presented earlier. Insofar as obtaining a speedy and heavy reinforcement for Johnston, Ewell's mission is a failure; indeed, it is doubtful that it has accomplished anything of substance at all.

Davis has two reasons for refusing to give Johnston the troops he wants. The first is the belief that the main Federal push in 1864 will be by Grant against Lee and that consequently Sherman represents a comparatively minor threat. To a degree this is a valid assessment: Grant in fact is massing huge forces in Virginia and along the North Carolina coast, altogether 160,000 troops as opposed to barely half that number of Confederates; and Lincoln, the Northern public, and Grant and Sherman themselves look to Grant to win the war in Virginia. Davis's strategic perception, however, is warped by a serious misconception. He believes (perhaps because he wants to believe) that the Federals lack the means to conduct large-scale offensives in the East and in the West simultaneously, and so he assumes that their one big effort will of course be where Grant personally commands. Encouraging Davis in this assumption are reports from a variety of sources, both Northern and Southern, official and private, that the Union XI, XII, and XXIII corps, as well as Burnside's IX Corps, have been transferred from the West to the East.[15]

Davis's other reason for turning down Johnston's plea for substantial reinforcements is a familiar one: his deep distrust of Johnston. This has become deeper still as a result of reading certain reports and letters that came to Richmond before and during Ewell's visit. The first of these documents is a report dated March 29 by Brigadier General William M. Pendleton, chief of artillery for the Army of Northern Virginia, whom Bragg had sent to Dalton to check on Johnston's claim that his artillery is so inefficient as to be practically worthless in the field. Some of Pendleton's findings do support Johnston: many of the Army of Tennessee's cannons are too small to be effective, and most of the horses assigned to pull them are thin and worn down. On the other hand, measures are under way to replace the inadequate pieces with more potent ones; a much-needed chief of artillery has been provided with the appointment of Brigadier General Francis A. Shoup, "said to be an excellent officer," to that post; and the condition of the horses is not worse "than in other commands at all similarly situated." Therefore, concludes Pendleton, with the addition of 500 horses, "soon to be furnished," the Army of Tennessee's artillery "will be capable at an early day, I am satisfied, of effective service."[16]

The second document is a report mailed for Dalton on April 11 by Lieutenant Colonel Arthur H. Cole, who was sent by the Quartermaster Department to investigate Johnston's assertion that his field transportation is insufficient for a long advance. On this point, as such, it backs Johnston fully: in order to have enough supplies for a move through East Tennessee into the Nashville area, the Army of Tennessee needs 900 wagons and 3,600 mules "over and above that on hand." However Cole's report also contains statements that are damning to Johnston's competency as an administrator: Johnston's chief quartermaster "has never estimated" the number of additional animals needed to remedy the existing deficiency. "On my arrival here I found that no one in this army knew what transportation was on hand, nor what was needed for campaign"; "of the 400 or 500 fine [artillery] horses impressed [for Johnston's army] . . . I find 100 at least used by officers, wagon-masters, clerks, &c."; and "I find every day I am furnishing him [Johnston] information concerning his transportation he never had before."[17] No one, least of all Davis, can read Cole's report without concluding that although Johnston is correct in claiming that he has insufficient transport for a Tennessee campaign, he is strangely ignorant about supply matters for a man who once was quartermaster general of the United States Army.

The third document takes the form of written comments by Bragg on another report from Pendleton. On April 15, while Ewell was conferring with Davis and Bragg, Pendleton met with Johnston in Dalton, having returned there to investigate further the situation in Georgia. During the meeting, which lasted the greater part of the day, he repeated the now-standard arguments of Davis and Bragg in favor of an immediate offensive, and Johnston again expressed his customary reasons for why that was impracticable. Moreover, for the first time, Johnston backed his views with the testimony of his chief of cavalry, Major General Joseph Wheeler, who also was present. According to Wheeler, who gave the estimated size of every major Federal unit in Tennessee, Alabama, and Georgia, Sherman had available a total force of 103,000, not counting "about 15,000 negro troops and 5,000 unassigned (but armed) Tennesseans." Impressed by Wheeler's findings, Pendleton emphasized them in a memorandum that he delivered to Davis in Richmond on April 21. Davis read it, then promptly passed it on to Bragg. The next day, Bragg sent it back with an "indorsement" declaring that Wheeler's figures were much too high, that Sherman at a "very liberal esitmate" had only 70,000 men, of which he could use no more than 60,000 in the field. Since Bragg's woefully mistaken calculations supported what Davis already believed, their effect was to neutralize in the president's mind the impact of Wheeler's far-more-accurate data, which, incidentally, is neutralized still more by Wheeler himself, who in an April 16 letter to Bragg states that 15,000 reinforcements would enable the Army of Tennessee to advance.[18]

The fourth and perhaps most influential document is another letter from John Bell Hood, the general who provides Johnston with his "greatest comfort." Addressed to Bragg on April 13 and marked "Private," it surely is read by Davis. In it Hood states that he

is sorry to inform you that I have done all in my power to induce General Johnston to accept the proposition you made to move forward. He will not consent. . . . I regret this exceedingly, as my heart was fixed upon our going to the front and regaining Tennessee and Kentucky. . . . When we are to be in a better condition to drive the enemy from our country I am not able to comprehend. To regain Tennessee would be of more value to us than a half dozen victories in Virginia.[19]

Nothing more is needed to confirm Davis's long-existing suspicion that Johnston simply does not want to carry the war to the enemy, that he is obstinately intent upon awaiting the Federal advance, and that accordingly, any troops sent to Dalton now would remain idle until that happens. But as before, there is nothing that Davis can do about what he perceives as Johnston's almost insubordinate recalcitrance. Removing him from command remains inexpedient, and as he told Ewell, it is dangerous to "force a plan of campaign upon any general commanding an army." Besides, it now is too late for the army of Tennessee to take the offensive, because, according to Cole's report, it could not possibly be ready in time to beat Sherman to the punch. All that can be hoped is that Johnston will be able to do what he proposes to do—defeat the enemy attack south of the Tennessee, then counterattack north across that river.

Ewell reports Davis's refusal to provide strong reinforcements for the Army of Tennessee to Johnston at Dalton on April 29. Johnston is not surprised. He already knows the outcome of Ewell's mission, and it is merely what he expected. After all, with a few exceptions, when has Davis ever granted Johnston what he has requested? And had not Wigfall warned him that "every effort would be made to produce your defeat"? Again thoughts of resignation flit through Johnston's mind. But no: to do that on the eve of battle would demoralize his army, which he considers to be "my true friend." So he will stay on, hoping that Davis will realize in time that the Confederate forces in Georgia face terrible odds, that their only chance of defeating the enemy is to stand on the defensive, and that they will not be able to do even that unless they are strengthened by every soldier that possibly can be detached from Beauregard and Polk. "The U.S.," Johnston writes Wigfall, "have the means of collecting two great armies—here & in Virginia. Our government thinks they can raise but one, that of course in Virginia."[20]

Part Three: The Armies

An April 30 report to Secretary of War Seddon from Colonel John S. Preston, superintendent of the Bureau of Conscription (and father of Hood's fiancée, Sally "Buck" Preston) makes it clearer than ever before that a Northern loss of will to go on with the war is the South's sole realistic hope of winning it. The report states that in spite of the new conscription law and all other efforts, since December the Confederate army has been able to add a mere 18,144 men to its ranks—8,036 returned deserters, 7,513 conscripts, and a pathetic total of 2,325 volunteers. Obviously the prediction of War Department clerk Jones back in January that the Confederacy would have 400,000 "effectives" in the field by spring has proved to be wishful thinking. The harsh fact is that the Southern army's overall strength is little more than it was at the beginning of the year—about 250,000 men—and that a statement made in the *New York Tribune* on March 17 is all too true: "The Rebels are now at the end of their chain. As a thousand fall, or are disabled by wounds or disease, there is no more to take their places."[21]

Yet, as such, the war continues to go well for the South. Besides the defeat of Banks in Louisiana and Forrest's capture of Fort Pillow, on April 20 a small Rebel army backed by an ironclad has retaken Plymouth, North Carolina, from the Federals and has killed, wounded, or captured nearly 3,000 of them. Coming on the heels of the successes in February and March, these spectacular victories seem to demonstrate that the Confederate army, in spite of everything, retains sufficient strength to hold the Yankees at bay. "Our military situation is very cheering," comments Secretary of State Judah P. Benjamin at the end of the month; and one of Johnston's soldiers writes his girlfriend in Mississippi that "in all probability this spring and summer will prove it vain for the North longer to dispute our rights." Northern Democrats would agree. The *New York World,* the *Chicago Times,* and other journals of the "peace party" report the defeats in Louisiana, Tennessee, and North Carolina with ill-concealed glee and declare once again that the war is a failure. They reinforce this contention by publishing stories from "special correspondents" asserting that Lee with "upwards of 95,000 men" plans an offensive, that Sherman will have to retreat soon to Nashville because he has a mere 60,000 troops against Johnston's 75,000, and that the defenses of Mobile, Savannah, and Wilmington make these blockade-running ports virtually impregnable.[22]

Yet, as Sergeant Robert Bliss of the 16th Alabama points out in a letter to his father from Dalton on April 24, all that has happened so far in 1864 are mere "side shows that are being enacted prior to the larger ones in Virginia and Northern Georgia." With regards to Virginia, Southerners are confident that Lee will be able to do to Grant what he has done to all of his predecessors—hurl him back in bloody, humiliating defeat. What they are unsure about is Georgia and the Army of Tennessee. Too many times that army has disappointed their hopes and expectations; even its only clear-cut victory, Chickamauga, turned into the ashes of defeat at Missionary Ridge. Will it do better under Johnston than it did under Bragg? Can it defeat, or at least stop, Sherman? All intelligent and informed Southerners realize that the outcome of the war might be determined by the answers that events give to these questions. Even Lee, accused by some as being obsessed with his beloved Virginia and blind to the importance of the West, believes that "upon the defense of the country threatened [by the Federal forces at Chattanooga] depends the safety of the points now held by us on the Atlantic."[23]

On Tuesday, April 19, Johnston holds a grand review of the entire Army of Tennessee except for units that either are engaged in keeping an eye on the enemy to the north or else are stationed at various places to the south. That evening Captain Key describes the review in his diary:

> Boots and saddles, the name by which artillerists designate harnessing, sounded at 8 o'clock and Swett's, Semple's and Key's batteries moved to the large field south of Dalton. The whole army was out for review, General J. E. Johnston was the inspector, with hundreds of ladies. The army presented itself in the best condition that I have ever witnessed, and the thousands of hardy soldiers marching to the notes of the shrill fife and bass drum or the harmonious melodies of brass bands looked grand and cheering. I supposed from other information that the infantry numbered about 40,000 to 42,000, and 3,000 artillerists.[24]

Key's estimate of the Army of Tennessee's infantry strength is accurate. The official returns for April 30 show a little over 36,000 "effectives" in the four divisions of Hardee's Corps and the three of Hood's Corps. But since "effectives" in Confederate parlance refers solely to enlisted men who are equipped and ready for immediate combat, the addition of officers and detachments would bring the total up to at least 40,000, a figure confirmed by the "present for duty" column of the April 30 return, which lists 41,279 infantry of all ranks and units. Moreover, since the "aggregate present" column shows a total of almost 50,000, there probably are as many as 8,000 men who are serving as teamsters, musicians, clerks, cooks, hospital orderlies, and in other auxiliary capacities. Many of them are amputees or are hobbled with a stiff arm or leg, have fingers missing on the right hand (the left does not count), or suffer from some other infirmity that makes them unfit for combat. Indeed, as a rule, the only fully able-bodied men not bearing arms are the half-dozen or so in each regiment who are assigned the task of carrying wounded comrades to the rear; they are the steadiest and sturdiest soldiers in their outfits, for they must go into battle *without* weapons.

All seven of the infantry divisions are roughly equal in size, with between 5,000 and 7,000 troops each, which makes them slightly larger than their Federal counterparts. The brigades, of which there usually are four to a division, average around 1,500; but too many of their regiments are woefully understrength, so much so that some of them have been consolidated with other small regiments. Yet, even with consolidations, few regiments number over 300, and when Colonel John Cooper Nisbet arrives with his freshly recruited 66th Georgia of more than 1,000 men, the veterans sarcastically dub it the "bloody old 66th Brigade."[25]

Slightly over half of the infantry are equipped either with Enfield or Springfield rifle muskets. Except for a comparative few manufactured in Southern

Men of the Fifth Georgia, Army of Tennessee (taken early in the war) (*Photographic History*, 10:121)

factories, the Enfields come from England via blockade runners, whereas the Springfields are Yankee-made and usually have been captured. Both are single-shot muzzleloaders that have a "killing range" of three hundred yards and can be effective up to five hundred yards. They are similar in length (54 inches for the Enfield, 56 for the Springfield), in weight (8 pounds for the Enfield, 9 for the Springfield), and in caliber (.577 for the Enfield, .58 for the Springfield), which means they can use the same cartridges so long as the former does not become too badly fouled. By and large, both Northerners and Southerners prefer the Enfield because they consider it more reliable and accurate and less difficult to maintain; but the two rifles function equally well in combat. Most of the Army of Tennessee's remaining infantry are armed either with a .54-caliber Mississippi Rifle or, to a lesser extent, a .69-caliber musket that has been converted into a rifle; some regiments have smoothbores. The latter can be as deadly as rifles at close quarters when loaded with "buck and ball" (shotgun pellets plus a regular bullet) but are hopelessly outmatched at any range in excess of two hundred yards. Hardee's Corps, it should be noted, possesses the greater proportion of Enfields and Springfields.

Curiously, almost incredibly, most of the infantry hitherto has had little or no training in marksmanship; either there was not enough time and spare ammunition, or else their generals shared the prevalent popular notion that the typical Southerner was a huntsman already skilled in the use of firearms. In any case, starting in March the troops, at Johnston's order, have been practicing regularly on the firing range. Brigadier General Arthur Manigault, commander of an Alabama–South Carolina brigade in Hindman's Division of Hood's Corps, recalls:

> Each regiment had its own target, a large one not easily missed even at the greatest distance at which we fired (500 yards), laid off in squares and properly numbered and lettered. A company at a time from each regiment would practice, each man firing three shots a day. As one company would get through, another would take its place, and so on, from eight o'clock in the morning until four in the afternoon. Each man was obliged to fire his own rifle, so as to become as familiar with its quality and pecularities as possible. It took us several weeks to get through, but was regarded rather as a pastime by the men, the greater number taking much interest in it, and I think that they learned much more of their weapons, their capability, and how to handle and direct them, in those few weeks, than they did in the previous two and a half years.[26]

Man for man, most of Johnston's foot soldiers match Sherman's troops (who also are spending more time on the range) in firepower. The big exception occurs when the former encounter one of the growing number of Yankee companies and regiments that are equipped with repeating rifles. That can make a decisive difference, especially when attacking such a unit.

Key's estimate of the number of artillerists in the Army of Tennessee likewise is accurate. At the end of April they total 3,227 "present for duty," serving 144 cannons organized into 11 battalions and 34 batteries (including the cavalry). This is a high proportion of guns relative to the size of the army, perhaps too high. Moreover, as Pendleton reported, many pieces are too small and short-range to cope effectively with the Union artillery, and all suffer from the afflictions common to Confederate-produced and -supplied cannon: namely, low-grade powder, which causes them, in the words of one Confederate soldier, to make "a tremulous bell metal ring" when fired instead of the "sullen low bass" boom of the Yankee guns; shells that wobble while in flight and often fail to explode because of defective fuses; and inferior design and construction, as a result of which the 12-pounder Napoleon, the standard cannon, weighs 300 to 400 pounds more than Federal models of the same type and therefore is less mobile. The men who serve these guns are brave, experienced, and capable enough. Yet, because of their inferior equipment and ammunition, rarely have they matched, much less dominated, in battle their Union counterparts, who possess a much larger quantity of the more powerful, more accurate, and longer-range types of cannon. The best the Southerners can hope for is that the rugged terrain and thick forests of northern Georgia will reduce the Federal advantage.[27]

To compensate in part for the artillery's weakness, the Ordnance Bureau has distributed to all the major Confederate armies British-made Whitworth sniper's rifles, of which about one hundred have gone to the Army of Tennessee. These weapons mount telescopic sights and fire a .45-caliber cardboard-encased cartridge that is three inches long (two inches of powder, one of lead). They produce a loud "pop" when fired and, in the hands of a crack shot, have a fair chance of hitting a man a mile and a half away, which compares favorably with the effective range of all except the most powerful field artillery. Consequently, although slow to load (the cartridge has to be rammed down a barrel, whose bore is hexagonal) and quick to foul, a few of them are capable of putting out of action the crew of an enemy battery. As might be expected, the sharpshooter company of Cleburne's Division possesses more Whitworths than any other such outfit—twenty, plus ten Kerr rifles, which are also British imports but not as good.[28]

Key's account of the grand review, it might have been noticed, does not mention the cavalry. Presumably most of it was absent on picket duty; quite possibly, too, he does not consider it worth mentioning. Universally in both armies the men who fight on foot—infantry and cannoneers—despise those who serve on horseback. They consider them useless in regular battle ("Cavalry never have and never will fight," sneers artillerist Lieutenant Andrew J. Neal), resent the fact that they rarely suffer heavy losses (Sergeant Bliss of the 16th Alabama dubs Roddy's Cavalry Brigade the "Life Insurance Company"), and envy their freer and apparently easier existence. That the foot soldiers have such an attitude is understandable but also unfair. As one Confederate trooper points out in an Atlanta newspaper in response to criticisms of the mounted forces, the primary job of cavalry is, not to fight, but to provide the commanding general with timely and accurate intelligence, to screen their own army's front, flanks, and rear, and to disrupt the enemy's communications. He might have added that during combat it is extremely difficult to get men who are equipped with sabers, revolvers, and short-range carbines and who make vulnerable targets on their steeds to attack or even stand against masses of infantry backed by artillery, especially when their horses offer a ready means of escaping from such potentially fatal situations. Deprived of that option and provided with the proper training and weapons, cavalrymen are just as capable of fighting hard as are infantry and artillerymen; this is amply demonstrated by Forrest's troopers, who actually are mounted infantrymen armed with regular rifles and who do not even bother to carry sabers.

According to the April 30 returns, the Army of Tennessee's cavalry corps contains three divisions with eight brigades, two independent brigades, and a battalion of four batteries of light artillery, all totaling an "aggregate present" of 10,000 men, of whom 8,500 are "present for duty." However, only six brigades and 2,400 troopers are operational. Hard campaigning throughout the summer and fall of 1863 and well into the winter has resulted in the loss or breakdown of large numbers of horses, especially in those units that accompanied Longstreet into East Tennessee and have just recently returned. Therefore most of the cavalry is posted in rear areas, either to rest their mounts or to await new ones. In addition, many men have gone home on leave to obtain horses, for it is Confederate practice to have troopers provide, insofar as practicable, their own steeds. Although several brigades soon will be ready for active duty, for the time being, Johnston's cavalry is, as he has often warned Richmond, dangerously weak.

It also suffers from other deficiencies. Discipline off the battlefield is sloppy, with the men of the First Kentucky being far from unique in their attitude toward their colonel's orders: "We obeyed them if it suited us." Warfare and the wide-ranging, relatively unrestricted life of the cavalryman has had a demoralizing effect on some troopers, who have few compunctions about robbing civilians of food, clothing, and horses when they feel the need or merely the desire. A surprising number of the rank and file have no weapons, and those who do carry a motley array of breechloading Sharps and Burnside carbines (captured from the Yankees), muzzleloading rifles, shotguns, and revolvers of all types—a state of affairs that makes for problems in supplying ammunition. Finally, absenteeism is chronic, and desertion is high; as a result, many regiments are scarcely bigger than a squadron, and most brigades are not as large as a regiment should be.

Such weaknesses, however, are common to nearly all Confederate cavalry but are largely offset by certain strengths that likewise typify Southern horse soldiers. The majority of them, vividly described by Sherman, are "young bloods of the South" who are "splendid riders, first-rate shots, and utterly reckless." They hold themselves superior to their Yankee counterparts, and since this belief is not mere conceit, it tends to make them so in fact. More importantly from the standpoint of military effectiveness, they have, on the whole, better leaders than do the Federal troopers, notably at the division level and in their corps commander, Major General Joseph Wheeler.[29]

Called Little Joe and the War Child because he is only five feet five inches tall and twenty-seven years old, he also is known as Fighting Joe: as often as not he rides into battle with his men, has suffered several wounds, and has had a half-dozen horses shot from under him and twice that number of staff officers shot down beside him. A native of Augusta, Georgia, he graduated from West Point in 1859 and was a second lieutenant in the Mounted Rifles when he resigned from the "old army" in April 1861. For a while he commanded an infantry regiment; then, in July 1862, Bragg put him in charge of the Army of Tennessee's cavalry. In that capacity, Wheeler performed competently during the Kentucky invasion, smashed a large Union wagon train at Murfreesboro, did a good job of covering Bragg's retreat into Georgia prior to Chickamauga, and after that battle, conducted a devastating raid against the enemy's supply columns north of Chattanooga before joining Longstreet in his futile attempt to take Knoxville. Wheeler lacks the panache of Stuart and the genius of Forrest, but he is aggressive, possesses iron nerves and endurance, and gives Johnston something that Sherman needs—a capable, experienced commander for all of his mounted forces. Unfortunately, Wheeler suffers from two weaknesses that are characteristic of cavalry generals in both armies: the inability to exercise effective control over his troopers except when personally present, and, worse, a penchant for making exaggerated claims about what he can accomplish and what he has accomplished. Also, just as Bragg owes his position to Davis, Wheeler owes his to Bragg and hence can be counted on to act accordingly should the occasion arise.[30]

Altogether the Army of Tennessee, not counting "an immense number" of slaves employed as servants by officers, now has 63,807 "aggregate present," 54,500 "present for duty," and 43,887 "effectives." As such this constitutes a formidable force, especially since the great bulk of it is made up of tough veterans led by experienced officers. Even so, if it is to have a reasonable chance of withstanding the much larger, better equipped, and equally battle-hardened host that Sherman is gathering, it must have reinforcements, conduct its operations with skill, and fight with utmost determination. Presumably Davis, once he is sure that Johnston needs and will use them, will provide the reinforcements. The skill, of course, must come mainly from Johnston. No one doubts that he possesses it; the question is whether he has enough or, to be precise, if it is the right kind. As for the determination, probably Private William Honnel of the 24th Mississippi best describes the mood of the vast majority of the soldiers of the Army of Tennessee when he writes his sister on April 24: "Our army is in good health and in tolerable good spirits and if we have this thing to decide by fighting it may be that the sooner the better."[31]

The army with which Sherman proposes to invade Georgia is not as big as he had hoped and expected it to be, but it is big, very big. Not counting the thousands of men assigned to garrison and other rear-area duty, it contains as of April 30 a grand total of about 110,000 troops, of whom nearly 99,000 are, according to Sherman, available for "offensive purposes. It is supported by 254 cannons and is accompanied by approximately 25,000 noncombatants in the form of teamsters, medical personnel, civilian railroad operators and repair crews, and black camp servants hired by officers and sometimes by groups of enlisted men. Only Grant in Virignia has more men at his disposal, and not since Halleck's ponderous campaign against Corinth in the spring of 1862 have the Federals concentrated such a powerful force in one place.[32]

The main component of Sherman's host is Thomas's Army of the Cumberland; with its 73,000 soldiers and 130 guns it alone outnumbers the Confederates at Dalton. A distant second in size is McPherson's Army of the Tennessee; because so many of its divisions are absent, it totals only 24,500 men and 96 cannons. As for Schofield's Army of the Ohio, it actually is little more than the XXIII Corps, which provides 11,362 for its total field strength of 13,559; the remainder consist of cavalry; and it has only 28 artillery pieces.

Eighty-five percent of Sherman's front-line troops are infantry, organized into seven corps. Of these corps, Sherman makes little effort to conceal his belief that Logan's XV Corps, which Sherman himself once headed, is best at marching and fighting. Its men, all of whom are midwesterners, principally from Illinois, Iowa, Missouri, and Ohio, heartily concur. Most of them have followed Grant from Shiloh to Chattanooga. Not only have they never known defeat; they consider it impossible. Ferocious on the battlefield, their conduct off of it can be, and ofttimes is, atrocious. Their discipline is feeble, and one of them admits: "I do honestly think our corps in one respect [is] composed of the meanest set of men that was ever thrown together. That is, while on the march they make it a point to abuse every man or thing they see. They always feel 'Bully.'"[33] Tough, rollicking "Black Jack" Logan is the ideal general to lead them.

The Army of the Tennessee's other two corps, the XVI and XVII, are of comparable quality and character. They, too, are made up almost entirely of rugged young men from the prairie states who have served in Grant's campaigns and whose know-how, morale, and confidence are accordingly high. Their sole serious deficiency is that both are at half strength. Each corps has a division

Men of the 125th Ohio, Army of the Cumberland (*Photographic History*, 3:117)

stranded with Smith in Louisiana and another posted along the Mississippi, with the result that each can contribute only two divisions, totaling about 10,000 infantry. Even the XV Corps will field a scant 11,500 troops owing to the need to leave one of its divisions in northern Alabama to guard the railroad. Because of its size and because it lacks cavalry and other auxiliary components, the Army of the Tennessee in actuality is more an extra-large corps than an army, and throughout the coming campaign the Confederates will refer to it as "McPherson's corps."

In round numbers the IV, XIV, and XX corps of the Army of the Cumberland contain, respectively, 20,000, 22,000, and 20,000 infantry present for duty in the field (a division of the XX Corps protects the Nashville and Chattanooga). Apart from some United States regulars and a few Pennsylvania and several dozen Kentucky regiments, the troops of the IV and XIV corps, like those of the Army of the Tennessee, come from the Midwest (only Iowa is unrepresented, but to make up for that the IV Corps has the 8th Kansas). They constitute the essence of the Army of the Cumberland; most of them have fought in the parched fields near Perryville, in the cedar thickets along Stones River, and among the hills and forests surrounding Chattanooga. Men of the Army of Tennessee taunt them about their defeat at Chickamauga, but they answer proudly that it was they who drove the Rebs off Missionary Ridge while the XV and XVII corps were being stopped cold by Cleburne. There are no better soldiers in the Union army, and in private even veterans of the XV Corps admit that they "will do."

The first two divisions of the XX Corps consist mainly of New York and Pennsylvania regiments and a few from other eastern states and from the Midwest. The third is entirely midwestern except for a regiment each from

Massachusetts and Connecticut. The men of the Army of the Tennessee and the IV and XIV corps never let pass an opportunity to deride the easterners from the oft-defeated Army of the Potomac as "paper collar" and "white glove" soldiers, but in fact they are every bit as tough as the westerners. If some of them, the remnants of the old XI Corps, broke at Chancellorsville and again on the first day at Gettysburg, it was because of bad luck and bad leadership, not because of any inherent defects. As for the veterans of the former XII Corps, they held their own against Lee's finest at Antietam and Gettysburg and are capable of doing the same against Johnston's.

Besides being small, Schofield's three-division XXIII Corps is the least experienced of all of Sherman's corps. Not only does it contain a whole division of raw recruits (5,000 Indianans), but its other two divisions consist predominantly of midwestern, Kentucky, and Tennessee regiments that have never participated in a major battle. However, apart from the Indianans, the XXIII Corps has undergone enough rugged campaigning in the mountains and snows of East Tennessee to qualify as veterans, and all it needs is a good dose of combat (which it is likely to get soon), and it will be quite adequate. Certainly Schofield is determined more than ever to make a good showing: the Senate, because of the intrigues of the political enemies he made in Missouri, has again refused to confirm him as a major general.

The typical regiment in Sherman's host numbers 300 to 500 men; a brigade, 1,000 to 1,500; and a division, 4,000 to 6,000. Many long-service regiments, however, have far fewer than 300. For example, the 73rd Illinois, called the Preacher Regiment because it contains so many preachers and divinity students, musters a mere 183, and many of the eastern regiments are even smaller. Other regiments are up to an effective strength only because they were able to recruit while on veteran furlough or because they sent detachments home to obtain new men. Thus the 21st Michigan, which had dwindled to under 100 after Chickamauga, now has 352 muskets, thanks to recent enlistments. Most of the recruits are teenagers, and according to the colonel of the 1st Michigan Engineers, who has 300 of them, it is "surprising how quickly they work into soldiers. At first the 'old ones' had a great deal of fun out of their awkwardness, but they now 'have to look to their laurels'—the 'green ones' they find are pretty sharp." Observers agree that putting enlistees into veteran regiments produces better results than the practice, prevalent in the North until now, of constantly forming new regiments. Not only do the recruits "learn the ropes" more quickly, but there is less illness among them.[34]

Most of the Union infantry, like the Confederates, are equipped with Springfields or Enfields, mainly the former. As yet only a few regiments possess repeating rifles, notably Spencers. This weapon fires eight .52-caliber copper-encased bullets without reloading—one from the chamber; the rest as they come from a spring-operated tube, which is inserted through the butt end of the stock and is activated by pushing forward a lever which also serves as the trigger guard. Using preloaded tubes carried in a special cartridge box, a soldier can easily get off fifteen rounds or more in less than a minute, as compared to the two or, at most, three a minute he can fire from a muzzleloader. However, the Spencer does not have the killing range of the Springfield and the Enfield, and troops equipped with a Spencer tend to fire too fast and tend not to take good aim, thereby quickly exhausting their ammunition and creating supply problems. For these reasons most high-ranking generals take a dim view of the Spencer as an infantry weapon. The men in the ranks, on the other hand, like it and are eager to obtain it. Many officers, individual soldiers, and companies and several regiments have purchased Spencers or the fifteen-shot Henry rifle with their own money.

Proportionate to army size, Sherman's 254 cannons represent a smaller entity than Johnston's 144. Sherman has deliberately reduced his artillery in order to increase mobility and decrease supply requirements; surplus guns, nearly 300 in number, have been returned to arsenals, installed in forts, or placed in reserve at Chattanooga and Nashville. He also is taking along just four types of cannon: 12-pounder Napoleons, 10- and 20-pounder Parrots, and 3-inch Rodmans. The first, the basic artillery piece of the Federals as well as the Confederates, has a bronze 3.6-caliber smoothbore barrel and is most effective at close range (under half a mile). The Parrots and Rodmans, whose barrels are wrought iron and rifled, have greater range and accuracy and so are better for counterbattery fire and for softening up enemy positions, yet can also devastate infantry at short range. Moreover they are much lighter, so that in the words of one Federal general, "we could jump them across a rough country where the teams could hardly move a Napoleon."

Serving the 254 cannons are 6,292 cannoneers (officers and men) organized into 50 4-gun and 6-gun batteries: 24 for the Army of the Cumberland, 19 for the Army of the Tennessee, and 7 for the Army of the Ohio. Eighteen additional batteries constitute the reserves in Chattanooga and Nashville, ready to make good any losses or to provide reinforcements. Superior in number, quality, and mobility, with ample supplies of ammunition, and manned by well-trained and experienced crews, Sherman's artillery gives him a great asset, notwithstanding the less-than-ideal terrain of northern Georgia's mountains and forests.[35]

Sherman's greatest liability is his cavalry. It is numerous enough—6,000 presently in the field and another 6,000 in the process of being mounted, equipped, and organized. But instead of being concentrated in a single corps under one commander, as is the case with Johnston's mounted forces, it is separated into four divisions, each with its own commander. To be sure, according to the organizational chart, three of these divisions belong to the Army of the Cumberland and form a corps headed by Brigadier General Washington Elliot. In actuality, Sherman himself exercises the sole central control over his cavalry, an arm with which he has had little experience and for which he has even less understanding or sympathy, as he demonstrated in the Meridian expedition. Furthermore, one of the division commanders, Major General Stoneman, nominally attached to the Army of the Ohio, is a conceited incompetent; another, Brigadier General Kenner Garrard, has never before commanded cavalry in the field and soon will demonstrate little aptitude for it; and the remaining two, Brigadier Generals Hugh Judson Kilpatrick and Edward McCook, although experienced and aggressive, suffer from serious deficiencies of both intellect and character. Finally, the Union horsemen are no better disciplined than their Confederate counterparts and, in spite of some excellent brigade and regimental officers, generally inferior to them in tactical skill and dash. Only in the Spencer carbine—a shorter-barreled version of the regular Spencer, with which many of them are equipped—do they possess an advantage; and even this will be largely negated by terrain and the longer range and greater accuracy of the short Enfields favored by Wheeler's cavaliers.[36]

Besides the standard components of infantry, artillery, and cavalry, Sherman's forces contain (or to be precise, the Army of the Cumberland provides) two regiments of engineers, two pontoon trains, a signal-corps detachment, and at least two thousand civilian railway workers, which in a modern army would be part of the engineer corps. Thus Sherman possesses ample strength and means to carry out a successful campaign, provided he manages well, obtains adequate supplies, and does not experience too much bad luck. By the same token, even with all possible reinforcements and great skill in the conduct of operations, Johnston stands small chance of holding back, much less driving back, Sherman. Yet, in spite of the heavy odds in their favor, the Federal soldiers will have to fight as hard as they ever fought—perhaps harder—if victory is to be won in Georgia.

They know this. As April, which has been unseasonably cold and wet, draws to a close, they sense that they are on "the eve of great events" and that soon they will be advancing to do battle with the Rebs at Dalton, "who calculate to fight us so long as they can concentrate an army," and that consequently "the contest will be desperate and bloody." Nevertheless most of them welcome the prospect of active campaigning. They are tired of repetitive drilling and the monotonous camp routine of "wash, iron, scrub, bake—wash, iron, scrub, bake." They are eager to be on the march again, "penetrating further and further into enemy country," on to Atlanta, maybe Montgomery, perhaps even Savannah or some other place on the sea. They also believe that there can be "no doubt but what we will succeed," that "Victory gained under these circumstances"—that is, deep in the interior of the South—"will carry dismay to the heart of every traitor," that the war cannot "last more than a year longer," and that once it is over, they can resume their "separate destinies."

Of course they also realize that they stand a good chance of dying or being mangled or falling prisoner. But most of them have faced this prospect before, and they are prepared to face it again: after all, that is why they are soldiers. Therefore they enjoy what life has to offer while waiting to start to kill and be killed. A rollicking, almost festive mood prevails in their camps. In particular they are seized by a veritable mania for dancing. Nearly every company has one or more fiddlers, and in the evening the "sound of music and dancing" is heard "all along the line."[37]

Toward the end of the month the long-anticipated orders come from Sherman. All excess personal baggage is to be disposed of; only that which is absolutely essential is to be retained. No tents are to be allowed except ones for the sick, wounded, and headquarters officers. Regiments and batteries will be limited to one wagon and an ambulance each; companies, to a packmule for transporting officers' gear. All of the wagons assigned to brigades and divisions will carry nothing but food, forage, ammunition, and clothing; the same restrictions apply to corps and army trains. In all Sherman has 5,150 wagons and 860 ambulances pulled by 32,600 mules and 12,000 horses. This gives him about 50 wagons for every thousand men, a higher proportion than Grant has in Virginia (40 for every thousand) and one exceeded during the Civil War only by the Army of the Cumberland when it made its long overland march from Murfreesboro to Chattanooga with 70 wagons for every 1,000 soldiers.[38] Although Sherman wants to be as mobile as possible (hence the limitations on regimental, battery, and company transport), he also wants his army to be able to get along without regular transfusions of supplies from the railroad should that prove either desirable or (dismal thought) necessary.

At once the troops begin stripping for the action they now know is near. "A busy day," writes Sergeant Lyman Widney of the 34th Illinois in his diary for April 30, "everybody packing boxes with extra clothing and the many trinkets possessed by every soldier. The larger portion of our personal property has been shipped home by express as we have found by experience that government warehouse is a knapsack 'Inferno' and we may well 'abandon hope' for all that enters there."[39]

Sherman also would like to rid his army, if he could, of those "infamous lying dogs" called reporters. As it is, he has applied to them his ban against civilian railroad passengers, denied them access to the telegraph, warned them that they are to observe strict silence concerning troop dispositions and movements, and backed up this warning by arresting as a spy a *Chicago Journal* correspondent who published a story stating that "our lines now extend from Knoxville to Huntsville," as if the Confederates could be ignorant of that obvious fact. The understandable consequence of Sherman's restrictions and attitude is that no more than a dozen journalists decide it is worthwhile to accompany his army in the forthcoming campaign, and one of them, Joseph Miller of the *Cincinnati Commercial* (the paper that had reported Sherman to be insane back in 1861), notified his editors that for "specific military intelligence" on operations in Georgia they will do best to consult Southern newspapers, "which not infrequently are more frank and intelligible than what a correspondent under restrictions can send you."⁴⁰ As a further consequence, the campaign to Atlanta will not receive nearly as much newspaper coverage as will the one against Richmond. But then, the eyes of the North are focused on the latter in any case. Even Sherman, as we have seen, expects the war to be decided by Grant in Virginia, not by himself in Georgia.

On April 25, Grant, who already has postponed the starting date of the Union offensive from that date to April 30, postpones it again, telegraphing Sherman: "Will your veterans be back to enable you to start on the 2d of May? I do not want to delay later." Sherman promptly answers that although the "veteran divisions"—by which he means the two divisions of the XVII Corps now at Cairo—"cannot be up by May 2 . . . I am willing to move with what I have." However, "every day adds to my animals and men. If you can, give me till May 5."

While waiting for Grant to respond to this request, Sherman instructs Thomas, McPherson, and Schofield to get ready to move by May 2. Then, on April 27, still not having heard from Grant, Sherman telegraphs him: "In view of the fact that I will have to take the initiative with 20,000 less men in McPherson's army than I estimated, I intend to order all McPherson's disposable force . . . to Chattanooga to start from a common center. I go forward tomorrow."

At noon the next day Sherman boards the train for Chattanooga. Before leaving, however, he delivers a final admonition to Quartermaster Donaldson: "I am going to move on Joe Johnston the day General Grant telegraphs me he is going to hit Bobby Lee; and if you don't have my army supplied, and keep it supplied, we'll eat your mules up, sir—eat your mules up!" He also sends a message to Memphis, where Washburn and Sturgis, the new commanders, are preparing an expedition against Forrest, who still is in West Tennessee: "We want you to hold Forrest and as much of the enemy as you can over there, until we can strike Johnston. This is quite as important as to whip him."

Sherman reaches Chattanooga the next morning. Awaiting him is a telegram sent the day before by Grant: "Get your forces up so as to move by the 5th of May." Sherman immediately wires back: "I will be all ready by May 5."[41]

Around Dalton the men in gray also are getting ready. First, after the grand review on the nineteenth, Johnston required all officers' wives and other female guests to leave the army. Among the former are Mrs. Johnston, who has gone to Atlanta, and Hardee's wife, who soon will follow. Next, on April 26, Johnston ordered all surplus blankets and clothing sent to the rear. Soon after, Captain Key ships a box of blankets to the Reverend D. K. Marshall of Atlanta, and Private Angus McDermid sends home, via a friend, his favorite coat, with instructions to his parents to "ceepe it in my green chest and dont let no body ware it."

Meanwhile Wheeler's troopers already are skirmishing daily with probing Yankee cavalry. On the morning of April 28 they counterattack a Federal force that surprised and seized an outpost in the village of Tunnel Hill, driving it back. During their stay there, members of the 10th Ohio Cavalry burned down its few buildings and shot thirteen Confederate captives. They did this in reprisal for the murder of a number of their comrades several days before by one of Wheeler's outfits, probably the 1st Tennessee Cavalry. They acknowledge that their victims were innocent of this crime but believe that "we had to do it [retaliate] or else the rebles [*sic*] will never stop killing our men." Word of the nasty little massacre at Tunnel Hill causes some of Johnston's soldiers to talk of raising the "black flag."[42]

On the morning of April 30, Lincoln writes Grant:

> Not expecting to see you again before the spring campaign opens, I wish to express in this way my entire satisfaction with what you have done up to this time, so far as I understand it. The particulars on your plan I neither know nor seek to know. You are vigilant and self-reliant; and pleased with this, I wish not to obtrude any constraints or restraints on you. While I am very anxious that any great disaster or capture of our men in great numbers shall be avoided, I know these points are less likely to escape your attention than they would be mine. If there is anything

wanting which is within my power to give, do not fail to let me know it. And now, with a brave army and a just cause, may God sustain you.[43]

In other words, Lincoln has confidence in Grant—and through him in Sherman—to do all that possibly can be done to win the war in the next several months. Lincoln does not even ask to know what the "particulars" of Grant's strategy are—a marked contrast to Davis's attempt to impose his "particular plan" on Johnston. All Lincoln wishes to do is to assure Grant of his support and, despite the tactful statement that it is not necessary, to impress on him the need to avoid a major defeat. Another Bull Run, Fredericksburg, or Chancellorsville, or even another Peninsular Campaign in which the Army of the Potomac reaches but does not take Richmond, would be too much for Northern morale. It would collapse and, with it, all prospect of Republican and Union victory in 1864.

On the afternoon of April 30, Sherman climbs to the top of Lookout Mountain and surveys the country lying to the south. With him is his chief of engineers, Captain Orlando M. Poe. That evening Poe describes the visit in a letter to his wife in Detroit, then comments: "Where the birds are now making so merry and warbling songs in welcome of new-born spring, will be heard the shriek of shell, the whistle of bullet, & the horrid music of terrible war. We are going into battle with the highest hopes of success—but God help us if we fail!"

That same evening, in a camp atop Rocky Face Ridge, Private William Honnell of the 24th Mississippi writes his sister: "We are in front building breastworks our duty is verry hard and we are looking for a fight any day but there is no telling when it will come off but I think it will not be before long and if we can whip them here it might bring about peace but we will have to wait and see the issue."[44]

CHAPTER FIVE

MAY

Part One: From the Tennessee to Snake Creek Gap

ON MAY 1 the editor of the *Augusta* (Ga.) *Constitutionalist* tells his readers: "Atlanta is thus the great strategic point. A crushing, decisive victory in Northwest Georgia will inevitably crush the power of the enemy, and break down the war party of the North. A substantial victory now will lead to peace. If on the contrary, we meet with a reverse of a serious character in Georgia, the war will be hopelessly prolonged." Therefore, the editor concludes, "the approaches to the Gate City—every one of them—must be made a second Thermopylae."

A "second Thermopylae"? In his patriotic fervor the editor overlooks a certain ominous historical fact: at the first Thermopylae the gallant Spartan six hundred indeed held the pass against the Persian horde—held it, that is, until the Persians outflanked them.

This, of course, is what Sherman intends to do to the Confederates holding Rocky Face Ridge. The trouble is, he has had to give up not only his original plan of swinging McPherson's army south toward Rome, but also the revised version of it he made on learning that A. J. Smith's two divisions would not be available—namely, to have McPherson cut across northeast Alabama to Georgia, where he would be in position either to move against Johnston at Dalton or head for Rome should Johnston retreat. Without the XVII Corps's two divisions, which are still at Cairo, McPherson simply is not strong enough, with at most 23,000 bayonets, to operate safely so far from the rest of the army. Another plan is needed.

Fortunately, one already is at hand. It comes from Thomas, who had proposed it to Sherman during their conferences in Chattanooga at the end of March and the beginning of April. The product of the reconnaissances ordered by Thomas after the demonstration against Dalton in February, it calls for McPherson's and Schofield's armies to "demonstrate on the enemy's position at Dalton by the direct road through Buzzard Roost Gap" while Thomas marches the entire Army of the Cumberland through Snake Creek Gap, an undefended mountain pass about thirteen miles south of Dalton, and cuts Johnston's railroad communication line at Resaca on the north bank of the Oostanaula River, thereby "turning his position completely" and forcing him "either to retreat

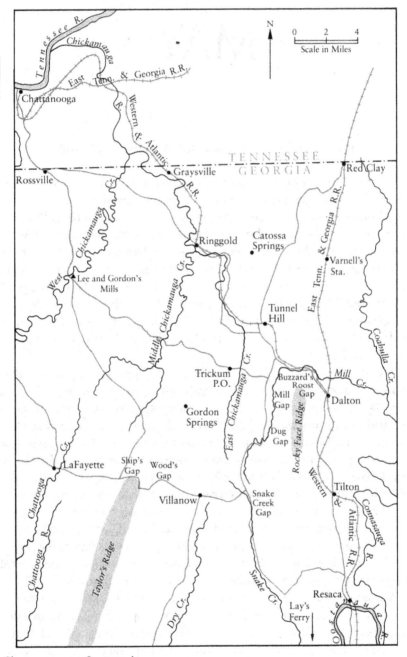

Chattanooga to Oostanaula

towards the east through difficult country, poorly supplied with provisions and forage," or else attack Thomas at Resaca, in which case the Army of the Cumberland would be strong enough to defeat him.[1]

Sherman, on first hearing this plan, had rejected it because (so he told Thomas) he wanted the Army of the Cumberland "to form the reserve of the united armies, and serve as a rallying point for the two wings, the Army of the Ohio and that of the Tennessee, to operate from." Now, however, having no alternative and no time to develop one, he adopts it, but with two major modifications. Instead of the Army of the Cumberland, he will send the Army of the Tennessee (which he has ordered to Chattanooga) through Snake Creek Gap, leaving Thomas and Schofield—three-fourth of his entire army—to press frontally against Buzzard Roost Gap and Rocky Face Ridge. Moreover, when McPherson (so Sherman instructs him on May 5) emerges from Snake Creek Gap, he will not occupy and hold Resaca; he will merely destroy the railroad and then return to the gap, ready to pounce on Johnston when he retreats southward, as he must do in order to restore his communications with Atlanta. What with Thomas and Schofield assailing the Confederates from the north and McPherson from the west as they try to cross the Oostanaula at Resaca, they will be crushed or at least so badly battered that they will not be able to offer further significant resistance short of Atlanta.[2] Ironically, after having planned a campaign designed in essence merely to compel Johnston to withdraw to Atlanta, the absence of four divisions he had intended to use for that purpose has forced Sherman to adopt a stratagem that, if successful, might destroy Johnston's army in a matter of days!

"We are having splendid weather here," writes Private Charles Dunham of the 129th Illinois to his father in Pontiac, Illinois, on May 1. "The trees are leaved [*sic*] out and I tell you what—it makes me feel as if I ought to be home at work."

A different kind of work than that referred to by Private Dunham lies ahead of him and the hundred thousand or so men whose long columns wind through the "small valleys and green hills" around Chattanooga during the early days of May. This they know; their only uncertainty is over what kind of work it will be—"a big fight or a foot race"—for a lot of them think that the Confederates won't make a stand until they get to Atlanta. In any case the Union men are, writes Dunham three days later, "cheerful and ready to give the rebs the best we have got—that is of blue pills," by which he means lead bullets.[3]

Most of them being veterans, they are stripped down to what they have learned through hard experience are the essentials: rifle, cartridge box, cap pouch, canteen ("water sometimes is more important than food"), haversack, and knapsack, around which is rolled a wool blanket, a shelter half, and a black rubber sheet that can double as a poncho. A bayonet dangles from their belts, along with a hatchet, a tin cup, and perhaps a small skillet or oyster tin, with these last items being used respectively for cooking food and brewing coffee. Their sole spare clothing, except for some who cling to their overcoats in the belief that the army is merely engaging in a demonstration and soon will return to camp, are a couple of pairs of socks and perhaps a change of underwear. "Never, as you value your expectations of seeing home again," counsels one old soldier, "attempt to carry extra clothing on a summer campaign." Personal items such as writing papers, diaries, letters from home, watches, money, Bibles, and cards are distributed among their knapsack and pockets. Although the standard headgear is the short billed kepi, many of them, especially among the western troops, wear wide-brimmed "slouch hats" that provide better protection against sun and rain. Apart from a relative few who have invested in boots, their feet are shod in squaretoed high-topped leather brogans. After five months spent mostly in camp, they presently are suffering from blistered feet, and Private Chauncey Cooke's 25th Wisconsin is not the only regiment in which, as he records in his diary for May 3, "many of the boys are badly crippled and will have to take to the ambulance tomorrow." But soon those feet will become as tough as the leather that covers them, capable of marching and marching and marching—marching far further than anyone presently foresees.[4]

Before, beside, and behind the trudging infantry ride the majors, colonels, and generals; unless they are staff officers or are in the cavalry or artillery, where everybody rides, captains and lieutenants must walk too. Both accompanying and following the infantry are horse-drawn batteries, ambulances, and hundreds of wagons, each wagon pulled by six mules. Up ahead or on separate roads, the cavalry jog along with their own trains of cannons, caissons, and wagons. In the wake of all, moving slowly through clouds of dust, are immense herds of cattle, driven by the drovers of the commissary. At the end of each day's march, men specially assigned to the task slaughter hundreds of the cattle, always selecting the most decrepit-looking for the purpose, then distribute hunks of bloody meat to the soldiers to be cooked, more or less, over their campfires. The carcasses remain where they lie, adding their stench to that of the dung being produced constantly, day and night, by all of these tens of thousands of men, horses, mules, and still-living cattle. By their very nature, armies on the march are not pleasant things, least of all for the civilians in their path, particularly if they are enemy civilians. "Not many minutes after coming into camp," comments Private Cooke in his diary on May 3, "every fence and movable thing in sight is pulled down to make the fires. God pity this south land when we are done with it."[5]

Two divisions of Schofield's Army of the Ohio—to be exact, of the XXIII Corps—travel by trains from Knoxville to Cleveland, Tennessee, where they pick up Brigadier General Alvin P. Hovey's brand-new division of Indiana recruits. On May 5, Schofield's troops, now afoot, cross into Georgia at Red Clay, fifteen miles due north of Dalton. Also moving down from Cleveland is Howard's IV Corps, which reaches Catoosa Springs, Georgia, near the northern end of Rocky Face Ridge on May 4. "This was," Private Benjamin Smith of the 51st Illinois notes in his journal, "a famous health resort before the war, a sort of Saratoga in the South." Now its once-handsome hotels "are only fit to house familiar ghosts."[6]

South of Chattanooga, Palmer's XIV Corps makes the shortest and easiest march, retracing the route it took in February to Ringgold. To the west of it, Hooker's XX Corps passes over the battlefield of Chickamauga as it moves into position to link up with Palmer's right. "I see," writes Private Judson Austin of the 19th Michigan to his wife on May 3, "several graves where the rebs buried their dead & it was done a little human but where our boys were pretended to be covered up their skulls & feet were still to be seen above the ground. . . . I send you a bunch of wild flowers that I picked within a step of where one of our soldiers was pretended to be buried." Several days later, following behind the XX Corps, the troops of the XV and XVI corps likewise take note of the "ghastly, ghostly sight" of the unburied or partially buried Union dead, some of whom have been rooted out and gnawed by hogs.[7]

At 10 P.M. on May 4, Sherman telegraphs Grant that he will start his offensive, as ordered, tomorrow, "but I hardly expect serious battle till the 7th." He adds: "Everything very quiet with the enemy. Johnston evidently awaits my initiative. I will first secure the Tunnel Hill, then throw McPherson rapidly on his communications, attacking at the same time in front cautiously and in force."[8]

On the morning of May 5, Sherman travels to Ringgold. He is accompanied by four aides-de-camp, three inspector generals, a medical director, and his chiefs of artillery, engineers, quartermaster, commissary, and ordnance, altogether twelve men, far fewer than the staff of a twentieth-century division commander. His "entire headquarters transportation," he informs Quartermaster General Montgomery C. Meigs in Washington, "is one wagon for myself, aides, officers, clerks, and orderlies. I think that is as low down as we can get until we get flat broke." Sherman himself "will dispense with tents" in hopes of setting an example for the whole army. "Soldiering as we have been doing for the past two years, with such trains and impediments, has been a farce, and nothing but absolute poverty will cure it."[9]

At Ringgold, Sherman learns that the Army of the Tennessee still is passing through Chattanooga on its way by train and foot from its camps in Alabama and Middle Tennessee. Accordingly he telegraphs Halleck to inform Grant— who yesterday sent the Army of the Potomac across the Rapidan into the same Wilderness where Hooker came to grief a year ago—that "McPherson is one day behind" but that "I will attack Tunnel Hill on Saturday [two day's hence], and, in the mean time, will occupy Johnston's whole attention."

By the night of May 6 most of McPherson's troops reach Lee and Gordon's Mills, ten miles south of Chattanooga and a dozen miles west of Ringgold. His wagon train, however, is at least a day's march behind, and Brigadier General Kenner Garrard's cavalry division, which is supposed to cover the flanking move, still is in Alabama, having been delayed by bad roads and the need, overlooked by Sherman in his planning, to bring along forage in slow-traveling wagons. Even so, Sherman orders Thomas to have the XIV Corps advance at dawn and seize Tunnel Hill. He will not delay any longer, particularly since Grant probably now has engaged Lee in battle (in fact the Army of the Potomac has just finished two days of ferocious fighting with a staggering loss of 18,000 men).[10]

In due course the order to Thomas passes down the chain of command to Colonel Dan McCook, commander of a brigade in the XIV Corps and formerly a law partner of Sherman's in Kansas. McCook in turn tells Major James T. Holmes, acting commander of the 52nd Ohio, that his regiment, originally McCook's own, will lead the advance. "When you get 'em started," he exhorts Holmes, "keep 'em on the hop."[11]

That night something occurs in the camps of the XIV Corps which its men will remember as long as they live—which is not much longer in many cases. Knowing that the campaign is about to begin and that he will not be able to use his candles any more, a soldier in the 37th Indiana cuts them in pieces, places them in and around his tent, and lights them. Others do the same, then someone climbs a tree and puts lighted candles along the branches, with the result that he, too, attracts a host of imitators. Before long, thousands of candles are burning in the tree tops, producing, in the words of Sergeant George Puntenney of the 37th Indiana, "a most beautiful sight."[12]

Johnston does not need the strange spectacle of a forest of giant Christmas trees in May to realize that the Federals are in great strength at Ringgold and that Sherman's long anticipated offensive is under way. He also has a good idea of what Sherman intends to do: namely, try to outflank him. Where Johnston is mistaken is in his assessment of how Sherman will go about doing this: he believes that Sherman plans to do what in fact he had planned to do until recently—march a large force, perhaps his whole army, to Rome. Therefore Johnston has ordered Wheeler to have his scouts keep an eye out for an enemy movement in that direction, and he has telegraphed both Davis and Polk, asking that Loring's Division in Mississippi and Reynolds's Arkansas Brigade at Mobile be sent as quickly as possible to Rome.

For a change, Johnston has gotten what he wants from the president and the bishop—indeed, much more. Davis, perceiving the obvious threat to Johnston's army posed by a Union thrust toward Rome, has directed Polk to place his department under the command of Stephen Lee and to "move with Loring's division, and any other available troops," to that town. In turn Polk, interpreting these instructions liberally as well as literally, not only has set out for Rome with Loring's Division and Reynold's Brigade but also has ordered French's Division and Jackson's Cavalry Division to follow him there. Thus what Johnston has been urging in vain since December—the reinforcement of his army by Polk's—now is taking place. It does so, however, against the intent of Davis, who neither desires nor expects Polk to go to Georgia with practically all of his infantry and close to half of his cavalry and who will be annoyed when he learns of what the bishop has done. Later Davis will claim that he wanted the balance of Polk's forces, in particular the cavalry, to remain in Alabama-Mississippi, in position to strike at Sherman's communications from the west, and that he acquiesced in their unauthorized transfer to Georgia only because he believed that this surely would enable Johnston to defeat Sherman, then mount an invasion of Tennessee and Kentucky.[13]

Meanwhile, the threat that is causing the Confederates to concentrate their strength in northern Georgia has failed to materilize. Wheeler's scouts can find no sign of a Federal move toward Rome; instead they report that Union cavalry are continuing to reconnoiter the approach to Tunnel Hill, that Sherman's men are repairing the railroads leading to Ringgold and Red Clay, that Howard's corps is at the latter place, and that an enemy column (Schofield) is moving from Cleveland toward Varnell Station. This information gives Johnston pause. Could it be that Sherman is planning a frontal assault against Rocky Face in the hope of duplicating Missionary Ridge? Or in view of the forces at Red Clay and on the Cleveland road, does Sherman propose to go around the northern end of Rocky Face and strike directly at Dalton? Or, a more subtle strategy yet, is Sherman merely feinting against Dalton from the north and west while using Taylor's Ridge, a mountain that parallels Rocky Face to the west, to conceal the march of a strong column that will turn east and attempt to penetrate the southern end of Rocky Face at Dug Gap?

Of these three possibilities, the least dangerous is the first; in fact, Johnston would welcome a frontal assault on Rocky Face at Buzzard Roost, for he is confident that he would win the same sort of easy, one-sided victory that Lee had won at Fredericksburg in December 1862, a victory that caused Johnston to comment enviously to Wigfall: "What luck some people have. Nobody will ever come to attack me in such a place." On the other hand he fears a Federal lunge at Dalton via the Cleveland road and so has instructed Wheeler to reinforce the cavalry already guarding that approach. In addition, since the presence of enemy forces to the north at Red Clay and on the Cleveland road might be designed to draw his attention away from a strike toward Rome, Johnston also has ordered Brigadier Will Martin's Cavalry Division to move "at once to the vicinity of Rome" and has telegraphed Major General William W. Loring, whose lead brigade has reached Montevallo, Alabama, to rush it to the same place and "not wait to assemble" his entire division. As for an enemy movement behind and then across Taylor's Ridge toward Dug Gap, Johnston is not concerned about that because he has directed General Mackall to transmit a dispatch to Wheeler instructing him to reconnoiter the country around Taylor's Ridge: should Wheeler's scouts discover that the Federals in fact are trying to get at Dug Gap, then there will be ample time to deploy sufficient troops to hold it.[14]

As Johnston's orders to Wheeler make evident, the campaign already has begun for the Confederate cavalry. The infantrymen, on the other hand, continue their regular routine, although they have been told to be ready to move at any time. Lieutenant Rennold's diary between May 1 and 6 refers to drills, digging trenches, washing clothes, seeing "a man on a wooden horse," and nightly prayer meetings. Granbury's Texans, having been shifted to a new camp, even "make brush arbors and fix everything nice." On the night of Friday, May 6, Captain Key, having heard a report that Lee has defeated Grant, writes in his diary: "Oh, how this cheered my heart and made me feel as if the war was on its last legs."[15]

At 3 A.M. on May 7 the buglers of McCook's brigade sound reveille. By daylight the brigade is on the road, followed by the rest of Brigadier General Jefferson C. Davis's division. Skirmishers from Major Holmes's 52nd Ohio precede the column. Soon they spot Confederate vedettes and exchange shots with them. "I had the honor," Holmes proudly writes thirty-some years later, "of commanding the line that fired the first shot of the Atlanta Campaign." A mile from the village of Tunnel Hill the Ohioans encounter fifty to a hundred dismounted cavalry supported by a battery, which opens fire. Between salvos a Reb shouts, "Bring on your God damned nigger wool!" Either he is unaware or does not care that except for some garrison troops, there are no blacks in Sherman's army. Indeed, there never will be, for he considers them incapable of equaling whites as soldiers and does not want any.

Davis personally directs Holmes to work his regiment around the enemy's left. As he does so the Confederates, who have no intention of making a stand, remount their horses and gallop away. During the afternoon the XIV Corps occupies the region around Tunnel Hill, and the IV Corps moves up on its left. The tunnel itself, much to Sherman's relief, has not been either blocked or destroyed; only the track has been removed. That can be replaced in no time at all, whereupon trains can pass through.

While Palmer's and Howard's units deploy, their bands play "Hail Columbia," "America," and "The Star Spangled Banner." Behind the Confederate fortifications, Lieutenant Lot D. Young of the Kentucky Brigade listens to these familiar pieces. They sound "sweeter than I had ever heard them."[16]

The XXIII Corps, which marched to Red Clay yesterday, approaches Rocky Face from the north, and McCook's cavalry spreads out across the Cleveland road to protect its left flank, for Stoneman's division, the other main component of Schofield's little Army of the Ohio, still is en route through Tennessee. To the southwest the XX Corps, having passed down the west side of Taylor's Ridge on the sixth, turns east and crosses the ridge by way of Gordon's Gap. It does this unopposed. Is it also unobserved? At present this makes little difference from a Federal standpoint: its assignment is to line up on the XIV Corps's right, which it does, with its own right covered by Kilpatrick's cavalry.

By the end of the day, all of Sherman's forces are more or less where he wants them to be, except for the Army of the Tennessee and Garrard's division. Although they have marched a hard eighteen miles, nightfall finds McPherson's troops around Gordon Springs, still a long way from Snake Creek Gap. As for Garrard, he has not quite reached Trenton, Georgia, twenty miles northwest of Gordon Springs, near the Alabama line. Nevertheless, Sherman feels optimistic. In a "Memorandum of movements for the 8th of May, 1864," which he distributes during the night to Thomas, Schofield, and McPherson, he instructs the last-named "to move through Villanow and occupy Snake Creek Gap to its strongest point, and get up his [Garrard's] cavalry, if possible, for the next day's work." While McPherson does this, Thomas is to "threaten Buzzard Roost Pass" and "get, if possible, a small force on Rocky Face Ridge," and Schofield is "to feel . . . along down Rocky Face to the enemy's signal station if possible."[17]

Johnston responds to the Union advance by sending Stewart's Division from Hood's Corps and Bate's Division from Hardee's Corps into Buzzard Roost

Gap, posting Cheatham's Division atop the northern end of Rocky Face, and placing Stevenson's and Hindman's divisions of Hood's Corps astride the Cleveland road in Crow Valley to the east of Rocky Face. Cleburne's and Walker's divisions he holds in reserve near Dalton, ready to move when and where needed. These, however, are just precautionary measures: he doubts that the Federals will oblige him with a frontal attack; instead he continues to expect them to try to outflank him, probably by way of Rome. Hence he is alarmed when, early in the afternoon, Wheeler's scouts west of Taylor's Ridge report that one of McPherson's divisions is south of Lee and Gordon's Mills on the road to LaFayette, a village about thirty miles northwest of Rome, and that the rest of "McPherson's corps" will be coming up during the night. Johnston promptly telegraphs this intelligence to Polk at Demopolis, Alabama, adding that "the urgency for the concentration on Rome is still greater." He sends a similar telegram to Loring at Montevallo; and he informs Major Genreal Martin, whose cavalry division now is at Rome, that the enemy is preparing to march a large force "by our left upon Rome or the railroad in our rear" and that therefore "it will be necessary to have this force under your close observation." In addition he cancels an order, sent in the morning, to Brigadier General George Cantey's Brigade, which has just arrived from Mississippi, to come up from Resaca to Dalton; instead, it is to stay at Resaca and "keep close observation on all routes leading from LaFayette to Resaca or to [the] Oostenaula on your left." (In 1864 the standard spelling of Oostanaula was Oostenaula. Other such inconsistencies of spelling will appear throughout this work for the same reason.)

Thus by the end of the day, Johnston is aware that McPherson is heading south, well beyond the left flank of his army at Dalton. For this very reason, however, Johnston is all the more convinced that Rome is the chief danger point. Although his instructions to Cantey seem to recognize the possibility of a Union thrust through Snake Creek Gap at Resaca, they are clumsily worded (Chief of Staff Mackall wrote them) and do not specifically mention that gap, conceivably a serious omission in view of the fact that Cantey has just arrived at Resaca and can know little of the local geography. Furthermore, a dispatch from Hood, received by Johnston at 2:40 P.M., stating that a "not large" enemy wagon train "has been reported moving to our left" in the valley between Rocky Face and Taylor's Ridge, has resulted in an order to Wheeler to send "a good regiment of cavalry" to that area but in no move to bolster the defense line along Rocky Face south of Buzzard Roost. Consequently, only two small infantry regiments hold Dug Gap, the place where the Federals almost broke through in February before being driven back by Granbury's Texans.[18]

May 8 is a bright, hot Sunday. Sergeant Widney of th 34th Illinois, tongue in cheek, invites some comrades to go with him to Tunnel Hill's little brick church. One of them answers that he can't: his "boiled shirt and paper collar" are packed in a knapsack that is piled in a field with forty thousand others just like it, and he doesn't have time to look for it. Another excuses himself on the grounds that he wouldn't be able to find a boy to take care of his rifle while he escorted his girlfriend to the service. A third claims that he expects a visit from the folks on top of Rocky Face, and a fourth asserts that Sherman might want him to carry a message up the ridge.

Most of the morning passes without any attempt at a major forward movement by the Federals gathered north and west of Rocky Face. Then, toward noon, Harker's brigade of Newton's division of the IV Corps attacks the northern end of Rocky Face. Spearheaded by Colonel Emerson Opdycke's 125th Ohio, its men swarm up the steep slope, grabbing bushes and roots to pull themselves along. They drive away the thin Confederate skirmish line that feebly opposes them, reach the crest, and then begin working their way south along it, in some places having to go in single file because it is so narrow. Of necessity, progress is slow, and enemy resistance stiffens; but by nightfall they have cleared three-fourths of a mile of the ridge. From its top they can see the Confederate lines and camps to the south and east: this is why Sherman last night instructed Thomas "to get, if possible, a small force on Rocky Face Ridge," an assignment now accomplished.[19]

Thomas performs his other mission, to "threaten Buzzard Roost Pass," equally well. Late in the afternoon, after Harker has gained his lodgment on Rocky Face, a division each from the IV, XIV, and XX corps advance toward Buzzard Roost, meeting only light opposition from Confederate skirmishers, until they are about one-half mile from the gap. Here they halt. They have to. Between them and the entrance to the gap is an artifiical lake that the Rebels have created by damming Mill Creek with stones, logs, and dirt. The sole passageway across the lake, which is too deep to wade, is along the trestle-supported railroad track. The gap itself is occupied by a fort bristling with cannons, and more artillery lines the high, steep cliffs on either side, as do large numbers of entrenched gray-clad infantry. Gazing across the lake at Buzzard Roost, the Union soldiers can also see why it is so-named: buzzards are roosting on it. "What do you think they are doing?" one of them asks a comrade. "Counting us," comes the reply. Truly, the place potentially is what Thomas calls it, "a slaughter pen."[20]

At about the same time that the Federals advance toward Buzzard Roost, six miles to the south Geary's division of the XX Corps moves from the vicinity of Trickum Post Office toward Dug Gap. Its commander, Brigadier General John

Buzzard's Roost Gap *(Harper's Weekly)*

W. Geary, is a forty-four-year-old Pennsylvania politican, former territorial governor of "Bleeding Kansas," veteran of many battles in both the East and the West, and at six-feet-six, probably the tallest general in the Union army. Along with more than a few other generals in both armies, he is very ambitious and seeks to promote his future political prospects with present military exploits; consequently he does not hesitate to claim maximum credit for everything he has done and sometimes has not done.[21]

Geary's orders from Thomas, relayed via Hooker, are to attack Dug Gap and take it if he can, but at the very least to keep the Confederates so busy there that they will not be able to interfere with McPherson's march through Snake Creek Gap. Geary approaches the gap shortly before 4 P.M. and promptly pushes forward two brigades to seize it. His troops encounter stubborn resistance from the Confederate defenders, who, although evidently not large in number, take cover behind rocks, logs, and trees and even roll boulders down upon the attackers as they climb and crawl up the precipitous sides of Rocky Face. Twice, panting and sweating—for it is terribly hot—they reach the top; but each time, after a fierce hand-to-hand struggle, they are forced to fall back. Although they heavily outnumber their opponents, only a comparative few of them can get onto the narrow crest at one time, and that is not enough.

Perceiving this and anxious to seize the gap before the arrival of Confederate reinforcements deprives him of what appears to be an excellent opportunity to do so, Geary sends the 33rd New Jersey to attack the ridge a half-mile to the south, where the defenders seem to be very few. However, on approaching the designated point, the Jerseymen see that it is physically impossible to scale the stone palisade in front of them. So they swerve to their left, where they find an opening up which two or three men abreast can climb. Supported by a battery that rakes the ridge line with shellfire, some of them reach the top and raise a shout of triumph. Geary's assault troops thereupon

Geary's assault on Dug Gap (J. B. Brown, *Mountain Campaigns in Georgia or War Scenes on the W & A* [Atlanta: Western & Atlantic Railroad, 1890]).

again go up the ridge at Dug Gap, again a few make it to the crest, but again they simply are too weak to hold on and must retreat, as do the Jerseymen for the same reason.

Defending Dug Gap are two regiments of Arkansas infantry and Colonel Warren Grigsby's Kentucky Cavalry Brigade. The latter consists of men who rode with John Hunt Morgan during his glory days and were lucky enough to escape being captured with Morgan in Ohio back in July 1863. Yesterday they were the ones who discovered and reported McPherson's march; today one of their regiments warned of Geary's approach. The problem is that the Arkansas regiments, who formerly were cavalry themselves, total a mere 250, and the Kentuckians can put only 800 on the firing line, for like all cavalry fighting on foot, one man out of every four has to be detailed to hold the horses in the rear, which in this case is down at the base of Rocky Face. Furthermore, although these badly outnumbered Confederates—Geary has 4,500 available troops—have fought superbly and, with the aid of the terrain, have managed to beat back the Yankee assaults, both they and their ammunition are approaching exhaustion. Unless they receive reinforcements, another Union attack has a good chance of succeeding.

Reinforcements are on the way, and none could be better: they are Granbury's and Lowrey's brigades from Cleburne's Division. Leading them—in fact, far ahead of them on their galloping horses—are Hardee and Cleburne, who headed for Dug Gap after Johnston, alerted by the outbreak of heavy firing from that quarter, ordered Hardee to look to its defense. The two generals ride up to the top of the gap and see that the situation is precarious. At once an order goes back to Granbury, who is in the lead, to come at the double-quick. Doffing blanket rolls and knapsacks, the Texans head for the gap as fast as they can, but (writes Captain Sebron Sneed of the 6th Texas to his wife a short time later) they are so tired from rapid marching that the "double quick" resembles more "the speed of a slow dog trot." When Hardee sees them approaching, he waves his cap and shouts, "Here are my fighting Texans!" He then tells Cleburne that the position now is safe, and he rides away. Granbury's men, followed soon by Lowrey's, take over the defense of the gap, and the Arkansans and Kentuckians retire to the base of the ridge for a well-deserved rest. For a while the Federals shell the crest of the ridge—Sneed finds the screeching projectiles "frightening"—but they do not make another assault, and with the coming of darkness their cannons cease firing. The fight—the first real one of the campaign—is over, and what could have been, against less resolute resistance, a calamitous Union breakthrough has turned out to be a one-sided Confederate victory. According to a postwar account by Colonel William Breckinridge of the 9th Kentucky, the Arkansans and Kentuckians lost "not a score," whereas Geary reports that the two brigades he employed suffered 357 killed, wounded, and missing. Yet Geary also states that in spite of these heavy casualties and in spite of being repulsed three times, he would have persisted in the assault had he not received word that its strategic purpose had been accomplished: McPherson is "in full possession" of Snake Creek Gap.[22]

To be precise, Brigadier General Thomas Sweeny's division of Dodge's XVI Corps is at the south end of Snake Creek Gap, having marched over twenty miles via Ship's Gap and Villanow. In doing so it met no Confederates, which is fortunate, for Snake Creek Gap is a narrow, rugged, four-mile-long gorge bordered by steep mountains. One enemy brigade backed by a battery could have blocked or at least greatly impeded passage through it. The XVI Corps's other division, Brigadier General John Veatch's, and two of Logan's XV Corps's divisions reach the north end of the gap during the evening; but Logan's third division (his fourth remains in northern Alabama guarding the railroad) still is on the way with the Army of the Tennessee's wagon train; and Garrard's cavalry continues to lag so far behind that during the night Sherman orders Kilpatrick to join McPherson with one of his brigades. Consequently McPherson's full force will not be available until morning; and since Kilpatrick cannot possibly reach him in time, he will have to rely on his only cavalry regiment, the 9th Illinois Mounted Infantry, to screen his advance. On the other hand, the Confederates seem to be unaware of McPherson's presence in the gap. Hence at 8 P.M. he issues orders to Dodge and Logan to have their troops ready at 5 A.M. for a "bold and rapid movement on the enemy's flank or lines of communication" at Resaca. Tomorrow, if all goes well, Johnston will be cut off from Atlanta and forced into precipitate, disastrous retreat.[23]

A 2 P.M. dispatch from McPherson notifies Sherman that the Army of the Tennessee is on its way into Snake Creek Gap. This is good: that part of his plan seems to be working. Not so good is the apparent weakness of the Confederates defending Buzzard Roost Gap and the northern half of Rocky Face: they are not even using artillery! Could it be that Johnston has left only a small covering force around Dalton and that he has marched south with the bulk of his army to pounce on McPherson? On Sherman's order, Schofield climbs to the top of that part of Rocky Face seized by Harker's brigade and endeavors to ascertain if the Confederates are holding the Dalton area "in force." His first report, marked 3:30 P.M., announces that Crow Valley is "strongly occupied by infantry." But his second, sent five hours later, states: "I am not able to say whether the enemy is in force at Dalton." After reading the latter, Sherman at midnight instructs Schofield "to feel the enemy's position from your direction" in the morning and "at the earliest possible moment get a look into the enemy's lines. . . . We must not let Johnston amuse us here by a small force whilst he turns on McPherson."[24]

Johnston has not, Sherman would be relieved to know, turned on McPherson, nor does he intend to. Instead, his army remains near Dalton, and his primary concern continues to be Rome and Crow Valley. As regards the first, he has sent more telegrams to Loring and Polk, urging them to hasten; as for the second, the enemy's seizure of the upper portion of Rocky Face and the presence of his cavalry (McCook's division) on the Cleveland road has increased his fear that Sherman might strike at Dalton from the north. The result is that Johnston has instructed Wheeler to reconnoiter between Tunnel Hill and Ringgold with a view to finding out if the Union forces are concentrated west of Rocky Face or to the north and east of it.

Then, shortly after dark, a message arrives from Cantey at Resaca: "Cavalry scouts report Yankees in vicinity of Villanow today." There is a road from Villanow to Resaca, and it passes through Snake Creek Gap (it is, in fact, the road being used by McPherson). Quickly Johnston sends orders to Grigsby's Kentucky Brigade, the only cavalry available on his left, to march to Snake Creek Gap without delay. However, he is not greatly alarmed, if alarmed at all. He still believes that Rome is the probable Union target to the south and that McPherson's "corps" is aimed at it. Moreover, during the morning, Breckinridge's 9th Kentucky also has sighted Yankee cavalry at Villanow. Thus it appears likely that any Federal thrust via Snake Creek Gap against Resaca will take the form of a cavalry raid. If so, Cantey's and Grigsby's brigades should more than suffice to repel it. But if Sherman does try to send an infantry column through Snake Creek Gap, Grigsby will be able to delay it long enough for reinforcements to reach Cantey. In sum, there does not seem to be any particular danger at Resaca, certainly no immediate one.[25]

Grigsby's troopers are just getting ready to eat when the order to go to Snake Creek Gap arrives. Nevertheless they obey with a "cheerful alacrity" that perhaps is explainable in part by their having gone through the knapsacks of Granbury's Texans and taken (in Captain Sneed's bitter words) "everything worth carrying away."

At 10 P.M., after gulping down some food, they are on the way. The distance from Dug Gap to the southern end of Snake Creek Gap is ten miles, ordinarily no more than a two-hour march for cavalry unencumbered by wagons and artillery. But darkness, a rough and unfamiliar road, and incompetent civilian guides make for slow going. By the time the Kentuckians pass into Sugar Valley south of Snake Creek Gap it is dawn. Up ahead they see troops camped at the mouth of the gap. Having been told that a company of Georgians had been placed there as pickets, Grigsby assumes they are fellow Confederates. He quickly finds out otherwise. With a sudden loud crash, rifle bullets pour out of a nearby forest; these are followed by advancing blue-jacketed skirmishers (it is the 9th Illinois Mounted Infantry, fighting dismounted). The unexpected attack throws the Kentuckians into "confusion," but they soon rally and even drive back the Yankees with a counterattack. But then another enemy regiment assails them: it is the 66th Illinois Infantry, sharpshooters armed with privately purchased fifteen-shot Henry repeating rifles. This is too much; also Grigsby realizes that he is too late: the Yankees, lots of them, are through Snake Creek Gap. He orders his troopers to fall back; all they can do now is try to slow as much as possible the enemy's march toward Resaca.

Around midmorning (sources either do not mention the time or disagree if they do) Sweeny's and Veatch's divisions of Dodge's corps emerge from the gap, followed at a long interval by Logan's three divisions, less two brigades that have been left at the upper end of the gap to guard both it and the wagon train. The Federals, with the 9th Illinois in the van, advance slowly, extremely slowly. Grigsby's troopers offer "considerable resistance," compelling Dodge to deploy a strong infantry skirmish line in support of the inadequate cavalry. The skirmishers for their part have to struggle through underbrush so dense that they can barely see one another, much less the enemy, who might be and frequently are waiting in ambush just ahead. The whole column frequently halts while detachments of the 9th Illinois scout the countryside to the north in case a large Confederate force lurks there, ready to pounce. Not until after 2 P.M., after covering a mere five miles, do they reach a crossroads about two miles from Resaca. Beyond this crossroads, which is formed by the intersection of the road they are following with a road that runs south from Dalton to Lay's Ferry on the Oostanaula River, there is a treeless ridge known as Bald Hill which is occupied (Dodge estimates) by 1,400 Confederate infantry. Acting on prior instructions from McPherson, Dodge stations Veatch's division at the crossroads in position to defend against an attack from the north; then he orders Sweeny to seize Bald Hill. In a combined frontal-flank assault spearheaded by the 66th Illinois with its Henry repeaters, Sweeny easily and quickly does so. In fact, the Confederates flee in panic. From the top of the hill Sweeny's soldiers look across a valley filled with dead pine trees and behold Resaca, less than a mile away. Named after the 1846 Battle of Resaca de la Palma in Mexico, it consists of a dozen or so wooden buildings beside a railroad track. On a hill east of the village the cannons of a log-and-dirt fort guard a railroad bridge that spans the nearby Oostanaula. If the Federals can destroy this bridge, they will slice Johnston's lifeline to Atlanta.

Within the fort—to be precise, inside one of its dugouts—Brigadier General Cantey worriedly watches the approaching Yankee legions. Quartermaster clerk Robert Patrick, who works in Cantey's headquarters and sometimes even rides in his buggy, considers him "a poor dependence for a commander," an opinion that seems to be confirmed by the fact that he did not so much as post pickets in Snake Creek Gap and therefore did not learn that McPherson's army had passed through it until so notified by Grigsby's troopers. To defend Resaca and its vital railroad bridge he has approximately 4,000 troops. Two-fifths of them belong to his own brigade and consist in large part of raw recruits: they are the ones who skedaddled from Bald Hill. Another two-fifths are members of the 66th Georgia and an attached battalion, who have been detached from Walker's Division to garrison Resaca. Most of the remainder are Grigsby's dogged but dog-tired Kentuckians, part of whom are patrolling the countryside to the north in case the Federals head that way. Such a force with such a commander should not be able to hold out long against McPherson's five veteran divisions.

McPherson, however, does not know this, nor could he possibly know it. What he does know is that there seem to be more Rebels at Resaca than Sherman and he anticipated, that his maps are worse than worthless because the actual roads around Resaca "run the wrong way," that he lacks sufficient cavalry to remedy this deficiency by scouting, that prisoners claim that Wheeler is heading for the north end of Snake Creek Gap with the intent of blocking it, that he has heard nothing all day from Sherman about the situation at Dalton, and that because of the hilly, wooded terrain he has not been able to establish signal-flag communication with Hooker, who is to warn him if enemy forces head toward Resaca from the north. The possibility of this happening bothers him most of all. As he later tells one of his staff officers, if Johnston should come down on his left flank and rear, he could cut him off from Snake Creek Gap like "you cut off the end of a piece of tape with a pair of shears." It was to guard against this that he had Dodge station Veatch's division at the crossroads; now, as a further precaution, he has him send an eighteen-man company of the 9th Illinois Mounted—all that is available in the way of cavalry—up the road to Dalton with instructions to look out for the enemy and, if possible, to tear up some of the railroad track north of Resaca.

Around 4 P.M., Logan's corps reaches the crossroads and halts. McPherson thereupon orders Dodge to advance Veatch's division to Sweeny's left, then have it "feel" for the railroad. Nearly an hour later, two of Veatch's brigades, each massed in a column and preceded by skirmishers, move slowly forward, wade a stream called Camp Creek, and start across an open field, at the end of which lies the railroad, less than half a mile distant. They draw artillery fire from the fort but encounter no other opposition.

While Veatch's brigades advance, McPherson stands on a tree stump atop

Bald Hill, peering through his binoculars at the Confederate fortifications. They look strong, their cannons are booming away briskly, some of their shells fall near him, and presently he sees a large number of gray-clad soldiers emerge and head toward Veatch's right flank. How many other Rebels wait behind those ramparts? A division? Half of Johnston's army? Or perhaps the enemy hopes to lure him into Resaca, then swoop down from the north with overwhelming force to cut him off from Snake Creek Gap and his wagon train. No, attacking Resaca simply is too risky: he stands to lose far more than he probably can gain. He steps down from the tree stump, walks slowly down the hill to where his staff waits, and tells his adjutant general, Lieutenant Colonel William Clark, to notify Dodge, who is personally directing Veatch's advance, to turn back: The Army of the Tennessee will withdraw to Snake Creek Gap.

By now Dodge's striking force has dwindled to one brigade, that of Brigadier General John W. Fuller, because the other brigade that advanced across Camp Creek, Colonel John W. Sprague's, has been halted to guard against the enemy column that McPherson saw emerge from the fort. Fuller's brigade, Dodge accompanying it, continues forward, and its skirmishers report that the railroad is only a short distance ahead. Suddenly a Confederate regiment and battery (at least that is what Dodge thinks they are) open fire on Fuller's right flank. Dodge orders Fuller to charge the battery, then swing his brigade farther to the north. But before this can be done, McPherson's order to retreat arrives. Dodge passes it on to Fuller, whose troops halt, then head back to the west side of Camp Creek, as does Sprague's brigade. Some of Fuller's troops had gotten within two hundred yards of the railroad and cannot understand why they are withdrawing. Watching them, Colonel Breckinridge does not understand either: only a thin line of Kentuckians defends the railroad north of Resaca.[26]

The Army of the Tennessee trudges toward a "yellow sun" that soon sinks out of sight, leaving behind pitch darkness. Its soldiers feel frustrated, tired, and terribly hungry: "Oh, dear, my belly is rubbing my backbone!" It is nearly midnight before they reach Sugar Valley and encamp near the south exit of Snake Creek Gap. While they light their fires, Kilpatrick—"a little fellow about 5 feet 5"—gallops by with an escort, but his main force still is on the way. Still later the eighteen-man detachment from the 9th Illinois Mounted also rides in. It was able to reach the railroad north of Resaca but found it so heavily patrolled by Rebel cavalry that all it could do was tear down a short stretch of telegraph wire.

Thus ends McPherson's "bold and rapid movement on the enemy's flank or line of communications." His total loss is six killed, thirty wounded, and sixteen captured.[27]

While McPherson marches to Resaca and then marches back, west and north of Rocky Face the XX, XIV, and IV corps skirmish with the Confederates and bombard their lines with artillery but make no attacks. In fact the XIV Corps in front of Buzzard Roost cannot attack even if it wants to, for an attempt last night by some of Davis's troops to eliminate the artificial lake blocking its way by destroying the dam on Mill Creek has failed owing to the presence of too many Rebel guards. Only Harker's brigade engages in serious fighting as it endeavors to resume its advance along the crest of Rocky Face with a view to gaining a point overlooking the enemy position in Buzzard Roost Gap. Soon, however, it encounters some of Cheatham's Tennesseans barricaded behind boulders. Not even the cannons that were laboriously hauled up to the top of the ridge during the night can blast through this obstacle, with the result that Harker's division commander, Brigadier General John Newton, notifies Howard shortly before noon: "We are butt up against the enemy and may not advance farther for some time." The Federals thereupon rake Cheatham's position with heavy rifle and artillery fire from the valley below. This barrage, although it inflicts few physical casualties, subjects the Tennesseans to terrible psychological strain, and at least one of them cracks under it. He is a member of Captain James Hall's outfit and is "considered one of the bravest men in the regiment." But after a cannonball knocks down the stone wall sheltering his company, he becomes so demoralized that a few days later he shoots off one of his own fingers in the hopes of getting a discharge, with what success, Captain Hall does not record. To counter the Yankee battery that probably fired that wall-toppling cannonball, Cheatham summons three sharpshooters armed with Whitworths. Their first shots, notes Hall, cause "consternation among the gunners," who at once start hitching horses to their cannons; and by the time several more rounds have been fired, they are "in full retreat to the rear." The distance is too great for Hall to tell whether any of them have been hit, but he has no doubt that "they were badly scared."[28]

East of Rocky Face, Schofield enters Crow Valley with two divisions, his object being to implement Sherman's order to "feel the enemy's position" in that area. For a while he meets scant opposition; then he comes in view of a "strong line of rifle-pits" extending from Rocky Face across the valley to a fortified hill on the west. His first thought is to attack the enemy's left, but he abandons the idea upon learning that Harker's advance along the top of Rocky Face has been stymied and that McCook's cavalry, covering his own left, have been driven back by Wheeler. Instead Schofield contents himself with a "strong demonstration" that lasts until evening. At 9 P.M. he informs Sherman that the Rebel works in Crow Valley are being held by a "force about equal to my own," and Sherman in turn orders him to establish a "strong defensive position."[29]

Even as Schofield pens his dispatch to Sherman, Johnston returns to his head-quarters in Dalton accompanied by Hood, with whom he has spent the after-noon viewing the skirmishing in Crow Valley. Here Johnston reads telegrams from Grigsby and Cantey, sent earlier in the day, stating that an enemy force, size not indicated, is moving against Resaca. He also reads some reports from Wheeler's scouts to the effect that "Logan and Dodge under McPherson are on an expedition to Resaca."

Johnston does not know what to make of these messages. They would seem to indicate that Sherman indeed is trying to cut Johnston's communication line at Resaca and that Sherman is employing more than just cavalry to do it. But how can Johnston be sure? Perhaps the Federals who are approaching Resaca are merely some of Hooker's troops carrying out a feint designed to cover the movement of McPherson on Rome, a supposition that would seem to be supported by telegrams from Cantey and Martin which refer to Hooker as the one who is menacing Resaca. After deliberating on these matters, Johnston tells Hood to take a train to Resaca and look over the situation there. At the same time he orders Walker's and Hindman's divisions and Cleburne's two brigades at Dug Gap to proceed as rapidly as possible to Resaca, where Hood will assume command. Toward midnight, Cleburne, with Granbury's and Lowrey's brigades, begins marching to Resaca, followed at long intervals by Walker and Hindman.[30]

When, around midnight, Sherman lies down for his customary three or four hours of sleep, he feels pleased with the day's developments and optimistic about tomorrow's. According to the last word received from McPherson, a dispatch marked 2 P.M., the Army of the Tennessee was encountering light opposition and was "within two miles of Resaca"—news that caused him to exclaim, "I've got Joe Johnston dead!" Presumably by now McPherson has destroyed the railroad at Resaca and has ducked back safely into Snake Creek Gap. Furthermore, in view of the enemy's stout resistance at Buzzard Roost and in Crow Valley, there can be little doubt that Johnston's army remains concentrated at Dalton, that Johnston intends to fight strictly on the defensive, and that so far at least, Johnston is unaware of McPherson's movement. This being the case, and since the Confederate lines around Dalton are virtually impregnable, perhaps a modification in the plan for defeating Johnston is in order. Instead of waiting for him to retreat in reaction to having his commu-nications line broken at Resaca, why not take advantage of his passivity and evident determination to hold on to Dalton by swinging most or all of Thomas's and Schofield's forces through Snake Creek Gap from where they then can move with McPherson to Resaca, thereby cutting Johnston off from Atlanta? Such a maneuver, successfully executed, would guarantee the destruction of Confederate power in Georgia even as Grant is destroying it in Virginia, a work that seems to be well under way, according to a recently arrived telegram from Halleck stating: "The Army of the Potomac had hard fighting on the 5th and 6th, driving the enemy from every position. On the 7th they [the enemy] had retreated some ten miles. General Grant is in pursuit." In a special order to his troops announcing Grant's victory, Sherman declares, "Let us do likewise," and that is what he both hopes and expects to do—soon.

At seven on the morning of May 10, Sherman telegraphs Halleck outlining his new plan:

> Johnston acts purely on the defensive. I am attacking him on his strongest fronts . . . till McPherson breaks his line at Resaca, when I will swing round through Snake Creek Gap, and interpose between him and Georgia. . . . Yesterday I pressed hard to prevent Johnston detaching against McPherson, but today I will be more easy, as I believe McPherson has destroyed Resaca, [from where] he is ordered to fall back to mouth of Snake Creek Gap.

Also during the morning, Sherman asks Thomas's advice on the best way to carry out the new plan: should they leave the XXIII Corps to cover Ringgold along with Stoneman's cavalry, "which should be near at hand," and then send the entire Army of the Cumberland by way of Trickum, Villanow, and Snake Creek Gap to join McPherson in "interposing ourselves" between Resaca and Dalton? Or would it be better to "cut loose from the railroad altogether and move the whole army on the same objective point, leaving Johnston to choose his course"? In any event, Thomas will order all of his troops to be ready to march tonight with three days' provisions, for "I expect to hear from McPherson."[31]

A short time later (probably between 9:30 and 10 A.M.) Sherman does hear from McPherson. He hears from him in the form of a dispatch delivered by Captain Joseph Audenried, one of his aides-de-camp who accompanied the march through Snake Creek Gap. Sent some twelve hours ago, it states that "the enemy have a strong position at Resaca naturally, and, as far as we could see, have it pretty well fortified"; that the Confederates there "displayed considerable force, and opened on us with artillery"; and that after "skirmishing till nearly dark, and finding that I could not succeed in cutting the railroad before dark, or getting to it, I decided to withdraw the command and take up a position for the night between Sugar Valley and the entrance to the gap" because "there are a half dozen good roads leading north toward Dalton down which a column of the enemy could march" and because "General Dodge's men are all out of provisions" and their wagon train is still far to the rear. If he had possessed, McPherson continues, "a division of good cavalry I could have broken the railroad at some point," but as it was, he has managed only to tear down "a small portion of telegraph wire" near Tilton. Finally, "I shall be compelled to rest my men tomorrow forenoon, at least, to enable them to draw provisions," and when he does move forward again, "I would like a division of Hooker's command to hold the entrance to the gap and the roads at Sugar Valley" so that he can employ his full force in conjunction with Kilpatrick, who "is very anxious to make the attempt to cut the railroad."

Sherman's disappointment and bafflement on reading McPherson's dispatch register themselves in his reply: "I have yours of last night. . . . I regret beyond measure you did not break the railroad, however little, and close to Resaca, but I suppose it was impossible." His plan for defeating, even destroying, Johnston's army, which seemed to be succeeding, suddenly and strangely has gone askew. Well, there is nothing to do except adopt a new one or, to be precise, adjust the new plan that he already was beginning to implement to the unexpected outcome of McPherson's thrust (which seems to have been more like a feeble shove) at Resaca. McPherson, so Sherman instructs him in his reply, must remain where he is and fortify his position. Meanwhile a "comparatively small force" will be left to hold the enemy in check at Dalton; the rest of the army, led by Hooker's corps, will march to and through Snake Creek Gap; in fact, Brigadier General Alpheus S. Williams's division of the XX Corps is on the way there now. Should Johnston attack McPherson with all or most of his army, which Sherman considers unlikely, McPherson is to "fight him to the last and I will get to you."[32]

As a courier gallops off to deliver this message to McPherson, Sherman's attention turns to the matter of what "comparatively small force" he will leave on the Dalton front. His first choice is Schofield's XXIII Corps, which on his orders, already is withdrawing from Crow Valley to a new line running northward from Rocky Face. Schofield, however, protests: "To leave my small command here . . . would simply result in my being idle or being whipped." Reading this, Sherman recognizes that Schofield has a valid point. Furthermore, as Thomas observes in his reply to Sherman's earlier query about the best way to shift the army to the Resaca area, once McPherson is reinforced by Hooker, he will be in no danger because "Johnston will be compelled to hold a large part of his force in Buzzard Roost as long as it is threatened." Sherman therefore informs Thomas that instead of the XXIII Corps, Howard's much stronger IV Corps, supplemented by McCook's and Stoneman's cavalry, will be left behind while the rest of the army moves south: first, Major General Daniel Butterfield's division of the XX Corps, which is to start at once; then, on the morrow, Geary's division, the XIV Corps, and the XXIII Corps in that order. Howard's task will be to keep the Confederates concentrated at Dalton by demonstrating against Buzzard Roost; should they "detect the dimunition" in Union strength around Rocky Face and attack him, he is to retire slowly to Ringgold and "defend that point at all costs," because it now is the railhead from which the army draws all of its supplies.[33]

In the evening, Sherman telegraphs Halleck that McPherson has failed to cut the railroad at Resaca and that "according to his instructions, he drew back to the debouches of the gorge" (Snake Creek Gap). As a consequence and since Buzzard Roost Gap "is naturally and artificially too strong to be attempted," he intends to "feign on Buzzard Roost, but pass through Snake Creek Gap, and place myself between Johnston and Resaca, when he will have to fight it out." However, he adds, "I will be in no hurry," as he is certain that Johnston "can make no detachments."[34]

Sherman's order to McPherson to remain at Snake Creek Gap is superfluous: McPherson does not so much as think of doing otherwise, for he believes that by now Johnston surely has sent a large portion, if not most, of his army to Resaca and that consequently he, McPherson, is in dire danger of being attacked by a superior enemy force. Therefore, in spite of the fact that his provision wagons arrive, Kilpatrick's cavalry joins him, Williams's division from the XX Corps reaches the north end of Snake Creek Gap, and his reconnaissance patrols encounter only small parties of Rebel cavalry west of Resaca, McPherson does not try again to cut the railroad but instead spends the day constructing a fortified line across Sugar Valley so as to cover all approaches from the north and east. The closest he comes to using in an aggressive fashion the 20,000 or more troops he now has available is to send Dodge's two divisions and one of Logan's to occupy the Resaca-Dalton crossroads. When in the evening some civilians report that the Confederates plan to attack him tomorrow morning, he has no doubt that they are telling the truth. "I shall be on my guard and fight them to the very best of my ability," he informs Sherman in a 6:30 P.M. dispatch.[35]

Johnston has no more intention of attacking McPherson at Snake Creek Gap than McPherson has of attacking Resaca. At 8 A.M., Hood had telegraphed Johnston from the latter place: "R[esaca] all right. Hold on to Dalton." Accordingly he has ordered Hood to rejoin the main army, instructed Cleburne to return to Dug Gap with Granbury's and Lowrey's brigades, and halted Hindman's Division near Dalton and Walker's at Tilton. Moreover, during the course of the day the Federals have withdrawn from Crow Valley and seem to have relaxed their pressure against Rocky Face. Consequently, by the end of the day, Johnston still cannot figure out what Sherman is trying to do, so he continues to regard Rome as the prime danger spot in the region south of Dalton. This is why, having learned that a brigade of Loring's Division has reached Rome, he has ordered Loring to send it at once to Resaca by rail but to keep his other two brigades at Rome until French's Division, on the way from Alabama, was within a day's march of the town.

However, sometime after nightfall, Grigsby reports that McPherson's "corps" is entrenching in Snake Creek Gap. Why this information comes so late— Grigsby's scouts have had McPherson's troops under close observation all day—cannot be explained on the basis of the available sources. In any case, it causes Johnston to change his mind about the relative dangers to Rome and Resaca: At 9 P.M., Mackall telegraphs Polk, who now is at Rome: "General Johnston wishes you to concentrate your troops at Resaca. Assume command of that place and of the district . . . and make the proper dispositions to defend the passage of the [Oostanaula] river and our communications."36

A tremendous thunderstorm rages throughout the night. The rain pours through the tents of Chauncey Cooke of the 23rd Wisconsin and all of the other troops that McPherson has stationed at the Resaca-Dalton crossroads "like sieves" and some men are lying in puddles that are two inches deep. Then an order from McPherson to fall back to the mouth of the gap turns into a rumor that the Confederates are about to attack, with the result that sentinels rush about shouting "To arms! To arms! The rebs are coming!" Already as wet as "drowned rats," Cooke and his comrades sling on their cartridge boxes and knapsacks, fasten their dripping blankets and shelter halves to their belts, and after grabbing their rifles, fall into line and begin marching. They wade through mud and water in a pitch darkness that is sporadically illuminated by flashes of lightning. Many stumble over rocks and roots, falling full length in the mire. After about four miles they halt near a big corral of wagons. Some build fires (soldiers learn to do this even in the rain) and dry their blankets and themselves as best they can. Others work at building log breastworks "cheerfully, and without a murmur," according to a general's official report. But twice now they have turned their backs on the enemy without, so far as they can tell, any reason to do so. "It's pretty hard," comments Private Cooke, "to tell what Sherman's trying to do."37

Shortly after 9 A.M., on May 11, Johnston, who also finds it "pretty hard to tell what Sherman's trying to do," receives another telegraphic message from Cantey: "Enemy advancing on this place in force." Johnston immediately sends Hood back to Resaca, alerts Cleburne to be ready to move there, orders Cheatham to withdraw his division from Rocky Face and replace Cleburne at Dug Gap, and telegraphs Polk, urging him to "send all the troops you can to Resaca with dispatch. . . . The enemy are close upon it." However, at 3 P.M., Hood telegraphs from Resaca that "no enemy is within four miles"; at about the same time the rest of Loring's Division, accompanied by Polk, begins arriving there. As a consequence, Johnston keeps Cleburne at Dug Gap and holds Cheatham's troops along the road between that point and Dalton. Since, evidently, Resaca is in no immediate danger, he will refrain from committing any more of his army to its defense until he hears from Wheeler, whom he has directed via Mackall to move his cavalry "around the north end of Rocky Face" and to "try to ascertain" the location of the enemy's left and whether the Federals "are in motion toward the Oostenaula." Until Johnston has definite intelligence that Sherman's main force is heading south, he cannot dismiss the possiblity that the strangely inert Union column in Snake Creek Gap is a mere decoy designed to lure him away from Dalton.[38]

One of the reasons Johnston remains unsure as to whether Sherman is shifting most of his army to the south is that this shifting is taking place very slowly. The only major Federal unit to reach Snake Creek Gap during the day is Butterfield's division, which has started its march before dawn. For the rest, Geary's division remains in front of Dug Gap, the XIV Corps waits until late afternoon before pulling back from Buzzard Roost while the IV Corps slides over to take its place, and the XXIII Corps stays put north of Rocky Face until after dark and the arrival—at last!—of Stoneman's cavalry. As he had telegraphed Halleck yesterday evening, Sherman is in no hurry. He believes, so he informs McPherson, that Johnston "can't afford" either to abandon his strong position at Dalton or to detach sufficient force to attack McPherson successfully. Therefore, McPherson is to continue strengthening his defenses and to "threaten the safety of the railroad all the time"—but not too much because, "to tell the truth, I would rather he [Johnston] should stay in Dalton two more days," at the end of which time "he may find a larger party than he expects in an open field" and so have to "move out of his trenches."[39]

Late in the afternoon, however, Sherman's confidence that Johnston is strategically paralyzed suffers a jolt. First, a dispatch comes from McPherson, who states that his scouts report that Cleburne's and possibly another enemy division are at Tilton; next, observers atop the northern half of Rocky Face have spotted Cheatham's Division moving southward. Could it be that Johnston is evacuating his lines around Dalton after all? To find out, Sherman orders Thomas to have the Confederate defenses "felt at once." In due course, several regiments from Stanley's division of the IV Corps move toward Buzzard Roost Gap deployed as skirmishers. As soon as they enter the gorge, they are, in the words of Captain Ira Read of the 101st Ohio, "greeted by a perfect shower of musket balls and cannister" from the front and both flanks. They struggle forward a few yards, then literally go to ground, every man sheltering himself as best he can behind rocks, trees, and anything else available, until it is dark and safe to withdraw.[40]

Obviously the Confederates, enough of them anyway, still hold Buzzard Roost Gap. Nevertheless Sherman concludes that as much as he would prefer it, Johnston will not oblige him by remaining two more days at Dalton, that on the contrary he is pulling out of Dalton and heading south toward Resaca. Since a telegraph wire has now been strung part of the way between Tunnel Hill and Sugar Valley, he has this message tapped out to McPherson: "The indications are that Johnston is evacuating Dalton. In that event Howard and the cavalry will pursue, and all the rest will follow your route. I will be down early in the morning."[41]

McPherson has spent the day, as he had the previous one, fortifying. Besides nearly all of his own 23,000 troops and Kilpatrick's cavalry, he has most of Williams's division, which has arrived in Sugar Valley early in the morning singing "Come, Johnny, Fill the Bowl," and Butterfield's division, which is hard at work in Snake Creek Gap improving the so-called road. Yet the only portion of this force that has moved out toward Resaca is Kilpatrick's, on the lookout for the enemy's supposedly impending morning assault. Probably this reconnaissance is what has caused Cantey to telegraph Johnston at 8:30 A.M. that the Federals were advancing on Resaca, thereby realerting Johnston to the danger there; if so, then from the Union standpoint it would have been better to have kept Kilpatrick close to Snake Creek Gap and made no reconnaissance at all.

On the other hand, had McPherson in fact moved against Resaca early in the day, he would have had, as on the previous two days, a fine chance of taking it, given the garrison's weakness and his own great superiority in numbers. By the end of the day, however, Resaca's defenders and their defenses are much stronger. All of Loring's Division has arrived, as has Polk; and as he gazes about in the evening, quartermaster clerk Patrick notes that "everything is stripped for the fight and the hills and knobs overlooking the town, on which we have batteries of heavy ordnance, are covered with troops." Atop one hill he sees, "together upon their horses," Polk, Hood, Cantey, and several other generals, "calmly

Confederate defenses at Resaca (*Photographic History*, 3:109)

surveying the scene." All along the line, riders gallop "from point to point, bearing dispatches," and on "an eminence" near where he sits, writing in his diary, "men are working hard, throwing up an embankment, behind which to plant a battery." There is, he concludes, "evidently a heavy thing on hand," whereupon he closes his diary, opens up a bottle, and proceeds to get drunk.[42]

At about 8 P.M., Polk and Hood take a train to Dalton, where they confer until midnight with Johnston and Hardee. Then Polk accompanies Hood to the latter's headquarters. There, in the parlor, by the dim light of a single candle and using a horse bucket for a font, Polk baptizes the one-legged general who, unable to kneel, remains standing, his head bowed. To Lieutenant William Gale, Polk's son-in-law and a member of his staff, it is "one of the most imposing ceremonies I ever witnessed."[43]

In the morning the XIV Corps sets out early enough—5 o'clock; but it marches "very slowly" according to a member of Major Holmes's 52nd Ohio. The road, which runs due south through the valley between Rocky Face and Taylor's

Ridge to Snake Creek Gap, is narrow, crooked, hilly, and so muddy that the trudging infantry have to halt again and again to await the extrication of some bogged-down wagon. Not until noon does the head of the column approach Dug Gap, a mere five miles from its starting point near Tunnel Hill and more than ten miles from its ultimate destination, Sugar Valley. Frustrated by the consequent delay to his XXIII Corps, Schofield thereupon notifies Sherman and Thomas that since the XIV Corps "seems to find difficulty in getting along," he will make a detour by way of the road from Trickum to Villanow, which he expects to reach around 5 P.M. However, at sunset, a good two hours after 5 P.M., Schofield's troops still are at least five miles from Villanow; and the XIV Corps, its progress stymied by Hooker's ammunition train, has not even reached Snake Creek Gap, much less passed through it. Only Geary's division, which left its position at Dug Gap upon being relieved by McCook's cavalry around noon, has managed to get to Sugar Valley by nightfall. According to the map, it should be an easy day's march from the Tunnel Hill area to Sugar Valley via Snake Creek Gap, but marches are made on roads, not maps, and they are all the harder to make if the roads are bad and if too many men, horses, mules, wagons, and cannons are trying to use them simultaneously.[44]

Sherman's southward march cannot and does not go undetected. At 9:30 A.M., Johnston wires Polk, who has returned to Resaca: "The enemy in our front is moving rapidly down the valley toward Snake Gap or Villanow." As the telegraph key raps out this message, 2,000 of Wheeler's troopers, backed by Hindman's Division, advance dismounted into Crow Valley. They encounter two road-weary brigades of Stoneman's division and easily drive them back until checked by infantry sent by Howard, who fears he is about to be assailed by the bulk of the Rebel army. Wheeler thereupon notifies Johnston that insofar as he can tell, the Federals have only cavalry and two infantry divisions north and west of Rocky Face. His report, along with other intelligence to the same effect, convinces Johnston that Sherman has sent most of his forces toward the Oostanaula. Yet Johnston still is uncertain as to the exact target. If it is Resaca, why was no serious attempt made to take it when it would have been easy to have done so? And why have so many Union troops—30,000 at last report—stayed so long in Snake Creek Gap, apparently doing nothing except build fortifications? After pondering these questions, Johnston decides that Sherman's objective probably is Calhoun, a railroad village about six miles south of Resaca. By seizing it, the enemy could trap him either north of the Oostanaula or within its horseshoe curve south of Resaca. To guard against both possibilities, he directs Walker to hasten his division to Calhoun and look to the crossings of the Oostanaula.

This done, Johnston next issues orders to Hardee, Hood, and Wheeler:

wagon trains will start southward at once, all infantry in the lines around Dalton will pull out as soon as it is dark and march to Resaca, and the cavalry will take their places during the night and then provide a rear guard in the morning against Union pursuit. Thus Dalton, which for nearly six months has been the base and headquarters of the Army of Tennessee, is to be abandoned because it is no longer tenable. Abandoned, too, is any hope that Johnston might have had of so badly crippling Sherman's forces in a defensive battle that he would be able to go over to the offensive. For the time being, Johnston's sole concern is and must be saving his own army from being trapped and destroyed.

In the evening, Johnston boards one of the last trains to leave Dalton and travels to Resaca. At Resaca he is ninety miles by rail from Atlanta.[45]

Late in the afternoon, Sherman and his staff ride up to McPherson's headquarters tent in Sugar Valley. As he dismounts, Sherman says to McPherson, who has stepped forward to greet him, "Well, Mac, you have missed the opportunity of a lifetime." According to an officer who is standing nearby, these words are spoken "not ungraciously"; but McPherson realizes that he is being rebuked for having failed to cut the railroad at Resaca on May 9. He makes no reply, at least none that has been recorded, and Sherman and he go inside the tent, presumably to discuss future operations.[46]

A couple of hours later, Thomas, who also has reached Sugar Valley, notifies Sherman that the signal station atop the north end of Rocky Face reports that long lines of wagons are moving south from Dalton. Now there can be no doubt whatsoever that Johnston is—or soon will be—pulling out of Dalton and retreating toward Resaca. Promptly Sherman sends orders to Palmer and Schofield to keep marching until they reach Sugar Valley; tomorrow morning the entire army will advance to Resaca and "interpose" itself between that place and the enemy. In response, the XIV Corps files through Snake Creek Gap in pitch darkness, "each man following the sound of his comrade's footsteps ahead," and the XXIII Corps, which had stopped to rest near Villanow, resumes its roundabout trek.[47]

As the sun rises on May 13, skirmishers from Stanley's division cautiously enter the gorge at Buzzard Roost Gap. They anticipate little if any opposition—fires burning in Dalton during the night had provided ample proof that the Johnnies were evacuating—but there might be a rear guard. To their relief, they find the enemy fortifications vacant and the enemy himself nowhere in sight. Looking about the gorge, they see (in the words of an Illinois soldier) "as wild a place as it is possible to imagine," with "huge rocks sticking up on every side like pointed monuments in a grave yard." In fact it is a graveyard, but one without graves. Lying about are the unburied corpses of their comrades who had been killed in yesterday's fighting, "stripped of every vestige of clothing, their nude forms exposed to the hot blistering sun." Moving on through the gorge, they enter Dalton, where they discover little of military value but do find, in still-intact warehouses, large quantities of tobacco, "home-made hatchets," peanuts, and even some cigars. They also come across an execution ground—eighteen or twenty posts with as many graves beside them—and stocks that had been used to punish Southern soldiers guilty of serious breaches of discipline by requiring them to stand for hours without being able to move their hands or feet. Pointing at the stocks, Brigadier General August Willich, a somewhat eccentric German-born officer, exclaims: "Phoys, you don't know what ees the greatest bunish-ments to these poor devils [Confederates placed in the stocks]. Dey can't scratch when de lice bites them!"[48]

A little after 9 A.M., Howard telegraphs Thomas that he has occupied Dalton and that as soon as he can re-form his troops, he will push on to Resaca with Stoneman covering his left and McCook his right. "The railroad," he adds, knowing that this will be of particular interest, "is entirely uninjured up to this point." Therefore he will turn Dalton into a supply depot at once. By noon he is about ready to begin marching, but he wires Sherman, "I think the rebels mean to avoid a fight at Resaca."[49]

Sherman agrees. Not only does he assume that Johnston intends to retreat south of the Oostanaula he also believes (as does Thomas) that the bulk of the Confederate army still is en route to Resaca and that, therefore he will be able to "interpose" between it and Resaca. However, he soon discovers the same thing that McPherson had before him: namely, that owing to what he later terms the impractical nature of the country," marching through Sugar Valley is slow going, made all the slower by the miserable road. Not until 10 A.M. does the van of his column reach the Dalton-Resaca crossroads, two miles from Resaca, and then a half-hour passes before Kilpatrick's troopers ride forward to re-connoiter.

Almost at once they meet enemy infantry posted in a dense grove of thickets. One regiment charges but turns aside on encountering heavy rifle fire. Kil-patrick thereupon orders a regiment armed with Spencers to attack on foot. As it advances, he plunges ahead into the thicket astride his horse and waving his sword, presumably endeavoring to inspire his men with his own bravery—the only quality that no one doubts he lacks. Less then ten feet away a Rebel rifleman pops up and puts a bullet through Kilpatrick's left thigh. Soon after-ward some of Logan's troops see him being carried to the rear on a stretcher.

The wound is not serious—no bone has been broken; no amputation will be required—but it will be a while before the dashing little general will be able to do any more dashing.

The Spencer regiment's overwhelming firepower flushes the enemy from the thicket grove, whereupon Kilpatrick's troopers fall back, in the sarcastic words of an Ohio footsoldier, to "a safer place." There simply are too many Confederates out there for cavalry to handle. During the next two hours the XV Corps deploys in line of battle, supported by Veatch's division on the right and a portion of the XX Corps on the left. Then, a little after 1 P.M., it begins advancing, preceded by a strong skirmish line. Fire from the Confederate skirmishers, reports Logan, is "rapid and effective"; nevertheless the Federals steadily push onward across hills and gulleys covered with young pines and thick underbrush. About 3 P.M. they emerge from these woods into some open fields and behold, less than half a mile ahead, a range of "commanding hills" crested with infantry and artillery. Logan orders a halt, brings up a battery that quickly silences the enemy cannons, then sends his troops forward again. They encounter little resistance and, at about 4:30 P.M., occupy the hills, one of which is the Bald Hill seized by Sweeny four days earlier. From it, looking out across the valley of dead trees, they can see, as did Sweeny's men, Resaca, the railroad bridge, toward which a train is puffing, and the Confederate fortifications. The latter, however, no longer are confined to the hill east of the village. Now they consist of a line of formidable-looking earthworks running along the hills and ridges on the other side of the valley and extending far to the north; moreover, they are swarming with troops and bristling with artillery.[50]

Sherman is mistaken in his assumption that Johnston intends to retreat south of the Oostanaula. Johnston believes that he must make at least a temporary stand at Resaca or else risk being attacked in the rear and flank while crossing a river. Moreover, he knows that the Federal forces are divided and so calculates that if he can concentrate his own full strength at Resaca in time, he will be able to repulse, perhaps even destroy, any Union column venturing out of Snake Creek Gap to attack him at Resaca. Contrary to Sherman's wishful thinking, Johnston already has on hand at Resaca most of his army: Polk's troops, Cleburne's and Major General Carter P. Stevenson's divisions, most of Cheatham's Division, and part of Walker's Division, which he has decided to retain there for the time being. The rest of his infantry—Bate's, Stewart's, and Hindman's divisions and a brigade of Cheatham's—is on the way and should arrive by evening. By then, certainly by tomorrow morning, he will be ready to give Sherman all the fighting he wants and maybe more.[51]

Sherman promptly abandons, as he must, his plan to "interpose" between Johnston and Resaca and orders his forces to form and fortify a line opposite the enemy defenses. By evening they are deployed as follows: Veatch's division on the right and close to the Oostanaula; next, straddling the road from Snake Creek to Resaca, the XV Corps; then Butterfield's division, with Geary's and Williams's to its rear in reserve; and finally the XIV Corps on the left, supported by two divisions of the XXIIII Corps. Kilpatrick's cavalrymen, now under the temporary command of Colonel Eli Murray, picket the north (actually in large part west) bank of the Oostanaula, Sweeny's division remains near the Dalton-Resaca crossroads, Hovey's division of the XXIII Corps guards the northern entrance to Snake Creek Gap, and even farther to the rear, Garrard's laggard cavalrymen screen the road from Villanow. As for Howard, McCook, and Stoneman, they still are well to the north of Tilton, their "pursuit" slowed to a crawl by a skillful rearguard action conducted by Wheeler with the backing of Maney's Brigade of Cheatham's Division. "The 'rebs,'" Howard subsequently writes his wife, "arrange barricades of rails and logs along the road. When driven from one, another force has unobstrusively moved a half or three quarters of a mile [further] on" and done the same thing.[52]

Thanks to Wheeler's delaying tactics, Bate's, Stewart's, and Hindman's divisions experience no difficulty reaching the Resaca area late in the afternoon. As soon as they arrive, Johnston completes his dispositions: on the left and in front of Resaca, Polk's Corps (for such in essence it now is, although it remains officially designated the Army of Mississippi); in the center, also facing west, Hardee's Corps (Cleburne, Cheatham, and Bate); and on the right, which bends back across the railroad to the Conasauga River, Hood's Corps (Hindman, Stevenson, and Stewart). Altogether Johnston has (not counting Wheeler's rear guard and Walker's detachment at Calhoun) close to 50,000 troops on hand. They are well entrenched or rapidly becoming so, and their immediate flanks rest on sizable rivers. To be sure, there are two potentially serious weaknesses in his position: the Federals are within artillery range of the railroad bridge (already their cannons are firing at it but so far causing no damage), and they could cut his communications line by thrusting a force across the Oostanaula to Calhoun. However, Polk's men should be able to hold their strongly fortified line (if they don't, part of Walker's Division is in reserve and Cleburne is nearby); and although Walker at Calhoun reports enemy activity along the Oostanaula, there is no indication as yet that the Yankees are crossing it or even preparing to do so. Hence, until there is good reason to do otherwise, he intends to defend Resaca in hopes that Sherman will make a costly frontal assault or, better still, leave himself open to a devastating counterblow.[53]

Sherman, Johnston would be happy to know, continues to assume that the Confederates are in the process of retreating south of the Oostanaula; already, as can be seen from Bald Hill, their main wagon train is across the river.

Therefore he believes that they merely are trying to gain time by pretending to offer battle at Resaca. Consequently, although his plans for tomorrow call for an attack, his primary concern is pursuit. To that end he has issued urgent orders that the pontoon train be brought down through Snake Creek Gap to Sugar Valley as speedily as possible—he wants it there by morning—and that two bridges be laid across the Oostanaula near Lay's Ferry, four miles south-west of Resaca. Then, once the bridges are down, Kilpatrick's and Garrard's cavalry divisions will cross them, the former for the purpose of cutting the railroad south of Resaca and the latter with a view of operating against Rome. Finally, when Johnston does pull out of Resaca and supposing he does not do so sooner, Schofield will lead his corps across the bridges and endeavor to impede the fleeing Confederates so as to give the rest of the army a chance to overtake and defeat them. As regards tomorrow's attack at Resaca, its chief objective will be to put the enemy under such pressure that he will be unable to break away until nightfall, by which time Kilpatrick's and Garrard's troopers should be on the other side of the Oostanaula. Sherman, because he believes that Johnston will not attempt a long stand at Resaca, ignores a proposal from Thomas merely to feint an attack there while sending McPherson and Hooker across the Oostanaula to the hills west of Calhoun, where they would be in position to do what McPherson was supposed to do out of Snake Creek Gap: pounce on the flank of the Confederates when they retreat south.[54]

Part Two: Resaca

Between midnight and dawn the Union pontoon train passes through Snake Creek Gap. Escorting it is the 58th Indiana under the command of Colonel George P. Buell, who also heads the Army of the Cumberland's pioneer brigade. When they had set out from Chattanooga on the morning of May 12, the Hoosiers of the 58th were glad to be going to the front, for lately they had been engaged in the convictlike labor of breaking stone for macadamizing the streets of that town. Now they are not so sure but what they would prefer to be back wielding the sledgehammers. They had marched eighteen miles on the twelfth and have been on the road—a rough and often steep road—since 4 A.M. of the thirteenth, with only a two-and-one-half-hour halt to eat and rest. Nevertheless they keep trudging along like the mules pulling the wagons that carry the pontoons—or, to be precise, the strange-looking wooden frameworks that, according to the pontoniers who march along with them, will be covered over with canvas, when the time comes, to form the pontoons. A desire to see how this is done helps keep them going.

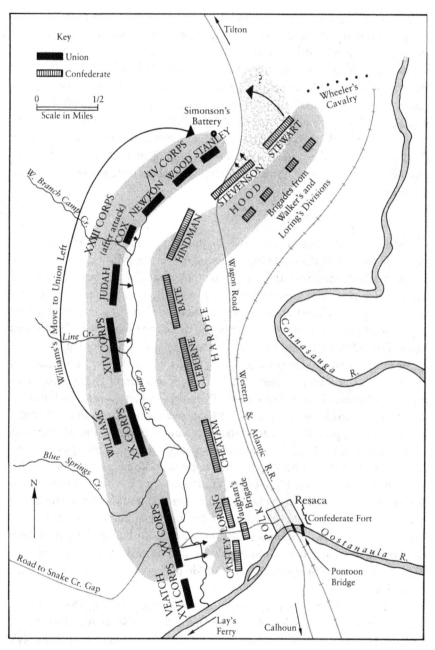

Battle of Resaca, May 14

At sunrise, Buell's column enters Sugar Valley, having covered nearly fifty miles in less than forty-eight hours. Bone-tired, both the soldiers and the pontoniers squat in a field beside the road, preparing and eating breakfast. To the west they hear cannonading. Then, after just an hour's rest, Buell orders them back on the road, because orders have arrived to get the pontoons to Lay's Ferry on the Oostanaula as quickly as possible. But there is no guide, and they waste several hours wandering about in the dense thickets until, finally, they reach the east bank of Snake Creek about a mile from where it flows into the Oostanaula. Here the pontoniers start assembling their canvas devices, and those Hoosiers who have not fallen asleep from sheer exhaustion satisfy their curiosity.[55]

"A battle usually comes between two breadths of sleep," comments Sergeant Nixon B. Stewart of the 52nd Ohio. Around 6 A.M. the skirmishers and sharpshooters of both the armies that face each other west of Resaca begin firing, and soon cannons here and there follow suit, producing the sound heard by Buell's men as they breakfasted in Sugar Valley. Neither side, however, attempts an attack. Johnston is content to remain on the defensive until he has a better idea of the Federal strength and intentions; Sherman still is positioning his forces and waiting for Howard to come up. As he does so, he makes two modifications in his plan of operations. One, a minor one, is to instruct Garrard to try to cross the Oostanaula near Rome rather than at Lay's Ferry, after which he is to "strike the railroad anywhere north of Kingston" or, failing in that, "threaten Rome" so as to prevent Johnston from receiving supplies and reinforcements from that direction. The other and more important modification takes the form of an 8 A.M. order to McPherson to "effect a lodgement" with one of his divisions on the opposite bank of the Oostanaula at Lay's Ferry, for Schofield has had to deploy so far to the north of the river that it now is impracticable to carry out the original plan of having him cross it when Johnston starts retreating, which Sherman continues to assume he will do before the day is over. McPherson immediately sends Sweeny's division toward Lay's Ferry; and Garrard, after notifying Sherman that he will "do the best I can," sets out for Rome around noon.[56]

At 11 A.M., Howard's corps, coming down from Tilton, arrives within supporting distance of Schofield on the Union left. As soon as it does, Cox's and Judah's divisions of the XXIII Corps and Baird's and Johnson's of the XIV Corps move forward with orders from Sherman to strike what he assumes is the Confederate right. Preceding each division, in accordance with the standard practice of both armies, is a skirmish line. This is provided by having one or two companies from the lead regiments go forward, widely spread and taking advantage of every bit of cover, to try to ascertain where the enemy is and how strong. Should the enemy forces counterattack, the skirmishers will delay them as long as possible, then scamper back to their own main line. When the actual charge takes place, they will lie down until the assault passes over them, then leap up and join it. When extra-strong opposition is expected or when a powerful enemy attack seems likely, whole regiments will be deployed in what are called "strong lines of skirmishers." These consist of a single dispersed rank, whereas a regular "line of battle" is formed by the companies of a regiment (with few exceptions ten in number) aligning themselves in two ranks, each company in a standard, prescribed spot:

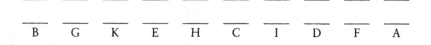

B   G   K   E   H   C   I   D   F   A

This usually suffices for defensive purposes, especially if the troops are behind breastworks or other types of fortifications. For attacks, on the other hand, a "double line of battle" usually is employed, meaning that the regiments of each brigade are drawn up in two lines of battle:

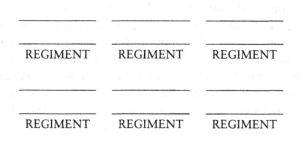

The assumption (or hope) behind this formation is that the first line will reach, then the second line will take, or break through, the enemy defenses. Since in practice this rarely happens, commanders sometimes will attempt to achieve success by sheer mass or weight of numbers and so will attack in "columns of brigades" wherein all the regiments of a brigade advance one behind another in lines of battle in a narrow but deep column:

REGIMENT

REGIMENT

REGIMENT

REGIMENT

REGIMENT

REGIMENT

Variations in these attack formations can be and are made, but whatever type is used, the role of the officers and the noncoms is to direct, control, and inspire. Hence as a regiment advances, its commander will be behind its center, his two senior officers will be to the rear of each wing, the company officers will be in front of their units, and the sergeants and corporals will act as file closers, ready to shove back into line anyone who falters. All regimental officers, including the commanders, are on foot, for they will not live long if mounted. Often also on foot are brigade commanders, who with their staffs follow in the immediate rear of their units. All regimental and brigade orders are delivered either by voice or bugle calls. On the other hand, division commanders, who usually remain mounted and well to the rear, transmit their orders by means of verbal or occasionally written messages borne to the brigadiers by mounted aides; only in extreme situations will they or a corps commander gallop forward to take direct charge of an assault. At the head of each regiment, two soldiers specially selected for outstanding courage and character carry the regimental flag and the national banner; theirs is a post of honor and also extra hazard, for enemy fire focuses on the colors, and the casualty rate of those who hold them is high. During battle every effort is made to keep the flags from falling to the ground or being captured; by the same token, seizing an enemy standard is an achievement surpassed only by the taking of a cannon or battery. Not only do the flags symbolize the regiment and the cause it is fighting for; they also serve the very practical function of a guide while advancing and a rallying point on defense or after a repulse: "Rally 'round the flag, boys, rally 'round the flag!" is more than just a rousing patriotic song.

These rows of men marching forward almost shoulder to shoulder offer excellent targets. Casualties can be and frequently are hideous: more than three-fourth's of a regiment, half or more of a brigade, as many as one-third of a division. Yet no one has found a practical alternative to such tactics. If attacks were made in loose, dispersed formations similar to the skirmish lines, they would lack the firepower and physical power needed to overcome defenders who likewise are massed in close ranks and usually behind some sort of cover. It also would be impossible for the division, brigade, and even regimental commanders to exercise effective control over their units, something they have difficulty doing in any case in the din and confusion of battle. Hence every assault in essence is an attempt to beat the odds, odds created by rifles that can inflict significant losses at 500 yards and become deadly at 300 yards and by cannons that can flatten a dozen men at any range from a mile to a few feet. Sometimes, as at Missionary Ridge, the attempt succeeds—if the enemy is overwhelmingly outnumbered, or he is poorly positioned, or his troops are of poor quality—but much more often than not it fails. Nevertheless, commanders continue to make frontal assaults in the hope of getting lucky and because most of the time there is no other way to do it if it is to be done at all. The best alternative—a flank attack—is difficult to execute successfully because its very effectiveness causes the enemy to take special precautions against it.[57]

Control (or rather the lack of it) becomes a serious problem the moment Schofield and Palmer start advancing. Even to get within sight of the Confederate defense line, about which nothing is known except that it is somewhere up ahead, the troops, who are formed in two lines of battle, must pass over hills and through gulleys so thickly overgrown with underbrush that (to quote from Brigadier General Absalom Baird's report) "an individual alone could make his way through it only with difficulty," and it is "utterly impossible . . . for a regiment, much less a brigade commander, to see and control the extremities of his command." Then, after about a half a mile, Baird's division, which constitutes the left half of Palmer's assault force, reaches the crest of a ridge overlooking a valley through which runs the narrow, shallow stream called Camp Creek; on the other side of the valley, atop another ridge about a quarter of a mile away, the Rebel works at last are visible.

Baird, an experienced and competent thirty-nine-year-old West Pointer from Pennsylvania, wants to halt in order to re-form his division and reconnoiter the enemy's position with a view to ascertaining its strength. Before he can do so, however, Brigadier General Henry Moses Judah's division of the XXIII Corps plunges by and even through his ranks. Seeing some of his regiments being carried along by Judah's troops, Baird feels compelled to order his division to charge too. It cannot, however, catch up with Judah, who also is far ahead of

Cox's division on its left. Consequently Judah's battle lines attack alone and unsupported. They are "met with a terrific fire from the [enemy] batteries and the rifle pits," writes Colonel Lyman Spaulding, whose 23rd Michigan is part of the first line. In spite of this they continue advancing "on the run" until they reach Camp Creek, whereupon they take "refuge." The air is "full of bullets and bursting shells," and Spaulding finds it "impossible to shout orders" loud enough for them to be heard.

Baird's division, as it scrambles down the "almost vertical slope" of the ridge, likewise encounters such withering rifle and artillery fire that it takes shelter beneath the "muddy bank" of Camp Creek. One officer tries to keep the attack going by yelling, "You are the men who scaled Missionary Ridge, and you can carry this!" but nobody budges. It is just as well, for opposing Baird are Cleburne's fighters, who had held their sector on Missionary Ridge back in November against several times their number of Grant's best.

On Judah's front a slackening of the Confederate fire enables most of the 23rd Michigan and the other lead regiments to crawl out of Camp Creek and make their way back up the ridge and to the rear. Here Spaulding meets Judah, who, in an excited manner, announces that he intends to renew the assault. Brigadier General Milo S. Hascall, senior brigadier of the division and Spaulding's commander, strongly protests: another attempt to carry the enemy's works will merely increase casualties. At first, Judah insists on attacking again, but then he listens to reason and orders the division to fortify the ridge, which it immediately starts doing.

While these things are transpiring, Schofield's other assault division, Cox's, approaches the Confederate lines to the north; thus the slackening of the fire against Judah's men. Brigadier General Jacob D. Cox is a tall, slender thirty-two-year-old Ohio lawyer who owes his rank to political connections (he has had it since May 1861) but who has earned it (and more) with excellent service both in the East and in the West, for he possesses what he himself considers to be the essential requisites of military leadership: "a bold heart, a cool head, and practical common-sense." The reason his division lags so far behind Judah's is that it has had a harder and longer way to go: on its front the Confederate works curve off to the northeast and can be reached only by crossing the two upper branches of Camp Creek, the western one of which is guarded by a strong, well-manned line of entrenchments.

Like Baird, Cox decides to attack at once in order to support Judah. However, it takes two, three, and finally four assaults just to dislodge the Rebels who are covering the west branch of Camp Creek, so stubbornly do they adhere to their well-located rifle pits. By then Cox knows that Judah has been repulsed; Cox also has had a chance to study what one of his officers accurately calls the "stronger defenses" of the enemy overlooking the eastern branch of Camp Creek. Therefore, he orders his troops to convert the rifle pits that they have seized into trenches for themselves. Noticing that the Confederates appear to be moving out of their works to his left, he deploys a regiment—all he dares spare—to protect that flank. After about an hour, during which the enemy continues to mass forces to the north and east, three brigades of the IV Corps arrive and relieve his division, which is nearly out of ammunition because the rugged terrain has prevented its wagon train from coming up.

Sherman's attempt to push back Johnston's right thus ends around 3 P.M. in total futility: Schofield and Palmer did not even encounter it per se, but instead merely butted against Cleburne's, Bate's, and a portion of Hindman's divisions in the center-right. Judah's headlong charge has produced approximately 700 dead and wounded, Cox has lost 66 killed and 486 wounded, and Baird's casualties total 135. As in every battle a stream of wounded head for the field hospitals in the rear, some on their own, others helped by comrades or carried on stretchers. First Assistant Surgeon James T. Reeve of the 21st Wisconsin, a part of the XIV Corps, finds it "very queer so many wounded in a right shoulder joint" and sees "one man whose left leg was entirely grounded to a jelly & his right one nearly as bad." Sergeant Widney of the 34th Illinois, after participating in a charge designed to enable Baird's troops to extricate themselves from Camp Creek, notices one soldier throw himself on his face and groan with "so much distress" that he assumes he is badly wounded and so asks him if he can be of any aid. "I am not hurt," the soldier answers, "but my little brother is lying dead in the weeds out there."[58]

Their blind infantry assault having failed, the Federals now do what they should have done in the first place: They bring up artillery to bombard the Confederate works. On orders from Thomas and Schofield, battery after battery comes up "in beautiful style," to quote a Confederate general who watches them. They take position on the wooded hills west and north of the upper reaches of Camp Creek, less than a mile from Johnston's defense line, and then open fire. Soon Cleburne's, Bate's, and Hindman's troops, as they crouch in their fortifications, are deluged with showers of shells that make an unnerving "tick, tick, tick" sound as they slice through the leaves. Trees and underbrush burst into flames that spread to some of the Confederates' log-and-rail parapets, "near smoking us out," comments a Mississippi soldier. Years later, Lieutenant William McMurray of the 20th Tennessee recalls that he counted between eleven and twenty-two shell explosions a minute in the sector held by his brigade of Bate's Division and states that it was "the most terrific artillery fire I was under in the war." One shell lands in the 20th Tennessee's rifle pit, where it lies sizzling viciously until two men grab it and toss it out just before it explodes. Others, however, are less lucky. A single shell kills six and mangles five members of the 24th Mississippi, causing one officer to flee in terror. Here and there whole regiments abandon their trenches and hug the ground behind them. Many cannoneers do the same, for their guns are the special targets of the Federal bombardment, and Confederate counterbattery fire is practically nil. Were Palmer and Schofield to attack now, their chance of success would be considerably greater. But Sherman does not order them to, nor does he have any thought of doing so. Before making any more offensive moves, he wants to extend his left so that it covers the Confederate right, which he now realizes stretches much farther to the north and east than he had assumed. Besides, the longer Johnston remains at Resaca, the more time there will be to establish the bridgehead on the Oostanaula at Lay's Ferry and thus make it possible to rapidly pursue and possibly intercept the Confederates when they do retreat, as he still expects them to do.[59]

That bridgehead is in the process of being established. Brigadier General Thomas Sweeny, commander of the division that McPherson has assigned to perform the tasks, is a forty-three-year-old County-Cork Irishman and regular army officer whose right arm had been shot off by the Mexicans at Churubusco and who dreams of someday leading a rebellion to overthrow English tyranny in his native land. His beard is a fiery red; so is his temper; and according to one of his soldiers he speaks three languages: "English, Irish-American, and Profane," being most eloquent in the last. Like numerous other regular army officers, Sweeny believes that he deserves a higher rank and command, and he strongly resents being subordinate to Dodge, whom he considers an amateurish "political general" and whose orders he does not hesitate to ignore or even defy if he thinks they are wrong, which he frequently does. Hence Sweeny welcomes the mission to cross the Oostanaula: it provides both an opportunity to operate independently of Dodge and perhaps to gain a long-overdue promotion.

The south bank of the Oostanaula at Lay's Ferry is guarded by what appears to be a large force of dismounted Rebel cavalry backed by a 4-gun battery atop a commanding hill. Therefore, instead of attempting a direct crossing, Sweeny deploys skirmishers and artillery along his side of the river and sends a detail from the 7th Iowa to carry Buell's now-assembled pontoon boats down the east bank of Snake Creek to where it empties into the Oostanaula about 300 yards downstream from Lay's Ferry. Sweating and cursing, the Iowans lug the cumbersome contraptions through the dense woods and shortly after 4 P.M. shove them into Snake Creek 100 yards from its mouth. Buell's pontoniers then climb into them, followed by six companies of the 81st Ohio and one company of the 66th Illinois, all under the command of Captain William H. Chamberlin of the 81st and all armed with Henry repeaters. Once everybody is aboard, fifteen men to a boat, the pontoniers start paddling, and the canvas flotilla heads toward the Oostanaula. As it does so, Sweeny's troops at the ferry open up such a devastating fire across the river that the Confederates on the other side immediately "take to the woods." A short time later, Chamberlin's riflemen land, charge into the woods, capture sixty cowed Rebels, and then deploy in a defensive perimeter. The sole casualties in the operation are three pontoniers, shot by snipers when their boat catches on a snag.

Sweeny plans to ferry an entire brigade across the river, then have Buell's men lay their bridges. But before he can do this, a report arrives from the cavalry (Kilpatrick's, now under the de facto command of Brigadier General Corse of Sherman's staff) that the Confederates are building a bridge, maybe two of them, at the Calhoun Ferry three miles upstream to the southeast. If this report be true (there has been earlier intelligence to the same effect), then the enemy soon will be able to send a force across the river that could cut his division off from the rest of the Union army and attack it from the rear. Consequently Sweeny orders Chamberlin's detachment (much to its puzzlement) back to the north bank, posts two brigades along the roads from Calhoun Ferry and Resaca, and sends another brigade toward Calhoun Ferry with instructions to "ascertain whether or not the enemy has constructed bridges, and to prevent his crossing, in case he should have done so." Eager as he is to establish the bridgehead, Sweeny wants to make sure he can do it without undue risk of having his division trapped and overwhelmed: that scarcely would lead to promotion![60]

However, there is another Union division commander who is facing a far-greater immediate danger than Sweeny. He is Major General David S. Stanley of the IV Corps, whose "splendid presence" causes his troops to refer to him proudly as "Our Stanley." His division occupies the extreme left of Sherman's line, being deployed just beyond the Tilton-Resaca road and facing southeast. This means that it is "in the air," vulnerable to a flank attack by the Confederates, whose right wing under Hood stretches east almost to the Conasauga.

Johnston, who has spent most of the day with Hood, knows this and plans to take advantage of it. It is precisely the sort of opportunity he had been hoping for. About 4 P.M. he orders Hood to attack the Union left flank as soon as possible, crush it, and then sweep on until he reaches the road between Resaca and Snake Creek Gap. If all goes well, Sherman will be cut off from the gap and will be faced either with annihilation or capitulation.

Stewart's and Stevenson's divisions move out of their works and form a double line of battle. As they do so, two of Walker's brigades come up from the south side of the Oostanaula (Johnston is unaware of what has been happening at Lay's Ferry) to reinforce Stewart and another of Walker's brigades, and one of Loring's brigades moves into reserve behind Stewart and Stevenson. Johnston is putting everything he can into this attack, which by good fortune will be conducted by the best general in the Confederacy for such an enterprise: Hood of Gaines' Mill, Hood of Second Manassas, Hood of Antietam, Hood of Chickamauga.

The thirty-four-year-old Stanley, who like so many of the Northern generals is an Ohioan, has an extremely low opinion of most other generals which he accompanies with an excessively high opinion of his own talents. However, he is capable, steady, and certainly experienced enough to know what to do when scouts bring word that the Confederates are massing in large numbers on his front and flank: he sends a courier to Howard to notify him of the impending assault, and he orders his chief of artillery, Captain Peter Simonson, to post the six Napoleons and Rodman cannons of the 5th Indiana Battery so as to cover the rear of Cruft's brigade on the extreme left.

The courier quickly reaches Howard and delivers Stanley's message. Faced with the horrifying prospect of suffering the same fate he had at Chancellorsville, Howard gallops off to see Thomas, who is with Sherman only a short distance away. Howard informs Thomas of the "alarming condition of things" on the left and asks for "immediate reinforcement." At once Thomas directs Hooker to send one of his divisions to the IV Corps's assistance. Hooker selects Williams's division, whose men are lounging in the rear, watching medical orderlies dig graves for future occupancy. Soon the division is on the way, guided by one of Howard's staff officers and with Hooker himself riding at its head.

About 5 P.M., Hood's battle lines begin advancing. Observing them, an Illinois soldier notes that they are "formed in admirable order, their flags floating gaily, many of their officers mounted, and a light line of cavalry riding in the rear and upon either flank."

In order to present as broad a front as possible, Stanley has strung out his division in a single rank, with wide gaps between each pair of regiments. Even so the Confederate right reaches far beyond his left. Thus what happens is inevitable. Charging forward with their shrill, chilling "rebel yell," Hood's troops sweep through, over, and around Cruft's brigade and Whitaker's next to it. Many Federals flee in panic, leaving behind knapsacks and even rifles, although others resist stubbornly, falling back only when in danger of being surrounded. Ultimately, however, all of them give way, unable to withstand the gray flood that threatens to engulf them.

The triumphant Confederates—to be specific, three brigades of Stevenson's Division—occupy the shallow trenches hitherto held by Cruft's and Whitaker's brigades, then pause to regain their breath and regroup, after which they again surge forward, swarming down the side of a heavily wooden hill toward an open field beyond. Suddenly they are struck with shells and shrapnel from Simonson's six cannons situated on a hill at the other end of the field, about a half-mile distant. At four-hundred-yards range Simonson's gunners switch to canister—cast-iron pellets approximately the size of golf balls which have been packed into tin tubes that explode on being fired from a cannon, creating the effect of a giant shotgun blast. Scores of Stevenson's men go down, their heads crushed, bodies ripped, arms and legs mangled. Those still on their feet halt, then swerve to the right, where they take shelter in a forest to the north of the battery. Simonson, realizing that they will be sure to make another charge, rapidly turns his pieces in that direction. At the same time the officers of Cruft's and Whitaker's brigades frantically try to rally their men but manage to collect only a few hundred in a ragged line on either side of the battery.

Soon Stevenson's troops emerge from the forest, advancing at a quick pace. Simonson's gunners double-shot their cannons with canister, then fire, reload, and fire again with a speed that an Illinois infantryman finds "marvelous to witness." Each salvo tears holes in the ranks of the attackers, who waver, then turn and run back into the forest, ignoring the pleas of their officers to keep going. Six cannons have repulsed 5,000 infantry.

A short time passes. Then, blurry in the twilight, the gray lines advance again. Stanley calls on Simonson's gunners and the handful of infantry supporting them to hold on just five minutes longer—help is on the way. Hardly does he finish speaking when seventeen-year-old Private Joseph Kimmel of the 51st Ohio looks back and sees "not more than 1/2 mile away, the army of Gen. Joseph Hooker, with the old general himself at their head." It is, of course, Williams's division, 7,000 veterans of Cedar Mountain, Antietam, Chancellorsville, and Gettysburg. Moreover, while Hooker might be riding at their head, they are commanded by their commander, the ferociously mustachioed Brigadier General Alpheus S. Williams, at fifty-three one of the oldest but also one of the best combat leaders in the Union army.

The Confederates rush forward. One of them, shooting into their flank, yells at a small group of Stanley's troops, "We don't care anything about you; we are after that battery!" Simonson's cannons belch forth canister even faster than before, but the gray mass keeps coming. Then, just as it seems the battery will be overuun, Williams's lead brigade arrives and, in the proud words of its commander, Colonel James S. Robinson, puts on a display of "Army of the Potomac fighting." Its five regiments are formed in as many ranks. At Robinson's order the first rank fires a volley and drops to the ground, the second does the same, and so do the third, fourth, and fifth. Shocked, staggered, and shredded, the Confederates turn and flee. Robinson's troops follow, still blasting away with their devastating volleys, until the bugles call a halt.

It grows dark. Fighting, apart from scattered flareups, ceases on this part of the battlefield. Stevenson's Division retires to the railroad, leaving behind piles of corpses in front of Simonson's battery. "Every one of you are heroes," Hooker tells the cannoneers. Stewart's Division likewise pulls back, having advanced two miles against little opposition and with few casualties. Evidently it has swung so far to the right that not only has it become separated from Stevenson's Division but also it has found nobody to fight! One of its brigade commanders, Brigadier General Alpheus Baker, was so drunk that Stewart had to order him to the rear.[61]

At almost exactly the same time that Hood's attack on the Union left gets under way, on the Union right the men of Brigadier General Charles Woods's and Brigadier General Giles Smith's brigades of the XV Corps wade across Camp Creek, rifles and cartridge boxes held over their heads, intent on capturing the Confederate-held hill beyond the creek. Sherman and McPherson had not planned for them to attempt this until tomorrow; indeed, up until now the Federals west of Resaca have been confining their activities to skirmishing and lobbing an occasional shell at the Oostanaula railroad bridge but never quite hitting it. However, around 4 P.M., McPherson had learned that enemy forces were moving from this part of the front to the north, whence the sound of heaving firing could be heard, and therefore had ordered Logan to attack the hill so as to prevent the Rebels from shifting more troops from this sector and in the hope of taking advantage of any weakening in their lines at Resaca.

Once across the creek, Woods's and Giles Smith's brigades—some 2,500 tough veterans from Ohio, Illinois, Iowa, and Missouri—re-form their ranks, then start up the hill. A "storm of lead and iron," to quote Logan's report, meets them, but they neither slow nor stop; in a few minutes they swarm over a row of piled-up logs that hitherto has sheltered two of Cantey's regiments. In fact the Confederates had weakened their line at this point in order to bolster Hood's attack, and now they have paid the penalty.

Ahead, about four hundred yards distance, lies the main and last fortifications between McPherson's forces and Resaca: red-dirt ramparts zigzagging along a low ridge and anchored by redoubts mounting cannon. If the Federals break through this line, they will cut Johnston's direct line of communications and retreat and so will threaten the very existence of his army. Polk at once orders Cantey, whose ad hoc division has been reinforced by Vaughan's Brigade from Cheatham's Division, to retake the hill. Starting at 7:30, Vaughan's Tennesseans make three separate assaults supported by a fierce artillery bombardment that seems to envelop the whole hill in fire. But Woods's and Giles Smith's

Alpheus S. Williams (*Photographic History,* 10:189)

men, aided by Captain Louis Voelker's 6-gun "German Battery," beat each of them back. "It was," later comments a Missouri soldier, "all the same to us whether we died here or some other place." Finally, after the third repulse, by which time it is pitch dark, Polk calls off the attack, and Vaughan's troops and the rest of Cantey's command withdraw to the main Confederate line. The hill now belongs to Sherman. Ironically, however, its impromptu capture is his sole substantial success of the day. All of the things that he has planned and expected to accomplish—drive back Johnston's right, sweep down from the north upon Resaca, and bridge the Oostanaula at Lay's Ferry—remain undone.[62]

The loss of the hill depresses the normally cheerful Polk; he fears that the Federals as a result have it "in their power at any moment . . . to burn our bridges and completely cut us off." Johnston, on the other hand, feels pleased about what has happened today and is optimistic about tomorrow. Along with Hood he has observed the assault on the Union left from a railroad cut behind Stewart's Division. He could see little from this position and has had to rely on the scanty reports that have drifted back from the front, all of which have spoken of big gains and slight resistance, but none of which has mentioned Stevenson's repulse or the fact that Stewart in effect has struck a blow in the air. Hence, as the advent of night brings fighting in this sector to an end, he instructs Hood to resume his offensive in the morning, directing it toward the mouth of Snake Creek Gap. Then, still accompanied by Hood, Johnston begins to ride back to headquarters in Resaca—and to bad news. First he meets a staff officer who informs him that the enemy have "effected a lodgement" on a hill near Resaca and the Oostanaula bridges. Next, shortly after reaching head-quarters, a message arrives from Major General Will Martin, commander of the cavalry assigned to guard the Oostanaula: Federal infantry, believed to be two divisions strong, have crossed the river at Lay's Ferry on a pontoon bridge!

At once Johnston cancels the resumption of Hood's offensive in the morning, calls back the brigade that had been sent from Cantey's Division to strengthen Hood, orders Walker to hasten with his entire division to the road between Lay's Ferry and Calhoun, directs his engineers to lay a pontoon bridge across the Oostanaula east of the railroad bridge, and sends Wheeler, whose caval-rymen have been screening the far right, to the south side of the Oostanaula to guard the railroad bridge and the adjoining wagon bridge. In sum, Johnston shifts from planning to cut off Sherman from Snake Creek Gap to endeavoring to prevent Sherman from cutting him off from Atlanta: that is, from thoughts of victory to concern with survival. As with Sherman, the day has not turned out as Johnston had hoped and, for a brief while, even thought.[63]

The night is chilly, almost cold. By unspoken mutual consent, firing ceases. Instead of shooting bullets and shells at each other, the blue- and gray-clad soldiers, where they are close enough to do so, exchange taunts.

"Johnny Reb! Oh John! Got anything to eat over there?—got any corn bread!"

"Yes; come over and get some. Say! are you Hooker's men?—where's Old Joe?"

"O, he's around; you've heard of Old Joe, have ye?"

"Say, Yank, did you make anything on the left today?"

"Yes; we made a hell of a noise."

"Say, got any commissary [whiskey] over there?—Pass over your canteen."

"What is Confederate money worth?"

"What nigger commands your brigade? Have the niggers improved the Yankee breed?"

Many of the troops in both armies spend much, sometimes all, of the night strengthening their defensive works. Among them are the men of the 9th Tennessee, who have been told by Cheatham, "Boys you'll have to stay here another day, [so] you'd better get down in the ground as deep as you can." Doing this, however, creates a dilemma for Captain Hall's company. They know from the "dreadful experience" of today's Yankee bombardment that Cheatham has given them good advice. But in a few hours it will be Sunday, and they do not wish to profane it by working unless absolutely necessary. After discussing the matter, they decide to compromise: they will dig as hard as they can until midnight, then lie down and sleep, hoping that since "we had been protected by an overriding Providence" during the day, they would continue to be protected "as long as we lived in obedience to his law." Accordingly they labor "with all our might" until midnight, then loan their pick and shovel to the company on their left who, not possessing the same religious scruples, had asked to borrow them. By now they have an adequately deep trench topped by a log placed in such a way that they can poke their rifles beneath it and fire without exposing their heads. It will have to do; the rest is up to God, so they go to sleep. The company on the left keeps digging.[64]

From midnight until morning, Sherman issues orders for May 15, pausing only once for a few hours of sleep: Howard and Hooker are to "attack in the morning directly south down upon Resaca." McPherson will mass his forces west of Resaca, for if Johnston attacks, it probably will be there in an effort to regain the hill lost yesterday evening. Palmer's corps will extend its front to the right so as to cover a sector left open by the massing of McPherson's troops but otherwise will remain on the defensive. As for Schofield, he is to move his corps (which now has all three divisions up) to the "extreme left, where it belongs." Sherman states in his final instructions for the day to Thomas:

> I want to hear the sound of that line [Howard and Hooker] advancing directly down the road [from Dalton] on Resaca until it comes within range of the forts. Whilst this advance is being made McPherson's guns will make the [railroad] bridge and vicinity too hot for the passage of troops. I am very anxious this advance should be made today, that we may secure a line whose left rests on the Coonesauga.

Basically Sherman proposes to do today what he had tried to do yesterday. As a consequence his plan is a blend of overoptimism and overconservatism. It

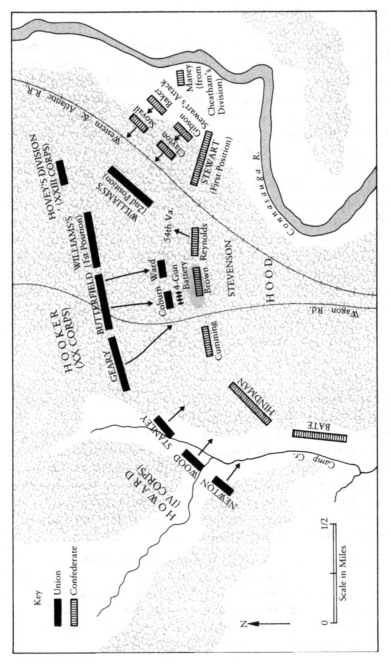

Battle of Resaca, May 15

Logan's artillery shelling the railroad at Resaca *(Harper's Weekly)*

assumes that Howard and Hooker will have no particular trouble advancing "down the road on Resaca" and that McPherson's artillery will be able to interdict the Oostanaula bridges, something it so far has not come close to doing. On the other hand it does not seek to exploit Logan's success in capturing the hill west of Camp Creek by making a strong assault on Johnston's left; instead, McPherson's primary mission merely is to hold against an anticipated Confederate attack. Furthermore among all Sherman's directives for May 15 there is only one reference to the crossing at Lay's Ferry, and it comes practically as an afterthought in a morning message to Thomas: "I have sent Corse down to see what progress Sweeny is making." Evidently Sherman is unaware that Sweeny had crossed, then (so to speak) uncrossed, the Oostanaula yesterday. Also Sherman still thinks of the bridgehead at Lay's Ferry as a means of facilitating the pursuit of Johnston's army when it retreats from Resaca, not as something that could provide a springboard for cutting its supply line and blocking that retreat. One gets the impression that even if Sweeny had maintained the Lay's Ferry bridgehead, Sherman's plan of operations would be the same.[65]

At daylight the skirmishers, sharpshooters, and artillerymen of both armies set to work. Wherever the battle lines already are in close contact, the rifle firing is continuous and ferocious. One of Captain Hall's men who has left his knapsack on the back of the trench subsequently finds it so riddled with bullets that he has to throw away the brand new shawl that he had folded up inside it—there is not a piece of it left "as large as a man's hand." But far worse, as usual, is the Union cannon fire. The rampart of Hall's trench is "battered down almost to the ground," and a solid shot strikes the head log, "cutting it in two and rolling it down on the men." Luckily no one in the company is seriously injured, and during a lull in the bombardment, Hall and his men even hold their customary Bible reading and prayer meeting. In contrast, there is a sudden outcry from the company on the left who had borrowed the pick and shovel. Hall calls over to ask what has happened and gets the reply that two men have been killed and another wounded. A solid ball has torn through the earth and hit them as they lay on the bottom of their trench. "If they had quit work at midnight when we did," reflects Hall, "their trench would have been two feet shallower . . . and this ball would have made its way two feet under them."[66]

Johnston spends most of the morning inspecting his lines and awaiting developments. What he does today—attack, retreat, or simply hold—will depend on what Sherman attempts and whether or not Martin's so-far-unconfirmed report that two enemy divisions have crossed the Oostanaula at Lay's Ferry is true. Johnston is, however, certain of one thing: Sherman's entire army is at or near Resaca. Yesterday he had received a telegram from President Davis stating: "It is reported that Grant is to be re-enforced from the enemy in your front. You will appreciate the importance of extreme vigilance, so that if you cannot prevent the execution of such a purpose, you may give the earliest information of the movement." Therefore, at 10 A.M., upon returning to his headquarters, Johnston replies as follows to this message, with its insulting insinuation that his army is not doing enough to prevent Sherman from sending troops to Virginia: "We are in the presence of the whole force of the enemy assembled from Tennessee and North Alabama. I think he cannot re-enforce Grant without my knowledge (nor do I think he will), as my whole line is engaged in skirmishing. Yesterday he made several assaults that were repulsed." Johnston does not bother to promise to provide "the earliest information" in case Sherman does reinforce Grant. If Davis thinks Johnston would not do that as a matter of course, Davis should relieve him of command immediately.[67]

Over on the Federal side, Howard and Hooker require all the morning and more to carry out deployments for their assigned attack down the Resaca road. Meanwhile the only Union offensive action occurs on the far left. Stoneman's cavalry, taking advantage of the withdrawal of Wheeler's troopers to the south bank of the Oostanaula, dash across the Conasauga into the Confederate rear and sweep through the hospital tents of Hindman's Division, destroying medical supplies, capturing hospital attendants, and according to some Confederate accounts, even shooting the wounded. Wheeler quickly sends back one of his brigades, which, along with some of Stewart's infantry, drives off the rampaging Federals and takes thirty of them prisoner: "Splendid looking villains," comments one Southern soldier in his diary.[68]

But if nothing of consequence occurs during the morning around Resaca, a very important development takes place five miles to the southwest at Lay's Ferry: Sweeny's division reestablishes and this time retains the bridgehead. During the night, two staff officers who had been sent by him to investigate the cavalry's report that the Confederates were building a bridge across the Oostanaula at Calhoun Ferry had returned with word that it was a false alarm: the Rebs were merely constructing fortifications on the south bank; there was no sign of them on the north bank. Hence, on Sweeny's orders, Rice's brigade returns to Lay's Ferry with Buell's pontoon train and, in essence, repeats yesterday's operation, using the same means to drive away the same enemy defenders. By late morning, one bridge has been laid, and two brigades have crossed; and at noon, Corse so notifies Sherman, adding: "There will be another bridge across soon."[69]

Around 1 P.M., Sherman's attack "down the road" gets under way. Initiating it is Howard, who has been instructed by Thomas to cover the main thrust which is to be delivered by Hooker. Three of Howard's brigades "leap" their works and advance toward Hindman's Division which holds a hill just beyond the road at a point where it curves slightly to the northeast. Immediately, to quote Brigadier General William B. Hazen, the commander of one of the brigades, "a concentrated fire of great violence" hits them. One-hundred and twenty of Hazen's men go down in thirty seconds, and he orders the rest to return to their fortifications. The other two brigades suffer a similar experience and react likewise. In soldier's slang, "it don't pay" to attack on this part of the front. Accordingly, Howard's troops proceed to emulate those of the XIV Corps to their right by laying down a heavy and constant fire on the enemy lines. The Confederates answer in kind; one of their sharpshooters puts a bullet through the arm and side of Brigadier General Willich, the same who had mocked the "poor devils" who had to stand in the punishment stocks at Dalton, unable to scratch their lice bites. Perhaps it is one of those "poor devils" who shot him, thereby ending Willich's active service.[70]

While Howard's assault is being blasted back, the XX Corps finishes deploying along a front facing southeastward across the Dalton-Resaca road: Geary's division is on the right, Butterfield's is in the center, and Williams's is on the left and slightly to the rear in order to guard the flank, for the XXIII Corps has yet to come up. Hooker's objective, as assigned by Thomas, is a "commanding hill" that anchors the Confederate line at the point where it bends away from the road toward the Conasauga. If it can be seized. Johnston's entire right will have to fall back toward Resaca, which, of course, is what Sherman wants.

The actual attack will be made to the west of the road by Geary's and Butterfield's divisions, with the three brigades of each formed in column of battle. In theory such a huge mass of troops—they number at least 12,000—concentrated on such a narrow front should be unstoppable. As they wait to ascertain whether this theory will prove true in practice, Geary's and Butterfield's men listen to their officers read the latest bulletin from Virginia: Grant has won another big victory, capturing a whole Rebel division and its commander at a place called Spotsylvania Court House. All cheer, but doubtless many share the feelings of Private Henry Noble of the 19th Michigan, who scrawls in his pocket diary: "I cannot say I crave the privilege [of going into battle], but had rather keep out if we are not needed. But if they need us I shall do my duty faithfully and if I fall I feel confident that it will be well with me. *I put my trust in God* and hope for the best."

About 1:30, Geary and Butterfield begin advancing. As was the case yesterday with the attacks by the XIV and XXIII corps, there has been no reconnaissance, so the Federals, from Hooker down to the rawest private, have only an approximate idea of the location of the Confederate lines and none whatsoever of their strength. The Federals simply plunge ahead through underbrush and dense clusters of small pine trees, up and down hills, across and through ravines. With each step their ranks become more uneven and broken, companies and regiments wander off course, brigades get mixed up with other brigades, the two divisions overlap, and some commanders lose contact with their units, in fact, they cannot even see them. The inevitable outcome is a disjointed series of charges made by bunches of blue-clad soldiers who, as soon as they come within effective range of the enemy, are either driven back or forced to go to ground.

There is, however, one about-to-be notable exception. It is Brigadier General William T. Ward's brigade of Butterfield's division. Just east of the Dalton road it beholds, about eighty yards in front of the hill that Hooker has been ordered to capture, Captain Max Van Den Corput's "Cherokee Battery" of four 12-pounders behind the low embankment where Hood has recently posted it for the purpose of silencing a Union battery that has been "annoying" Hindman's line. Stimulated by so inviting a target—perhaps by whiskey too—Ward, "in his shrill, familiar squeak," orders his brigade to charge and take the battery. At once it rushes forward, Colonel Benjamin Harrison's 70th Indiana in the lead (or at least among the leaders). Corput's guns fire salvos of canister, and a torrent of lead rains down from the Rebel infantry on the hill; but Ward's troops, most of whom are in their first battle, keep going and swarm over the embankment, shooting and bayoneting the cannoneers, some of whom try to fight back with their long-poled barrel spongers. One "big red-bearded" Confederate crawls out from under a gun carriage and begs for quarter, only to be struck down by a dozen bayonets when the attackers notice that he has tattooed on his arm "Fort Pillow." "I shall never," writes Private Robert Strong of the 105th Illinois, "forget his look of fear."

Taking the cannons is one thing; keeping them is another. From the top of the hill and both flanks the Confederate infantry—tough Tennesseans of Brown's Brigade of Stevenson's Division—pour volley after volley into the presumptuous Federals, who scramble back over the embankment and seek shelter on the other side. Then someone—probably a clever Rebel playing a Yankee trick—shouts, "We're being flanked!" Most of Ward's men immediately take to their heels, leaving behind only a handful who either did not hear the fake order or who are too frightened to flee. Later, another of Butterfield's brigades, Colonel John Coburn's, also "captures" the 4-gun battery but then abandons it too. Still later, Colonel David Ireland's brigade of Geary's division does not even try to reach the battery: instead it lies down fifteen yards away and opens fire on the enemy breastworks atop the hill, inflicting few casualties but forestalling an attempt by the Confederates to retrieve the cannons, which thus remain in the limbo of no man's land. "Come on—take those guns!" taunts Brown's Tennesseans. "Come and take 'em yourselves!" the Federals yell back.

Hooker's assault is a bloody failure, its sole success is the putting out of action, at least for the time being, of four semiobsolescent enemy cannon. His loss totals about 1,200, of which number 156 are in Harrison's 70th Indiana alone, and some are the product of Union troops' firing on their own comrades in other units. This is nearly as many men as in Brown's whole brigade, which bore the brunt of the attack and did most of the fighting on the Confederate side. The Tennesseans have organized themselves into three-man firing teams, in which the best shot does all the firing while the other two keep him supplied with loaded rifles. In this way they have created a barrier of lead that the chaotic and uncoordinated Federal thrusts have not been able to penetrate.[71]

Johnston, concerned over the prolonged roar of musketry and artillery to the north, arrives at Hood's headquarters around 3 P.M., just as the fighting in that sector subsides. Hood tells him that the Federals, in spite of strong and determined assaults, have been totally repulsed by Hindman and Stevenson, who have not even had to employ their reserves. This news, along with a recently received message from Walker stating that there has been no sign of an enemy movement toward Calhoun, causes Johnston to reactivate his plan to smash Sherman's left flank and cut him off from Snake Creek Gap. Via Hood, Johnston orders Stewart, provided Stewart himself has not been attacked before then, to wheel his division to the left (west) and strike the enemy flank. In addition, Johnston directs Stevenson and Hindman to assail the Federals in their front and detaches a brigade each from Hardee's and Polk's corps to add weight to Stewart's thrust.

Major General Alexander P. Stewart forms his division into a double line of battle consisting of Clayton's Alabama Brigade and Gibson's Louisiana Brigade on the left and Stovall's Georgia Brigade and Baker's Alabama Brigade on the right. Stewart also stations the brigade on loan from Hardee (Maney's Tennesseans of Cheatham's Division) and a small body of cavalry on his extreme right so as to cover that flank. Then, shortly before 4 P.M., he learns that a "heavy movement of the enemy" is taking place on his front. He notifies Hood of this development but receives no reply. So exactly at 4 P.M. he orders all of his brigades to make a half wheel to the left, then advance straight ahead. The command "Forward, guide left, march!" rings out, and the attack begins.

As it does so, Johnston receives a new dispatch from Walker: the "Federal right" is crossing the Oostanaula! At once Johnston tells Hood to suspend the attack; the Confederates must now concern themselves with their own left and rear, not Sherman's. Hood in turn sends Lieutenant Colonel Edward Cunningham, his inspector general, to notify Stewart. A few minutes later, Cunningham gallops up to Stewart and informs him that the attack has been called off; but he arrives too late: Stewart's troops already are engaged.

To be precise, they are heavily and bloodily engaged. Instead of an exposed enemy flank, they have encountered Alpheus Williams's division, the same that had driven Stevenson's Division from the field yesterday. Hooker, learning that the Confederates were massing for an assault on his left, had ordered Williams to move up in line with the rest of the XX Corps. This was the "heavy movement by the enemy" that Stewart had reported to Hood prior to advancing. Williams's troops, also formed in two lines of battle, occupy a row of hills that parallel the railroad, some three hundred yards to their front, at a point where it curves to the east. Geary's division, which has relieved Butterfield's battered brigades, anchors their right, and two batteries of rifled artillery back them up. Hovey's division of the XXIII Corps should be on their left. Williams had requested Hovey to put it there, and he had agreed; but when the raw Indiana recruits who constituted it started forward, they came under enemy shellfire and promptly went to ground, where they still remain in spite of all orders and pleas to get up. Thus Williams's division meets Stewart's assault unaided except by some of Geary's adjoining units to the right.

Williams's veterans prove to be fully up to the task. Waiting until the gray-clad lines emerge from a forest on the other side of the railroad, they deliver the same sort of rapid successive volleys that had devastated Stevenson's men yesterday. Hit first and hardest are Clayton's Alabamans: because of the half wheel to the left, they are ahead of Stovall's Brigade on their right. Although, in the words of one of their colonels, "the almost utter impossibility of success" immediately becomes "apparent to everyone," they press onward, stopping twice to lie down and not firing a shot. Then, about eighty yards from Williams's line, they open fire while continuing to advance. But, writes Captain James Wemyss of the 36th Alabama, the "scathing and fatal fire" of the enemy, who can be "only imperfectly seen on account of the small pines and other dense undergrowth," simply overpowers them. Except for some who rush forward and are shot down, they halt, fire a few more shots, and then turn and run back in "inevitable retreat." Behind they leave most of their dead and badly wounded, a sign of rout, because both armies make it a point of honor never to do this if at all possible.

Stovall's Georgians emerge next from the woods. A terrible blast of bullets and canister strikes them too, but instead of forging ahead like Clayton"s Alabamans, they promptly flee, except for several hundred who, à la Hovey's panic-stricken Hoosiers, fling themselves to the ground and remain there. In brief, their assault ends almost as soon as it begins. Later their commander, Brigadier General Marcellus Augustus Stovall of Augusta, Georgia, attributes their miserable performance to having encountered, while moving through the woods, "a thicket almost impenetrable" which had thrown their ranks "into confusion and so made it impossible for them to enter the fight with that order so desirable." What Stovall does not explain is why the same thicket had not had the same effect on Clayton's men.

Or, for that matter, on another brigade of Alabamans, that of Alpheus Baker, who evidently is sober today. Baker's Brigade follows in Stovall's wake and finds that the thicket indeed is bad: it is, Baker subsequently reports, "impossible to see more than ten paces ahead, and almost equally impossible to hear," and so the advance is "not made in good order." Passing through Stovall's fugitives, Baker's four regiments leave the woods and at once come under "a severe fire" which they return but "with not equal effect I think." Nevertheless they keep going, halting occasionally to fire and reload. During these pauses the Reverend J. P. McMullen, an elderly Presbyterian preacher serving as a missionary-chaplain, exhorts the troops to pray while they fight. Suddenly a bullet strikes him dead. Almost simultaneously his son, a soldier in the 40th Alabama, is killed also. Scores of others go down, and although some of them get within thirty yards of the Yankees, fifteen minutes after they have begun their charge, all of Baker's men who are still able to walk stream back toward the rear. They carry with them the flag of a Georgia regiment, picked up from the dirt by Sergeant L. D. Rickey of the 42nd Alabama. Accompanying them is Sergeant William Murray, colorbearer of the 52nd Georgia, who until now has stayed on the battlefield trying in vain to rally the remnants of his regiment. They, too, leave behind many dead and wounded, 250 according to Baker.

Stewart, who has had three horses shot from under him, sees that the attack, which he was ordered too late not to make, is a failure. Therefore he calls back Gibson's and Maney's brigades before they become seriously engaged and orders all of his forces back to their original line. After they retreat and the firing ceases, about forty Georgians stand up and approach Williams's line, one of them waving a white flag. Captain Julian Hinkley of the 3rd Wisconsin is astonished. Never in his three years of service has he seen "Confederate soldiers who might have escaped come in and give themselves up as prisoners."

Stewart's loss totals approximately 1,000 killed, wounded, and captured. Close to half of this number, as might be expected, come from Clayton's Brigade. In addition, the 54th Virginia of Stevenson's Division, which also received belated word that the attack had been canceled, suffered 100 casualties while assailing Geary's division. The Confederates have paid a stiff price for making an assault that had practically no chance of success and that would have been meaningless even had it succeeded. In contrast, Williams has lost only 48 killed, although his 366 wounded indicate that the return fire of Clayton's and Baker's Alabamans was not ineffective. Williams feels proud of his men, not one of whom "left the ranks unless wounded," and has nothing but contempt for Hovey's Hoosiers, one of whose colonels he calls "a damned cowardly son-of-a-bitch." However, this does not prevent Schofield from subsequently asserting in his official report that Hovey's division of "new troops, now for the first time under heavy fire, advanced gallantly over an open field swept by the enemy's artillery, formed on the left of the Twentieth Corps, engaged the enemy, and assisted in his signal repulse."[72]

Over at Lay's Ferry a second pontoon bridge now spans the Oostanaula, and all three of Sweeny's brigades are across, two of them having easily beaten off a feeble attempt by one of Walker's brigades to drive them back. However, Sweeny makes no attempt to advance beyond the bridgehead, for he believes, as do Corse, Dodge, McPherson, and Sherman, that he faces Walker's entire division, if not more. Actually, Sweeny could move on to the outskirts of Calhoun, for Walker has withdrawn his division to there out of fear that the "enemy can throw any number of troops over" the river. Thus, as so often happens in war, the Confederates are spared the possible consequences of their mistake by a counterbalancing mistake on their opponent's part.[73]

Even so, when shortly before dark Johnston meets with Hardee, Hood, and several division commanders in a field behind Stewart's Division, he informs them that the army will withdraw to the south bank of the Oostanaula during the night. There is no other choice. Enemy troops, reportedly two divisions strong, have crossed the river at Lay's Ferry on a pontoon bridge and now menace Calhoun and the rail line to Atlanta. Also, Sherman has established an entrenched line from the Oostanaula to the Conasauga. What, therefore, is to prevent the Federals from "detaching 40,000 and striking our communications, holding on at the same time to their works with a force equal to ours?" Nothing, "for we [cannot] send a force sufficient to beat the force in our rear and at the same time hold [our] position."

None of the generals gainsay this analysis. How can they? It is only too accurate. Johnston thereupon gives verbal instructions as to the timing and manner of the withdrawal, a difficult and dangerous operation to perform when in close contact with a powerful enemy. Later, at headquarters in Resaca, Mackall and other staff officers issue detailed written orders: the wagon train, most of which already is on the south bank, will cross the Oostanaula on the pontoon bridge; the troops will use the railroad and wagon bridges; skirmishers will be left behind in the front-line fortifications to cover the pullout, then will follow once the main force has crossed; and as soon as everybody is over, the engineers will take up the pontoon bridge and destroy the other bridges. The only thing of substance not being removed are the four 12-pounders in front of Stevenson's position. Although Stevenson declares that he could secure them with a night attack, Johnston tells him to leave them there. They are not worth the casualties they would cost.[74]

General Geary places a higher valuation on the cannons. Getting hold of them would be useful both to his military career and to his political aspirations, which extend all the way to the White House. Hence, shortly after dark, he sends the 5th Ohio, under the command of Lieutenant Colonel Robert Kilpatrick, to remove the guns and bring them to his headquarters. Aided by fifty men from the 33rd New Jersey and by some troops from the 19th Michigan, the 20th Connecticut, and the 85th Indiana of Butterfield's division, who are there for the same purpose, a five-company work party of the 5th Ohio digs openings in the embankment, then drags the pieces away with ropes, all the while being covered by rifle fire from other units. On examination the cannons prove to be brand new, the product of the arsenal in Atlanta, and have names inscribed on them, one being "Minnie, the Belle of Alabama."

Geary promptly claims credit for this "important achievement," which receives considerable publicity in the press, including a drawing in *Harper's Weekly*. It is, however, another officer in the XX Corps who ultimately benefits most from the "capture of the four-gun battery." He is Colonel Harrison of the 70th Indiana, whose troops, he stresses in his report, were the first to lay hands on the guns. During the years ahead, "Little Ben," as his men call him because of his stumpy stature, will continue to assert this; in 1892 it will help him become, like his grandfather, William Henry ("Tippecanoe") Harrison, president of the United States.[75]

Starting around midnight, Hardee's Corps crosses the Oostanaula on the wagon bridge, Hindman's and Stevenson's divisions march over the railroad bridge, as do Polk's troops following them, and Stewart's Division, formed in line of battle, acts as rear guard. According to Brigadier General Arthur Manigault, a brigade commander in Hindman's Division, the crossing is made "in much confusion," and "Bragg would have managed much better." Nevertheless no serious hitches occur, and Lieutenant Thomas Mackall, General Mackall's cousin and aide, notes that the soldiers do "not seem at all alarmed, rather noisy and in very good humor." By 3:30 A.M. all the wagons, artillery, and infantry (except for inevitable stragglers) are across, whereupon the engineers, who already have taken up the pontoon bridge, set fire to the railroad and wagon bridges. Then and afterward, General Manigault wonders why the Union batteries on the ridge overlooking Resaca did not shell the troop-choked bridges, thereby causing "demoralization and confusion" that "might have been serious in their consequences." They had the range, for during the day one of Walker's regiments had suffered a direct hit while passing over the railroad bridge; and he considers it "very likely" that the Federals knew what the Confederates were doing. Yet, as Lieutenant Mackall comments in his journal, the Federals remained "remarkably quiet."[76]

The explanation is simple. Sherman does not know or even suspect that Johnston is evacuating Resaca. Having begun the day with the assumption that Johnston was retreating, Sherman ends it expecting, or at least hoping, that the Rebel army will stay at Resaca. "We have been fighting all day," he telegraphs Halleck at the end of the day, "pressing the enemy, and gaining substantial advantage at all points. . . . We intend to fight Joe Johnston until he is satisfied, and I hope he will not attempt to escape." Consequently, Sherman's plan for tomorrow is to "strengthen the line of circumvallation, so as to spare a larger force to operate across the Oostanaula, below Resaca"—in other words, to do exactly what Johnston feared Sherman would do if Johnston were to remain at Resaca.

The XV Corps is in the best position to detect and disrupt Johnston's retreat. However, Sherman has ordered it to remain on the defensive, and Logan also thinks that the Confederates will not attempt an "immediate evacuation" of Resaca. Therefore, after it becomes dark, Logan has a redoubt built on the hill captured yesterday evening by Woods's and Giles Smith's brigades, and he places two 12-pounders and two 20-pounder Parrotts in it; these guns, he is confident, will be able to destroy the Oostanaula bridges "in an hour" come morning, so short is the range. Then, around midnight, Logan hears a flareup of fighting to the north, occasioned by the removal of the 4-gun battery by Hooker's troops. Thinking that the Confederates might be attacking the Union left, he orders his skirmishers to "press the enemy constantly at all points" so as to prevent Johnston from drawing reinforcements from the Resaca sector.

Shortly after 3 A.M. the skirmishers discover that the enemy trenches are empty. Cautiously, they push on toward Resaca. As they do, flames spurt up from the bridges and buildings in the village. Realizing what this means, they advance rapidly, overtaking and capturing dozens of Rebel pickets and stragglers. The skirmishers reach the bridges at the first glimmer of daylight. The railroad bridge is fully afire and cannot be saved, but the Confederates who are assigned to burn the wagon bridge are having trouble. A volley drives them away, and Logan's men put out the flames on this bridge by dousing them with river water scooped up in haversacks. A few repairs and Sherman's army can use it to cross the Oostanaula in pursuit. The Battle of Resaca is over and with it the first phase of the campaign.[77]

During the nine days that have passed since Major Holmes's 52nd Ohio set out on the road to Tunnel Hill, Sherman twice has compelled Johnston to abandon tactically strong defensive positions and has penetrated Georgia to within eighty-five miles of Atlanta. On the other hand, Johnston twice has escaped potential disaster and has preserved his army as a formidable fighting force. The question is, could both generals have done better than they did?

In Sherman's case the answer must be a definite yes. His first and by-far-greatest mistake was not to execute Thomas's original plan of operations, the essence of which was to send at the *outset* a *powerful* force through Snake Creek Gap into Johnston's rear. He could have done this in three different ways: he could have (1) thrust, as Thomas proposed, the entire Army of the Cumberland through Snake Creek Gap; (2) employed two of its corps under

Thomas's personal command, which still would have provided ample strength to take and hold Resaca while holding the Confederates in check at Dalton; or (3) if determined, as he obviously was, to entrust the Snake Creek Gap assignment to McPherson, bolstered the understrength Army of the Tennessee with one of Thomas's corps, as ultimately he did anyway, but too late. All three of these approaches were practicable; any one of them almost certainly would have blocked Johnston's direct line of communication and retreat. One has to conclude that had "Slow Trot" Thomas, as some members of Sherman's entourage disparagingly call him, been in command of the Union army in Georgia, the North probably would have won the campaign in less than a week. (For an analysis of a viewpoint contrary to the one presented here, see Appendix A.)

Sherman himself blames McPherson for the failure of the Snake Creek Gap maneuver to achieve decisive results. In a June 9 letter to brother John, Sherman asserts that "had McPherson fallen on Resaca with the violence I had ordered Johnston's army would have retreated Eastward losing all his [*sic*] artillery & wagons," and three days later he writes Ellen: "Had my plan been executed with the vim I contemplated I should have forced Johnston to fight the decisive battle in the Oostenaula Valley between Dalton and Resaca; but McPherson was a little over-cautious."[78] What Sherman neglects to mention, obviously, is that he did not order McPherson to take and hold Resaca; instead, McPherson merely was to cut the railroad there, then fall back to Snake Creek Gap and wait to pounce on the Confederates when they retreated from Dalton. Moreover, although McPherson in truth was "over-cautious" and even, as Sherman states in the first edition of his *Memoirs,* "a little timid" at Resaca, if McPherson had possessed twice as many troops and adequate cavalry, which he could and should have, he would have possessed not only the strength but also, presumably, the confidence to fall on Resaca with "violence," take it, and then hold it. Possibly, too, Sherman would have deemed it safe to instruct him to do precisely that, rather than send him on what amounted to a hit-and-run raid.[79] In criticizing McPherson for being excessively cautious and not throwing his army across Johnston's line of retreat at Resaca, Sherman in effect criticizes him for not being bolder than Sherman himself was and for failing to do what he, McPherson, had not been either ordered to do or given the means to do.

But if Sherman wasted an opportunity for a decisive victory in the Snake Creek Gap maneuver, what is to be said about Johnston for allowing him that opportunity? Johnston's own answer is to deny that there was such an opportunity. The Confederates, he asserts in his postwar self-exoneration, *A Narrative of Military Operations,* had examined the country between Snake Creek Gap and Resaca "very minutely" and had "learned its character thoroughly," with the result that "we could calculate with sufficient accuracy . . . the time that would be required for the march" of Sherman's army from "Tunnel Hill to Resaca, through the long defile of Snake-Creek Gap, and by the single road beyond that pass. We knew also in how many hours our comparatively small force, moving without baggage trains and in three columns, on roads made good by us, would reach the same point from Dalton." Thus there never was any danger that the Confederates would be cut off at Resaca, a contention that Johnston seeks to support by pointing out that on May 9 two brigades prevented McPherson from taking the place, that by May 11 it was defended by thirteen brigades, and that by May 13 the entire Army of Tennessee was there waiting for Sherman.[80]

As he (and for that matter Sherman) so often does in defending himself, Johnston evades the real issue by ignoring certain inconvenient facts: (1) A large Union force was able to pass through the easily defended Snake Creek Gap unopposed and, until almost too late, undetected. (2) If this force had been as strong and aggressive as it should have been, it would without difficulty have taken Resaca and blocked his direct line of retreat, thereby obliging him to flee into the wilderness of northeast Georgia. (3) Even as it was, he was compelled to relinquish a tactically impregnable position at Dalton and make a night retreat to a strategically untenable position at Resaca, whence he again had to retreat at night after suffering severe losses in futile counterattacks. Although Johnston conducted both retreats in a timely and skillful fashion, only luck and the overcaution of the Federals saved his army from disaster.

Cleburne, in a report dated August 16, 1864, expresses the same opinion: Had the Federals taken full advantage of their penetration of Snake Creek Gap, "it is impossible to say what the enemy might not have achieved—more than probably a complete victory." Furthermore, he states: "I cannot imagine" why the defense of "this gap, which opened upon our rear and line of communications, was neglected." The only explanation that he has received has come from General Mackall, who "told me it was the result of a flagrant disobedience of orders, by whom he did not say." In any event, concludes Cleburne, "certainly the commanding general never could have failed to appreciate its importance."[81]

This last sentence sounds sarcastic. If it is, then the sarcasm is justified, for the evidence clearly demonstrates that in fact Johnston did not appreciate the importance of Snake Creek Gap. First and foremost, he did not fortify, garrison, or even picket the gap. Second, he initially ordered Cantey's Brigade, when it arrived at Resaca, to come up to Dalton, and he countermanded that order only after having learned that Union forces were moving toward the Oostanaula. Third, not until the night of May 8, after the Federals' near-breakthrough at Dug Gap (which he likewise neglected to defend adequately), did he send Grigsby's cavalry to reconnoiter Snake Creek Gap, by which time

William W. Mackall, Johnston's chief of staff (*Photographic History,* 10:273)

McPherson already was passing through it. Fourth, as late as the afternoon of May 9, while McPherson's troops were probing Resaca's defenses, Mackall, on Johnston's instructions, had notified Wheeler that "I do not think Resaca in any danger; we have 4,000 men there." And finally, if what Mackall told Cleburne is true—namely, that Snake Creek Gap was left undefended because of "a flagrant disobedience of orders"—then why does not Johnston cite the guilty party or parties in his report on the campaign or in any of his postwar writings? Certainly he never hesitates to blame others and to name names with regard to other occasions when his skill as a general is at issue. One has to conclude that

Mackall, in his allegation to Cleburne, was endeavoring to protect the reputation of his commander and friend and that Cleburne was not deceived, although some historians have been.

The truth of the matter is that Johnston was caught badly off guard by the Snake Creek Gap maneuver. The reasons why this was so have been indicated in the narrative: Johnston *hoped* that Sherman would attack frontally at Dalton, thereby providing him with an excellent chance to implement the strategy he had advocated since taking command of the Army of Tennessee, namely, crippling the Union army in a defensive battle, then launching an offensive into Tennessee. Not until it was almost too late did he awake to the danger at Resaca, and he was lucky—luckier then he deserved to be—that he was able to retreat there at all.

At the Battle of Resaca, May 13–15, it was Sherman's turn to indulge in wishful thinking and to make erroneous deductions. Thus, during the first two days, he acted on the premise that Johnston intended to continue retreating and that he was merely fighting a delaying action. Then, on May 15, Sherman went to the other extreme and acted as if Johnston were riveted to Resaca and would make an all-out stand there. As a consequence, Sherman delivered several hasty, costly, and useless attacks, made no serious attempt to seize or at least interdict with artillery the bridges across the Oostanaula, exposed his left flank to a potentially bad mauling, and worst of all, failed to derive or even to think of deriving all the benefits of the crossing at Lay's Ferry, benefits that could have included achieving what he had not achieved at Resaca itself—namely, cutting off Johnston from Atlanta. In contrast, Johnston, apart from his overambitious and wasteful counterattacks, waged a good defensive fight at Resaca, conducted a well-timed and well-executed retreat, and throughout displayed his prime virtue as a commander: impervious calmness under pressure. In so doing he did as much as was reasonably possible, whereas Sherman did much less than he could have.

Nevertheless, by mid May the trend of the campaign clearly favors Sherman. He is advancing and holds the strategic initiative, while Johnston is retreating and so far has done little except to react to Sherman's moves. Equally important, although Sherman has failed to "break up" Johnston's army, he has pushed it back toward Atlanta and made it impossible for the Confederates to transfer forces from Georgia to Virginia, unless Davis is willing to give up that city, which he definitely is not. That, as Sherman sees it, is the essential task assigned him by Grant, who of course will win—indeed, according to the news from Washington, seems to be on the verge of winning—the war by defeating Lee.

Sherman does not know it yet, but the reports of Grant's great victories in Virginia that he has passed on to his cheering troops are, to put it mildly, much exaggerated. Instead of waiting, as did Johnston at Dalton, for the Federals to come to him, Lee has struck first, catching Grant on the march, rolling up one flank and mangling the other, and inflicting on him worse punishment than Hooker suffered in the same Wilderness a year before. This has caused Grant, who is not as phlegmatic as he seems, to fling himself on his cot and weep in frustration (see Foote, *Red River to Appomattox*, 185–86). However, unlike "Fighting Joe," Grant has shrugged off defeat and continued his offensive, sliding by Lee's right to Spotsylvania Court House in a well-designed thrust that failed mainly because a Confederate corps commander found it necessary to keep marching instead of camping where orderd. In the days that ensued, Grant has managed twice to crack Lee's defenses, only to be denied further penetration by furious counterattacks. Both Grant and Lee seek quick and decisive victory and so throw all they have into the fray. As a result, the fighting in Virginia, in contrast to that in Georgia, has been hideous in its carnage: by mid May, Grant has lost close to 30,000 men. This is a butcher's bill of unprecedented size, the payment of which can only be justified to the Northern people by victory. That, in spite of the reports coming out of Washington, Grant has not won—not yet, at any rate.

Part Three: From the Oostanaula to the Etowah

"We are in possession of Resaca," Sherman wires Halleck on the morning of May 16 as soon as his telegraphers have their instruments operating in that village. "We saved the common road bridge, but the railroad bridge is burned. The railroad is good to this point, and our cars will run here today. Our columns are now crossing the Oostanaula."

Sherman hopes to overtake and defeat Johnston between the Oostanaula River and the Etowah River, thirty to forty miles to the south. There the country is more open and level than anywhere else in northern Georgia, whereas beyond the Etowah the terrain again becomes mountainous and heavily wooded. In addition, once he reaches the Etowah, Sherman's supply line will stretch nearly a hundred miles to Chattanooga. He would prefer, if possible, not to stretch it farther before engaging in a decisive battle. Accordingly, he has issued orders for a prompt and rapid pursuit, orders that are based on the assumption that Johnston intends to retreat south of the Etowah to Allatoona and not to attempt a stand unless pressed so hard that he will be forced to turn and fight.[82]

While the Northern soldiers wait to begin the pursuit, they explore Resaca's fortifications, curious to see what they have been up against the past couple of

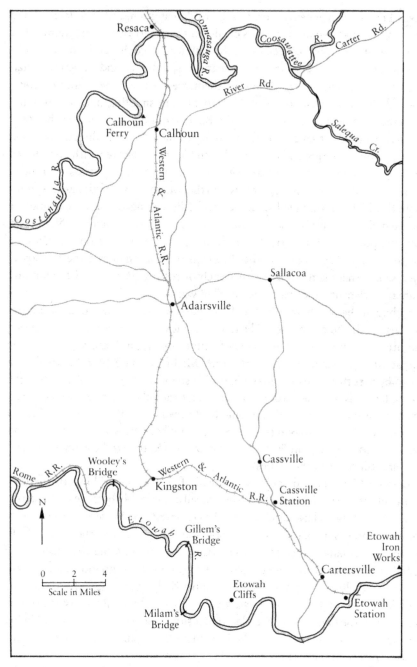

Oostanaula to Etowah

days. They find the enemy works to be of "great strength," well located and constructed, and two or more lines deep—in short, virtually impregnable. The trees near these works, especially in the vicinity of Judah's and Cox's assaults and of the 4-gun battery, have been scarred, splintered, and sometimes shattered by shells and bullets. Many of them are on fire, "the flames creeping upwards from the base like a living serpent, and shooting out fiery tongues from the topmost branches." Inside the Rebel redoubts and trenches the scene is "ghastly in the extreme." Dead and mangled men "lie in all directions and in every position"; the ground is "stained with blood and littered with abandoned clothing and equipment of all descriptions." To the rear are "masses" of dead horses and numerous new-dug graves. Further on, in the Confederate hospitals, more dead lie, intermingled with men so badly wounded that they cannot be moved and probably will die. Charles Benton, a soldier of the 150th New York, sees one body "stark and rigid" on an operating table made out of poles, "a rough affair at best" but one that "seemed to have answered the purpose." Everywhere there is the oppressive stench of rotting flesh and of human and animal excrement—the "patriotic odor" of war.

Although the Southern killed and wounded are numerous, much more numerous are the Northen ones. The latter lie thickest, as to be expected, among the brush-covered ravines and fields fronting the 4-gun battery. Some of the corpses, notes Henry Noble of the 19th Michigan, have been "burned to a crisp" by fires that have broken out in the brush during the night. Altogether the Union loss at Resaca, according to Sherman, totals about 4,000, of whom 600 are dead or mortally wounded. Confederate casualties probably come close to 3,000, including 500 to 600 prisoners, among whom are seven Georgians who surrender to Private John Peck of the 1st Ohio even though he is unarmed and they are still carrying their rifles!

Details of Federal soldiers bury the dead of both armies. This is the nastiest of all military tasks. Most of the corpses smell abominably because in the spasm of death the bowels have discharged. Others have so badly decomposed under the hot Georgia sun that they will not hold together and must either be carefully rolled onto a blanket or else have the ends of their trousers and coat sleeves tied together, then be gently dragged along the ground. Most go into mass graves: Yanks in one, Rebs in another. Sergeant James Kelly of Harrison's hard-hit 70th Indiana records in his diary: "Collected together and buried twenty-six of our regiment in one long trench. We placed in it side by side each wraped [sic] in his blanket our Comrade who had died for there [sic] country. We covered them with evergreen branches to break the fall of the clods."[83]

Stretcher bearers and ambulances carry the wounded, Northerners and Southerners alike, to the tents containing the Federal field hospitals. Here surgeons, their hands and bare forearms crimson with blood, stand over portable operating tables while using probes, tweezers, scalpels, saws, and other tools of their trade. They extract bullets, canister slugs, and shrapnel shards; then if it is a "painful wound," they apply a few grains of morphine with a blood-and-dirt-encrusted fingertip before bandaging it. When practicable, they set or resection broken bones, but in most cases the large, soft-lead Minie balls that inflict most casualties make amputation a necessity, with the result that gruesome heaps of severed legs and arms pile up outside the operating tents. Ether or chloroform renders patients unconscious during surgery; morphine, whiskey, or brandy alleviates their pain afterward. The use of the aforementioned drugs is about the only significant medical advance since Napoleon's time, and sometimes Confederate doctors have none to use. Men with deep wounds in the head or anywhere from the neck to the groin receive little or no treatment at all, because little or nothing can be done for them; with a few exceptions, sooner or later they will die in greater or lesser agony. Many who undergo operations and seem to be recovering end up dying too, for nothing is known about germs, and the surgeons routinely "clean" their instruments by wiping them with a blood-stained rag.[84]

Ambulances transfer the wounded after they have been treated (or not treated) to houses and buildings that have been turned into hospitals. Here they are tended by orderlies, many of whom are lightly wounded or convalescent soldiers. Among the latter is Private James Overholser of the 81st Ohio. He had become sick during the march through Snake Creek Gap and had been sent to a hospital despite his protest that he had been in one before and "knew how it was." Now he is fully recovered and eager to rejoin his regiment, but the chief surgeon—possibly because Overholser knows how it is—has placed him in charge of a ward. Here he takes care of sixty-three wounded, some of them Confederates who seem "surprised that they should receive such kind treatment from the North." One Reb is George Smart, a member of the 65th Georgia. He has an ugly shrapnel wound in his thigh but bears the pain "like a Christian" as he lies on the bare floor, his "old gray coat for a pillow." While dressing his wound, Overholser notices a book lying by his side. Since a book is "a rather unusual thing" among soldiers, Overholser picks it up to see what it is. As he does so, Smart asks him if he can please keep it, because it is a Bible his mother gave him. Overholser is so overcome with emotion that for a moment he cannot speak; he, too, has "a Christian mother away up North" who, he doubts not, "is praying for me." Then he hands the Bible to Smart, saying, "God forbid me doing so mean an act as to keep a Bible from a wounded comrade."[85]

Eventually trains will take all of the wounded, except those who can soon return to duty, to Chattanooga and from there to the big hospitals in Nashville,

Knoxville, and even Louisville and Cincinnati. If possible, the more serious cases go in special hospital cars equipped with bunks, whereas the majority ride in ordinary boxcars whose floors usually, but not always, have been covered with boughs and blankets. Whichever the mode of transportation, it is a slow, miserable trip. The cars have no springs, the rails often are worn and uneven, and thus many of the wounded suffer terribly from jolting and jouncing. Moreover, since all trains headed for the front have the right of way, the hospital trains frequently are shunted to sidings, causing them to take as long as forty-eight hours to travel the fifty-six miles to Chattanooga. Sometimes, too, derailments or collisions occur, with the result that wounded men suffer new injuries or the death they thought that they had escaped on the battlefield.[86]

At 10 A.M., Harker's brigade of the IV Corps enters Resaca. The village, notes "E. B." of the *New York Tribune,* "is a picture of desolation," with most of its few buildings "shattered by shot and shells." But "it was never, even in peaceful times, an inviting situation for persons fond of shade and averse to dust." Only a few old men and women stand at their doors, watching the Yankees as they march by singing "Cheer Boys Cheer." "They cheer all the time," Captain Poe writes his wife, "and are as eager to march after the retreating enemy, as any one could desire."

Harker's troops set to work repairing the partially burned wagon bridge and constructing a footbridge over the remains of the railroad bridge. By 1 P.M. they complete these tasks, and the IV Corps begins crossing the Oostanaula. As it does so, Colonel Buell's pontoniers arrive and rapidly put down a floating bridge. At 6 P.M. the IV Corps's advance, skirmishing all the way with Wheeler's cavalry, reaches the outskirts of Calhoun, where it halts for the night.

The XX Corps, followed by the XXIII Corps, crosses the Conasauga east of Resaca by means of bridges left intact by the Confederates, then heads south for Newton Ferry on the Coosawattee, a river that joins the Conasauga at this point to form the Oostanaula. However, finding it impracticable to cross at Newton Ferry, the XX Corps swings east to McClure's Ford and Fields' Mill, where the engineers build makeshift bridges out of boards stripped from nearby buildings, among them a church. Even so, by nightfall only a small portion of Hooker's troops have been able to cross and none of Schofield's, who perforce must wait their turn. Annoyed, Schofield sends Sherman a dispatch blaming his inability to cross on Hooker, who he says "started south but turned east." Two days ago, on observing Sherman and Hooker needlessly exposing themselves to enemy shellfire, Schofield had become aware of the deep personal animosity between the two. Hence he can be reasonably confident that any criticism he might make of "Fighting Joe" will not displease the commanding general.[87]

To the west the XV Corps and Veatch's division of the XVI Corps march to Lay's Ferry, cross on the pontoons there, then head toward Calhoun. Sweeny's division precedes them, with orders from Sherman to seize the Rome-Calhoun crossroads with a view to striking the Confederates as they retreat through Calhoun. Sweeny, however, moves so cautiously—for all he knows, the entire enemy army might be up ahead, and there are no cavalry to reconnoiter—that although he starts early in the morning, not until midafternoon does his entire division reach the crossroads. Here he encounters what appear to be, and in fact are, more Confederates than he can handle—Walker's, Bate's, and Cleburne's divisions. After some sharp skirmishing, during which one of his brigade commanders, Colonel Patrick Burke, is killed, he falls back, on orders from Dodge, and along with Veatch forms a defense line about a mile northwest of the crossroads. After dark the XV Corps arrives and extends this line to the right.[88]

Baird's and Johnson's divisions of the XIV Corps remain in Resaca, waiting for morning to follow the IV Corps. Davis's division, on the other hand, is on the way to Rome. Because of a garbled or misunderstood verbal message delivered by a courier from Garrard, Sherman has gotten the impression that Garrard has located a bridge, called Farmer's Bridge, across the Oostanaula and is operating as planned on the other side of that river. Consequently during the morning he instructed Thomas to send a "good division" from the XIV Corps to Farmer's Bridge, from where it is to move south and cut the railroad between Rome and Kingston. Thomas has assigned the mission to Davis, who has marched rapidly toward the supposed bridge only to learn from one of Garrard's staff officers that Farmer's Bridge spans, not the Oostanaula, but a creek flowing into it! After pondering this information, Davis has decided to continue his march until night and then, unless ordered to do otherwise by Thomas, to whom he has sent word of his change of plans, "push for Rome" tomorrow.[89]

In war, every decision automatically requires another one. Thus, having decided to evacuate Resaca, Johnston has to decide what to do next. One option would be to fall on the Federals as, divided and vulnerable, they cross the Oostanaula and Coosawattee. But, however attractive this might be in theory, the Army of Tennessee is in poor shape to attempt it in practice. As Major William Stiles of Cleburne's Division has written his wife the day before, "both man & beast are broken down" from almost incessant fighting and marching, lack of sleep, and inadequate food. "Our ration of meat," notes a Tennessee soldier in his diary for May 16, "is so small that it doesn't give us a full meal more than once a day and frequently not that." Furthermore, for Johnston to remain in the pocket formed by the Coosawattee and the Oostanaula, as he would have to do in order to launch a counteroffensive, would expose him to being trapped there by either McPherson or Hooker-Schofield cutting in behind him.

Another course open to Johnston would be to sidestep into Alabama, thereby putting Sherman on the horns of a strategic dilemma: should Sherman follow, he would be turning away not only from Atlanta but also from the railroad and into a semibarren country where it would be extremely difficult if not impossible for him to supply his army. On the other hand, should Sherman push on toward Atlanta, then Johnston could march toward Middle Tennessee, whereupon Sherman would have to hasten north to defend Nashville and Kentucky. However, although this stratagem looks brilliant on a map, it suffers from two fatal flaws: first, Sherman could counter it by stationing Thomas at Rome to keep an eye on Johnston while moving with McPherson and Schofield against Atlanta; and second, under no circumstances would Davis permit Johnston to uncover Atlanta, the holding of which Davis considers second in importance only to the retention of Richmond.

Johnston's third alternative is the one he chooses: to continue retreating until he finds another place on the road to Atlanta where he has a good chance of holding Sherman in check and inflicting heavy losses on him. This is, he believes, his only realistic choice. Because of Sherman's "great numerical superiority," Johnston later explains, it would be "expedient to risk [offensive] battle only when position or some blunder on the part of the enemy might give us [the Confederates] counterbalancing advantages." Therefore, he is "determined to fall back slowly until circumstances should put the chances of battle in our favor, keeping so near the U. S. [Sherman's] army as to prevent its sending reenforcements to Grant, and hoping by taking advantage of positions to reduce the odds against us by partial engagements" and to gain time during which Union strength will be "materially reduced . . . by the expiration of the terms of service of many of the regiments which had not re-enlisted." He also is "confident" (he afterwards will claim) that Davis will "see the expediency of employing Forrest and his cavalry to break the enemy's railroad communications," something Johnston has been and will continue urging the president to do.

When he evacuated Resaca, Johnston had hoped that Calhoun would provide one of those positions where it would be "expedient to risk battle." But on arriving there, he finds a "large creek" which would divide his army and be a "great impediment" to its operations. Consequently, at 1 A.M. on May 17 his army, most of which has been able to secure much-needed rest and food, begins retreating toward Adairsville, seven miles to the south. According to Johnston's maps, north of that village there is a valley so narrow that he can easily defend it and the high ridges flanking it on the east and west. Here he will offer Sherman battle.[90]

Sherman's objective on May 17 likewise is Adairsville, but he does not antici-pate a battle. He continues to assume, as he telegraphs Halleck in the morning, that Johnston intends to "retire on Allatoona, beyond the Etowah," and that if by some chance Johnston does make a stand, it will be at Kingston. In that event, "I will break his railroads right and left, and fight him square in front." Everything, Sherman declares, "has progressed and is progressing as favorably as we could expect; but I know we must have one or more bloody battles, such as have characterized Grant's terrific struggles."[91]

The IV Corps resumes its pursuit at sunrise and soon, with bands playing, passes through Calhoun, which "E. B." of the *New York Tribune* describes as a "pretty little town" of about four hundred inhabitants "when they haven't run away," as most of them have. South of Calhoun, however, it encounters Wheeler's cavalry, who employ the same tactics they had used in covering Johnston's retreat from Dalton: every half-mile or so they make a stand behind a log barricade erected across the road. The only way Colonel Frank Sherman's brigade, which is in the van, can drive them from these barriers is to deploy into a heavy line of skirmishers, part of which engages them in front while other parts work around their flanks—a difficult, time-consuming process. As a result, Howard's column advances at a sporadic crawl, not so much chasing the Confederates as following them.

Late in the afternoon, Colonel Sherman's brigade finally comes within sight of the outskirts of Adairsville and also under a heavy artillery and sniper fire that drives it to cover. Colonel Sherman rides back and tells Howard that he has encountered an entire Rebel division "behind good substantial earthworks" and supported by cavalry and at least a battery. Howard, who has been repeat-edly urged by General Sherman to make better time, refuses to believe him: "*It is not true.* I have information through my scouts every few minutes, and you only have part of a brigade of mounted infantry in your front. Your brigade *must move forward.*" The colonel returns to the front, but far from moving forward, it is all he can do not to fall back, and his troops suffer a large number of unnecessary casualties. Not until Howard gets a personal taste of the Con-federate shellfire does he admit that the enemy indeed is "making a strong stand, here at Adairsville." He thereupon deploys his corps for an attack, but before he can deliver it, Thomas instructs him to postpone it until morning, as it soon will be dark.

This is a prudent decision. Not only is there little daylight remaining, but the Union forces are widely scattered and badly strung out. McPherson, who has taken a road that veers toward Rome, is eight miles to the west of Adairsville; Baird's and Johnson's divisions of the XIV Corps, their march impeded by Howard's wagon train, are far to the rear, as is the XX Corps, which did not complete its crossing of the Coosawattee until early afternoon; as an inevitable consequence the XXIII is even farther behind. Nor is the cavalry any better situated. Most of Stoneman's division, having had to wait for Hooker and Schofield, has yet to cross the Coosawattee, McCook is following it, Kilpatrick's division remains near Resaca, and Garrard, after finally crossing the Oostanaula at Lay's Ferry (something that could have been done two days earlier), is moving at a leisurely pace toward Rome, evidently in no haste to carry out orders from Sherman to "strike" the railroad between that town and Kingston. In brief, it would be both premature and dangerous for Sherman to engage immediately in offensive battle at Adairsville. Therefore, during the evening he tells Thomas to bring up the XX Corps and Baird's and Johnson's divisions as fast as possible, sends orders to McPherson and Schofield to move in the morning toward Adairsville from the west and east respectively, and directs Stoneman to break the railroad between Cassville and Cartersville tomorrow. He still doubts that Johnston intends to make a stand at Adairsville: in Sherman's opinion, Johnston is just conducting a rearguard action there to protect his wagon train. But if the Confederates do stay and fight, Sherman will assail them in front and on both flanks and will cut them off in the rear![92]

The truth is that Johnston no longer plans to give battle at Adairsville. The valley, where he proposed to give it, has proved on personal inspection to be wider than depicted on his maps—too wide, indeed, for the front of his army when "properly formed for battle," even though it has been substantially reinforced during the day by the arrival of most of Brigadier General William H. Jackson's cavalry division and an infantry brigade from Polk's Army of the Mississippi. Furthermore, Johnston has gotten word that strong enemy columns are advancing east and west of Adairsville, thereby posing a threat to his communications line. Hence he has decided to wait until night before resuming his retreat; as Sherman suspects (although for the wrong reason), Johnston is merely conducting a rearguard action north of Adairsville, using for that purpose Cheatham's Division, in order to keep the Yankees at bay until after dark.

The question is, where and by what route shall the Confederates retreat?

Johnston believes he has the answer, a brilliant one. At 6 P.M. he meets with Hardee, Hood, and Polk; Mackall also is present. Pointing on a map to the road from Adairsville to Cassville, about eleven miles to the southeast, he asks how long would it take for the entire army to march that distance by this route alone. Hood asserts that it cannot be done: the army would become so badly jammed up that it barely could move, and the enemy easily would overtake it. Hardee thereupon declares that since this is the case, the only thing they can do is stay and fight. And why not? According to the latest scouting reports, McPherson's "corps" is near Rome, and another Union corps has left for Virginia. Thus the Southerners now have something like equal numbers and should be able to defeat Sherman.

Johnston then points to the map again. Besides the road to Cassville, another road, paralleling the railroad, runs from Adairsville to Kingston, seven miles due west of Cassville. Let Hardee and most of the cavalry take that road while Hood and Polk march to Cassville. Sherman no doubt will divide his army likewise, sending half and possibly more toward Kingston and the rest toward Cassville. By doing so he will expose himself to a devastating counterblow: Hardee, on reaching Kingston, will turn east and join Hood and Polk at Cassville. Then the united Confederate forces will pounce on the part of the Union army that is advancing on Cassville and will overwhelm it before the other part can come to its aid. Such a defeat will force Sherman to retreat or at the very least to halt and assume the defensive. Moreover, it will happen at a bad time for the Federals, because just arrived is a dispatch from Stephen D. Lee in Mississippi stating that "Forrest will start for Middle Tennessee on the 20th, from Corinth, with 3,500 picked men." Thus before long, Sherman, with his army crippled and unable to advance south and with his lifeline to the north being ravaged by Forrest, will have to abandon his campaign altogether![93]

Johnston's generals enthusiastically express their approval of this plan with its glittering promise of a great, perhaps decisive, victory. Then Polk asks Johnston a nonmilitary question: Is he ready now to be baptized? Recently the bishop-general has received a letter from Mrs. Johnston, now residing in Atlanta, asking him to "lead my soldier nearer to God," and Polk has been discussing the matter with the commander. Johnston replies yes, he is; and sometime later, Polk, using an improvised altar, baptizes Johnston in the presence of Hood, Hardee, and several staff officers. To General Mackall it is "a very solemn scene," but not being a religious man himself, he feels "as if I were parting from an old friend."[94]

Scouting reports are not the only reason that the Confederates believe that McPherson is near Rome. Since late afternoon the sound of firing has been heard coming from there. McPherson, however, has nothing to do with it; instead, it is occasioned by Davis's division. In the morning, having received no response to his request to Thomas for new instructions, Davis has decided to continue on toward Rome, subsequently explaining that by so doing he believed that the "main object of the expedition could best be obtained": that is, he could achieve his overdue promotion to major general. Marching rapidly an hour before sunset, he has approached the west bank of the Oostanaula opposite Rome just as a courier from Thomas has arrived bearing an order to turn back and rejoin the XIV Corps! What with his troops already skirmishing with Confederate pickets, he could not have complied with this order even had he wanted to; therefore, he has persisted in his advance, confident that he can quickly take the town.

Ordinarily he indeed would have, for the regular garrison consisted of a mere 150 cavalry. However, two brigades of French's Division and Ross's Brigade of Texas cavalry, the last of Polk's troops from Mississippi, were in the process of passing through Rome. As a consequence, night finds Davis still on the west bank of the Oostanaula, held at bay by Ross's Texans behind fortifications guarding the bridge, while in Rome itself, French's troops load themselves and as many supplies as possible into trains heading toward Kingston. Joining them in the evacuation are hundreds of civilians, some by train, others in wagons piled high with household goods and bundles of clothing. Only a comparative few remain, people who either figure they have nothing to lose or else cannot stand the prospect of becoming homeless refugees and so decide to stay and hope for the best.[95]

During the night the rain, which has been falling throughout most of the day, ceases, leaving behind a dense fog. When it clears at sunrise, the Federal pickets perceive that their gray-clad foes have gone. Soon the IV Corps begins marching toward Adairsville. Along the way some of its soldiers pillage and then burn an octagon-shaped mansion they have dubbed the "gravel house" because its cement walls are studded with small stones. They do this because yesterday the house had provided a stronghold for Confederate sharpshooters, but in the opinion of "E. B." of the *Tribune* it should have been spared for use as a hospital.

No more than three or four families remain in Adairsville itself, a village normally containing about three hundred inhabitants. In it is a factory that had manufactured rifles until its machinery was moved to Dawson, Georgia, after the Battle of Missionary Ridge. Lying on the ground outside of it are several amputated legs, an indication that yesterday it had served as a hospital. One of the legs, notes "E. B.," belonged to a tall man; another to a short one. Howard's troops find only one dead Rebel in the village but pick up a few stragglers, one of them a lieutenant who states that he has been studying Lincoln's Amnesty Proclamation and has "come to the conclusion that he could swear it all straight through."[96]

As Johnston expected he would, Sherman assumes that the entire Confederate army is retreating down the railroad toward Kingston and accordingly issues orders for all of his forces to concentrate four miles north of there by nightfall, ready to attack in the morning if the enemy should make a stand, which he continues to regard as unlikely. However, only the IV Corps and Baird's and Johnson's divisions of the XIV Corps, which has finally caught up, manage to advance that far. The other main columns—McPherson's, Hooker's, and Schofield's—are respectively six, ten, and eighteen miles from Kingston when evening comes. The reason Schofield remains so far back is that after marching most of last night in an effort to make up for the long delay in crossing the Coosawatee, he had decided that his men needed rest and so had encamped early in the afternoon. This pause also had given him a chance, with Sherman's permission, to relieve Judah from command of his division for having mishandled the May 14 attack at Resaca and to replace him with Brigadier General Milo S. Hascall, a thirty-four-year-old West Pointer who is a "thorough soldier." Schofield would also like to get rid of Hovey, whom he considers "utterly inefficient and worthless as a division commander," but cannot because Sherman is afraid of offending Grant, who "esteems" Hovey and had promised him a division out of gratitude for his fine performance as a brigadier at the Battle of Champion's Hill during the Vicksburg Campaign.

In the evening, Sherman receives messages from McPherson, Hooker, and Schofield reporting and explaining their inability to get closer than they are to Kingston. Sherman is disappointed but reacts philosophically. After all, as he observes in a reply to Schofield, "the roads are not suited to one concentric movement on Kingston, and we must approach the game as near as the case admits of." More disturbing is a dispatch from Hooker, whose corps is on the road between Adairsville and Cassville. It states that his troops have encountered enemy pickets three miles north of Cassville, that a captured Rebel soldier has declared that Walker's Division was drawn up in line of battle near that town, and that the same prisoner has also asserted that the Confederates do not intend to fight at Kingston, "as it is no place," but that "they will make a stand at Hightower bridge" on the Etowah. Could it be, then, that Johnston did not retreat to Kingston with all or even the bulk of his army? After pondering the matter, Sherman concludes that this is not likely in view of the "broad, well-marked trail" left by Johnston's troops on the road to Kingston and that probably the enemy force at Cassville is merely a detachment covering the Confederate wagon train as it uses a different route to reach the Etowah. Therefore, during the night, Sherman instructs McPherson, Hooker, and Schofield to continue toward Kingston tomorrow: "Johnston may . . . fight us this side of the Etowah, trying to fall on one or other of our columns," but until "we ascertain the course of the enemy after reaching Kingston we cannot do better."[97]

While issuing these instructions, Sherman receives a dispatch, marked 8:30 P.M., from McPherson containing a report from Garrard: during the afternoon various detachments from Garrard's division have cut the railroad between Rome and Kingston, have skirmished with strong Confederate cavalry and infantry pickets near Kingston, and have ridden to a few miles of Rome without meeting any resistance—one indication that "Rome is almost entirely evacuated." On the basis of this report, comments McPherson, it would seem that "Brig. Gen. Jeff. C. Davis has been attacking Rome since yesterday, and is in possession of the place."

McPherson's surmise is correct. The last Confederates left Rome during the morning, burning behind them the bridges over the Oostanaula and Etowah, which join here to form the Coosa River. Crossing the Oostanaula on rafts, in canoes, and even by swimming, McCook's brigade occupied the town, where many of its men proceeded to get drunk on left-behind Rebel whiskey and to ransack, loot, and occasionally burn abandoned shops and houses, some of which appeared to have been pillaged already by Southern troops before they departed. In a dispatch to Thomas, now on its way, Davis boasts that he has captured ten cannons, an "immense amount of stores," a train of boxcars, and—completely intact—the Noble & Co. Ironworks and Machine Shop, one of the few Confederate facilities of its kind. Undeniably Davis's unordered and countermanded expedition has been justified by success; perhaps it will help him gain a sorely desired second star for his shoulder straps.[98]

Johnston has several good reasons to feel pleased by the way things have gone today and optimistic about tomorrow. Except for one of Cleburne's brigades and some of Jackson's cavalry that have been left at Kingston to hold the Federals in check, his entire army is deployed along the bank of Two Run Creek about one mile northwest of Cassville: Hood on the right, Polk in the center straddling the Adairsville road, and Hardee on the left covering the route from Kingston. This army, moreover, now numbers between 70,000 and 74,000 troops—the largest force ever assembled by the Confederacy in the West. And best of all, Sherman appears to have fallen for this stratagem: according to scouts and a Yankee prisoner, the enemy's XIV Corps has gone to Rome, McPherson's "corps" is moving toward the Etowah via Kingston, and Howard's,

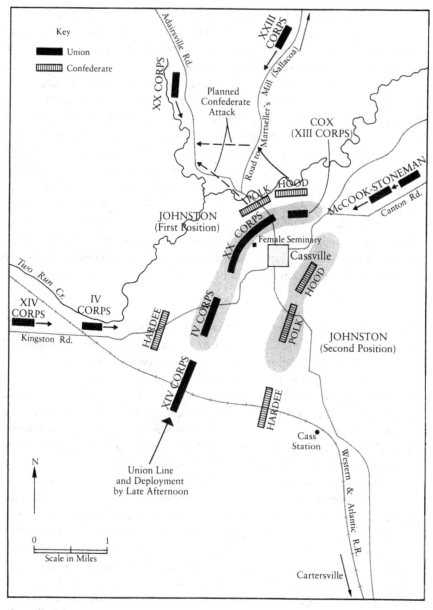

Cassville, May 19

Hooker's, and a third corps (presumably Schofield's) are approaching Cassville from the direction of Adairsville. Thus Johnston is in an excellent position to crush or at least maul this last column by falling on it with his own concentrated and superior strength—a truly Napoleonic stroke.[99]

Notwithstanding this promising situation, Johnston remains his usual wary and noncommittal self. When at an evening conference at his headquarters, Hood, Hardee, and Polk all urge that the army march forth this very night and attack the enemy column advancing on Cassville from Adairsville, he does not answer either yes or no, nor does he present any alternative plan or issue any directives for tomorrow other than to indicate that the army will give battle. Apparently he believes it is better to allow the Federals to walk into his trap, rather than to seek them out. Possibly, too, he wishes to give his troops a full night's rest before engaging them in battle: during last night's march, notes Lieutenant Rennolds in his diary, "the men began to give out for the first time." In any case, instead of being Napoleonic, Johnston chooses to act like a Micawber on horseback and wait until morning to see what turns up.[100]

The sun that rises on May 19 promises a hot, muggy day—a promise it amply fulfills. Between 7 and 8 A.M., Johnston dictates a general order to be read to all the troops. It praises them for their "firmness in combat, patience under toil," and for the "courage and skill" with which they have "repulsed every assault of the enemy." It declares that "by marches by day and by marches by night you have defeated every attempt upon your communications," which as a result "are secured." It concludes by announcing that the army now will "turn and march to meet" the advancing enemy columns: "Fully confiding in the conduct of the officers, the courage of the soldiers, I will lead you to battle."

While clerks prepare copies of the order for distribution, Hood, Hardee, and Polk enter Johnston's headquarters tent with the intention of urging again the plan proposed last evening by Hood. But before they can do so, reports arrive that Union infantry are pushing back the cavalry on the Adairsville road in front of Polk's position. At once the generals ride to the right of Polk's line, near where Hood's Corps is bivouacked. Here Hood asks Johnston's permission to advance up a country road about a mile to the east of the Adairsville road and attack the flank of the oncoming enemy, which the Confederates mistakenly believe to be Howard's corps. Johnston replies that Hood may do this "if you desire." Hood thereupon rides off to put his troops in motion, and Johnston gives Polk and Hardee their instructions: Polk will continue to cover the Adairsville road and be ready to move forward when Hood attacks; Hardee will continue to guard the western approach to Cassville and support Polk's left.

Then, satisfied that his generals understand what they are to do, Johnston returns to his headquarters to await developments.

Hood rides at the head of his corps across an open field until he reaches the country road he has mentioned to Johnston. He finds this road, which runs north to the village of Sallacoa, in the possession of some Confederate cavalry; no enemy is in sight. Everything, it seems, is going right, and Hood has every reason to believe that soon he will have an opportunity to deliver a crushing blow against the Yankees. But then, about 10:30 A.M., Colonel Taylor Beatty of Hood's staff calls his attention to a "dark line" off to the right. Hood looks and perceives "a body of the enemy," which he supposes to be cavalry, on the Canton road to the east of Cassville and to the rear of his corp's bivouac. Skirmishers from Hindman's Division engage the Federals, who respond with rifle and artillery fire, "doing some mischief" according to General Manigault. Ordering all units to halt, Hood sends Major John Hamilton of his staff to notify Johnston of the enemy presence on the Canton road. Shortly after Hamilton's departure, General Mackall gallops up, having been sent by Johnston upon receiving word from Hardee that a large Union force is advancing on him from the west. Mackall informs Hood of the situation on Hardee's front and passes on instructions from Johnston not to get too far from Polk's right and, if he attacks the Federals advancing down the Adairsville road, to do it "promptly and hard." Hood answers that he, too, is being threatened by an enemy force that has appeared without warning on the Canton road and that as a consequence he must fall back to protect his rear. A little later, Hood withdraws to the Canton road, across which he places Hindman's Division facing east.

Mackall, deciding to wait until he sees where Hood deploys his corps, sends a courier to inform Johnston of Hood's retreat and the reason for it. The courier reports to Lieutenant Mackall, who conveys the message to Johnston. "It can't be!" exclaims Johnston, who adds that Armstrong's Brigade, a unit belonging to Jackson's recently arrived cavalry division, had reported that no enemy were on the Canton road. Procuring a map, Johnston examines it, then mutters, "If that's so, General Hood will have to fall back at once." Presently General Mackall arrives and confirms that Hood has done exactly that. Johnston thereupon summons all of the corps commanders and Wheeler. After a brief discussion, he orders the army to take up a new position along a ridge a half-mile to the east and south of Cassville. For the Confederates, advance has turned into retreat; attack, into defense.[101]

Who are the Federals on the Canton road, and why are they there? They are McCook's cavalry division followed by Stoneman's. Both are endeavoring to carry out orders from Sherman, relayed to them by Schofield, to cut the railroad between Cass Station and the Etowah, then to attack the Confederate wagon train that Sherman assumes is retreating by that route. They no more expected to encounter Johnston's army east of Cassville than Johnston expected them to appear on his left and rear. By happening to come along where and when they did, they unknowingly have saved the Union column that was moving down the Adairsville road from a damaging if not devastating attack. It is the most valuable service that will be performed by Sherman's cavalry during the entire campaign.[102]

Having entered Kingston early in the morning without opposition, Sherman more than ever is convinced that Johnston has retreated or is in the act of retreating south of the Etowah. Hence Sherman has ordered Thomas to follow the railroad east to the Cassville area with the IV Corps and Baird's division of the XIV Corps, sent McPherson with his army and Johnson's division of the XIV Corps to seize the Etowah crossings south of Kingston and intercept a Confederate division that he mistakenly thinks is heading in that direction, and instructed Hooker and Schofield to link up with Thomas at Cassville prior to moving on to Cartersville. In sum, he is thinking in terms of pursuit, not battle.

Around noon, Stanley's division, in the van of the IV Corps, approaches Cassville and beholds three enemy battle lines drawn up along some high ground east of Two Run Creek. Such a formation usually signifies that a major attack is about to be launched, and sure enough, the gray mass surges forward as if to do exactly that. However, after crossing the creek and advancing a short distance beyond, it suddenly halts, then turns around and goes back to its original position. This seemingly inexplicable retrograde action puzzles but also relieves Stanley's troops, who were bracing for a ferocious, Chickamauga-style charge by the Rebs; it also puzzles but (so some say later) disappoints the Confederates who have made it. Having listened to the stirring words of Johnston's general order, they were all set to hurl themselves against the Yanks.

During the next several hours the IV Corps deploys, then pushes slowly toward Cassville while the Confederates fall back without offering serious resistance. At 3 P.M., Thomas sends a dispatch to Sherman, who still is in Kingston, notifying him that "I have seen at least one division in Stanley's front" and stating: "If Hooker and Schofield will move upon Cassville I think we can capture the troops in Stanley's front." Obviously Thomas also believes that Johnston is retreating and that the Confederates at Cassville are merely a rear guard covering that retreat.[103]

By midafternoon Johnston has established his new line; the demonstration against Stanley, which was carried out by Hardee's full corps and not just a division, was designed to gain additional time for doing this. Laid out under Johnston's personal direction, this line is about three miles long and slants from the northeast to the southwest, with Hood on the right, Polk in the center, and Hardee on the left covering Cass Station. Except for the extreme left, all of it runs along a 140-foot-high ridge that overlooks a densely wooded valley beyond which lies Cassville. The west slope of this ridge is gentle and comparatively free of timber and brush; it provides a good field of fire. Against an infantry assault it would be an excellent defensive position.

But not, in the opinion of Brigadier General Francis Shoup, Johnston's chief of artillery, against an infantry assault preceded and supported by an artillery barrage. Riding along the line with Johnston, Shoup points out that the sector of Polk's front designated for French's Division is exposed to enfilade fire from a ridge about one mile to the northeast. Johnston considers the matter briefly, then he tells Shoup that the Federal guns will be too distant to cause severe damage but that if they do so, French's troops can either take shelter in traverses (trenches dug at right angles to the main one) or else withdraw to the rear, where they would be both protected and in position to reoccupy their works as soon as the enemy lifts his barrage, which he will have to do in order to avoid hitting his own advancing infantry. Then, having thus decided, Johnston rides on to inspect his left flank where, because it is open to being turned, he has stationed Cleburne's stalwarts.[104]

The XX Corps moves on Cassville from the north by way of the Adairsville road and Gravelly Plateau, a rugged stretch of terrain to the west of that road. Had Hood's attack taken place, it first would have struck Butterfield's division. As it was, late in the morning, Butterfield's lead brigade under Colonel James Wood saw Confederates massing to the left, whereupon it fell back and hastily fortified. However, when the enemy showed "no disposition to attack" and after a while withdrew, Butterfield resumed his advance, although very cautiously. As far as Hooker is concerned, the Confederates have more than a rear guard at Cassville, maybe a lot more; so he proceeds accordingly.

Around 5:30 the XX Corps comes into line with the IV Corps, and soon afterward, Cox's division of the XXIII Corps, moving down the Sallacoa Road, takes position on Hooker's left northeast of Cassville. Sherman, who now is present, thereupon orders a bombardment of the Confederate-held ridge east of Cassville. The purpose of this bombardment is merely to provide cover for the infantry who move forward and occupy a line from which an assault can be made in the morning should the enemy forces remain to fight. Sherman doubts that they will. In spite of the large numbers of gray-clad troops seen and encountered today, Sherman still believes, so he telegraphs Halleck in the evening: "The enemy has retired south of the Etowah" and that only "Hardee's Corps" is in his front.

Until darkness makes accurate aim impossible, upwards of forty Union cannon pound the Confederates, quickly silencing the few guns that attempt to reply. Particularly effective, according to Captain Simonson, he who staved off Hood's flank attack at Resaca on May 14, is the "cross-firing" of Battery B of the Pennsylvania Light Artillery, posted on a high ridge southwest of Cassville, and a section of Battery C of the First Ohio Light Artillery, stationed on a hilltop next to the Cassville Female Seminary just north of the town. In addition, one of Cox's batteries is able to fire straight down the Rebel works from the northeast, thereby enfilading them.[105]

Shoup's warning about the vulnerability of French's sector proves fully justified, for it is here that the "cross-firing" referred to by Simonson hits. Two of French's batteries lose several horses and men before they can even unlimber, and when they fire back, salvos of solid shot from the guns near the Female Seminary promptly silence them. In the trenches, his troops hug the ground. "The shells are bursting over our heads constantly," a soldier in Loring's Division, which is to the left and much less exposed, scrawls in his diary. Nor is it much better in the rear, where Johnston thinks that French's men could safely wait out a bombardment. In Sears's Brigade, posted in reserve, Captain William Chambers's regiment alone suffers five wounded, and Brigadier General Claudius Sears himself is struck in the foot by a shell fragment.[106]

Alarmed by the storm of artillery fire that is sweeping his position, Polk sends one and then another staff officer to investigate. Both report that the position is untenable. A little later, Hood, while riding with his staff along his line, personally comes under a barrage that, according to General Manigault, knocks one battery "to pieces" and probably does the same to some others. As a result, Hood wastes no time in responding to a request from Polk to come to the McKelvey house, a clapboard cabin about a mile south of Cassville where the bishop has established his headquarters. On meeting, Hood and Polk quickly agree that their positions are untenable and that they must so inform Johnston, whom Polk also has asked to join him.

Toward 9 P.M., Johnston enters the cabin, accompanied by French. Polk announces that he will not be able to hold his part of the line for more than an hour after the Federal batteries open up in the morning, and Hood declares that two hours is the most he can hope to stand. In support of these contentions, Captain Walter J. Morris, Polk's chief engineer, points to a sketch map that he has made during a reconnaissance of the front and states that French's sector is subject to cross and enfilade fire and cannot be defended; that both Hood's and Polk's troops are exposed to plunging fire because the enemy's guns are on higher ground; that as a consequence it would be useless to dig traverses or seek shelter behind the ridge; and that owing to its location, the Federal artillery can bombard the Confederates until attacking infantry reach "a line very close to the crest of the ridge" occupied by Polk's Corps. French, on being asked by Johnston, sustains Morris to the extent of saying that the extreme right of his front, where it curves outward, is indeed exposed to enfilade fire.

In spite of these powerful arguments, Johnston for a while rejects the idea of a withdrawal. How embarrassing that would be so soon after proclaiming to the army that he will lead it into battle; how embarrassing also to be told that a defense line he himself chose is indefensible! So adamant is he that French leaves the conference with the impression that the army will stay where it is. Hood and Polk, however, continue to insist that their lines are fatally exposed. But, adds Hood, if a battle is to be fought at all tomorrow, it should take the form of an offensive that would begin with a flank movement against the Union left so as to force the removal of the enfilading cannons posted there. Polk, although he feels that it might be too late now for any sort of attack, agrees with Hood.

Ultimately, after more than an hour of discussion, Johnston decides to order a retreat, starting at once, south of the Etowah. He does so, he claims in his *Narrative,* "in the belief that the confidence of the commanders of two of the three corps of the army, of their inability to resist the enemy, would inevitably be communicated to their troops, and produce that inability." This is a plausible reason, although it should be observed that corps commanders normally engage in direct communication only with their division commanders and staff officers and that Longstreet's lack of confidence in Lee's plan to break the Union center at Gettysburg with a frontal assault obviously did not impair the fighting spirit of Pickett's Virginians. But in all likelihood other considerations as well explain Johnston's change of mind. First, prior to going to the McKelvey cabin, he has received a dispatch from Brigadier General Sul Ross of Jackson's cavalry stating that the enemy are across the Etowah at Wooley's bridge west of Kingston, which of course means that Sherman is in position potentially to do what he had attempted to do at Resaca—namely, cut the Confederate lifeline to Atlanta. Second, the latest word from Stephen D. Lee in Mississippi is that the threat of a Union thrust from Memphis has caused the cancellation of Forrest's planned raid into Middle Tennessee and thus has materially reduced the strategic advantage to be gained from blocking Sherman's advance into Georgia. And finally, although Johnston still believes that he can, as he did at Resaca, hold at Cassville for at least a day or two and inflict severe losses on the Federals, he cannot help but realize that his position here not only is exposed to vicious, possibly demoralizing artillery fire but also that it is vulnerable on both flanks and even in the rear: Cox already overlaps Johnston's right, his left can be turned by McPherson coming in from the west, and there is that mysterious Union force on the Canton road that forced Hood to cancel his attack and that, for all Johnston knows, may now be moving to interpose between the Confederates and the Etowah.

Hardee, who Johnston belatedly has invited to the conference, arrives just as it ends. On being told by Johnston that the army is going to retreat, he expresses astonishment and asks why. Before Johnston can answer, Hood speaks: "General Polk, if attacked, cannot hold his position three-quarters of an hour; I cannot hold mine two hours." Hardee grumbles but makes no overt objection. It is becoming obvious to him that Johnston places little value on his opinion and that he looks mainly to Hood for counsel—to Hood, sixteen years Hardee's junior, who was a cadet at West Point while Hardee was commandant.[107]

Between midnight and 2 A.M. the Confederates pull out of their works, covering the movement with skirmishers and employing details of axmen to chop down trees so as to conceal the sound of wagons and cannons being hauled away and to create the impression that they are strengthening their fortifications. From generals down to privates they are surprised and in some cases indignant over retreating right after having been told that they had stopped retreating; but as the night goes on, word circulates that there is no alternative. The Yankees, again taking advantage of their superior numbers, again are threatening to cut the Rebels off from Atlanta. Notwithstanding considerable confusion among the wagons and having only one regular road on which to march, by dawn the Confederates reach Cartersville, eight miles to the south.[108]

It also is dawn before the Federal soldiers around Cassville discover that the Confederates are gone. They feel neither surprised nor relieved, for like Sherman they had assumed that the Rebs were retreating in any case. Major Eli Griffin, whose 19th Michigan has occupied Cassville during the night along with other troops of Butterfield's division, strolls about the place in the daytime. Most of the inhabitants are gone, having fled two days before when it became apparent that their town was likely to become a battlefield, some of the streets and buildings are barricaded, and there are earthworks around the

Female Seminary and Cherokee Baptist College. Nevertheless Griffin finds it "to be a beautiful town and the ladies quite sociable, what were left. . . . Roses in blossom and things look like living more than any place in Ga. we have yet seen." Sergeant Oliver Haskell agrees that it is "nice looking," but then he adds in his diary that "many of the citizens left their houses [along] with the rebles [*sic*] and the boys tore their things to pieces." A little later men of the XXIII Corps, while passing through, tear up the pieces left by the cavalry, grab and gulp all the food they can find, and in several cases parade about in women's clothes. Finally, toward noon, Alpheus Williams enters the town with a detachment from his division with orders to clear out stragglers and stop the pillaging. He discovers that "some rascal" has set fire to one of the main buildings and that the flames are threatening the "whole place" with destruction because water is so difficult to find. Fortunately many of the soldiers in the detachment are former New York City firemen who, by using wet sheets and tearing down endangered buildings, manage to save most of the town, at least for now. Even so, Cassville, which Griffin found so beautiful early in the morning, is a shambles. (Today only a historical marker indicates where Cassville once was, the town having been almost totally destroyed by Union forces in October and November of 1864 in retaliation for guerrilla attacks in the area.)

Williams attributes the pillaging and near-incineration of Cassville to "irritation" on the part of Northern troops over being fired at from the "close hill" outside the town. A better explanation comes from Sergeant David Nichol of the Pennsylvania Light Artillery in a May 21 letter to his father: "Our men has [*sic*] no mercy whatever—take any thing they can lay their hands on, leave the country bare wherever they go. The houses near the road suffer the most—I have seen women crying & begging for them to leave a little for the children, but their tears were of no avail. Some of our soldiers are a disgrace to the service." Yet, concludes Nichol, expressing the common sentiment among Sherman's men, "Such is war & the sooner the aristocracy or rather the ones who brought it on feels the effects, the sooner we will have peace."[109]

When Sherman, who is spending the night in Kingston, learns that the Confederates have abandoned their defenses at Cassville, he assumes, as he has all along, that their main body already is south of the Etowah and that there is no likelihood of a serious encounter north of that river. Accordingly he instructs Thomas and McPherson to encamp their forces nearby, respectively at Cassville and Kingston, and sends only Schofield in pursuit, with instructions to "push the enemy [rear guard] past Cartersville." Thus if Johnston intends to make a stand at Cartersville, which topographically is a good place to do so, he could give Schofield and his undersized "army" a nasty surprise.

But Johnston has no such intention. His sole desire is to get safely over the Etowah, a desire shared by his men who, notes Lieutenant Mackall, are "dispirited & fagged" after more than twenty-four hours of marching and skirmishing with little or no sleep. During the morning, most of the Confederates pass through Cartersville and begin crossing the Etowah via the railroad bridge, a wagon bridge, and two pontoon bridges. Despite mix-ups on the north bank and pileups on the south bank, by midafternoon the whole army is across except for the cavalry rear guard. The engineers thereupon remove the pontoon bridges and set fire (by mistake according to Lieutenant Mackall) to the railroad bridge, which burns down to its stone pylons. Shortly before sunset, Schofield's troops come into view, "burning everything as they go," notes Albert Porter of the 33rd Mississippi in his diary. As they draw near, Wheeler's troopers dash across the wagon bridge and then set it aflame, destroying it. At 8:45 P.M., Schofield reports to Sherman that he has reached the Etowah, that both bridges are gone, and that "the enemy appears to have but slight defensive works" on the other side.[110]

Thus ends the third phase of the campaign, although because of its brevity and lack of major fighting it could be regarded as merely the aftermath of the series of maneuvers and engagements that has compelled the Confederates to retreat first from Dalton and then from Resaca. During it, Sherman has tried but failed to bring Johnston to battle, and Johnston has tried but failed to give him that battle. The reasons for Sherman's failure are obvious and to a degree inevitable. The sheer size and lopsided organization of his army have made it impossible for it to move swiftly on the few and poor roads; as Sherman himself points out in a letter to his wife on May 22, "I can't move about as I did with 15 or 20,000 men."[111] Because it was so widely dispersed and because of his own poor utilization of it, Sherman's cavalry has played practically no role in the pursuit; its sole significant contribution has been accidentally to cause the aborting of Hood's attack at Cassville. Above all, Sherman has suffered from the inherent disadvantage of the pursuer against the pursued: Johnston has been able to make his nocturnal retreats unconcerned about what lay ahead and knowing exactly where he wanted to go, whereas Sherman has had to spend the better part of each day looking for and catching up with his quarry, with the result that for several days (May 18–20) he literally lost track of the Confederate army.

Johnston, for his part, has conducted his retreat skillfully, suffered minimal losses ("we find very few stragglers, take very few prisoners," comments an officer of the XV Corps in his diary for May 20).[112] Thanks to the arrival of all of Polk's forces, Johnston has crossed the Etowah with an army considerably stronger than the one he had at the outset of the campaign. On the other hand his great caution, although on the whole justified, has allowed the Federals, marching as they have in dispersed, strung-out, and hence potentially vulnerable columns, to advance from the Oostanaula to the Etowah in four days with only a few skirmishes and trifling casualties. As a consequence they now stand less than fifty miles from Atlanta.

Part Four: From the Etowah to Pumpkinvine Creek

The Confederates continue retreating until they reach the vicinity of Allatoona, whereupon they halt and encamp. Allatoona is another little railroad village whose sole importance derives from its location in Allatoona Pass. A long narrow gorge, through which the railroad runs, and the high hills that flank it make Allatoona a position naturally stronger than even Buzzard Roost and Rocky Face. Nothing would suit Johnston better than if Sherman were to assault him here; but while Johnston hopes that this will happen, he has seen enough of Sherman's mode of operating not to take it for granted. Suffice for the moment that his army occupies a place where it is out of immediate danger and can obtain needed rest.

Johnston establishes his headquarters in a house about one and a half miles north of Allatoona and near the railroad. Presently the telegraph clicks out a message, for Johnston, dated May 18 and in cipher, from President Davis. When decoded it reads: "Your dispatch of the 16th [announcing the retreat from Resaca to Calhoun] received; read with disappointment. I hope the re-enforcements sent will enable you to achieve important results."[113]

Only a few lines, but there is much between them. Davis is not merely disappointed; he is angry that Johnston has retreated so far into Georgia without attempting to defeat Sherman in all-out battle, he expects Johnston to make such an attempt now that he has been strengthened by Polk, and he surely will be angrier still on learning that Johnston has retreated thirty more miles, the distance from Calhoun to Allatoona, still without fighting a battle.

Never one to allow himself to be hurried in such matters, particularly when dealing with Davis, Johnston waits until the following day, May 21, before answering:

> Your dispatch of the 18th was received yesterday. I know that my dispatch [reporting the retreat from Resaca] must of necessity create the feeling [of disappointment] you express. I have earnestly sought an

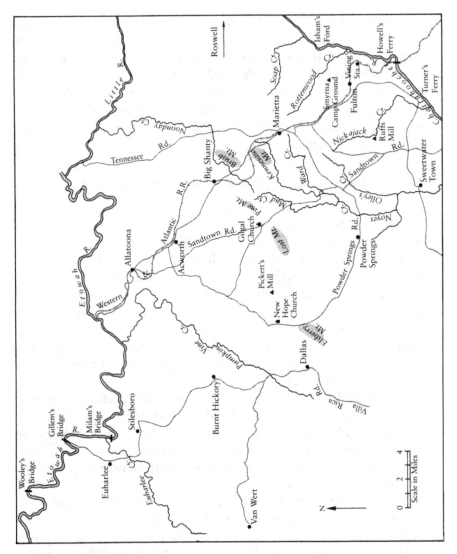

Etowah to Chattahoochee

opportunity to strike the enemy. The direction of the railroad to this point has enabled him to press me back by steadily moving to the left and by fortifying the moment he halted. He has made an assault upon his superior forces too hazardous.[114]

On reading this two days later, Davis cannot help but reflect that Lee had not found it "too hazardous" to strike Grant's 120,000 men with his 60,000 in the Wilderness, inflicting on the Yankee commander losses that would have turned back anyone else. And Davis's feeling that Johnston is not doing all he could and should do to defeat Sherman becomes stronger after he talks with Colonel Henry Brewster toward the end of May. Brewster, a volunteer aide on Hood's staff, brings to Davis a letter from Hood, dated May 24, stating: "Colonel Brewster has been with us since we left Dalton and can give you an account of the operations of this army since the enemy made their appearance in our immediate front. . . . I think it would be well for you to have a conversation with him in relation to our affairs, etc., etc." Exactly what Brewster tells Davis is not known, but the gist of it can be deduced from what Davis subsequently says to Mary Chesnut in Columbia, South Carolina: Johnston failed to fight at Dalton because he had no plan, Johnston repeatedly has rejected the urgings of Hood and Polk to attack, "all this delay is breaking Hood's heart," and "so much retreating would demoralize General Lee's army." Yet, in spite of Johnston's avoidance of battle, so ominously reminiscent of his conduct in Virginia in 1862 and in Mississippi in 1863, Davis feels he has no choice other than to hope, as he writes Lee on May 20, that "the future will prove the wisdom of his [Johnston's] course."[115]

Ever since December the people of Atlanta have been told again and again by their newspapers and by self-appointed spokesmen of the Army of Tennessee that Johnston is a great general, that his forces are strong and ready, and that he will stop and defeat the enemy in the mountains of northern Georgia. And when Johnston had retreated, first from Dalton, then from Resaca, these same sources had assured them that this was the "result of plans formed months ago" and that he was just waiting for the right time and place to attack and destroy Sherman. To be sure, not everyone believed this: editor John Steele of the *Intelligencer* felt obliged to chide those pessimists who were saying that "It looks mighty black for us up there." But on May 20, to quote Mary Mallard writing that day to an aunt, word had circulated through the city that "General Johnston has issued his battle order saying that he will give battle and will fall back no further." Hence, when the news arrives on May 21 that Johnston has retreated again, this time south of the Etowah, and that his wagon train is heading for the Chattahoochee, a mere six miles to the north, Atlantans are shocked, alarmed, and for the first time give serious consideration to the possibility—some feel it is more than that—of having the Yankees reach and even occupy their city. The very next day the newspapers publish a proclamation from Mayor James M. Calhoun: all the "male citizens of Atlanta, capable of bearing arms, without regard to occupation, who are not in the Confederate or State service," are to report at noon on May 26 to the city marshal for the purpose of being "organized into companies and armed." Men "not willing to defend their homes and families," adds Mayor Calhoun, "are requested to leave the city at their earliest convenience, as their presence only embarrasses the authorities and tends to the demoralization of others." What the proclamation of course does not mention is that Calhoun's own family already has left the city. But it is not the only one, and many other people are either getting ready or planning to do the same, even though the *Atlanta Southern Confederacy* staunchly declares that "our position is strengthened" by Johnston's retreat because it has shortened his line of communications.

Almost as depressing as the bad news from the front are the wounded that arrive from there every day. They lie in long rows both inside and outside the large brick railroad station near the Five Points, waiting to be transferred to Macon, if they can be moved, or to one of the local hospitals if they cannot. Most of them are dirty, blood-soaked, and in pain, but surprisingly cheerful. Women from the churches and Soldiers Aid Committees (one of the latter is headed by the wealthy slave trader Robert A. Crawford) do all they can to make the wounded as comfortable as possible. Among these volunteer nurses is Mary Mallard, who finds that one of the greatest needs is old sheets: "When limbs are amputated and the clothing cut off a foot or two above the place, something cooler and lighter than their blankets is necessary to throw over them."

A flow of refugees with "sad faces" crowds still more the already overcrowded city, adding to the gloom and anxiety. North of the Chattahoochee, reports the *Appeal* in the same issue that contains Mayor Calhoun's proclamation, "the roads are filled with the fleeing, and vehicles of every imaginable description are brought into requisition." Most of these "runagees," as one correspondent wryly dubs them, are from nearby Marietta, where on May 21 a "stampede" occurs when the army begins evacuating the hospital and removing stores. All seek to save themselves and as much of their property as they can carry away from Sherman's oncoming and apparently unstoppable horde, about whose depredations they have heard terrifying tales. Perhaps some have also heard that their own Southern troops are not necessarily the most pleasant visitors either. Quartermaster clerk Patrick writes in his diary for May 21 while traveling with Johnston's wagon train toward Chattahoochee:

> This morning, when the train was passing the house of a farmer a lady gave to the men all the milk, butter and butter-milk she had. They were not satisfied with this. They took all the chickens she had, robbed all the nests they could find, went to the stables and took all the fodder and not content with this, pulled down the fences and turned their horses in upon the fields of wheat. I am sorry to say this has been the case all along the road by our Army.

"War," concludes Patrick philosophically, "is a terrible thing."[116]

Sherman spends most of May 20, 21, and 22 sitting at a desk next to a window in the inner room of a small building on the south side of Kingston's main street. Here he reads and answers dispatches, issues orders, and writes letters. Two of the letters are to Ellen, the first he has sent her since late April. His campaign, he informs her, "has been rapid, skilful, and successful." By sending McPherson through Snake Creek Gap, he has spared his troops the "terrible door of death that Johnston had prepared for them in the Buzzard Roost." Although "forced to attack at Resaca," he had been able to fight with "as little disadvantage as possible" by catching the "strong and weak points of the enemy." Johnston, he estimates, has lost "about 6,000 men" whereas his own loss is "less than 4,000," and the only reason Johnston has escaped destruction is his familiarity "with all the byways" and because of McPherson's "timidity" in Snake Creek Gap.

As for Sherman's next move, that will be to force the enemy "behind the Chattahoochee," after which he will "take Atlanta and disturb the peace of central Georgia and prevent reinforcements going to Lee." He plans to accomplish this by heading "due south to Dallas and thence to Marietta and the Chattahoochee Bridge." That way he will avoid the main roads, which lead to Allatoona "among hills that afford strong positions" in a country he had traveled through as a young officer twenty years ago. "I have no doubt we must have a terrible battle at some point near the Chattahoochee," but "I think I have the best army in the country, and if I can't take Atlanta and stir up Georgia considerably I am mistaken."[117]

Sherman's main concern, as usual, is logistical. His railroad supply line now stretches eighty miles back to Chattanooga, and he believes that it is dangerously exposed to Johnston's cavalry, which he frankly and rightly regards as superior to his own "in quantity and quality." Only by posting infantry detachments along the railroad can he adequately protect it, but in so doing he reduces his army as he advances while Johnston increases his as he retreats. To replenish the front-line strength already lost in this fashion so as to provide an ample margin for the future, he therefore orders Brigadier General John E. Smith's division of the XV Corps at Huntsville to come to Georgia, directs the XVII Corps (now en route to Huntsville) to march directly to Rome and then join the rest of the Army of the Tennessee as it moves toward the Chattahoochee, and summons nine regiments of the XXIII Corps from Kentucky and East Tennessee. Because the departure of John Smith's division and the XXIII Corps troops greatly weakens protection of the railroads in Tennessee and Kentucky, Sherman also appeals to the War Department to send one-hundred-day regiments from the Northwest to take their place: "Back us up with troops in the rear, so I will not be forced to drop detachments as road guards, and I have an army that will make a deep hole in the Confederacy." These regiments, the ultimate and in fact only tangible outcome of Governor Morton's January call for an all-out effort to win the war by autumn, are low in numbers and quality, but at least they will give rebel raiders and guerrillas something to think about. In response to Sherman's plea, which Lincoln seconds with telegrams to the governors of Indiana, Illinois, Iowa, and Wisconsin, Morton sends all of the available Hoosier militia south, and his counterparts in the other states promise to do what they can, which, as it turns out, is not much.[118]

Supply also is Sherman's prime concern when it comes to his planned thrust to the Chattahoochee. For the first time since the campaign began, his army will be leaving the railroad and depending entirely on wagon transport for an indefinite, but he hopes short, period of time. Hence on May 20 he directs Thomas, McPherson, and Schofield to "send to the rear all wounded and sick, as also all worthless men and idlers"; to collect sufficient provisions to furnish subsistence to their commands "independent of the railroad for twenty days"; and to have the whole army "ready to march by May 23, stripped for action": this means, he explains, that "the wagon trains should rather be diminished than increased, as we can safely rely on getting much meat, and forage, and vegetables in the country to which we prepare to go," namely, central Georgia. As a result of this order, trains chug day and night into Kingston, Cass Station, and Cartersville to unload supplies and take away the unfit, among whom, according to Chauncey Cooke of the 24th Wisconsin, are hundreds of men "who are sick and dying from want of sleep" and sheer exhaustion. Replacing them, as well as several regiments whose enlistments have expired, are recruits, newly arrived regiments, and soldiers returning from furlough and hospital. These additions, Sherman calculates, will give him 80,000 to 85,000 infantry when he crosses the Etowah.

Sherman's May 20 directive also states that during the march to the Chattahoochee, "Brigade quartermasters and commissaries will . . . forage and graze, but indiscriminate plunder must not be allowed." No doubt Sherman is reacting to the conduct of his troops at Cassville and elsewhere, conduct that General Hascall of the XXIII Corps considers so "barbarous" as to "disgrace and render worthy of defeat any army in the universe." Thomas, McPherson, and Schofield likewise are concerned. Thomas publishes a circular forbidding "all straggling from the ranks, entering of houses or barns," and the "burning of buildings, unless done by order from competent authority." McPherson instructs Logan and Dodge to organize "regular foraging parties" that "will invariably be in charge of reliable officers." Schofield issues a special field order reprimanding the colonel of the 124th Indiana, Hovey's division, for letting his men commit "acts of violence and depredation on the defenseless inhabitants of the country through which we are passing" and declaring that he is "determined to enforce discipline and suppress disorderly and disgraceful conduct by every means" in his power. All three assert that field officers will be held individually and directly responsible for the behavior of their troops.[119]

Finally, Sherman deals with what might be termed a morale problem. He has learned that many of the soldiers, misunderstanding the restrictions he has placed on newspaper reporters' transmitting stories from the army, think that he has forbidden the writing of letters home, something they resent and often vow to defy. Consequently on May 20 he issues a circular "assuring all officers and men that, on the contrary, he encourages them . . . to keep up the most unreserved correspondence with their families and friends wherever they may be." What he does discourage, he explains, "is the maintenance of that class of men who will not take a musket and fight, but follow the army to pick up news for sale, speculating upon a species of information dangerous to the army and to our cause, and who are more used to bolster up idle and worthless officers than to notice the hard working and meritorious whose modesty is generally equal to their courage, and who scorn the cheap flattery of the press."

The circular elicits a predictable reaction from Northern newspapers: by unfairly discriminating against and restricting reporters, they charge, Sherman is denying the public its "right to know," which is especially important (so affirms the *New York Times*) in a "People's War" like this one. Yet on the whole the press's reaction is mild. So far at least, Sherman has been too successful to be denounced, as he otherwise would be, as a bungler trying to cover up his bungling. In any case the correspondents with his army are beginning to file stories, sending them either through regular channels or by ingenious means that circumvent Sherman's orders. Besides, the campaign in Georgia is not all that important anyway; it is in Virginia where the war is being decided and which accordingly commands the primary attention of both the newspapers and their readers.[120]

Both Sherman's and Johnston's troops welcome the pause in the campaign; both spend it for the most part in the same way: catching up on their sleeping and eating, reading newspapers and mail from home, writing letters, drawing new equipment and clothing (particularly shoes) or repairing old, and in general cleaning up. The last involves not merely washing themselves and their uniforms but also the more difficult task of trying to get rid of lice. That "friend of man," writes Private Strong, sticks "closer than a brother." They "get into the seams of our shirts and pants and drawers, and when not engaged in laying eggs . . . sally out and forage our defenseless bodies." During active campaigning, the soldiers use every chance they get to peel off their shirts and kill the lice by cracking them between thumb and forefinger. Now, with the time and facilities to do it, they strip themselves naked and boil all of their clothes, during which process they stand about covered by blankets, rubber ponchos, or nothing at all. Once everything is thoroughly boiled and dried out, they dress again and enjoy the bliss of not being constantly bitten, for a few days, anyway.[121]

Not everybody, however, is able to take it easy. The Northern and Southern cavalries patrol, respectively, the north and the south banks of the Etowah. Cox's division marches up the river and burns the Etowah Iron Works—actually a useless endeavor, for the machinery is en route to Atlanta, having been removed by Georgia militia. Kilpatrick's division, now under the acting command of Colonel William Lowe, is posted along the railroad to guard it against raiders and guerrillas. And a brigade from Sweeny's division goes to Rome to garrison it and relieve Davis's division, which Sherman has ordered to link up with the army's right as it moves toward the Chattahoochee. Sweeny himself takes advantage of the lull to try to further a cause dearer to his heart than preservation of the Union: by flag of truce he sends a letter to Cleburne proposing that after the war they join in raising a Fenian army to liberate their native Ireland from English tyranny. Cleburne answers that both of them will have had enough of fighting, once this war is over, to last them for the rest of their lives.[122] (Two years hence Sweeny will head a Fenian "invasion" of Canada which is such a fiasco that it would be totally farcical were not some men killed during it.)

On Sunday, May 22, religious services take place in each army. Polk, again wearing his bishop's robe over his uniform, preaches to a large assemblage which includes the recent converts Johnston and Hood. Sherman, on the other hand, remains in his office; when he hears the church bell in Kingston ringing, he tells Corse to send a squad to arrest whoever is doing it. The squad returns with the Reverend E. P. Smith, a member of the Christian Commission. Corse asks Smith, "You were ringing the bell?" "Yes, it is Sunday and I was ringing it for service," Smith replies. Corse relays this answer to Sherman, who looks through the doorway at Smith, then says to Corse, "Sunday, Sunday! Didn't know it was; let him go." Smith conducts his service in the church, which is filled with soldiers, among them Howard. Sherman remains at his desk.[123]

That night, as they lie down to sleep, the Union soldiers know that their brief vacation from war is about to end and that in the morning the advance south-ward will resume. They are ready, and they are confident. Some, like Israel Atkins of the 23rd Michigan, think that the Confederates "are as good as whipped" and "making for Atlanta as fast as they possibly can." Others, not so optimistic, fear, as does Colonel James Robinson of Williams's division, that "our troubles are just commencing."[124]

Among the Confederates there is a wider range of attitudes. At one extreme can be found men like the one who left behind this note on the north bank of the Etowah: "Yanks, the rebellion will be crushed. You've got men, we haven't." At the opposite extreme are those who would agree with Lieutenant Andrew Neal, who writes his mother on May 20 that if the Yankees "would give us a fair fight we could sweep them from the face of the earth." But probably the sentiments of the vast majority are both conveyed and described by Sergeant Robert W. Banks of the 37th Mississippi in a May 23 letter to his parents: "The Army of Tennessee has been forced to fall back because of Sherman's superiority in numbers. It may turn out for the best—let us trust so at all events. Remember that McClellan once said, beware of *Johnston's retreats*. The troops are in fine spirits and eager for a decisive fight."[125]

"We are now all in motion," Sherman telegraphs quartermaster Donaldson in Nashville on May 23, "like a vast hive of bees, and expect to swarm along the Chattahoochie in five days." During the day, McPherson with the XV and XVI corps crosses the Etowah west of Kingston on Wooley's bridge; Thomas with the IV and Baird's and Johnson's divisions of the XIV Corps crosses on Gillem's bridge and by means of a ford southeast of Kingston; and the XX Corps passes over a pontoon bridge further south near Milam's bridge, which is the only one along the river, other than the Cartersville bridges, which the Confederates have destroyed. Waiting to use the pontoon bridge when Hooker's troops get through with it is Schofield. Needless to say he is annoyed at again being blocked by the XX Corps, particularly since it is he who is responsible for the pontoons being there in the first place. "I do not wish to utter a word of complaint," he complains to Sherman, "but this frequent conflict between General Hooker's orders and mine causes great trouble."

Sherman's immediate objective is Dallas, a crossroads village about fourteen miles south of the Etowah from Milam's bridge, the same distance southwest of Allatoona, and sixteen miles west of Marietta, his ultimate and main goal. To reach Dallas he has instructed McPherson to swing through Van Wert and approach it from the west, while Thomas moves on it from the north and Schofield and Stoneman cover the army's left flank and rear. As his telegram to Donaldson indicates, Sherman does not anticipate serious resistance before getting to the vicinity of Marietta. Operating on the assumption that Johnston has no intention of fighting a full-fledged battle until he is close to Atlanta, Sherman believes that the Confederates will either fall back to Marietta or, more likely, withdraw to the south side of the Chattahoochee.

Beyond the Etowah the country is rolling, the soil is rich, and the broad fields remind Harvey Reid of the 22nd Wisconsin of his home state. Every acre appears to be sown with wheat, rye, or corn; but none are sown with cotton although gins are everywhere. Noting this, the Northern soldiers conclude that all the talk about starving out the Rebels is nonsense. By the same token they see no reason why they should not enjoy this land of plenty. Foraging parties, authorized as well as not authorized, spread out, collecting cattle, pigs, chickens, eggs, hams, and other edibles from the prosperous-looking farms and plantations, most of which have been abandoned by their owners. Whenever there is a halt, the cavalry and teamsters take their horses and mules into the fields, where they trample what they do not eat. The civilians who remain usually vow that they are Unionists, and in truth this section of Georgia had opposed secession in 1860–61. Those who are persuasive enough in their professions of loyalty, states Reid, "have their property protected as far as possible." But, Reid adds, "such is the general license given that few can save anything that a soldier can use. . . . Strict orders are issued against plunder and killing pigs, chickens and so forth but there are few company or regimental commanders who will report a man." Thus the recent orders of the Federal commanders forbidding such behavior and warning field officers that they will be held responsible turn out to be no more effective than similar decrees in the past and for the same reason: they are not enforced at the level where they need to be enforced.

The weather is scorchingly hot, the narrow roads are dusty, and canteens soon become empty. "I never saw so many stragglers as today," comments Captain Charles W. Wills of the veteran 103rd Illinois in his diary that evening. "For 12 miles no water was to be had. . . . Saw no cases of sunstroke, but two of my men from heat turned blue with rush of blood to the head, and had to leave the ranks." At sundown the Union columns halt wherever they can locate water. By then McPherson, whose flank is covered by Garrard's cavalry, has reached Euharlee Creek, about five miles west of Van Wert; Thomas, with McCook's troopers in the van, is at the village of Euharlee, less than four miles from Gillem's bridge, waiting for Hooker to come up; and Stoneman, whose division has crossed the Etowah ahead of the main army, patrols the area east of Stilesboro. Schofield, of course, waits impatiently for Hooker to complete his crossing on the pontoon bridge.[126]

Sherman's thrust west of the Allatoona Mountains does not catch Johnston off guard. It is an obvious move in view of what Sherman had done at Dalton and Resaca, and on the evening of May 22, Brigadier General Ross has informed Johnston that there has been considerable enemy activity around Milam's and Gillem's bridges. Therefore, on the morning of May 23, when his cavalry reports that large Union forces are crossing the Etowah at both those places and also at Wooley's bridge, Johnston promptly orders Hardee and Polk to march for Dallas. The distance from Allatoona to Dallas, as already noted, is sixteen miles, exactly the same as it is to there from Milam's bridge, where Hooker is crossing, and only about four miles less than from Gillem's bridge, over which Thomas has passed. Theoretically this would seem to mean that Thomas and Hooker's columns, who have had an earlier start, should be able to reach Dallas ahead of Hardee and Polk, or at least at about the same time. However, the latter have no river to cross, are not encumbered by large wagon trains, need not worry about running into an ambush, and above all do not halt at sunset. Instead they keep marching until after it is dark, rest for a few hours, and then resume marching. Their troops, like the Federals, suffer badly from heat during the day, then are soaked by the rain that falls during the evening. Ignorant of the purpose of the march and knowing only that they are heading generally southward, they figure that they are retreating again. In Captain Samuel T. Foster's company of the 24th Texas Cavalry (Dismounted) of Granbury's Brigade, "some say we are going to Florida and put in a pontoon bridge over to Cuba and go over there." Meanwhile Johnston, who remains at Allatoona with Hood's Corps, orders Wheeler to go to the north side of the Etowah and reconnoiter the Cartersville area so as to make sure that Sherman is not trying to trick the Confederates into leaving Allatoona undefended. During the night, Wheeler with 800 men crosses the river near the former railroad bridge.[127]

The Federals resume their advance early on the morning of May 24. After a few miles the terrain assumes, in the words of a *Cincinnati Commercial* correspondent, "a rough aspect"; and still further, "mountains and great hills appear, not in parallel ranges, but a succession of mounds, knobs, hills and mountains. It looks as if a dozen each had been thrown down on a level tract of country," and they "are usually covered with timber and thick underbrush. Truly this may be called a mountain fastness." Open fields become rare, as do farms and inhabitants. Most of the latter are women and children of the "poor white trash" type, who exist in squalid log cabins, are comically yet pathetically ignorant, and in some cases are literally starving. From now on, Sherman's troops find little in the way of provisions to take from the countryside, although they take it nevertheless.

During the day, McPherson marches via Van Wert to a branch of Raccoon Creek about eight miles west of Dallas. His wagon train, which extends all the way back to Euharlee Creek, is joined by Davis's division coming down from Rome. Hooker, taking the lead for the Army of the Cumberland, advances through Stilesboro to Burnt Hickory, a hamlet seven miles north of Dallas which derives its name from the hundreds of charred, branchless, eerie-looking hickories that surround it. Howard and Palmer follow; and Schofield, after crossing the Etowah in the morning, proceeds to an area northeast of Burnt Hickory, where he covers the Union left along with Stoneman.

Early in the afternoon some of McCook's troopers capture a Rebel courier who is carrying a dispatch from Johnston to one of his cavalry commanders. It states that the entire Confederate army is moving toward Dallas. Then, in the evening, Thomas receives word from Garrard that his cavalry, riding far ahead of McPherson, has been attacked a quarter of a mile from Dallas by a portion of Bate's Division of Hardee's Corps. Both of these highly significant items of intelligence pass on to Sherman, who has left Kingston and is accompanying Thomas. Even so, Sherman remains confident that if Johnston attempts to make a stand at all north of the Chattahoochee, it will be at Marietta. His orders for tomorrow are to push on to and past Dallas.[128]

It is not going to be that easy for Sherman. After crossing the Etowah, Wheeler has ridden all the way from Cartersville to Cass Station without sighting any Federals except a large wagon train, part of which he has burned, the remainder of which (seventy wagons) he has brought back with him. In addition, Jackson's cavalry has spotted long dust trails heading southward from Milam's and Gillem's bridges, and it has clashed with Yankee cavalry between Van Wert and Dallas. As a consequence, Johnston has decided that Sherman's army is moving to the west in an attempt to outflank him and so has ordered Hood to follow Hardee and Polk to the Dallas area. Nightfall finds Johnston and his staff in a tent pitched by the roadside, four miles east of Dallas. Although again forced to relinquish a strong (in a sense, too strong) defensive position by a turning movement, he now blocks Sherman's way to Marietta and intends to give him battle, if he wants it, tomorrow.

On the morning of May 25, Hardee's Corps forms a line astride the Atlanta-Marietta road directly east of Dallas, Polk's Corps takes position on Hardee's right, and Hood's Corps advances to New Hope Church, a log Methodist meeting house at a crossroads northeast of Dallas. Observers atop Elsberry Mountain report dust columns approaching from the north, and early in the afternoon, Hood's pickets capture a Yankee who says he belongs to Geary's division of Hooker's corps and that "Fighting Joe" is headed in their direction. Hood thereupon deploys his now-standard battle line: Hindman on the left, Stevenson on the right, and Stewart, bolstered by one of Stevenson's brigades, in the center around New Hope Church. Many of the Confederates, remembering Cassville, doubt that there will be a battle but nevertheless start digging rifle pits and erecting barricades of logs and rocks. Only some of Stovall's Georgians do not bother to fortify, perhaps because they have ready-made, if somewhat inauspicious, cover behind the tombstones in the New Hope Church cemetery.[129]

Just like the Yankee prisoner said, Hooker is headed toward New Hope Church. To be precise, he intends to go there as soon as he feels it is safe to do so. During the morning he marched, Geary's division in the lead, down from Burnt Hickory and crossed Pumpkinvine Creek on a bridge that he saved from destruction by personally leading a charge of his and Geary's escorts that drove away some Confederates before they could do a proper job of setting it afire. Then came a hint of trouble. A short distance beyond the bridge, Hooker found a road branching off to the east from the direct road to Dallas, a road not on the Union maps. On the mistaken assumption that it also led to Dallas and with Thomas's concurrence, Hooker went by this road with Geary while Williams's and Butterfield's divisions continued on the main, in fact the only, road to Dallas. After proceeding about a mile and a half, Geary's troops began to encounter such stiff resistance from Rebel skirmishers that they thought they were being opposed by a brigade, whereas it was only a 250-man regiment. Pushing on, they took several prisoners who said that Hood's whole corps was up ahead at a place called New Hope Church and that Hardee was nearby. This intelligence was as alarming to Hooker and Thomas as it was unexpected. Not only did they, like Sherman, assume that there would be no serious opposition from the enemy until well past Dallas; they also realized that Geary's division now was at least five miles from the rest of the Army of the Cumberland and,

Charge by Hooker's escort *(Harper's Weekly)*

therefore, in "dire danger" of being crushed should Hood attack with his full force. Quickly Geary deployed his men in preparation for a desperate stand, Hooker sent couriers to Williams and Butterfield with orders to hasten to Geary's support, and "almost in a whisper" Thomas instructed Captain Henry Stone of his staff to ride back as fast as possible and "hurry up the Fourth Corps." Thus, as the afternoon sun beats down hotly, Hood and Hooker each await the attack of the other, the first in hope of victory, the second in fear of being overwhelmed before help arrives.

Captain Stone reaches Howard at 2:20 P.M. and delivers Thomas's message. Howard, who already has gotten word of the emergency from another member of Thomas's staff, is three miles from the Pumpkinvine Creek bridge and six miles from where Geary's division at this very moment might be fighting for its existence. To Stone it seems he "never saw men moving so slowly" as Howard's troops, but when he urges Howard to march them faster, the one-armed general replies that doing so will "use them up." Stone then rides ahead and sees Williams, easily recognizable even at a distance because of his flamboyant mustache, riding at the head of his division toward the road to New Hope Church. He gallops up to Williams and tells him about Geary's precarious situation, whereupon the "gallant old soldier" at once speeds his march.

Having done all he can to bring help fast, Stone heads back to report to Thomas. On the way he overtakes a courier who is carrying a note from McPherson to Sherman, whom he sees "dismounted by the roadside, showing great impatience." While Sherman rapidly reads the note, Stone informs him of Thomas's message to Howard and that Williams soon will be up. Sherman scratches a few words with a pencil on the envelope of McPherson's note, hands it to Stone to deliver to Thomas, and then "somewhat testily and fretfully" says: "Let Williams go in anywhere as soon as he gets up. I don't see what they are waiting for in front now. There haven't been twenty rebels there today."

Between 4 and 5 P.M., Williams and Butterfield reinforce Geary, the former taking position to the front and the latter on his left and slightly to the rear so as to guard against a flank attack. Hooker, acting on instructions from Sherman relayed to him by Thomas, orders all three division commanders to form their troops for an advance and assault. Still sure that at most no more than a small Confederate delaying force is in Hooker's front, Sherman proposes to overwhelm it and then push on without further delay toward Dallas and Marietta.

Shortly after 5 P.M. the bugles sound "Forward," and Williams's division advances in three battle lines of a brigade each, with Williams and Hooker riding behind the first line. A few minutes later, Butterfield also moves out, as does Geary. In spite of dense woods, underbrush, and rocky grounds, Williams's Army of the Potomac veterans preserve "beautiful order," and he feels proud of them. The skirmishers soon meet steadily stiffening opposition from their Confederate counterparts but keep going. After about a mile, Williams commands "Double Quick," and his men break into a trot. Then, as they near the foot of a slope, a hurricane of bullets, shrapnel, and canister strikes them: to Williams it seems to come from "all directions except the rear." They lurch forward a few more steps, then take shelter behind trees, boulders, logs, anything that looks like it can stop a bullet. Geary's and Butterfield's troops do likewise. The Federals had hoped, when they began the attack, to catch the Rebs "in the open" and have "a fair fight." Now, up ahead, through gaps in the foliage, they can see piles of logs and red dirt billowing forth bluish-white clouds of smoke. All they can do is fire back as fast as possible, and this they do.

After a while the sky darkens; then thunder and lightning mingle with the roar of the cannons and rifles. The noise, thinks musician Albert Porter, who is well to the rear with other Confederate noncombatants, "beats everything I heard at Resaca." Robinson's brigade, which forms the first line of Williams's division, fires off all of its ammunition, sixty rounds per man, in little more than half an hour. Brigadier General Thomas Ruger's brigade takes its place, and before long its men are scrounging cartridges from the dead and wounded. Eventually

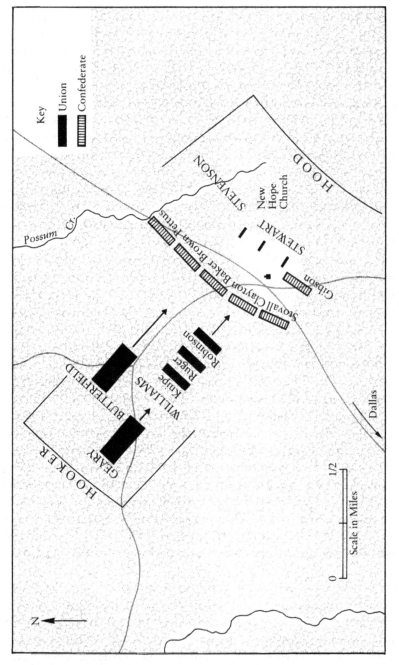

Battle of New Hope Church, May 25

Williams's attack at New Hope Church *(Harper's Weekly)*

they drive away the cannoneers of a 6-gun battery—about the only graybacks discernible—but the "sickening thud" of Minie balls hitting human flesh and bone continues to be heard again and again and again in their ranks. Yet few of them flee or seek to escape in the manner of Private Martin Jones of the 19th Michigan over on Butterfield's part of the line: he "accidentally" shoots himself in the foot, then heads for the rear to have his wound treated. Actually, as bad as it is, a man is safer up front than farther back. Thus when Captain Julian Hinkley of the 3rd Wisconsin goes to the rear with a legitimate wound, he discovers that there are "a thousand bullets flying, to every one nearer the front." The fact is that most of the troops on both sides are firing too high, for they have only an approximate idea of where the enemy is.

Facing Hooker's three divisions are all of Stovall's and Clayton's brigades and parts of Gibson's and Baker's brigades of Stewart's Division—about 4,000 men versus approximately 16,000. But the Confederates are behind cover, even if it only be a tombstone; also they are backed by sixteen cannons, all of which are on the firing line, whereas at most only a third of Hooker's force is in position to shoot at their unseen foes. "It is fun," writes Lieutenant Neal to his sister a week later, "for our troops to stand in their trenches and mow down their [the Yankees'] lines as they advance." Sergeant John Curry of the 40th Alabama fires sixty rounds, forty from his own cartridge box, the rest as they are handed to him by his company commander. When he ceases, the barrel of his rifle is so hot that nobody can hold it. Johnston, who has joined Hood at his headquarters during the afternoon, sends word to Stewart asking if he needs help. Stewart, who is riding up and down immediately behind the firing line in spite of pleas from his men to go to a safer place, replies that none is necessary; and he is right.

At 7:30 it starts raining, a steady, drenching downpour. This and the coming of darkness put an end to fighting except for sporadic exchanges between the pickets. Stewart's troops raise a "prolonged cheer of victory"; Hooker's fall back slowly and sullenly. The latter's casualties total about 665 killed, wounded, and missing, nearly half of them in Williams's division, who have had what they dished out to Stewart's Division at Resaca handed back to them on the same bloody platter. Stewart reports a loss of "between 300 and 400," with over a tenth of it being in Eldridge's Artillery Battalion, presumably the unit that served the 6-gun battery silenced by Ruger's brigade. Both Johnston and Hood praise Stewart warmly for his division's stalwart defense. A forty-two-year-old West Pointer and former college professor in his native Tennessee, Stewart hitherto has performed ably but not spectacularly as a brigade and division commander in all of the Army of Tennessee's major battles. Now "Old Straight," as his men call him, is in line for promotion to lieutenant general should a vacancy at that rank occur.

Hooker, in contrast, receives no commendations from Sherman. On meeting him shortly after the repulse, Sherman brusquely tells him that by waiting most of the afternoon for Williams and Butterfield to come up instead of pressing forward with Geary, Hooker has given the Confederates time in which to reinforce and fortify. Angered by this unfair and obviously prejudiced criticism, which also implicates Thomas, Hooker replies sarcastically that yes, maybe fifty more men have joined Hood during the afternoon. Apart from the basic fact that he detests Hooker, Sherman feels frustrated over having his plans so unexpectedly and, as he sees it, unnecessarily upset. Even now he finds it difficult to believe (so he writes McPherson at 9 P.M.) that "there is anything more than Hood's Corps" in the Dallas area. Yet, he admits, it is possible that Johnston's "whole army" is there and thus "we should act on that hypothesis." During the night he orders all of his forces to concentrate around New Hope Church in expectation of battle tomorrow.[130]

The sound of the fighting at New Hope Church carries all the way to Atlanta, twenty-five miles distant. It is a disturbing, ominous sound, one never heard before in the city; to quote the *Appeal,* it causes a "commotion." Frantic women pack clothing and food in preparation for flight, some of them in their haste

Alexander P. Stewart (*Photographic History,* 10:249)

putting their "preserves in bandboxes and their bonnets in butter kegs." Groups of excited men stand on the street corners, repeating and creating all sorts of rumors. Crowds besiege the provost marshal's office on Whitehall Street, clamoring for passes to Macon, Augusta, and Mobile. Only a small number of people, though, actually leave. Most Atlantans still hope, like Mary Mallard, that "General Johnston will be successful in driving them [the Yankees] away from the city." They just want to be ready and able to flee in case he fails. Thus Mary Mallard herself sends "all our winter clothing, comforts, my sewing machine, and most of Mr. Mallard's books to Augusta to Brother Joe, so that if the army does not make a stand at this place, we will not lose everything." She also makes plans, should the enemy get much closer, to take her children and "the servants" to one of her family's Liberty County plantations near Savannah. That should be far enough away to be safe from the Yankees.[131]

During the night the Union troops west of New Hope Church work "like beavers" with axes, spades, picks, bayonets, and sometimes even tin cups and bare hands. By sunrise on the twenty-sixth, most of them stand in broad, shallow trenches behind three-to-four-feet-high log breastworks covered in front by a thick rampart of dirt and topped by a head log. The latter is a thick tree trunk (it had better be thick, for a Minie ball can penetrate six one-inch pine boards at 600 yards) separated from the parapet by poles that slant to the rear of the trench. Through the narrow slot between the head log and the parapet a rifleman can aim and fire with virtual immunity to all except the best-aimed enemy bullets. Should a cannonball or shell dislodge the head log, then the poles cause it to slide down harmlessly. For Federal and Confederate alike, entrenchments of this type now are standard, as are rifle pits—ditches about three and a half feet deep, with the excavated dirt piled in front and likewise topped by a head log resting on skid poles. Adequate breastworks and rifle pits can be constructed in an hour or less, after which, if there is time, the soldiers heap tree branches ("tangle foot") in front of their line and clear away any underbrush that might obscure their aim or offer concealment to attackers. Through bloody experience the rank and file of both armies have learned that "it don't pay" to attack such defenses frontally, and also that it can be fatal to be without them when attacked.[132]

As soon as they can spot targets, the skirmishers and sharpshooters open fire and keep it up all day, with the cannons occasionally adding their roar to the crackling of the rifles. Neither side, however, attempts a major assault. Johnston is content to remain on the defensive; Sherman needs to bring up and deploy his forces, particularly those of McPherson, who does not enter Dallas (which the Confederates make no attempt to hold) until the afternoon. By evening the XV Corps, Veatch's division of the XVI Corps, and Davis's division occupy a line two miles east of Dallas, while Thomas's and Schofield's troops face toward New Hope Church and its vicinity. A one-mile gap, guarded by only a thin screen of pickets, exists between McPherson's left and Thomas's right, but the junglelike forest conceals it, as it does a similar interval between Hardee at Dallas and Polk and Hood at New Hope Church. Bolstering the Confederate right is Cleburne's Division, which Johnston has detached from Hardee's Corps and stationed to the right rear of Hood's Corps. "Some of the boys," Captain Foster of the 24th Texas, Granbury's Brigade, records in his diary for May 26, "go to the breastworks in front of us to see what soldiers are there, because they have no confidence in any of them except the Arkansas troops. . . . We find Georgia troops in our front, and our boys tell them that if they run that we will shoot them, and no mistake."[133]

At the end of the day, Sherman, who still is skeptical that the whole Confederate army confronts him, issues his orders for tomorrow: all of the batteries of Hooker, Howard, and Schofield that can be brought to bear will bombard the enemy from early morning until 9 A.M. Then, at 10, Howard, supported by two divisions of the XXIII Corps, will wheel southward and assail the Confederate right north of New Hope Church. As he does so, McPherson will "move straight toward the enemy at New Hope Church, and make connection with General Hooker's right." Sherman hopes in this way to drive back both flanks of the Confederates, thereby forcing them to retreat and uniting his own army for a resumption of the advance on Marietta.[134] It is, to say the least, not a realistic plan, being based on the assumption that in all likelihood only Hood's Corps faces him and that Johnston intends to make his stand along the Chattahoochee.

At daylight on May 27, Hooker's, Howard's, and Schofield's artillery opens up, and the Confederates respond in kind. Next, Howard orders Brigadier General Thomas J. Wood to pull his division out of the battle line; it is to spearhead the attack against the enemy's right. Wood protests that his men have just completed fortifying their position at "some loss" and deserve to enjoy the benefits of their labor. Howard answers that he is about to undertake a "hazardous attempt" and needs Wood's division to make it a success. Wood thereupon withdraws his division, and Stanley's division takes its place, always a ticklish process when in close proximity to an aggressive enemy. Meanwhile Thomas and Howard personally reconnoiter the area designated by Sherman for Howard's attack and discover that Wood will have to advance across an open field that is exposed to enemy cross fire. Consequently, Thomas directs Howard to shift Wood to the left of the XXIII Corps, both to avoid the field and in hopes of flanking the Confederate right. In addition, Thomas detaches

Brigadier General Richard W. Johnson's division of the XIV Corps to support Wood, for obviously the divisions of the XXIII Corps that have been assigned this task no longer can perform it. Angered over being deprived of the command of yet another of his divisions, Palmer immediately asks Thomas to relieve him—"you believe me unfit"—and let him go home to Illinois, where he would prefer to be anyway. Thomas manages to calm him down, but Palmer's resentment against the West Pointers continues to simmer, ready at any moment to boil up again.

Wood's division, once it reaches the rear, forms into an assault column consisting of all three of its brigades, each brigade in a double line of battle. On its left and somewhat to its rear, Johnson's division likewise deploys into a column of brigades. Then, at 11 A.M., one hour behind schedule, both divisions begin marching in a generally eastward direction, Howard and his staff accompanying them. Their route takes them through "dense forests and thicket jungles, over a country scarred by deep ravines and intersected by difficult ridges." Since it is impossible to see more than a few yards in any direction, Wood hands a pocket compass to the commander of his lead regiment, Lieutenant Colonel Robert Kimberly of the 41st Ohio, and tells him to use it to guide the column. Another of Wood's officers, Colonel William Gibson, commanding the wounded Willich's brigade, endeavors to keep on the right path by having the buglers blow frequent blasts. He merely disgusts his troops, who grumble, "If we are expected to surprise the enemy, why don't they stop those damned bugles?"

After marching one and a half miles, which takes as many hours, Howard guesses that he has gotten beyond the enemy's flank. Hence he orders Wood to swing south and Johnson to cover the left; he also sends word to Brigadier General Nathaniel McLean, commander of the Third Brigade of Cox's division, which now is on his right, to fill in the gap now existing between his column and the Union left. But when Wood's skirmishers go forward, they come upon a large field at the far end of which are piles of red dirt with men in gray behind them. Obviously the Confederate lines, arching northeastward from the New Hope Church area, do not end here. So Howard resumes his march.

Manning the defenses seen by Wood's skirmishers is Cleburne's Division, with Lowrey's and Govan's brigades on the front line and Polk's and Granbury's in reserve. Furthermore, scouts sent out by Govan have long since spotted Howard's column (no doubt Gibson's bugle calls made that easy enough to do), and Cleburne has passed the word on to Johnston. On receiving it, Johnston jumps to the conclusion that Sherman has abandoned his offensive and is beginning to retreat northeast to the railroad. Therefore he orders

Hardee and Hood to advance in hopes of catching the Federals in the highly vulnerable act of pulling out of their entrenchments. In due course, several of Hardee's and Hood's brigades assail the Union positions west of New Hope Church and east of Dallas, overrun their skirmish lines, and then learn the hard way that there are plenty of Yanks in the main lines who show no disposition to depart—in fact, just the opposite. However, as a result of these otherwise useless sallies, Johnston realizes that instead of retreating, Sherman is trying to turn his right flank. Accordingly he sends Stewart to back up Cleburne, who along with Hindman shifts farther to the right, and makes ready to move other units to the endangered flank should this prove necessary.

If Howard, groping through the forests northeast of New Hope Church, is experiencing frustration, then so is McPherson in the equally dense woods around Dallas. Hitherto, in spite of reports from Garrard's cavalry that the enemy was in strong force on his front, he has shared Sherman's optimistic belief that little serious opposition would be encountered short of Marietta. Now he knows differently. Indeed, he has discovered that the Confederates east of Dallas are so numerous and well entrenched that it would be virtually impossible to drive them back, much less turn their flank as ordered by Sherman. In addition, and to make matters worse, since their lines appear to extend beyond the Villa Rica road to the south and since the long gap between him and Thomas to the north is covered only by Davis's stretched-out division, both of his own flanks are potentially vulnerable to being turned.

News of McPherson's situation reaches Sherman late in the morning, probably in the form of a verbal report from Corse, whom he has sent to observe the Army of the Tennessee's operations. This has two major consequences. First, it finally makes Sherman accept as definite what he should have recognized no later than yesterday evening: namely, that he is up against Johnston's entire army and that his plan to compel it to retreat to or beyond the Chattahoochee by striking for Marietta via Dallas is not succeeding and will not succeed. Next, it causes him to formulate, with characteristic quickness, a new plan with a less ambitious but more realistic objective. At 1:15 P.M. he communicates its essence to McPherson: "We don't want to turn the enemy's left flank but his right, so that we can get our concentrated army between him and the railroad." To that end, McPherson is to "work up so as to connect with General Hooker," and Thomas will continue "working around the left" so as to put the army, once reunited, in position to move northeast to the railroad, "of which we want to make use."

What this means is that Sherman, having failed to reach Marietta by a long-

Oliver Otis Howard *(Harper's Weekly)*

range flanking move, now proposes to make a short-range one designed to place his forces on the railroad somewhere above that town. As a consequence, Howard's march no longer is part of an attempt to drive the Confederates back from New Hope Church with a pincers attack on their flanks but instead has been transformed into an operation that, if successful, will open the way for the army to return to the railroad once it is united. Johnston, in assuming when he learned of Howard's movement that this was Sherman's intent, merely was premature.

After marching another mile or so, Howard again halts his column, this time on the west bank of a narrow, twisting branch of Pumpkinvine Creek known locally as Pickett's Mill Creek because its northward flow turns the wheel of a grist mill owned by the Widow Pickett. Then, while his hot and weary troops rest—much of the way they have literally had to rip through the underbrush and climb up and down a seemingly endless succession of steep, rocky ridges—Howard rides southward with Wood on another reconnaissance: perhaps *now* he has gotten beyond the enemy's right! Coming to a clearing, he peers through his binoculars and sees more mounds of red dirt. But they are fresh ones, the Confederates behind them still are digging, and they do not extend off to the left. He considers the matter, then decides to go ahead and attack. Although not the ideal situation that Thomas and he hoped, even expected, to find—a totally open enemy flank—it comes close enough and offers an opportunity, too good to be passed up, to do to the Confederates in this Georgia wilderness what Stonewall Jackson had done to him in a Virginia wilderness a little over one year ago.

Riding back, Howard orders Wood to swing his division about so that it faces south, instructs Johnson to do likewise on Wood's left, and notifies McLean that he is to deploy his brigade at the edge of an open space on the right, where its job will be to feint an advance so as to draw the enemy's fire away from Wood's attack. McLean, it so happens, had commanded a brigade in Howard's old XI Corps at Chancellorsville, and Howard regards him as one of those responsible for the disaster he suffered there. In turn McLean, a political general from Ohio, hates Howard and resents having to serve under him again, even temporarily. Of all the brigade commanders in Sherman's army, a worse one to assist in Howard's attack could not have been found, but he is the only one available.

Wood soon is ready to move forward, but McLean, manifesting, to put it mildly, an uncooperative attitude, takes an extremely long time getting his four (two Kentucky and two Tennessee) regiments into position, and Johnson takes

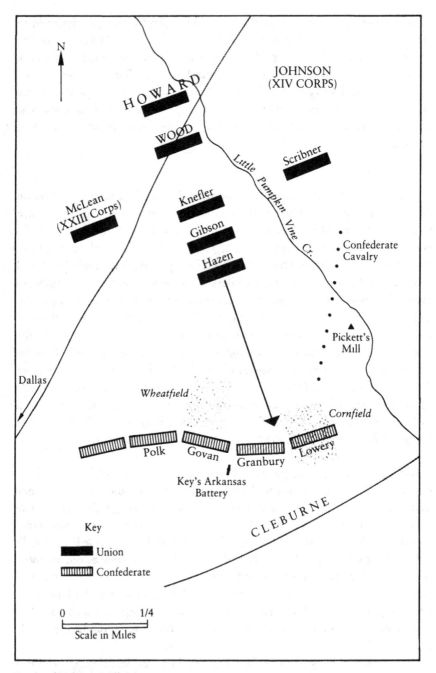

Battle of Pickett's Mill, May 27

just as long deploying his troops, if not longer. Probably Johnson's heart is not in this attack; it rarely is in any attack. Although a West Pointer, brave enough and intelligent, he is a cautious, unaggressive commander temperamentally more suited to be the college professor he will become after the war than the general he now is. He still is deploying when, at 3:35, Howard sends Colonel Thomas J. Morgan of his staff to Thomas with a note that reads: "I am . . . now turning the enemy's right flank, I think." Twenty-five minutes later, according to Lieutenant Colonel Joseph S. Fullerton, keeper of the IV Corps's headquarters journal, Morgan returns and states that "General Thomas says that Major General Sherman wishes us to get on the enemy's flank and rear as soon as possible." In other words, Howard is to go ahead with the turning movement as ordered: he is to attack.

Nevertheless Howard hesitates. A favorite aide has just been shot down at his side by an enemy sharpshooter, shells are landing among Wood's troops (ominous evidence that the Confederates know of their presence), and a prisoner asserts that Hindman's and Cleburne's divisions are up ahead. Finally, a little before five, Wood rides up to Howard and asks, "Are the orders still to attack?" Howard glances at him, then replies, "Attack!" It is the only thing he can do without disobeying Sherman.

Or so he thinks. What he does not know, because he cannot know, is that Sherman suddenly has decided to call off the attack. Why, he never explains; as a matter of fact, he never explains anything about today's operations. Probably, though, Howard's difficulties have brought him to the conclusion, to quote from a dispatch he sends to Schofield at 5 P.M., that "it is useless to look for the flank of the enemy, as he makes temporary breastworks as fast as we travel." In any case, at approximately the same time that Howard orders Wood to attack, Sherman instructs Thomas to direct Howard to halt where he is and establish a defensive position—in other words, not to attack.

Wood's first two battle lines consist of Hazen's brigade. There could be no better choice to lead an assault. The bullet-headed thirty-three-year-old Hazen is one of the ablest combat commanders in the army, so recognized since he held the key Union position on the first day at Stone's River. His troops, although a meager 1,500 in number, are tough veterans from Ohio, Kentucky, and Indiana who never have failed to perform their assignment in battle. One of them is Hazen's twenty-one-year-old topographical engineer and personal protégé, Lieutenant Ambrose Bierce. Young Bierce already has learned much about men in war; today he will learn more.

"At 4:30 P.M., precisely," Wood orders Hazen to advance. Then he turns to Howard and says, "We will put in Hazen, and see what success he has." Howard nods in assent. Hazen hears Wood's words and sees Howard's nod; they are, he

William B. Hazen (*Photographic History,* 10:89)

later writes, "a revelation." Hitherto he had assumed, because of the division's formation, that the attack would be made in columns, each brigade following the other in close succession in an effort to overpower any Confederate opposition by the sheer weight of concentrated numbers. Now, to his mingled alarm and disgust, he realizes that his brigade will attack alone and unsupported. Silently he rides to its head. As he does so, he glances at Bierce, who instantly understands what the glance means: a blunder, a "criminal blunder," is about to occur.

Hazen's troops move forward. The underbrush is so thick that they keep their flags furled to prevent them from being torn to shreds, Hazen and the other mounted officers send their horses to the rear and go on foot, and Hazen resorts to a compass in an attempt to maintain the correct direction. Nevertheless his second line, instead of following behind the first, angles off to the left. Actually, in any true sense, there are no lines, just (records Bierce) "a swarm of men struggling through the undergrowth of the forest, pushing and crowding." Suddenly there is "a ringing rattle of musketry," and up ahead bluish puffs of smoke drift across the green foliage. Enemy troops are in front; there can be no doubting that. The only questions are, how many and are they entrenched?

They are not many and they are not entrenched. They number fewer than a thousand troopers from Brigadier General John Kelly's and Brigadier General William Humes's cavalry divisions stretched in a long thin skirmish line to the right of the main Confederate front. The most they can hope to do is to delay the Federal onslaught until infantry help arrives. Knowing this, they fight tenaciously. Hazen and his men think they are infantry. Still, inevitably, they fall back before the attackers' superior manpower and firepower until they reach the top of a rocky, tree-covered ridge overlooking a ravine. If the Yankees take this ridge, they will be able to strike at the right and rear of Johnston's army.

Hazen's troops advance to the ravine and see, a hundred yards beyond it, the ridge. Cheering and firing, their flags now unfurled, they surge forward, expectant of victory. As they do so, Rebel infantrymen arrive on the ridge. They are Granbury's Texans, sent there on the double by Cleburne as soon as he received word that a strong Union force was threatening to turn the right flank. Taking cover behind boulders, trees, and logs, the Texans open fire. Scores of the Federals go down, but the rest keep coming, some of them yelling (according to Cleburne's report), "Ah! damn you, we have caught you without your logs." Then, twenty to thirty yards from the crest, they halt, unable to advance further against the bullets that are pelting them, in the words of Lieutenant Colonel Robert Kimberly of the 41st Ohio, "like hail in sheets." They find shelter wherever and however they can, then fire back rapidly in a desperate effort to blast the defenders off the ridge. Many of the Texans go down, and to their right the cavalry, who still are holding that part of the line unaided, start wavering. At once Granbury calls on Brigadier General Daniel Govan, whose Arkansans are on his left, for help. Govan sends Colonel George Baucum's 8th/19th Arkansas Consolidated Regiment. It counterattacks the Federals just as they are about to overrun the cavalry and drives them back. Soon afterward Lowrey's Alabama-Mississippi Brigade prolongs the Confederate right, in the process repelling some Yanks who have started to trickle around it. It also overlaps Hazen's left, which he pulls back in order to avoid being outflanked. There is no sign of Johnson's division, which was supposed to support the assault in this sector.

Hazen's men cling stubbornly to the slope of the ridge but suffer ever-mounting losses, their ammunition begins to run low, and they are approaching the limits of their physical and emotional endurance. Perceiving this and believing that the attack still can succeed if promptly supported, Hazen sends every member of his staff and several regimental officers to the rear with urgent pleas for reinforcements. None come. Finally, after fifty minutes of sustained combat, Hazen's surviving troops start falling back. He makes no attempt to stop them.

At this very moment Wood orders forward Gibson's brigade. Why he had not had it follow Hazen immediately, as originally planned, and why he has not responded to Hazen's calls for reinforcements, he never explains; nor, for that matter, does Howard. As to why he now has Gibson attack, according to his report he believes that "a second effort might be more successful than the first had been."

It proves to be a badly mistaken belief. Gibson's troops, first-class midwesterners, follow much the same route as Hazen's and suffer an identical fate. They manage to reach the ridge and start up it, only to be brought to a dead halt—in a great many cases quite literally so—by an invisible but impenetrable barrier of lead and iron. Here and there a few of them, caught up in the passion of battle, rush forward to within several yards of the enemy before being shot down, thereby achieving future praise in regimental histories but nothing else. Also like Hazen's men they have no support on either flank. To their left Scribner's brigade of Johnson's division, which at long last has moved forward, goes to ground on coming under enfilade fire from Kelly's cavalry, posted atop some hills adjoining the creek. To their right a Confederate rifled battery and two of Captain Key's howitzers, taking advantage of the continued quiescence of McLean's brigade, rake them at close range with shells, canister, and solid shot. After about an hour, again emulating Hazen's troops, they begin falling back—those, that is, who are able to.

Meanwhile Gibson's regimental commanders, being unable to locate him, have been sending officers directly to Wood with requests for reinforcements. One of these messengers is Captain Cyrus Askew of the 15th Ohio. He finds Gibson with Wood. Both are "laboring under terrible stress" and so excited that he doubts that they understand what he is saying. Then Howard rides up, dismounts, and asks Askew to describe the situation up front. He does so, whereupon Howard declares, "Go back and tell the men that I will have more troops sent in both on their right and left as soon as I can get them."

Askew turns, takes a few steps, and then suddenly a shell strikes the ground and explodes behind him. He looks back and sees Howard throw the stump of his amputated right arm over his eyes and hears him exclaim, "I am afraid to look down! I am afraid to look down!" He rushes to the general's side and tells him that a shell fragment has struck his left foot but has merely torn off the heel of the boot. Howard is "much relieved"; he feared that his foot had been mangled and that he would have to endure another amputation. As it is, the foot is so badly bruised and swollen that he can neither walk nor ride but must sit on the ground while receiving reports and issuing orders.

By now most of Hazen's survivors have straggled back to a clearing near Pickett's Mill where he endeavors to rally and reorganize them. This proves difficult. They are in a "bad humor" and complain of being "sold out." Eventually he collects a "small fragment," which Howard sends to the right to guard against an enemy counterattack. McLean, who should be covering that flank, is marching his troops back to their camp, alleging that they need rations!

At 6 P.M., almost exactly an hour after his attack got under way, Howard receives Thomas's dispatch, which is marked 5:15, conveying Sherman's order to cancel the attack and go over to the defense. Neither in his report nor in his *Autobiography* does Howard describe his reaction to this dispatch or otherwise comment on it. From one standpoint, comment is unnecessary; from another, this is merely the sort of thing that happens in war. Whatever the case, Howard immediately instructs Wood to send his remaining brigade, Colonel Frederick Knefler's, to the front with instructions to hold the Confederates in check until a regular defense line can be established around Pickett's Mill.

About 6:30, Knefler's brigade advances through the woods and into the ravine. At once it discovers, in Knefler's words, that the ravine is "completely enfiladed" by rifle and artillery fire. His troops are "thrown into disorder" and fall back to the woods, where they hastily erect a rail-and-stone barricade, then begin shooting at the crest of the ridge. After a while the 37th Indiana and the 78th Pennsylvania from Scribner's brigade join them; the rest of that brigade, however, remains to the rear with its commander, who according to Sergeant Puntenney of the 37th Indiana, is either drunk or becoming so.

Both Federals and Confederates pump bullets at each other across the ravine until it is totally dark. Then the firing ceases except for occasional flareups and an occasional Rebel shell lobbed into the area around the mill. One of these projectiles strikes General Johnson a glancing blow in the side but does not explode, and he is only "somewhat injured"—enough, though, to compel him to relinquish command of his division to Brigadier General John H. King.

For the next two hours, details of Knefler's troops, guarded by a screen of skirmishers, remove as many of Hazen's and Gibson's wounded from the ravine as they can. Up on the ridge, Captain Foster hears "the Yankees . . . moving among the dead leaves on the ground like hogs rooting for acorns." Then at 10 P.M., Knefler receives an order to withdraw; Howard's defense line has been completed. By coincidence, at that very moment, Granbury, who has obtained permission from Cleburne to "clear" his front, tells a bugler to sound the charge. The bugle rings out, and with a "regular Texas yell," Granbury's troops rush down the ridge and into the ravine, all the while screaming "like all the devils from the lower regions" and firing their rifles even though they cannot, Foster records, "see anything at all." Surprised by this sudden onslaught and shaken by the "demonic yells" that accompany it, the Federals fire a ragged, harmless volley, then flee. The Texans, following hard on their heels, catch and take many of them prisoner, or else come upon bunches of terrified bluecoats lying behind logs and crying, "Don't shoot! Don't shoot!" The chase continues until the Texans reach the other side of the ravine, where they take more captives but lose the trail. In the proud words of Cleburne's report (written, like all of his reports, by Captain Irving Buck, his adjutant and future biographer), "It needed but the brilliance of this night attack to add lustre to the achievements of Granbury and his brigade in the afternoon."

Granbury's Brigade returns to the top of the ridge, leaving behind pickets to watch out for any fresh attempt by the enemy to advance. It is a prudent but unnecessary precaution. Except for two unused brigades in Johnson's division, the Federals have no units capable of offensive action, and their commander is in a state of physical and emotional anguish. Lying on the ground near a field hospital, with his foot throbbing and unable to sleep, Howard gazes upon a scene that will always remain in his memory as "a sort of nightmare": An "opening in the forest, faint fires here and there revealing men wounded, armless, legless and eyeless; some with heads bound up with cotton strips, some standing and walking nervously around, some sitting with bended forms, some prone on the earth." Others, "in despair," have "resorted to drink for relief," and the "sad sounds from those in pain [are] mingled with the oaths of the drunken and the more heartless." For Howard "no perdition here or hereafter can be worse."

If Howard had been down in the ravine, he could have seen even-worse things. There, when the sun begins rising, Captain Foster, who is on picket duty, discovers that he is literally surrounded by dead Yankees. He counts fifty of them within a thirty-foot radius: "Men lying in all sort of shapes and positions just as they had fallen, and it seems like they have nearly all been shot in the head, and a great number of them have their skulls bursted open and their brains running out." Although he has seen "many dead men, and seen them wounded and crippled in various ways," including their "limbs cut off," he feels sick, almost faint, and leaves the place as soon as he can.

A little later Johnston rides over the battlefield, then congratulates the Texans on their fight and tells Granbury, "This shall no longer be called Granbury's, but shall be known as Johnston's brigade." Cleburne in his report estimates the Union loss to be at least "3,000 killed and wounded" and puts his own at 448, obviously very low in comparison but high enough to indicate that his troops were not in a mere turkey shoot, especially since most of these casualties are concentrated in Granbury's Brigade. To the Confederates, Pickett's Mill is a glorious victory won against enormous odds, for they believe that they have been assailed by the entire IV Corps backed by the XIV Corps.

Actually, of course, one elite Confederate brigade, occupying a naturally strong position and supported by parts of two other brigades, well-posted artillery, and a sizable force of dismounted cavalry, has repulsed a determined but disjointed assault by two small Union brigades (Hazen's and Gibson's) and then has driven off another brigade (Knefler's) which was about to withdraw anyway. Furthermore, the Federal loss comes to little more than half Cleburne's estimate, being approximately 1,600 killed, wounded, and missing. As might be expected, most of it is in Hazen's brigade (467) and in Gibson's brigade (681), whereas Knefler's brigade lost only about 250, mainly prisoners, and Scribner's lost no more than 125, of whom 102 were in the 37th Indiana and the 78th Pennsylvania, the only regiments of that brigade to be seriously engaged. According to Howard in his *Autobiography,* 800 of the nearly 1,400 casualties in Wood's division consist of men killed in action, an exceptionally high proportion, because the normal ratio of dead to wounded in Civil War battles is one to five, and are probably the consequence of many of Hazen's and Scribner's men being struck repeatedly: the Confederates found one Federal corpse with 47 bullets in it. "I could of walked 2 or 3 hundred yards," a sergeant in Lowrey's Brigade writes to his wife two days after the slaughter at Pickett's Mill, "on the bodeys of the ded yanks."[135]

At 6 A.M. on May 28, Sherman telegraphs Halleck to report on what he has been doing and what he plans to do, something that Sherman does nearly every morning and sometimes in the evening too, providing thereby a sharp contrast to Johnston, who rarely communicates on his own initiative with Richmond except to ask for or complain about something. Sherman informs Halleck:

> The enemy discovered my move to turn Allatoona [it was designed to do much more than that!], and moved to meet us. . . . Johnston has chosen a strong line . . . and thus far has stopped us. . . . I am gradually working around by the left to approach the railroad anywhere in front of Acworth. . . . We have had many sharp, severe encounters [Williams's and Wood's troops would second that!], but nothing decisive. Both sides duly cautious in the obscurity of the ambushed ground.[136]

Sherman could add, although it would be embarrassing for him to do so, that he has another reason besides Johnston's "strong line" for wanting to "approach the railroad": much to his dismay (indeed, at first he refused to believe it), his army is hungry. Soldiers are on three-fourth's rations, and on some days get "only enough to tease their appetites," horses and mules are gnawing the bark off of trees, and beef cattle are chewing on bushes. How can this be, particularly since Sherman had ordered his troops to take along provisions for twenty days? One answer is that because each regiment is limited to one wagon (Confederate regiments have at least three), it cannot carry with it that much food and so must rely on the divisional and corps quartermaster trains. A second answer, closely related to the first, is that these trains are experiencing great difficulty in distributing rations in the north Georgia wilderness where, to quote Sherman, there are "no roads of any consequence." And the third answer comes from Rufus Mead, commissary sergeant of the 5th Connecticut in Williams's division, who on June 4 writes his parents that "it is 20 miles or more to Kingston, our base of supplies, and it is difficult to get supplies fast enough." Thus, both because of and in spite of his huge wagon train, Sherman has found that he cannot maintain his army for a prolonged period of time when distant from the railroad. This discovery will be an important consideration in his operations during the remainder of the campaign.[137]

But before Sherman can shift to the railroad at Acworth, he first must do two things: unite McPherson with the rest of the army and secure access to the road to Acworth. Accordingly his orders for May 28 call for McPherson to vacate his lines around Dallas and take up a new position on Thomas's right; for Davis's division, once McPherson's movement is under way, to rejoin the XIV Corps, which then will take over the XXIII Corps's sector; and for Schofield to "move out to the main Acworth road" and cover Thomas's left. Meanwhile, since McPherson will not start pulling out of his works until night (it would be too risky to do it in daylight) and since Schofield cannot go anywhere until relieved by the XIV Corps, Howard (so Sherman directs him via Thomas) will protect his and the army's left flank against a turning movement by "barricading it" and, if need be, "refusing it"—that is, forming it at a right angle to the front line.[138]

Sherman's concern about his left is justified, more so than he knows. Even as he issues his orders, Hood's entire corps is on the way to try to outflank and attack it. During the previous evening, Wheeler had informed Hood that the Union left along Little Pumpkinvine Creek appeared to be "in the air." Hood at once had gone to Johnston and proposed that he pull his corps out of the line, swing around to the northeast, and if Wheeler's report proved true, crush the exposed enemy flank. Johnston had agreed and had ordered Polk and Hardee to be ready to join in Hood's attack once it got under way. As soon as it was dark, Hood's troops had withdrawn from their positions and Polk's had taken their place, the exchange occurring so silently that the Federals, in spite of being only seventy-five yards away in some places, had noticed nothing. By midnight Hood was marching toward what he and Johnston hoped would be a smashing victory in the morning.

Hood's march, however, has been a long one—five to six miles—and a slow one, with frequent halts; it simply is impossible for a large force to move quickly through such country at night. Not until around 6 A.M. does he approach the area where the supposedly vulnerable enemy flank lies. As he does so, Wheeler's scouts bring bad news: the Federals have fallen back to the other (north) side of Little Pumpkinvine Creek and have erected breastworks. Hood promptly orders a halt and sends Lieutenant B. H. Blanton to inform Johnston of this development and to ask for further instructions. Blanton delivers the message to Johnston at Cleburne's headquarters, where he is waiting anxiously for Hood's attack to begin. Disappointed, Johnston sends back an order for Hood to return and take position on Polk's right. Too little would be gained and too much might be lost by proceeding with the attack.

Later, in his report and his *Narrative*, Johnston will accuse Hood of doing the same thing he allegedly had done at Cassville—throwing away a golden opportunity to smite Sherman a stunning blow. In all likelihood, however, the only opportunity that has been thrown away is one of suffering a costly setback. Although Howard's forces in fact have not fallen back to the north side of Little Pumpkinvine Creek, they would have had ample time to discover the Confederate threat and prepare to defend against it while Hood's weary, sleep-starved troops were forming in the junglelike woods for an assault; they would also have had ample strength to hold Hood in check until, as on the first day at Resaca, reinforcements could come to their aid. Not even Lieutenant Mackall's postwar "journal," fabricated to support Johnston in his efforts to discredit Hood, describes Johnston as being dissatisfied with Hood's conduct on May 28.[139]

But if it is impracticable to attack the enemy's left, what about his right? After the cancellation of Hoods' foray, Johnston receives reports (probably from observers atop Elsberry Mountain) that the Federals around Dallas are moving northward. This erroneous information causes him to conclude, as he had yesterday, that Sherman is endeavoring to pull back. Therefore he orders Hardee to have Bate, whose division is on the Confederate left, "develop the enemy" east of Dallas and "ascertain his strength and position, as it is believed he is not in force." If this does prove to be the case, then Bate is to attack and take the Union works on his front.

Bate, whose men call him "Old Grits," is a thirty-seven-year-old Tennessean with a well-deserved reputation as a bold battlefield leader even though he needs a crutch to walk because of a crippling wound suffered at Shiloh, where he prevented a surgeon from amputating his shattered leg by threatening to shoot him if he tried. Bate has at his disposal his own division, three brigades totaling about 5,000 troops, and Jackson's cavalry, who are covering the left flank and number approximately the same. After consulting with his brigade commanders and Jackson, Bate issues the following orders: Armstrong's Brigade of Jackson's Division will charge first; if it encounters little or no resistance, four cannon shots will be fired in rapid succession and Bate's infantry, formed into three separate and widely spaced brigade columns, will attack too. On the other hand, should Armstrong find the Federals present in strong force, there will be no signal shots, and the whole operation will be suspended. Bate believes, however, that there will be little if any opposition, an opinion shared by his brigadiers and Jackson.

Around 3 P.M., Armstrong's troopers, dismounted, occupy the breastworks hitherto held by Bate's Division, now deploying to the right. Worried by the sharp rifle fire coming from the Union line, which he cannot see because of underbrush even though it is only a couple of hundred yards away, Lieutenant Colonel Frank Montgomery of the 1st Mississippi Cavalry climbs to the top of a nearby hill on which one of Bate's batteries is located. He peers through an embrasure, and instantly a half-dozen bullets hiss by his head, causing him to jump back. But he has gotten a view of the Yankee fortifications, and it was not a pleasant one. They are strong, filled with infantry, and packed with artillery. Returning to his regiment, he informs its commander, Colonel R. A. Pinson, of what he has seen. Pinson replies that he has just talked to Armstrong, who has told him that Bate is confident that the enemy have only a skirmish line around Dallas. Montgomery says no more and resigns himself to making an attack that he considers foredoomed. A soldier has no other choice.

At 3:45 a cannon shot signals the attack, and Armstrong's men—Mississippians and Alabamans who have served under Forrest and are accustomed to fighting as infantry—dash forward with a savage yell that an Illinois soldier opposite them thinks "the devil ought to copyright." Their onslaught is so sudden and swift that they capture numerous enemy pickets, overrun three cannons of the 1st Iowa Battery which is posted in front of the main Union line, and swarm through a gap in the Yankee entrenchments, which at this point are manned by two brigades of Harrow's division of the XV Corps. But they go no further. A counterattack by the 6th Iowa drives them out and retakes the

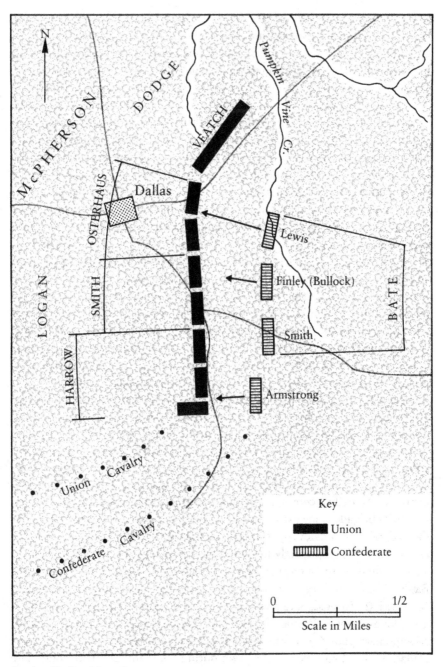

Battle of Dallas, May 28

cannons; and Logan, yelling "Give them hell boys!" personally brings up reinforcements. Realizing that they are hopelessly outnumbered and outgunned, all
of Armstrong's men who are still on their feet use them to scramble back to their
breastworks. They have discovered what Lieutenant Colonel Montgomery (who
is unscathed) already knew: Sherman's right still is held in "adequate force."

Bate now also knows it. He orders the signal cannons not to fire, and he
sends couriers to inform his brigadiers that there will be no attack. The message
quickly reaches Lieutenant Colonel Thomas B. Smith of the Tennessee Brigade,
who is acting commander of Tyler's Tennessee Brigade, but does not reach the
commanders of Finley's Florida Brigade and Lewis's Kentucky Brigade. Misled
by the tumult occasioned by Armstrong's charge, they assume that an all-out
attack is under way and that they have been unable to hear the four rapid
cannon shots signaling it. Hence they launch a series of fierce but uncoordinated assaults against the left of the XV Corps and the right of Veatch's division
of the XVI Corps. The Federals, whose fortifications along this part of the front
consist of a double tier of log-and-dirt ramparts, mow the Floridians and
Kentuckians down by the hundreds: "a heap of human beings, one over the
other, writhing in their blood," is how Private John Bueguel of the 3rd Missouri
describes it. Some of the Kentuckians, who rank among the best troops in the
Confederate army, make it to within fifty yards of the Union breastworks, and
none fall back until ordered to do so. Some of their wounded crawl away
through the weeds and brush, "leaving a bloody track behind them."

Around 6 P.M. the Southern onslaughts cease. Even the veterans of the Army
of the Tennessee are impressed by their ferocity. "Talk about fighting, etc.,"
Captain Wills of the 103rd Illinois jots in his diary, "we've seen it this p.m.
sure." Logan's soldiers believe they have been attacked by Hardee's whole
corps. They also claim to have killed and wounded 3,000 to 4,000 Rebels. This
is as absurd as Johnston's subsequent assertion that the Confederate loss is a
mere 300. Actually it comes to at least 1,000 and perhaps as many as 1,500: the
Kentucky brigade alone lost 51 percent of the 1,100 men it took into battle. On
the Federal side, Logan reports 379 casualties in his corps, which under the
circumstances is surprisingly high; and the commander of the only brigade of
Veatch's division to be engaged does not record any losses at all. In sum, the
Battle of Dallas, as it becomes known, is practically a mirror image of Pickett's
Mill, with the Confederates now being the ones to make a valiant but bumbling
and bloody assault. Furthermore, it was utterly unnecessary, for as Colonel
Montgomery points out, if the Federals in fact had only a skirmish line around
Dallas, it would have been withdrawn during the night, and Bate could have
occupied the Union works in the morning without firing a shot or losing a
man.[140]

Part Five: The Hell Hole

Bate's fiasco does accomplish one thing: It causes McPherson to request Sherman to postpone the leftward shift of the XV and XVI corps until tomorrow night. "I do not know," he writes Sherman at 6:25 P.M., "how I can move tonight; besides the effect on our men will be bad." After discussing the matter with McPherson, Sherman agrees and informs Thomas and Schofield of the change in plans. Both Sherman and McPherson fear that the Confederates, who obviously realize that McPherson is trying to withdraw, intend a full-scale night assault at Dallas, a fear that is seemingly confirmed by a captured Rebel officer who states that an attack will take place at midnight.

On orders from McPherson, Logan's and Dodge's troops remain in their trenches all night, on the alert, with no thought of sleep. But there is no attack, and with the arrival of morning the now-routine "heavy skirmishing" resumes all along the front. Several times during the day, bands of Confederates sally forth in attempts to recover their dead from Bate's assault but are driven off before they can reach them. "It is considered," comments Private John B. Brobst of the 25th Wisconsin in a letter he is writing to his wife, Mary, "a great victory when the dead and wounded fall in the hands of the enemy. We have got all ours taken care of, and a good share of the enemy's." An Ohio soldier in the XV Corps who helps bury some of the Southern slain writes that they are "very dirty, and mostly shot in the head and upper part of the body." In some places the Confederate corpses already are half-covered by dirt thrown up by the shells and bullets that have turned them into corpses.[141]

The day passes without any major offensive actions by either army. Sherman simply is waiting for night so that McPherson again can try to link up with Thomas; Johnston's strategy (so General Mackall informs his wife) is "to keep close up to the enemy" and "watch carefully." Although Johnston is aware of the long gap in the Union front between McPherson and Thomas, his own forces are similarly divided, and he dares not weaken either wing for fear of an attack or flanking move. In a sense he is like a wrestler who has caught a stronger opponent in a hold that might not bring victory but at least will prevent defeat as long as he can maintain it. By the same token, Sherman must break this hold in order to gain a new chance to use his superior strength to win.[142]

Though there are no large-scale assaults or flanking movements, there is plenty of fighting, fighting of a type that hitherto had been unprecedented in this or any other war except during sieges, but that now has been going on in this north Georgia wilderness (as it is in northern Virginia) since May 25 and will continue for many days to come. The opposing armies face each other along a front that runs, twisting and turning, approximately ten miles, from south of Dallas to northeast of Pickett's Mill. Except for a few sectors where they are either much closer or much farther apart, the main lines are between two hundred yards and a half-mile apart and are screened from each other by intervening timber and underbrush. Therefore, both sides employ strong skirmish or picket lines at all times to provide timely warning of an attack and to slow it down. Usually operating in teams of three—that way at least one man is always ready to shoot—the skirmishers have taken to occupying miniature rifle pits called "skirmish pits," often complete with a head log, from where they engage opposing skirmishers and fire at the enemy's main works if practicable. In addition, swarms of sharpshooters, the Confederates with their Whitworths and Kerrs, the Federals with equally deadly Ballards, station themselves in treetops or other vantage points from which they snipe away from dawn to dusk with such effectiveness that in many sectors it is the equivalent of suicide for anyone on the picket or front lines to expose himself for even a split second. As usual their favorite targets are officers and cannoneers; for example, Lieutenant Mackall records that Yankee sharpshooters had killed the colonel and a captain of the 1st Missouri and forty men and forty horses in an artillery battalion during the course of just one day.

Of course, the cannoneers do their own share of killing. Wherever and whenever they think they can do some, they set to work. Most of the time they fire single shots or salvos, with more or less long intervals between them; but if the enemy's main line is both visible and vulnerable, they unleash full-fledged bombardments designed to make it untenable. Thus an exposed salient held by Stanley's division suffers a steady pounding throughout the daylight hours which forces the defenders to spend each night repairing and further strengthening their fortifications; among other things they increase the dirt embankment from the normal four feet to twelve, having discovered that solid shot at close range can bore through less. Even where they are not subject to such intense fire, the troops constantly improve and expand their defenses, creating in the process a veritable maze of breastworks, trenches, traverses, communication ditches, and "sleep pits," the latter for sheltering oneself while in the so-called rear. So complex and extensive are these works and so easy is it to lose one's sense of direction in the all-encompassing forests and thickets, that there are numerous cases of men, squads, and even entire companies and regiments getting lost, taking up positions that face the wrong way, or wandering into or behind enemy lines.

Where the fronts are in close proximity (in some sectors, notably the Confederate one held by Cantey's Division, they are less than a hundred yards apart), pickets are impossible, and thus each side persistently endeavors to hold or, better still, force the other back to a safer distance. One method for doing this, rarely used because it rarely succeeds, is direct assault. Another, more practical and therefore more common, is to rush forward under cover of darkness while carrying logs that can quickly be piled up into a crude but servicable parapet atop high ground overlooking the enemy's position, leaving him little choice except to retreat. But the most common tactic, since it is the easiest and safest, is simply to blast away at the other side's entrenchments in hopes of making them untenable. Their superior artillery gives Sherman's men the advantage in this type of fighting; thus out of 126 Confederate shells fired one day at that part of the front held by Harrow's division of the XV Corps, only nineteen explode. Furthermore, some Rebel regiments, equipped with smoothbores or other inferior weapons, cannot cope with Yankee rifle fire and so must call for help from neighboring units armed with Enfields or Springfields. Yet on the whole the Southerners give as good as they get, and sometimes better, for example when some of French's troops kill twenty-one Federals "one after the other" in a single rifle pit. Small wonder that Sherman's soldiers have started referring to this area as "the hell hole."

Because they are so evenly matched and their defenses are so strong, little ground is gained or lost by either side. By the same token all of the tens of thousands of bullets, shells, and cannonballs that they fire at each other, while shredding and shattering countless trees and cutting down acres of brush, produce relatively few casualties. What they mainly do is subject the soldiers to the constant danger of dying. Writes musician Albert Porter of the 33rd Mississippi, for the time being in the front line: "The bullets are whistling over us constantly. A ball has just struck a man belonging to the 1st Mississippi. I heard the ball strike him very plainly. No doubt he died instantly, as the ball struck him in the side." And Henry Noble of the 19th Michigan notes in his diary: "Today we are lying behind a line of breastworks where the bullets are constantly whipping over our heads and scarcely an hour passes without someone getting wounded." In some ways the strain of this sort of warfare, which is compounded by sleeplessness, rain, mud, cold nights, and what Colonel Aden Cavins of the 97th Indiana describes as "the smell of gore and decaying men," is worse than a regular battle which, however horrible it may be, at least has the virtue of usually ending in a few hours. Some men crack under it, physically and emotionally, and are sent back to the hospitals; others seek to escape by pretending to be ill or skulking about far in the rear. Even veteran regiments have chronic malingerers and "coffee coolers," as they are called in the Union army, who somehow always seem to manage to stay or get out of any "hot place." But the vast majority, like Porter and Noble, neither of whom pretends to heroism, huddle behind their parapets or crouch in their rifle pits, grimly enduring. They are the sort of men who make this war or any war possible.[143]

During the afternoon of May 29, McPherson's reserve wagons and artillery pass through Dallas and head north along the Burnt Hickory road. Then, as soon as it is fully dark, his main force and Garrard's cavalry prepare to follow. But at 10 P.M., just as Logan's and Dodge's troops are about to leave their breastworks, firing breaks out along the skirmish line, and a few minutes later, pickets come running back, shouting "Boys, they're comin'!" At once they poke their rifle barrels beneath the headlogs and start shooting. In the flickering light created by the flash of their rifles and of the cannons that quickly open up also, it seems to them that large masses of Confederates are swarming toward them through the woods. They beat off one onslaught, but after a short time, there is another, then another, and again another. Captain Wills of the 103rd Illinois counts eight separate assaults on the XV Corps, and Private Brobst of the 25th Wisconsin enumerates four against the XVI Corps. "Braver men," he informs his wife, Mary, "never shouldered a musket than those rebels that came up to drive us out of our works. We piled up their dead and wounded in perfect masses." Finally, at daybreak, the attacks cease, and the Confederates disappear from view. Many Union soldiers, utterly exhausted, flop down and go to sleep instantly. Not a few officers, who have facilities for doing such, gulp down whiskey or brandy; one of them, Lieutenant Colonel Benjamin Myers of the 83rd Indiana, gets so drunk that in a "crazy fit" he makes a solo charge on the enemy and is killed. "I don't know when I have been so used up as this morning," Captain Wills writes in his diary, "and the whole command is not far from the same condition." For Joseph Saunier of the 47th Ohio, the night just passed is "the hardest one we had to endure during the war."

It has been a hard night, too, for Bate's and Cleburne's troops, who are the ones confronting the XV and XVI corps. However, this is not because they have been piled up in "perfect masses" while making gallant, repeated, but futile charges. On the contrary, apart from some routine skirmish-line probes, they have never attacked or even attempted to attack! Instead the intermittent but persistent storm of Yankee shot and shell that has swept over their lines has caused them to think that they were the ones under attack; so, like Logan's and Dodge's men, they have spent a sleepless night banging away with their rifles (the Confederate artillery, not having ammunition to waste, has prudently withheld its fire for observable targets). Probably what happened was that some of the Union pickets, worried about being left behind and captured when McPherson withdrew, saw or heard Confederate skirmishers advancing toward them, jumped to the conclusion that a full-scale assault was under way, and so ran back to spread the alarm, thereby touching off the "battle." In any event, there has been, again to quote Captain Wills, "a good deal more shooting than killing on both sides."[144]

Even so, this attack-that-was-never-made produces the same effect as Bate's attack-that-should-not-have-been-made: it prevents McPherson from withdrawing. Only Garrard's cavalry division, which likewise has spent the night battling largely imaginary assailants, manages to pull away on the extreme right and reach the Burnt Hickory road. The division is in terrible shape. The men have gone without sleep for seventy-two hours, and their horses are literally dropping from hunger, having had no forage for five days. "These old Alatoona [*sic*] Mountains," growls Sergeant Ben McGee in his journal-history of the 72nd Indiana Mounted Infantry, "are the most God-forsaken country we ever saw; two whippoorwills could scarcely get a living on a mile square, and if a third one should come on a visit, he would have to bring his rations or all three would starve to death."145

Thus the problem of extracting McPherson from the not-so-loving embrace of the Confederates persists. During the morning, Sherman goes to look into the matter himself and, around noon, rides along the Army of the Tennessee's front with McPherson and Logan. After this excursion, during which Logan suffers a slight wound in his left arm, Sherman orders McPherson to make another attempt to withdraw on the night of May 31: after last night's pyrotechnics the troops are too tired to try it tonight. In addition he directs Stoneman and Garrard to proceed by separate routes to Allatoona Pass and occupy it so as to open the way for the establishment of rail connections with Acworth once the army reaches that place. As to reaching it, Sherman has worked out, in conjunction with Thomas, a plan whereby Schofield will move out to the extreme left, northeast of Pickett's Mill, and seize the main road to Acworth once the Union forces are united and he can pull out of the position he presently occupies on Howard's right.

On the morning of May 31, Sherman sends detailed instructions to McPherson on how to make his next breakaway attempt, at the same time assuring him that "if the enemy follows, he will do so cautiously, and I feel no doubt will be easily repulsed." McPherson in turn issues even-more-detailed instructions to Logan, Dodge, and Davis: At 10 P.M., Colonel August Mersy's brigade of Sweeny's division will slide to the left and take over a fortified position on the Marietta road now held by Mitchell's brigade of Davis's division. Then at daybreak the XV and XVI corps will fall back division by division, starting on the right, to a new line of breastworks just east of Dallas that have been constructed by pioneer troops and that are manned by reserve infantry and artillery. Once this movement, which is to be screened at all times by the skirmish line, has been completed, then the rest of Davis's division will pull out to rejoin the XIV Corps, and the XV and XVI corps will take its place, in the process linking up with Hooker. The device of a staggered, division-by-division withdrawal evidently comes from Sherman, who prescribes it in his instructions to McPherson. As to the new defense line in the rear, that also might be Sherman's idea, the result of yesterday's visit to McPherson, although Logan's report hints that he originated it. Regardless of who deserves the credit, McPherson's plan to disengage avoids the danger inherent in the simultaneous retirement of all of his forces and enables them to retreat to previously prepared and already defended fortifications.

At 10 P.M., right on schedule, Mersy's brigade leaves its breastworks and marches by a newly cut road to Dallas, from where it then moves by way of the Marietta road to relieve Mitchell's brigade, which is located midway in the gap between McPherson and Thomas. Next, at daylight, the rest of the Army of the Tennessee begins vacating the line it has held, and which in a sense has held it, for so long. Although Johnston's observers atop Elsberry Mountain see Union troops moving north from Dallas, the Confederates make no attack or in any way interfere. In fact, if diaries and other sources are a valid indication, not even their skirmishers are aware that the Federals are pulling back. Thus by the morning of June 1, Sherman is well on the way to reuniting his army, the indispensable first step toward shifting it to Acworth and a new approach to reaching Atlanta.[146]

It now has been a month since Grant launched the offensive that was to knock out Lee, take Richmond, and decide the war. So far it has failed. Defeated in the Wilderness and stymied at Spotsylvania Court House, Grant, like Sherman, has been able to advance only by taking advantage of his superior numbers to carry out flanking maneuvers that have forced Lee, like Johnston, to retreat. Furthermore, a supplementary offensive designed to drive the Confederates out of the Shenandoah Valley, their Virginia breadbasket, has ended in a humiliating rout at New Market. And an attempt by Major General Benjamin F. Butler's Army of the James to cut off and perhaps seize Richmond from the south has had an even more humiliating outcome: Beauregard, hastily summoned from Charleston and with a much smaller force, not only has stopped Butler but has shoved him onto a narrow peninsula at Bermuda Hundred where he is, in Grant's words, "in a bottle strongly corked." But worst of all, in one month's time, Grant has lost close to 40,000 men. This is a staggering toll, especially since most of the casualties are first-class veterans who can be replaced in quantity out of the North's manpower reservoir but not in quality.

The last day of May finds Grant completing his fifth flanking march of the campaign, one that has taken him via Hanover Court House to the Chickahominy River near a village called Cold Harbor. Although Lee again has managed to get in front of him, Lee's army is stretched perilously thin. Grant knows this; he also knows that if he can smash through here, nothing will be able to stop him from reaching Richmond, which is only eight miles away.

May 31 also witnesses a flanking maneuver of the political kind. Its locale is Cleveland, Ohio, and it takes the form of a convention of ultra-Radical Republicans. They believe that Lincoln should not and cannot be reelected because of his immoral refusal to make the total elimination of slavery the be-all and end-all of the war, thereby causing it to drag on endlessly, even though, in the words of Wendell Phillips, "for three years the Administration has poured out the public treasure and blood of the country like water." Accordingly the convention forms a new political party, which it dubs the Radical Democracy, nominates for president John C. Frémont, the Republican standard-bearer of 1856, and adopts a platform that, among other things, calls for the confiscation of "the lands of the rebels and their distribution among the soldiers and actual settlers"—that is, former slaves. Few if any of the four hundred or so delegates, a hodgepodge of fanatics and malcontents, think that Frémont actually can win the election. What they hope to do is to pressure the Republican convention, scheduled to meet a week hence in Baltimore, to pass over Lincoln in favor of a candidate who would be more sympathetic to their ideas and aspirations. But even in this they have no chance of success: every Northern state delegation to the Baltimore convention is controlled by Lincoln loyalists. The only thing the Frémont movement conceivably can do is help the Democrats win a close election by depriving Lincoln of votes he otherwise would get. Some of the Radical Republicans, at least, are willing to let that happen: "If Mr. Lincoln is re-elected," Phillips warns, "I do not expect to see the Union reconstructed in my day, unless on terms more disastrous to liberty than even disunion would be."[147]

Democratic leaders, as the bloody month of May ends, feel both increasing bitterness and increasing hope. The bitterness derives from what they can only view as a deliberate and vicious campaign by the Republicans and Lincoln's administration to suppress their party by violence and persecution. Since January, no less than twenty Democratic newspapers have been destroyed, attacked, or threatened by mobs of Republican Union Leaguers and soldiers; at least a half-dozen others have been shut down for varying lengths of time, and their editors have been arrested by governmental officials. The most flagrant cases of the latter are the most recent: on May 10 a United States marshal arrested, on a charge of "conspiracy," Samuel Medary, the sixty-three-year-old editor of the *Columbus* (Ohio) *Crisis*; and eight days afterwards the commander of the Military District of New York imprisoned the editors of the *New York World* and the *Financial Chronicle* and suspended the publication of their papers for two days because they made the mistake of printing a proclamation, ostensibly issued by Lincoln but actually concocted by a gold speculator, in which the president supposedly announced that as a consequence of Northern military defeats, he was setting aside a day for "fasting, humiliation, and prayer" and was calling up 400,000 more troops, to be raised "by an immediate peremptory draft." Not until the editors proved that they had published the bogus proclamation in the sincere belief that it was genuine—some Republican editors did the same—were they released and their papers allowed to resume operation.

As for the Democrats' increasing hope, that comes from Virginia. They fully realize that if Grant wins there this spring or summer, they will lose in the fall. But so far he has not won, and they are beginning to think, like Ohio Copperhead Robert Dun, that "Grant has gone up 'like a rocket & will come down like a stick.'" Most of them are not inclined as yet to declare this openly: 1863 had demonstrated the danger of premature predictions of defeat. Thus for the time being they confine themselves to playing up Grant's enormous losses, pointing out that McClellan got to the gates of Richmond at far less cost, unctuously urging Lincoln to cease his "persecution" of the victor of Antietam and make him a sort of assistant commander to Grant, and asserting that the Confederates, given no choice by Lincoln's Emancipation Proclamation except to keep on fighting, are as strong as ever. But they are confident that if Grant does fail, then they will be vindicated in their contention that the Union can be restored only by peace. For this reason and because as a rule they already are agreed on their presidential candidate—it will be McClellan—they have postponed their nominating convention, originally scheduled for early July, to the end of August.[148] This is an unprecedentedly late date for such an event since some states hold their elections in October; but by then the outcome of Grant's campaign surely will be known and definite. And if it is defeat or even anything short of victory, then it will be victory for the Democratic party when Northern voters go to the polls.

CHAPTER SIX

JUNE

Part One: Acworth

JUNE 1 is another hot, sultry day, like every day since the terrible thunderstorm on the night of May 25. Sitting behind a breastwork on the XX Corps's front line, forty-four-year-old Sergeant Phinehas Hager of the 19th Michigan writes his wife in Otsego, Michigan:

> We are exposed to sharpshooters all through the day and we have been aroused by heavy firing every night since the 26th inst. . . . It is trying to the nerves to be in such circumstances. . . . The boys are very much tired out, and several have gone to the rear. I perceive that our men are very much affected by the circumstances under which we are placed. There is not half the levity and profanity that I have usually seen in camp. Few men can look upon death with indifference, especially upon death under such appalling circumstances. . . . O God! when will men cease to be such Demons?[1]

Late in the morning, Sergeant Hager and the other troops of the XX Corps behold a welcome sight: the arrival of the XV Corps. Riding at its head is Logan himself, "black and swarthy, with a heavy mustache, looking like the part Indian he was said to be," writes Major Stephen Pierson of the 33rd New Jersey, who adds that "never before or since did man look more handsome to me than he did." As quickly but as quietly as possible, Hooker's men withdraw from the positions they have held for the past week, and Logan's veterans move into them. The XX Corps then marches about six miles to the northeast and bivouacs in the rear of the Union left near Pickett's Mill. Meanwhile, at 5 P.M., Stoneman's cavalrymen reach Allatoona, which they find undefended and deserted, and secure control of the railroad between Acworth and the Etowah. When Sherman lies down for his customary short night's sleep, he knows that at last he can make his oft-postponed movement back to the railroad and out of what his troops have aptly dubbed the Hell-Hole.[2]

Johnston, thanks to his cavalry scouts and the observers atop Elsberry Mountain, realizes that the Federals have pulled out of the Dallas area and are shifting to the northeast. But does this mean that they are retreating? Reports that their horses and mules are starving point to this pleasing possibility. Or as seems more probable, are they again trying to turn his right flank? Owing to this uncertainty, he cancels a "Confidential Circular" that he had issued in the morning directing a retreat during the night to a new line along Lost Mountain, and he transfers Cleburne's Division from the far left to the far right.[3] As a result, Sherman still faces the problem of breaking free from Johnston's close embrace, whereas had he retained McPherson's forces at Dallas for just one more day, he would be able, come tomorrow, to march unhindered to Acworth and the railroad. War of course, abounds in such ironies.

The Confederates who enter Dallas find twenty or thirty of their wounded lying in hospitals, "limbs amputated and undressed for two days," their wounds crawling with maggots. Although some of the Confederate dead are "neatly buried," reports a "Special Correspondent" of the *Appeal,* others lie rotting on the ground. The same correspondent adds that "aside from taking everything which the people had to eat and acting haughtily and insultingly," the Federals while in Dallas had not been guilty of any "unusual brutality," and many had been "polite and gentlemanly," notably General McPherson. On the other hand a woman whose house Sherman occupied as headquarters has described him to the correspondent as "haughty and snobbish, even repulsive," with a "pug nose" and "short, red beard and mustache." All of the Yankees "boasted of their humanity, their superior power, and the justness of their cause" and spoke of the "capture of Atlanta and speedy end of this wicked rebellion . . . as early certainties."[4]

Rain begins falling early on the morning of June 2 and continues all day, becoming heavy at times. The troops on both sides welcome the downpour as a relief from the heat and humidity of the past week. Before the month ends, they will look back upon their reaction to the rain with wry amusement.

Along the front lines the skirmishing and sniping resume. Behind the Union left, Schofield's corps, which has been relieved during the night by the XIV Corps, moves up the Allatoona road with orders from Sherman to turn the Confederate right "so as to get on the waters of Allatoona Creek," about two miles northeast of Pickett's Mill. Butterfield's division supports the movement, having been detached from its own corps for this purpose.

Schofield's column encounters "obstinate" Confederate skirmishers and an "almost impenetrable" forest of loblolly pine "so dense that one cannot see two rods." As a consequence the going is slow and arduous, halts are frequent, and despite the use of compasses, whole skirmish lines become lost and have to be replaced with new ones. Not until evening, by which time the rain has turned into a torrential deluge, does Cox's division, which is in the van, reach Alla-toona Creek. Its first line crosses the stream and immediately comes under fire from strong enemy fortifications backed by artillery. At Cox's request, Hascall swings his division around to the left, hoping to outflank the Confederates, but he also finds himself confronted by well-manned fieldworks. His skirmishers, however, report that these works do not extend much further and can be turned. Hascall passes this information on to Schofield. Since Hovey's division is too far to the rear to come up before dark, Schofield sends a staff officer, then goes himself, to ask Butterfield (being junior in rank, Schofield dare not order him) to deploy his division on Hascall's left: if Butterfield will "put in" just one brigade, it will "give us a footing beyond his [the enemy's] parapet."

Butterfield, whose army nickname, sarcastically intoned, is "Dan the Mag-nificent," answers that his orders are merely to support Schofield, not engage in an attack. Behind his refusal to cooperate with Schofield is utter contempt for that general and his so-called Army of the Ohio. Understandably enough, Schofield resents Butterfield's recalcitrance; in his memoirs he retaliates by claiming that subsequent investigation has "demonstrated that our skirmishers were right, and that a single brigade on our left would have been ample to turn the enemy's flank and open the way to victory." In fact, however, Johnston has stationed not only Cleburne's Division but Walker's as well on his right after learning of Schofield's movement. Thus Butterfield has done the correct thing, although for the wrong reason. Were he to "put in" a brigade on Hascall's left, it might indeed gain a "footing" beyond the Confederate parapet, but it would also be exposed to a devastating counterattack.

Left with no other choice, Schofield orders Cox and Hascall to entrench and wait until morning to resume operations. Despite his feeling of frustration over not being able to achieve a "victory," Schofield has accomplished what Sherman wanted him to do—namely, extend the Union line two miles closer to the railroad. In addition, during the day, Garrard's troopers occupy the south bank of the Etowah opposite Cartersville, and Stoneman reports to Sherman from Allatoona that the "railroad is undisturbed up as far as Acworth." Thus the way is clear for rebuilding the Etowah railroad bridge and reestablishing rail com-munications for the Union army once it reaches Acworth. For Sherman at present this is the only thing that really matters.

It rains hard all night, so hard that Cox's boots fill with water, which he empties by sticking out one leg, then the other, while riding his horse. All that the soldiers in the trenches can do is lie in the red mud or stand, knee deep, in dirty water.

In the morning, Schofield puts Hovey's division in the line, then orders it to move out beyond the Confederate flank and seize the crossroads near Allatoona

Church. Hovey considers this assignment "extremely hazardous" because it puts his division in "danger of being cut off from the main army." Consequently he moves so timidly and slowly that it is almost sundown before he reaches the crossroads. Hascall and Cox then advance, only to find that the enemy has gone from their front. Nothing now stands between the Federals and the railroad at Acworth.5

Obviously Johnston has decided to make no further effort to block Sherman's shift to the railroad. In his *Narrative* he contends that the "great inequality of force" between his army and Sherman's had left him with only Wheeler's cavalry to hold the region between Pickett's Mill and the railroad. This is nonsense. Not only were Cleburne's and Walker's divisions available for that purpose, but during the day they were joined by Bate. The truth is that Johnston believes that Sherman is not retreating but instead is attempting to get around Johnston's right and cut him off from Marietta. That is why on the night of June 3 Johnston again issues the order he had canceled two days ago: the army will withdraw tomorrow night to a line running from Lost Mountain on the west to the railroad on the east.

Johnston's decision to pull back, even though there is no need to, comes in the wake of and is made in spite of another galling telegram from Bragg. Sent from Richmond on June 2, it is in response to a June 1 telegram from Johnston asserting that his army "in partial engagements . . . has had great advantage, and the sum of all the combats amounts to a battle." In it Bragg sarcastically comments that "General Lee, like yourself, has had no general battle lately, but in a series of partial engagements he has greatly damaged the enemy." Bragg's implication is clear: Johnston is not doing all he could and should do to stop Sherman.

Bragg's telegram also contains a passage in which he refers to "the assistance now on the way to you from S. D. Lee and Forrest." This, of course, is what Johnston has been hoping for since the campaign began. But why has he not been notified? Or if he is being notified now, why in such an offhand manner? Therefore in his reply to Bragg, Johnston ignores the statement about "partial engagements" and instead points out, with some sarcasm of his own, that he has "no knowledge of any assistance on way from S. D. Lee and Forrest. Please inform me what movements of these forces are being made. . . . Cavalry in the rear of Sherman, this side of the Tennessee, would do him much harm at present."

Shortly after this message goes off, two telegrams arrive from S. D. Lee himself. Both are in cipher; one cannot be decoded, and the other states that a strong Union expedition consisting of the XVI Corps and eighteen cannon is heading rapidly toward Okolona, Mississippi, with the result that Forrest's cavalry has been recalled from Alabama to oppose it. So much, then, for the "assistance now on the way to you from S. D. Lee and Forrest." If perchance Johnston had, as a consequence of Bragg's telegram, any second thoughts about retreating to Lost Mountain, they no longer exist.[6]

On the evening of June 3, as he usually does at the end of the day, Captain John C. Van Duzer, head of Sherman's telegraphic detachment, transmits a brief report on the military situation in Georgia to Major Thomas T. Eckert, chief of the military telegraph bureau in Washington. At the close of his message, Van Duzer requests the latest news from Virginia: "How is General Grant?"

The answer, when it arrives, will not be a happy one. At dawn on June 3 the bulk of Grant's 100,000-man army assailed Lee's 45,000 along a six-mile front near Cold Harbor, nine miles east of Richmond. There was nothing subtle about the attack. It simply attempted to break through by sheer weight of numbers. If it succeeded, almost certainly Grant would be able to drive on to Richmond: Lee had not a single regiment in reserve, for he had none to spare. Instead the assault failed horribly. In most sectors it was all over in less than ten minutes; in fact, some Confederate commanders did not realize that there had been an attack! More than 7,000 Northern soldiers, many of them wearing, pinned to their jackets, pieces of paper on which they had written their names and home addresses in expectation of being shot, lay in clusters, dead or wounded. The Southern loss is a mere 1,200. Meade conducted the attack and actually brags of the fact in a letter to his wife. But Grant conceived and ordered it, he accepts the responsibility, and he will get the blame for the slaughter.[7]

The rain continues on June 4, and so does Sherman's shift eastward. To that end he instructs McPherson, come tomorrow, to withdraw his forces from the New Hope Church area and swing around behind the rest of the army toward Acworth. Sherman believes, so he informs Thomas at 9:30 P.M., that "Joe Johnston is shrewd enough to see that we have begun such a movement, and will prepare the way"—that is, try to stop it.[8] Yet even as Sherman is writing the words "Joe Johnston is shrewd enough," the Confederate troops pull out of their fortifications and head for Lost Mountain, about six miles to the southeast. Once again the Federals notice nothing, even though at places the lines are so close that the opposing sides have taken to throwing stones and shovels and picks at each other! It is, Captain Foster records in his diary, "the darkest night of all the dark nights," with a pelting rain that turns the red-clay roads into quagmires of liquid mud three to twelve inches deep. Each step is an effort, men stumble and fall, shoes are sucked off their feet, wagons become stuck and can be extracted only by dozens of soldiers adding their strength to that of the mules. Yet the march goes on, "slosh slosh through the night," in the words of a Georgian. Just before daylight the Confederates reach their new positions. Soon afterward it stops raining, and when the sun rises, it reveals an army literally covered with red mud. Weary men wash the mud off their skin and uniforms as best they can, then they draw a whiskey ration that is both much needed and much welcomed. "We had last night," Hardee writes his wife, "the hardest marching I have known troops to encounter."[9]

Captain Wills and the other men of the 103rd Illinois are among the first to discover that "everything [is] gone this morning slick and clean" from the Confederate works, which were only eighty yards from their own. They go forward and find that these consist of three lines, "two of them very strong," with dirt ramparts nine feet thick at the base, seven at the top, and surmounted with head logs. The enemy camps, however, are less impressive. "The Rebels," writes Wills, "were awful dirty and the smell in their camps dreadful." Contributing to the stench are a number of dead Federals killed in Hooker's battle on May 25 and still lying between the lines, their bodies nearly decomposed. The graveyard at New Hope Church, where Stovall's Georgians had made their stand, is a shambles, the palings bordering the graves having been torn down to serve as beds. As word spreads that the Confederates are gone, the Union soldiers experience a sense of relief and joy: relief that the ordeal of the Hell-Hole is over; joy over what they deem to be another victory. They also feel confident about the future. "Well," comments Wills in his journal, "I expect another heat like this at the Chattahoochie river, and when we get them out of there, as we are bound to do, ho! for easy times!"[10]

Sherman, on learning that Johnston has retreated, instructs McPherson to proceed with his march to Acworth. McPherson does so, and on the following day, June 6, he deploys his forces along Procter's Creek south of the village. Sherman joins him there and, obviously relieved at again being in contact with the railroad, telegraphs Halleck: "All is well."[11] Exactly one month after the campaign had begun, its third phase ends. To whom, this time, should the honors go—Sherman or Johnston?

Sherman wastes no time in claiming them. In a June 6 telegram to Brigadier General John D. Webster in Nashville, a telegram he authorizes Webster to publish, Sherman asserts: "Johnston tried to head us off at Dallas but did not succeed. In all encounters we had the advantage." Three days later he elaborates on this statement in a letter to Ellen: "[Johnston] thinks he checked us at Dallas. I went there to avoid the Allatoona pass, and as soon as I had drawn his army there I slipped . . . round the main [Confederate] army," achieving "a perfect success."[12]

Either Sherman is trying to deceive others, even his own wife, or else he has managed to deceive himself; probably it is a mixture of both. The truth, of course, is that Johnston did head Sherman off at Dallas (or, to be more exact, New Hope Church) and that he did it so well that after three days of fighting, Sherman's overriding concern was to disengage and return to the railroad. Moreover, far from gaining the "advantage" in "all encounters," Sherman suffered severe defeats on May 25 and 27, and he owed his only victory to the blundering Confederate attack of May 28. Finally and most fundamental of all, Sherman's objective, in fact his expectation, was not merely to flank Johnston out of Allatoona but also to drive him to or across the Chattahoochee. That is why Sherman plunged blindly and bloodily into the hell-hole of New Hope Church, with the result that he soon was glad to settle for the lesser goal and call it a "perfect success."

Regarding Johnston, he performed well between May 23 and June 6. He anticipated Sherman's thrust around his left, acted quickly and effectively to intercept it, and then pinned down the Union army in an awkward and precarious position for nearly two weeks, in the process inflicting heavier losses on the Federals (about 4,500 casualties) than he himself suffered (approximately 3,000). By so doing he not only foiled Sherman's plans, but the defensive victories at New Hope Church and Pickett's Mill have revived his army's morale. This had sagged badly after the retreat from Cassville, and desertions had become so numerous, particularly among troops from northern Georgia, that Johnston had found it necessary to order sixteen would-be deserters shot *en masse* as a deterrent. Now, according to Lieutenant Colonel Columbus Sykes of the 43rd Mississippi, "the army is . . . ready and anxious to fight the enemy whenever 'Old Joe' gives the word."[13]

Johnston's sole serious mistake during the New Hope Church standoff was to order the operation that led to, but did not cause, Bate's ill-fated assault. Conceivably, too, he might be faulted for not exploiting the wide gap between Thomas's and McPherson's forces and for not trying harder to block Sherman's shift to Acworth; but this would be to hold him up to the mirror of military perfection, a mirror that rarely reflects a flawless image of even the greatest commander.

Unfortunately for himself, and even more so for the Confederacy, Johnston has not been equally successful in the campaign as a whole. Since it began a month ago the invaders have penetrated eighty miles into Georgia, compelled Johnston to abandon a half-dozen strong positions and two major rivers, and inflicted on his army of 65,000 to 75,000 men a probable loss of at least 9,000 while losing approximately 12,000 from an army of about 100,000. Sherman, moreover, soon will make good his losses, and then some, with the arrival of the two divisions of the XVII Corps, another division of the XV Corps, and miscellaneous units from Kentucky and Tennessee that have been relieved by 100-day regiments. Johnston, in contrast, cannot expect additional significant reinforcements other than the Georgia Militia: Davis and Bragg already have sent him all the troops they believe can be spared from elsewhere; in fact they think he has more than he should have. Thus if Johnston truly is endeavoring, as he later will claim, to wear down Sherman's strength by attrition until it no longer greatly exceeds his own, thereby enabling him to go over to the offensive, then he is failing. Instead by early June, Sherman is relatively stronger and Johnston is relatively weaker than either of them was when they had first clashed at Resaca in mid May.

To the toll taken by bullets and shells during the past two weeks must be added that of physical and psychological strain. "This is the severest campaign this army ever had," a veteran Ohio artilleryman tells his brother in a June 3 letter. Private McDermid, who is "black and dirty," would agree; writing to his parents on June 7, he declares that "it is awful hard soldiering up here and takes a right stout man to stand it." Many soldiers in both armies are not stout enough, and as Chauncey Cooke informs his mother, "the doctors are sending them back by the hundreds to rest and recruit." Among them is William Sloan of the 5th Tennessee Cavalry, who is so "tired out" that he has been ordered to a hospital in Atlanta where a physician "says I am overcome with general debility." The 96th Illinois has a hundred men "prostrated by sickness and exhaustion," twenty more than its combat loss. In the 63rd Virginia, reports Captain Thomas B. Hampton to his wife, "a great many . . . are Breaking down & falling into the hands of the enemy & some are running away."[14]

Seeking to escape the misery of the front lines, hundreds of soldiers fill the rear areas of both armies, Confederates as far south as the Chattahoochee, Federals all the way north to Kingston. Some hang around the hospitals, pretending to be ill or acting as volunteer nurses; others claim to be on foraging expeditions; still others hide out in remote cabins, away from the main roads and settlements. So serious is the problem in his army that Sherman on June 4 issues Special Field Orders, No. 17, declaring that the "only proper fate" for "skulkers" is to be "shot as common enemies of their profession and country"; instructing Thomas, McPherson, and Schofield to "at once organize guards and patrols" to arrest and punish stragglers; and stating that since the prime responsibility for keeping troops "at their places" belongs to the brigade and regimental commanders, he intends both personally and through his inspectors to give their performance in this regard his "full attention" so that "when the time comes for reports on which to base claims for reward and promotions no officer having a loose, straggling command need expect any favor."[15]

By this order, Sherman seeks not only to tighten discipline but also to curtail the plundering and the outrages being committed by his soldiers against the civilian population. These have continued unabated, indeed have grown worse, during the past two weeks. Captain Poe sometimes blushes, he informs his wife on the same day the order is issued, because "my duty brings me in contact with some of the thieves and pillagers of this army, whose ideas do not rise above a hen-roost, and whose notion of the proper way to subdue the rebellion are exemplified in the maltreatment of innocent women & children." In a similar, although less literate, vein, Private Ira Van Deusen of the 111th Illinois comments in a letter to his wife the following day that "you have no idea how the women & children suffer here whear we run there husbands & fathers from there houses & sometimes kill them at their one dorse [own doors] & then our men take everything they have & some places tair up everything in the house & tair up there gardens & paster [pasture] there wheat fields & burn their fences. . . . Any whear near whear we pas everything is destroyed."[16]

Whether Sherman's stern words and threats of even-sterner punishments will prove more successful in stopping or at least reducing such crimes and depredations than have the previous efforts of his army commanders along the same line must be considered (to put it mildly) doubtful. As we have seen already, too many of the Union soldiers truly do believe that "the proper way to subdue the rebellion" is to inflict suffering on the women and children of the South; too many of them are like Private Joseph Kimmel of the 51st Ohio, who is "determined never to go hungry longer than . . . necessary" and therefore goes foraging on his own in deliberate defiance of orders; and too many of the brigade and regimental commanders, not to mention company officers, are unwilling to risk the resentment, perhaps worse, of their men by enforcing strict discipline, Sherman's warning notwithstanding. When on June 6 several soldiers of the 96th Illinois, the same regiment that has one hundred of its members prostrated by sickness and exhaustion, are punished for taking food from civilians by being made to carry heavy fence rails on their shoulders, their comrades are so angered by what they consider to be such unjust and cruel treatment that they threaten to "take revenge" unless the men are "speedily released," which they are.[17]

Among the Confederates the problem of straggling and pillaging elicits the same remedies as in the Union army and with an identical outcome. Thus both Wheeler and Polk have issued orders on the subject very similar to Sherman's in language and tone. Wheeler's, dated May 31, describes civilians being "frequently robbed of their horses, provisions, and grain by mounted men" claiming to be Confederate cavalry and directs his commanding officers to suppress these "marauders" and to see to it that their troopers collect no supplies without proper authorization and payment. Polk's, published June 1, denounces the "burning of fence rails, the destruction of houses, and the pasturing of cattle in fields of grain" by his soldiers, particularly those assigned to the wagon train, and urges "commanding officers of every grade . . . to use every endeavor to suppress this lawless tendency to the destruction of the property of our own people which is so rife amongst the army at large." However, nine days after Wheeler's order, Captain Sidney Champion of the 28th Mississippi Cavalry will write his wife that "straggling *is the rule* of the hour & not the exception," and ten days later, Lieutenant Colonel Columbus Sykes, whose 43rd Mississippi serves in Polk's Corps, will inform his wife that "I have known our own soldiers to go to farms and destroy everything on the place."[18] (The 28th Mississippi Cavalry, to be sure, is part of "Red" Jackson's Division, but there is no factual or logical reason to believe that discipline in that division is worse than in Wheeler's Corps, as subsequent accounts will amply demonstrate.)

Individually, the vast majority of men in both armies are decent enough, probably more so on the average than in a present-day army. Collectively, however, they constitute a horde that has been hardened by war to the point where they regard suffering, their own and others', with varying mixtures of scorn, despair, and utter indifference.

In other words, they do not give a damn.

Sherman's objective remains the same as when he crossed the Etowah: Marietta and the Chattahoochee. Only his strategy for getting there will be different. Having failed in his attempt at a wide, bold sweep around the enemy flank, he now intends to push straight ahead, at all times keeping his army in contact with the railroad. He hopes and sometimes even believes that Johnston will fall back across the Chattahoochee rather than risk battle with that river to his back. Sherman also realizes that it is very possible that Johnston will make a stand north of Marietta, where mountainous terrain offers strong defensive positions. Should he do so, Sherman assures Halleck, "I will not run head on his fortifications."[19]

At Acworth, Sherman awaits two things before advancing: the arrival of the XVII Corps and the rebuilding of the Etowah railroad bridge. On June 8 the first requisite is fulfilled when, after an arduous journey from Cairo, Illinois, by steamboat, train, and foot, the XVII Corps's two divisions finally rejoin the Army of the Tennessee. They number 9,000 troops; another 2,000 remain at

Rome to garrison it, and 1,500 more have been left at Allatoona for the same purpose. Most of them are veterans of Fort Donelson, Shiloh, Corinth, and the battles that had led to the fall of Vicksburg. There are no better fighting men in either army, and some of their regiments, thanks to recruiting while on veteran furlough, are extraordinarily large for this stage of the war, numbering in one case (the 68th Ohio) 900 and in another (the 12th Wisconsin) 1,037.

Accompanying them is a unique unit: the 1st Alabama Cavalry (U.S.A.). Its enlisted men are pro-Union Alabamans, some of whom bear the marks of bites from dogs set upon them by Confederate patrols that had tried to ferret them out from the mountains, swamps, and forests where they had hidden until able to join the Federal army. Following the XVII Corps, notes Chaplain John J. Hight while watching it cross the Etowah on the pontoon bridge, are "a number of negro women and children in the train." Whoever would have thought that someday black and white Southerners would be part of an army invading Georgia?[20]

The commander of the XVII Corps, Major General Francis P. Blair, Jr., is a tallish forty-three-year-old native of Kentucky and graduate of Princeton whose sandy-hued beard is one of the longest worn by any general. His brother, Montgomery Blair, is Lincoln's postmaster general, and his father, Francis P. Blair, Sr., had served in Andrew Jackson's cabinet and has been a confidential advisor of presidents ever since. He himself until recently has been a congressman from St. Louis, where in 1861 he had led Missouri's Unionists in their successful struggle to keep that state under the stars and stripes. Like Logan, Geary, and numerous other politicians-turned-warriors, he hopes that the path of glory, which he has trod as a brigade and division commander in the Vicksburg Campaign, will lead to the White House. The officers and men of the XVII Corps have not yet made up their minds about him—he never before has served with, much less commanded, the corps—but one of them, Brigadier General Manning Force, notes that he "has the reputation of a gallant officer."[21]

By coincidence the same day that Sherman adds Blair to his army he loses another politician-general: Hovey. On the morning of June 8, Hovey asks Schofield for a leave of absence pending action on a letter of resignation that Hovey has sent to Lincoln: Hovey thinks that he should be a major general and that all ten of the Indiana regiments he recruited during the winter should be under his command, instead of only five. Schofield refers the matter to Sherman who, after vainly trying to persuade Hovey that he has not been "unfriendly dealt by," endorses his resignation and directs Schofield to break up Hovey's division, which has only 3,000 men present for duty owing to heavy losses from illness and fatigue. Schofield thereupon assigns one of its two brigades to Hascall, the other to Cox. As a result the XXIII Corps (alias the Army of the

Francis P. Blair, Jr. (*Photographic History*, 8:102)

Ohio) dwindles to a mere two divisions. But they now are large divisions and ably led; furthermore, Sherman and Schofield are rid of an incompetent and discontented general.[22]

The rebuilding of the Etowah railroad bridge has been under way since June 6. Colonel William W. Wright, head of the Railroad Construction and Repair Corps, personally supervises the 600 civilian workers he has assigned to the task. Altogether he commands 2,000 highly skilled laborers who have been distributed in detachments along the railroad with huge stockpiles of precut timber, ready to repair or rebuild bridges and trestles between Chattanooga and Atlanta. It had taken him just three days to restore the bridge over the Oostanaula, and he has promised Sherman that trains will be able to cross the

Etowah by June 12. Chaplain Hight watches Wright's crews in action along the banks of the Etowah in fascinated awe: "two sets of hands—one on each end—are working. Every man has his part assigned him. There is no confusion. No one seems to be in hurry, yet the work goes rapidly forward."[23]

By June 9, Wright can assure Sherman that the bridge will be completed on schedule. Sherman therefore orders Thomas, McPherson, and Schofield to "move forward tomorrow morning" and develop "the enemy's position and strength." He also writes Ellen, telling her that "Johnston may fight us at the ridge of hills just this side of Marietta" but that he expects that the "great battle" will occur "on or near the Chattahoochee, the passage of which he [Johnston] must dispute." In either case, he adds, echoing his assurance to Halleck, "I will not run hot-headed against any works prepared for us."[24]

Preparing works for Sherman to run against, hot-headed or otherwise, is exactly what Johnston has been doing since withdrawing from the New Hope Church area on the night of June 4. At first he had deployed along a front that slanted northeastward from Lost Mountain to Gilgal Church, covering the western approaches to Marietta. Then, after Sherman had reached Acworth and concentrated the Army of the Tennessee south of there, Johnston had shifted to a new position between Gilgal Church and Brush Mountain, a three-hundred-foot height due north of Marietta and east of the railroad. Here the Confederate battle line, writes Lieutenant Colonel Walter Roher of the 20th Mississippi to his "Dear Cousin Susan," runs

> not in a straight line, but in such a manner as to get the corn and wheat fields in our front, and at the same time have our line on higher ground than any in front of it, that being one of the most important considerations in a line of battle. We have not quite men enough to make two lines the entire distance, [therefore] about two brigades are placed on the front line, and one about one hundred and fifty yards to the rear. This last is the reserve line, and may be sent to any point along the front line that is hard pressed by the enemy. Hood is on the right, Hardee on the left, and Polk in the center.[25]

Again Johnston intends to adhere to the defensive, attacking only if there seems to be a favorable opportunity. Although Sherman now in fact outnumbers him no more than three to two, Johnston continues to believe (or at least professes to believe) that he faces two-to-one odds and thus has no practical alternative to the type of strategy that in any case he prefers for theoretical and temperamental reasons. Consequently he pays no heed to the public's unease over his repeated retreats and cares not, supposing he even knows, that all three of his corps commanders and a goodly number of his troops have misgivings about the same. Likewise he totally ignores another attempt by Bragg, via a June 7 letter, to prod him into offensive action by in effect warning him that the Confederacy is doomed unless Sherman is defeated soon. If anything, the letter merely makes Johnston all the more determined to follow his own course in Georgia regardless of what Bragg and Davis might think, say, or do. Reflecting his attitude toward them is his devoted aide, Lieutenant Richard Manning, who writes his mother on June 9:

> I understand that in consequence of the General not having provoked a *General Engagement* with Sherman that the *enemy* at Richmond (who I regard as the most dangerous that this army & its General have) are busy criticizing—blaming—abusing & undermining.
>
> What does the General think of all this? He thinks little of it—as of the rain & mud thru which he passes sleepless nights & anxious days. His world now is his army. For his army it is. He has made it.[26]

While Sherman and Johnston make ready to renew their duel in Georgia, in Baltimore on June 8 the national convention of the Union party (as the Republicans have styled themselves in order to attract War Democrats and Border State Unionists) does what was expected of it: it nominates, by acclamation, Lincoln for a second term. In addition, at Lincoln's behest, it selects as his running mate Andrew Johnson of Tennessee, a prewar Democratic senator from that state whose fiery opposition to secession and whose embattled service as its military governor have made him the most prominent Southern Unionist. The platform endorses Lincoln's policies, calls for a constitutional amendment emancipating all American slaves, and promises a relentless prosecution of the war until total victory has been achieved. (Lincoln's Emancipation Proclamation of January 1, 1863, applied only to areas then under Confederate control and did not include the Border States of Delaware, Maryland, Kentucky, and Missouri, in all of which slavery existed.)

Reaction to the convention's actions likewise is what could be expected. The *New York Times,* the de facto organ of the administration, declares that Lincoln "has done his duty wisely and nobly" and predicts that he will carry every state except possibly New Jersey and Kentucky. Other Republican journals generally follow suit; the major exception—a very major one—is the *New York Tribune,* whose Radical editor, Horace Greeley, announces that although he "accepts" Lincoln's nomination, he would have preferred someone else (whose name he does not reveal). Democratic newspapers, needless to say, denounce the nominees, their tone being one of disgust that, to quote the *New York World,* "in a crisis of the most appalling magnitude, requiring statesmanship of the highest order, the country is asked to consider the claims of two ignorant, boorish, third-rate backwoods lawyers for the highest station in the government." (Andrew Johnson in fact is not a lawyer; he is a former tailor. The *World* quickly corrects its error and, in common with other Democratic papers, heaps scorn on Johnson for his "effeminate" trade.) Confederate papers take the same line as the Democratic one; Atlanta's *Intelligencer* provides a fair sample as it asserts, "What a pretty pair of vagabonds—both coming from foul and putrid stock—both low, vulgar and unprincipled—both from the very dregs of society." The only notable difference between their editorials and Democratic ones is that they frankly avow what the latter dare not admit openly: that they look forward to Northern military defeat to produce Republican political defeat. "Lee, Beauregard, and Johnston," predicts the *Richmond Examiner,* "can both give the Yankees a [Democratic] President and make us [the South] well rid of them and their Presidents for ever."[27]

Part Two: Big Shanty and Pine Mountain

On the morning of June 10, Sherman begins advancing, the Army of the Tennessee on the left, the Army of the Cumberland in its accustomed place in the center, and the Army of the Ohio on the right, with Garrard's and Stoneman's divisions covering respectively the east and west flanks. A strong force of skirmishers backed by a battery of rifled cannon precedes each column. Sherman anticipates little or no serious resistance until he reaches Kennesaw Mountain immediately north of Marietta; he dismisses as exaggerated the reports from his cavalry that strong enemy forces, strongly fortified, hold Brush Mountain and Pine Mountain.

Indeed at first the only deterrence to the advance takes the form of rain and mud, the seventh straight day of both. Then, late in the morning, the IV and XIV corps encounter Confederate skirmishers about a mile from Pine Mountain. This elevation, which actually is a mile-long ridge that is only three hundred feet at its highest point, stands betwixt and dominates two of the roads leading to Marietta. Johnston therefore has posted Bate's Division and four batteries on it, even though it is a mile in front of his main defense line: he hopes that the Federals will be rash enough to assault it. Thomas, however, has no propensity for rashness; in any case, he has been instructed by Sherman to refrain from attacking fortified positions. Accordingly he orders Palmer and Howard to deploy their lead divisions and entrench. The total distance covered by the Army of the Cumberland during the day is three miles. Hazen's brigade, at the rear of the IV Corps, marches a mere four hundred yards before rebivouacking, and the XX Corps remains where it was in the morning.

Schofield's advance likewise makes little progress, coming to a halt on the Sandtown road one-half mile north of Gilgal Church when it is confronted by a line of Confederate works. Only McPherson achieves some significant progress as the XV Corps occupies and then moves a mile south of Big Shanty toward Brush Mountain. Big Shanty (the present-day town of Kennesaw) is another railroad station, exactly twenty-eight and a half miles by rail from the center of Atlanta; it has a hotel and some wooden shanties that once had housed the laborers who constructed the Western and Atlantic and thus gave the place its name.

Sherman arrives in Big Shanty at 11 A.M. He at once asks N. S. Townsend, head of the telegraph-wire repair crew, all of whom are civilians like the track repairmen, how soon the field telegraph can be in operation. Not wanting to disappoint Sherman, Townsend answers, "In an hour and one-half." Half an hour later, Sherman hears the key tapping away near his tent, whereupon he angrily exclaims to Townsend, "What did you mean, sir, by telling me 'an hour and one-half'?" Henceforth Townsend will always give Sherman the shortest, rather than the longest, time estimate.

Big Shanty sits at the top of a long, steep grade on the railroad. From it Sherman and the troops of the XV Corps can see not only Brush Mountain to the southeast but also Pine and Lost mountains to the southwest, Kennesaw due south, and on a hill beyond Marietta the Georgia Military Institute. On the summits of Brush, Pine, and Kennesaw the Confederate signal stations vigorously wigwag their flags, and along their sides, swarms of gray-clad men are cutting down trees and digging trenches. Such activity does not smack of a Rebel retreat, yet one can always hope. "General Sherman's staff," notes Captain Wills in his diary, "say that a general fight is not expected here."[28]

Even as the Northern host crawls a few miles closer, Atlanta observes a day of "fasting, humiliation, and prayer," so proclaimed by Mayor Calhoun and the city council. Mary Mallard attends a combined service of the Baptists, Methodists, and Presbyterians. She finds it "deeply solemn and interesting," with the highlights being addresses by a chaplain from the Army of Northern Virginia and by the preacher-colonel of one of Cleburne's Texas regiments, who stands in the pulpit garbed in his uniform and with a "pistol in his belt." At this and other gatherings, Atlantans "beseech almighty God to bless our arms with decisive victory"—that is, help Johnston's army defeat Sherman.

Atlanta's newspapers continue to assure their readers that sooner or later that army will do exactly that. Sherman (affirms the *Appeal* in an editorial echoed by the *Intelligencer,* the *Southern Confederacy,* and the rest) is only "*apparently* successful"; actually he has "gained nothing substantial to aid him in the accomplishment of his grand purpose, the capture of Atlanta." His advance, which has carried him one hundred miles from his base, has been made by "flanking and maneuvering," not by fighting. The Yankee soldiers have suffered huge losses, their rations are short (prisoners' haversacks contain only a little parched corn), and "their numerous deserters say that they want to 'get out of this mess.'" In contrast, the Army of Tennessee is "intact," it gets plenty to eat, its morale is spendid, and its soldiers possess total confidence in Johnston and ultimate victory. "Why, then, should we in the rear indulge in fear?"

Some Atlantans believe this propaganda; they desperately want to. Most of them, however, merely hope it is true while remaining skeptical. Johnston has retreated so often already, how can he be trusted not to do so again? If he does, the Yankees will be at the very gate of the city. Hence more and more people leave, and others prepare to flee should Johnston fall back to the Chatta-hoochee. The only ones who intend to stick it out no matter what either have nowhere else to go, or they lack the means to leave even if they do. Typical of the latter in situation and attitude, although she does not live in Atlanta itself, is the wife of Private Richard B. Jett of the 9th Georgia Battery, who lives on a farm near the Chattahoochee with her children and slaves. She can hear the sound of the cannon across the river, Confederate troops already have "destroyed lots of crops" in her neighborhood, and she expects "every day for the solgers to turn their horses in our fields." Should the "main army fall back here we will perish for what . . . our men leave the yanky [will] eat up clean." Since "I haint got the money to take us of[f] so we will hafter stand the test."[29]

Not far from Mrs. Jett's farm, at "Camp Brown" on the railroad three miles north of Atlanta, about 2,000 other Georgians are getting ready to "stand the test." They are those members of the militia who so far have answered Governor Brown's summons to arms. Most of them are state officials of one sort or another and thus are exempt from Confederate conscription; for that reason and because Brown hitherto has refused to mobilize them, they have acquired the somewhat derisive name of "Joe Brown's Pets." Most, but by no means all, are middle-aged, and according to one of them, Lieutenant William Dickey of Duncansville, writing to his wife, "a larger & heartier set of men you never saw." Furthermore, although attired in civilian clothes and laughably awkward in drill, they are well equipped with rifles, cartridge boxes, and the other basic accouterments of soldiers. Dickey, for one, thinks they will be "able to make a good fight if the test is ever made & they dont show the white feather."[30]

"Rain! rain! rain!" exclaims Major Henry Hampton of Hardee's staff in his journal entry for June 11. This makes the ninth consecutive day of rain, and two more will follow. The ground, Alpheus Williams informs his daughters back in Michigan, is "saturated like a soaked sponge." The Union forces find it difficult to move at all, and when they do, it is not very far. In the center the XIV and IV corps inch closer to Pine Mountain from the east and north, on the right the XX Corps goes into line between the IV Corps and the XXIII Corps, and on the left McPherson masses his army opposite Brush Mountain but makes no attempt to advance. Owing to what Hazen terms the "nearly impassable" roads, commissary wagons cannot reach some units, particularly in Hooker's and Schofield's corps, where men are offering twenty-five or fifty cents for a piece of hardtack and where Lieutenant Thomas Thoburn of the 50th Ohio has been reduced to eating—"with relish"—a weed known as sheep sorrel!

When not at his headquarters in Big Shanty, Sherman spends most of the time with his favorite corps, the XV, which is deployed astride the railroad. Major Thomas Taylor, commander of the skirmish line for Brigadier General Peter J. Osterhaus's division, notes that Sherman looks "cheerful" and speaks "confidently as to result. To look at him you would think he has no mightier cares upon his mind than when [he was] our Division and Corps commander, except that occasionally he leans his head on his hands." During the afternoon of the eleventh, Sherman's cheerfulness turns to joy as he hears the sound of an approaching locomotive. It belongs to Wright's construction train, and its arrival means that the new bridge over the Etowah has been completed, one day ahead of schedule to boot. Sherman tells the engineer to take his locomotive down the track and "sound the whistle as loud as possible." He does so, going almost to the skirmish line, then running backward and forward in mocking defiance of the Confederates, who respond with a futile shower of artillery shells. After three weeks of separation, Sherman once more has immediate contact with his railroad "cracker line," and he is determined, if at all possible, to retain it.

This is one of the reasons for leaning his head on his hands every so often. There is a heavy concentration of Confederate infantry on Brush Mountain, and Garrard reports strong enemy cavalry forces to the east of that height. Could it be that Johnston plans to try to turn Sherman's left flank with the object of getting behind him and seizing Big Shanty and/or the railroad? It would be a logical move for Johnston to make and, if successful, would be devastating in its consequences. Hence Sherman has cautioned McPherson to be on guard against a flank attack and has directed Thomas to reinforce McPherson in case of need. These, however, are merely precautions; he still believes that sooner or later Johnston will fall back and accordingly has

Union wagon train crossing the mountains of Georgia in a storm *(Harper's Weekly)*

ordered Thomas and Schofield to push on against Pine Mountain and Gilgal Church.[31]

Sherman's concern about the Confederate forces on Brush Mountain, although understandable, is unnecessary. Their mission is strictly defensive. Thanks to his cavalry scouts and prisoner interrogations, Johnston knows that Sherman has received 9,000 reinforcements in the form of the XVII Corps and that all of McPherson's "corps" is at Big Shanty. Johnston believes that this means that Sherman probably intends to strike southeastward around his right flank to Roswell on the Chattahoochee in another attempt to cut Johnston off from Atlanta. Consequently he has ordered Hood to pull his corps out of the fortifications along the north slope of Brush Mountain and deploy it to the east where, along with Wheeler's cavalry, it will be in position to counter such a thrust. In addition, Johnston has directed Polk to extend his corps to the right to take the place of Hood's withdrawn troops on Brush Mountain, even though this will stretch Polk's battle line to only a single rank. Counting Jackson's cavalry, who have been placed in the trenches along Lost Mountain to protect against a possible Union move in that direction, Johnston's front covers ten miles, and he is so pessimistic about being able to hold it that he has sent all of the wagon train except ordnance wagons and ambulances south of the Chattahoochee and has instructed the militia detachment at Roswell to burn the bridge there as soon as the enemy approaches.[32]

In sum, both Sherman and Johnston, as their armies again brace for combat, fear that the other plans to do what in fact neither has the slightest intention of doing. It is a curious situation, but one not uncommon to war.

"Papers report," Lieutenant Mackall tersely notes in his journal for June 12, "Forrest captured 200 wagons in N. Miss." This is the first inkling at Johnston's headquarters of what happened two days ago at a place called Brice's Crossroads in Mississippi. With just 3,500 cavalry, Forrest not merely defeated but routed 8,000 Union cavalry and infantry under Sturgis, the general to whom Sherman back in April entrusted the task of crushing that exasperatingly bothersome Confederate. Sturgis's loss in killed, wounded, captured, and missing totals well over 2,000; Forrest's, less than 500. The most spectacular victory of Forrest's career, it enhances his already awesome reputation for genius and invincibility.

June 13 brings Johnston definite word of Forrest's success in the form of a telegram from Stephen Lee. There could be no better news short of an announcement that Grant had suffered total defeat. It means—certainly it should mean—that Forrest now is free to turn against Sherman's supply line. At once Johnston telegraphs Bragg: "I earnestly suggest that Major General Forrest be ordered to take such parts as he may select of the commands of Pillow, Chalmers, and Roddey, all in Eastern Alabama, and operate in the enemy's rear." Likewise Polk and Hardee, presumably at Johnston's request, send telegrams, in their case to President Davis, urging that Forrest be ordered to "operate on the enemy's communications" between Chattanooga and Marietta. Perhaps the pleas of these two generals, friends of Davis's, will prove more effective in persuading the president to unleash Forrest than will those of Johnston, his enemy, hitherto have been.[33]

In his nightly report to Halleck for the thirteenth, Sherman refers to the "hard and cold rains" that have fallen for the past ten days, then states: "A gleam of sunshine this evening gives hopes for a change." June 14 fulfills these hopes. The sun emerges, the clouds disappear, cool winds blow, and the roads and fields start to dry. Atop Big Kennesaw, so called because it is the highest of that mountain's three knobs, "linen coated gentlemen and gaily dressed ladies" gather to view the battlefield below through spyglasses, the voices of the women "ringing out in merry laughter." To musician Porter, who is at a nearby hospital serving as a nurse and who yesterday had written in his diary that "the poor soldiers are coming in sick" from lying in "ditches" filled with mud and water, "it seems strange that they can laugh when there is so much misery and distruction [*sic*] all around."[34]

Sherman, who has postponed making a personal reconnaissance of the Pine Mountain area because of the bad weather, now proceeds to do so, his object being to discover a way to "dislodge" Johnston or "draw him out of his fortifications" without making a direct assault on that height. Sherman first confers with Thomas, who informs him that the XIV and IV corps have worked their way around to its base on the east side, whereupon he instructs Thomas to push both corps between Pine and Kennesaw mountains, a move he believes will produce a general enemy retreat. Then, toward 11 A.M., Sherman observes a party of Confederates standing near a battery on the crest of Pine Mountain, peering at the Union lines through field glasses. Turning to Howard, who accompanies him, he points to the group, says "How saucy they are!" and tells him to make them take cover. Howard replies that he would have done this already except that Thomas has directed him to employ his artillery only when absolutely necessary so as to save ammunition. This, answers Sherman, is right as a rule, but "we must keep up the *morale* of a bold offensive" and therefore orders Howard to have a nearby battery fire three volleys at the Confederates. Sherman then rides off to visit the XX Corps further down the line.

The groups that Sherman has spotted on Pine Mountain consist, among others, of Johnston, Hardee, and Polk. Johnston and Hardee are there because yesterday Hardee, who dislikes the placing of Bate's Division on the mountain so far in advance of the main line, has asked Johnston to inspect the position with a view to abandoning it. Polk is there for both military and religious reasons. The military one stems from the fact that during the morning he has carried out Johnston's orders to replace Hood's troops on the north slope of Brush Mountain and he wishes to study the terrain on his new front from the vantage point of Pine Mountain. The religious one results from his having received last Sunday, June 12, four copies of a recently published tract "Balm for the Weary and Wounded," by the Reverend John T. Quintard, chaplain at large to the Army of Tennessee and rector of Atlanta's St. Luke's Episcopal Church; once the inspection was over, Polk plans to present a copy each to Johnston and Hardee. All three generals stand behind the rampart of a fort occupied by Lieutenant René T. Beauregard's South Carolina Battery. Standing on top of the rampart, Colonel William S. Dilworth, presently commanding the Florida Brigade, points out to them the location of the Union works and batteries in the valley below. At the request of Dilworth, who fears that "a large crowd would be sure to attract the fire of the enemy," the staffs of the three generals are gathered a short distance to the rear. Only yesterday a Yankee shell barely missed Cleburne while he was visiting the mountain.

Approximately one-third of a mile to the north, Howard passes on Sherman's order to the nearest artillery officer. He happens to be Captain Peter Simonson, who held off Hood's attack on the first day at Resaca and who now is Stanley's chief of artillery. Simonson instructs the 5th Indiana Battery, the one he had commanded at Resaca, to fire several shots to establish the range, then fire by volleys.

Dilworth sees a puff of smoke issue from a Union cannon and at once jumps down from the rampart. A second later a solid shot shrieks overhead. This is no place for the commander of the army and two of his top lieutenants! Dilworth urges them to leave the battery and take cover on the other side of the mountain. None of them moves. He then implores them to at least separate. This they do. Johnston walks off to the left, Hardee to the right, accompanied by Dilworth and followed by Polk. A second projectile comes screeching in and is quickly succeeded by a third. Dilworth stops and looks back but cannot see Polk. Suddenly someone exclaims: "General Polk is killed!" Hardee turns to go back, but Dilworth catches him by the arm and tells him he must not expose himself. Then Johnston joins Hardee and Dilworth and, upon being informed of what has happened, also starts to go back. Dilworth pleads with him not to; it simply is too dangerous. Yankee shells are falling now in salvos, and there is nothing that can be done to help Polk in any case. Finally he persuades the two generals to go to his headquarters on the other side of the mountain; he will have Polk's body brought to them there.

After a while, litter bearers enter Dilworth's tent with Polk's corpse. It is a ghastly sight. A three-inch solid shot, probably the second one fired by Simonson's battery, has struck Polk in the left side and passed through his chest, mangling both arms and ripping away his lungs and heart. Johnston and Hardee are "almost overcome with grief," with the former crying, as he places his hand on Polk's head, "We have lost much! I would rather anything but this."

At noon the Confederate signal station on Pine Mountain wigwags a message to Johnston's headquarters, which are located in the Cyrus York house, three and a half miles west of Marietta: "Send an ambulance for General Polk's body." Time passes, but the ambulance does not arrive, whereupon the station's flags query: "Why don't you send an ambulance for General Polk?" Finally litter bearers have to carry the body to a hospital in Marietta, where Dr. J. N. Simmons removes the bloody shreds of Polk's coat. In its left pocket he finds the Book of Common Prayer and, in the right, four copies of Quintard's "Balm for the Weary and Wounded." The fly leaves of three of the booklets are inscribed, respectively, to Johnston, Hardee, and Hood, "with the compliment of Lieut.

Where Polk was killed: The crest of Pine Mountain *(Harper's Weekly)*

General Leonidas Polk, June 12, 1864." Written in the fourth is his own name. All are saturated with blood.[35]

Sherman returns to his headquarters in Big Shanty, an abandoned house, early in the evening. Last night a telegram from Stanton brought the pleasing news that the notorious Rebel raider John Hunt Morgan had been utterly routed while making a foray into Kentucky. Now there is another telegram from the secretary of war, but it is the reverse of pleasing: "We have received from General Washburn report of battle between Sturgis and Forrest, in which our forces were defeated with great loss. . . . Forrest is in pursuit."

What sort of being is this Forrest? A devil? It is incredible that he has so badly defeated Sturgis's 8,000 troops with less than half that force. Yet he has done it, and this means that he again is free to pounce on what Sherman, in a letter to brother John, calls the "long and single line of railroad to my rear . . . the delicate part of my game." Obviously something must be done to prevent that, and Sherman at once decides what it will be. A. J. Smith's divisions still are at Memphis; instead of sending them to Mobile as he had been planning, he will have them (he telegraphs Stanton) "go out from Memphis and defeat Forrest at all cost." If Smith and his stalwart infantry can't deal with Forrest, nobody can.

But even if they can't, they'll keep him so busy in Mississippi that he will not be able to go anywhere else. That is the essential thing.[36]

Back at his headquarters in the Cyrus York house, Johnston reports Polk's death to Richmond and announces it to the army. As Orderly Sergeant Robert Bliss of the 16th Alabama writes his father, the news produces "a universal feeling of sorrow," for although the bishop was not considered a good general, "no man had fewer enemies or was more highly appreciated for his worth." Johnston appoints William Loring, the senior major general of Polk's Corps, as acting commander. A veteran of the Mexican War and a pre-1861 regular army colonel, Loring is an experienced and capable combat leader, but he also is vain, petty, and quarrelsome. Johnston intends to retain him as corps commander only until he can replace him with someone he deems better qualified—preferably Mansfield Lovell, but failing in that, then, if he can, one of Lee's corps commanders in Virginia.

Before leaving Pine Mountain, Johnston authorized Hardee to withdraw Bate's Division, because clearly it is in imminent peril of being cut off. Hence, as soon as it is dark, Bate's troops fall back to the main Confederate line. They depart gladly; not only are they escaping potential entrapment, but maybe now they will get enough to eat, something they have not been able to do lately because of their semi-isolated position. Despite being at the base of the mountain, the Union pickets neither notice their going nor that they have gone.[37]

In Virginia, east of Richmond, other troops move through the night unbeknownst to their enemies. They belong to the Army of the Potomac, and they are marching across the James River on a 2100-foot pontoon bridge. Many Federals, three divisions of them, already have crossed by boat. In a maneuver as brilliant and bold as the one by which he got below Vicksburg fourteen months ago, Grant plans to have these forces link up with those of Major General Ben Butler on the other side of the James. When they do so, nothing but a few thousand Confederates under Beauregard will stand between Grant and Petersburg, twenty-three miles south of Richmond. Since all except one of the railroads that connect the Rebel capital and Lee's army with the rest of the South pass through Petersburg, its capture will leave Lee (who has not the slightest inkling of what Grant is doing, although he expects such a move) with just two choices: either abandon Richmond and retreat into southwest Virginia or else stay, fight, and be crushed. Grant could win the war—or at least come close to doing so—before the week is over.[38]

This same night of June 14, Clement L. Vallandigham stands in his room in the Hiron's House in Windsor, Canada, viewing himself in a mirror. He cannot recognize himself and hopes no one else can either. He is wearing a false moustache—a long fake beard covers his own short one, he has darkened his eyebrows, and a large pillow stuffed under his vest makes him look fat and somewhat shorter. Satisfied with his disguise, he slips out of the hotel, and escorted by four Ohio Democrats who have come to Windsor for this purpose, he boards the ferryboat to Detroit. Right after he lands, a United States customs officer comes up to him and says, "See here, old fellow, that won't do, you have got contraband there," and pokes a finger into his stomach. Vallandigham jumps back in alarm but relaxes when the officer apologizes: "Pardon me, I see I am mistaken; but I have to watch for tricks." Vallandigham bows, then he and his companions head for the railroad station. They purchase sleeping-car tickets on the next train to Dayton. Soon Vallandigham, lying snug in a berth, is on his way back to Ohio.

Vallandigham has decided to openly and brazenly defy Lincoln's banishment decree. His mother in Lima, Ohio, reportedly is dying, and he wants to see her. Otherwise, however, his motives are strictly political. The recent bloody repulses in Virginia have convinced him that Grant, too, has failed and that the Northern people now are ready to support a presidential candidate who is pledged to reunite the nation by means of peace rather than futile war. Consequently he is returning to the North and risking imprisonment—although he doubts that Lincoln will dare touch him—to do all he can to make sure that the Democrats choose such a candidate. That is why he will not stop off at his home in Dayton even to see his wife and children. Instead he will go on to Hamilton, Ohio, where the Democrats of his district are meeting tomorrow to select delegates to the party's national convention in Chicago. He intends to be one of the delegates—and much more besides.[39]

June 15 is another fair day, pleasantly cool. Just before dawn, Howard's pickets discover that the enemy has left Pine Mountain, whereupon they scramble to the top. Here some of them come upon a pool of clotted blood and, near it, a tree on which has been carved "Gen. Polk killed June 14, 1864." Correspondent David P. Conyngham and a surgeon companion examine the "mass of blood"; they also pick out pieces of rib and arm bones which they keep as souvenirs. Several Union soldiers dip their handerchiefs into the blood, "whether as a sacred relic, or to remind them of a traitor," Conyngham does not know which.[40]

Sherman, when he learns that the enemy has evacuated Pine Mountain, jumps to the conclusion that Johnston either is pulling back all along his front or is about to. Hence Sherman orders McPherson to "threaten to turn Kennesaw by the left," Schofield to try to take Gilgal Church and "threaten" Lost Mountain, and Thomas to push between Pine Mountain and Kennesaw and "break the center" of the Confederate line by seizing the road that runs along the ridge between Marietta and Gilgal Church.

What Sherman does not realize is that the main Confederate defense line west of the railroad occupies this ridge and covers the road. When the XIV and IV corps try to penetrate it, they meet with such stiff resistance that Thomas, ignoring an absurd order from Sherman to push on through the night, instructs them to halt and brings up artillery. At the same time, Geary's and Butterfield's divisions suffer large losses for little gain east of Gilgal Church, and to the west of it, Schofield's attempt to reach the intersection of the Marietta and Sandtown roads escapes a similar outcome only because it is so feeble. Mortally wounded during the fighting, a bullet through his chest, is Major Griffin of the 19th Michigan, who had admired the roses and sociable ladies of Cassville.[41]

The sole noteworthy Union success of the day comes on the extreme left. Here Walcutt's brigade of Harrow's division of the XV Corps, having been moved to the west side of Noonday Creek, charges across that stream in what Captain Wills of the 103rd Illinois terms "regular storm fashion" and overruns an outer line of enemy rifle pits, taking several hundred prisoners, most of them from the 40th Alabama. Because his assignment merely is to threaten Johnston's right, McPherson makes no attempt to exploit this coup, and at nightfall, Harrow's division returns to its original position south of Big Shanty. Writing to his wife four days later, Colonel Cavins of the 97th Indiana, Walcutt's brigade, opines: "If there had been one corps to make the charge instead of one brigade, we would have crushed the right flank of the rebel army, but the golden opportunity is passed." Cavins cannot know that Hood's whole corps guards the Confederate right.[42]

By the evening of June 15, Sherman, although willing to concede the possibility that the Confederates have "a second line of earthworks" covering Kennesaw Mountain, nevertheless considers it unlikely and still believes that Johnston is either retreating or about to retreat. Therefore he renews his order to Thomas to press ahead on the center. Thomas, however, again disregards an utterly impractical command from Sherman and on June 16 proceeds with his own plan of blasting the enemy's line with artillery. His gunners bring up battery after battery, fortify them, and then open fire. Enterprising as ever, Captain Simonson endeavors to get a better view of the Confederate works by crawling forward to the skirmish line, rolling a log in front of him. Suddenly he stops moving and lies flat on his face. Approximately fifty-five hours after one of his guns eviscerated Polk, he too is dead, a bullet through his head. In the evening some soldiers of the 101st Ohio capture a Rebel sniper who states that he had shot three times at Simonson before hitting him.

The Federals, however, have other skilled artillerists. Some of them in the XX and XXIII corps discover that the Confederate position around Gilgal Church forms a salient vulnerable to enfilade and cross fire. They take the appropriate measures, and at sunset, shells begin to rain down on Cleburne's troops, who are holding the Gilgal Church sector, from what seems to them every direction except the rear. In addition, Cox's division works around to the west side of the salient, and to its right, Hascall's division advances toward the Confederate entrenchment that is covering the area between the church and Lost Mountain. Since only Ross's dismounted Texas cavalrymen hold this line, the XXIII Corps now is in position to turn Johnston's left.

Schofield, although he claims otherwise in his report, does not realize this. But Johnston does, and he reacts as usual. On his order, Hardee's Corps begins withdrawing as soon as it is dark. While doing so, a stray Yankee shell explodes near Brigadier General Lucius Polk, commander of Cleburne's Tennessee brigade, mangling a leg so badly that it has to be amputated. Lucius Polk is a nephew of the recently deceased bishop-general Polk. Several days later, General Mackall comments in a letter to his wife that it is "singular that two of the name should be hit by chance shots so soon after the other."[43]

Unaware (also as usual with him in such cases) that the Confederates, or at least a large portion of them, are finally making the retreat he has assumed they have been making for the past several days, Sherman feels so frustrated by the night of June 16 that he starts to contemplate doing what he has promised he would not do—"run head on" against the enemy's fortifications around Kennesaw. "I have," he telegraphs Halleck at 9:30 P.M., "been along" the Confederate line and "am now inclined to feign on both flanks and assault the center." Such an attack, he admits, "may cost us dear but in results would surpass an attempt to pass around."

But then, about three hours later, while conferring with Thomas, presumably about an assault on Johnston's center, word arrives from Hooker that the Confederates have withdrawn on the XX Corp's front. No doubt feeling both vindicated and relieved, Sherman at once writes out an order to Thomas:

> Get down to your command as soon as you can this morning, and if you can put your whole army between the two wings of the enemy, do it; or if he shows a force on Kenesaw, push his center and try to get on the Marietta and Vining's Bridge road—that is, to the rear of Marietta. . . . We can get between him and his base without uncovering ours.

For a while on June 17, a cool day with an ominously cloudy sky, something like the pursuit that Sherman envisions takes place. On the right the XX and

XXIII corps move down the Sandtown road, opposed only by a small delaying force of cavalry, and in the center the IV Corps advances two and a half miles in less than two hours. Then the situation suddenly and drastically changes. On approaching Mud Creek, a narrow but steep-banked stream running almost due south into the Chattahoochee, Hooker's and Schofield's forward units discover the Confederates, by all appearances lots of them, dug in along high ground on the opposite side. About the same time, Howard's van comes upon an open field beyond which lies a forest wherein can be seen that only-too-familiar sight—mounds of red dirt.

Hooker and Schofield deploy their troops, and Schofield sends Hascall to look for a way to outflank this new enemy line. Howard, on the other hand, has no such happy option. His instructions from Thomas, which in turn reflect Sherman's order to try to reach "the rear of Marietta," are to "attack the enemy as soon as you can," provided, that is, "his works are not too strong." After pondering the matter for an hour or so, Howard concludes that the only way to ascertain whether or not those works are too strong to attack is to attack them. Accordingly he directs Wood to advance across the open field, Newton to support Wood's left, and Stanley to stand by in reserve.

Wood receives Howard's attack order at approximately 10 A.M. Nearly three hours later, Fullerton records in his journal that there is "heavy skirmishing in Wood's front." Then at 1:50 P.M., Fullerton notes that "General Wood's skirmishers report that the enemy has breastworks about 150 yards in their front." Not until almost 4 P.M. does Wood commence "to move his main line," whereupon Howard instructs Stanley to "give Wood any assistance he may need." Wood, however, needs no assistance and for a very simple reason: his skirmish line cannot (will not?) advance. Finally, at 6:30 P.M., on Thomas's orders, Howard has his artillery shell the forest containing the enemy works. After more than half an hour of "terrific fire" by the big guns, Wood's skirmishers charge across the field to the edge of the forest, then they halt and dig in, even though all the Rebs in their immediate front (members of Walker's Division) have fled.

Sherman himself has been watching this remarkable display since 9:30. When he had first arrived on the scene, he had found "Stanley and Wood quarreling which should not lead," with the result that "I swore, and said what I should not." Now he feels like swearing again. He believes that Johnston is on the run, that only a rear guard covers his retreat, and that the Army of the Cumberland, in particular the IV Corps, should have swept by Marietta and on to the railroad. But he does not swear; instead, as darkness descends, he tells Thomas and Howard that he is displeased with what he has seen today; then he returns to Big Shanty. Here he vents his feelings in a telegram to Halleck. Last night Johnston "abandoned six miles of as good fieldworks as I ever saw"; as a result the Union right "now threatens his railroad to Atlanta"; yet in spite of having "worked hard today to get over to that road," he could not: "the troops seem timid in these dense forests of stumbling on a hidden breastwork."[44]

That they are. If Sherman wants to know why, all he has to do is ask the survivors of Hazen's, Gibson's, and Knefler's brigades, the very same men whom Howard has ordered in the morning to cross the open field into the forest where those red mounds are. They could tell him why: all they would have to say is "Pickett's Mill."

It was Howard's cannonade, not Wood's skirmishers, that drove Walker's troops from their trenches in the forest. It also has alerted Johnston to the potentially fatal defect in his army's new alignment. With Hardee's Corps facing west and Loring's (Polk's) facing north, the right-flank division of the former (Walker's) and the left-flank division of the latter (French's) both can be subjected to a devastating enfilade fire by the Union artillery. Obviously, therefore, another and more defensible line is needed, and Johnston has ordered his chief engineer, Lieutenant Colonel Stephen Presstman, to mark it out. Until that is done, Johnston can only hope that the Federals are unable to take advantage of the vulnerability of his present line.

During the night his hope is realized. It rains heavily and continues to rain all through June 18. Once more the roads turn into quagmires, the fields into swamps, and Noonday and Mud creeks, normally easily waded, become full-fledged rivers deep enough to swim a horse. Anything resembling a major military operation, especially an offensive one, is impossible. The Union troops remain where they are but wish they were somewhere else, preferably some place that is dry. Presstman has ample time to lay out the new defense line, and Johnston orders Hardee, Hood, and Loring to withdraw to it during the night.[45]

Unable to attack the enemy's army, Sherman, resentful over what he considers a wasted opportunity to drive the Confederates pell-mell across the Chattahoochee, instead devotes this otherwise inactive day to attacking his own army, or at least that considerable portion of it known as the Army of the Cumberland. He does so in a letter to Grant, the first one he has written him since the campaign began.

It begins by stating that "I have no doubt you want me to write you occasionally letters not purely official, but which will admit of a little more latitude than such documents possess." Therefore he will explain more fully and frankly than he has in his dispatches to Halleck why his progress in Georgia perhaps has been "slower than you calculated." One reason is McPherson's failure at

Resaca. "My first movement against Johnston was really fine, and now I believe I would have disposed of him at one blow if McPherson had crushed [the Confederate garrison] at Resaca, as he might have done . . . but Mc. was a little over cautious . . . the truth was I got all of McPherson's army, 23,000, eighteen miles south of Johnston's rear before he knew they had left Huntsville." With this "single exception McPherson has done very well," as has Schofield, allowing for the smallness of his army. As to the cavalry, it is "dwindling away," is "always unable to attempt anything," and both Garrard, who is "over-cautious," and Stoneman, who is "lazy," have had "fine chances of cutting in [behind Johnston] but were easily checked by the appearance of an enemy."

But (and here is the crux of the letter):

> My chief source of trouble is with the Army of the Cumberland, which
> is awful slow. A fresh furrow in a ploughed field will stop the whole
> column, and all begin to intrench. I have again and again tried to impress
> on Thomas that we must assail and not defend; we are on the offensive,
> and yet it seems the whole Army of the Cumberland is so habituated to be
> on the defensive that, from its commander down to its lowest private, I
> cannot get it out of their heads. I came out without tents and ordered all
> to do likewise, yet Thomas has a headquarters camp in the style of
> Halleck at Corinth. . . . He promised to send it all back, but the truth is
> everybody there is allowed to do as he pleases, and they still think and act
> as though the railroad and all of its facilities were theirs.

The chronic slowness of Thomas and his Cumberlanders, Sherman goes on, "has cost me the loss of two splendid opportunities which never recur in war." The first was at "Dallas" (he means New Hope Church), where "there was a delay of four hours to get ready to advance, when we first met Johnston's head of column, and that four hours enabled him to throw up works to cover the head of his column, and he extended the works about as fast as we deployed." The other occurred yesterday, when "I broke one of his [Johnston's] lines, and had we followed it up as I ordered at daylight, there was nothing between us and the railroad back of Marietta," but the Army of the Cumberland moved so slowly that "we only got to a creek to the south [*sic*] of it by night, and now a heavy rain stops us and gives time [for the enemy] to fortify a new line."

Still, in spite of everything, "I have all the high and commanding ground, but the one peak [Kennesaw Mountain] near Marietta, which I can turn, our supplies of food have been good, and forage moderate," and there are "strong guards along the [rail] road" who "make prompt repairs." Thus Grant "may go on with the full assurance that I will continue to press Johnston as fast as I can overcome the natural obstacles and inspire motion into a large, ponderous and slow (by habit) army."[46]

The exaggerations, distortions, and falsehoods in this letter should be apparent to all who have read this far. Some of them, no doubt, stem from simple ignorance and honest misunderstandings. Others, however, are the product of personal prejudice and represent a craven and dishonorable attempt to forestall censure from Grant for having failed to achieve decisive results in Georgia by putting the blame on others—notably Thomas, whom he knows Grant dislikes. One cannot wonder if four weeks of vainly trying to reach the Chattahoochee, on whose banks he had expected his troops to "swarm" long before now, have not reduced Sherman to an emotional condition akin to the one that had afflicted him in Kentucky and Missouri in the autumn of 1861. The sole difference is that then he had been excessively pessimistic about the enemy's capabilities and intentions, with the result that he had imagined that he was about to suffer, owing to the fatuity of his superiors, calamitous defeat, whereas now he tends to be unduly optimistic on both counts and thus believes that only the slothfulness and timidity of his subordinates have denied him glorious victory. It also is a crucial difference, for it saves him from being the sort of opponent that a commander of Johnston's temperament could best cope with, namely another Johnston!

Part Three: Kennesaw

Night comes. The rain continues, and the Confederates retreat. By morning they occupy their new line. Hood's Corps covers the area east of the railroad where it bends around Kennesaw Mountain, Loring's Corps holds the mountain itself, and Hardee's Corps takes position south of it on a chain of hills overlooking Nose's Creek, another tributary of the Chattahoochee. Not counting Wheeler's cavalry, who picket the right flank, and Jackson's on the left, the Confederate front extends seven miles and is both anchored and dominated by Kennesaw. This mountain forms a two-mile-long ridge that slants southwestward from the railroad and consists of three distinct knobs: Big Kennesaw at the northeast end, 691 feet above ground level; Little Kennesaw in the middle, almost 400 feet high; and Pigeon Hill at the lower end, only about 200 feet in elevation. From their signal station on Big Kennesaw, Johnston's observers can see all the way to Atlanta, twenty miles south, and equal distances in all other directions; no Union movement in the entire surrounding region, unless at night, can go undetected. Little Kennesaw, "being bald and destitute of timber," also "affords a commanding view," to quote from the diary of General French, whose division occupies the mountain. On the northwest, facing the enemy, the mountainside is steep, rocky, and heavily wooded. All in all, Kennesaw provides a naturally stronger defensive position than either Buzzard Roost or Allatoona.[47]

Union trenches before Kennesaw Mountain (*Photographic History,* 3:117)

At daylight, Thomas and McPherson notify Sherman that the Confederates are gone from their fronts. Elated, Sherman telegraphs Halleck: "Enemy gave way last night in the midst of darkness and storm. . . . The whole army now is in pursuit as far as Chattahoochee. I start at once for Marietta, and leave orders for railroad and telegraph to be brought up." Once again Sherman has leaped to the conclusion that Johnston is doing what Sherman wants him to do.[48]

Later in the morning, Captain William Chambers, standing in line of battle with Sears's Brigade of French's Division about fifty feet beneath Big Kennesaw's summit, watches the Federals approach through the still-falling rain. First come their skirmishers, followed closely by "heavy lines of infantry and sections of artillery." Behind them are "thousands of tents" and, "parked on a hundred open fields," countless wagons. By 10 A.M. the enemy's skirmishers begin engaging the Confederate pickets, and soon afterward his cannons go into action. The first shot from the battery facing Sears's Brigade falls at the base of the mountain. Believing that they are too high up to be reached by artillery fire, Chambers and his comrades cheer derisively. Then a second shot hits half-way up on the side, and although they cheer again, the cheer is fainter. Next, in rapid succession, two more projectiles screech toward them. One strikes the cliff above their heads; the other cuts in two a member of the 40th Mississippi. At once they scramble for cover, finding it on the crest behind a ledge.

By noon the Union bombardment, writes French in his diary, is "severe"; and before the day is over, thirty-five men of the Missouri Brigade, holding Pigeon Hill, are *hors de combat,* including its commander, Brigadier General Francis Cockrell. Hence French quickly agrees when his chief of artillery, Major George Storrs, proposes placing batteries on top of Little Kennesaw despite an assertion from the engineers that this is impossible because the mountain is too steep and rugged. Locating a spur to the rear of the height, Storrs has a pathway cut through the brush on the mountainside, then he assembles a hundred men who use ropes to drag gun after gun to the top until all three of French's batteries have been brought there. Come tomorrow, French will be able to give the Yankees a taste of their own bitter medicine.[49]

Though Sherman's artillery can reach Kennesaw, even its highest point, his infantry cannot. McPherson's troops become bogged down in mud "six to eight inches deep"; Thomas's find the mountain, in Howard's words, "unassailable"; and Schofield's, although they manage to wade chest-deep across Mud Creek, are unable to cross rain-swollen Nose's Creek. Sherman, who in the morning has telegraphed Halleck that the "army is in pursuit as far as the Chatta-hoochee," wires him again in the evening to admit that "I was premature in announcing that the enemy had abandoned his position."[50] Johnston, he now realizes, merely has pulled back to yet another defense line, the very thing Sherman had hoped (without any foundation for doing so except his own wishful thinking) to prevent. Again a strong sense of frustration mounts within him. Will he ever be able to get out of these damnable rain-soaked mountains and forests to the Chattahoochee and the flatter, more open country beyond, which leads to Atlanta?

In Virginia on this June 19, a Sunday, Grant has far greater cause to feel frustrated than does Sherman in Georgia. Grant's bold and brilliant plan to transfer the Army of the Potomac south of the James River and take Petersburg, thereby forcing Lee to relinquish Richmond and retreat to ultimate destruction in southwest Virginia, has failed. It should not have. By every rational calcula-tion, by all the laws of probability, it should have succeeded. On June 14, just as he intended, Grant got the Army of the Potomac across the James without Lee's knowing it. For the next three days Lee had believed, or at least had had to consider it possible, that most of that army, if not all of it, remained north of the James and thus posed an immediate threat to Richmond. Consequently on June 15, Beauregard, commanding Confederate forces south of the river, had only 2,200 troops to hold Petersburg against 16,000 Federals; the following day, 12,000 as opposed to 60,000; and on the seventeenth, 14,000 facing 80,000. Had the Union legions simply moved forward en masse, they would have swamped Beauregard's men and walked into Petersburg. Instead an incredible combination of bumbling, timidity, inaccurate maps, and sheer bad luck prevented a determined, sustained, and coordinated attack. Meanwhile, having definitely established that Grant's main force indeed was south of the James, Lee had redeployed his army accordingly. When on June 18 the Federals finally had mounted a full-fledged attack, Petersburg's fortifications—immense works fronted by deep ditches and studded with cannons—were well manned. Seeing this and fearing another Cold Harbor slaughter, whole brigades of Northern soldiers had defied orders to charge: "We have had enough of assaulting earthworks." A Maine regiment, made up of artillerists converted to infantry who had never before been in combat, had rushed forward and in less than half an hour had lost 632 of its 850 men. Finally Meade, who had ordered the assault, had called it off and notified Grant that "our men are tired and the attacks have not been made with the vigor and force which characterized our fighting in the Wilderness."

There is an obvious reason why that is so. Feeble as it has been, the thrust against Petersburg has cost the Army of the Potomac 11,000 casualties, making its total toll since May 1 a horrendous 66,000. This is more than Lee's whole strength at the beginning of the campaign and averages out to 1,300 a day. Worse, most of these losses have taken place in veteran units, the ones that had nearly shattered the Army of Northern Virginia at Antietam and had defeated it at Gettysburg. Thus not only has Lee foiled Grant's attempt to crush him or at any rate take Richmond; he also has inflicted such terrible physical and moral damage on Grant's forces that it has become questionable whether they remain capable of taking effective offensive action. Petersburg would seem to indicate that they do not. Lee himself is so confident of being able to continue to hold Grant at bay, despite being outnumbered two to one, that he has sent off two elite divisions under Jubal Early to parry another Yankee invasion of the Shenandoah Valley, the loss of which would make it next to impossible for Lee to feed his army and would also enable the Federals to move against Richmond from the west.[51]

June 20 brings more rain, more mud, and more skirmishing, which turns into a ferocious little battle during which Whitaker's brigade of Stanley's division retakes, then holds, at the cost of 250 casualties, some tactically advantageous hills that had been seized by the Confederates in a surprise assault. (Ten days later, Brigadier General Walter Chiles Whitaker of Kentucky, who habitually goes into battle with a giant whiskey flask dangling from his waist, takes leave of absence "on account of ill-health.") At 1 P.M. on the twenty-first, Sherman telegraphs Halleck disgustedly: "This is the nineteenth day of rain [this month] and the prospect of clear weather [is] as far off as ever. The roads are impassable, and fields and woods become quagmires after a few wagons have crossed." Such conditions, Sherman decides, make it useless to attempt any major offensive operations. Hence he orders both Thomas and McPherson to hold where they are; not "until we can move our army with some skill and rapidity," he informs Thomas, "will there be any point in attacking the enemy."[52]

On the other hand he has work for Schofield to do, regardless of the weather and roads. Yesterday, Cox's division had made it across Nose's Creek, and last night, Schofield had notified Sherman that "I regard it as certain that there is now no material obstacle between us and Marietta, nor on the Sandtown road as far as the next creek [Olley's Creek]." If this be true, then the way is open to Johnston's rear or to the Chattahoochee or both. Accordingly, Sherman instructs Schofield to continue moving down the Sandtown road, provided that while doing so, he can preserve contact with Hooker, whose corps remains on the right of Thomas's front.

This proviso turns out to be the rub. Schofield finds that he cannot proceed down the Sandtown road without separating himself dangerously from the XX Corps, which although it has crossed Nose's Creek, does not move much beyond it because of Sherman's order to Thomas to suspend offensive operations for the time being. Moreover during the day, enemy cavalrymen appear west of Marietta and around Powder Springs in such numbers and with such aggressiveness that Schofield suspects that they are backed by infantry. The consequence is that by nightfall he no longer is certain that "no material obstacle" lies between him and Marietta. On the contrary, as he writes Sherman at 8 P.M., Schofield now thinks that while he "might perhaps" turn the Confederate left by pushing east along the Powder Springs–Marietta road, "I take it for granted . . . that the enemy now occupy that road in force."

It is a good thing he takes this for granted, for it is true. Johnston has been keeping a wary eye on the slow but persistent Union advance down the Sandtown road. Yesterday, when a large force of Federals had crossed Nose's Creek, he had concluded that he had no choice, other than to abandon Kennesaw and retreat, except to extend his left in order to counter this threat to his left and rear. Therefore early on the morning of June 21, Hood's Corps pulled out of its position on the right and bivouacked on the Powder Springs road west of

Marietta. Replacing it is Loring's Corps, its front now stretched beyond the railroad, and Wheeler's troopers, most of whom have been put into trenches. In thus redeploying his army, Johnston knows that he risks having his weakened right attacked or turned by McPherson, who remains concentrated along the railroad and who hitherto has carried out all of Sherman's major flanking maneuvers. But since Sherman has shown no inclincation in a week and a half to move by Johnston's right, and since in fact he is as usual moving by his own right, Johnston considers it an acceptable risk. Besides, to repeat, it is his only alternative if he is to continue to hold on to Kennesaw.[53]

"The sun *does* shine this morning and I *do* hope it will continue to do so for the next six months." Thus Captain Bryan D. Paddock of the 1st Michigan Light Artillery starts his diary entry for Tuesday June 22. No doubt he expresses the sentiments of the soldiers of both armies. For nearly a month they have spent most of their time marching, fighting, eating, and sleeping in rain and mud, standing in trenches knee- and sometimes hip-deep in water, and going for days without being able to take off and dry their soaked uniforms, with the result that in many instances their pant legs have become moldy in their boots. Little wonder that they sometimes declare that they would prefer one big bloody battle to such interminable misery; at least it would get things over with, one way or another. Besides, such a battle could scarcely produce greater loss than the sum total of hundreds of men who each day go to the rear suffering from pneumonia, influenza, and rheumatism, not to mention the large and growing numbers who have broken down from physical or mental strain, often both. Musician Porter's diary for June 13 notes that "there are 5 sick men to one killed and wounded," and in all likelihood that ratio also exists among the Federals and has, if anything, increased since then.[54]

To Sherman the cessation of the rain means that he now can make a full-fledged effort to pry Johnston loose from his Kennesaw stronghold. Therefore early in the morning he directs Thomas to have Hooker move east toward Marietta and orders Schofield to advance on the Powder Springs–Marietta road "till you support Hooker's right" while simultaneously protecting his own right by leaving a force at the Cheney house, where the Powder Springs road intersects the Sandtown road. "If Johnston fights for Marietta," he explains to Schofield, "we must accept battle, but if he gives ground we must be most active"—that is, intercept him before he reaches the Chattahoochee. Obviously Sherman clings to the hope that Johnston will retreat without accepting battle, much less offering it.[55]

What happens next cannot be understood unless we take into account the state of mind of "Fighting Joe" Hooker as it has evolved by the third week of June 1864. So far his corps has made every major Union attack, save Howard's ill-fated foray at Pickett's Mill; as a consequence it has suffered about 5,000 casualties, far more than any other corps in Sherman's army. Although proud of the performance of his troops, who have adopted as their own the nickname given them by the Rebs—"Hooker's Ironclads"—Hooker believes that they have been required to bear a disproportionate share of the fighting and hardships of the campaign; as he has told Geary on the twentieth, "one only wonders that there is a man" left alive. By the same token, Hooker resents, as do many other veterans of the Army of the Potomac and also of the Army of the Cumberland, Sherman's flagrant favoritism toward the Army of the Tennessee. In all likelihood he would agree with Colonel Robinson of Williams's division that a charge by Lee's Army of Northern Virginia would "break its line." Finally the events of the past seven weeks have deepened Hooker's already low opinion of Sherman. Hooker believes, not without cause, that Sherman bungled the Snake Creek Gap maneuver, that Sherman obstinately ordered the XX Corps to make the useless and costly assault at New Hope Church on May 25 and then just as obstinately refused to admit his error, and that since then Sherman has wasted the better part of a month floundering about in the woods and mud below Kennesaw Mountain. Hooker, in short, sees himself and his corps as having been victimized in the past by a malevolent and incompetent commander and as being in danger of having the same thing happen in the future.[56]

Such is Hooker's mood as he proceeds to execute Sherman's order, transmitted to him by Thomas, to move against Marietta from the west (something he himself, incidentally, had recommended to Thomas yesterday evening). Advancing eastward from Noses's Creek early in the afternoon, Hooker deploys his divisions—Butterfield on the left, Geary in the center, and Williams on the right—along a line that runs south from the IV Corps to Kolb's farm on the Powder Springs road. About the same time, Hascall's division of the XXIII Corps goes into position on the other side of that road, with Strickland's brigade facing east and the other two brigades slanted off to the southwest to protect the right flank. Still further to the right, Cox's division entrenches around the Cheney house to guard against a Confederate thrust from the south or west.

So far only enemy pickets have been encountered, but then Geary's division comes under heavy shelling, and skirmishers report that they have taken prisoners who state that Hardee's and Hood's corps are massed in a forest up ahead, poised to attack. At once Hooker and Schofield order their troops to dig in, which they do, using bayonets, tin plates, and bare hands; and the 123rd

New York of Williams's division and the 14th Kentucky of Hascall's go forward
to reconnoiter. Also, Hooker sends a dispatch to Thomas, urging him to relieve
Butterfield's and Geary's divisions with other units so that "my line may be
sufficiently contracted to render it safe," adding "if done at all it should be done
at once." Obviously Hooker considers his situation extremely precarious.

The forest that supposedly conceals Hardee's and Hood's corps covers a
cluster of hills on both sides of the Powder Springs road about a mile east of the
Kolb farm. Overrunning and capturing some Confederate skirmishers, the
123rd New York and the 14th Kentucky enter the forest, where their advance
patrols come upon a huge host of gray-clad infantry forming into lines of battle.
The patrols quickly withdraw to the edge of the forest while messengers hasten
back to report what has been seen. Then, on receiving orders to hold up the
impending enemy assault as long as possible, they hastily construct a log-and-
rail barricade.

Confirmation that the Confederates are massing on the Powder Springs road
for an attack causes Schofield to direct Cox to leave one of his brigades at the
Cheney house and to place the other three in line next to Hascall's division,
thereby extending the Union right all the way to the Sandtown road. On the
other hand it makes Hooker even more sure that he is in imminent peril of being
crushed by vastly superior enemy forces. Consequently he renews his request to
Thomas that Butterfield and Geary be relieved so that he can concentrate his
corps: "Concurrent testimony of prisoners represent that the whole rebel army
lies between my immediate front and Marietta, and that they are marching in
this direction. . . . My line is too long to make an obstinate defense."

Alarmed by this message, Thomas rides over to Hooker's sector to examine
the situation himself. He finds the XX Corps occupying a "very strong" position and as "well together" as the IV Corps. With regards to the "whole rebel
army" being between Hooker and Marietta, that is beyond belief: it would
mean that Johnston has left nothing to oppose McPherson, Palmer, and Howard!
Hooker, Thomas concludes, has been "stampeded"; therefore at 4:30 P.M.,
Thomas has his chief of staff, Brigadier General William Whipple send Hooker
a note stating that "the major general commanding says" that at present he
"cannot relieve any portion of your corps" and "you will necessarily have to
hold on with your breast-works, as he thinks you will be able to do, without
danger, Schofield being on your right. You now have as strong lines as General
Howard."

Thomas's skepticism about the strength of the Confederate force that is
menacing Hooker is justified: it consists solely of Hood's Corps. Early in the
afternoon, about the same time that Hooker and Schofield were deploying, it
marched west on the Powder Springs road about a half-mile beyond Mt. Zion

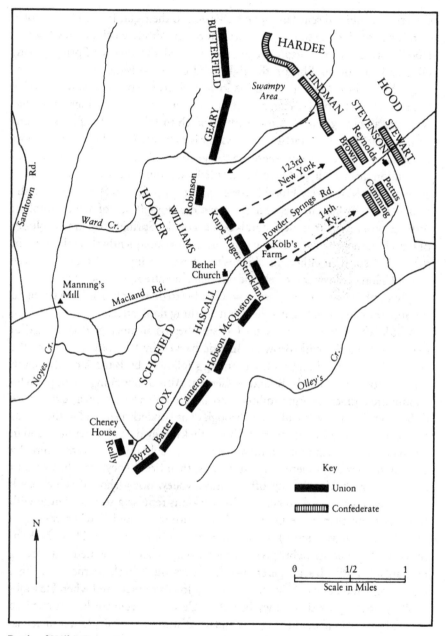

Battle of Kolb's Farm, June 22

Church. Here Hood sent Hindman's Division to the right, formed Stevenson's astride the road, and retained Stewart's in reserve directly behind Stevenson's. Hood's orders to Stevenson are to strike down the Powder Springs road, Hindman supporting him on the right, and drive the Federals toward Manning's Mill. Since Manning's Mill is located nearly two miles west of Kolb's farm, evidently Hood does not expect to encounter strong resistance. Why that is so we can only guess. A subsequent dispatch to Johnston that he was counterattacking after repulsing a Union assault is palpably false, his official report devotes only part of a vague sentence to the events of June 22, his memoirs fail to mention them at all, and no other Confederate source provides a satisfactory explanation. Most likely Hood believes, given his orders to Stevenson and the arrangement of Stevenson's and Stewart's divisions (both of which imply a turning movement), that the Federals on the Powder Springs road are in column of march, rather than in line of battle, and that consequently their flank is "in the air." If so, then either his skirmishers have not informed him about the actual Union deployment, or else he has made no attempt to ascertain it and is simply gambling that at long last he will be able to do what he has been trying to do since the campaign began—deliver a crushing flank attack.

A little after 5 P.M., Stevenson's Division begins advancing. It is formed in two lines of battle, with Brown's Brigade backed by Reynolds's north of the Powder Springs road and with Cumming's followed by Pettus's on the south side. Almost immediately Brigadier General Alfred Cumming's troops, who mainly are former Georgia militia with little combat experience, experience difficulties. They have to advance through dense underbrush, and in the words of Colonel George Gallup of the 14th Kentucky, they do so "reluctantly and in much disorder, resembling a mob more than . . . soldiery." The 14th Kentucky waits until they are a mere thirty feet away, then fires. They are "thrown into confusion" and, after letting off a "heavy volley, not a shot of which took effect," fall back out of range. The Kentuckians repulse a second charge with equal ease but then come under enfilading fire from the left when the 123rd New York gives way and so have to retreat to a new position. Here the Kentuckians continue to fight, giving ground only when threatened with being outflanked, until Hascall peremptorily orders them back to the main line. Cumming's and Pettus's brigades, however, do not pursue, and when Hascall's artillery open up on them, they flee. A single Union regiment has stopped an assault by two Confederate brigades and has disrupted Hood's plan, if such it is, to turn the Federal right. The losses of the 14th Kentucky total 12 killed and 48 wounded, whereas Gallup claims that 69 dead Rebels subsequently are found on its front.

North of the road, where the terrain consists mainly of cleared fields, Brown's and Reynolds's troops quickly drive off the 123rd New York and emerge from the forest far ahead of Cumming's and Pettus's column. Shouting what Williams terms their "peculiar yell," they advance (later writes Samuel Toombs of the 13th New Jersey) "steadily and in good order" toward Knipe's and Ruger's brigades who occupy a low ridge overlooking the Kolb farm. Then, as soon as they come within optimum (from the standpoint of killing) range, one of Geary's, two of Williams's, and two of Hascall's batteries open up with a cross fire of shell and canister. Their hitherto even ranks dissolve, to quote Williams's report, into a "confused mass," and when Knipe's brigade and two regiments of Ruger's rake them with several rapid volleys, the survivors either run back into the woods or seek shelter in a ravine, where one of Williams's batteries pounds them with plunging shot, piling up corpses in heaps. Williams's troops achieve ample revenge for New Hope Church; they do it, moreover, against the same Confederates that Robinson's brigade had cut to pieces with its Army of the Potomac style of fighting at Resaca.

Hardly has Stevenson's attack been broken up than Hindman's division emerges from a forest opposite Robinson's brigade and Geary's right. Artillery fire quickly brings its left wing, William Tucker's and Deas's brigades, to a "standstill" (in Williams's words), then drives it back in "utmost disorder." On the right, Walthall's Mississippians advance only a few yards before flopping to the ground; and although Manigault's men make a determined effort to reach the Union works, they find their path blocked by a "creek with a boggy, miry margin on each side," with the result that after making a costly attempt to cross it, they likewise either take cover or take to their heels. Cannons alone, according to Williams, have repulsed Hindman's Division, not a single unit of which has come within rifle range.

This ends Hood's assault. He has lost at least 1,500 killed, wounded, and missing, two-thirds of them in Stevenson's Division, which again has demonstrated, as it did at Resaca, a lack of offensive punch. Federal casualties, in contrast, number at most 250, with 86 of them being in Knipe's brigade and 72 in Strickland's, and even these are mainly in the 123rd New York (48) and the 14th Kentucky (70). What will be known as the affair at Kolb's farm is more a one-sided slaughter than it is a battle.[57]

Sherman spends most of the day in Palmer's and Howard's sector—a peculiar place to be, in view of the fact that the main Union effort is taking place well to the south, and he notified Schofield early in the morning that "I will probably meet you today about Mrs. Kolb's." At 5:30 P.M., having heard "some cannonading" from that direction, he signals Hooker: "How are you getting along?

Near what house are you?" But no answer comes, and in the evening Sherman returns to Big Shanty still unaware that the Confederates have made a major assault on his right. Then, at 9:30, Hooker's reply, which, since it is marked 5:30, must have been badly delayed in transit, arrives: "We have repulsed two heavy attacks and feel confident, our only apprehension being our extreme right flank. Three entire corps are in front of us."

Sherman cannot comprehend what he reads. Wouldn't "two heavy attacks" have produced more than the brief and not particularly loud cannonading that he heard late in the afternoon? Why should Hooker be apprehensive about his right flank? Has not Schofield obeyed the order given him in the morning by Dayton in person to support the XX Corps in the Powder Spring road? And most incredible of all, how can there be three enemy corps—in effect Johnston's whole army!—in front of Hooker?

Sherman promptly sends two messages. One, to Hooker, reads:

> Dispatch received. Schofield was ordered this morning to be on the Powder Springs and Marietta road in close support of your right. Is this not the case? There cannot be three corps in your front. Johnston has but three corps, and I know from personal inspection that a full proportion is now and has been all day on his right and center.

The other message is to Thomas. In it Sherman, after quoting his 5:30 query to Hooker and Hooker's late-arriving reply, again asserts that all three Confederate corps cannot possibly be facing Hooker. "Still," he continues, "it is very natural the enemy should meet Hooker." Therefore if Schofield, despite orders, is not covering the XX Corps's flank, Thomas should "send a staff officer at once and notify him of the necessity" and, if need be, call on Palmer and McPherson for reinforcements: "Tomorrow, if need be, we must bring matters to a crisis."

As these dispatches go forth, one arrives from Thomas. It contains the reassuring information that Schofield has a division with Hooker at the Kolb house but also the startling news that Hooker has reported that "the concurrent testimony of prisoners captured represents that the whole rebel army lies between him and Marietta," that both Hooker and Schofield state that the enemy is advancing against them, and that "just before dark" he received a signal message that "reports heavy musketry firing on Hooker's front." Consequently, although Thomas believes that Hooker and Schofield are exaggerating the threat, he has taken steps to form a reserve; and should the enemy attack, "I will hold him in check, and think that McPherson will then have a fair chance to overwhelm any force between him and Marietta."

While Sherman ponders these words, which still leaves the situation on the right vague, he receives a second message from Thomas, written at 10 P.M. in response to Sherman's dispatch of half an hour ago. Thomas repeats, in essence, that adequate measures have been taken to repel a Confederate thrust along the Powder Springs road, and he again urges Sherman to have McPherson move against Marietta: "The enemy cannot possibly send an overwhelming force against Hooker without exposing his weakness to McPherson." However for some reason he makes no mention at all of the fight at Kolb's farm, nor does he provide any information about the size and identity of the attacking Confederate force and the number of casualties on both sides. Not until toward midnight does Sherman finally get a specific and accurate account of the engagement. It comes in the form of a 9 P.M. report from Schofield:

> I have pushed forward on the Marietta road until I connect with General Hooker's right. . . . The fighting has been heavy . . . and has been decidedly to our advantage. . . . Prisoners say the whole of Hood's corps left their right and came to this side of Marietta yesterday. They made an assault upon me and also upon Hooker this evening with the evident purpose of breaking our lines, yet their assaults were hardly strong enough for the force named. Prisoners all agree that Hood's whole corps was in our front today, and do not know that any force but cavalry took their place on the enemy's right. My loss is about 100, that of the enemy much larger.

Sherman can now lie down for his short night's sleep knowing that his right is in no immediate danger and that Hooker and Schofield at most face only Hood's Corps and already have repelled an attack by it without difficulty. What Sherman does not know but resolves to find out in the morning is why Hooker has claimed that he was beset by Johnston's entire army and why he has expressed concern about his flank, in spite of its being supported by Schofield. Hooker had better have an explanation—a good one.[58]

At daylight on June 23, Sherman sets out for Kolb's farm. On the way he passes through Butterfield's division, formed in reserve behind the rest of the XX Corps, and learns from Butterfield that it had not been engaged in yesterday's battle. At Kolb's farm, Sherman finds the XXIII Corps on the Powder Spring road, "its head of column abreast Hooker's right." He then meets with Schofield and Hooker in a "little church," as it has started to rain. He shows Schofield the signal-message that Hooker sent yesterday at 5:30 P.M., stating, "We have repulsed two heavy attacks, and feel confident, our only apprehension being from our extreme right flank." Schofield becomes "very angry," and "pretty sharp words" pass between him and Hooker, with Schofield declaring that his "head of column (Hascall's division) had been, at the time of the battle, actually in advance of Hooker's line; that the attack or sally of the enemy struck his troops before it did Hooker's," as Hooker knew at the time; and that he could show Sherman that Hascall's dead are "lying farther out than any of Hooker's." Sherman thereupon asks Hooker, who has "pretended not to have known" that Hascall was on his right, why he had called for help to protect that flank when he had had Butterfield's division available for that purpose; Sherman also tells Hooker that the "enemy's sally must have been made by one corps (Hood's)," not by three. With this the meeting ends, but as the generals ride away from the church, Sherman warns Hooker that "such things must not occur again," whereupon Hooker goes into a "sulk," even though Sherman has treated him "more gently than the occasion demanded."[59]

Such, at any rate, is the account that Sherman gives in his *Memoirs*. Unfortunately for the convenience of the historian and for Sherman's reputation for veracity, the only things in it that can be considered true or at least probable are that Sherman went to the Kolb farm on the morning of June 23, that he saw Butterfield's division in reserve and Hascall's on the Powder Spring road, that he talked to Schofield and to Hooker (but separately and not together), and that he dressed down Hooker, who in turn manifested resentment. Everything else in the account is either demonstrably false or highly questionable. Butterfield's division was (as we know, and as Sherman easily could have ascertained) on Hooker's left and so could not have reinforced his right on June 22, and it is inconceivable that Butterfield, Hooker's close friend, would have told Sherman otherwise.[60] Schofield, in his autobiography and in notes he made on Sherman's *Memoirs*, states that he has no recollection of having met with Sherman and Hooker in the church but has the "impression" that Hascall conferred with them there; thus if anyone was "very angry" at Hooker and exchanged "pretty sharp words" with him, it had to have been Hascall. Schofield also comments that Sherman did not show him Hooker's 5:30 P.M. signal-message but merely gave him a verbal description of it and that if he had been able to read it, he would have told Sherman that it simply meant that Hooker was concerned about the *army's* flank and not his own, for Hooker was fully aware that the XXIII Corps was in position on his right and could not possibly "have meant by his dispatch what General Sherman understood it to mean." Moreover, since Hooker in a message sent to Thomas at midnight on June 22 gives due credit for Hascall's assistance in repelling Hood's assault, it is impossible to believe that during his conference with Sherman and Hascall, Hooker at first denied, then "pretended" hitherto not to have known, that Hascall was on his right (which, incidentally, seems to rule out even Hascall as the one who became "very angry" at Hooker).[61] Finally, although a minor matter, the rain that Sherman says caused him to hold his alleged meeting with Hooker and Schofield inside the "little church" must have been confined exclusively to that spot, for the unanimous testimony of diaries and letters is that June 23 was sunny and dry. In fact, Sherman himself mentions in a telegram to Halleck on the night of June 23 that "the weather is now better, and the roads are drying up fast."[62]

Some of the manifold and manifest flaws in Sherman's account, such as the rainfall, can be attributed to faulty memory. Most of them, and the main ones, however, are the product of his intense personal animosity toward Hooker, a feeling that had not subsided ten years later when he wrote his *Memoirs*. Thus, in addition to perpetrating the falsehoods described above, he also in the *Memoirs* denounces Hooker for violating the chain of command by sending his 5:30 P.M. signal-message directly to him instead of by way of Thomas, totally ignoring the fact that Hooker had done it in response to a direct inquiry from Sherman himself.[63]

The sole legitimate complaint that Sherman can bring against Hooker is for reporting that the whole Confederate army was between him and Marietta. Yet even in this regard some things can be said by way of explanation if not extenuation. First, as Sherman and Thomas both noted, concentrating a powerful force against the Union right was a logical move for Johnston to make, and that possibility no doubt worried Hooker from the outset on June 22. Second, Butterfield's division in fact did encounter the left of Hardee's Corps, and while advancing toward Marietta, Geary's and Williams's troops skirmished not only with Hood's pickets but also with Ferguson's cavalry, which organizationally belonged to the Confederate Army of Mississippi (Polk's, now Loring's, Corps). Thus Hooker had some basis in reality for his fantastic assertion that he faced all three of the enemy's corps, and this claim, combined with his dislike and distrust of Sherman and his feeling that the XX Corps too many times already had been recklessly exposed to disaster, caused him to become, as Thomas put it, "stampeded." In the battle itself, however, he had been "Fighting Joe" at his best, so much so that in a letter written two days afterward, Colonel Robinson of Williams's division proclaims enthusiastically: "Hooker is *the* commander. I wish you could see him when a fight is underway. His enthusiasm is enough in itself to inspire any man." Any man, that is, except Sherman.[64]

North of the Powder Springs road, Geary's and Williams's divisions remain behind what have become full-fledged breastworks; and south of it, Hascall's merely advances a short distance beyond the Kolb house before fortifying also. Up ahead, through intervals in the forest, Hood's men can be seen in strong entrenchments that are steadily growing stronger. Attacking them would be obvious and costly folly; therefore the question is, Can they be flanked?

Sherman orders Schofield to find out. During the afternoon, skirmishers from Colonel James W. Reilly's brigade of Cox's division move down the Sandtown road from the Cheney house toward Olley's Creek. They find the crossing guarded by dismounted and barricaded cavalry (they are Ross's Texans) backed by artillery. At 8 P.M., Schofield sends Sherman a dispatch notifying him that the Confederates hold a line that "extends much beyond the point to which my line would reach" so long as his left remains anchored to the Powder Springs road. In other words, far from being able to outflank the enemy, his own flank is in potential peril.

While Schofield's message is on the way, Sherman returns to his headquarters. It has been an irksome and discouraging day. In addition to the blowup with Hooker, Rebel raiders have cut the railroad and telegraph near Dalton; an attempt by detachments of McCook's cavalry to do likewise to Johnston's communications south of the Chattahoochee has come to naught when they couldn't even get across the river; and worst of all, "progress" in what can now only be called the Siege of Kennesaw continues to be measured in yards and feet. "The whole country," Sherman telegraphs Halleck at 9:30, "is one vast fort, and Johnston must have full fifty miles of connected trenches, with abatis and finished batteries. . . . As fast as we gain one position the enemy has another all ready."

Then Sherman receives Schofield's message stating in effect that the Confederate left reaches a mile beyond the Union right, for that is how far the crossing of Olley's Creek is from the Cheney house. Thus there can be no turning of Johnston's south flank unless Sherman extends his own line a substantially greater distance in the same direction. The obvious solution would be to shift the Army of the Cumberland farther to its right so as to enable Schofield to do the same. The following morning, however, Thomas reports that "the enemy's entrenchments in front of Howard and Palmer are very strong," that his troops are "much fatigued," and that "Howard's and Palmer's fronts are now so much extended that it will be exceedingly difficult for them to mass a sufficient number of men to make an effective move on any point." Far from endorsing further movement southward, Thomas suggests that "if Schofield and Hooker were moved up on the Powder Springs and Marietta road it would contract our lines and enable us to strengthen them."[65]

So that is that. There simply seems to be no safe and practical way to get around Johnston's left. Some other means, therefore, will have to be used to pry the Confederates off of Kennesaw. But what means?

One, in line with Thomas's proposal of two days ago, would be for McPherson to strike at Marietta from the north and/or east, taking advantage of the transfer of Hood's Corps to the other side of the town. A second would be to continue pounding the enemy with artillery and inching forward with infantry, seeking to wear him down until he is forced to retreat. And a third would be to assault his lines in the hope of somewhere breaking through.

Sherman rejects the first alternative out of hand. He does so for the same reason he consistently has refused to employ McPherson's forces against Johnston's right flank and instead has kept them concentrated along the railroad—namely, the fear of being cut off from his vital iron lifeline by a sudden enemy thrust to or above Big Shanty. This fear is so great that it outweighs the fact that Hood's Corps no longer faces McPherson and a report from Blair that the enemy trenches east of Marietta appear to be either empty or held only by cavalry.[66] The second alternative also is unacceptable to Sherman. It would be tantamount to accepting a stalemate that might enable Johnston to send reinforcements to Lee. This must not happen or even have a chance of happening. If it did, it would mean that Sherman had failed in his strategic mission of helping Grant win the war in Virginia by tying down the enemy in Georgia; it would mean failing Grant.

This leaves the third alternative, which Sherman chooses. He announces his choice in his reply to Thomas's report on the impracticality of stretching the Army of the Cumberland's front:

> Your note received. Schofield reports he can't go ahead . . . and is far outflanked. I suppose the enemy, with his smaller force, intends to surround us. But I propose to study the ground well, and the day after tomorrow break through. . . . According to Blair his [Johnston's] right is now at Roswell Factory, and according to Schofield his left is . . . across Olley's Creek; so our best chance is to break through.[67]

For the second time in a week, frustration has caused Sherman to propose what he promised he would not do when he set out from Acworth: "run head on" against the Confederate fortifications. The first time, June 17, an enemy retreat spared him and his men the probable consequences. Will he and they be so fortunate again?

As usual, Johnston is unhappy with his military situation. As usual, he has cause to be. His infantry, reduced now to about 43,000 effectives, occupies a line that now stretches eight miles, and he dares not stretch it further. East of Marietta, Wheeler's troopers are so "very thin in the trenches" that Brigadier General Winfield Scott Featherston, acting commander of Loring's Division, doubts they can "do much good" if attacked by a strong force (Blair's report on

the weakness of the Confederate defenses in this sector is absolutely correct).
And southwest of the town, nothing but Ross's small cavalry brigade covers the
left flank along the Sandtown road, down which the Federals, reportedly a
division, persistently probe. Keenly aware of these things, Johnston considers it
merely a matter of time before he will have to abandon Kennesaw and retreat to
the Chattahoochee.[68]

He does not, however, intend to fall back until he deems it absolutely necessary. He knows the effect that another withdrawal, especially one from a
position as strong and as close to Atlanta as Kennesaw, would have on the army,
on the public, and above all on Davis. It might even lead to Johnston's removal
from command.

Johnston's friend Senator Wigfall, who is traveling to Texas with his wife and
two daughters, knows and fears the same thing. On the evening of June 24,
leaving his family with Mrs. Johnston in Atlanta, he visits Johnston at his
Marietta headquarters. Wigfall tells Johnston that he has heard rumors in
Richmond that the president is so displeased by the general's frequent retreats
and failure to engage Sherman in a decisive battle that he intends to replace him
with Hood! Can Johnston, Wigfall asks, forestall such a calamity by defeating
Sherman or, at the very least, halting him north of the Chattahoochee?

Johnston answers that he cannot promise to do either. Sherman's vastly superior numbers (so Johnston describes them) enable him to carry out flanking
moves that compel the Confederates to retreat so as to safeguard their communications, and Sherman's constant entrenching makes it virtually impossible to
attack him successfully. Therefore the best, if not the only, way to turn back
Sherman is to attack and destroy his supply line with cavalry, and since most of
Johnston's own cavalry must be used to cover his flanks, that cavalry will have to
come from Alabama and Mississippi. Unfortunately, in spite of his repeated
requests and notwithstanding Forrest's recent victory at Brice's Cross Roads,
Davis has refused to order Stephen Lee to send a strong mounted force to operate
in Sherman's rear. Instead, Davis and Bragg have responded with curt, even rude,
rejections, with the latest and the rudest one having come just today.

Johnston hereupon shows Wigfall two documents. One is a copy of telegram,
dated June 22, from Stephen Lee to the War Department stating that "a formidable expedition is organizing under A. J. Smith against this department," that it is
estimated to number 20,000 troops, and that all he has to oppose it are 9,000
cavalry. The other is a copy of a June 23 memorandum from Davis to Bragg
regarding Lee's telegram. In it, after commenting that "the within indicates the
propriety of concentrating the force of General S. D. Lee for the defense of his
department," Davis declares that back in early May, he had authorized Polk to
take his "infantry alone" to Georgia, that he had done so on "the supposition that

the enemy would be met at Dalton or in front of it," and that the "retreat of the Army of Tennessee has exposed the country for the protection of which General Polk's troops were posted." Therefore, he concludes, "General S. D. Lee should get and keep in hand all the force he has left," and Johnston should be notified of the "condition of things" in Mississippi "so that he may not count on aid from General Lee, but rather perceive that the drafts upon the Department of Alabama, Mississippi, and East Louisiana have already been too great."

In effect, Davis is saying that if anyone deserves assistance, it is Stephen Lee, not Joseph Johnston!

Wigfall can draw his own conclusion from what Johnston has told and shown him, and he does so: Once more, Davis, out of obstinacy and personal spite, is denying Johnston the means needed to gain victory and thereby is exposing the Confederacy to another terrible, perhaps fatal, disaster in the West. Before leaving Johnston's headquarters, Wigfall promises to do all he can to pressure the president to send Forrest, or at least Morgan, to raid the railroads that feed Sherman's army. Johnston, for his part, resolves to continue, despite past rebuffs, his efforts to persuade Davis that he (Johnston) has retreated out of necessity, not out of choice; that the solution to stopping Sherman's army lies in its rear, not its front; and that it would be better, if need be, to sacrifice Mississippi rather than lose Atlanta and Georgia. Should Johnston succeed, then all still could turn out well; if not, then at least (but how important to him!) no one can justly blame him for the consequences. Meanwhile he will hold on to Kennesaw as long as he can without risking the safety of his army. Who knows? Maybe Sherman will commit a bad blunder.[69]

A couple of miles to the west, Sherman dictates an attack order to aide-de-camp Captain Lewis M. Dayton. He does so in his new headquarters, a tent (borrowed from Thomas) on "Signal Hill," an elevation about a half-mile south of the Marietta–Lost Mountain–Dallas road and behind the center of his army. He has had Van Duzer's men string telegraph wires to McPherson's, Thomas's, and Schofield's headquarters. If these function properly (soldiers cutting trees keep breaking them), he will become the first commander to conduct a battle by means of electricity.

When finished, the order calls for McPherson to "feign . . . a movement of his cavalry and one division of infantry" toward Marietta from the north but to "make his real attack at a point south and west of Kennesaw"; for Thomas to "assault the enemy at any point near his center, to be selected by himself"; and for Schofield to "feel well to his extreme right and threaten that flank of the enemy with display and artillery, but attack some one point of the enemy's line as near the Marietta and Powder Springs road as he can with prospect of success." All of these assaults are to begin "at 8 A.M. precisely" on June 27; each "will endeavor to break a single point of the enemy line, and make a secure lodgment beyond"; and the attacking columns shall be prepared to advance "toward Marietta and the railroad in case of success."[70]

In due course, Thomas, McPherson, and Schofield read their respective copies of the order. They dislike what they read. Thomas still favors taking advantage of Hood's departure to strike at Marietta from the north and east. McPherson, who at Resaca had demonstrated a reluctance to attack fortified positions even under the best of circumstances, considers the present circumstances far from good. And Schofield fears that an attack on "some one point of the enemy's line" near the Powder Springs road has no "prospect of success" whatsoever but has a superb prospect of bloody failure.[71]

Thomas probably manifests his misgivings, if not by words, then by his manner; but if so, Sherman ignores him. On the other hand, McPherson, more than likely remembering Sherman's criticism of his lack of aggressiveness at Resaca, not only says nothing but also advises his generals to do the same. As for Schofield, he is saved from protesting Sherman's order—supposing he would have the courage to protest it, which is doubtful—by Sherman himself. While visiting the right wing of his army on June 25, Sherman takes a look at the Confederate works covering the Powder Springs road and notes that they have been strengthened by embrasures for three batteries. He also sees for himself what Schofield reported two days earlier—namely, that the enemy line extends well beyond the XXIII Corps's flank. Hence, no doubt to Schofield's relief, Sherman decides to exempt the XXIII Corps from participation in the June 27 assault. Instead, starting tomorrow, Schofield will have Hascall demonstrate against the Rebel entrenchments south of the Powder Springs road while Cox moves down the Sandtown road and across Olley's Creek. This, Sherman hopes, will cause the Confederates to send troops to their left, thereby weakening their center and making it more vulnerable to a breakthrough.[72]

The attack order still stands for McPherson and Thomas; their only choice is to determine how best to execute it. In McPherson's case that problem is simplified by the fact that Sherman has stipulated where he wants him to strike—south of Kennesaw. Therefore, beginning on the night of June 25 and continuing through the next day, McPherson transfers the XV Corps from north of Big Kennesaw to west of Pigeon Hill, where it takes the place of Davis's and Baird's divisions of the XIV Corps. Its target, he instructs Logan, will be the west and south slopes of Pigeon Hill. A breakthrough there will enable it to reach Marietta via the Burnt Hickory road and at the same time will cut off the retreat of the Confederates on Kennesaw.

Thomas, on the other hand, has been authorized by Sherman to select himself his point of attack. Accompanied by Captain Henry S. Stone, Thomas spends much of June 25 searching for that point, sometimes going beyond the picket line. Stone does not see any place that appears to "afford the slightest prospect of success," and he gets the impression that neither does Thomas. Finally, Thomas chooses a sector, just south of the Dallas-Marietta road, where the opposing lines are close, but not so close as to preclude the deployment of a large assault force out of range and, more important, out of sight of the enemy. Next, on the morning of June 26, Thomas notifies Palmer and Howard that a division each from their corps will deliver the attack. In Palmer's case he also designates the division—Davis's—but leaves it up to Howard to select the one he wishes to employ, which turns out to be Newton's. Like the XV Corps, neither of these divisions so far during the campaign has made a full-fledged assault, which probably is why they are chosen to make one now.[73]

While McPherson and Thomas prepare for the main event in the center, Schofield and Cox conduct their sideshow on the right. During the afternoon of June 26, Colonel James W. Reilly's brigade establishes itself on the north bank of Olley's Creek at the Sandtown road crossing and pounds with artillery the Confederates who are entrenched along the other side. Simultaneously another of Cox's brigades, Colonel Robert K. Byrd's, crosses Olley's Creek a mile above Reilly's brigade and occupies a hill that connects with a series of heights that appear to Cox to run beyond the extreme left of the main Rebel line. Cox thereupon orders Byrd to fortify the position; then Cox reports what he has done and seen to Schofield, adding that he has encountered only dismounted cavalry. Schofield passes on this information to Sherman by telegraph, and Sherman wires back, directing Schofield to construct a "good bridge" over Olley's Creek where Byrd has crossed it and to resume operations in that quarter in the morning. Schofield, who already has started building the bridge, in turn instructs Cox to dislodge the Confederates at the Sandtown road crossing come tomorrow morning. What was intended to be a mere demonstration designed to draw enemy troops away from the center (which, incidentally, it has not done) shows promise of becoming something much more than that.[74]

Other than the skirmishing and cannonading along Olley's Creek, the front is unusually, one might say unnaturally, quiet on June 26, which happens to be Pentecost Sunday. Troops of both armies who are able and so inclined attend religious services. Here and there, opposing pickets arrange informal truces, a practice that has become common in recent weeks. After all, killing another Yank or Reb is not going to make any difference in the greater scheme of things, so why risk one's life trying to do it? Even the rival artillery batteries cease dueling. They might as well. Most of the Union projectiles pass harmlessly over Kennesaw, and the Confederate guns on the mountain are too high up to do much serious damage below. Actually, about all their firing achieves is a spectacular show which, along with the equally spectacular view, draws crowds of civilian sightseers to the summit of Big Kennesaw. Most of them are women, largely from Atlanta. Yesterday, in a letter to his wife, Captain Poe commented:

> By using a glass I can see . . . quite a bevy of Georgia's "fair daughters," on the top of the Mtn. looking with the greatest complacency upon the attempt to kill some of the "vile Yankees." One of them is standing upon a projecting rock, and occasionally waves her handkerchief in defiance. She is *wearing black.* I can't help wondering whether for a husband, father, or brother. . . . I must acknowledge a sort of admiration for her courage though I feel very sure that we have not got a sharpshooter along our whole line who would attempt deliberately to shoot her.

Sometime during the day, Sherman writes Ellen to tell her what he intends to do tomorrow. "My lines," he explains, "are ten miles long, and every change necessitates a large amount of work. Still we are now all ready and I *must* attack direct or turn the position. . . . This is Sunday and I will write up all my letters and tomorrow will pitch in at one or more points."

Across the lines, Hardee, against whose troops Sherman plans to "pitch in," also writes his wife: "My lines are strong and I feel perfectly confident of whipping the yankees whenever and whosoever [sic] they come."

The day ends with a beautiful sunset. To Sergeant Stewart of the 52nd Ohio, who will participate in tomorrow's attack, the trees and woods seem to have been "set on fire." They remind him of Moses' burning bush:

> And the angel of the LORD appeared unto him in a flame of fire out of the midst of a bush; and he looked, and, behold, the bush burned with fire, and the bush was not consumed. And Moses said, I will now turn aside, and see this great sight, why the bush is not burnt. And when the LORD saw that he turned aside to see, God called unto him out of the midst of the bush, and said, Moses, Moses. And he said, Here am I.[75]

Some of Logan's, Newton's, and Davis's troops have learned what they are going to do tomorrow morning from friendly staff officers or couriers. Others suspect it from such signs as the clearing out of the field hospitals with the obvious purpose of making room for new patients—lots of them. But most do not know it until just before dawn on June 27, when their officers line them up and tell them to get ready for an attack. Whenever and however they find out, they are surprised and not at all pleased. They had assumed that Sherman, using the same method he had used at Dalton, Resaca, Cassville, and Allatoona, would flank Johnston off of Kennesaw. But they will do their best; they only hope that Sherman knows what he is doing.

They eat breakfast, stack knapsacks and haversacks, fill cartridge boxes and canteens (fire and water are the absolute necessities), make sure their rifles are in good working order, tighten their belts, give a tug to their caps or hats, and then march to the jumping-off points for the attack. In the XV Corps sector, Logan has designated three brigades to make it: Walcutt's of Harrow's division and Giles Smith's and Joseph Lightburns's of Brigadier General Morgan L. Smith's division. Each brigade forms a double line of battle, with Walcutt's on the left, Giles Smith's in the center, and south of the Burnt Hickory–Marietta road and facing almost due north, Lightburn's on the right. Altogether they number 5,500 men and occupy a one-third-mile front. Harrow's other two brigades and Osterhaus's division stand in reserve, ready to bolster success or salvage failure. Although he does not show it, Logan anticipates the latter, having confided to his wife in a letter yesterday that a "bloody road" lies before his corps.

About a mile to the south, Newton's division, 5,000 strong, assembles behind the outer works of Stanley's division. Nathan Kimball's and George D. Wagner's brigades are to the left, and Harker's is to the right; they are drawn up in "column of divisions," which means that their regiments have lined up in five rows of two companies each, one regiment after the other. This, the narrowest and deepest formation in the drill book, has been expressly ordered by Howard. He hopes that it will facilitate the movement and concealment of Newton's division over the first third of the distance to the Confederate lines, "the ground being favorable for this," and then will enable it to make a "sudden rush of numbers" over the enemy works. The rank and file, however, take a different view of the matter. "Damn these assaults in column," growls one of Newton's soldiers. "They make a man more afraid of being trampled to death by the rear line than he is of the enemy."

To Newton's right, Davis, who evidently is acting under direct orders from Thomas, selects McCook's and Colonel John G. Mitchell's brigades, approximately 4,000 men, for what he terms (sarcastically?) "the distinguished duty" of delivering his division's assault, with Morgan's brigade being held in reserve. Davis then goes forward with McCook and Mitchell and shows them their objective. It is a hill, about 600 yards distant, that forms a westward-facing salient in the enemy front. Much of the ground leading to it is rocky and covered with trees and brush, but the Confederate works on top of it appear to

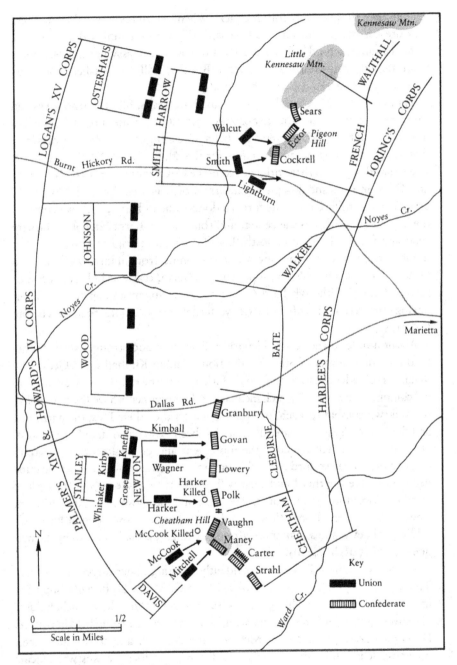

Battle of Kennesaw Mountain, June 27

be unprotected by abatis, and Davis therefore considers it more vulnerable than any other available point of attack.

After seeing where they are to try to go, McCook and Mitchell return to their brigades and deploy them in four lines of battle, a regiment to each line, to be preceded by a fifth regiment acting as skirmishers. Basically it is the same formation used by Hooker at Resaca and New Hope Church and by Howard at Pickett's Mill. Whether it will be more successful today than it had been on those occasions remains to be seen.

The sun now is fully up—a hot sun that will soon send the temperature soaring to a hundred degrees.[76]

At 8 A.M., precisely on schedule, McPherson's artillery, fifty-one pieces according to Confederate count, opens up on Kennesaw, causing one Union soldier to hope (in vain) that it will blow the Rebs to "smithereens." Simultaneously Logan's assault brigades move forward. The going is difficult. They have to cut or crawl through dense clusters of briars and brush that are interwoven with snakelike vines, slosh across shallow but muddy-banked Nose's Creek, and in the case of Lightburn's brigade, wade a knee-deep swamp. The skirmishers cannot keep ahead of the main line, and the main line quickly turns into the usual formationless swarm. Finally they reach relatively open terrain. Twenty paces ahead they see rifle pits. The gray-clad men in them fire. The Northerners fire back, then, with a wild yell, charge.

Thomas's cannons also go into action at 8 A.M., concentrating on the salient hill and the area adjoining it. Some of his infantry, however, still are deploying, and so he defers the order to charge. While they wait to advance, McCook's troops gaze at the hill they have just been told they are to take. There is, later writes Major Holmes of the 52nd Ohio, an "ominous stillness" in their ranks, for all know that "many must fall" getting there. Sensing their mood, McCook strides up and down in front of them, reciting the stanzas of Thomas Babington Macaulay's "Horatius at the Bridge":

> Then out spoke bold Horatius,
> The captain of the gate,
> To every man upon this earth
> Death cometh soon or late;
> And how can man die better
> Than facing fearful odds
> For the ashes of his fathers
> And the temples of his gods?

Several hundred yards to the north, Harker's troops also stand poised to charge, their rifles uncapped and bayoneted, for Harker has ordered them to rely solely on cold steel. They have no idea at all of what they are going up

Dan McCook: "To every man upon this earth / Death cometh soon or late."
(Harper's Weekly)

against, because timber and brush totally screen the enemy's line on their front. In his headquarters journal, Fullerton notes that "we are about to make an assault upon works we know little about." Harker, a twenty-seven-year-old West Pointer who recently has received a brigadier's commission for outstanding leadership and bravery at Chickamauga, has given his private papers to a member of his staff, telling him "I shall not come out of this charge today alive."

Finally, at about 9 A.M., an hour late, all of Thomas's infantry are in position, and he orders the attack to begin. Signal cannons roar, bugles blare, and with a cheer the assault columns rush forward. On the right, Mitchell's brigade heads for the south angle of the salient hill, and McCook's aims for its apex. On the left, Harker's brigade advances toward a point north of the hill, as does Wagner's. Kimball's brigade, however, remains behind, its assignment being to reinforce Wagner and Harker should their onslaughts falter. Soon all four columns come under shellfire, and the skirmishers, after plunging across a muddy rivulet, come upon the Confederate picket line.

Over around Pigeon Hill, Logan's troops by now have routed, killed, captured, or even "trampled underfoot" the Rebel pickets; in one rifle pit alone they bayonet and club to death nine Georgians, members of Mercer's inexperienced brigade. Up ahead, however, Logan's men behold a veritable maze of knobs, cliffs, and ridges, all of them steep and rocky, and all surmounted by log-and-dirt fortifications filled with gray-clad infantry, fronted by abatis and supported by artillery. Nevertheless they plunge onward. Advancing across an open field, Lightburn's brigade attempts to storm Pigeon Hill from the south. Withering fire from Walker's Division rips its ranks, as do shells from some of French's cannons atop Little Kennesaw. Lightburn's force abruptly halts, then falls back to the cover of some woods. Even though the din of battle continues, the groans and screams of the wounded who have been left behind in the field can still be heard.

West of Pigeon Hill, Walcutt's and Giles Smith's brigades cross a gorge, claw through tangles of heaped-up tree limbs, and climb over huge rocks as they endeavor to reach the Rebel works, which here are manned by Cockrell's stalwart Missouri brigade. Some of the attackers make it to the abatis; a few somehow get through it, only to be shot down or forced to surrender; but most of them do not. In some places they find themselves confronted by cliffs so steep that it would be difficult to climb them even if there were no enemy at the top shooting at them or, here and there, rolling boulders down upon them. The closest any of them come to breaking through occurs when some of Walcutt's men, swerving to their left, seize an undefended spur of Little Kennesaw between Cockrell's and Sears's brigades; however, a counterattack by the Missourians and Mississippians quickly drives them off, and that is that. Realizing

Charles Harker: "I shall not come out of this charge today alive." *(Harper's Weekly)*

that they cannot go forward, yet reluctant to retreat, the Federals get behind rocks and trees, from which cover they fire back at the virtually invulnerable Confederates. After a while, Logan rides forward to see for himself what is happening, and on finding that "many men were being uselessly slain," he orders Walcutt and Giles Smith to withdraw to the other side of the gorge and entrench. As the pullback takes place, one of Cockrell's Missourians yells tauntingly, "Why don't you come on up, Yanks, and draw your Georgia?"

Newton's and Davis's skirmishers, like Logan's, quickly overrun the Confederate pickets and push on. Marching in quickstep, the four assault columns follow in their wake, scarcely slowed by the brush, webs of vines, and "slashings" of felled trees that they encounter. Mounted officers, however, find it expedient to dismount. The sole exception is Harker, for whom it is a matter of pride and honor always to ride into battle. Once through these obstacles, the columns halt briefly to realign, then start up the incline, first at the double-quick, then running.

Waiting for them are Cheatham's and Cleburne's divisions: unknowingly the Federals have chosen to attack the troops in Johnston's army that are least likely to give way before any attack. Furthermore these troops occupy trenches anchored by redoubts bristling with cannons and so deep that in order to fire over the head-logged parapets, which consist of six to nine feet of hard-packed red Georgia clay, they have to climb up onto a one-and-a-half-foot-high firing step. The only weak point in the Confederate defenses along this part of the front is the salient hill, which is held by Maney's Brigade of Cheatham's Division (henceforth it will be known as "Cheatham's Hill"). Unlike the rest of the line, as Davis has noted, it is not protected by a regular abatis but merely by a flimsy pile of cut saplings, the consequence of a lack of large trees in the vicinity. Potentially even more dangerous for the defenders, about thirty to sixty yards in front of Maney's trench the ground drops off sharply, creating a space in which attackers can neither be seen nor shot, thus providing them with an opportunity to reach the trench, which is on the topographical rather than the military crest of the hill, in a quick, overwhelming rush.

At present, however, Maney's Tennesseans have no trouble at all seeing and shooting at the oncoming Yankees. Listening to the bullets buzz about them, it occurs to Major Holmes that "if I should hold out my hand I could catch several of them—a handful—immediately"; but he refrains from attempting the experiment. All around him he hears the "sickening sound" made by the "thud of a minie ball through human flesh." A soldier in his regiment who has never before quailed in combat suddenly whirls about, his face "as white as death's." Holmes raises his sword and says "Stop, Joe." Without a word the soldier turns around and goes forward again. Afterward he has no recollection of the incident.

Panting, sweating, and already half-exhausted, the Federals continue to ascend the hill, leaving behind an ever-lengthening trail of dead and wounded. Then Mitchell's brigade, moving toward the south angle of Cheatham's works, runs into branches and brush "cross-lapped in a manner" that makes it impossible to advance in line. At the same time a Confederate 4-gun battery, posted to the south of the hill and concealed by brush piles, opens up, catching the brigade in a deadly enfilade fire. Mitchell's men lurch forward a few more yards; some of them actually scale the Rebel ramparts and are promptly killed or captured. But in the end, all who still are on their feet lie down on the ground, then start crawling back toward the drop-off and, they hope, safety. Survival, not victory, is their only goal now.

Because McCook's brigade is attacking the western apex of the salient, which the Confederates afterwards dub "The Dead Angle" or "Devil's Elbow," neither the masked 4-gun battery to the south nor a 2-gun section north of the hill can fire at it without endangering Maney's troops. This, and the absence of obstructions as formidable as those encountered by Mitchell's brigade, enables a comparatively large number of its men, mainly from the 52nd Ohio, which is in the rear rank of the assault column, to reach the base of the parapet. On the other side the Tennesseans, realizing that they will be trapped and slaughtered in their trench should the Yanks get on top of the parapet, fire their rifles as fast as they can, not even bothering to aim but simply thrusting the barrel beneath the head log and pulling the trigger. Soon some rifles become literally too hot to handle, or else they fill up with molten lead from bullet shavings. Their possessors thereupon discard them and resort to throwing stones at the bluecoats.

In the face of such fierce resistance, only a handful of McCook's men manage to climb onto the parapet, one of them being the colorbearer of the 52nd Ohio, who plants his flag on the top, shoots down a Rebel captain who tries to seize it, and then goes down himself, riddled with bullets. Standing a few yards away, near the south angle, McCook urges them on. "Colonel Dan," a soldier cries, "for God's sake get down—they will shoot you!" "God damn you, attend to your own business!" McCook snarls back. Then he falls, a bullet through the chest. As four men carry him to the rear, he gives his last order: "Stick it to them!" Twenty days hence, one day after being promoted to brigadier general, he will die at home in Steubenville, Ohio.

McCook's successor, Colonel Caleb Dilworth of the 85th Illinois, orders a retreat, which in fact already is under way. Most of the troops scramble down the hill, in Holmes's words, "breathing hard through fear and physical exhaustion." Reaching the drop-off below the crest and perceiving that it offers shelter from the hail of lead that continues to pelt them, they flop flat on the ground, hugging it as if it were life itself, which in a sense it is. Many other survivors from both McCook's and Mitchell's brigades remain behind on top of the hill, either unable or afraid to flee. Eventually 200 of them, according to the adjutant of the 1st Tennessee, accept Confederate summonses to "come over"— that is, to surrender. Others lie motionless, pretending to be dead and waiting until it is dark and safe to crawl away.

After repulsing the assault, some of the Tennesseans shout in exultation, "Chickamauga! Chickamauga!" Not since then have they shot so many Yankees or seen so many others run. Most of the Tennesseans, though, are in no condition to celebrate. Never before has Sam Watkins of the 1st Tennessee, a veteran of numerous battles, beheld "so many broken down and exhausted men," who like himself are "sick as a horse" and "wet with blood and sweat," their tongues "cracked for water" and "faces blackened with powder and smoke." Nevertheless they remain at their posts, because the Federals are only a few yards away below the crest and they might charge again. Another attack, however, does not occur. Thomas, Palmer, and Davis all think that McCook's brigade has been, in Thomas's words, "compelled to fall back and reorganize" and do not learn the truth until several hours later. By then the Confederates, realizing that the hill is the weak point in their defenses, have hurried up reserves and dug no fewer than three new trench lines, bolstered by artillery, behind Maney's position.

At least McCook's and Mitchell's brigades have secured a foothold—or, to be more exact, a belly hold—near their objective. Wagner's and Harker's troops are not even that successful. As they emerge from the belt of timber and brush that hitherto has screened the Confederate works from their view, rifle and artillery fire from Vaughan's brigade of Cheatham's division and Polk's, Lowrey's, and Govan's brigades of Cleburne's division literally blows away the heads of their narrow columns, which quickly dissolve into haphazard clusters of men following their regimental flags. Still they push onward until they come up against not merely one but three rows of obstacles: first, chest-high "tanglefoot," then sharp-pointed pine poles planted four inches apart and slanting forward at a forty-five-degree angle, and finally chevaux-de-frise—logs crisscrossed with pointed stakes that have been inserted through holes bored with augers. Most of the attackers lie down and begin firing at the enemy trenches, providing cover for small groups of comrades who frantically strive to pull down, climb over, or wiggle through these barriers. Some of them get through and even reach the Confederate parapet, but they are either shot down or forced to surrender. Concluding that it is suicidal as well as useless to persist any longer in the assault, Harker's troops start to drift rearward. Harker, still astride his white horse, tries to rally them by waving his hat and shouting, "Come on boys!" Then a bullet tears through his arm and chest, and he tumbles from his saddle.

His men, several of whom are killed in the process, carry him back to the Union lines, where in the evening he dies, his prebattle prophecy fulfilled. Soon after he goes down, his brigade flees (to quote one of its members, Captain John Tuttle of the 3rd Kentucky) "like an immense herd of infuriated buffaloes running over and trampling each other under foot." Wagner's troops likewise break into pell-mell flight, not stopping until they are brought up short by the leveled bayonets of one of Stanley's brigades posted in the rear.

Less than an hour has gone by since Newton's and Davis's assaults began. Shortly after 10 A.M., Thomas, evidently misled by a no-longer-true message from Colonel Opdycke, who is in command of Newton's skirmishers, to the effect that Wagner's brigade is "within a few feet of the enemy's works" and a fresh column could be "led through it over the enemy's works," directs Howard to have Newton send in Kimball's brigade. Newton does so, and Kimball's troops repeat the experience of Wagner's and Harker's. As Kimball subsequently reports, his lead regiment, the 74th Illinois, is "swept away"; only twelve of its men get to the Confederate trenches to be killed or captured. Ten minutes after it has advanced, Kimball's brigade retreats. Newton, deciding that it had been amply "demonstrated that the enemy works were too strong to be taken," thereupon orders all of his troops to fall back to the main Union line, which they do except for skirmishers who occupy the rifle pits formerly held by the Rebel pickets.

Kimball's repulse ends the assault but not the fighting. Sharpshooters on both sides set to their murderous work, and Thomas's artillery, which of necessity had to stop firing when the infantry moved forward, resumes its bombardment, and Hardee's guns respond. After a while, shells and wadding ignite brush fires in front of Govan's Brigade, threatening to burn alive the scores of Union wounded who are lying there. Realizing their plight, Lieutenant Colonel Will Martin of the 1st Arkansas ties a white handkerchief to a ramrod, then climbs atop the parapet, where he waves his improvised flag of truce and shouts across the battlefield: "Come and get your wounded; they are burning to death; we won't fire a gun till you get them away. Be quick!" The Federals also cease firing, and groups of them come forward to join with Cleburne's men in removing the wounded and, in many cases, plundering the dead. "Such," comments Sergeant Bliss of the 16th Alabama, writing his mother two days later, "is the effect of war." Once the wounded have been carried to safety, both sides return to their positions, and the fighting resumes.[77]

At 10:45 A.M., Thomas telegraphs Sherman that Newton's and Davis's assaults have been repulsed. Almost simultaneously, McPherson reports the same regarding Logan. Sherman now knows that his attempt to break through the

Confederate center is a failure, at least so far. Should he persist? At 1:30 P.M. he queries Thomas: "Do you think that you can break any part of the enemy's line today?" Ten minutes later Thomas answers: "From what the officers tell me I do not think we can carry the works by assault at this point today, but they can be approached by saps and the enemy driven out." (Saps are zigzag trenches dug toward enemy fortifications until they get so close as to make them untenable. They require much time and great labor and normally are used only in formal sieges, such as at Vicksburg.)

Sherman ponders Thomas's proposal, then at 2:45 P.M. he responds: "Is there anything in the enemy's present position that if we should approach by regular saps he could not make a dozen new parapets before one sap is completed? Does the nature of the ground warrant the time necessary for regular approaches?" In other words, Sherman doubts that saps would succeed and fears that resorting to them will prolong the stalemate around Kennesaw that he had hoped to break with his assault.

Thomas's reply is blunt:

> The division commanders report the enemy's works exceedingly strong; in fact, so strong that they cannot be carried by assault except by immense sacrifice, even if they can be carried at all. I think, therefore, the best chance is to approach them by regular saps, and if we can find a favorable position to batter them down. We have already lost heavily today without gaining any material advantage; one or two more such assaults would use up this army.[78]

By implication, Thomas is telling Sherman that so long as he refuses to try to flank Johnston off of Kennesaw, he will have to resort to the arduous, tedious, and dubious methods of siege warfare. This (as Thomas doubtlessly knows) Sherman will not do, both for the reasons previously given and also because his temperament forbids it. Hence by midafternoon, Sherman is left with the second of the alternatives he had described yesterday to Ellen: "I *must* attack direct or turn the position." The only question is where and how to do it.

Shortly after 5 P.M. the answer to the first part of that question arrives in the form of a telegram from Schofield relaying a dispatch from Cox. In it Cox, who during the morning drove Ross's cavalry from the Sandtown road crossing of Olley's Creek and then marched down that road, states that he has occuped a ridge overlooking the valley of Nickajack Creek, a stream paralleling the Chattahoochee and little more than a mile from it, and that he believes that if reinforced by Hascall's division, he possibly could turn the enemy's left flank. Sherman at once orders Schofield to go and see for himself if what Cox says is true. If it is. . . .

Schofield does so and at 7 P.M. telegraphs confirmation:

General Cox's position overlooks the Nickajack Valley and seems to control the ridge between the creeks [Olley's and Nickajack], so that the enemy cannot extend his line along the ridge without [first] displacing us. It threatens the enemy's left rear and seems to me more important than I first supposed. I think it should be held by my whole force if you propose to move in that direction.

Schofield's message leaves no doubt that Johnston can be flanked on the south. But doing it requires a much stronger force than Schofield's little corps and also an extension of the Union right by more than three miles, the distance from the Cheney house to the ridge held by Cox's division. Such a force and such an extension can be provided only by shifting all of McPherson's army to the west side of Kennesaw, which means leaving the railroad. Dare Sherman risk it? He remains reluctant. When at 8 P.M. he reports to Halleck on the day's fighting, he states: "I cannot well turn the position of the enemy without abandoning my railroad, and we are already so far from our supplies that it is as much as the road can do to feed and supply the army. There are no supplies of any kind here."[79]

Yet the more he thinks about the matter, the more it becomes apparent that the sole realistic answer to how Johnston's position can be turned is to abandon the railroad and swing his entire army around to the right. Therefore he studies his map, looking for a point in Johnston's rear which can be reached quickly from Cox's position while at the same time maintaining at least a wagon-road connection to the north. Finally he finds it: Fulton, a railroad hamlet about seven miles south of Marietta.

At 9 P.M., Sherman telegraphs Thomas: "Are you willing to risk the move on Fulton, cutting loose from our railroad? It would bring matters to a crisis, and Schofield has secured the way." Thomas answers with questions: "How far is Fulton from the crossing of Olley's Creek? Will we have to cross any other streams of much size? When do you wish to start?" Sherman replies: "According to Merrill's map, it is about ten miles. Nickajack the only stream to cross. Time for starting, day after tomorrow." Thomas wires back: "What force do you think of moving with? If with the greater part of the army, I think it decidedly better than butting against breastworks twelve feet thick and strongly abatised." The sarcasm contained in these words is obvious, as is their implication, namely, that Thomas has a low opinion of the way in which Sherman has been conducting operations during the past two weeks. Sherman responds: "If we move on Fulton we must move with the whole army, leaving our railroad, on the chance of success." Then, indulging in some sarcastic innuendo of his own, he adds: "Go where we may we will find the breastworks and the abatis, unless we move more rapidly than we have heretofore."

Sherman waits ten minutes for Thomas's reaction to this. None comes, and at 9:50 P.M., Sherman has his telegraph operator tap out a closing message: "I will see you tomorrow. In mean time make such preparations as you can."[80]

So, after trying to break through Fortress Kennesaw by direct frontal assault, Sherman decides to try to go around it. It is a decision that many of his troops, if they knew of it, would wish he had made about fourteen hours earlier or at any time prior to 8 o'clock on the morning of June 27.

"I tell you the men were mowed down like grass." Thus writes a young soldier in McCook's brigade to his parents in Illinois. He tells the terrible truth. Logan's killed and wounded total 586; Newton's, 654; and Davis's, 824. Add 17 missing from Logan's corps and approximately 300 prisoners from Newton's and Davis's divisions; add also 57 and 200 casualties suffered respectively by the XVI and XVII corps while demonstrating against the Confederate right; and allow 300 more for backup units of the IV and XIV corps and skirmishers of the XX and XXIII corps; then Sherman is substantially correct when in his report he puts the cost of the assault at "nearly 3,000." To be sure, as Civil War butcher bills go, this is rather modest. Lee paid a much higher price at Malvern Hill and Cemetery Ridge, and it is trifling compared to the charges recently run up by Grant in Virginia. Nevertheless it is high enough, particularly in McCook's and Mitchell's brigades. The ground in front of Maney's position, writes Captain Hall, is "completely strewn with dead bodies"; and Colonel Melancthon Smith, Hardee's artillery chief, notes that many of the corpses have been "hit by three or four bullets" or have literally been torn asunder by exploding shells, producing rivulets of blood ten feet long. Moreover, because of the columnar assault formations that they employed, most of the losses in Newton's and Davis's divisions are concentrated in the lead regiments. Thus 357 of Mitchell's 414 dead and wounded come from the 113th and 121st Ohio; four regiments have contributed 183 of the 231 casualties in Harker's eight-regiment brigade; the 49th Indiana has lost approximately 150 of Wagner's 215 total; and more than one-third (72) of Kimball's 194 casualties have occurred in the 74th Illinois. The sole exception to this pattern is the 52nd Ohio, which in spite of being in the rear at the start of the assault, has suffered more than one-fourth of the 410 killed and wounded in McCook's five regiments. In the XV Corps, because of its linear deployment, losses are more evenly distributed among regiments, as well as being lower overall. Even so the casualties of Walcutt's brigade, 246, exceed those of Giles Smith's by nearly 100, with all but 39 of the former being in three of its five regiments, notably the 97th Indiana which, according to its commander, Lieutenant Colonel Cavins, went into battle with 200 men and came out of it with 66 killed or wounded and its flag "all torn into ribbons by shot and shell, and . . . covered with blood and brains."[81]

Johnston's loss comes to about 700. Probably close to half of this total, however, derives from pickets overrun at the outset of the Union onslaught, as witness the fate of the 63rd Georgia, which suffered 123 casualties in this fashion. The main Confederate battle line, therefore, was able to shoot down approximately ten Yankees for every man it lost, a ratio rarely if ever equaled in any major engagement of the Civil War. Even the 1st and 27th Tennessee, which bore the brunt of the fighting at the "Dead Angle," had only 12 killed and 17 wounded.[82] Little wonder the Confederates hope that Sherman will make more such attacks. Nothing, in fact, would suit them better.

In his campaign report, written three months later, Sherman accepts the "entire responsibility" for the assault and its failure. During the days and weeks immediately following it, however, he not only endeavors to justify the assault but also puts the blame for its outcome on others—to be precise, the troops who made it. "It was no mistake," as he writes Halleck on July 9;

> I had to do it. The enemy and our own army and officers had settled down into the conviction that the assault of lines formed no part of my game. . . . Had the assault been made with one-fourth more vigor, mathematically, I would have put the head of George Thomas' whole army right through Johnston's deployed lines on the best ground for go-ahead. . . . Had Harker and McCook not been struck down so early [!] the assault would have succeeded.

In a letter on the same day to Ellen he repeats that he was "forced to make the effort" and that it would have succeeded had not his troops become "so used to my avoiding excessive danger and forcing back the enemy by strategy that they hate to assault." In the same vein, but even more harshly, several days after the battle he tells Brigadier General Mortimer Leggett of Blair's corps that his division, which merely engaged in some skirmishing on June 27, "did all he asked and more than he expected, while no other division in the army had done what he asked." Finally, in the aforementioned letter to Halleck and in his report on the campaign, Sherman asserts that the attack, despite its failure, "produced good fruits, as it demonstrated to General Johnston that I would assault and that boldly" and so caused Johnston to become "more cautious" and give ground "more freely."[83]

Sherman's rationalizations and accusations perhaps helped him soothe his conscience; they even have convinced a few historians. They all, however, dissolve in the acid of basic facts: eight Union brigades (counting Kimball's), totaling about 15,000 troops, advanced blindly across a third of a mile (more or less) of rugged bullet-and-shell-swept terrain against an exceedingly strong fortified line that was protected (except in one place) by nearly impenetrable barriers and held by an equal if not superior number of some of the South's toughest fighting men. No similar attack made under comparable conditions succeeded throughout the Civil War, and there is no reason to believe that this one, especially in view of the way it was conducted, could have, would have, or should have been the exception even if it had been delivered with "one-fourth more vigor, mathematically" or if McCook and Harker had gone through it unscathed. As for its demonstrating to both the Union soldiers and to Johnston that Sherman would "assault and that boldly," thereby ridding the former of the notion that he would always flank and causing the latter to become "more cautious" and more willing to retreat, one merely need point out that another two months will pass before Sherman will attempt another major frontal attack and that it is difficult to conceive of anything, least of all an easy victory, that could increase Johnston's caution and his propensity for retreat. The best comment on the assault at Kennesaw comes from General Newton, who on seeing Sherman at Howard's headquarters following the bloody repulse of his division, went up to him and said, "Well this is a damned appropriate culmination of one month's blundering." Sherman made no reply; he just bit his lip.[84]

On the evening of June 27, Johnston, with manifest satisfaction, reports his first clear-cut major success of the campaign to Bragg: "The enemy advanced upon our whole line today. They assaulted French, Cheatham, Cleburne, Stevenson, Quarles, by whom they were repulsed. . . . Their loss is supposed to be great; ours known to be small."

Yet, pleasing as the victory is, Johnston realizes that his strategic situation remains unaltered, which is to say precarious. Only Wheeler's cavalry and some thinly stretched troops of Loring cover Marietta on the east. West of the town he has extended his line as far southward as he dares; indeed, during the Union assault he has found it necessary to send one of Cheatham's brigades, which had been posted in reserve, to plug a gap between Hardee's and Hood's corps. Worst of all, Johnston knows, thanks to a stream of accurate dispatches from Ross, that Federal infantry have pushed down the Sandtown road to a point where they reach beyond Hood's left and actually are closer to the Chattahoochee than his own army is. To counter this threat he has directed Major General Gustavus Smith, field commander of the Georgia State Militia, to bring as many of his men as he can to the north side of the Chattahoochee and join Jackson's cavalry in "a demonstration calculated to deter the enemy from any further attempt to extend his right flank toward the river." But if the

Federals cannot be prevented from extending their right and if instead they execute a strong turning movement against his left, then he will have no choice except again to retreat. Should that displease the "enemy at Richmond," so be it. He will not endanger the existence of his army merely to appease a pig-headed president and his toadying military advisor. Besides, it is Davis, not Johnston, who possesses the power to foil Sherman. As he has explained this very day in a dispatch to Bragg, a dispatch that repeats in essence what he has told Wigfall, he lacks the manpower to stop Sherman; his own cavalry are too weak to break Sherman's supply line, and therefore cavalry from elsewhere (meaning Mississippi) must do it. Perhaps the logic of these facts—he so regards them—will induce Davis to do in time what he should have done long ago: namely, order Stephen Lee to send Forrest into Georgia. At least Johnston can hope so. Meanwhile, he will keep an eye on his left flank.[85]

Sherman's answer to Thomas's question as to when the flanking move will start—"the day after tomorrow"—proves, as have so many of his time schedules, to be over-optimistic. He plans to assign McPherson the key role in the move, swinging him around from the left to the right. Not only will this be safer and quicker than ponderously shifting the whole army southward, but as always he prefers to employ the Army of the Tennessee, which he calls his "whip-lash," for flanking maneuvers, despite the fact that so far the blows it has struck have been more like flicks than slashes. But when on June 28 he asks McPherson, "How long will it take you to load up and be ready to move for ten days, independent of the railroad?" McPherson replies that he won't be able to move until "the cars bring me six days' rations and five days' forage." Although guerrilla bands and Confederate cavalry detachments operating north of the Etowah have not done any serious damage to the railroad, they have (to quote the report of Lieutenant Colonel Langdon C. Easton, Sherman's chief quarter-master) "interrupted to a great degree the passage of trains" and have delayed the stockpiling of supplies at Allatoona, which is being turned into a major depot. Perforce Sherman will have to wait a bit while McPherson accumulates additional provisions.[86]

   That night a telegram arrives from Halleck which makes waiting easier: "Lieutenant General Grant directs me to say that the movements of your army may be made entirely independent of any desire to retain Johnston's forces where they are. He does not think that Lee will bring any additional troops to Richmond, on account of the difficulty of feeding them."[87]

   Suddenly Sherman finds himself relieved of what hitherto he has considered his most essential task, the one he must perform even if unsuccessful at everything else: namely, keeping such strong and constant pressure on Johnston that the Confederates will be unable to transfer troops from Georgia to Virginia. Now he can conduct operations solely on the basis of his own situation and not worry about how they might affect Grant. Moreover, and of even greater significance, by freeing Sherman to act independently in Georgia, Grant in effect is admitting that he has no expectation of overcoming Lee in the near future. This means that Sherman's campaign, which both he and Grant have deemed secondary to the one in Virginia, henceforth will possess equal status. Indeed, should the stalemate at Richmond and Petersburg persist long enough, conceivably Sherman's campaign could acquire primary importance, for if a decision cannot be reached in the East, it will have to be achieved in the West.

While McPherson's quartermasters load up their wagons, what might be termed a tidying up of the battlefield takes place. On the evening of June 28, in Logan's and Newton's sectors, the Confederates agree to a truce so that the Federals can remove their dead and any remaining wounded. For two hours, Yanks and Rebs mingle in friendly, even jolly, fashion, with some of the latter even assisting the former in their grisly work (many corpses and some of the wounded have been, in the words of a Union surgeon, "nearly devoured" by maggots). Then, when the wounded have been carried away and the dead have been buried in a large pit, the men in blue and the men in gray return to their respective positions. As they part, a Confederate calls to one of Logan's soldiers, "I hope to miss you, Yank, if I happen to shoot in your direction." "May I," comes the reply, "never hit you Johnny if we fight again."

Arranging a truce on the "Dead Angle" of the salient hill takes longer because the opposing sides are so close together—in some places a mere thirty yards—that neither dares ask for it out of fear that the other will take advantage of it. Finally, on the morning of June 29, the Confederates offer one, and the Federals promptly accept. It has become a virtual necessity for both. Scores of bodies lie between the lines, rapidly putrefying under the Georgia sun. They present, records Colonel Melancthon Smith, "a most revolting appearance, as black as negroes—enormously swollen, fly blown, emitting an intolerable stench." So awful is the smell that some of Maney's Tennesseans literally are sick to the stomach and cannot eat.

While Union work details carry away the dead, officers and men from both armies meet halfway between the lines, where they engage in "friendly conversation," exchange newspapers, swap Northern coffee for Southern tobacco, and even drink from each other's canteens—the sign of comradeship. Among the Confederates are Cheatham and Hindman. Sergeant Widney is startled by

Cheatham's clothes, which are not at all what he expected of a Southern general. Cheatham is attired in "nothing but a rough pair of gray pants tucked under the tops of an unpolished pair of boots, a blue flannel shirt and rough felt hat." On the other hand, Hindman, a short, thin man, "wears an abundance of gold lace and cord," and his "auburn hair flows in ringlets over his shoulders." Learning who they are, a goodly number of Yanks crowd around the Rebel generals, soliciting and obtaining their autographs. After a while, Cleburne also shows up. He has, reports *New York Herald* correspondent Conyngham, a "tall, meager frame" with an "ugly scar across his lank, gloomy face." None of the Union soldiers approaches Cleburne, and one of them, a survivor of Pickett's Mill, views him with "loathing."[88]

Around 5 P.M., after the rotten, stinking carrion that once had been strong young men has been hauled away, dumped in holes, and covered with some red dirt, the friendly enemies shake hands, wish each other "personal good luck," and return to their trenches. Along most of the front the opposing pickets, agreeing that there is no point to it, refrain from firing at each other. Not so, however, at the "Dead Angle." Fearful of a sudden rush by their too-close foe, Maney's Tennesseans stand on the alert, shooting at anything blue they see (or imagine they see) and, when it becomes dark, tossing out flaming, turpentine-soaked cotton balls to light up the night and prevent the Yanks from sneaking up on them or destroying the chevaux-de-frise that they have thrown out in front of their works by means of ropes. Opposite Maney's men, Union sharp-shooters blaze away at the space between the Confederate head logs and para-pet, in some cases using mirrors rigged to their rifles so that they can aim accurately without exposing themselves to enemy fire. Slowly but surely their bullets are chewing away the head logs and inflicting heavier losses on Maney's men than they had suffered in the June 27 assault. Meanwhile, at the bottom of the hill, other members of McCook's brigade (for so it still regards itself) are digging a tunnel, their object being to get under the Johnnies on top and, writes Lieutenant Colonel Allen Fahnestock of the 86th Illinois in his diary, "blow up the Rebble works" with gunpowder.[89]

By the morning of June 30, as a result of "extraordinary exertions" by the quartermasters, McPherson has received, or is in the process of receiving, the required ten days' rations. Sherman accordingly issues orders designed to prepare the way for turning Johnston's left flank. After nightfall, Thomas will have a division of the XX Corps relieve Hascall's division south of the Powder Springs road. Tomorrow, Schofield will advance his entire corps and occupy the area between Olley's and Nickajack creeks, securing as he does so the crossing

View of the city of Atlanta from the north *(Leslie's Weekly)*

over Nickajack's of the road leading to Fulton. At the same time, Stoneman and McCook are to march down the west bank of Sweet Water Creek to Sweet Water Town, a mere two miles from the Chattahoochee and only twelve miles due west of Atlanta. Once these moves are accomplished, McPherson then can either cut around Johnston's flank toward Fulton or, if that proves impracticable, head toward the Chattahoochee: this is why he will be taking along his pontoon train as well as ten days' provisions.[90]

Sherman tells telegrapher Van Duzer that he expects to be "in Marietta or across the Chattahoochee in five days, sure." Nevertheless, when on this last day of June he writes Ellen to inform her of his plans, his mood is grim, as grim as that muddy, bloody, frustrating month itself has been: "It is enough to make the whole world start at the awful amount of death and destruction that now stalks abroad. Daily for the past two months has the work progressed and I see no signs of a remission till one or both and all the armies are destroyed. . . . I begin to regard the death and mangling of a couple thousand men as a small affair, a kind of morning dash—and it may be well that we become so hardened." For, he adds, "The worst of the war is not yet begun."[91]

Late in the afternoon there is a short but heavy shower. It brings welcome relief after six straight days of torrid temperatures, and it washes away the summer haze from the valley of the Chattahoochee. Climbing to the topmost branch of a pine tree that is being used as a signal station, one of Howard's staff officers views "the rebel city of Atlanta," seventeen miles to the southwest. With the "naked eye" he sees six church spires rising above its trees, and with a "good telescope" he sees the windows of the houses, "a large white hospital with a red flag flying above," lines of earthworks north of the city, a "long row" of rifle pits on the west side, and trains "coming & going from the city . . . bringing the rebellious host their meals & carrying back the wounded & sick."

So there it is, Atlanta, only a day's march away. But when the staff officer turns his gaze to the east, he sees the smoke of Confederate camp fires, hundreds of them, extending mile after mile, and he reflects that "we need not flatter ourselves that we are about to contend with any mere handful of men."[92] Seeing Atlanta is one thing, but perhaps taking it will turn out to be something else.

CHAPTER SEVEN

JULY

Part One: To the Chattahoochee

NEWS, WHICH has lost nothing in the telling, of the Yankee's bloody repulse at Kennesaw on June 27 brings joy and revived hope to Atlanta. The *Appeal* assures its readers on July 1 that Sherman "has been successfully halted in his mad career . . . and Gen. Johnston has said to him, 'Thus far shall thou come, and no farther.'" Editor Steele of the *Intelligencer* takes the same view, declaring on July 2 that Sherman "seems now to be in the condition of a wounded snake that spitefully turns and bites itself when it no longer can drag its slow length along." Both newspapers confidently predict that it merely is a matter of time before what the *Appeal* calls the "grand raid upon Atlanta" will fail like Grant's attempt to take Richmond. Although less optimistic—she still thinks Johnston might retreat again—Mary Mallard, who a few weeks ago was preparing to become a refugee, feels there is no "immediate danger" and on July 1 urges her mother in Liberty County to visit her: "I want you to come while we are enjoying our vegetables."[1]

This very same day, Hascall's division, leapfrogging Cox's, moves southward to and beyond Ruff's Mill, within easy artillery range of Nickajack Creek, the last stream between the Union army and the Chattahoochee. Sherman, as soon as he learns of Hascall's advance, instructs McPherson to reinforce Schofield with Morgan L. Smith's division of the XV Corps in the morning and to go into line on Hascall's right with the entire Army of the Tennessee the following day. Once that is done, Sherman predicts in his nightly report to Halleck, Johnston will be forced "to move his army down from Kennesaw, to defend his railroad crossing and the Chattahoochee."[2]

For a change, Sherman correctly forecasts Johnston's course of action. Johnston has long expected the Federals to prolong their right toward the Chattahoochee, thereby threatening to turn his left. Furthermore, he believes nothing can be done to stop them, that he already has stretched his line as far as he dare without exposing it to calamitous breakthrough. Evidently he remains ignorant of the smallness of Schofield's force and does not realize that the only connection between Hascall's division and the rest of Sherman's army is Cox's division, which is deployed in a skirmish line three miles long. Evidently, too, it does not occur to Johnston to employ the strategy that Lee has been using and will continue to use so successfully to hold his twenty-six-mile front around Richmond and Petersburg—namely, detaching strong striking forces to counter enemy flanking moves while relying on the strength of his fortifications to beat back any frontal assault. The only thing Johnston can think of doing is to make another retreat.

In essence this is what, on July 1, at his headquarters outside of Marietta, he tells Confederate Senator Benjamin Hill of Georgia. Like Wigfall, Hill has come to find out Johnston's views on the military situation and what he plans to do about it. Unlike Wigfall, Hill is a supporter of Davis. For that reason, Wigfall and Governor Brown, after the former's conference with Johnston, urged Hill to join with them in trying to persuade the president to unleash Forrest or Morgan against Sherman's supply line. Perhaps Davis will be more willing to listen to a friend than to foes. Hill has agreed, saying he would go to Richmond in person, but not until he himself has talked with Johnston.

Hood also is present; Hardee, significantly, is not. Johnston tells Hill what he has told Wigfall and has written to Bragg: Sherman's entrenching tactics make it impossible to attack him with any reasonable prospect of success; Sherman's greatly superior numbers enable him to flank the Confederates from their defensive positions; and thus the only way Sherman can be stopped and turned back is to cut his railroad supply line between Dalton and Marietta. This, Johnston states, "could easily be done." Five thousand cavalry "in one day could destroy the railroad to an extent that as to require two weeks or a month to repair it," in which case Sherman either would have to attack and be defeated or would have to retreat and guard against the Union flanking moves. Forrest or Morgan or both should be sent to do the work. Stephen Lee has 15,000 cavalry in Mississippi and Alabama: "if Forrest with one-third of that force were sent into Sherman's rear," that would suffice.

Supposing, Hill comments, the president agrees to send Forrest or Morgan against Sherman's communications, is there still time for such an operation to succeed before Sherman can reach Atlanta? Yes, answers Johnston. Maybe, remarks Hood, but the hour is very late. In any event, both generals declare, it had better be done soon if done at all. How long, Hill next asks, can Johnston hold on north of the Chattahoochee? Calculate that for yourself, responds Johnston. It has taken the enemy more than thirty days to advance from "New Hope to the present position, only a few miles." Hood, however, is less optimistic. The defense line now based on Kennesaw, he points out, is the strongest in the country. When (he does not say if) it is abandoned, the army will "go back much more rapidly." Not so, counters Johnston; he has other strong positions to his rear and will be able to keep the enemy "for a long time," a month or more, north of the Chattahoochee.

Some "free conversation," as Hill subsequently terms it, follows. During it he discovers, to his astonishment, that Johnston is not aware that the railroad bridges over the Chattahoochee between Georgia and Alabama are unprotected, and he has only a vague knowledge of the geography of that area. Also when Hill warns that if Sherman gets across the Chattahoochee, he will be in position to cut off both Johnston's army from its main supply base in Alabama and Lee's army from its south Georgia granary, Johnston dismisses this danger with the offhand comment, "Well, before the enemy shall get the position you mention of course we shall have a bloody fight"—the only time during the entire meeting that he speaks of fighting or in any way implies an intention of giving battle to save Atlanta.

As Hill leaves, he promises Johnston that he will go "at once" to Richmond and urge Davis to send Forrest or Morgan against Sherman's supply line. Johnston himself already has done the same. So too, with his sanction, have Governor Brown and, this very day by telegram, Major General Howell Cobb, leader of the pro-Davis faction in Georgia. Rarely if ever has a military commander striven harder to persuade the head of his government that he is incapable of defeating by his own efforts the army he opposes.[3]

On the morning of July 2, Morgan Smith's division relieves Hascall's at Ruff's Mill, thereby enabling Schofield to thicken his perilously thin line—about 13,000 troops spread out over five miles. Later in the day, Stoneman's cavalry crosses to the west bank of Sweetwater Creek, and a detachment goes to the Chattahoochee opposite Campbellton, sixteen miles below the Western and Atlantic railroad bridge and the same distance southwest of Atlanta. Then, as soon as it becomes dark, Blair's, Dodge's, and the rest of Logan's corps head south along the Sandtown road. Garrard's troops occupy the trenches north of Kennesaw, covering Big Shanty, with orders to "fall back gradually toward Allatoona" if assailed by "superior and overwhelming" enemy forces. At the same time, Thomas prepares either to resist a Confederate attack (which is what Sherman wants) or to "press the enemy close and . . . break his line and reach the railroad below Marietta" should Johnston retreat (which is what Sherman expects).

Johnston already has informed his army that it "will change position tonight." At 10 P.M., Loring's corps and, an hour later, Hardee's and Hood's evacuate their trenches, leaving behind the customary skirmishers and, what also is becoming customary, a goodly number of men who have decided to call it quits. When the first glimmer of dawn appears above Cheatham's Hill, the troops of the 52nd Ohio hear a voice calling from the enemy works: "Don't shoot down there, they are done gone from here." The Buckeyes shout back, "Come over"; and a "tall, lank Johnny Reb" scrambles down the hill and surrenders. Some of the 52nd go forward and confirm that the enemy troops indeed have gone. The survivors of McCook's brigade feel a sense of relief, yet they are disappointed. The tunnel they have been digging is within thirty feet of the crest of the hill, and they expected to complete it and pack it with gunpowder today, then blow up the Rebs tomorrow. It would have been a glorious way to celebrate the Fourth.

All along the front other Union troops discover that the enemy has gone. Some of them scramble to the summit of Big Kennesaw and unfurl the United States flag. A great cheer arises from the fields and forest below, and the bands play "The Star Spangled Banner" and other appropriate music. The Siege of Kennesaw—two grinding weeks of incessant digging and fighting, rain and mud, blood and death—has ended.[4]

Sherman assumes that the Confederates are heading for the other side of the Chattahoochee and hopes to catch them while they are crossing it. Again he assumes and hopes too much. Despite being slowed by roads muddy from yesterday afternoon's heavy rainfall, they already have reached their new defense line. It is six miles south of Marietta and centers on Smyrna Camp Ground, a collection of wooden buildings used by the local Methodists for summer revivals. As soon as they have had a chance to eat and rest a bit, they set to work and in a few hours are (to quote Manigault) "in a condition to resist an attack" along a six-mile front stretching from Nickajack Creek on the left to Rottenwood Creek on the right.[5]

Thomas's troops march through and around Marietta in pursuit, picking up along the way hundreds of Rebs who have stayed behind to be taken prisoner, some with rifles still in their hands. Those who pass through the town are impressed by its tree-lined streets, lovely courthouse square, and beautiful houses, "more beautiful even than the palatial residences of Michigan Avenue" in Detroit, writes John Boardman, a Michigan artillery officer, to his father. But, Boardman continues, "there is an air of desolation" about the place. Nearly all of the houses and stores are empty; no one can be seen on the streets except Union soldiers and "a few Negroes," some of whom cry out "I'se been looking for you for six months, Massa." Although Alpheus Williams and other generals try to keep their men in line, stragglers soon begin to plunder and ransack, sparing as a rule only the few dwellings that remain inhabited.

South of Marietta, Thomas's columns at first encounter only token resistance from squads of Wheeler's cavalry. Then, late in the afternoon, shells start falling along the roads, and the advance guards report that there are well-manned rifle pits up ahead. At once Hooker, Palmer, and Howard order their lead divisions to halt and deploy. All obey except Butterfield's division. It no longer is commanded by Butterfield, who has taken sick leave because of acute diarrhea and because, in Alpheus Williams's opinion, he is "disgusted and tired." Butterfield's replacement, by virtue of seniority in rank (his only virtue), is Ward; and Ward is drunk. He rides along at the head of the division in a stupor from which he emerges occasionally to shout, "Forward there!" Fortunately, Hooker gallops up with his staff and, on beholding Ward, asks: "What ails you? Are you drunk, or are you crazy, or are you a fool?" Ward merely stares at him with, in the words of an observer, "his drunken, half shut eyes." Hooker thereupon places Colonel Coburn in command of the division with orders to entrench on the spot. (Incredible as it may seem, Ward soon will resume command and retain it until the end of the war.) It is a mile ahead of the rest of the Union army, and only Hooker's timely intervention has prevented it from being, as one soldier puts it, "gobbled" by the Confederates.[6]

Sherman, who earlier in the day had been infuriated when he discovered that Garrard's cavalry were not out in front chasing the presumably fleeing Confederates, at first is unwilling to believe that Johnston has established a new line north of the Chattahoochee; not until he makes a personal reconnaissance does he accept the fact. Even so, he remains confident that Johnston soon will resume retreating. "The more I reflect," Sherman notifies Thomas, "the more I know Johnston's halt is to save [gain] time to cross his material and men. No general, such as he, would invite battle with the Chattahoochee behind him." Thomas, therefore, is to press Johnston's front while McPherson and Schofield operate against his left with the object of getting "the enemy started in confusion toward his bridges," for "we have now the best chance ever offered, of a large army fighting at a disadvantage with a river to his rear."[7]

July 4 is appropriately torrid. Marching from Marietta to join the rest of the XV Corps at Ruff's Mill, more than half of the men in Harrow's and Osterhaus's divisions fall by the roadside from heat exhaustion; some die. Despite Sherman's order to "press" the supposedly retreating foe, most of the morning passes with little activity on Thomas's front other than bands playing and troops cheering in celebration of Independence Day. Not until around noon do several brigades of the IV Corps attack the Rebel rifle pits east of the railroad. Sherman, who has conducted another personal reconnaissance, insists that the pits are held only by unsupported skirmishers. They prove instead to be backed by artillery and a battle line of infantry, both concealed by a forest—exactly what Howard and his officers tried in vain to tell Sherman was the case. The assault force, losing heavily, manages to seize the rifle pits but cannot advance further. Watching the Yankee charge, Private Edward McMorries of the 1st Alabama thinks that "nobody but a set of drunken fools would have attempted such a thing." As a matter of fact a goodly number of Howard's troops, who by no means share his teetotaler sentiments, are either drunk or getting that way. On the other hand in the XV Corps, notes Major Thomas Taylor of the 47th Ohio in his diary: "Everybody very sober today—cause: Supply of whisky exhausted."[8]

Off to the southwest, around Ruff's Mill, matters go better if not more merrily for the Federals. There Dodge's corps crosses Nickajack Creek in a sudden attack that routs several regiments of Stevenson's Division and forces all the Confederates in this sector to fall back. In addition, Stoneman's troopers, supported by a detachment from Blair's corps, advance toward Turner's Ferry on the Chattahoochee until brought to a halt one-half mile from it by what appears to be a sizable force of entrenched enemy infantry but which actually is merely a few hundred Georgia militia huddling in their "ditches" and hoping, as one of them confesses in a letter to his wife, that the Yankees won't attack.

Sherman, who feels "disappointed so little had been done today," learns of Dodge's success around midnight. Immediately he notifies Thomas that come tomorrow, "I want you with your whole army to press steadily down on the enemy while McPherson cuts in on his flank," and Stoneman threatens "to cross the Chattahoochee and break the Atlanta and West Point Railroad." Again finding himself unable to push straight ahead, Sherman again resorts to a flanking movement.

And again he is too late. Having received, during the evening, reports from Hood that a division from "Blair's Corps" was advancing in his rear and reports from Major General Gustavus Smith that his militia would have to withdraw at daylight from its position on the Turner's Ferry Road, Johnston has reissued the retreat order he had sent out in the morning, in anticipation of an enemy thrust around his left, but had canceled when it had failed to occur. As a result, Hardee's and Loring's corps are marching through the night toward the Chattahoochee, and Hood's awaits the morning in order to do the same.[9]

Johnston, however, has no intention of crossing the Chattahoochee, at least not at present. Two weeks ago, General Shoup came to Johnston's headquarters to make an "audacious proposition." Was he correct, he asked Johnston, in assuming that the army after a while would retreat once more? It was, answered Johnston, "but a question of time, and that a short time." Did Johnston have any "specific plans" for what he then would do? None, came the reply, other than to get across the Chattahoochee as best he could. Shoup thereupon requested the authority to "gather a sufficient number of negroes" to construct "a line of works covering the railroad crossing" of the Chattahoochee that could

Francis A. Shoup, soon after the war when he had become an Episcopal priest (*Photographic History,* 10:261)

be "held indefinitely by one division against Sherman's entire army." Such a line, declared Shoup, would enable Johnston either to concentrate his own forces for an overpowering attack on Sherman or to crush him, should he try to outflank it by crossing the river, or, "as a more brilliant movement," to "march out upon his communications, capture his depots and press on into Tennessee and Kentucky," thus compelling his army to "disperse." To Shoup's delight, Johnston on hearing this directed Shoup "to proceed at once to put the plan into execution." Shoup did so, sending agents "down all the railways to gather gangs of negroes from the plantations, with tools and provisions, and bringing them to the Chattahoochee with the utmost dispatch." Three days after meeting with Johnston, Shoup had "something like a thousand able-bodied hands" hard at work and a week later they had constructed a line of fortifications that began on the right at the Chattahoochee a mile above the railroad bridge and curved around to the south and west until it returned to the river three miles below the bridge.[10]

Hardee's and Loring's troops behold these fortifications at sunrise on July 5. They don't like what they see. Instead of the familiar tried-and-true trenches and embankments, protected by abatis and other obstacles, there is a row of wedge-shaped, fully enclosed, log-and-dirt redoubts eighty yards apart and connected by palisades of upright saplings and trees ten to fifteen feet high. No one has explained to the troops, or for that matter their generals, that the redoubts, which are virtually shellproof, have been placed in such a fashion as to have interlocking fields of fire and that the palisades are primarily for the purpose of facilitating the movement of troops from one point to another. All they can envision is standing behind this flimsy stockade while the Yankee artillery, in quartermaster clerk Patrick's words, knock it "northwest and crooked." By the end of the day, most of the palisades have been torn down and replaced with regular fortifications.[11]

A slow start and Wheeler's cavalry delay the Union pursuit. Not until midmorning, about a mile south of Vining's Station, does the van of Palmer's corps encounter enemy skirmishers and shellfire. Sherman, still sure that Johnston is "merely opposing us to gain time to get his trains and troops across the Chattahoochee," orders Thomas to have Palmer "fiercely assault." Fortunately, before the command can be executed, Sherman conducts another of his personal reconnaissances and does a better job of it than he did yesterday. Peering from behind a tree across a valley, he sees a line of "strong redoubts" fronted by wicked-looking abatis. He also happens upon a "poor negro," one of Shoup's laborers, who tells him what the Confederates have been doing along the north bank of the Chattahoochee. Thus informed, Sherman cancels the attack and orders his army to go into line opposite Johnston's new position.[12]

Sherman sets up headquarters in Vining's Station. Nearby, west of the railway, there is a high knob. On it a half-mummified corpse dangles from a tree, a rope around its neck. Deserter? Spy? Suicide? No one knows. From the top of the knob the Chattahoochee can be seen and beyond it, "glittering in the sunlight," the church spires of Atlanta, exactly 8.5 miles to the southeast. Through his field glasses Sherman observes, on the other side of the river, lines of fortifications, troop camps, and long trains of covered wagons. Johnston, he concludes, has left only one corps—Hardee's—on the north bank and plans to make his actual stand on the south bank. So the problem, as Sherman sees it, is how to get his own army across the river without heavy losses, perhaps a terrible repulse. His solution is, and can only be, another flanking movement. When and where to make it are the only questions.

Concerning when, the answer is easy: as soon as the two sections of the railroad that the Confederates have torn up north of Marietta and at Vining's Station can be replaced and as soon as the Chattahoochee, still swollen by the June rains, has returned to its normal, rather shallow depth. With regard to where, he already has sent Garrard to Roswell, a factory town twelve miles north of Vining's Station, with instructions to seize the bridge that spans the Chattahoochee at that point. If all goes well, within a few days his troops finally will swarm along the banks of that river.[13]

"Atlanta will not and cannot be abandoned." So proclaims the *Southern Confederacy* on July 5. News that Johnston had fallen back to Smyrna Camp Ground reached the city on Sunday evening July 3. With it came the report, soon confirmed, that the army was transferring munitions and other supplies from the warehouses around Five Points to Macon. The next day the *Appeal*, which on Saturday had been so confident that Johnston had stopped Sherman at Kennesaw, admitted that "since our last issue . . . the situation in our immediate front has been somewhat changed" owing to "a heavy movement of the enemy around" the Confederate left. Now, on July 5, Atlantans learn that Johnston has retreated again, this time to the very banks of the Chattahoochee, a mere six miles away. Nevertheless, reports the *Southern Confederacy,* "there is but little manifestation of uneasiness or excitement visible upon the faces we meet in the street"; and William Dickey, a member of the Georgia Militia, writes his wife that "the People about Atlanta are just about as much unconcerned about the war now as they were weeks & months ago." Maybe they believe that indeed "Atlanta will not and cannot be abandoned." Perhaps they feel reassured by letters from soldiers at the front, such as the one that appeared in the July 4 *Appeal* stating that "the army is satisfied with the situation" and urging civilians to, "like we do, trust to Providence and Gen. Johnston." More likely, however, they simply are waiting to see what happens next. If Johnston holds north of the Chattahoochee, all yet can turn out well. But if he does not. . . .[14]

On July 6 and 7, per Sherman's instructions, Schofield's corps marches to Ruff's Station, Schofield himself reconnoiters the river above Pace's Ferry north of the railroad bridge, and construction crews repair the breaks in the railroad, after which trains start rolling into Vining's Station. All the while, Stoneman's patrols spread out along the right bank of the Chattahoochee between Nicka-jack Creek and the Campbellton ferry, doing their best to give the impression that Sherman intends to cross downstream from Johnston's bridgehead. Up the river, Garrard's troopers arrive too late at Roswell to forestall Wheeler's cavalry from burning the bridge but in plenty of time for themselves to burn three textile mills, a dozen related buildings, and some houses. They also take into custody the workers in the now-smoldering mills—four hundred or so women, mostly young. Sherman, on being advised of the presence of these females, has them sent to Marietta, where they are quartered in the Georgia Military Institute pending shipment north, where he believes they "can find employment in Indiana." In Captain Wills's estimation there is "hardly one who is passably handsome," but they are women, and a Hoosier soldier assigned to guard them records that "some of them are tough and its a hard job to keep them straight and keep the men way from them." According to Sergeant McGee of the 72nd Indiana, while still in Roswell some of Garrard's troopers, after getting drunk, have not stayed away from the women.

On the evening of July 7, Schofield notifies Sherman that he has found "a pretty good crossing near mouth of Soap Creek" at Isham's Ford, one that appears to be guarded by "only a squad of cavalry and one or two pieces of artillery" (the correct spelling of the creek's name is Sope, but since "Soap" is used in all contemporary references, that spelling has been retained here). However, since Wheeler's main force seems to have gone from the area north of the railroad, "I take it for granted that I can cross at Roswell" instead. Sherman responds with an order to cross tomorrow at Soap Creek. Garrard, he explains, will secure a "lodgment at Roswell," whereupon he will be reinforced by one of McPherson's divisions "to hold fast all he makes" and so provide "plenty of room" for passing over the river above Johnston's defense line.[15]

Later in the evening, in a tent pitched in the yard of the Campbell house south of the Chattahoochee, Johnston meets with his corps commanders. Among them is a new face, the lean, dark-bearded one of Stewart, who earlier in the

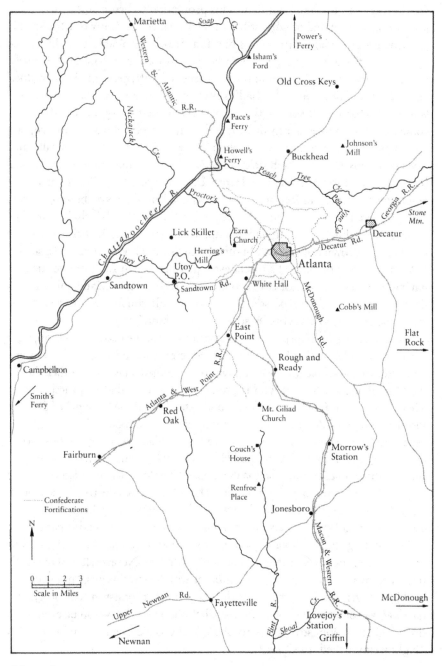

Atlanta Area

day, having been officially notified of his promotion to lieutenant general, has just assumed command of what still is officially called the Army of Mississippi, relieving Loring, who returns to his division. Stewart probably owes his elevation to the influence of Bragg, whom he had written to in March, fulsomely congratulating him on his appointment as chief of staff; certainly Stewart does not owe it to Johnston, who had "respectfully" requested that Lieutenant General Richard S. Ewell of the Army of Northern Virginia be given the command (Johnston evidently did not realize that Ewell, who had had a superb record as a division commander early in the war, had become physically and psychologically unfit for high field command by the summer of 1864). Taking over Stewart's former division is Henry D. Clayton, whom President Davis, ignoring a request from Johnston that Mansfield Lovell receive the assignment, had promoted to major general along with Edward C. Walthall, who has replaced the ailing and marginally competent Cantey. Finally, Brigadier General John C. Brown now heads Hindman's Division, Hindman having gone on sick leave, in part because of a recent eye injury but mostly out of resentment at having been passed over for corps command. According to Manigault who, as do many others, finds him personally obnoxious, Hindman was "anxious to get away, and everybody else equally so to get rid of him."[16]

The conference in Johnston's tent has been called at the request of Hood, who begins it by declaring that his position on the left behind Nickajack Creek is unsafe and that the whole army should withdraw immediately to the other side of the Chattahoochee. Shoup, who is present, reacts with alarm to these words. They indicate that Hood has no more understanding of the "design" of Shoup's fortifications than do the troops, who continue to remodel them, despite a general order explaining their function. In addition, Shoup wonders if Johnston understands it either, for he has allowed Hood's Corps to entrench along a line that runs for three miles *outside* the fortifications! Therefore, when called on for his opinion, Shoup states that Hood "ought to be moved across the river" and at least one other corps as well, but that the fortifications should be "held at all hazards" and provisioned "so as to stand a siege, if necessary, of a considerable period."

The meeting ends without a decision as whether to retreat south of the river, as urged by Hood, or to implement Shoup's proposal. Nevertheless Shoup feels disturbed by the "tone" of the discussion: it was, he later writes, "not such as I could have wished." Were he to see the telegram that Johnston sent Bragg two days ago announcing the retreat to the Chattahoochee, he would be even more disturbed. In it Johnston refers to Shoup's cherished chain of redoubts as a "slightly entrenched" position.[17]

> Out of the hills of Habersham,
>   Down the valleys of Hall,
> I hurry amain to reach the plain,
> Run the rapid and leap the fall,
> Split at the rock and together again,
> Accept my bed, or narrow or wide,
> And flee from folly on every side
> With a lover's pain to attain the plain
>   Far from the hills of Habersham,
>   Far from the valleys of Hall.

So begins "The Song of the Chattahoochee" by Georgia poet Sidney Lanier. North of Atlanta the river, whose name means flowered or marked stone in the language of the Creek Indians, has long since come out of the hills of Habersham County up near the North and South Carolina borders and has almost attained the plain, with the result that although it is four hundred to five hundred feet wide, it tends to be shallow and normally can be easily waded in summer. This summer, however, the June rains have made it unusually wide and deep, and that part of it into which Soap Creek empties is no exception. Here, on the afternoon of July 8, it is three hundred yards across, and its swift-flowing yellow water is higher than a man's head. In addition, on the south bank atop a commanding hill there is a detachment of Confederates with a cannon.

Schofield knows all of this. But he also knows something the Confederates do not: upstream about a half-mile there is a submerged stone fish dam spanning the river. Carefully keeping his troops out of enemy sight, he sends Cameron's brigade of Cox's division to the dam. At 3:30 P.M., fifty soldiers of Colonel John Casement's 103rd Ohio, having removed their pants, walk along its top to the other side and occupy a ridge, where the rest of the regiment soon joins them. A half-hour later, twenty-five of Buell's pontoon boats, packed with men of the 12th Kentucky from Hascall's division, emerge from the mouth of Soap Creek and head for the south bank. The Confederates, who number only a few score and appear to be militia, find themselves beset front and flank. After firing a couple of harmless shots with their virtually harmless 6-pounder, they flee, leaving behind the "pop-gun." While more of Hascall's troops cross in the boats, the 58th Indiana, which has taken over the job of laying pontoons as well as escorting them, sets to work. By dusk it has one bridge completed and another under way. Cox thereupon marches the rest of his division to the other side and establishes an entrenched line.

Up at Roswell the ever-prudent Garrard, worried about being so far from the main army and fearful of being pounced on by Wheeler, whom he credits with having 15,000 troopers, postpones his crossing attempt until tomorrow. Even so, with scarcely a fight and without a casualty, the Federals have breached the last major natural barrier between them and Atlanta.[18]

Johnston does not receive definite word of the Union crossing at what the Confederates call Cavalry Ford until around midnight, and then it comes from one of his provost marshal officers. The news puzzles more than it alarms him. As Sherman has guessed he would, Johnston assumes that the Federals will try to outflank his bridgehead by crossing the river somewhere below it—an assumption that is strengthened by the presence of McPherson's "corps" in that area, the activity of Stoneman's cavalry, and the fact that by moving against Atlanta from the west, Sherman would be in position to cut it off from Alabama. Hence Johnston merely orders Wheeler to watch the enemy force that has crossed at Cavalry Ford and, should it advance, to "impede its march as much as you can."[19]

At daylight on July 9, under the covering fire of the Chicago Board of Trade Battery and three companies of riflemen, four dismounted companies of Colonel Abram Miller's (formerly Wilder's) brigade of Garrard's cavalry start wading the Chattahoochee at a ford near the burned Roswell bridge. As they go forward, Garrard shouts at them: "Bully boys! bully boys! *Whisky in the morning!*" The river here is only two to three feet deep and about two hundred yards wide, but the current is strong, and it is hard to stand upright on the slick, stony bottom. Across the way a small force of Confederates, who earlier had been observed sleeping on the porch of a white house, rush down to river's edge and open fire. Their bullets go high, and Miller's men blaze back with their Spencers, ducking down under the water whenever they need to reload them. As they approach the shore, the would-be defenders run back up the bank, except for several who surrender. The rest of Miller's brigade then follows and digs in atop a hill overlooking the ford. The Federals now are across the Chattahoochee at two places.

Sherman learns of Garrard's success at 10 A.M. At once he sends Garrard an order to "hold fast all you have made" until reinforced by Newton's division and Dodge's corps, both of which already are on the way. Sherman believes, as he has told Thomas, that Johnston now will be "forced in strategy" either to attack McPherson and Thomas or else to "abandon this bank of the Chattahoochee altogether," for he "will not attempt to hold both shores after we have secured a crossing." As usual, Sherman expects Johnston to retreat.[20]

This time Sherman's expectation is fully justified. Upon receiving word of the enemy crossing at Roswell and after determining the size of the Union force at Cavalry Ford, Johnston orders another nighttime withdrawal. "Shoup's line," he explains to his staff, "cannot be held by [a] small force" so as to release the "major part of [the] army to operate" on the south bank. Starting at dusk, the

Confederates begin pulling back, and then, beneath a "half-full moon," they cross the Chattahoochee on bridges covered with sand and leaves. By 4 A.M. all of them except stragglers and deserters are on the other side, whereupon they set fire to the railroad bridge and adjoining wagon bridge while either removing or, in the case of the one at Pace's Ferry, cutting loose their pontoons. Then, leaving behind strong detachments to guard the crossings between Pace's Ferry and Turner's Ferry, they march south two miles along the railroad and bivouac.

Johnston establishes his new headquarters at the Dexter Niles house, the now-abandoned residence of a slave dealer from Boston, on the Marietta Road; it is three miles from the center of Atlanta. In the morning he summons Shoup and tells him that he is "sorry that he had been obliged to abandon" his fortifications but that the enemy had already crossed the river in "considerable force" and that it was "best to be on this side." Shoup refrains from reminding Johnston of the strategy that they supposedly had agreed on for utilizing the fortifications, but he feels betrayed. After the war, Shoup will go so far as to assert that "the abandonment of the works at the Chattahoochee River . . . was, in my opinion, the final turning point in the fate of the Confederacy." Actually it was naïve of Shoup, particularly after two months of active service under him, to think that Johnston would be daring enough to defend the bridgehead with a small portion of his army while using the main part of it for offensive operations. Also there was an inherent flaw in Shoup's plan, namely, that Sherman, by fortifying his own lines opposite the bridgehead, could contain the Confederates within it, thus freeing most of his own army for action elsewhere. Johnston's true mistake—supposing what is doubtful, that he seriously intended to make a prolonged stand at the Chattahoochee—was in assuming that Sherman would attempt to cross downstream and therefore in failing to station adequate forces upstream. By the same token, in bloodlessly flanking Johnston from his last defense line north of the Chattahoochee, Sherman has made his best, as well as his easiest, move of the campaign.[21]

Atlanta learns about Johnston's fallback as soon as it occurs. "I can give you no idea of the excitement in Atlanta," reports a correspondent for the *Mobile* (Ala.) *News*, who then does his best to give an idea:

> Everybody seems to be hurrying off, and especially the women. Wagons loaded with household furniture, and everything else that can be packed upon them, crowd every street, and women, old and young, and children innumerable, are hurrying to and fro, leading pet lambs, deer, and other little household objects of affection, as though they intend to save all they could. Every train of cars is loaded to its utmost capacity, and there is no grumbling about seats, for even the fair ones are but too glad to get even a standing place on a box car. The excitement beats anything I ever saw.

Mary Mallard and her family go to Augusta. Mary lies on a mattress on the floor of a boxcar, for on the way to the depot she has been thrown from a wagon and has suffered severe bruises and a dislocated collarbone. Hardee's wife and Wigfall's daughters take a train to Macon, the latter riding in a car packed with wounded soldiers. Mrs. Johnston, after joining her husband at his headquarters for a wedding anniversary "jollification," returns to Atlanta but with instructions from him to be ready to go to Macon at a moment's notice. The *Intelligencer,* which back in 1861 had declared that "so-far as civil war is concerned, we have no fears of that in Atlanta," and the *Southern Confederacy,* which only a few days ago had predicted that Sherman would not be able to "outflank General Johnston and the Chattahoochie [*sic*]," also leave for Macon. The only newspaper left in Atlanta is the *Appeal.* A veteran of several flights from the Yankees since departing Memphis in 1862—wags call it "The Moving Appeal"—it continues publishing and defiantly asserting that the city "must be and will be defended." But as if to mock that statement, the evacuation of munitions, military stores, and the factories and shops that produce them also continues, with most of them being shipped to Macon.

Although by July 12 one of Hardee's couriers finds Atlanta "nearly deserted," thousands of people remain. A few, such as Mayor Calhoun and the men of the fire brigade, have duties that require them to stay. Many more, mostly women and children, simply have no place else to go or are incapable of making the effort. Among them is the pregnant Julia Davidson, who keeps urging her husband, presently in a hospital, to get out of the army, by desertion if necessary, and come to her. Some, like Samuel Richards, an English immigrant who operates a stationery store on Whitehall Street, have decided "to stay at home, Yankees or no Yankees. We hear and read terrible tales of them, but I don't think they are as bad as they are said to be," he writes in his journal. Others—Northerners, Unionists—look forward to Sherman's coming, but needless to say they conceal their sentiments in public. Slaves who have not been taken off with their fleeing masters also conceal themselves; they are there, but how many and exactly where, no one seems to know.

Atlanta itself has become, to quote from one of the final issues of the *Intelligencer* prior to its removal to Macon, "almost exclusively a military camp" where "hundreds of horsemen and footmen . . . dashing hither and thither, the roar of wagons rolling on the streets and the cracking of whips, the grinding of wheels, the shouts of drivers, the braying of mules and the rapid foot falls of couriers create a medley of sounds that seems strange and almost bewildering." Soldiers on leave (or often without leave) throng the saloons and brothels—none of these have refugeed—or reel drunkenly along the sidewalks, yelling, shooting pistols into the air, taunting and sometimes roughing up male civilians of military age, "requisitioning" food from houses that are occupied, and occasionally ransacking those that are not. An increasing number of people in and around Atlanta would agree with the Georgia soldier who recently wrote his wife: "I had almost as leave have the Yanks around my hous [*sic*] as our own men, except they would not insult ladies."[22]

It now is thirty days since Sherman began his advance from Acworth. During those days his army has suffered a bloody repulse in a hopeless attack, endured rain and mud and heat and dust, and lost about 9,000 men in combat and approximately the same number from disease, illness, and fatigue while gaining a mere fifteen miles, an average of one-half mile per day. But it also has given the Confederates one bad drubbing (Kolb's farm); compelled them to abandon a series of extremely strong positions; inflicted on them losses in killed, wounded, prisoners, and deserters little less than their own; subjected them also to enormous hardship and sickness; and driven them to the very outskirts of Atlanta. Clearly the pluses outweigh the minuses. The only pertinent question that needs to be asked is whether the same results, or perhaps better ones, could have been achieved more quickly and at smaller cost.

From June 10 through June 20 the incessant rain and consequent mud made it impossible for Sherman to do other than he did, and he can be faulted only for trying to do more than that—namely, pursue and rout the Confederates on the erroneous assumption that they were retreating or were about to do so. But after the rains ceased on June 21, by which time it was obvious that Johnston was standing fast at Kennesaw, Sherman should have done one of two things: (1) adopted Thomas's suggestion of having McPherson strike at Marietta from the east or (2) what he eventually did anyway—outflank the mountain from the west. Concerning the first alternative, the evidence, although not conclusive, is impressive that the Confederate lines east of Marietta were weakly held, mostly by dismounted cavalry; that Johnston greatly feared a Union move from that direction; and that if a strong, vigorous one had occurred, almost certainly Johnston, finding himself beset on three sides, would have beat a hasty retreat. The reason that Sherman refused to attempt such a move, as we have seen, was the same one that caused him to make his disastrous June 27 assault: fear for the safety of his supply line and his forward base at Big Shanty. This was an unjustified fear, as events soon demonstrated, and it cost him unnecessary delay, useless casualties, and possibly an opportunity to badly maul and demoralize the Confederate army. As he himself admits in a July 12 letter to Grant, "My operations have been rather cautious than bold."[23]

Even so, he has reached and breached the Chattahoochee, and with one short lunge he can either take Atlanta or force its defenders to risk destruction in a fight to save it. Thus, he is fulfilling his strategic mission.

The same cannot be said for Johnston. He has failed to stop the Northern army, much less defeat it. Neither has he, despite his subsequent claims to the contrary, significantly reduced the Union strength, and his own losses are proportionately heavier. Even his success in checking the invaders in the New Hope Church–Kennesaw region for more than a month owes more to weather, terrain, and Sherman's supply problems than it does to Johnston's military skill, which has displayed itself chiefly in timely, well-conducted retreats. To be sure he argues and will forever argue, as do his apologists, that given the odds against him, he could not have done otherwise; that his only practical course has been to conduct a passive defense and retreat when the Federals employ their hugely superior numbers to outflank him. Perhaps this is true—the matter will be discussed as such later—but the undeniable fact is that his own army now literally has its back to the walls of Atlanta. If it retreats again, it will be either into the city or beyond it.[24]

Part Two: The White House of the Confederacy

On the evening of July 10, Jefferson Davis sits in his office listening intently while Senator Hill recounts his conversation with Johnston nine days ago and urges that Morgan or Forrest be sent to attack Sherman's supply line. When Hill finishes, Davis informs him that Morgan's raid into Kentucky has been a fiasco that has left him with only a few hundred demoralized men. As for Forrest, a recently received dispatch from Stephen Lee, who now is a lieutenant general and formally in command of the Department of Mississippi, states that 12,000 to 15,000 Federals, "mostly veteran troops," are advancing southward from Memphis and that another Union army, estimated to be 20,000 strong, is moving against Mobile from New Orleans. To counter the first threat, Lee has less than 9,000 men, mainly Forrest's cavalry; to defend Mobile, a mere 4,000 troops.

Then, having demonstrated to Hill how badly mistaken Johnston is about the availability of Morgan and Forrest, Davis asks him, "How long did you understand General Johnston to say he could hold Sherman north of the Chattahoochee River?" Hill answers that it was a month or more—"a long time." Davis thereupon reads to Hill a telegram that has just arrived:

Atlanta, July 10, 1864

On the night of the 8th [*sic*] the enemy crossed at Isham's, or Cavalry Ford; entrenched. In consequence we crossed at and below the railroad and are now about three miles from the river, guarding the crossings.

J. E. Johnston[25]

Hill's account of his meeting with Johnston merely brings Davis closer to doing what he already is thinking of doing: remove Johnston from command. He considers Johnston's claim that Sherman has "greatly superior numbers" to be false. According to figures recently furnished by Bragg, Johnston as of June 10 had about 65,000 men, whereas if Johnston's own statements, relayed by Hill, about Union losses are at all true, Sherman cannot have much more than 75,000 troops.[26] In any case, Johnston has been sent all the reinforcements, and more, that the Confederacy can spare; he comes as close to matching his opponent's strength as a Confederate commander can reasonably hope; and certainly he is less outnumbered than is Lee in Virginia, who has been able not only to stop Grant but also to detach substantial forces to carry the war into Maryland, where this very day Jubal Early, after routing a Federal army near Frederick on July 9, is marching on Washington itself!

Davis also disbelieves Johnston's contention that although he has constantly sought an opportunity to strike an offensive blow against Sherman, he has been unable to because of Sherman's entrenching tactics. Surely, during more than two months of campaigning, Sherman has exposed himself to attack in the open somewhere, sometime, someway. Besides, Davis has Hood's communications, and a number of other statements from those in a position to know, among them Hardee—all to the effect that Johnston has had a number of opportunities to attack to advantage but that every time he has refused to avail himself of them. Here, too, the contrast to Lee is damning. Right from the start, Lee pounced on Grant, and even now, while defending a twenty-six-mile line with fewer than 40,000 men, he lashes out fiercely whenever the enemy tries to outflank him.

Likewise Davis doubts Johnston's oft-repeated declarations that he lacks sufficient cavalry of his own to break Sherman's supply line in Georgia. Johnston's June 10 returns show that he has 27,390 "aggregate" cavalry, 12,231 of them "effective." On the other hand, Johnston has told Hill that Sherman's mounted arm numbers less, that it is "very inefficient," and that it will "not fight our cavalry except with infantry support." This would seem to indicate that Johnston could safely detach 5,000 troopers, the force he says could do the job in one day, to wreck the railroad between Dalton and Marietta. Moreover, the person who is best qualified to judge the matter agrees. In a letter of July 1 to Bragg, which Davis had read, Wheeler asserts that he has pleaded with Johnston for permission to make a large-scale raid into Sherman's rear, only to be denied.[27]

Finally, Davis rejects the view, which has become the basis of Johnston's entire strategic argument, that Atlanta and Mississippi cannot both be defended successfully and that since the former is more important, the latter should be sacrificed in order to save Atlanta by sending Forrest against Sherman's supply line in Georgia. Davis believes that to abandon Mississippi (and with it Alabama) to being overrun and devastated by the Yankees would have a demoralizing effect on the South as a whole and would lead to the disaffection of the people and troops of those states. Besides, as Davis sees it, the defense of Atlanta cannot be separated from the defense of Mississippi. Supposing Forrest were to go into Georgia. Almost surely the Federal army that is presently invading Mississippi would either pursue him or reinforce the three divisions already protecting Sherman's communications or both. As a consequence, Forrest, redoubtable as he is, could do little damage and would risk destruction himself. Meanwhile the other Union forces in Mississippi and those in Louisiana would be free to lay waste the grainfields of the Tombigbee Valley, demolish the factories, arsenals, and storehouses at Selma and Montgomery, seize Mobile, and isolate Mississippi and Alabama from the rest of the Confederacy. Johnston's army, which draws most of its food and material from this region, would have to abandon Atlanta and withdraw toward Augusta, its only remaining source of supplies, merely to stay in the field. Most of Georgia in turn would be left at the mercy of the Yankees.[28]

These things must not be allowed to happen. If they do occur, the South will lose a war that it at present is winning. In Virginia, Grant, despite his physical proximity, is no closer to taking Richmond than he had been at the beginning of May. In Maryland a Confederate column menaces the enemy's own capital. In Mississippi, Forrest twice has routed invading forces, and there is no reason to think he cannot succeed again. In Kentucky the people at long last are rising up against an abolitionist thralldom that is being shakily maintained by draconian military measures. West of the Mississippi the Missourians seem to be doing the same, and in Arkansas the Union garrisons huddle in a few fortified towns, afraid to venture forth.

But the best signs of approaching Southern victory come from the North itself. Grant's unsuccessful campaign and the horrendous losses accompanying it have sent morale plummeting and, with it, support for an apparently hopeless war. The Democrats scarcely bother to conceal their glee over his failure as they confidently predict that they will win the fall elections on a platform calling for peace. The Republicans, in contrast, are so pessimistic that some of their top leaders, such as Greeley, refuse to endorse Lincoln's candidacy, and others in desperation urge that Grant be nominated in his place. If existing trends persist, the Republican party might disintegrate soon, making it impossible for the North to continue its bloody effort to restore the Union by force.[29]

Only in Georgia is the war going badly. Only there has the South failed to hold its own. Only there does it face the prospect of losing something it cannot afford to lose.

It has been seven months since Davis, most reluctantly, appointed Johnston commander of the Army of Tennessee. He had done so in the hope that Johnston would either drive the Federals at Chattanooga northward or, at the very least, prevent them from advancing further southward. Johnston has done neither. Instead, following the same pattern of retreat and avoidance of battle that he had displayed in Virginia in 1862 and in Mississippi in 1863, he has allowed them to penetrate Georgia to the very gates of Atlanta. His failure jeopardizes the Confederacy's successes everywhere else. It jeopardizes, in fact, the existence of the Confederacy itself.

Secretary of State Benjamin, who had opposed giving Johnston the command in the first place, and Secretary of War Seddon, who had advocated it, are both urging Davis to remove him. So, too, are many congressmen, newspapers, and a growing number of influential men in Georgia and other states. Davis himself believes that Johnston deserves to be dismissed. Nevertheless he hesitates to do it. Johnston has powerful friends both in and outside of Richmond who already are accusing the government of malignantly refusing to provide him with the means to repel Sherman. By most accounts, Johnston, despite his retreats, retains the confidence of his army and much of the public, even in Georgia. Deposing a commander in the midst of a campaign, perhaps on the eve of a decisive battle, is fraught with risk, for it could lead to defeat rather than victory, a defeat for which he, Davis, would get the blame. Last but most important, who will replace Johnston if he is removed? This is a question that Davis is not yet prepared to answer.

Hence, he has sent Bragg to Atlanta. Bragg's mission is to investigate the military situation in Georgia and to ascertain what plans, if any, Johnston has for countering Sherman. Until he hears from Bragg, who left yesterday, or unless events occur that require immediate action, Davis will postpone a decision about Johnston. Meanwhile he can only hope that Johnston, out of necessity if nothing else, will finally stand and fight for Atlanta. As Johnston himself has told Hill, according to Hill's account, "All, then, is lost by Sherman's success, and all is gained by Sherman's defeat."[30]

Part Three: Along the Banks of the Chattahoochee

Unlike Davis, Sherman knows what he will do about Johnston and Atlanta. He will implement the strategy that he outlined to Grant in April: upon crossing the Chattahoochee, cut the railroad between Atlanta and Montgomery, then "feign to the right, but pass to the left and act against Atlanta or its eastern communications, according to developed facts." Moreover, he already has put this plan into operation. As the consequence of orders he issued late in June after electing to outflank Kennesaw, 2,500 blue-clad cavalry under Major General Lovell H. Rousseau, the stalwart commander of the District of Tennessee, have ridden into Alabama for the purpose of "breaking up" the Montgomery and West Point Railroad at Opelika, after which they are to join Sherman in Georgia if possible or, if not, to make for Union-held Pensacola. If successful, Rousseau's raid will totally eliminate Johnston's rail communications with Alabama, for Opelika is the junction of both the direct and the indirect lines linking Atlanta to that state.[31]

Sherman also has decided exactly how he will "feign to the right, but pass to the left." Stoneman with his division will pass down the right bank of the Chattahoochee to the Campbellton area, cross it, and then destroy the Atlanta and West Point Railroad around Newnan. This foray, along with Rousseau's, will cut the direct line between Montgomery and Atlanta, and even if it fails, it should strengthen Johnston's evident assumption that the Federals intend to strike at Atlanta from the west. Meanwhile the XV and XVII corps, presently on the right near Turner's Ferry, will join the XVI Corps at Roswell on the left. Then, as soon as Stoneman returns from his raid, McPherson will swing the Army of the Tennessee east of Atlanta toward Stone Mountain. As he does so, Schofield and Thomas will advance on his right toward the city from the north. Should Johnston try to counter McPherson's move, the way will be open for them to take Atlanta. On the other hand, should Johnston concentrate his forces to resist them, McPherson can get astride the Georgia Railroad between Stone Mountain and Decatur, thereby cutting off Atlanta from Augusta and blocking Johnston's retreat in that direction. With his communications severed to the east by McPherson and to the west by Rousseau and Stoneman, Johnston will have to evacuate Atlanta or stand a siege in it or attack in an attempt to drive the Union army away from it. Sherman expects him to do the first.

A further advantage of Sherman's plan, which he points out to McPherson in a July 10 letter describing it, is that a move on Atlanta from the west would again take his army away from the railroad and expose his forward supply depots, whereas by striking from the north and east, "we are all between the enemy and our base, and now that he has destroyed his own bridges [across the Chattahoochee] he can't get over without fighting us." The only serious threats to his supply line, Sherman believes, are Johnston's cavalry, guerrillas, and Forrest. The first will be guarded against by McCook and Stoneman (after he returns from his expedition against the Atlanta and West Point), both of whom will patrol the Chattahoochee below the railroad bridge. With regard to the second, Sherman orders Major General James B. Steedman (at Chattanooga) and the other rear-area commanders to arrest "all suspicious persons and families" and send them north and to "shoot without mercy all guerrillas." As he explains to Brigadier General John E. Smith, whose XV Corps division has been brought from Alabama to garrison the Resaca-Allatoona area, "the safety of this army must not be imperilled by citizens. If you entertain a bare suspicion against any family send it to the North."32

Concerning Forrest, the matter of most concern to Sherman, Stephen Lee's report that another powerful Union expedition has headed south from Memphis is correct. It consists of 14,000 infantry, cavalry, and artillery under A. J. Smith. Sherman wants Smith to "follow Forrest to the death, if it cost 10,000 lives and breaks the treasury." To that end he has directed Smith to "pursue and kill Forrest" and has promised Brigadier General Joseph A. Mower, commanding Smith's infantry, "my influence to promote him to a major general" if that goal is achieved. In addition, Sherman has ordered Major Generals Henry Slocum at Vicksburg and E. R. S. Canby at Baton Rouge to move, respectively, against Jackson, Mississippi, and Mobile, Alabama. If the combined expeditions of Smith, Slocum, and Canby cannot keep Forrest pinned down in Mississippi, nothing can.33

However, just in case "that devil Forrest" should get loose in his rear, Sherman, in conjunction with Donaldson, Easton, Wright, and McCallum, has taken measures to soften the impact. Enough provisions and munitions are being accumulated at Chattanooga to last his army for two months without additional shipments from Nashville. There are huge and growing stockpiles of the same at Dalton, Resaca, Kingston, Cartersville, Rome, Acworth, Big Shanty, Marietta, Vining's Station, and above all Allatoona, which has been turned into what Sherman calls a "second Chattanooga." Two divisions of infantry (Steedman's and John Smith's) and one of cavalry (Kilpatrick's, now headed by Colonel William Lowe) guard these depots, all of which have been fortified, as have the bridges over the Oostanaula and Etowah. Wright's construction crews, who have rifles as well as picks and shovels, and the 1st Michigan Engineers stand ready both to fight for and to repair the railroad wherever needed. Perhaps Davis is more justified than he knows in refusing to send Forrest into north Georgia. By the same token, Sherman is justified in writing Grant on July 12 that he feels "less timid about the roads to our rear."34

Sherman intends to make what he hopes and expects will be his final thrust to Atlanta as soon as Stoneman returns from his raid, which he has been told should take no longer than five days. This delay provides, among other things, a chance for the Union troops to rest and refit. They need it. "It has been a long campaign," Captain James Zearing, a surgeon in Dodge's corps, informs his wife, "Puss," on July 11, "the troops have been on the watch or the march night and day." Many are "thin and haggard," their uniforms are rags, and their shoes are falling apart. What poet and hospital nurse Walt Whitman calls "the great disease of the army"—diarrhea—is widespread, along with its more deadly brother, dysentery. Scurvy, too, has appeared, causing Captain Wills to note in his diary: "I have seen several black-mouthed, loose-toothed fellows hankering for pickles!" Thousands of men have been hospitalized with these and other afflictions, notably malaria and typhoid, and thousands more are, in the words of an Illinois soldier, "in reality fit subjects for the hospitals." Even the perfectly well suffer the misery of lice, chiggers, flies, and heat so terrible that Corporal John Barnard of the 72nd Indiana Mounted Infantry thinks he might "dry up & blow away"—all six feet, six inches of him.

Although the continued arrival of fresh regiments from the North and from inactive theaters has kept Sherman's overall strength close to 100,000, the combination of battle, sickness, and exhaustion has drastically reduced the size of many of the units that began the campaign. Thus Wills's 103rd Illinois is down to 7 officers and 190 enlisted men, the 11th Pennsylvania of Geary's division can muster only 250 of its original 573 rank and file, and the 63rd Indiana, which early in May numbered 873 troops, now has only 360 fit for duty, which, reports the *Indianapolis Sentinel*, is a "little above average" for regiments in Cox's division. Furthermore, actual combat strength is much lower. Writing to his wife on July 11, Sergeant Phinehas Hager of the 19th Michigan notes that while his company lists 64 men on its roll, it can put a mere 28 on the fighting line. Of the other 36, he explains, 17 are convalescing from wounds after having been released from hospital, 12 are "sick with disease," and the "ballance [sic] are Teamsters, hospital attendants, &c." Assuming that the situation in Hager's company is more or less typical of all such units, which seems reasonable, probably Sherman has no more than 60,000 infantry available for actual combat: a figure, it is interesting to note, that accords with Confederate estimates.[35]

Like the Federals, the Confederates are weary and ragged, prey to the "bloody flux," scurvy, and lice, and in the words of one of them, "so dirty I am ashamed to be seen"; like them, too, their ranks are depleted, with the typical size of a brigade being 1,200 but sometimes much less. Unlike the Federals, however, the Confederates have not been able to make good their losses by reinforcements. Despite the relatively low casualties in the fighting around Kennesaw, by July 10 their total strength has shrunk to 60,000 officers and men present for duty, 10,000 fewer than a month before. Moreover, 3,000 of this decline has occurred since June 30 during a period of little serious combat. Even after making due allowance for other factors, this can only mean that large numbers have deserted.

Without exception, Union accounts of the advance from Kennesaw to the Chattahoochee describe picking up "scores" and "hundreds" of willing Rebel prisoners after each of Johnston's withdrawals. These accounts, furthermore, are confirmed in substance by Confederate sources, notably a letter of July 6 by Celathiel Helms of the 63rd Georgia, who informs his wife that "the men . . . are going to the Yankees by the tens and twenties and hundreds a[l]most every night." Many of the deserters, of course, simply are men who are unable or unwilling to endure longer the hardships and perils of war, reasons that cause some Yankees likewise to "go over" to the enemy. But perhaps an equally large number of the deserters, again to quote Helms, are "all out of heart." In the words of another Georgia soldier, writing to his sister on July 11, they feel that "if we cant stop them [north of the Chattahoochee] it is not reasonable we can stop them at any other place." Indeed, some of the Confederate troops have begun to doubt that Johnston will even attempt to hold Atlanta: "Everything indicating," notes orderly William Trask in his diary for July 10, "the giving up of Atlanta." Also, probably at least a few Southern soldiers would agree with James Watkins, a member of the Georgia State Guard serving in Stevenson's Division, that "our Confederacy is about to go up the spout." Finally and significantly, the deserters tend to come from Tennessee, Kentucky, Alabama, and—as the above quotations suggest—above all Georgia, states that are either occupied or invaded by the Yankees. Thus what happened on a small scale in Mississippi in February during Sherman's Meridian Expedition is beginning to happen on a much larger scale in Georgia in July as Sherman again marches, seemingly irresistible: a sense of futility and despair among many of the Confederate soldiers, coupled with a desire to look to the safety of their homes and families rather than go on with a losing fight for a lost cause. This, to be sure, is far from being the prevailing mood, and militiaman William Dickey probably comes closer to the truth when he writes his wife on July 13 that although "there is some demoralization in the army," it "is very confident the most of them." Yet if Sherman's marching continues, it could become so.[36] The symptoms already are present.

As they wait for active operations to resume, Yanks and Rebs alike "catch up" on their sleep, wash their uniforms (a Wisconsin soldier beholds "fully 500 naked men scattered along the river bank attending to boiling clothes"), draw (if they are lucky) new uniforms and shoes, write letters and read newspapers, pick and eat the abundantly growing blackberries, go fishing (on July 14, Lieutenant Chesley Mosman of the 59th Illinois catches "46 fish and a turtle"), and—their favorite activity—go swimming in the Chattahoochee; even Sherman, his lean body stripped, takes a dip while his amused soldiers look on. Along the river between Pace's Ferry and Turner's Ferry, where picket lines face each other, informal truces become the rule. During them, reports Alpheus Williams to his daughters, men from both armies "bathe on the opposite banks of the river and meet on a neutral log in the center of the stream and joke one another like old friends, making trades in tobacco, coffee, and the like, and exchanging newspapers." Occasionally some of them swim over to the other side and visit the enemy's camp, even staying overnight, and during one evening, Union troops serenade Iverson's Georgia Cavalry Brigade with "national, humorous or sentimental songs," eliciting a response in kind. It would almost seem that when not trying to kill each other, these Northerners and Southerners like each other.

They all feel that the campaign is approaching its climax, that in the next few days or weeks it will be decided. They disagree as to what this decision should be, which is why they normally try to kill one another; but they share a common hope that it will bring the war to an end. "Army operations are necessarily slow," Sergeant Hager of the 19th Michigan writes "My Darling" on July 11, "but still the time is coming ever nearer & every day, when this war will end. Keep up your courage. I expect to spend next winter with you." This same day, a few miles to the south, Private John Crittenden of the 34th Alabama writes "Dear Bettie": "I do hope that this year will end this war and that we may all get home again. But I fear that many of us will have to fall before Peace will be made."[37]

On the morning of July 12, Jefferson Davis stares aghast at the latest telegram from Johnston. Dated July 11, it reads: "I strongly recommend the distribution of the U.S. prisoners, now at Andersonville, immediately."

Andersonville is one hundred miles south of Atlanta. If Johnston fears the imminent liberation of the thousands of Yankee prisoners there, that can only mean that he intends to retreat again, abandoning Atlanta. That must not be allowed to happen. He must be replaced. But, again, by whom?

Davis telegraphs Lee at Petersburg:

> General Johnston has failed, and there are strong indications he will abandon Atlanta. He urges that prisoners be removed immediately from Andersonville. It seems necessary to remove him at once. Who should succeed him? What think you of Hood for the post?

Lee quickly answers:

> I regret the fact stated. It is a bad time to relieve the commander of an army situated as that of Tennessee. We may lose Atlanta and the army

too. Hood is a bold fighter. I am doubtful as to the other qualities necessary.

In the evening, Lee sends Davis a letter elaborating his views on the subject of Johnston, Atlanta, and Hood. In it, after repeating his misgivings about removing Johnston, Lee states:

> Still if necessary it ought to be done. . . . If Johnston abandons Atlanta I suppose he will fall back on Augusta. This loses us Mississippi and communications to the Trans-Mississippi. We had better therefore hazard that communication to retain the country. Hood is a good fighter, very industrious on the battlefield, careless off, & I have had no opportunity of judging his action, when the whole responsibility rested upon him. I have a very high opinion of his gallantry, earnestness & zeal. Genl Hardee has more experience in managing an army.
> May God give you wisdom to decide in this momentous matter.

In essence Lee is telling Davis that dire necessity alone would justify the removal of Johnston; that it would be a lesser evil to give up Atlanta than to lose the Army of Tennessee, for only it stands between Sherman and the Carolinas and Virginia, which is what Lee means by "country"; and that if Johnston is removed, it would be better to replace him with Hardee than with Hood. Davis ponders this advice, then decides once more to postpone a decision about Johnston. He will wait until he hears from Bragg.[38]

On the morning of July 13, Bragg, accompanied by two staff officers, steps from the train in Atlanta's arcaded brick railroad station. He is a tall, skinny, ungainly man of forty-seven whose gray, spiked hair and beard make him look like "an old porcupine" in the opinion of one female observer. Six months ago he had left Georgia in disgrace after having resigned as commander of the Army of Tennessee. Now he returns as the president's chief of staff and with instructions from Davis to "confer with Genl Johnston in relation to military affairs there." What he reports to Davis concerning those affairs will in large measure determine whether Johnston will retain his post and, if he does not, who will take his place.

Bragg's first act is to telegraph Davis: "Have just arrived without detention. Our army all south of the Chattahoochee, and indications seem to favor an entire evacuation of this place. Shall see General Johnston immediately." He next goes to Johnston's headquarters where (so he later reports) he spends most of the day with him, "ascertaining the position of his army, its condition and strength, and in obtaining from him such information" about the Federals as he has. Bragg also listens to Johnston explain in "more detail" his past operations. What Bragg hears and learns confirms his worst fears and suspicions. That

Braxton Bragg (*Photographic History*, 10:243)

night he again telegraphs Davis to inform him that according to Wheeler, the Federals have "crossed two corps to this side of the river," that they also have just crossed it near Newnan, and that Johnston's army is "sadly depleted." "I find," he concludes, "but little encouraging." (This telegram is marked "1 P.M.," but since it refers to the Federals crossing the Chattahoochee "this evening," obviously it was sent on the night of July 13, possibly at 1 A.M.)

This message reaches Davis sometime on July 14, probably late in the morning. It strengthens his determination to remove Johnston but leaves him still unsure as to a replacement. Lee obviously considers Hardee preferable to Hood, an opinion that carries great weight. Moreover Davis has a June 22 letter from Hardee in which "Old Reliable" had complained about Johnston's retreats and predicted that "if the present system continues," the army would reach Atlanta "before a serious battle is fought." This sounds as though Hardee, if given the command, would fight for Atlanta. Perhaps, therefore, he should be the one to replace Johnston. With this in mind, Davis sends the following telegram to Bragg: "The selection of a place must depend upon military considerations so mainly that I can only say that if C. is thus indicated adopt advice and execute as proposed." This cryptic language can only mean that Davis and Bragg have arranged to communicate on certain matters in a way that they alone can comprehend. One of those matters, of course, would be a successor to Johnston. What Davis is telling Bragg is that when or if the military situation around Atlanta warrants it, he is authorized to relieve Johnston and appoint Hardee in his stead.[39]

While this message travels the wires to Atlanta, Bragg spends the day conferring with Johnston's corps commanders at his headquarters, then in a private interview with Hood at his headquarters, during which Bragg receives a memorandum from Hood. On the following day, July 15, Bragg transmits a series of telegrams to Davis. One summarizes what Bragg has garnered from his conferences with Johnston and the corps commanders:

I have made General Johnston two visits, and been received courteously and kindly. He has not sought my advice, and it was not volunteered. I cannot learn that he has any more plan for the future than he has had in the past. It is expected that he will await the enemy on a line some three miles from here [Atlanta], and the impression prevails that he is now more inclined to fight.

A second telegram replies to Davis's proposal that Hardee replace Johnston:

I am decidedly opposed, as it would perpetuate the past and present policy which he has advised and now sustains. Any change will be attended with some objection. This one could produce no good.

A third wire announces that "Lieut. Col. H. W. Walter [one of Bragg's aides] leaves here this evening, bearer of a letter for you." In this letter, after repeating in detail the substance of his telegraphic report on his meetings with Johnston, Bragg addresses the subject of future strategy in Georgia, how it is to be implemented, and—the main point—by whom. Even if the Federals do not move directly against Atlanta, they are in position to devastate Alabama and Mississippi, whereupon, "our army will melt away." There is but one way to avert this calamity: "offensive action." Throughout the whole campaign "General Hood has been in favor of giving battle, and mentions to me numerous instances of opportunities lost." Hardee, on the contrary, "generally favored the retiring policy, though he was frequently non-committal." Furthermore he does not have "the confidence of the army to the extent of the present chief." Therefore, "if any change is made, Lieutenant-General Hood would give unlimited satisfaction, and my estimate of him, already high, has been raised by this campaign. Do not understand me as proposing him as a man of genius, or a great general, but as far better in the present emergency than any one we have available."

Accompanying the letter is Hood's memorandum to Bragg. It also states that Johnston has passed up "chances to strike the enemy a decisive blow" and, after declaring that the only way to prevent Sherman from taking Atlanta and splitting the Confederacy is to "attack him, even if we should have to recross the river to do so," the letter concludes thus:

> I have, general, so often urged that we should force the enemy to give us battle as to almost be regarded reckless by the officers high in rank in this army, since their views have been so directly opposite. I regard it as a great misfortune to our country that we failed to give battle to the enemy many miles north of our present position. Please say to the President that I shall continue to do my duty cheerfully and faithfully, and strive to do what I think is best for our country, as my constant prayer is for our success.

This is nothing more nor less than a bid for command of the Army of Tennessee. It is a bid, moreover, supported by a deliberate attempt to convey a false impression about Hardee's attitude without mentioning him by name. In speaking of "officers high in rank in this army" who have "almost" come to regard him as "reckless" because of his advocacy of giving battle, Hood clearly implies Hardee, the only such officer (other than Johnston and Hood himself) who has participated in the army's councils of war throughout the campaign. Yet Hood knows full well that Hardee had joined with him in urging an attack at Cassville and that Hardee had opposed the retreat from there that Johnston had made at

Hood's insistence, and it is highly unlikely that Hood is ignorant of Hardee's dissatisfaction with Johnston's conduct of operations, for reticence in expressing criticism of his commanders never has been one of Hardee's traits.

Obviously Bragg and Hood, who meet again in private on July 15, are collaborating for the purpose of assuring Johnston's dismissal and Hood's assignment as his successor. Hood is motivated by ambition and by a sincere and not necessarily mistaken belief that he possesses what Hardee lacks—the ardor and determination needed to turn the tide of war in Georgia before it sweeps over Atlanta. Bragg, who in all probability has initiated and masterminded the collaboration, shares this belief. It is easy for him to do so because he hates and despises Hardee. Hardee might be "Old Reliable" to others, but to Bragg he is the man who after Perryville and Murfreesboro had slandered him in public and private, who had intrigued with other high-ranking malcontents to have Davis remove Bragg as commander of the Army of Tennessee, and who had been a prime cause of the dissension in that army which had culminated in the disaster at Missionary Ridge and his own disgrace. It would require a nobler man than Braxton Bragg to forgive such wrongs, especially since he is to a high degree right in thinking that Hardee had committed them. Now, if Davis will only follow his advice, Bragg will have his revenge, and with it the satisfaction of knowing that he has done his duty to his president and his nation. How nice it is to be able to combine the two.[40]

On July 16, Davis reads Bragg's telegrams as they arrive. What they relate makes it all the more necessary to remove Johnston. On the other hand they make the matter of replacing him all the more difficult. How can Bragg's statement that Hardee "has advised and now sustains" Johnston in his perpetual retreats be reconciled with Hardee's June 22 letter criticizing Johnston on precisely that score? Is Hardee lying? Or is Bragg mistaken about Hardee?

Davis cannot answer these question. But they raise another question, one he has asked himself before and which he now must ask again. Regardless of whether he upholds or opposes Johnston's conduct of operations, is Hardee the right man to take command of the Army of Tennessee in this moment of crisis? Seven months ago, when offered it on a regular basis, Hardee had declined it on the grounds of "my inability to serve the country successfully in this new sphere of activity." How can Davis have confidence in a general who evidently lacks confidence in himself?

Davis decides to give Johnston a last chance. If Johnston is about to give battle to Sherman or if he will provide definite assurance backed by a definite plan for doing so in the near future, he will remain in command. If he does neither, then he will be removed. Accordingly, Davis sends Johnston what in effect is an ultimatum: "A telegram from Atlanta of yesterday [one of Bragg's,

conveying a report from Wheeler] announces that the enemy is extending entrenchments from river toward railroad to Augusta. I wish to hear from you as
to present situation, and your plan of operations so specifically as will enable
me to anticipate events."

Johnston receives the message sometime during the evening. Davis already
has made his dissatisfaction with Johnston abundantly clear. Wigfall and others
have warned him that the president intends to relieve him. Despite his subsequent claim to the contrary, Johnston knows that Bragg's visit is not a routine
one, and he also knows about the private meetings between Bragg and Hood.
And just yesterday, Johnston received a telegram from Senator Hill in Richmond stating: "You must do the work with your present force. For God's sake
do it."

Even so, Johnston's response to Davis's attempt to get him to commit himself
to a definite course of action is as vague and evasive as ever: "Your dispatch of
today received. . . . As the enemy has double our number, we must be on the
defensive. My plan of operations must, therefore, depend on that of the enemy.
It is mainly to watch for an opportunity to fight to advantage. We are trying to
put Atlanta in condition to be held for a day or two by the Georgia militia, that
army movements may be freer and wider."

Either Johnston does not think that Davis will dare remove him, or else he
does not care if he does. All that is certain is that no matter what, Johnston will
not abandon the strategy he has pursued from the outset: adhere to the strategic
defensive, engage in the tactical offensive only if there appears to be an opportunity to strike the enemy a hard blow with minimal risk and loss, and trade
space for time in the hope that Forrest will be sent to attack and break Sherman's supply line. It is the only strategy that he believes offers a realistic
prospect of success given the enemy's superior strength and cautious mode of
warfare. If the president wants a different strategy, let him name a different
commander.[41]

Sherman also engages in telegraphic conversation on July 16. At the other end
of the line are Grant and Halleck. In the morning, Grant warns Sherman that
Early, whose army skirmished with hastily assembled defenders manning the
fortifications of Washington before (wisely) withdrawing, has returned to Virginia with "possibly 25,000 troops" and that since Lee has all the men he both
needs and can feed to hold Richmond-Petersburg, it is "not improbable that you
will find in the next fortnight re-enforcements in your front to the number
indicated above." Such being the case, Sherman, on getting to Atlanta, should
"set about destroying the railroads as far to the east and south" as possible,

"collect all the stores of the country for your own use," and then "select a point that you can hold until help can be had. I shall make such a desperate effort to get a position here which will hold the enemy without the necessity of so many men. If successful, I can detach from here for other enterprises, looking as much to your assistance as anything else."

That afternoon, Halleck repeats Grant's warning about Johnston's being reinforced from Virginia and likewise advises Sherman to "prepare a good line of defense" and to stockpile supplies. In sum, after having been told three weeks ago that he no longer needed to concern himself with preventing Johnston from transferring troops to Lee, Sherman now is being told that he faces the prospect of Lee's sending troops to Johnston and that therefore he, Sherman, should make ready to fight for his very life. The grand strategy that Grant and he had formulated in March and April has been reversed by events. Far from the war's being won in Virginia, the object has become to save it from being lost in Georgia. If lost there, it is lost everywhere.

We do not know if Sherman grasps the significance of Grant's and Halleck's messages; we can only assume that he does, given the fact that they are tantamount to a confession of failure in Virginia. In any case, they do not alarm him. He has about 90,000 troops of all arms available for field duty, whereas he estimates Johnston's force (accurately enough) at no more than 60,000. Moreover, before any large number of Lee's troops can reach Georgia, Sherman expects to have Atlanta or, the equivalent thereof, to have cut all the city's railroad communications. Hence in his 11 P.M. reply to Grant and Halleck, he assures them that they need not be alarmed either: "I had anticipated all possible chances and am accumulating all the stores possible. . . . I do not fear Johnston with re-enforcements of 20,000 if he will take the offensive; but I recognize the danger arising from my long line [of supply] and the superiority of the enemy's cavalry in numbers and audacity. I move tomorrow from the Chattahooche toward Decatur and Stone Mountain. . . . All well."

Last night, Sherman learned the outcome of Stoneman's expedition against the West Point railroad: another failure by Sherman's cavalry, which probably accounts for his remark about the superior "audacity" of the Confederate troopers. Stoneman managed to seize a usable intact bridge over the Chattahoochee about ten miles from the railroad at Newnan, but when he tried to cross it, he met artillery fire and so merely burned it and then withdrew to a camp near Villa Rica, where his men—described by Chaplain Hight of the 58th Indiana as "far from presenting a bold appearance"—busied themselves at reshoeing their horses and picking blackberries. But at least Stoneman made his raid, if such it can be called, within the allotted five days, and thus Sherman, as he had indicated to Grant and Halleck, can begin his strike at Atlanta come morning. At Roswell, Dodge's corps has built a "double track" bridge across the Chattahoochee and waits to use it along with Logan's and Blair's corps. To the south at Pace's and Powers's ferries, Thomas is ready to cross via trestle bridges and pontoons. Schofield and Garrard, of course, already are on the opposite bank and, as Bragg notified Davis, have pushed out toward the railroad to Augusta. Finally, according to Sherman's calculations, by tomorrow Rousseau should reach Opelika and start wrecking the rail connections between Georgia and Alabama. All indeed is well.[42]

Early on Sunday morning July 17, Davis studies Johnston's reply to his request for precise information about his plans. It is not what Davis hoped for, merely what he might have expected. Again Johnston declares that he is impossibly outnumbered, that as a consequence he must stand on the defensive, that his future movements depend on what the enemy does, and that all the while he will "watch for an opportunity to fight to advantage," as if he were more likely to find that opportunity in the six miles that now separate him from Atlanta than he has been during the hundred miles he has retreated during the past two months! The only new thing in the reply is the most alarming thing, namely, that he is "trying to put Atlanta in condition to be held for a day or two by the Georgia militia, that army movements may be freer and wider." Why is not Atlanta already in condition to be held by the Georgia militia: hasn't fortifying been going on there for months? What if the Georgia militia can't hold the city for a day or two? So far only a few thousand of them have been assembled there, and Governor Brown has had to request firearms for those still unmobilized. And what is meant by "freer and wider" army movements? A retreat toward Augusta or toward Macon? Certainly that can't be ruled out, for nowhere in his reply does Johnston say what Davis has wanted him to say: that Johnston intends to fight for Atlanta in an all-out, determined effort to keep it out of Yankee hands.

Johnston must be removed at once; it would be folly to wait any longer. And Hood will replace him. Whatever else he might be or might not be, Hood is a fighter who can be depended on to do all he can to save Atlanta. Even if Hood fails, that will be better than letting Atlanta fall without a real struggle, by default so to speak. Should that happen, all that has been gained so far this year by the South at such heroic cost will be disgracefully lost. In particular it would undo the effect of Jubal Early's just-completed raid into Maryland, a raid that took his fast-marching veterans to within musket range of Washington's fortifications and forced Grant to rush a whole corps of his army to the Yankee capital to save it from capture! Proof of how shattering that foray has been to

Northern morale, which was already crumbling beneath the weight of corpses piled up by Grant in his vain attempts to overpower Lee, is present right now in Richmond. At the Spotswood Hotel, waiting to see the president of the Confederacy, are Colonel James F. Jaquess, commander of the 73rd Illinois, a regiment in Sherman's army, and James R. Gilmore, a well-known journalist with Washington connections. They claim to have come to Richmond strictly in a private capacity, but they bear a letter from Lincoln and could not have come without his knowledge and permission. They also say that they want to "discover some way by which this war may be stopped." Very well: Davis will be glad to tell them how it can be stopped. But when he does so, he wants to feel confident that Sherman will not be marching virtually unopposed into Atlanta.

In the afternoon, on instructions passed down from Davis, General Samuel Cooper, adjutant of the Confederate army, sends the following telegram to Johnston:

> Lieut. Gen. J. B. Hood has been commissioned to the temporary rank of general. . . . I am directed by the Secretary of War to inform you that as you have failed to arrest the advance of the enemy to the vicinity of Atlanta, far in the interior of Georgia, and express no confidence that you can defeat or repel him, you are hereby relieved from the command of the Army and Department of Tennessee, which you will immediately turn over to General Hood.

That evening, Davis and Secretary of State Benjamin meet in the latter's office with Gilmore and Jaquess. The Northerners state that they are appalled by the hideous loss of life in the war and hope to open the way for official peace negotiations. To that end, Lincoln has authorized them to tell Davis that the South can have peace; all it has to do is agree to return to the Union and abolish slavery. Davis promptly and flatly rejects these terms; they are nothing but a proposal for Southern surrender. The South, he declares, is fighting, not for slavery, but for independence; "and that, or extermination, we will have." Gilmore and Jaquess argue that the South cannot win, citing as proof the enormous odds against it and its precarious military and financial plight. Davis answers by pointing to Lee's success in stopping Grant, Early's raid, and the North's own monetary problems. To be sure, Davis concedes, Sherman has penetrated deep into Georgia; but that merely has made his army more vulnerable. "So, in a military view, I should certainly say our position is better than yours." He concludes the interview by reaffirming the South's determination to fight on until its independence is acknowledged by the North: "We will govern ourselves. We *will* do it, if we have to see every Southern plantation sacked, and every Southern city in flames."[43]

At 10 P.M., as he sits in his office at the Dexter Niles house discussing with Colonel Presstman plans to strengthen Atlanta's defenses, Johnston receives Cooper's telegram relieving him of command and appointing Hood as his successor. After reading it, he sends a note of congratulations to Hood, whose headquarters are near Turner's Ferry, then composes a farewell to the Army of Tennessee, praising its courage and endurance and declaring that although "no longer your leader, I will watch your career, and will rejoice in your victories." Not until morning does he react to his dismissal with a telegram to Richmond. Addressed to Cooper, it in fact is directed at Davis:

> Your dispatch of yesterday received and obeyed. Command of the Army and Department of Tennessee has been transferred to General Hood. As to the alleged cause of my removal, I assert that Sherman's army is much stronger compared with that of Tennessee than Grant's compared with that of Northern Virginia. Yet the enemy has been compelled to advance much more slowly to vicinity of Atlanta than to that of Richmond and Petersburg, and has penetrated much deeper into Virginia than into Georgia. Confident language by a military commander is not usually regarded as evidence of competency.

Clearly Johnston feels aggrieved, although it would be amazing if he were surprised. He believes, and he will always maintain, that he has done the best that could be done, given the Confederacy's overall military situation and the enemy's superior strength. He believes and will forever contend, too, that he is the victim of Davis's stupidity, stubbornness, and vindictiveness. On the other hand he cannot help but feel a certain sense of relief at being relieved. No longer does he bear the burden of defending Atlanta; no longer will be he blamed should it fall. Both that burden and that potential blame now belong to Hood. Johnston indeed will watch—with great interest—the Army of Tennessee's future career under its new commander. Whether he will also be able to rejoice in its victories is another matter.

An hour after Johnston learns of his downfall, Hood learns of his elevation, likewise via a telegram from Cooper. Accompanying it is a message from Seddon, obviously speaking for Davis: "You are charged with a great trust. . . . You will, I know, act to the utmost of your capacities to discharge it. Be wary no less than bold. . . . God be with you."

Hood spends the night in "deep thought." Little wonder. It is one thing to say what an army commander should do; it is another to be the commander who has to do it. Moreover, whatever he does, it will have to be done quickly: Sherman's host has spent the day crossing the Chattahoochee and even now is advancing on Atlanta. At 1 A.M., Johnston's note of congratulations arrives, whereupon Hood replies: "I accept your congratulations. . . . I desire to have a conversation with you, and for that purpose will be over early in the morning." Shortly before sunrise he sets out for the Dexter Niles house. As he nears it, he meets Stewart heading for the same destination. Stewart asks Hood to join Hardee and him in urging Johnston to "retain command of the Army until the impending battle should have been fought." Hood agrees; to do otherwise would, to say the least, create a bad impression.

Hence, on reaching the Niles house, Hood telegraphs the War Department that "I deem it dangerous to change the commander of this army at this particular time, and to be the interest of the service that no change should be made until the fate of Atlanta is decided." This done, he meets in private with Johnston and urges him to pocket the dismissal order and "fight the battle for Atlanta." Johnston answers that the president has ordered him relieved and that the order must stand unless countermanded. Hood, Hardee, and Stewart thereupon telegraph Davis, asking him to suspend the order at least until a decision has been reached at Atlanta. While waiting for a reply, Johnston, at Hood's request, issues orders through Mackall. At 5:20 P.M. the reply comes, addressed to all three generals:

> Your telegram of this date received. A change of commanders, under existing circumstances, was regarded as so objectionable that I only accepted it as the alternative of continuing in a policy which had proved so disastrous. Reluctance to make the change induced me to send a telegram of inquiry to the commanding general on the 16th instant. His reply but confirmed previous apprehensions. There can be but one question which you and I can entertain—that is, what will best promote the general good; and to each of you I confidently look for the sacrifice of every personal consideration in conflict with that object. The order has been executed, and I cannot suspend it without making the case worse than it was before the order was issued.

In other words, to restore Johnston to command after having removed him would make the president look ridiculous and would assure what the removal is intended to prevent—namely, the fall of Atlanta.

This settles the matter. Hood issues an announcement of his assumption of command, and Johnston goes to Atlanta, from where on the following evening he travels to Macon with his wife.[44] Hood and he will never set eyes on each other again.

The news that Johnston is out and Hood is in as commander makes a strong impact on the army, and most of it is negative. In telling Davis that Hood's appointment "would give unlimited satisfaction," Bragg was deceiving either himself or the president, most likely the latter. Hardee, who late in June resentfully had written his wife that "Hood, I think, is helping the General [Johnston] to do the strategy, and from what I can see is doing most of it," considers himself insulted at being passed over in favor of a general far junior to him in seniority and years; only the crisis of the moment prevents him from tendering his resignation. Stewart, although he is a friend of Bragg's and is critical of Johnston's conduct of operations, obviously is alarmed by the change. Clayton, now commanding Stewart's former division, at first refuses to believe it, and one of his brigadiers orders the arrest of anyone who spreads such a false, enemy-inspired rumor. French, on meeting Hood at the Niles house, frankly declares that he is sorry that Johnston has been relieved. Cheatham, according to orderly Trask, is "surprised" and expresses "regret." Brigadier General Clement H. Stevens of Walker's Division writes Johnston: "We would hail with joy your return to command us." Cleburne, if his official report on the campaign is any indication, has little regard for Johnston but, given his close personal relationship, presumably thinks that Hardee should have succeeded him. Walker, on the other hand, probably is delighted that Hardee, the sponsor of Cleburne's despicable proposal to make slaves into soldiers, is not the successor. As for Hood, Walker believes (so he writes his wife) that "he is brave," but "whether he has the capacity to Command armies (for it requires a high order of talent) time will develop," scarcely an enthusiastic endorsement. If there is any general in the Army of Tennessee who welcomes Hood's accession to command, it is Wheeler; after all, he helped to bring it about.[45]

The army's rank and file, with relatively few exceptions, react to the change with "astonishment," "shock," "indignation," "dissatisfaction," "outrage," "sorrow," and "gloom." Some men actually weep and talk about refusing to fight and going home, and while marching past the Niles house on the evening of July 18, Walker's Division presented arms in salute, not cheering only because Johnston has requested them not to. Since taking command seven months ago, "Old Joe" has, Lieutenant Robert Gill of the 41st Mississippi informs his wife on July 18, "made himself very dear to the soldiers." They like his jaunty yet dignified manner, his frequent visits to their trenches, and the way he had (in the words of Captain Foster) "always been looking after our comfort and safety" and seeing to it that there was "something to eat." Many of them, to be sure, are worried about retreating so often and so far; like Benjamin Seaton of Granbury's Brigade they feel that "we have gone as far as we ought to go unless we intend to give up all our country and not fight anymore and that is not the idey [*sic*]—it is victory or death." Also, according to Colonel Sykes, their "general opinion is that Atlanta [will] be given up," an assessment supported by numerous other sources. Nevertheless the vast majority of the soldiers retain, like Sergeant Joel Murphee of the 57th Alabama, "the utmost confidence" in

Johnston and believe that the retreats, discouraging as they may be, have been necessary because, as Sergeant John Hagan of the 29th Georgia explains to his wife, "the Yankee army is So much Stronger than ours & then have a corps or two which they can Send on eather [*sic*] flank & then we have to fall back to prevent them from getting in our rear." They also think that Johnston has done the right thing in staying, as a rule, on the defensive, for this has enabled them (so they think) to inflict much larger losses on the enemy than they themselves have suffered—30,000, even 40,000, some of them calculate. "If we can keep this up," Captain Hall predicts to his daughter, "we win."

The trouble is, they are not sure that Hood will "keep this up." They know his reputation and how he got it—by attacking. They know as well that all of the army's large-scale assaults during the campaign, not counting Bate's blundering charge at Dallas, have been made by Hood and that all have ended in such bloody repulses that there are troops in his corps who call him a "butcher." And they sense that he has been put in command for the specific purpose of making a supreme effort to save Atlanta and that almost certainly a desperate battle to decide that city's fate will take place soon. Therefore, while they hope that "Old Peg Leg" will lead them to victory and although, as one of them puts it, they are fighting "for the cause, not the general," they would feel better about their prospects if "Old Joe" still were in charge. He could be trusted not to do anything foolish.[46]

Part Four: Peachtree Creek

There are no peach trees along Peachtree Creek. The name comes from the Indians; it refers to a giant "pitch tree" that had once stood on its bank. Two streams—called Peachtree Creek North and Peachtree Creek South—join northeast of Atlanta to form the creek, which flows in a generally westward direction until it empties into the Chattahoochee not far from the railroad bridge. It is not wide, and its muddy, sluggish waters are not deep, but its banks are high and steep and "fringed with briar patches and almost impassable undergrowth," to quote a newspaper correspondent. It is, in short, a formidable obstacle to both advance and retreat, the last natural obstacle of any consequence between the Federals and Atlanta, five miles to the south.

By the evening of July 18 the Army of the Cumberland, the IV Corps in the lead, has reached Buckhead, less than two miles from the creek, Schofield is three miles to the east at Johnson's Mill, and the XV Corps and Garrard's cavalry are astride the Georgia Railroad, where detachments are tearing up track. Sherman himself has established headquarters at a house near Old Cross

Keys on the Peachtree road leading due south into Atlanta where it becomes Peachtree Street. His mood is optimistic. So far all has gone according to plan, with only light resistance from Rebel cavalry being encountered. Tomorrow, he telegraphs Halleck at 7 P.M., he will make a "bold push for Atlanta," with McPherson moving toward it from the east via Decatur, Schofield advancing from the north to the same town, and Thomas pushing south across Peachtree Creek. In addition, Sherman has ordered Garrard to head eastward along the Georgia Railroad, destroying it "as far as deemed prudent." Should the Confederates attack, he expects it will not be "until we reach below Peachtree Creek." The absence of serious opposition, however, causes him to wonder whether they will try to defend Atlanta at all. "It is hard to realize," he comments in an afternoon dispatch to Thomas, "that Johnston will give up Atlanta without a fight, but it may be so. Let us develop the truth."[47]

Hood spends July 19, his first full day of actual command, assessing the situation. The bulk of his army—about 55,000 effectives including the cavalry and Smith's militia—occupies a line south of Peachtree Creek that runs from the Chattahoochee railroad bridge to just beyond the Peachtree road, with Stewart's Corps on the left, Hardee's in the center, and his own former corps, which on recommendation of Hardee he has placed under the acting command of Cheatham, on the right.* Jackson's cavalrymen guard the crossings of the Chattahoochee to the west; Wheeler's troopers and Smith's militiamen cover the eastern approaches to Atlanta. According to the reports Hood has received, on the Federal side, Thomas is beginning to cross Peachtree Creek, and McPherson and Schofield are approaching Decatur, a village six miles due east of Atlanta. This information delights Hood. It means that Sherman has "committed a serious blunder," that he has split his army so widely that neither half can support the other, thereby providing a golden opportunity to smash each half separately. At once Hood formulates a plan to exploit the blunder. Stewart's and Hardee's corps will attack Thomas's forces just after they cross Peachtree Creek but before they can entrench, the object being to drive them

---

*Why Hardee recommended Cheatham rather than the better-qualified Cleburne for temporary command of Hood's old corps is not known, but probably it was simply because Cheatham was senior in rank. In any case, the oft-contended proposition that Cleburne (or Forrest) should have been named to command the Army of Tennessee is historically irrelevant. Doing so probably never entered the head of Davis, who was firmly committed to reserving high commands for West Pointers and who did not depart from that policy until the final months of the war out of sheer necessity. Also there is no factual evidence that Cleburne's proposal to use black troops in the Confederate army (which Cheatham supported) had anything to do with his failure to achieve higher rank and command.

into the pocket formed by the juncture of the creek with the Chattahoochee. Then, with their retreat blocked by the two rivers and being cut off from the rest of the Federal army, they will have to surrender or be obliterated. While Stewart and Hardee deliver this blow, Cheatham will join Wheeler and the militia in fending off McPherson and Schofield. Once Thomas has been disposed of, the whole Confederate army will turn against them and complete the destruction of Sherman's host. Atlanta will be saved—and with it the Confederacy.[48]

Hood's information about Thomas's movements is correct. During the day, portions of Davis's, Geary's, and Wood's divisions have crossed Peachtree, and Stanley is over the north branch. Only Davis has encountered strong opposition, with McCook's old brigade, still under Colonel Dilworth, suffering 245 casualties in taking a hill overlooking the Howell's Ferry crossing, a loss that makes Major Holmes, who now commands the 52nd Ohio once again, feel more depressed than he had after the June 27 assault. On the other hand, either Wheeler or perhaps Mackall, who remains on as chief of staff, has failed to keep Hood posted on McPherson and Schofield. They are not merely advancing on Decatur; they already are there, ransacking the place and ripping up more of the Georgia Railroad. Since Hood's plan in part is based on the assumption that there is no immediate threat to Atlanta from the east, this lack of accurate intelligence could prove troublesome.

Sherman, who is with Schofield at a house north of Decatur, now knows that Hood is in command of the Confederate army, having learned it from a copy of yesterday's *Appeal* that Dodge has procured from a spy. Sherman believes that the change from Johnston to Hood indicates that the enemy means to fight for Atlanta, not evacuate it as he was half-expecting. If so—and Schofield, a West Point classmate, says Hood is "bold even to rashness"—then where and how? As Sherman sees it, there are two possibilities. One would be for Hood to make a stand inside Atlanta's fortifications. In that case, he will swing his forces between Atlanta and the Chattahoochee, cutting or threatening to cut its communications to the west and south. The other possibility is that Hood will attack, and this is the one that worries Sherman. He is aware of the great gap between the two wings of his army, and he fears that Hood might attempt to exploit it by concentrating against, not Thomas, whose Army of the Cumberland he deems strong enough to withstand anything the enemy can throw against it, but McPherson and Schofield, who are weaker and farther from their base than is Thomas. Therefore, several times during the day, Sherman has urged Thomas to get across Peachtree Creek as quickly as possible so that he will be in position to send assistance to the left, and also has ordered him to shift Howard's corps to the southwest so as to close the gap between the two wings.

At 8 P.M., Sherman receives a dispatch from Thomas stating that both of these things are in the process of being accomplished and also that "an Atlanta paper of today has been captured by Wood's force which reports Opelika was captured." Sherman feels much relieved, indeed delighted, on reading this message. The news about Opelika can only mean that Rousseau has reached there and presumably has cut railroad communications between Alabama and Atlanta. And now that Howard is moving to the left, there is little danger that McPherson and Schofield will be overwhelmed. "Good for Rousseau!" he writes Thomas, then instructs him to "move for Atlanta at daylight," adding that should the enemy attack east of Atlanta, McPherson, Howard, and Schofield will be "ample to fight the whole of Hood's army, leaving you to walk into Atlanta, capturing guns and everything."[49]

A curious situation exists as July 19 draws to a close. Hood, unaware that the Federals already are in Decatur, believes that there is no particular danger east of Atlanta. Sherman, assuming that Hood, if he attacks at all, will do so against the weakest portion of his army, thinks that east of Atlanta is the only place where he might face a serious danger. Perhaps tomorrow will reveal which commander suffers most from his mistake.

Around midnight, Hood, who has transferred army headquarters to a house just north of Atlanta on the Peachtree road, meets with the corps commanders and Smith to explain to them their roles in his plan. The attack will start at 1 P.M. Hardee will lead it off, his assault divisions advancing *en echelon* from his right, and Stewart will continue it, employing the same formation. The objective is to roll up the Federals and drive them back toward Peachtree Creek and the Chattahoochee, trapping and destroying them. Hardee and Stewart are to keep one division each in reserve to ensure and exploit victory. While they attack, Cheatham with Hood's former corps will guard Hardee's right flank, cover the northeastern approaches to Atlanta, and place batteries in position to rake the entire area around the headwaters of Peachtree Creek, thereby preventing McPherson and Schofield from going to Thomas's aid. Smith's militia will man Atlanta's east-side fortifications and support Wheeler in checking any Union advance toward the city from that direction.

Having learned from "long experience" that nothing is more important than that orders be fully understood before the time comes to execute them, Hood then asks the corps commanders if they comprehend their assignments. They all answer yes. Assured on that score, Hood then tells Hardee and Stewart that although troops will encounter "hastily constructed works" held by the Federals who already have crossed Peachtree, most of the enemy will be "caught in the act of throwing up such works" and thus will be vulnerable to "a bold and persistent attack." This being the case, it is important that their men charge and carry these works, at the "point of the bayonet" if necessary. Again Hardee and Stewart signify that they understand. Hood thereupon dismisses the generals, and the conference ends. Twelve hours hence he will fight his first battle as an army commander, if all goes as scheduled.[50]

Dawn of July 20 promises and delivers another fiercely hot day; it is enough to make one long for the rains of a month ago.[51] A mile or so south of Peachtree Creek, Hood's troops make ready for combat. Yesterday they dug in along a line that runs for five miles from the Western and Atlanta tracks on the left to the south fork of the creek on the right. Stewart's Corps is west of the Howell's Mill road (sometimes called the Pace's Ferry road), Hardee's is to the east of it, and Cheatham's is on Hardee's right. The terrain consists of low hills and ridges, cut by ravines and small streams; and except for some scattered fields near the creek, everything is covered by the usual pine forests and dense underbrush. Neither army can see the other. The Confederates, however, know that the Federals are along Peachtree, whereas Thomas's troops merely sense that the Rebels are somewhere up ahead and have not the slightest idea how many and how far.

During the morning, Thomas resumes crossing the creek. The XIV Corps is the first to get over in full strength, but instead of advancing, Palmer orders it to entrench along a front extending from the mouth of the creek on the right to the Howell's Mill road on the left. Made wary by the rough experience of McCook's brigade yesterday, he has a hunch that the Confederates might attack, and he does not intend to be caught in the open. Similar considerations of prudence cause Thomas to modify Sherman's order to fill the gap between the army's two wings with the IV Corps. If executed literally, this would leave both the Peachtree road and the Army of the Cumberland's left flank unprotected. Hence Thomas has Wood's division recross the creek via the bridge that it built yesterday and sends it, along with Stanley's division, to link up with Schofield's right. At the same time he replaces Wood's division on the south bank of the creek with Newton's division. Howard accompanies Wood and Stanley on their march after notifying Newton that for the time being he will take his orders directly from Thomas. Howard also tells Newton that "from present appearances the battle will be fought by the forces on your left"—that is, Schofield and McPherson.

The XX Corps completes its crossing last. First, Williams's division passes over on bridges built by Geary's pioneers, then moves west to the Howell's Mill

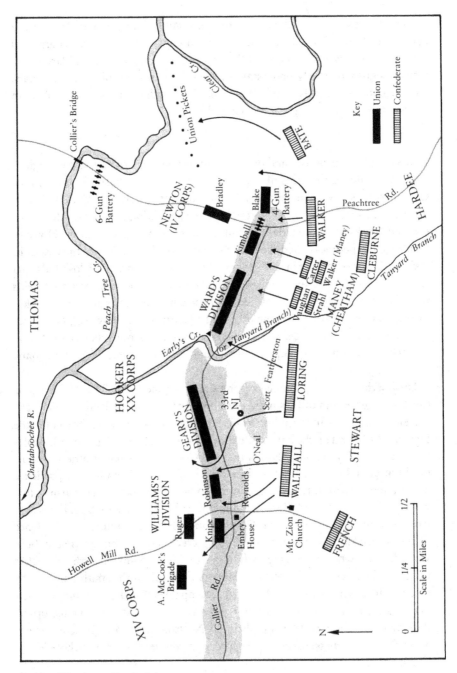

Battle of Peachtree Creek, July 20

road. Next, Ward's division marches across the Peachtree-road bridge and halts in a valley to the right and rear of Newton's division, from which it is separated by a northward-flowing tributary of Peachtree called Early's (or Tanyard) Creek. Thus, as noon approaches, most of Thomas's troops are south of Peachtree, but they do not form a continuous line and, except for the XIV Corps on the right and Newton's division (which has occupied some works thrown up by Wood's division near the Peachtree-road bridge), they remain unfortified. In short, they are exactly where and, in the case of the XX Corps, in the condition that Hood wants them to be.

Unfortunately for Hood, the same does not hold true for Sherman's left wing. Although it is advancing from Decatur on Atlanta at the ponderous rate of one mile every three hours, it is advancing and in overwhelming strength: Logan's corps, followed by Dodge's on the Decatur road, and Schofield's and Blair's corps on parallel roads to the north and south respectively. Only Wheeler, with 2,500 dismounted troopers and a 4-gun battery, stands in Sherman's way. Obviously this is not enough, and Wheeler has sent a message to Hood so informing him.

The message reaches Hood at his Peachtree-road headquarters about 10 A.M. It leaves him with no choice other than to slide his army to the right so as to prevent McPherson's and Schofield's columns from marching virtually unopposed into Atlanta. Accordingly he orders Cheatham to move his corps a division front (one mile) to the south with the object of covering the Decatur road. Since this shift will open up an equally wide gap on Cheatham's left, Hood instructs Hardee and Stewart also to sidestep to their right, but only a half-mile each. This, of course, will create a gap between Hardee and Cheatham, but that should be no problem since it can be covered by Cheatham's artillery and no Federals are reported in that area anyway. Just to make sure, however, Hood further directs Hardee to maintain contact with Cheatham, presumably by means of a picket line, and to post a staff officer on his left flank to notify Stewart exactly where to halt his shift. Confident that the redeployment of his army will not take long, Hood still expects the attack to be made at 1 P.M. as scheduled, and at 11 A.M., he so notifies Wheeler, to whom he has sent 1,000 reinforcements from Jackson's cavalry. Around noon, Hood rides with his staff to Stewart's headquarters on the Howell's Mill road. Observing him, a reporter for the *Savannah Republican* notes that his eyes are flashing with "a strange indescribable light." It is the expression of a general who anticipates victory.

But then things begin to go wrong. For some reason—inexperience as a corps commander, concern about defending what amounts to a five-mile front, or sheer inefficiency within his command—Cheatham is slow to move, and when he does so, he moves, not one mile, but two miles to his right. As a consequence Hardee finds himself facing a dilemma. How can he both slide eastward a half-mile and still stay in contact with Cheatham, even with just a picket line? After considering the matter and without referring it to Hood, who presumably has informed him that he has gone to Stewart's headquarters, no more than a five-minute gallop away, Hardee decides to follow Cheatham, and shortly before 1 P.M. he begins doing so, again without notifying Hood.

Stewart, seeing Hardee marching east, becomes alarmed. He believes that the rightward shift is unnecessary and that in any case it now is too late to make it if the Yankees are to be caught in the open. Hence he sends a staff officer to Hood with a request that he stop Hardee and order an immediate advance against the enemy. Hood, however, ignores Stewart's plea. Understandably enough, Hood's model for conducting a battle is Robert E. Lee; could there by a better one? Lee's practice is to tell his corps commanders what he wants done, then let them find a way to do it. Hood can only assume, or at least hope, that Hardee—who is, with the debatable exception of Longstreet, the most experienced corps commander in the Confederate service—knows what he is doing. Besides, to interfere at this juncture might merely make matters worse by intensifying Hardee's manifest resentment over not being named Johnston's successor. Thus 1 P.M. and then 2 P.M. pass with Hardee's and Stewart's corps still sliding to the right—or, to be more accurate, lurching to the right, as perforce they halt whenever Cheatham halts, which is often.

Meanwhile Newton's and Geary's divisions slowly advance, the former down the Peachtree road, the latter toward a ridge along which runs a lane called the Collier Ridge road that connects the Peachtree road with the Howell's Mill road to the west. Thomas, having been told by Rebel prisoners that Hood's entire army is in his front, has instructed Newton to find out how much in the way of opposition lies ahead, and Hooker has ordered Geary to do the same. Hooker also directs Ward and Williams to send out skirmishers to occupy the ridge on either side of Geary but otherwise to stay put; he has no intention of advancing in full strength until the XIV Corps moves forward so as to cover his right flank. Palmer, on the other hand, insists that the XX Corps advance first, for he is more than ever convinced that there is a large force of Confederates up ahead, just waiting to pounce. Thomas, who is at Peachtree-road bridge supervising Newton's operations, sends chief of staff Whipple to try to put an end to this military prototype of an Alphonse and Gaston act. It is getting toward mid-afternoon, and Thomas is not appreciably closer to Atlanta than he was at sunrise.

Three-fourths of a mile from the bridge, Newton reaches the eastern end of the same ridge that Geary is occupying. Here he halts to wait for Ward's division to come up on his right. Uneasy about his exposed position, Newton deploys Kimball's and Colonel John Blake's brigades respectively east and west of the road, where they rapidly throw up a backward-curving barricade of rails and logs and place a 4-gun battery between them. To cover his left flank and rear, he retains Colonel Luther P. Bradley's brigade (formerly Harker's) in march column on the road behind Kimball and Blake, sends two regiments to establish a picket line running eastward to Clear Creek, and stations six cannons near the bridge. These preparations demonstrate that Newton, a thirty-one-year-old West Pointer who, like Thomas, is a native of Virginia, has lost none of the defensive skill that he had displayed a little more than a year ago as an acting corps commander at Gettysburg.

To the west, Geary, on reaching his portion of the ridge, likewise orders a halt, in this case to wait for both Ward and Williams to advance. While waiting, he masses Colonel Charles Candy's and Colonel Patrick H. Jones's brigades along the ridge behind an improvised rampart of rocks and logs, brings up several batteries to support them, and keeps Colonel David Ireland's brigade on another ridge to the rear as a reserve. In addition, Geary moves the 33rd New Jersey three hundred yards forward to a hill which he thinks will provide an "important outpost." Despite taking these precautions, he thinks that there is little danger of an enemy attack: three Rebels captured by his skirmishers have assured him that there are "no large bodies of [our] troops within two miles." Major Pierson, on the outpost hill with the 33rd New Jersey, disagrees. The woods up ahead seem to him "ominously quiet."

Shortly before 3 P.M., Hardee finally ceases his rightward shift. His corps now is approximately one mile from its original position and extends well to the east of the Peachtree road. Stewart's Corps has followed and, in the form of Loring's Division, is close by on the left. Noticing this, Hardee sends a staff officer to Loring to tell him that he had not intended for Stewart to move more than the half-mile to the right stipulated in Hood's order and had left behind another staff officer to so inform Stewart, but that through "some misunderstanding" that officer had failed to perform his assignment. Loring passes this message on to Stewart who, on receiving it, declares that it is too late to countermarch his corps and that the attack must be made at once or not at all.

Hardee, who agrees, deploys his corps with Bate's Division to the right, beyond the Peachtree road; Walker's in the center, astride the road; Cheatham's, now commanded by Maney, on the left; and Cleburne's in reserve behind Walker and Maney. Loring's Division and Major General Edward Walthall's Division (formerly Cantey's) form between Early's Creek and the Howell's Mill road; they are to advance once Hardee's assault gets under way. French's Division, which takes position to the left and about four hundred yards to the

William J. Hardee: "Old Reliable" (*Photographic History*, 10:247)

rear of Walthall's, is not to attack until the Federal front begins to crumble or unless it is ordered to do so. All three of Stewart's divisions have only two brigades in line of battle, for he has had to detach a brigade from each to cover the army's left flank. But what they lack in numbers they are to make up in spirit. While awaiting the word to advance, their commanders tell them what Stewart has told them to: they are to drive the Yankees to the creek and then down it. If they encounter breastworks, they are to fix bayonets and storm them. They are to stop for no obstacles. The assault will be desperate.

If Hardee's troops hear similar words from their officers, the available sources fail to record the fact. By the same token, there is no evidence to support Hood's subsequent assertion, based on an inference drawn from an alleged statement made to him by Cleburne, that Hardee warns them to be on the "lookout for breastworks." Besides, the veterans among them have no need for such a warning; they will be on the lookout for breastworks in any case.

At approximately 4 P.M., Hardee orders the attack to begin. This is three hours later than scheduled. Yet the delay and the shift to the right that caused it have cost the Confederates little and, potentially, have gained them much. Thomas's forces still are on the south bank of Peachtree Creek or close to it. Except for Palmer's corps and portions of Newton's and Geary's divisions, they have not so much as a semblance of defensive works, both Newton and Geary have their flanks in the air, neither Ward's nor Williams's divisions are formed for battle, and Hooker is lolling about with his staff under the shade of some trees, waiting for Palmer to move out so that he can then go forward too. As for Thomas himself, he has just been notified by Newton that a large Confederate force is up ahead on the Peachtree road, and Thomas in turn has instructed Newton to strengthen his makeshift fortifications, but Thomas does not know that he is about to be assailed by nearly two-thirds of the enemy army. In sum, the Union situation along Peachtree Creek is much like Hood hoped it would be.

His own, on the other hand, actually is improved. Had they advanced from their original positions, Hardee's Corps would have been overlapped on the right by Newton's and Ward's divisions, and Stewart's Corps would have gone straight against Palmer's fully deployed, well-entrenched, and on-the-alert troops. Now, thanks to the sidestep to the east, Stewart will be assaulting Hooker's un-aligned, unready, and mostly unprotected corps, and Hardee can throw the full weight of his 15,000 veterans against Newton's 3,200. Not since Chickamauga have chance and circumstance so favored the Army of Tennessee. Perhaps Peachtree Creek can be another less costly but more rewarding Chickamauga.

Bate's Division, in accordance with Hood's plan to attack *en echelon* from right to left, advances first. Theoretically it is in position to sweep around

Newton's weakly guarded left, cut him off from the creek, and start the process of rolling up the Union line. Doing so proves to be another thing. Since the Confederates have not conducted a reconnaissance—either they felt there was no time, or they feared it would tip off the Federals to their intent—Bate only knows there are Yankees somewhere ahead. Moreover, his division is so far to the east that it does not face Newton's front, and the countryside in his sector is covered with almost impenetrable thickets that makes it impossible to see more than a few yards in any direction. As a consequence he literally cannot find the enemy and instead flounders about looking for him. Eventually some of Lewis's Kentuckians, advancing along the creek bank, drive most of the Union pickets who are stationed there to the other side, but then fall back when they come under fire from two of Newton's cannons near the bridge.

To the south along the Peachtree road the "dusky gray columns" of Walker's Division come over a hill so quickly that Kimball's and Blake's troops have to throw aside the shovels and axes with which they are improving their defenses and grab their rifles. Both sides open fire simultaneously; to a Union artilleryman it sounds "something like the heavens and earth had suddenly come together." Stevens's Georgians charge once, then again, and each time withering fire repulses them with heavy casualties, among whom is Stevens himself, mortally wounded by a bullet in the head that knocked him from his horse, just east of the road and in front of the 40th Indiana. Next Brigadier General States Rights Gist's Georgians, South Carolinians, and Mississippians, taking advantage of a sheltering ravine, bypass the Union left and head for the bridge over Peachtree. So, too, do some of Bate's Kentuckians. Should the Confederates seize the bridge, they will trap Newton's division south of the creek. Realizing this, his men begin having "visions of Andersonville." But the six cannons posted by Newton and four more brought up by Thomas in person scour the ravine with canister, causing both Gist's troops and the Kentuckians to run back "like a flock of sheep." As they flee, Bradley's brigade, having rapidly deployed along the road, pumps more death into them. This ends the assault on Newton's front, left, and rear.

On his right, two of Maney's brigades, Vaughan's and Colonel John Carter's, go forward west of the road; the other two, Strahl's and Maney's own, under the command of Colonel Francis Walker, remain in reserve. Then, on reaching a woods, the Tennesseans halt. Before going further they want to know what lies ahead, and so they send skirmishers to find out. Too often in past battles— Fort Donelson, Shiloh, Perryville, Murfreesboro, Chickamauga (above all, Chickamauga)—they have rushed headlong against the Yankees, only to be slaughtered to no avail, even at Chickamauga where, supposedly, they won. For that reason they consider, in the words of one of Lee's Virginia paladins, "storming works as belonging to an early part of the War and played out now."

Such, for the time being, is Hardee's attack. Stewart's does much better, at least at first. Exploiting the gap between Newton and Geary, one of Loring's brigades, Featherston's Mississippians, sweeps up the valley of Early's Creek and drives Ward's skirmish line from the ridge; the other, Brigadier General Thomas M. Scott's Alabamans and Louisianans, overruns Geary's outpost hill, capturing many of the 33rd New Jersey and its state flag, then utilizes a ravine to get onto the right flank and into the rear of Candy's and Jones's brigades, many of whose troops flee in panic, abandoning a 4-gun battery. Loring's assault, however, has been delayed by the failure of Maney's Tennesseans to advance on schedule. As a result, Ward's brigadiers, acting on their own initiative, are able to rush their men forward in time to parry Featherston's thrust beyond the ridge. In the brutal open-field fight that ensues, they first stop him, then push him back to and off the ridge where the farm lane, being sunken, provides them with a natural parapet that they strengthen with fence rails. Almost simultaneously Geary's reserve brigade—Colonel David Ireland's New Yorkers and Pennsylvanians—mounts a counterattack that forces Scott's Brigade to retreat after a bitter, bloody seesaw struggle during which Hooker personally helps rally Candy's and Jones's brigades and establishes a firm line in his center. Meanwhile, a belated and tentative attack by Vaughan's and Carter's brigades against Newton's right and Ward's left soon ceases when the Tennesseans—who, as they feared, find the enemy "posted behind breastworks"—start taking too many casualties to "make it pay," as one of them comments subsequently in his diary. Maney's other two brigades merely advance a short distance, then lie down below the crest of a hill.

Walthall's assault, which falls principally on Williams's division, benefits least from the advantage of surprise. As soon as fighting broke out on Newton's front, Williams realized that the Confederates had launched a major offensive, so he ordered forward Robinson's and Knipe's brigades; Ruger's brigade already had been sent to support the left of the XIV Corps. Robinson and Ruger, however, are deployed amidst such dense underbrush—Williams's map shows "Open Fields"—that Walthall's troops, who come on "yelling like demons," get within point-blank range before they can be seen, then deliver a murderous volley. A fierce, "almost hand-to-hand" struggle follows, during which Brigadier General Edward O'Neal's Alabama and Mississippi Brigade turns Williams's left by way of a ravine and Reynold's Arkansans (the same who held Dug Gap against Geary in May) cut around his right, enfilading it, and also strike the flank of the XIV Corps along the Howell Mill road. For a moment it seems as if they might break through to the creek, but before they can penetrate further, Union artillery cross fire rakes their ranks, forcing them back. Still they fight on doggedly, giving as good as they get, until the Federals threaten to swing in behind their flanks from both east and west, whereupon they retreat, "not in very good order," admits O'Neal in his report. Killed on the Howell Mill road while directing the fire of one of his batteries is Major William L. Preston, Walthall's chief of artillery, who is the brother of Hood's fiancée, Sally ("Buck") Preston.

It now is late afternoon, yet there still is enough July daylight left, thinks Loring, to shove the Yankees into Peachtree Creek. Hence he notifies Stewart that if reinforced and supported by Hardee, he will attack again. Stewart in turn orders Brigadier General John Adams's Brigade to Loring and sends a staff officer to Hardee with a request for his cooperation. At once Hardee instructs Cleburne to attack, but before Cleburne can do so word arrives from Hood that Wheeler is in dire need of reinforcements. Hardee thereupon orders Cleburne to march to the east side of Atlanta and cancels the attack. It is just as well. Newton's troops, every other one of whom carries either a shovel or an axe, now have full-fledged entrenchments, and Thomas has massed artillery and brought reinforcements from Palmer's corps to support them. An assault by Cleburne would be extremely costly, unlikely to succeed, and even if successful, incapable of producing decisive results, especially so late in the day and against veteran well-led troops.

Hood's urgent summoning of a division from Hardee is in response to a dispatch from Wheeler stating that he needs help quickly. Wheeler's alarm is understandable. McPherson is a mere two and a half miles from the center of Atlanta. He arrived there via the Decatur road about 1 P.M., at which time one of the 20-pounder Parrotts of Captain Francis DeGress's First Illinois Light Artillery fired three shells into Atlanta, two of which hit buildings and one of which killed a young girl when it exploded at the corner of Ivy and East Ellis streets. Little stands in McPherson's way. Cheatham's line, although in some places stretched to a single rank, does not reach to the Decatur road. Wheeler's own force of around 3,500 cavalry can only hope to do what it has been doing— try to harass and delay McPherson's 25,000 infantry. And the 700 militia who man Atlanta's eastern fortifications are nothing but a façade that would crumble at the first hard shove.

The main thing holding back McPherson is McPherson. He shares Sherman's belief that if the Confederates fight for Atlanta, it will be against him. Hence instead of pushing on toward Atlanta, he has halted to deploy his forces in a line of battle running from north of the Decatur road, where it connects with Schofield, to about a mile south of it. This has taken most of the afternoon and has resulted in Brigadier General John W. Fuller's division (formerly Veatch's) of the XVI Corps being on the right, Logan's corps in the center astride the

Decatur road, and Blair's corps on the left. But even then McPherson's advance has not resumed. Fearful of being enfiladed from the south by some Confederates on a bald hill (earlier a sharpshooter posted there had shattered the left knee of division commander Brigadier General Walter Gresham), Blair has ordered Leggett's division to take the hill. For some reason the order has miscarried, and Leggett has not assaulted. Learning of this as evening approaches, McPherson thereupon has decided to postpone further movement toward Atlanta until tomorrow. He has made this decision, ironically, at approximately the same time that Hood has received Wheeler's call for help. As McPherson was outside of Resaca on May 9, so he is outside of Atlanta on July 20, preoccupied with being attacked rather than with attacking, more concerned with what the enemy might do to him than with what he might do to the enemy.[52]

Hood is still at Stewart's headquarters, where he has awaited the outcome of the attack on Thomas. He feels deeply disappointed by its failure—and also frustrated. It should have succeeded. Stewart, in bitter words, has told him that it would have succeeded if Hardee had done his part. But Hood can't think about that now. Sherman is at the very door of Atlanta, and something must be done about this quickly and decisively. Already he has a plan, a plan worthy of Lee. What Hood needs to know is whether it is feasible. Hence, after ordering Hardee and Stewart to fall back to their breastworks as soon as it is dark, he heads back to his own headquarters. There he will confer with Wheeler, whom he has instructed to come "as soon as you can safely leave your command" after the arrival of Cleburne's Division.[53]

Sherman has spent the day with Schofield and Howard northeast of Atlanta, the only place along his entire front where nothing of consequence happened or, for that matter, could have happened. Moreover, although only two to three miles away, he could not hear the sound of the battle along Peachtree Creek and is completely unaware that it has occurred. On the other hand the noise of McPherson's skirmishing did reach him, with the result that he was strengthened in his assumption that most of Hood's army probably was east of Atlanta. In fact, at 3:25 P.M., even as Hardee and Stewart prepared to strike, he sent a dispatch to Thomas stating that "All your troops should push toward Atlanta, sweeping everything before them." And at 8 P.M., in a letter giving McPherson his instruction for tomorrow, he declares that owing to Thomas's slowness and excessive caution, "our only good chance of entering Atlanta by a quick move if

possible is lost" and that in the morning the Union forces will find the Confederates behind "good parapets."

Not until around midnight does Sherman learn the truth in a dispatch from
Thomas marked 6:15 P.M.: "The enemy attacked me in full force at about
4 P.M., and has persisted until now, attacking very fiercely, but was repulsed
handsomely by the troops all along my line. Our loss has been heavy, but the
loss inflicted on the enemy has been very severe." Sherman now realizes that he
was mistaken in thinking that Hood's main effort, if he fought at all, would be
east of Atlanta. This in turn means that McPherson must have faced only a
small force during the day, a perception that is soon confirmed by an 8:45 P.M.
note from that general admitting that there is not "much of anything but cavalry
in front of us" and endeavoring to excuse his lack of progress on the grounds
that this cavalry possesses "four pieces of artillery" and are "armed with short
Enfield rifle's," as if that gave it some sort of unnatural advantage!

Sherman responds by informing McPherson of Thomas's battle and then
states: "I was in hopes you could have made a closer approach to Atlanta . . . ,
as I was satisfied you had a less force and more inferior works [opposed to you]
then will be revealed by daylight, if, as I suppose, Hood proposes to hold
Atlanta to the death." This is a rebuke, a gentle one, but nevertheless a rebuke
and a deserved one. Twice now McPherson, because of his excess of caution,
has muffed opportunities to decide the campaign.[54]

For Rufus Mead, commissary sergeant of the 5th Connecticut, Knipe's brigade,
July 20 has been "the saddest day I ever saw." He has spent most of it with his
team and wagon near a hospital north of Peachtree Creek. It was "sickening" to
look at "the suffereing [sic] & dying conditions of the poor fellows that lay there
wounded in every part of the body, some crazy & raving. . . . Doctors were
busy cutting off limbs which were piled up in heaps to be carried off and
buried, while the stench was horrible."

The XX Corps has close to 1700 killed, wounded, and missing. Williams's
division contributes the most to this total, 627, with all but 39 coming from
Robinson's and Knipe's brigades; his division, Williams sadly writes a friend, is
"reduced in number to a brigade." Ward's loss is 561, fairly evenly distributed
among his brigades, and Geary's is 476, of whom 164 are missing and nearly
half (233) are in Ireland's brigade, whose counterattack sealed off the Confederate breakthrough on Geary's front. Newton's casualties, in stark contrast, are a
mere 102, and Johnston's division of the XIV Corps, the only one to be
engaged, has lost between 80 and 100 men, 41 of them in the 104th Illinois,
which bore the brunt of Reynolds's charge up the Howell's Mill road, and had,

in the words of one of its officers, "fully half of Cos. A, B, C, D & E . . . killed, wounded, or dragged off to the rebel hells called prisons." Altogether the Union casualties amount to about 1,900, approximately 10 percent of the troops who fought in the battle.

Confederate losses must be estimated, as complete reports on the battle exist only for Stewart's Corps. They show a total of slightly more than 1,400 killed, wounded, and missing: 1,062 of them in Loring's Division—"Our steps were marked with blood," later and truly writes one of its soldiers—and 344 in Walthall's. (French's Division merely engaged in some long-range skirmishing, losing 19.) For Hardee's Corps, the sole official casualty return comes from Cheatham's (Maney's) Division: 277 killed and wounded (there is no enumeration of missing and captured), with all except 33 being in Vaughan's and Carter's brigades, which suffered almost equally. (By contrast one regiment alone of Scott's Brigade, the 57th Alabama, lost 157 of its "about 330 aggregate.") Since neither Bate's nor Cleburne's divisions participated heavily in the fighting and since only two of Walker's brigades and two of Maney's assaulted, in all probability Hardee lost about 1,000, most of them in Stevens's Brigade wherein the 66th Georgia had one-fourth and the 1st Georgia Confederate one-half of their men put out of action. If so—and unless it can be demonstrated that the Confederates lied to themselves in reporting casualties, it has to be considered so—then the sum cost of Hood's attempt to smash Thomas is approximately 2,500, not counting (as is Confederate practice) lightly wounded men who remain with their units and are still capable of performing duty. This is no more than 10 percent of the combined strength of Hardee's and Stewart's corps, no more than half of whose troops were fully engaged in the fighting.*

Such, then, are the butcher bills for both armies. The Federals can pay theirs

---

*William T. Sherman, "The Grand Strategy of the Last Year of the War" (in *Battles and Leaders of the Civil War,* ed. Robert U. Johnson and Clarence C. Buel [New York: Century Co., 1887], 4:253), puts the Confederate loss at 4,796, and most historians have followed him. Such estimates of enemy casualties, however, tend to be grossly exaggerated, reflecting wishful thinking. For example, Knipe in his report on Peachtree Creek claims (in effect) that his brigade inflicted 1,500 casualties on the Confederates attacking it. Since these Confederates came principally if not entirely from Reynold's Brigade, this would mean that it lost three times the number of men it took into the battle! Even worse exaggerations of Union losses appear frequently in Confederate reports, as witness Featherston's boast that his division killed and wounded at least 1,000 and "perhaps 2,000 or 3,000" Federals at Kennesaw Mountain on June 27. The actual loss of the Union force (Leggett's division) that skirmished with him that day was 10 killed and 76 wounded (38 OR 3:563, 880). Jacob D. Cox, *Atlanta* (New York: Charles Scribner's Sons, 1882), pp. 211–14, in effect contends that the Confederates did lie to themselves regarding casualties, but he bases this allegation on a statement by Johnston on the inaccuracy of Confederate records in general, which is not the same thing. As a rule, official Confederate figures on unit losses are confirmed by the letters and diaries of members of those units.

more easily: they have more men, and they have won the battle. The Confederates, on the other hand, have paid a stiff price or, in the case of Loring's Division, an exorbitant one, for defeat. Many of them blame Hood, and so will most historians. He attacked too late, they assert, to catch Thomas in the vulnerable act of crossing Peachtree, thereby allowing him time to entrench his entire force on the south bank, and even worse, he hurled his troops in reckless, hopeless frontal assaults against those entrenchments. The result was a futile slaughter, the first of a series to come.

Although understandable, most of this criticism is unfair because it is based either on ignorance or on an ignoring of certain facts. Hood never intended to strike Thomas while he was crossing Peachtree; he wanted to trap all of his troops south of the creek. In any case, Thomas had crossed in full strength during the early morning, and thus an attack at 1 P.M. or, for that matter, a much earlier time, would have made no difference. Delaying the attack in order to shift to the right, as we have noted, actually had improved the Confederate prospects of victory. Finally, only two of Newton's and one of Geary's brigades were behind defensive works when assaulted, and these did the latter little good; all of the rest of the Federal units east of the Howell's Mill road were in the open, exactly as Hood had hoped they would be.

The basic reason for the Confederate defeat is twofold: (1) Hardee's attack, on which depended the success of the whole operation, was made blindly (thus virtually eliminating Bate's from the battle), was uncoordinated (the separate charges of Stevens and Gist and the slowness of Vaughan and Carter to advance), employed only a third of his available force, and in the case of the Tennesseans was delivered in a half-hearted fashion that wasted any chance of turning Newton's right and Ward's left. These failures, far more than the rudimentary breastworks of Kimball's and Blake's troops, explain why Newton was able to repulse so easily Hardee's much stronger force while losing a mere 102 men. (2) Stewart's soldiers came close to breaking through; they did something rare for an attacking force in the Civil War: inflict on a larger enemy greater losses than they themselves incurred. Yet, with all due credit to the ferocity and skill of their assault, they achieved these things mainly because they struck the XX Corps while it was unready and unaligned, for the most part unentrenched and undeployed, and in terrain that enabled them to outflank their opponents or approach unseen to a murderous range. In his report, Loring gleefully describes how "as the enemy fled in confusion from his works, the steady aim of the Mississippi, Alabama, and Louisiana marksmen of my command produced great slaughter in his ranks"—a description that is confirmed by a soldier of the 111th Pennsylvania (Ireland's brigade), who records that eighty of his regiment's "scarcely more than two hundred were lost" in thirty minutes to Confederates who "swarmed like bees" down a ravine into its rear at the same time it was attacked in front by "fire . . . at our breasts." Once Hooker's troops recovered from the shock of the initial impact, brought up their full strength, and solidified their front, Stewart's Corps—actually just four brigades attacking nine—simply could not sustain its hitherto devastating assault.[55]

In brief, where the Confederates had the advantage in strength, they did not fight well; and where they fought well, they were too weak. And because they did not fight well enough where they were strong enough, they lost. This in essence is the story of Peachtree Creek.

Part Five: Bald Hill

It still is dark on the morning of July 21 as Cleburne's Division (now reduced to three brigades by the dismantling of Polk's Brigade and the distribution of its regiments to other commands) deploys southward from the Georgia Railroad. His troops, finding the rifle pits left behind by Wheeler's cavalry too shallow, hastily deepen them. Soon they are glad they did so; at the first glimmer of daylight the Yanks opposite them open up with a nasty sniping fire and even nastier artillery fire. On the right, Granbury's Texans—who for the past month, while Granbury has been on sick leave, have been commanded by Brigadier General James A. Smith, a thirty-three-year-old West Pointer from Tennessee—suffer in particular from a Union battery which enfilades their position from a hill eight hundred yards to the north. A single shell kills seventeen of the eighteen men in a company of the 18th Texas, and Captain Foster gets tossed into the air by another shell that explodes between him and another soldier and slays three men ten feet away. Never before has Smith, a veteran of Shiloh, Perryville, Murfreesboro, and Chickamauga, seen "such accurate and destructive cannonading."

To the right of the Texans is the bald hill that Blair had ordered Leggett to take yesterday afternoon only to have the order go astray. This morning, Blair has repeated the order, and Leggett, a burly Ohioan who is a former law partner of Jacob Cox's, intends to execute it. He assigns the task to Force's brigade, his strongest one. About 7 A.M., Force's troops, having formed under the cover of a woods, charge the hill and quickly reach the top, sending its defenders, Brigadier General Samuel W. Ferguson's cavalry brigade, scurrying. Although not high, the hill dominates the surrounding countryside, and possession of it opens the way for a general advance of the XVII Corps. Accordingly, Blair directs Brigadier Giles Smith, whom McPherson has assigned to take the place of the wounded Gresham, to attack the Confederates north of the hill with his division. Initially Smith encounters little resistance: the enemy troops on his front—Brigadier General Alfred Iverson's Georgia cavalry brigade—fire a wild, ragged volley, then in the words of Captain Foster "break and run like good fellows." Their flight exposes the right flank of the Texas Brigade and, thus, of Cleburne's whole division. "Leave here," shouts a cavalry colonel as he rushes by, "you all will be captured." Ignoring his advice, the Texans counterattack, hurl back Smith's Federals, and then, with the aid of Key's and Swett's batteries, force them to withdraw to their own works. As a consequence of Smith's being repulsed, Leggett makes no attempt to advance beyond the bald hill, even though no enemy is south of it. Instead he plants a howitzer battery on the crest from where, shortly before 9 A.M., it begins lobbing shells into Atlanta, which is clearly visible a scant one and a half miles away.[56]

People in Atlanta who have stayed on in the hope that Sherman somehow would be held at bay have lost that hope with the failure of Hood's attack along Peachtree Creek, a failure made all too evident by the streams of wounded and stragglers pouring into the city. The shells from Leggett's howitzers merely increase what a cavalry captain calls the Atlantans' "wild state of excitement." They run about the streets "in every direction," women and children scream whenever one of the Yankee missiles explodes, and would-be refugees turn the Union Depot into a scene of "Pandemonium" as they clamor to get aboard the outgoing trains, which is hard to do, because casualties and patients from the Fair Grounds hospital, the last to be evacuated, take precedence. Drunken men, both military and civilian, crowd the saloons around Five Points, getting drunker. Others, among them blacks, lurk about, alert for opportunities to plunder abandoned houses and stores. Last night a fire destroyed a block-long brick building on Whitehall Street across the way from Samuel Richards's stationery shop.[57]

North of Atlanta, Thomas sends forward pickets, but makes no attempt to advance, nor does he intend to, until he is sure that the bulk of Hood's army no longer is on his front. Made extra wary by what happened yesterday, he thinks it quite possible that Hood will attack again; so Thomas's troops have spent the night working in shifts to construct full-fledged fortifications. In the XX Corps and Newton's division, discovery that the Confederates have withdrawn produces a victory celebration, during which Hooker rides along his line congratulating his men, who respond with enthusiastic cheers. When he reaches Ward's division and learns that it has captured seven Rebel banners, he doffs his hat and bows to it, eliciting more and louder cheers. No one present, least of all Hooker, foresees that "Fighting Joe" is enjoying his final moment of glory.

After the celebration comes the nasty job of clearing away the human wreckage of the battle. It is another torrid day, and already the sickening odor of death taints the air. Details collect what seems like hundreds of mangled, gray-clad corpses, most of them with three to five wounds, then bury them in long, shallow pits. The details also carry to the Union hospitals numerous enemy wounded, among them a young woman wearing a uniform and a cartridge box. "She was shot," writes Judson Austin of the 19th Michigan to his wife later in the day, "in the breast & through the thy [*sic*] & was still alive & as gritty as any reb I ever saw. I hope our women will never be so foolish as to go to war or get to fighting."

Another 19th Michigan soldier, Sergeant Hager, informs his wife: "We have punished the rebels pretty severely. I don't see how they can have a particle of courage to hold out. They have to fall back every few days and their army must be getting smaller very fast." Despite their own heavy losses, Thomas's troops hope for more "open field" battles like yesterday's: "The army in front of us has got to be whiped [*sic*]," comments Private Henry Dean, also of the 19th Michigan, in his diary, "& if Hood will fight it soon will be accomplished."[58]

Fight is precisely what Hood intends to do. Yesterday's frustrating failure at Peachtree Creek, he believes, has "rendered urgent the most active measures, in order to save Atlanta even for a short period." The greatest danger lies east of the city. There, not only are McPherson's forces within cannon range; also they are in a position potentially to cut the Macon railroad, his last fully functioning supply line now that Rousseau's raiders have wrecked the Montgomery railroad around Opelika. On the other hand, east of Atlanta also lies the greatest opportunity. From Wheeler, Hood has learned that McPherson's left flank is in the air and that large numbers of his wagons are parked in and around Decatur. If he can get around McPherson's exposed flank and into his rear, Hood will be able to rout McPherson's army, capture his wagon train, and then proceed to accomplish what he attempted yesterday—drive Thomas down Peachtree Creek and pin him against the Chattahoochee.

But if this is to be done, it must be done rapidly, while the two wings of Sherman's army remain separated and before McPherson can swing south of Atlanta to the Macon railroad. Accordingly Hood has formulated another plan of attack. He will, come night, withdraw Stewart's and Cheatham's corps, along with Smith's militia, to Atlanta's inner defenses. At the same time he will send Hardee's Corps and Wheeler's cavalry circling around McPherson's left to

Decatur to strike at both his wagon train and his rear. Obviously Hardee again will be cast in the key role. In view of "Old Reliable's" poor performance yesterday, Hood has misgivings about this. Yet what else can he do? Stewart's Corps is neither in condition nor in position to make the move; Cheatham lacks experience commanding a corps; and one of his divisions, Stevenson's, has demonstrated a lack of offensive punch both at Resaca and Kolb's farm. On the other hand, Hardee's troops, as Hood observes in his memoirs, are "comparatively fresh," having "taken but little part in the attack of the previous day," and one of his divisions, Cleburne's, already is opposite McPherson's left.

During the morning, Hood prepares to implement his plan. Having been notified by Colonel Presstman, whom he asked to look into the matter, that Atlanta's existing fortifications are too close to the city, poorly situated, and virtually nonexistent on the west side, Hood orders the engineers to stake out a new line that will remedy these rather alarming deficiencies. He also keeps close watch on Thomas and the Union forces northeast of Atlanta and is relieved to find that the former has no aggressive intent and that the latter are advancing so slowly that there is no immediate danger that the gap between the wings of Sherman's army will be closed. Only McPherson, Hood's target for tomorrow, threatens to ruin everything; about 9 A.M. a dispatch arrives from Cleburne stating that the Federals have driven back Wheeler and are trying to turn his right flank. At once Hood orders Hardee to hasten Maney's Tennesseans to Cleburne's support. While waiting for them to come, Cleburne holds on desperately in what he later will call the "bitterest fight of my life," his line raked from both left and right by Union artillery. Finally, early in the afternoon, the Tennesseans appear, and Cleburne has Maney deploy them to the south of the bald hill, leaving Wheeler's troopers to defend the interval between the two divisions. Thus, thanks to Cleburne—and also once again to McPherson's lack of aggressiveness—Hood preserves his front east of Atlanta and, with it, the ability to carry out his new plan.

But Hood pays a price to achieve these things. Not only will Cleburne's, Maney's, and Wheeler's men have to wait until it is dark before they dare disengage from the enemy and begin marching to Decatur, but they are bound to be very weary and frazzled by then. Furthermore, Leggett's Federals atop the bald hill observe large numbers of Confederates (Maney's Tennesseans) passing to the south. As a result, Blair, on orders from McPherson, switches Giles Smith's division from Leggett's right, where its place is taken by Harrow's division of the XV Corps, and deploys it on his left, thereby extending the Union line southward also. Finally, the movement of enemy forces in that direction causes McPherson—who is already uneasy about his left flank, which is screened by only a few cavalry vedettes left behind by Garrard who has headed east at Sherman's direction to tear up more rails of the Georgia Railroad—to feel almost sure that Hood is getting ready to hit that flank. In a 3 A.M. dispatch, McPherson expresses his concern to Sherman, adding: "I will simply remark . . . that I have no cavalry as a body of observation on my flank, and that the whole rebel army, except Georgia militia, is not in front of the Army of the Cumberland."

Late in the afternoon at his headquarters, Hood gives the corps commanders, plus Wheeler and Smith, their instructions. As soon as it is dark, Stewart, Cheatham, and Smith are to withdraw to the new line around Atlanta and entrench, with Stewart guarding the western and northern approaches and Cheatham the eastern one. At the same time, Hardee will assemble his corps in the city, then march south on the McDonough road to Cobb's Mill, from where he will proceed northeastward to and, if necessary, beyond Decatur, putting himself in position to strike McPherson's rear at daylight. Wheeler, with all of his available cavalry, will accompany Hardee and provide guides. Cheatham, once the Federal left starts to crumble under Hardee's onslaught from the east, will join in the attack from the west, assailing what by then should be the enemy's flank north of the Decatur road. Stewart's primary assignment is to prevent Thomas from going to the aid of McPherson and Schofield; only when Hardee and Cheatham succeed in driving the Federals toward Peachtree Creek will Stewart go over to the offensive. To forestall a possible lunge by McPherson toward the Macon railroad, Shoup will mass his artillery southeast of Atlanta.

After making sure that each of his generals understands "not only his own duty, but likewise that of his brother corps commanders," Hood dismisses them, and they leave to carry out his orders. If Hood's plan works as he has conceived it, tomorrow he will win the most spectacular victory of the war.[59]

Sherman's objective on July 21 is to close the dangerous gap between the wings of his army, in the process getting his army nearer Atlanta so that he can subject it to a converging artillery fire which, he believes, will destroy the city and force Hood to evacuate it, supposing that he does not do so anyway after the failure of his attack at Peachtree Creek. Hence Sherman concentrates on pushing Howard forward, with the result that Stanley's and Wood's divisions advance two miles over difficult terrain against stubborn resistance from strong Confederate skirmish lines. This puts them within long-range cannon fire of Atlanta but still leaves them separated from the rest of the Army of the Cumberland to the west and the XXIII Corps to the south. Schofield, worried by his exposed right flank, asks Howard to send a brigade to cover it. Howard, however, replies, "I would prefer not to extend further to the left" because

"Hood is great for attacking." Schofield then takes the matter to Sherman, who responds by having Sweeny's division sent to support the right of the XXIII Corps.

As Sweeny's troops march to their new position, they pass a mansion on the porch of which stands a woman dressed all in white, who looks "almost angelic" to Private Edwin Brown of the 81st Ohio. She has placed three clean tubs of water by the side of the road, and "about twenty darkies, little and big," keep them filled for the thirsty soldiers tramping by in their dirty, sweat-stained, nearly black jackets. They thank the woman on the porch, and she silently bows to them while twilight shadows the red hills and green pine forests east of Atlanta.[60]

Toward evening it rains, a short but hard shower that brings welcome relief from the day's heavy heat. When the sky becomes dark, Stewart's Corps starts its withdrawal. Through some mix-up, instead of stopping at the line marked earlier in the day by Presstman's engineers, it keeps going until it reaches Captain Lemuel Grant's fortifications on the northern outskirts of Atlanta. Apart from some formidable redoubts protecting the main roads, these prove to be, in the words of Colonel Sykes of the 43rd Mississippi, "a badly constructed line of trenches" so inadequate that his men, as well as those of other units similarly situated, work all night converting them into proper defensive works.

While Stewart's troops ply pick, shovel, and axe, Bate's and Walker's divisions march via the Peachtree road into Atlanta and then out of it on the McDonough road. According to Hood's plan, Cleburne's, Maney's, and Wheeler's forces should be accompanying them. They are not. It is after midnight before they are able to pull out of their works, march into the city by way of the Decatur road, and assemble at the Five Points. Obviously they cannot reach Decatur, fifteen miles by the route Hood has prescribed, in time to launch an attack at daylight. Realizing this, Hood and Hardee hold an impromptu conference. The outcome is a modification in the plan. Instead of going all the way to Decatur, Hardee will send Wheeler there to capture or destroy McPherson's wagon train while his own corps moves against the Union rear from the Cobb's Mill area. Since Hardee now has little more than half as far to march, he should be able to make his attack at dawn and Hood so instructs him.[61]

The entry of Hardee's Corps and Wheeler's cavalry touches off a panic in Atlanta, where it is taken to mean that Hood is evacuating the city. Civilians—"woefully scared," observes a Tennessee soldier—throng the streets leading southward, fleeing in wagons, on horses and mules, or even on foot, taking with them all that they can carry, desperate to escape Sherman's "vandals," lurid stories of whose atrocities in northern Georgia they have been reading in the newspapers for weeks. Gangs of soldiers, many of whom also believe that the army is retreating, plunder shops, stores, and saloons in the Five Points. According to orderly Trask, they carry off "clothing of all kinds,—notions of every description,—cigars, tobacco, and whiskey," the latter being "gulped" on the spot. Among their victims is Samuel Richards: "cavalry robbers" break into his stationery shop and take "everything they took a fancy to." The proprietor of another store, a woman, tries to prevent troopers of the 7th Alabama Cavalry from entering it by threatening to shoot them; contemptuously they snatch her pistol away and drag her out onto the street by her hair. Not until 3 A.M. do Maney's troops, following in the wake of Cleburne's, set out on the McDonough road. Dawn will be breaking in a couple more hours.[62]

Between 3 and 4 A.M., Sherman receives a series of messages from Schofield, all to the effect that the "enemy have abandoned their lines" on his front. This intelligence, along with an earlier report from McPherson that Confederate regiments had been seen moving southward, causes Sherman, who as always is eager to believe that his opponents are doing what he wants them to do, to conclude that Hood has evacuated Atlanta and in all likelihood is retreating toward East Point, junction of the Macon and Montgomery railroads five miles southwest of the city. Delighted, he sends staff officers galloping off to inform Thomas, Howard, and McPherson of what has happened and to instruct them to pursue vigorously, with the first two passing to the west and the third to the east of Atlanta. As for Schofield, his little Army of the Ohio will have the honor of marching into Atlanta itself. (But not if Hooker can help it; on learning that the Confederates are pulling out of the city, he orders his troops to push forward and claim the prize for themselves and for him.[63])

Shortly before dawn, Hood establishes a command post atop a hill on the eastern edge of Atlanta near the Decatur road across from Oakland Cemetery. Here he eagerly awaits the sound of Hardee's guns. As soon as the Union left gives way, Hood will send forward Cheatham's Corps, which has moved into the fortifications astride the Decatur road.

Hood is going to have to wait much longer than he expects. By 5 A.M., Bate's Division, leading Hardee's column, is at Widow Parker's house, less than three miles southwest of Decatur on the Fayetteville road, and Walker's Division is a mile further down the road near the Aker's house. But Cleburne has yet to reach

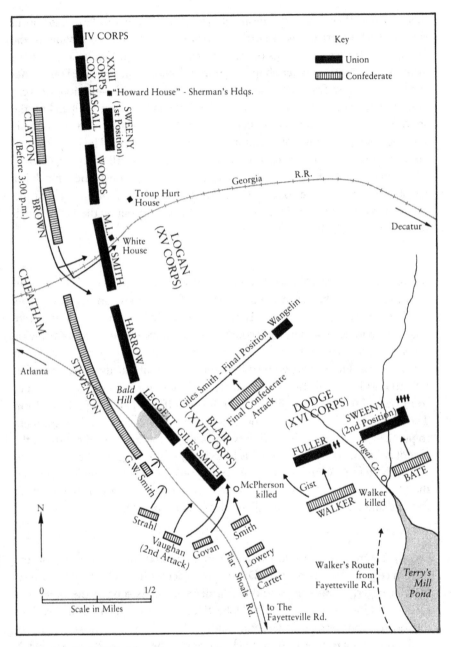

Battle of the Bald Hill, July 22

Cobb's Mill, and Maney is far behind him. To a late start their divisions have added a slow march. Cleburne's troops are, states Brigadier General Daniel Govan in his report, "much wearied by the operations of the 20th, the subsequent maneuvering and intrenching upon the Augusta railroad, and the fight of the 21st"; and the "loss of another night's rest" has placed a "heavy tax upon their powers of endurance." Maney's Tennesseans are in little better condition, and to make bad enough worse, the dust on the road is ankle-deep, the night is hot and humid, and Wheeler's troopers, many of whom have sacks of Five Points plunder attached to their saddles, are constantly cutting through the plodding infantry, producing additional delays and aggravation. Hundreds of men, unable or unwilling to go on, drop by the roadside, where they join large numbers of stragglers from Bate's and Walker's divisions. To Colonel Thomas Roy, Hardee's chief of staff, it is "the most tedious and harassing night march I ever experienced."[64]

Not until daylight—full, bright, hot daylight—does Hardee, as usual riding with Cleburne, reach Cobb's Mill. Here he calls a halt. The troops need to eat, rest, and draw additional ammunition; and he needs information. Cleburne and he go to the nearby house of William Cobb, owner of the mill, where they are joined by Wheeler and Walker. Wheeler states that his scouts report no enemy forces between the mill and Decatur, information that is confirmed by local civilians. Judging from this that he has gotten beyond the Union left and that he is in position to strike it in both flank and rear, Hardee issues instructions for the attack. Wheeler will continue on to Decatur from where, after disposing of McPherson's wagon train, he will turn west along the Decatur road, wreaking all the havoc he can. Bate and Walker, who are to begin the attack, will deploy their divisions parallel to the Fayetteville road, then move northward along the line of Sugar Creek, bearing to the left. In order to give their thrust more power, Maney's Brigade (still commanded by Colonel Walker) will reinforce Bate, whose division has been seriously understrength since the Dallas fiasco. Cleburne, after forming to Walker's left, will advance up the east side of the Flat Shoals road, and Maney's three remaining brigades will do the same west of it. At this point, Walker asks permission to take a different route because the country around Sugar Creek is an enormous briar patch. "No, sir!" answers Hardee in an exasperated voice. "This movement has been delayed too long already. Go and obey my orders!" The conference then ends. Walker rides away seething with anger. A staff officer's efforts to calm him and a verbal message from Hardee, delivered by an aide, apologizing for his "hasty and discourteous language," are to no avail. Hardee, Walker vows, "must answer me for this."[65]

Sherman, Schofield, and Cox draw rein in front of a white two-story frame house situated on a wooded knoll about three-fourths of a mile north of the Decatur road and two miles from Atlanta. Across an intervening valley, Sherman sees something that he had not expected to see. It is a line of strong fortifications filled with Rebel troops. Looking down into the valley, he sees other Confederates building an abatis of trees and saplings. Hood has not evacuated Atlanta after all. On the contrary he appears to be preparing to make a fight for it.

Sherman promptly sends messages to Thomas, Howard, and McPherson, notifying them that enemy forces still hold Atlanta and canceling the pursuit order. Instead the city is to be invested on the west, north, and east, then bombarded. If that does not force Hood out, at least it will keep him occupied while McPherson swings around to the right flank to strike the Macon railroad. In addition, not content with having torn up the Georgia Railroad between Stone Mountain and Decatur and dispatched Garrard to wreck more of it further east, Sherman decides it would be a good idea to wreck it west of Decatur as well, for he is determined to make it absolutely impossible for Hood to receive reinforcements from Virginia via Augusta. Moreover, it so happens that there are plenty of troops available for that purpose: Sprague's brigade from Fuller's (formerly Veatch's) division of the XVI Corps already is at Decatur, guarding the wagons there, and Howard's and Schofield's advances have so contracted their fronts that Sweeny's division, which hitherto has filled the gap between them, has been squeezed out of line. Therefore, learning that Dodge has orders to form on Blair's left, Sherman writes McPherson: "Instead of sending Dodge to your left, I wish you would put his whole corps at work destroying absolutely the railroad back to and including Decatur. I want the road absolutely and completely destroyed . . . and as soon as Garrard returns, if the enemy still holds Atlanta, I will again shift you around to the extreme right."

Sherman believes that McPherson has extended unnecessarily far to the south. Sherman expects Hood (so he informs Thomas) to "make Atlanta his right and East Point his left" and to remain strictly on the defensive behind Atlanta's fortifications while endeavoring to "operate on our [rail]road with cavalry." Despite having been warned by Schofield and McPherson that their West Point classmate Hood is "a brave, determined, and rash man," Sherman feels there is little if any danger of his making another attack.

Not so McPherson. Long before getting Sherman's message that Hood had not evacuated Atlanta, McPherson saw for himself the enemy "industriously engaged in strengthening his works" around the city, works that run southward well beyond Blair's front. This is why he has ordered Dodge to move Sweeny's division to the south and mass it behind the XVII Corps and has instructed

Fuller to place Colonel John Morrill's brigade (formerly Fuller's own) on the XVII Corps's left. Repeatedly and "with great earnestness," he predicts to his staff that the biggest battle of the campaign will take place today.

Hence, on receiving Sherman's order to employ the XVI Corps in ripping up rails, McPherson rides off to see Sherman and ask him for a cancellation. He finds him at the white house on the knoll. Because its present inhabitant is a local whiskey distiller named Thomas C. Howard, the Federals call it the Howard house. Actually it belongs to one Augustus Hurt, whose older brother, George M. Troup Hurt, has an unfinished brick residence a short distance to the south, not far from the railroad. Before the day is over, both houses will be historic.

McPherson tells Sherman that Dodge's corps is not needed to destroy the railroad back to Decatur, because the pioneers can do the job just as well, and that except for Sprague's brigade at Decatur, all of the XVI Corps either is already on the left flank or is on the way there. Sherman, although he believes that McPherson again is being excessively cautious, withdraws the order. McPherson in turn agrees that if the Confederates do not attack by 1 P.M., they probably will not attack at all, in which case at least one division of the XVI Corps can be spared for destroying track. He then leaves and rides along the length of the line held by Logan's and Blair's troops, who are waiting for pioneer detachments to reverse the evacuated Rebel works before advancing. Around noon he and his staff join Logan, Blair, and their staffs for lunch in an oak grove. After eating and while smoking a cigar, he receives a pencil-written note headed "12 M" from Sherman: "As General Sweeny's division has already moved over to the left . . . you will leave his division where we designated, and send Fuller's division back on the line of the railroad between here and Decatur, to destroy it as directed." McPherson writes out a copy of the note, then hands it to a staff officer to deliver to Dodge. If the Confederates were going to attack, surely they would have done so by now.[66]

East of Sugar Creek, Bate's troops are floundering through underbrush, muck, and knee-deep water. They have no idea of where they are going or what they will find when they get there, if they ever do. Bate himself is unsure as to what he is supposed to do. His orders have been changed from what they originally were, and the staff officer he has sent to Hardee for an explanation has not returned. Furthermore, because of straggling, his division musters a mere 1,200 muskets—the average size of a brigade; and the brigade from Maney's division that is supposed to bolster him has yet to appear. All he can hope is that Hardee is right about there being no Yankees in front. The division could not stand another Dallas slaughter. Although Bate doesn't think it was his fault, the Kentuckians and Floridians blame and hate him for it.

West of the creek, Walker has managed to get through the briar patch, but now he faces a far worse obstacle—a huge, deep, utterly impassible lagoon filled with dead trees which is known as Terry's Mill Pond. His volatile temper explodes again. Pulling out his revolver, he aims it at Case Turner, a fifty-year-old employee at Cobb's Mill, who is serving as a guide. Only the intervention of Major Joseph Cumming, Walker's adjutant, prevents him from firing. Turner, fearful that his reprieve might be a short one, tells the irate general that he can get around the pond by skirting its west side. Walker thereupon issues orders for the division to take that route and then, after reholstering his revolver, extracts from a saddlebag a canteen of peach brandy.[67] He needs it, or conversely, perhaps he has had too much of it already.

Cleburne's Division also encounters rough going as it moves up the east side of the Flat Shoals road with Govan's Brigade on the left, Smith's on the right, and Lowrey's 500 yards behind the latter. The troops literally have to claw and grope their way through a jungle of wild blackberry bushes (later they will refer to this advance as the "Blackberry Charge"), and it is impossible to maintain their alignments or even to be sure in what direction they are going. To make matters worse, during one of the frequent halts to try to straighten things out, Carter's Brigade, which Hardee at the last moment has decided to use to bolster Cleburne's assault, gets mixed up with Lowrey's Brigade, thus creating further confusion and delay.

As it had done two days ago at Peachtree Creek, Hardee's Corps is making its attack in a disorganized, pell-mell, virtually blind fashion and for the same reason: already hours behind schedule, Hardee feels that he cannot take the time to conduct a reconnaissance for the purpose of ascertaining the location and strength of the enemy lines and the best way of approaching them. He can only trust that the advantage gained by taking the Federals by surprise and from the rear will compensate for all else. Also this time he is determined to go in with his full strength. Thus when a dispatch arrives from Wheeler proposing that instead of going to Decatur he pursue Garrard's raiders, he replies curtly: "We must attack, as we arranged, with all our force."[68]

In Atlanta the exodus continues, for the prevailing belief is that Hardee's movement to the south is designed merely to cover a retreat and that the Yankees will march into the city before the day ends. The *Appeal,* once again moving, also leaves except for a small hand press, which will continue to print a one-sheet bulletin. In addition the office of the Southern Press Association remains open, keeping Atlanta in touch with the rest of the Confederacy—for the time being, at any rate.

Some Atlantans, those who for whatever reason are staying, stand on rooftops and hills, gazing off to the southeast where, so rumor has it, there might be a battle, a big one. They see little other than dust clouds, little puffs of smoke where presumably pickets are popping away, and an occasional large billow produced by a cannon. Only on the bald hill are troops visible, troops whose dark uniform jackets and striped flags mark them as Yankees. It is not a reassuring sight.

Hood is not among the spectators. Sometime ago he received a dispatch from Hardee reporting his position and in effect stating that the attack had been delayed but would be made as soon as possible. No doubt disappointed and quite likely disgusted as well, Hood thereupon returned to his new headquarters, the home of J. S. Thrasher on Whitehall Street. He stayed there back in November, recovering from his amputation at Chickamauga. Now he awaits the start of a battle that could prove far, far more important than that one. Two days ago, in its next-to-last regular edition, the *Appeal* predicted that "the greatest battle of the war will probably be fought in the immediate vicinity of Atlanta" and that its result would determine "that of the pending Northern Presidential election. If we are victorious the Peace party will triumph: Lincoln's Administration is a failure, and peace and Southern independence are the immediate results."[69]

These are the stakes that Hood is playing for today.

Having ridden across a seemingly endless expanse of oozy mud, Walker draws rein atop a slope north of the millpond and raises his field glasses to examine some woods about 250 yards ahead. A Union picket, spotting what obviously is a Rebel officer, takes aim, then fires. Walker tumbles to the ground, still clutching his field glasses. In the prewar army he had been known as "Old Shot Pouch" because of his propensity for getting wounded. This time he is dead.

Perhaps the shot that has killed him is one that McPherson, Logan, and Blair hear off to the southeast at "ten or fifteen minutes past twelve," as best Lieutenant Colonel William Strong, the dashingly handsome twenty-two-year-old inspector general of the Army of the Tennessee, can recall five years later. It is followed by another shot, then a "a rattling volley of small arms," which soon swells into "rapid and incessant firing from Dodge's Corps." Mounting their horses, Logan and Blair leave for their corps, and McPherson, accompanied by several of his staff, rides off to see about Dodge. It sounds as if the Confederates are attacking after all, and in the rear at that.[70]

The Confederates indeed are attacking: rather, they are trying to. Bate's troops are splashing through the eastern extension of the millpond. Often they have to stop and rescue comrades from hip-deep slime by pulling them up onto the logs and brush piles that fill the pond. All semblance of formation is gone. They are merely a mob of exhausted men floundering about in a quagmire. To their left, Walker's Division, now under the command of Brigadier General Hugh Mercer, is in little better shape. Stevens's Brigade (probably commanded by Colonel Nisbet) has managed to get into line, more or less, with Bate's Division, but Gist's Brigade has veered off to the west, and Mercer's own brigade lags far behind the other two. Although Mercer is a West Pointer who is doing his best, he is fifty-five, in poor health, and has spent most of the war commanding the garrison of his hometown of Savannah.

Hood's plan assumes, as does Hardee, that both divisions will be able to move forward unopposed, swing to the west, and fall upon the rear of an unsuspecting and unprotected enemy. Once this assumption was valid; now it is not. Some thirty minutes ago Sweeny's division, on the way to support Blair in accordance with McPherson's orders, halted a half-mile south of the Georgia Railroad and just to the east of Sugar Creek. Warned by a cavalry vedette of possible danger to the south, Sweeny prudently sent out skirmishers to reconnoiter in that direction. Soon they reported that a large Confederate force was advancing on them, whereupon Sweeny formed both of his brigades (Brigadier General Elliott W. Rice's and Colonel August Mersy's) in a line of battle bolstered by six cannons posted near the left flank, which is bent back so as to face east.

West of the creek, Colonel John Morrill's brigade of Fuller's division, with Fuller exercising direct command, also is ready for combat, as are the six Rodmans of the 14th Ohio Battery atop a hill overlooking the creek. The brigade spent the morning bivouacked about three-fourths of a mile to the rear of Giles Smith's division, waiting for it to occupy the abandoned Confederate works before taking position on its left. So little did either Dodge or Fuller anticipate an enemy attack that they were lunching in the latter's tent when the sound of shots (probably the same ones first heard by McPherson, Logan, and Blair) came from the south. At once Dodge hastened off to investigate, and Fuller ordered his troops to deploy, which they quickly did despite having to make their way around dozens of careening wagons driven by panic-stricken teamsters fleeing the oncoming Rebels.

Soon, about three hundred yards away across a shallow valley, gray masses emerge from a forest, the same one that Walker had briefly scanned from the other side with his field glasses. They pause, as if surprised by the presence of the Union battle lines. Actually they are merely forming their ranks prior to charging. From contact with Sweeny's skirmishers they already know that an enemy force stands in their way. They just hope that it is not a large one, or at least that it has not had time to entrench.

Bate's Division advances first in two lines of battle, bearing towards Sweeny's center. The Union batteries lacerate it with shellfire. Halfway across the valley it halts, with the obvious intent of delivering a softening-up volley before charging. Realizing this, Sweeny's troops fire first. For a couple of minutes both sides blaze away at each other. Then Bate's men surge forward. A devastating cross fire of canister hits them. It is too much. They break and run back into the woods. Except for some long-range skirmishing, this ends their participation in the battle. They are too weak in body, spirit, and numbers to make a successful assault on an enemy that, although fighting in the open, outnumbers them and possesses artillery support. Maney's Brigade, which was to provide extra weight to their attack, still is far to the rear, having been blocked by the millpond.

Next Stevens's Brigade moves against Sweeny's right and Fuller's left, only to falter and then retreat when it comes under fire from the six Rodmans of the 14th Ohio Battery. After a while it again advances, this time with officers urging their men on with drawn swords and with the color-bearers flaunting their flags. But before it gets more than half-way across the valley, Fuller orders two of his regiments to charge its exposed left flank, and Dodge directly commands two of Sweeny's regiments to do the same against the right flank. These counterattacks rout the Georgians, inflicting heavy casualties and netting well over 500 prisoners, among them Colonel Nisbet.

There is a short lull; then Gist's Brigade appears on the field, heading straight for the gap between Fuller's right and the rear of Giles Smith's division. Should it get through, it could be disastrous for the Federals. Grabbing the flag of the 27th Ohio, which he had once commanded, Fuller runs forward and points with his sword to where he wants a new front formed facing west. His troops quickly respond and then pour a devastating enfilade fire into Gist's column, as do the Rodmans, driving it back. Gist, waving his hat, tries to rally his men for another charge, only to fall from his horse badly wounded. His brigade thereupon scurries to the cover of the woods, leaving the ground over which it has advanced and then retreated littered with dead and wounded, particularly in the sector defended by the Henry-toting 64th Illinois. Among the slain are thirteen Rebels stacked in a heap in a fence corner.

Next Mercer's Brigade moves forward, but not far nor for long. Instead it halts and then falls back on discovering (to quote the report of its acting commander) "the enemy drawn up in three lines of battle" atop a hill and "supported by five batteries." Its total loss in its "attack" comes to "about 15 killed and wounded."

Less than forty-five minutes after they have begun, Bate's and Walker's assaults end in dismal failure. Nowhere did they get within a hundred yards of the Union line. On the surface it would seem that six Confederate brigades were unable even to reach, much less breach, an unfortified position held by three Union brigades. Actually, owing to straggling, skulking, and the small size of Bate's force, the number of Rebel combatants probably did not exceed Sweeny's and Fuller's combined strength of 5,000; perhaps, indeed, it was smaller. In addition the Federals were rested, skillfully commanded, and enjoyed the enormous advantage of artillery support, whereas Bate's and Walker's troops were weak from fatigue, their attacks were uncoordinated, and of necessity they had to rely solely on small arms. They stood so little chance of success that it would have been remarkable had they achieved it.[71]

Success also is eluding Wheeler at Decatur. He has seized the town, and with it a batch of Yankee prisoners; but his main target, the wagon train, has escaped, albeit in a veritable stampede. Moreover Sprague's brigade and two batteries, although falling back to avoid encirclement, are holding him in check and preventing him from wreaking havoc in the Union rear as envisioned by Hood's plan. Incidentally, Wheeler's troopers are making no saber charges against Sprague's infantry, whom they outnumber at least three to one; instead, as usual, they are fighting on foot. Besides, they long since have discarded their sabers, which are more a hindrance than a help in a rifle pit.[72]

McPherson has watched the attack on Dodge from a knoll to the right of Fuller's brigade. After its repulse he sends Lieutenant Colonel Strong to check on Blair's situation. Strong soon returns with word that Blair fears that the enemy is "feeling" for the gap between Fuller and Giles Smith. McPherson thereupon sets out on the same road that Strong has just traveled to see Blair himself. Along the way he orders Strong to go to Logan and have him send Colonel Hugo Wangelin's brigade to plug the gap. This leaves McPherson with only his orderly and a signal officer.

Suddenly, only a few yards away, a band of Rebels emerges from the underbrush on the south side of the road. Several of them yell "Halt!" and an officer raises his sword, signaling McPherson to surrender. He draws rein, doffs his hat as if in salute, then wheels his horse about and gallops into the woods on the other side of the road. The Confederates fire. One of their bullets rips through McPherson's lungs near his heart. His horse carries him a short distance, then he falls heavily to the ground, face downward. He is dead, or soon will be. Both the orderly and the signal officer lie nearby, knocked senseless from their saddles by low-hanging tree limbs. When the latter recovers consciousness, he notices that his watch has been smashed and that it reads two minutes past 2 P.M.

Where McPherson died (*Photographic History*, 3:131)

The officer with the lifted sword is Captain Richard Beard of the 5th Confederate, a ninety-one man "regiment" of Tennesseans that has recently been transferred from Polk's defunct brigade to Granbury's. According to Beard's subsequent testimony, Corporal Robert Coleman of that regiment has fired the fatal bullet at McPherson; probably this is the truth, for what it may be worth. In any case, several of the Tennesseans stop to remove McPherson's watch, sword belt, field glasses, and dispatch book; then they hurry on, leaving behind a diamond ring and a wallet stuffed with large-denomination bills. They are more concerned with the live Yankees than with a dead one, even if he is a general. Cleburne's Division, spearheaded by Govan's and Smith's brigades, is about to penetrate the gap between Blair and Dodge.[73]

Sherman paces up and down the porch of the Howard house, listening to the rumble of cannon fire in the vicinity of Decatur. The sound worries him, and he already has had Schofield send one of Cox's brigades in that direction. Then Lieutenant Colonel William Clark, McPherson's adjutant, gallops up, his horse glistening with sweat, and shouts that McPherson is "killed or a prisoner."

"McPherson dead! Can it be?" Sherman exclaims, his voice like a groan. Clark answers that McPherson had been seen riding up a road leading to Blair's corps, that firing had been heard, and that McPherson's horse, bleeding from bullet wounds, has been found. At once Sherman orders him to inform Logan that he is now in command, as its senior major general, of the Army of the Tennessee. Logan, on receiving this message, turns over the XV Corps to Morgan Smith, then gallops off on his huge black horse to find out what is happening on the left. Three years and one day ago, while still a congressman, he had picked up a discarded musket on the battlefield of First Bull Run and had tried to rally fleeing Union troops. Today he might have to do more rallying, this time of troops belonging to an army of which suddenly he is the commander.[74]

Prior to advancing, Hardee and Cleburne had assured Govan that the Federal entrenchments parallel the Flat Shoals road and that he would take them in the flank, after which nothing would bar his way. Hence he is unpleasantly surprised to find that the enemy troops have what in his report he calls "other works . . . designed to protect [them] from the very movement" his brigade is making. But nothing can be done other than attack and take these works. He gives the order, and his Arkansans rush forward, determined to do precisely that.

Colonel William Hall's Iowa brigade of Giles Smith's division mans these works. Its four regiments are veterans of every major battle of the Army of the Tennessee, starting with Shiloh. Although sadly reduced in numbers, they constitute one of the best fighting units in the whole Union army. Aware that their position on the extreme left is both crucial and vulnerable, they have been fortifying it since yesterday. The result is a semicircular log-and-dirt rampart facing southeast and bending back to the north. In front of the rampart is a cleared "killing ground" fifty yards wide, and beyond that there is an abatis of interlaced tree branches and saplings. Braced by four cannons, the position is virtually impregnable to frontal assault.

The Iowans hold their fire until the on-charging, shrilly yelling Rebels reach the abatis, then pour forth a deadly torrent of bullets supplemented by canister. The enemy's first line seems "to crumble to the earth," as even those who are not killed or wounded fall to the ground. A second line suffers the same fate, but not until it breaks through the abatis. The Iowans continue firing as "fast as

"Black Jack" Logan (Tomes, *War with the South,* vol. 3)

eager and experienced soldiers" can load and pull the triggers of their rifles, the barrels of which become so hot that cartridges begin flashing when inserted. A third Confederate line, consisting of both Arkansans and some of Smith's Texans, gets to within a few yards of the rampart, then stops, unable either to advance or retreat. Lying down, it raises several white flags. But then more of the Texans spill around the left (northern) flank of the rampart, cutting off and capturing most of the 16th Iowa and two cannons. Hall's remaining force, its position now totally untenable, falls back in good order to the west. Govan does not pursue; he cannot. He has lost too many men, and it will be some time before those who are left will be in shape for more fighting.

Smith's troops press on, heading toward the bald hill. Along the way they scoop up Federal stragglers, wagons, ambulances, and several abandoned cannon. Lowrey's Brigade follows on the left, with Carter's Brigade in support. At the same time Vaughan's and Strahl's brigades advance against the Union works along the Flat Shoals road. Blair's corps is in danger of being hit simultaneously in both front and rear. Should the Confederates succeed in doing this, they will shatter the Federal left.

They fail. Seeing Smith's brigade approaching from the east, Leggett's division jumps over to the other side of its works, its rear toward Atlanta. A ferocious struggle ensues, during which a bullet penetrates Manning Force's left cheekbone and upper jaw, shattering both. Even so, his troops hold onto the bald hill, and Smith's begin to falter: there simply are not enough of them. Smith desperately calls for reinforcements; none come. Instead, Walcutt's brigade from Harrow's division of the XV Corps, having swung around to face south, assails his right flank. Smith orders a retreat; then he goes down with a painful wound. Most of his men manage to escape, taking him with them; but a charge by two of Walcutt's regiments captures practically the entire 17/18th Texas and the 5th Confederate along with their colors. In addition, a sally by the 64th Illinois along the road where McPherson has met his fate enables a party led by Lieutenant Colonel Strong to retrieve the general's body.

Hardly has Smith's assault been repulsed than Blair's corps discovers another Confederate force approaching from the southwest. It is Strahl's Brigade. Leggett's men return to the east side of their fortifications, while Hall's and Colonel Benjamin Pott's brigades of Giles Smith's division form in the open at a ninety-degree angle to Leggett's line. The Tennesseans charge up and across the Flat Shoals road, meet what Lieutenant Rennolds calls a "too destructive" fire, and quickly fall back—wisely, for they are but a single brigade attacking two divisions.

Next it is Lowrey's turn. Passing through the remnants of Smith's brigade, his Mississippians and Alabamans move toward the Union line south of the bald hill. During their advance, scores of them have fallen from the ranks, "completely exhausted from fatigue, lack of sleep and the oppressive heat," and their formation is "scattered and thin." Nevertheless they rush forward, in Lowrey's words, "with great impetuosity, as though they bade defiance to Yankee breastworks."

Hall's Iowans and Pott's brigade await them; emulating Leggett's troops in the same situation, they have taken cover behind the front side of their parapets after having beaten off Strahl's assault a mere five minutes ago. Colonel William Belknap, the stalwart red-bearded commander of the 15th Iowa, cautions his men not to fire until each has marked a target. When they do squeeze their triggers, a whole row of Confederates collapse as if cut down by a giant scythe, and the survivors flee back into a forest. Elsewhere a single volley fells one-third of the 32nd Mississippi. Yet Lowrey's troops rally and charge again and yet again, being joined in the fray by Carter's Brigade. The ground in front of the Iowans, who bear the brunt of these desperate sallies, becomes covered with gray-clad bodies. Colonel Harris Lampley of the 45th Alabama runs up to the 15th Iowa's parapet, sword in hand, then turns around and, finding that he is alone, curses his regiment for being a bunch of cowards. Belknap grabs him by his coat collar, drags him over the parapet, then yells at him: "Look at your men! They are all dead! What are you cursing them for?" In a few places the Confederates actually enter the Federal works, only to be shot or captured like Lampley, who, although unwounded, soon dies of "chagrin." Finally what is left of Lowrey's Brigade falls back out of range into the forest, as does Carter's. Carroll Clark of the 16th Tennessee, while going to the rear to have a wound tended, comes upon "at least two hundred" skulkers hiding in a creek bed. Years later, describing the scene, he comments that "many old soldiers never paid for the salt put in their bread." This cannot be said of Lowrey's Mississippians and Alabamans today; they have lost 578 killed, wounded, and missing, nearly half the number they took into the battle.

It now is midafternoon. Except on the extreme left, where Hall's brigade has given ground in order to escape from being surrounded, Blair's corps has maintained its position through hard and skillful fighting and because of the disjointed, piecemeal nature of the Confederate assaults. Along with Dodge's corps it so far has totally frustrated Hood's attempt to smash the Army of the Tennessee.[75]

Hood has been on Oakland Cemetery hill since 2 P.M. (about the time Cleburne's Division penetrated the gap between Dodge and Blair), again eagerly looking and listening for signs that Hardee is hitting the Union left and crushing it. They have not come. Instead, to quote his memoirs, he first "discovered with astonishment a line of battle composed of one of Hardee's divisions advancing directly against the entrenched flank of the enemy." Next, according to the same source, he heard a "roar of musketry occurring only at intervals," and this strengthened his impression that "the desired end was not being accomplished"— a very valid impression, needless to say. And all the while the Yankees on the bald hill have remained there, flags flying and cannons lobbing shells into Atlanta.

Around 3 P.M. a staff officer whom he has sent to find out what Hardee is doing, if anything, returns with word that the attack has achieved some gains, but that in general it has been "checked in consequence of our troops coming in contact with different lines of entrenchment" (or so Hood summarizes the report in his memoirs). When he hears this, Hood concludes that Hardee has failed—for the second battle in the row—to perform his assignment. Accordingly he orders Cheatham and Shoup to create a diversion east of Atlanta so as to prevent the Federals from concentrating against Hardee. This done, he goes into the city and establishes his command post near the railroad depot, an act that suggests that he feels that the battle, to all intents and purposes, is over.

But then, toward 4 P.M., word arrives that Hardee is "driving" the enemy! And this is true. Govan's Brigade, resuming its advance east of the Flat Shoals road, and Vaughan's Brigade, attacking from the south and west, have succeeded in doing what Cleburne and Maney hitherto have failed to accomplish: namely, hit Giles Smith's division simultaneously in front, flank, and rear. The result has been devastating. Describing the assault by Vaughan's Brigade, Captain Alfred Fielder of the 12th Tennessee writes in his diary:

> our regiment was the first to strike the [enemy's] works and A. M. J. Fielder [his brother] who bore the colors was the first man upon the works [and] waving his colors he called out "Boys follow the flag of your country" and over he leaped and right well did the Regt. follow as also did the 13th and 14th Tennessee which was on our right side and the 11th and 29th Tenn. swung around correspondingly so as to enfilade the left side of their [the Federals'] works. The enemy commenced retreating up their works as soon as we charged them and we having an enfilading fire upon them and they being in great confusion and huddling together we mowed them down with awful havoc. They would jump first on one side of the works and then on the other but we being on both sides and pouring in them such a galling fire they continued steadily to give way firing back at us as they went. Squads of them would occasionally throw down their arms and throw up their hands and run to us and surrender. I suppose we had driven them 400 yds up their works filling their ditches in places with their dead and wounded when I was disabled having received three wounds.

The Federals rolled up by Vaughan's Tennesseans belong to Giles Smith's division. More of Smith's troops, trying to hold trenches to the east, have suffered the same fate at the hands of Govan's Arkansans. The whole Union front south of the bald hill has crumbled.

Hood responds to the good news from Hardee by ordering Cheatham to make not a mere demonstration, but a full-fledged attack. Perhaps the enemy's left wing can be crushed after all, and Sherman can be driven, if not into Peachtree Creek, back from Atlanta, his army badly mangled. *

Cheatham, having moved out from Atlanta's fortifications, deploys his corps in lines of battle from north of the Georgia Railroad to south of the bald hill, with Clayton's Division (formerly Stewart's) on the left, Brown's (Hindman's) in the center, and Stevenson's on the right. In keeping with the Army of Tennessee's standard practice, Stevenson's Division or a portion thereof advances first. A few well-directed volleys from Leggett's division (which again goes over to the east side of its works) and Walcutt's brigade easily repulse it, and it fails even to dislodge the Union pickets and pioneer troops who are occupying the former Confederate trenches west of the bald hill. To the south, Gustavus Smith, despite having no orders to engage the enemy, assumes that a general attack is under way, and so he advances with the militia and a battery. The latter (according to Smith) silence some Union guns but, on seeing Stevenson's troops retreat, refrain from making an "isolated attack" and merely hold their position while (in the words of James Watkins) "the bullets whis [sic] about" until, on orders from Hood, they return to the fortifications, having lost "about 50 men killed and wounded."

A mile or more to the north, what was Hindman's Division, now under the command of John C. Brown, advances along the railroad, with two of its brigades (Manigault's and Colonel Jacob H. Sharp's) north of it and the other two (Deas's under Colonel John G. Coltart and Walthall's under Colonel William Brantly) on the south side. Watching the Confederates approach, Major Taylor of the 47th Ohio is impressed by their "beautiful battle flags" and the steadiness of their ranks. Apart from the two South Carolina regiments in

---

*As noted previously in describing it, Hood's plan for July 22 called for Cheatham to attack once the Union left gave way under Hardee's onslaught from the rear. Contrary to what practically all historians have stated, Hood never intended Cheatham to assault from the west at the same time Hardee struck from the east, but rather to have him exploit the expected consequences of Hardee's strike by turning the left flank of the Federal forces (Schofield and Howard) north of the railroad. For this reason it is unfair to criticize Hood for not ordering Cheatham forward when Hardee's attack got under way. Furthermore, since both Clayton's and Brown's divisions of Cheatham's Corps were posted north of the railroad until shortly after 3 P.M., only Stevenson's Division and the militia were available for an attack from the west on Blair in any case, and given their low offensive capabilities and the two-mile (at least) front they were covering, it is doubtful that an attack by them would have accomplished much even if Hood had decided to throw them into the fray.

Manigault's Brigade, they consist entirely of Mississippians and Alabamans and number approximately 3,500 rifles. This is the first time they have made an attack since Kolb's farm exactly one month ago.

For a while it seems that they will repeat that bitter experience. The south column makes no headway at all against three regiments of Colonel James S. Martin's brigade (the other three have gone, unnecessarily, to reinforce Dodge), and Manigault's Brigade, leading the assault north of the railroad, becomes stalled in front of the works held by Colonel Wells S. Jones's five Ohio regiments (Lightburn's brigade). Then, suddenly and spectacularly, the course of the fighting changes. Between the Union brigades there are a deep railroad cut and a wagon road. Furthermore, north of this road (it is the one to Decatur) a two-story white house stands just beyond the left flank of Jones's brigade. Jones, perceiving the potential danger represented by the house, the road, and the railroad cut, has urged Morgan Smith and Lightburn (who now commands Smith's division) to destroy the first and barricade the other two; but Jones is ignored. Smith and Lightburn never explain why; presumably they think that the four artillery pieces that they have posted north of the cut will suffice to secure this section of the front.

Now their men pay the price for Smith and Lightburn's obtuseness. Some of Manigault's Carolinians climb to the second floor and the upper porch of the white house and then start firing down into the trenches of Jones's Ohioans. Others, concealed by dense billows of smoke from the four cannons, rush forward and seize them, shooting and capturing most of their crews, then swing around to Jones's rear. As they do so, several regiments of Sharp's Mississippians slip through the railroad cut and hit Martin's regiments in the flank and from behind, capturing two more Yankee guns. Lightburn's entire line gives way, carrying with it part of Harrow's division on the left. The Confederates pursue, taking scores of prisoners and enjoying, to quote Lieutenant Gill of the 41st Mississippi, "the pleasure of shooting at Yankees as they run without being shot at much." For a while a few of Jones's troops make a stand in the Troup Hurt house, but a charge by parts of Manigault's and Sharp's brigades drives them out and forces Captain DeGress, whose 4-gun battery of Parrotts has been stationed by the house despite his repeated protests that they were unsafe there, to order his cannoneers to spike their pieces and abandon them—the last resort and greatest humiliation for artillerists.

Thanks to the blundering of Morgan Smith and Lightburn, two Rebel brigades have torn a huge hole through the center of the XV Corps—Sherman's own, beloved, and hitherto invincible XV Corps. If the Confederates can exploit their success, they might be able to do what Hood has ceased to think possible: drive back, perhaps even crush, the Union left wing.

Brigadier General Charles Woods, whose XV Corps division holds the sector north of the Troup Hurt house, reacts to the routing of Lightburn's troops by pulling back his two remaining brigades—the third, Wangelin's, long since has gone to try to plug the gap between Dodge and Blair—and then deploying them and two batteries so that they face south, in position to resist an enemy turning movement. While Woods is forming his new line, Morgan Smith gallops up and orders him to attack the Confederates around the Troup Hurt house. At the same time, Sherman summons Schofield to send him *"all"* of his artillery, then personally leads it, twenty pieces in all, to a hill near the Howard house. Sherman also sends a courier to Logan with orders to have the XV Corps recover its lost ground "at any cost." Logan, who by now is with Dodge, at once heads northward with the three regiments from Martin's brigade and Mersy's brigade of Sweeny's division. "Forward, forward," he shouts, "and yell like hell!"

Within half an hour the Federals have four brigades and at least twenty-eight cannons either in position or on the way to seal off the breach in the XV Corps's line. What, on the other hand, are the Confederates who made the breach doing?

They are retreating. Manigault and Sharp have been ordered by Brown to fall back, and although the order astonishes and puzzles them, they are obeying it. It also astonishes and puzzles the historian, for no report exists from Cheatham, Brown, or any other Confederate explaining it. Perhaps Cheatham, unaware of the success gained by Manigault and Sharp, has directed Brown to withdraw for the purpose of forming for another assault; conceivably Brown, worried by the lack of support on his flanks, has acted on his own; or quite possibly a miscommunication or misunderstanding has occurred somewhere along the chain of command. In any case, after retiring about one-fourth of a mile, Manigault and Sharp get an order to reoccupy the enemy works north of the railroad. This they quickly do, driving away some of Lightburn's troops who had returned to their trenches.

Once Manigault and Sharp are back in the works, however, they come under an increasingly heavy and accurate enfilade fire from Woods's and Schofield's batteries to the north (Sherman himself directs the latter), and they sense that the Federals are gathering their strength for a counterattack. Manigault begins to worry. As far as he can tell, only his and Sharp's brigades are doing any fighting, and unless they get help soon, they will be overwhelmed. Hence he sends a series of ever-more-urgent messages to Brown, describing the situation and asking for reinforcements.

After a while these arrive—two brigades. But they belong to Clayton's Division, not to Brown's, and they are not where they should be. Clayton's orders from Cheatham, presumably relayed from Hood, are to attack the Federals north of the bald hill (Harrow's division), presumably to provide support for Hardee's onslaught; otherwise they would serve no purpose. To get into position to do this, Clayton has formed three of his brigades into a column which then has headed southeast across the railroad, leaving behind a fourth brigade (Baker's) to guard against the Yankee forces around the Howard house. On the way and without Clayton's knowledge, Brown has directed the lead brigade (Stovall's, commanded by Colonel Abda Johnson) to move eastward. As a consequence the brigade following it, Holtzclaw's, under Colonel Bushrod Jones, has gotten lost in the woods and has ended up north of the railroad. It is these two brigades that have joined Manigault and Sharp. Clayton's remaining assault brigade, Brigadier General Randall L. Gibson's Louisianans, one of the best in the Army of Tennessee, has halted somewhere in the rear, understandably at a loss as to where to go. Owing to Brown, who as a division commander seems to have gone beyond the limits of his capability, Clayton's attempt to attack the Federals north of the bald hill has ended before it could begin.

Stovall's Brigade, following a brief struggle with a small number of Lightburn's troops, occupies the works earlier captured by Sharp, whose brigade now is on the north side of the railroad. At Manigault's suggestion, Bushrod Jones deploys his brigade along a northward-facing line that runs at a right angle from the Troup Hurt house. Scarcely has it gotten into position when the Union counterattack descends in full fury. Wood's division sweeps in from the north, and a mixed force consisting of portions of Lightburn's division and Martin's and Mersy's brigades advance from the east, urged on by Logan astride a big black horse. "Black Jack! Black Jack!" his troops shout. "McPherson and revenge!"

All the while Woods's and Schofield's cannons shower the area between the Troup Hurt house and the railroad with shells, their aim being, later writes Manigault, "accurate in the extreme." Even so, the Confederates maintain their position, and Manigault sends word to Brown that if reinforced, they can continue to hold it. But instead of reinforcements Manigault receives, once again, an inexplicable order from Brown to retreat. Since there is "nothing left for us but to obey," Manigault passes on the order, and both his and Sharp's brigades pull back. In doing so they uncover the right flank of Bushrod Jones's brigade. Seeing their opportunity, Woods's and Mersy's troops rush forward, swarm around the Troup Hurt house, and recapture DeGress's four Parrotts. Clayton thereupon orders Jones to withdraw: a superfluous command, because Jones's men already are in full flight. South of the railroad, Stovall's Brigade, assailed on both flanks, likewise scurries rearward.[76] The XV Corps, content with having restored its front and its reputation, makes no attempt to pursue.

Around the bald hill, as the sun starts to set, the fighting mounts to a climax. Having expelled Giles Smith's division from its entrenchments, Vaughan's Tennesseans and Govan's Arkansans start doing the same to three Ohio regiments of Scott's brigade of Leggett's division. Leggett, declaring that "the hill must be retained at all hazards and at whatever cost," orders the Ohioans to form a new line facing southward and running eastward from the breastworks of Force's brigade (now commanded by Colonel George Bryant of the 12th Wisconsin) atop the hill. They quickly do so, whereupon the remnants of Smith's division, having rallied, take position on their left at the edge of a cornfield along a front slanting to the southeast; and Wangelin's brigade deploys so as to cover its flank. In spite of this eastward extension of the XVII Corps's line, a half-mile gap still exists between it and the XVI Corps, but fortunately for the Federals, the woods and underbrush screen it from the Confederates.

Besides, their attention is focused on the bald hill, which Hardee is determined to take. To do so, he has brought Walker's (Maney's) and Mercer's brigades from the XVI Corps's front and has placed them on Govan's right in position, he hopes, to take the defenders of the hill in the rear while Vaughan and Govan continue assailing them from the south. In addition he has ordered his artillery to provide close-range support for the assault and has collected fragments of Lowrey's, Smith's, and Gist's brigades to exploit it should it succeed. This is his last chance to achieve victory: soon it will be dark, and he knows it.

Hardee's attempt to take the bald hill from the rear speedily fails. As Walker's and Mercer's brigades move across the cornfield, they come under such an intense fire from Giles Smith's division that, Captain Hall records, they begin "dropping by the score." Nevertheless the Tennesseans drive back Smith's right near the base of the hill. Mercer's Georgians, on the other hand, go to ground about a hundred yards from the Union line and can be "induced to go no farther," to quote the report of their acting commander, Lieutenant Colonel Cincinnatus S. Guyton of the 57th Georgia. As a result, Walker's troops are exposed, in Hall's words, to "a terrific hail of bullets and cannon shot fired from that part of the enemy's line on our right which we had failed to capture"; and they are forced to fall back. Left behind, lying in a furrow, is Hall himself, shot in both thighs, and next to him is his brother Junius, "killed instantly by a bullet through the heart." Colonel Walker also is among his brigade's 53 dead, by far the highest number suffered by any of the Tennessee brigades this day.

Charging up the south slope of the bald hill, Govan's Arkansans reach the rail barricade that Leggett's Ohioans have hastily thrown up. Literal hand-to-hand combat—rare in Civil War battles—ensues. Men go down because of bayonet thrusts, blows from clubbed muskets, and even fists; and officers slash at enemies with their swords, which are normally considered "mere playthings," later writes Lieutenant Henry Dwight of the 20th Ohio. When some Rebs grab an unfortunate Buckeye around the ankles, he is "almost dismembered" as his comrades try to save him from captivity by holding onto his head. Finally those Confederates who are able to do so fall back to the shelter of nearby woods. Some of them desperately endeavor to renew the assault, sallying forth in small packs, but to no avail. Hosea Garrett, color-bearer of the 10th Texas, on getting to within ten paces of the Union line, stops to look around him and discovers that there are "not more than a half a dozen men with me." On the Confederate left, Vaughan's Brigade takes cover in abandoned Federal trenches. Harrying the Yankees from both sides at the same time is one thing; going up against them straight on is another, especially when they are behind breastworks and backed by cannons. "Several of our boys acted badly and played out of the fight," notes thrice-wounded Alfred Fielder in his diary the following evening.

The sun now is a dying ember in the western sky, and still the fighting continues around the bald hill. Confederate snipers force Leggett's troops to keep their heads low unless they want them shattered with a .577-caliber hunk of lead. Hardee's and Shoup's artillery pounds the hill from what seems like all directions, leveling whole sections of parapets, mangling the men behind them, and causing some of the defenders to fear that they might be "shot from it." But as night descends, the bombardment slackens, then ceases; and the bald hill remains securely in Union possession. What will be called by the Confederates the Battle of Decatur and what the Federals and the historians (who generally follow the winners) will name the Battle of Atlanta, but which should be entitled the Battle of the Bald Hill, ends.

"I don't want to see another day like this," John Bates, one of Fuller's soldiers writes in his diary. He then adds, "I am tiard so good knight."[77]

At 10:30 P.M., Hood telegraphs Richmond a brief report. It states that Hardee's Corps "attacked the enemy's extreme left today at 1 o'clock" and "drove him from his works, capturing 16 pieces of artillery and 5 stands of colors"; that Cheatham "attacked the enemy at 4 P.M. with a portion of his command" and forced him back, "capturing 6 pieces of artillery"; that "we captured about 2,000 prisoners"; that "Wheeler's cavalry routed the enemy in the neighborhood of Decatur"; and that "our loss is not fully ascertained" but that "prisoners report McPherson killed." "Our troops," it concludes, "fought with great gallantry."

The telegram conveys an impression of victory, and this is the impression it creates in Richmond and throughout the South.[78] Actually, of course, Hood has failed in his attempt to crush Sherman's left wing and sweep the rest of the Union army into Peachtree Creek and thus to turn the tide of the war in Georgia. Indeed, he has not even realized, although he sincerely believes otherwise, his minimal objective of foiling a Federal thrust from the east against the Macon railroad, for Sherman was not attempting such a movement; his plan was to swing the Army of the Tennessee around to the west of Atlanta for that purpose. All Hood in truth has accomplished in this, the largest and bloodiest battle of the campaign, is to drive a part of Blair's corps from its position south of the bald hill, a position from which it soon would have departed in any event.

Logan, in a report written in September, attributes Hood's failure on July 22 to "the lateness of the hour at which the attack was made, a lack of concert in his movements, the opportune presence of a portion of the Sixteenth Corps in the rear of the left of our line, but more than all of these to the splendid bravery and tenacity of the men and the ability and skill of the officers of the Army of the Tennessee." He also states that the Army of the Tennessee lost 3,722 killed, wounded, and missing (1,801 of whom were in the XVII Corps), whereas the Confederate loss was "at least 10,000."[79]

On the whole this remains a valid assessment of the battle and needs to be qualified on only two points. The first is the "presence of a portion [Sweeny's division and Fuller's brigade] of the XVI corps" on the left rear of the XVII Corps. This was "opportune" but not a mere matter of luck. Sweeny and Fuller were there when Bate and Walker attacked because of orders from McPherson and because McPherson had prevailed on Sherman to suspend an order by him that would have sent them to Decatur. On the other hand they were not there for the purpose they served—to block the Confederate strike against the rear of the Army of the Tennessee—but rather to extend the left of the Army of the Tennessee, around which Hardee already had circled. Furthermore, had Hardee's attack begun a half-hour earlier, Sweeny's division would not have been present; and if it had started at least an hour later, Fuller's brigade would have been on the way to Decatur in pursuit of Sherman's renewed order to McPherson to employ it in ripping up tracks—an order that McPherson had passed on to Dodge, who received it even as his troops were beating off Bate's and Walker's onslaughts. Thus McPherson's prudence saved the Federals from a potential disaster, yet he does not deserve high marks for his generalship. Although no doubt a man of sterling character, highly intelligent, and with great personal charm, his record throughout the campaign demonstrates that in commanding what in effect was a large corps, he had reached and perhaps exceeded the limits of his military ability: he worried too much about what might be "on the other side of the hill."

The other point in Logan's evaluation of the battle that requires amendment is his estimate of Confederate casualties. Sherman himself did this in his report, lowering it from "at least 10,000 men" to a "full 8,000 men," a figure that most historians, including Southern ones, have accepted. But again a close examination of Confederate sources and an application of what might be termed the laws of probability suggest a substantially smaller figure. Hardee's chief of staff, Colonel Roy, states that Hardee's Corps, which evidently did not have more than two-thirds of its men engaged owing to straggling, lost 3,299. Of this number, according to official reports, 1,388 came from Cleburne's Division and 619 (not including missing) from Maney's. No figures are available for Walker's and Bate's divisions, except 168 for Mercer's Brigade and 135 (missing are not included) in the Kentucky brigade, but probably Walker's Division contributed the majority of the remaining casualties in Hardee's Corps if for no other reason than that it had more men to lose. Cheatham's casualties probably total at most 2,000, with "over 1,000" in Brown's Division according to Manigault; approximately 600 in Clayton's Division, where Stovall's and Bushrod Jones's brigades, the only ones heavily engaged, lost 298 and 128 respectively; and the rest in Stevenson's Division. If one adds the 50 killed and wounded in Smith's militia and—a generous estimate—150 casualties for Wheeler's cavalry, the Confederate loss for July 22 comes to about 5,500. This, to be sure, is a high figure, particularly considering the number of troops involved in Hood's attack, which could not have exceeded 35,000 of all arms and probably was less; yet compared to such hecatombs as Shiloh, Antietam, and Murfreesboro, where Confederate armies of around 40,000 lost respectively 10,694, 13,724, and 11,739 men, it is not inordinately so.[80] It simply represents a greater price in blood than Hood and the Confederacy can afford to pay without its being redeemed by victory.*

In his report and memoirs, Hood attributes his defeat—or as he puts it, his "partial success"—to Hardee's not executing his orders to march to Decatur before attacking, thereby failing to strike the Federals in the rear as planned.[81] This accusation is as absurd as it is unfair. Not only did Hood himself agree to a modification of Hardee's original instructions when it became apparent that they could not be implemented, but even had this modification not occurred,

---

*The above estimate of 5,500 Confederate casualties would seem to be supported by Colonel Beatty, who in his diary for July 23 states that "our loss in yesterday's fight was about 5,000 it is said." Possibly the reason Southern historians have accepted Sherman's 8,000 figure is that many of them believe that Hood wantonly wasted his troops in reckless attacks, or else they believe that the Confederates fought with such spirit and determination on July 22 that they could not but have suffered extremely heavy losses. The estimate that because of straggling, no more than two-thirds of Hardee's Corps took part in the fighting derives from Oldham's Diary, July 23, 1864.

Hardee still could not have reached Decatur with his entire corps by daylight or, for that matter, before midafternoon. (Wheeler's cavalry did not approach it until about 1 P.M.) Furthermore, it is doubtful that an attack by Hardee from around Decatur would have achieved the devastating results that Hood envisioned. Hardee would have encountered Sprague's brigade at Decatur, he would have had to deploy his virtually exhausted troops along a line facing west, and they then would have had to advance in line of battle four miles before making contact with the Federal rear. All of these things would have given the Army of the Tennessee ample time to take effective countermeasures. Indeed, given the physical condition of his men and the low offensive potential of some of his units, it is conceivable that Hardee would have been repulsed and then cut off from the rest of the Confederate army.

The fundamental reason for Hood's failure on July 22 is that he tried to do too much with too little in too short a time. Once it had become known that Cleburne's and Maney's divisions would be so late in beginning their march that they could not possibly reach the enemy rear by daylight, Hood should have canceled, instead of merely modifying, his plan; and he should have adopted a new, less ambitious one whereby Bate's and Walker's divisions would have sought to strike the flank and rear of the Union left south of the bald hill, while Cleburne and Maney assailed it from the front, which they were already in position to do. This way Bate and Walker would have advanced into the gap between the XVI and XVII corps instead of running up against, first, Terry's Mill Pond and then Sweeny and Fuller; and Cleburne and Maney would have been able to assault Blair from the west while he was being attacked from the east, thereby almost surely routing his corps at the very outset of the battle. As it was, after spending most of the night and part of the morning marching ten to twelve miles, two of Maney's brigades (Strahl's and Vaughan's) ended up where they had started from, and Cleburne's Division found itself still confronted by the XVII Corps, only from a different direction. Hood's plan for July 22, both in its original and in its modified forms, could be used as a classic example of a commander's not making sufficient allowance for the factors of time, distance, fatigue, and what is called the "friction of battle."

Sherman's sole contributions to the Union victory were to make a battle possible by providing Hood with the opportunity to go around his left flank and, following the Confederate penetration along the railroad, to summon Schofield's artillery, which was hardly a stroke of genius. Beyond these things he did nothing significant and failed to do some things that might have been momentous. Although he should have realized from the strength of Hood's attacks east of Atlanta that the bulk of the Rebel army was in that sector, he did not (contrary to the claim in his *Memoirs*) order Thomas to "make a lodgement" in Atlanta or even to feint an assault from the north. Instead he merely alerted Howard to be ready to move to the left if needed and sent what proved to be unneeded reinforcements from the XV and XXIII corps to bolster the XVI Corps and protect the rear. As a consequence the Army of the Cumberland, with its 40,000 fine infantry, spent the day skirmishing with and entrenching in front of Stewart's Corps, which at most numbered 10,000 men defending a haphazardly fortified line at least four miles long. To be sure, Thomas and his soldiers, having experienced the fierce surprise onslaught of July 20 and having been told in the morning that Atlanta had been evacuated and then that it had not, were more concerned (as their extremely cautious movements amply demonstrate) with being attacked than with making an attack; but had they been explicitly ordered to storm Atlanta, almost surely they would have advanced against the city's fortifications in such force as either to carry them or at least to compel Hood to abandon his attempt to crush the Union left.

Sherman also rejected proposals from both Schofield and Howard that their forces be used to launch a counterattack against Cheatham's exposed left flank, thereby cutting off his corps from Atlanta: "Let the Army of the Tennessee fight it out!" he answered Howard. In his *Memoirs,* Sherman attempts to justify this course of nonaction by asserting that he was afraid that "if any assistance were rendered by either of the other armies, the Army of the Tennessee would be jealous" (i.e., resentful). This, of course, is sheer nonsense. Actually it was he who resented using "other armies" to aid his favorite army, and therefore he was unwilling to do so unless it became, as it did during the Snake Creek operation, absolutely necessary. Because of this attitude, which probably in part explains his failure to have Thomas make at least an attempt to enter Atlanta from the north, Sherman on July 22 practiced to an excess the basically sound philosophy of command he once expressed to a newspaper correspondent, namely, that "fighting is the least part of a general's work, the battle will fight itself." Had he directed Thomas to strike for Atlanta and/or had he adopted Schofield's and Howard's advice, the Battle of Bald Hill might have been more than just another, albeit big, defensive victory. It could have been a decisive triumph, producing the fall of Atlanta and the virtual destruction of Hood's army. Not being that, Atlanta remains in Confederate hands and the Army of Tennessee, although badly injured, remains dangerous.[82]

Part Six: Ezra Church

During the night the men of the XV, XVI, and XVII corps work much and sleep little while they strengthen their old fortifications and construct new ones

"After the battle of Atlanta—Forty-five dead in one place" (Drawing by Lieutenant Henry Dwight, 20th Ohio. Ohio Historical Society)

in anticipation of a renewal of the enemy's offensive come morning. They need not worry. The Confederates have neither the means nor the will to attempt again tomorrow what they have not been able to do today. Their sole concern now is to protect against the putative thrust of the Union left wing toward the Macon railroad. To that end Hardee's forces withdraw to the southwest and, by appropriate coincidence, entrench along Intrenchment Creek.

At dawn the only Rebels that Logan's troops can see are dead and wounded ones. Around the bald hill these lie piled in heaps and sprawled in rows. Numerous clusters of blue-clad corpses mingle with the gray ones on ground that is "literally red with blood." After a while the Confederates propose a truce for burying the dead and removing the wounded. Logan, after checking with Sherman, grants it with the stipulation that it be limited solely to his sector. During the rest of the morning the enemies again join in clearing away the human debris of battle. If they can find friends and relatives, they bury them in individual graves with headboards to identify them. Most of the bodies, however, are dumped into shallow pits and are covered with a thin layer of dirt; one such mass entombment in front of the XV Corps is marked by a fence rail that has been stuck upright into the ground and inscribed with charcoal "24 Rebs." Little emotion is shown because little is felt. "We cook and eat, talk and laugh with the enemy's dead lying all around us as though they were so many logs," notes Captain Foster. For his "album," Lieutenant Henry Dwight of the 20th

Ohio draws a sketch of Confederate corpses stacked like logs in front of his regiment's breastworks.

Wounded who are collected by the Federals go to field hospitals in the rear. John Bates of Fuller's brigade describes one of them in his diary: "Here lay the Union troops on one side and the Rebels on the other. Arms and legs under the [operating] table. Some [of the wounded] praying and some laffing and some dying and some dead all on one acre of ground." The Confederates take most of their seriously wounded into Atlanta to be shipped south by train. A seemingly endless procession of "enormous, black-covered" wagons passes along Decatur, Fair, and McDonough streets. Watching them, Sarah Huff, who two days ago had had to abandon her house on the city's northern outskirts, sees "the blood trickling down from the wounds of the poor helpless victims." From the court-house, where many of them have been placed, comes a constant groan so loud that it can be heard blocks away. It cannot be heard only when a Yankee shell explodes nearby.[83]

After riding along the lines of the Army of the Tennessee, which greets him with cheers, Sherman again ponders the perpetual question of an army commander: What next? Two recent events influence his thoughts. One occurred recently in Mississippi. There, on July 14 outside of a town called Tupelo, A. J. Smith's 14,000 infantry and cavalry beat off an attack by close to 10,000 Confederates, half of them Forrest's troopers, under the command of Stephen Lee. During the battle the Confederates, who in Smith's words charged forward as if in a "foot race" and "yelling and howling like Comanches," lost 1,400 men, whereas the Union casualties were less than half that number. Moreover, although Mower's XVI Corps veterans failed to fulfill Sherman's behest that Forrest be killed, some Yankee put a bullet in "Old Bedford's" foot, forcing him to take to a buggy. But then something queer happened: the very next day Smith headed back toward Memphis with his victorious army. The reason, he alleges in his report, was that he had just learned "that much of our bread was spoiled when drawn from the commissary depot" at the outset of the expedition, an explanation that can be believed if one can also believe that a general of Smith's experience would be so careless as to draw bad bread in the first place and that it would take him ten days to discover this fact in the second place. A much more likely explanation is that, like Sooy Smith and Sturgis before him, he got cold feet and decided to get out of "Forrest country" while the getting was good. Smith already was starting to retreat before the Tupelo battle was fought, and it would not have been fought at all had not Lee, concerned about what proved to be a nonexistent threat to Mobile (Canby's column from New

Orleans, instead of numbering 20,000 as reported by Confederate intelligence, scarcely mustered 2,000 troops) believed that he needed to defeat Smith immediately and therefore, against Forrest's better judgment, ordered the wild assault on the entrenched Federals.

Sherman has learned about Lee's defeat and Smith's retreat from both Union and Confederate sources, among the latter being the last (July 21) regular issue of the *Appeal*. The paradoxical news puzzles him, but one thing is clear: Forrest still is on the loose and dangerous. Hence Sherman has telegraphed Washburn at Memphis, instructing him to "order Smith to pursue and keep after Forrest all the time." That "devil" must not be allowed to go on a rampage against the railroads in Tennessee while the campaign is coming to a climax in Georgia.[84]

The other event that enters into Sherman's calculations happened yesterday: Rousseau arrived safely in Marietta from his raid through Alabama. He brought with him, besides confirmation that he had destroyed a long section (thirty miles to be exact) of the railroad between Atlanta and Montgomery, 2,500 cavalry. So far Sherman has had to employ Stoneman and McCook to cover his right flank and the Chattahoochee above the railroad bridge. Now Rousseau's troopers can take over this assignment, freeing Stoneman and McCook for other more productive work—namely, a raid against the Macon railroad. If it succeeds, Hood, his last supply line to the rest of the Confederacy severed, will have to leave Atlanta or starve. But if it does not succeed, at least it will distract Hood and divert his cavalry, thereby facilitating what Sherman has decided will be his next main move.[85]

This is to do what he had planned to do anyway prior to yesterday's enemy attack: swing the Army of the Tennessee from the left to the right wing and use it to strike south of Atlanta from the west. This surely will force Hood either to evacuate the city in order to avoid being trapped or else to sally forth again to fight. Sherman doubts that Hood will do the latter. Instead, as he informs Logan, "the enemy, having failed in his assault on your flank . . . and having sustained most serious loss, will not again attempt it, but will await our action."[86]

Certain preliminaries, however, are necessary before "our action" can get under way. One is the return of Garrard from his raid. This occurs on the afternoon of July 24, whereupon he reports to Sherman that he has destroyed the railroad bridges over two wide rivers, six miles of track, two trains, depots and quartermaster supplies, and two thousand bales of cotton. (He does not mention that his troopers got drunk and, to quote one of them, left behind in Oxford and Covington "homes plundered, women insulted and every species of outrage committed.") Sherman congratulates Garrard on his success—the first time he has had any occasion to do that during the campaign—and notifies him that "I will give you time to rest and then we must make quick work of Atlanta."[87]

Another and much more important preliminary is selecting a permanent commander for the Army of the Tennessee. Logan performed well on July 22. Among Northern generals he has few peers as a combat leader. He combines prudence with dash, his troops admire him, and even a captured Reb found him impressive: "Don't he look savage!" he has exclaimed on beholding "Black Jack." The rank and file of the Army of the Tennessee want him to remain at their head, and so does he. Indeed, he expects to.

Sherman, however, takes a different view of the matter. To begin with, he distrusts "volunteers" for whom the path of military glory is merely the road to political office, and he fears (so he claims in his *Memoirs*) the potential consequences of the "natural rivalry" between Logan and Blair. Also, in common with nearly all of his fellow West Pointers, Sherman believes that only graduates of the Military Academy should hold high command: "The army," he wrote brother John back in December, "is a good school, but West Point is better." Therefore, after discussing various possibilities with Thomas, who likewise has misgiving about Logan, Sherman decides that Howard is "the best officer, . . . present and available for the purpose." Howard, to be sure, has done nothing in the campaign to distinguish himself and in fact has suffered more setbacks, whether they were his fault or not, than any of the other corps commanders (the first day at Resaca, Pickett's Mill, the utter failure of his assault on June 27, to list the main ones). But he is personally loyal, has ample experience, is an efficient administrator with the best staff of all the corps commanders, and can be relied on to execute orders promptly and energetically—qualities that Sherman values above all others in top subordinates. Furthermore the only other corps commander in the army who has a West Point certificate—unless Schofield, who already heads an "army," be so considered—is Hooker. This alone would suffice to cause Sherman to choose Howard to replace McPherson.

After his conference with Thomas, Sherman telegraphs Halleck that he wants Howard to head the "Army and Department of the Tennessee." If this meets with Lincoln's approval (only the president can appoint department commanders), Sherman will assign Howard to the post.[88] But before he can get a reply to this request, he suddenly finds himself confronted by another, a much more dramatic, problem involving his generals—a brawl, no less, between Dodge and Sweeny.

The one-armed Irishman long has resented having to serve under Dodge, whom he despises as a presumptuous amateur soldier who owes his position to political influence. Then, during the fighting on July 22, there occurred what for Sweeny was an intolerable insult: Dodge had issued orders directly to several regiments of Sweeny's division. On the morning of July 25, upon learning that Dodge and Fuller are touring the XVI Corps's lines, Sweeny invites them to his tent. As soon as they enter he breaks forth in a furious denunciation of "damned political generals" (Fuller had operated a publishing business in Toledo before the war) and declares that Fuller's brigade "broke" on the 22nd. The ensuing altercation at first is merely verbal, with "son of a bitch" being the most frequently used expression. Then suddenly Sweeny strikes Dodge in the chest, Dodge swings back, and Fuller wrestles Sweeny to the ground and chokes him until he is pulled away by some staff officers. Dodge thereupon places Sweeny under arrest (Sweeny sarcastically tells him that he cannot even do that in proper military style) and then notifies Logan, who in turn refers the matter to Sherman, at the same time asking that Corse be assigned to command Sweeny's division. Sherman, after due consideration, authorizes Logan to send Sweeny to Nashville for a court-martial and, although reluctant to part with his inspector general and troubleshooter, grants Logan's request for Corse. Later in the day, Sweeny departs for Nashville, never to return to active duty even though he is acquitted at his trial.[89]

The next day, Halleck telegraphs Sherman that Howard has been approved as commander of the Army of the Tennessee. On the morning of July 27, Howard assumes his new post, while Stanley takes over the IV Corps. Logan, who has asked Sherman to retain him at the head of the Army of the Tennessee at least until the campaign has ended, is bitterly disappointed. Dodge finds him sitting on the porch of Sherman's headquarters, tears in his eyes. Logan believes, not without cause, that he has been passed over because he is not a West Pointer. "West Point," he writes his wife ten days later, "must have all under Sherman who is an infernal *brute.*" Nevertheless Logan returns to the XV Corps; after all, the war is far from over, and there could be another opportunity, perhaps a better one, to become an army commander. "It makes no difference," he tells Dodge; "it will all come right in the end."[90]

If Logan is disappointed, Hooker is outraged by Howard's elevation. As soon as he learns about it he sends a note to Sherman asking to be "relieved from duty with this army. Justice and self-respect alike require my removal from an army in which rank and service are ignored." Sherman, after obtaining Thomas's endorsement, agrees. In the evening he telegraphs Halleck: "General Hooker is offended because he thinks he is entitled to the command of the Army of the Tennessee. I must be honest and say that he is not qualified or suited to it. . . . He is welcome to my place if the President awards it, but I cannot name him to so important a command as the Army of the Tennessee." At Thomas's recommendation, Sherman designates Slocum to head the XX Corps, an assignment, given the well-known enmity between Slocum and Hooker, that is like rubbing

Thomas Sweeny, fighting Irishman (*Photographic History,* 10:91)

John Fuller, fighting Ohioan (*Photographic History*, 10:91)

salt into "Fighting Joe's" wounded pride. Pending the arrival of Slocum from Vicksburg, Alpheus Williams will head the XX Corps, a post for which he is eminently qualified, having served brilliantly as a corps commander at Antietam and Gettysburg.

Hooker's reaction to having Howard, rather than himself, become commander of the Army of the Tennessee is understandable and, to a degree, justified. Not only is he much senior in rank to Howard; it was Howard's inertness that, as much as anything else, had caused Hooker's defeat at Chancellorsville. Moreover, as Alpheus Williams points out in a letter to his daughter on August 11, Hooker "certainly has been a superior corps commander. He is full of energy, always courteous and pleasant, and has a great facility of winning the confidence and the regard of all ranks." Even so, if not the fair thing, Sherman has done the right thing. Personal friendship need not exist between a commander and a top lieutenant, but if antipathy, distrust, and contempt exist, the consequences can be disastrous. Hooker, in thinking that Sherman would or could ignore the nature of their relationship, merely manifests his inability to view himself, or to appreciate how others view him, in a realistic manner. As Butterfield had written Hooker prior to leaving the army, "you never were, nor ever will be a politic man." And not being that, Hooker makes an abrupt exit from the stage of Civil War history, a stage where briefly he had held the limelight.[91]

Unbeknownst to Sherman, another of his generals also is unhappy about not becoming commander of the Army of the Tennessee. It is Schofield. Although already head of what is nominally an army, he knows full well that it actually is a corps and a small one at that; so he has hoped that Sherman's choice would fall on him, a hope encouraged by Blair who, as Sherman anticipated, was displeased by the prospect of serving under Logan. But Schofield carefully conceals his feelings—he is very good at that—and, like Logan, waits for the wheel of fortune to turn, prepared to give it a nudge if need be.[92]

Changes in command also are taking place in Hood's army. They start on the afternoon of July 24 when Bragg, just returned from Alabama, confronts General Mackall on the porch of Hood's headquarters at the Thrasher house. Mackall, the intensity of whose loathing for Bragg has increased with the removal of Johnston, declines to shake his proffered hand, whereupon Hood—who no doubt has intended to do so anyway—dismisses Mackall as chief of staff and designates Shoup as his replacement. "The removal of Mackall is a good move," Colonel Beatty comments in his diary, for "he always was opposed to fighting—always predicted disaster [and] he has been aptly termed the 'owl of the army.'" On the following day, Mackall joins Johnston in Macon, taking with him all of the headquarter records for use in waging the campaign that most interests both of them now: the one against Davis, Bragg, and their cohorts in infamy. Lieutenant Mackall soon finds a post on Clayton's staff and after a few more days terminates his journal. Fortunately for the historian, Shoup begins keeping one as chief of staff.[93]

Other changes, all of them either initiated by Bragg or the outcome of consultations between him and Hood, include disbanding Walker's Division and assigning Mercer's, Gist's, and Stevens's brigades respectively to Cleburne, Maney, and Bate, all of whose divisions badly need bolstering; summoning Major General Patton Anderson from Florida, where he is "no longer necessary," to take over Hindman's Division in place of Brown; having Davis order Stephen Lee to Atlanta to assume command of Hood's old corps, thereby returning Cheatham to his division; formally making the Army of Mississippi a corps of the Army of Tennessee, which of course is what it has been in practice since early May; naming Colonel Robert Beckham, chief of artillery in Hood's old corps, as Shoup's successor; and obtaining Major General Martin L. Smith to replace Presstman as chief engineer. Smith's experience in preparing the defenses of Vicksburg, Richmond, and Petersburg should prove useful at Atlanta.

Bragg and Hood also want to get rid of Hardee, who for his part has frankly told them that he wants to leave the Army of Tennessee because he feels humiliated serving under Hood. Accordingly on July 27, prior to going to Montgomery to confer with Major General Dabney H. Maury, the new commander in Alabama and Mississippi, Bragg writes Davis that "there does not exist that cordiality and mutual confidence and support" between Hood and Hardee that is necessary to success and that therefore it would be best if Hardee and Lieutenant General Richard Taylor (the nemesis of Banks's Red River Expedition into Louisiana back in February) exchange places: "With Taylor in Hardee's place this army would be invincible."

Concerning that army as such, Bragg in the same letter reports that it has lost only "about 3,000" since Hood has taken command, that the "arrival of extra duty men and convalescents, &c.," has increased its strength by "about 5,000" and more men are coming in daily, that the "militia are turning out largely," that on July 22 Sherman had been "badly defeated and completely failed [foiled] in one of his bold flank movements, heretofore so successful," and that the "moral effect" of this victory has been "admirable on our troops." Every one of these assertions is either false or misleading. Hood's losses, as Bragg surely knows, total at least 9,000 since July 17. The accession of 5,000 "extra duty men and convalescents" does not make up for these losses in quantity, and since many of the replacements are clerks, cooks, musicians, teamsters, orderlies, and what the front-line veterans call "dead heads," they are not equal in quality to the troops lost in the assaults of July 20 and 22. Although the militia in fact are growing in number—soon they will reach 5,000—most of them are old men or "slim barefooted boys" who can stand behind a rampart and pull a trigger but can do little else. Finally, Sherman had not been "badly defeated" or "foiled in one of his bold flank movements" on July 22, and although there are many Confederate soldiers who, like Lieutenant Andrew Neal, believe that Hood "gained victory" that day, there are many more, particularly those who had participated in the fighting on the 22nd, who know its terrible cost. Captain Foster, after listing his company's casualties at Bald Hill, wryly comments in his diary that "we look loansome [*sic*]."[94]

Bragg, more than any one else except Johnston, is responsible for Hood's being commander of the Army of Tennessee. Now he finds himself in the position of having to justify his handiwork. His method is to deceive Davis as to what Hood has done and is capable of doing at Atlanta.

Late on the morning of July 27, Sherman rides with Howard to a hilltop west of the Turner's Ferry road on the right flank of the Army of the Cumberland. Following them is the Army of the Tennessee, which has pulled out of its trenches before sunrise, leaving the XXIII Corps to guard what now is the Union left along the Georgia Railroad. Pointing to a wooded ridge running southward parallel to Atlanta's west-side fortifications, Sherman informs Howard that he is to march his forces "straight along" a road to the west of the ridge until he reaches a point beyond the Confederate left on the Lick Skillet road, which will enable him to flank it and "get hold of Hood's railroad" somewhere north of East Point. Hood then will have to choose between Atlanta and East Point, and since he will be trapped and isolated should he stay in Atlanta, that means he will evacuate the city and retreat to East Point. There will be, Sherman assures Howard, "little risk" in the movement because the ridge will screen it from the enemy; Hood will be unable to extend his lines southward rapidly enough to block it even if he does detect it; and he is unlikely to mount another attack.

Howard, noting that the road which he is to take is covered thickly with trees and being keenly aware of Hood's "enterprise" from previous experience (Resaca, Pickett's Mill), disagrees with Sherman's prognosis. Unless Sherman objects, he tells him, "instead of pushing out my right into the air," he will "carefully unfold" by having his divisions "take their place on Thomas's right, moving up in succession," so that each will protect the flank of the preceding division. Sherman, although again expressing doubt that Hood will give any trouble, agrees to let Howard have his way. As a consequence the Army of the Tennessee spends the rest of the day ponderously deploying southward. By nightfall, at which time Howard suspends operations, only Dodge's two divisions are in position along the ridge, their left connecting with the right of the XIV Corps at Proctor's Creek. Blair's corps, reduced by its heavy casualties on the twenty-second to little more than 4,000 troops, faces the ridge but is not yet on it, and Logan's corps is behind it in reserve. Confederate pickets have been encountered, convincing Howard all the more that there is a strong likelihood of his being attacked. If caution is the measure, he is a worthy successor to McPherson.[95]

While the Army of the Tennessee awaits morning to resume uncoiling to the south, the other part of Sherman's double thrust against Hood's communications gets under way. McCook, at the head of 4,000 cavalry, marches down the west bank of the Chattahoochee toward Smith's Ferry; Stoneman, with about 2,000 troopers, moves toward Covington; and Garrard's 3,000 horsemen halt near Flat Rock, sixteen miles west of Covington. According to Sherman's instructions, McCook is to cross the Chattahoochee, then proceed via Palmetto and Fayetteville to Lovejoy's Station, twenty-three miles south of Atlanta on the Macon railroad. Here he is to rendezvous with Stoneman who, after feinting toward Augusta, is to circle back to the west and south by the way of McDonough. Garrard's role is to serve as a decoy and then to block pursuit by Wheeler. Once McCook and Stoneman are able to join forces at Lovejoy's, which Sherman expects will be "during the day or night of the 28th," they are to destroy "substantially" two to five miles of track and pull down as much telegraph wire as possible. That done, McCook is to recross the Chattahoochee and return to Union lines. Stoneman, on the other hand, has sought and received Sherman's permission, should he think it practicable, to head with his division for Macon, sixty miles further south, and release the 1,500 Union officer captives who are being held there at Camp Oglethorpe, then to go on and do the same for the more than 30,000 enlisted men imprisoned at Andersonville. Although Sherman doubts, so he has informed Halleck in a July 26 telegram, that Stoneman can succeed in this enterprise, he believes that "even a chance of success will warrant the effort."[96]

Howard's wariness is justified. Hood, as soon as he learned around 4 A.M. that the Federals had withdrawn from south of the Georgia Railroad, concluded that Sherman, having failed (so he supposes) to cut the Macon railroad from the east, intended now to attack it from the west. Then, when pickets reported during the afternoon that the Army of the Tennessee was pushing toward the

Lick Skillet road, Hood promptly took countermeasures. On his orders, Hardee's Corps, shifting to the left, occupied the fortifications between the Peachtree road and the Decatur road, and Stephen Lee, who arrived yesterday in Atlanta to assume command of Hood's old corps, moved Brown's and Clayton's divisions to the Lick Skillet road, which they reached after dark. Hood plans, as he has explained to his corps commanders in an evening conference at his new headquarters (the L. Windsor Smith house on the southwest edge of Atlanta), to have Lee deploy Brown's and Clayton's divisions along the Lick Skillet road in the morning so as to check the Union advance. Meanwhile Stewart will pull Walthall's and Loring's divisions out of their works on Atlanta's northwest side and will march out on the same road until he gets well beyond the enemy's right flank. Then, early on the morning of July 29 and after being reinforced by French's and Bate's divisions, he is to strike the Federal right wing from the rear and crush it. In short, Hood seeks to do to the Army of the Tennessee on July 29 what he was unable to do a week earlier. To make sure that it is done this time, he has assigned the task to Stewart, whose troops performed so magnificently on the twentieth.

Hood also is aware, thanks to reports from Wheeler, of Stoneman's raid. Initially, on the basis of these reports, Hood thought it was a small affair and therefore instructed Wheeler only to "detach what force you can spare" to counter it. Then, as he learned of its true nature, he directed Wheeler to "go yourself in pursuit of the enemy" with "such force as you may deem sufficient." This Wheeler has done, taking two divisions totaling approximately 3,000 troopers.

Hood, who as yet does not know about McCook's expedition, assumes that Wheeler will dispose of Stoneman easily enough. His primary concern is with the situation west of Atlanta. Should his new plan succeed, it will cripple the Federals so badly that they will cease to be a threat to the city for the time being, if not permanently. There is no reason, moreover, why it should not succeed. Unlike the previous two attacks, ample time has been allotted for the units who are making it to get into position—twenty-four hours in the case of Stewart. Of even greater importance, the whole operation will be carried out by commanders who, unlike Hardee, believe in aggressive tactics. All that is necessary is that Stewart's and Lee's troops fight with spirit and determination. As Hood has stated in a general order issued to his army two days earlier, "You have but to will it, and God will grant us the victory your commander and your country expect."[97]

At early dawn on July 28, Howard resumes his deployment. By late morning all of Blair's corps is in position along the ridge facing east, and Wood's division of the XV Corps has gone into line next to it near a small frame building that

Stephen Dill Lee (*Photographic History*, 10:91)

the local Methodists who built it call Ezra Church or Chapel. Harrow's and Morgan Smith's divisions, formed in line of battle, advance southward until they reach another ridge that runs westward from the church and is about a half-mile north of the Lick Skillet road. Their skirmishers, who have been encountering stiff resistance from dismounted Rebel cavalry, move toward the road, which runs in a generally northwest direction from Atlanta.

Suddenly several cannon shots ring out, and Howard hears the "rattle of grapeshot" in the trees and sees limbs falling to the ground. He turns to Sherman, who has just ridden up, and says that there is going to be a battle and soon. Sherman answers that he does not think so, but Howard, convinced that he is about to be attacked, instructs Logan to have his troops fortify their positions. They do so, quickly erecting barricades of rails, logs, and (in the case of some of Wood's men) pews taken from the church. Sherman watches them a while, then he leaves after again telling Howard that he doubts that the Confederates will attack him but that if they do, Howard need not worry about his right flank: Davis's division of the XIV Corps has been ordered to move by way of Turner's Ferry toward East Point and thus will be coming up from the west at any time.

Off to the south, Stephen Lee rides along the Lick Skillet road at the head of Brown's (Hindman's) Division, which is followed by Clayton's. Lee is thirty, from Charleston, South Carolina, and was a West Point classmate of Howard's. Prior to serving as a cavalry and then a departmental commander in Mississippi-Alabama, he had been an artillery officer in Virginia and at Vicksburg, where he had become a prisoner until exchanged. Never before has he headed a large force of infantry, and his sole experience in conducting a battle had occurred two weeks ago at Tupelo, with results that have been described.

About 12:30 P.M., Morgan Smith's troops, on Logan's right, hear "fearful yells, fierce and numerous," coming from the woods to the south. They have heard that sound before—the last time was six days ago from the very same Confederates—and they know what it signifies. All along the ridge they either kneel or lie down behind their improvised parapets of rails and logs, rifles cocked. "Take steady aim," their officers caution them, "and fire low at the word."

They do not have to wait long. First the skirmish line comes scampering back, then swarms of Rebs appear, all screeching the "cornbread yelp." Three of Brown's brigades assail Smith's division. Repulsed, they try again and are repulsed again. Only on the extreme right do Brantly's Mississippians manage to seize a weakly held hill by charging it from the west. But a counterattack, organized and led by Major Taylor, quickly retakes the hill, "more by noise than numbers" according to Taylor. In his report, Brantly explains that his brigade

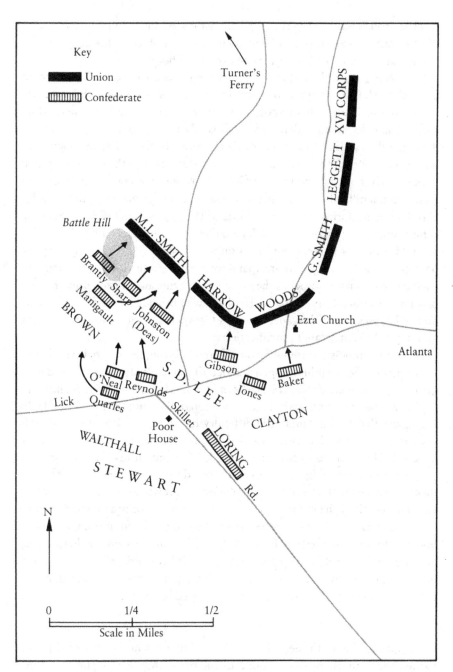

Battle of Ezra Church, July 28

had been too "weakened by the killed and wounded and the innumerable cases of utter exhaustion among the best men . . . as well as by the absence of a goodly number who had no legitimate excuse" to hold it.

Lee, seeing Brown's assault falter, tells his inspector general, Lieutenant Colonel E. H. Cunningham, to go to Clayton's Division and move it forward at once. Cunningham, without notifying Clayton or even Brigadier General Randall Gibson, its commander, orders Gibson's Louisiana Brigade to attack. Although the Louisianans, as one of them writes the following day, "smell the biggest kind of rot," they advance "at a quick step" against the Federals around Ezra Church (Harrow's and some of Wood's troops) and come in sight of their works atop a hill, whereupon they lie down and engage them in a fire fight for about an hour, during which two-thirds of the brigade's left wing is "used up completely." At Gibson's behest, Clayton then sends in Baker's Brigade, only to see it "driven back in confusion" as soon as it comes under fire. Perceiving the obvious—that his troops are incapable of charging, much less breaking, the enemy line—Clayton suspends the assault and withdraws Gibson's and Baker's brigades and puts Bushrod Jones's (Holtzclaw's) Brigade into a defensive position. Clayton's fourth brigade, Stovall's Georgians, is not with him, having been left behind in Atlanta's fortifications.

Despite the repulses suffered by Brown and Clayton, Lee still believes that he has caught the Federals in the open and that they need "only to be attacked with spirit to be put to utter rout." Hence he orders up Manigault's Brigade, hitherto in reserve; then he points to the highest portion of the Union-held ridge and tells Manigault that he will "find little difficulty in taking it." Brown seconds this assertion, declaring that Sharp carried a similar objective when his brigade attacked. Thus assured by his commanders, Manigault leads his men forward. Twice they go up the ridge; twice they are forced to retreat, even though some of them penetrate the enemy ranks. Concluding that it would be a waste of lives to continue attacking, he withdraws out of range, only to be ordered by Lee to go forward yet again. He obeys, resolved—not to do or die, for it is impossible to do—but to die while trying. Fortunately for him and his troops, before they advance far, Brown dashes up and countermands Lee's orders (which, however, does not prevent Brown from writing in his report three days later that "the greater portion [of] Manigault's brigade behaved badly").

Two miles to the north, near Thomas's headquarters in the rear of the XIV Corps, Sherman listens to the sound of the battle that he thought would not take place. When a member of General Richard Johnson's staff asks what it means, he replies: "Logan is feeling for them and I guess he has found them."

Then one of Howard's aides gallops up and reports that the Confederates are making a heavy assault on the XV Corps. "Good!" Sherman exclaims. "That is fine—just what I wanted, just what I wanted. Tell Howard to invite them to attack, it will save us trouble, save us trouble, they'll only beat their brains out, beat their brains out." As he says this, an idea occurs to him. Instead of having Davis's division merely cover Howard's western flank, why not use it to hit the Rebel flank? In that way Hood, who obviously has tried to ambush him, will be ambushed himself.

Accompanied by Palmer, Sherman rides to Davis's headquarters where, to his dismay, he discovers that Davis is sick in bed and that General Morgan, who has assumed command, has set out for Turner's Ferry some five hours ago. "I wish to God," Sherman says to Palmer, "Davis was in command of his division today." Hearing this remark, Davis emerges from his room, declares that he will resume command, then dresses and mounts his horse, only to faint and almost fall from the saddle. One of Davis's staff officers thereupon rides off to inform Morgan that the Confederates have attacked Howard's right and that he is to hasten to that point via the Turner's Ferry road.

Lee is frantically trying to rally his troops—Howard recognizes him riding back and forth—but to no avail. They refuse to go forward again, many head in the opposite direction, and still more huddle in ravines. Then Stewart appears on the scene, leading Walthall's and Loring's divisions. Lee informs him of what has happened, claims that the Federals are "still within easy range of the Lick Skillet road," and asserts that they "would yield before a vigorous attack." He also tells Stewart, or gives him the impression, that Hood wants him to "attack the enemy's right flank." This is a lie. Lee has just received a dispatch from Shoup directing him "to prevent the enemy from gaining the Lick Skillet road, and not to attack unless the enemy exposes himself in attacking us."

Stewart agrees to join in the battle. If there is an opportunity to defeat the Yankees here and now, as Lee says, then it should be exploited. "To succeed," Stewart had announced to his troops four days ago, "we must work hard and fight hard—and many of us must die." Besides, how can he continue his march to the west along the Lick Skillet road when, according to Lee, the Yankees are in position to seize it? He might be cut off from the rest of the army. Therefore he orders Walthall, whose division is in the van, to assault the Union right and push it back toward Ezra Church. *

*Hood (38 OR 3:632) states he ordered Stewart to assist Lee in the attack, but both Lee and Stewart in their reports (ibid., 763, 872) indicate that Stewart joined in the battle at Lee's request and because Stewart saw that Lee needed help. Moreover, Shoup's dispatches to

Walthall forms his troops between the road and the Poor house, with Cantey's Brigade (still commanded by Colonel O'Neal) on the left, Reynolds's Brigade on the right, and Quarles's Brigade behind Cantey's to provide both a reserve and protection for his left flank. At about 2 P.M., having been "informed that my right would be protected by troops of another command" (Clayton's Division), Walthall begins advancing. After going a "short distance," he beholds the enemy, "in strong position and large force on a hill."

The hill is the same one that Brantly's men have briefly held. Contrary to Walthall's impression, it is defended, not by a "large force," but by four regiments of Lightburn's brigade, so small in numbers that they do not even have a continuous line and so must rely on cross fire to cover the gaps in it. Furthermore they have been so busy fighting that they have had neither the time nor the energy to construct any kind of defensive works and indeed are in "the open." Conscious of the value and vulnerability of the hill, which anchors his right, and having seen no sign of Davis's promised division in that quarter, Howard has summoned ten of Blair's regiments and four of Dodge's to back up Lightburn's brigade and has posted no less than twenty-six cannons so that they can sweep the entire area to the west.

O'Neal's and Reynolds's troops attack with the same vigor and persistence they displayed eight days ago at Peachtree Creek. Only a detachment of 150 "mechanics" from the arsenal at Columbus, Georgia, which has been assigned to Reynolds's undersized brigade, fails to behave, Reynolds drily comments in his report, "with the coolness and courage of veterans." They charge repeatedly and, when not charging, maintain a heavy fire at close range. Equally stubborn, Lightburn's men return shot for shot, and then some. After being relieved by the 81st Ohio from Dodge's corps and retiring to the rear, Major Taylor's Buckeyes clean the powder-clogged barrels of their rifles by urinating down them.

All the while the support that Walthall had been promised for his right has been conspicuous by its absence. Finally Walthall calls both Lee's and Stewart's attention to this fact, with the result that Lee sends word that he will at once order in a brigade on Walthall's right. On hearing this, Walthall brings up Quarles's Brigade and puts it into line on his left. Its entrance into the fray so alarms Howard, who fears that the enemy might, "by continually throwing in fresh troops," wear his men down, that he reinforces Morgan Smith with two of Dodge's regiments and calls on Sherman for help from (he has no qualms on this score) the Army of the Cumberland. At first Sherman denies Howard's request on the grounds that Morgan soon will arrive with Davis's division, but when Howard renews it, Sherman sends him one of Palmer's brigades.

---

both generals during the afternoon demonstrate that Hood was not aware of what was happening on the Lick Skillet road (ibid., 5:919–20).

By the time it arrives, it no longer is needed. Walthall, still lacking support on his right, informs Stewart that he must retreat. Stewart agrees, but instructs him to hold on until Loring's Division can deploy behind him so as to resist a Federal counterattack, should that occur. This Walthall does; then he withdraws, his troops passing through Loring's lines. Suddenly Stewart reels in his saddle, struck in the head by a deflected bullet. A few minutes later, Loring also suffers a disabling wound, whereupon Walthall assumes command of both divisions. Soon afterward he receives a message from Shoup, addressed to Stewart and marked 3:25 P.M. It states that Hood "desires you to hold the enemy, but not to do more fighting than necessary, unless you should get a decided advantage." Walthall sends it back to Hood's headquarters without comment.[98]

For the Confederates the battle is over. It could be continued on the Federal side by Howard's launching a counterattack or by Morgan's making the flank movement that Sherman has directed or by having Thomas's and Schofield's forces attempt to storm Atlanta's defenses in hopes that Hood has so weakened them for his offensive against Howard that they can be carried. None of these things happens. Howard considers "sweeping the field" and then "making a bold push for Atlanta," but he quickly drops the idea. He has made a fine beginning as commander of the Army of the Tennessee, so why jeopardize it? Morgan, after getting the order to link up with Howard's right, spends the afternoon wandering about the woods and swamps southwest of Atlanta and finally bivouacs for the night, still far away. As for storming Atlanta, once it was clear that the Confederates had concentrated a large force against Howard, Sherman instructed Schofield and Stanley to explore the practicability of assaulting the city from the east, only to be told by the former that "the enemy has met me in strong works with a good deal of artillery, and men enough to resist assault," and by the latter that "I think any attack upon their main line, excepting by a regular, well-managed assaulting column," would fail. Stanley and Schofield are correct. Although by late afternoon Atlanta's fortifications are held by only four divisions and the militia, they now are extremely formidable and buttressed by large numbers of well-sited artillery—fifty-three cannons in Cleburne's one-and-a-half-mile sector alone. Moreover, Sherman's soldiers are in no mood for frontal attacks against these defenses. Yesterday a mere rumor that such an attack had been ordered caused a veteran of McCook's brigade, a soldier with an impeccable record, to shoot himself in the wrist.[99]

In the evening, Hood telegraphs the War Department a brief report on the battle: "The enemy commenced extending his right about 8 this morning, driving in our cavalry. Lieutenant Generals Stewart and Lee were directed to

Logan's troops repelling the Confederate attack at Ezra Church *(Leslie's Weekly)*

hold the Lick Skillet road for the day with a portion of their commands. About 1:30 o'clock a sharp engagement ensued with no decided advantage to either side. We still occupy the Lick Skillet road." This, of course, is nonsense and lying nonsense at that. It can only be explained, but not excused, by the well-known reluctance of all generals to admit defeat, particularly when they feel, as Hood must in this case, that the defeat is not their fault. The true tale of what will be called the Battle of Ezra Church lies in stark statistics. Howard's loss totals 632 killed, wounded, and missing, all but 70 in the XV Corps. In contrast, Walthall's Division alone has lost, according to his report, "152 officers and nearly 1,000 men," 514 of them in Quarles's Brigade; Brown's, 807; and Clayton's, 600, with all but 120 being contributed by Gibson's Louisianans. If one adds, by conservative estimate, 150 casualties for Armstrong's Brigade, which opposed Howard's advance toward the Lick Skillet road, and for Bushrod Jones's troops and Loring's Division, both of which saw some action late in the battle, then altogether the Confederate loss comes close to 3,000. This is nearly five times that of the Federals. Little wonder that the ground in front of Morgan Smith's division, where the fiercest fighting occurred, is dotted with pools of blood. George Girton of the 47th Ohio, who has seen many battlefields, "never saw the [Rebel] dead lying so thick in my life—they are almost in piles—looking as though they had been swept down whole ranks at a time." Virtually all of the gray-clad corpses, moreover, bear the marks of bullets; only a few of Howard's cannons saw action, and that not until toward the end of the battle.[100]

Historians will blame Hood for this slaughter. The true culprit is Stephen Lee. Disregarding his instructions and ignoring subsequent orders, he attempted to crush Sherman's supposedly vulnerable right flank with impromptu and disjointed attacks by his own and Stewart's troops long after the failure of the first one demonstrated that they stood no chance of success—the exact duplicate of his conduct two weeks ago at Tupelo, from which experience he obviously has learned nothing. What he should have done is what Hood had directed him to do—simply keep open the Lick Skillet road for the passage of Stewart's forces, which he could have accomplished easily enough by driving back Logan's skirmishers, then establishing a defensive line northeast of the road. It is extremely unlikely that Howard would have attacked, much less broken through, such a line. Also, since Logan's main force was a half-mile from the road and unable to see it because of the intervening forest, the Union artillery could not have prevented Stewart from using it, as in fact he did. Lee's attack served no necessary purpose and should never have been made.

Some historians also contend that Hood should have personally supervised Lee's and Stewart's movement, thereby maintaining control over it and preventing it from turning into the bloody fiasco that it became. This criticism, however ignores the strong possibility that Hood, had he been present, would have reacted as Lee did to the apparent opportunity to hit the Federals in the flank while they were still weak and unentrenched: Hood's report justifies Lee's decision to attack, and his memoirs approvingly quote Lee's explanation of why the attack failed, namely, that it was not made with sufficient vigor and cohesion. Moreover, why should Hood have been out on the Lick Skillet road at noontime on July 28? He was not expecting a battle that day but was planning one for the next day, to which end he was, as he should have been, at his headquarters, engaged in redeploying his army so that it could attack the enemy's rear and at the same time defend Atlanta from the enemy in front. Thus planning and engaged, he did not realize (as Shoup's afternoon dispatches to Lee and Stewart demonstrate) that a full-fledged battle was taking place near Ezra Church until it was nearly over. When he did learn about it and also that Stewart and Loring were *hors de combat,* he put Cheatham in command of Stewart's Corps and sent Hardee to take charge of affairs on the Lick Skillet road. By the time that Hardee arrived, which probably was toward dusk, the fighting had ended, and there was nothing he could do. It would have been the same had Hood gone there in person.

Hood's true mistake on July 28 was basically the same one that he committed on July 22—trying to do more than his army, unless favored by extraordinarily good luck, was capable of doing: namely, delivering a successful offensive blow against an enemy as strong, tough, and experienced as the Army of the Tennessee (or for that matter any comparable portion of Sherman's forces). Even had Stewart been able to march to Howard's rear, it is doubtful that he could have delivered a successful assault, given Howard's precautions, the proximity of the XIV and XX corps, and the presence of Davis's division in what would have become Stewart's own rear. Hood would have done better simply to have extended his lines out along the Lick Skillet road, which, falsely and significantly, is what he claims in his report to have been seeking to do. That way he would have accomplished at little cost all that he has achieved at an excessive price: blocking, for the time being, Sherman's push toward the Macon railroad. As it is, Hood has suffered, even though it is not his fault as such, another defeat, the third in a row and the most one-sided of all, a defeat that can only have a demoralizing effect on troops already depressed by futile attacks with heavy losses. When, after surveying the heaps of Rebel dead lying in front of Lightburn's brigade, Major Taylor asks a captured Confederate officer how many men Hood has left, he receives this bitter, sarcastic reply: "Hood has about enough left to make two killings."

Like Peachtree Creek and Bald Hill, Ezra Church is a battle that Sherman did not expect to fight and that was won more in spite of what he did than because of what he did. It also, from a strategic standpoint, is a frustrating affair for him, in that his attempt to get at the railroad between Atlanta and East Point has failed, as has his effort to hit the Confederates in their left flank while they assailed his right flank. Nevertheless, thanks to Howard's caution and the fighting skills of the Army of the Tennessee, he has gained another big defensive victory, which, in sharp contrast to Hood's troops, heightens the already high morale and confidence of his troops. The men of the XV Corps in particular feel elated over shooting down so many Rebs—they estimate the enemy loss as being at least 5,000—while suffering relatively few casualties themselves. "I am tired of seeing such butchery," Captain Wills writes in his diary, "but if they will charge us that way once a day for a week, this corps will end the war in this section. . . . We are in excellent spirits, and propose to take Atlanta whenever Sherman wants it."[101]

Part Seven: Brown's Mill and Sunshine Church

What Howard's infantry was unable to do Sherman now hopes, indeed expects, Stoneman's and McCook's cavalry to achieve: cut Hood's railroad lifeline to the south, compelling him either to evacuate Atlanta or to come out again to fight for it, most likely the latter. Shortly after 9 P.M. he telegraphs Thomas (wires have been run to his and Schofield's headquarters), directing him to form a reserve and have it ready to move at a moment's notice, for "our cavalry surely will reach the Macon road tonight, and tomorrow the enemy will do something desperate."

But Sherman's cavalry is not going to reach the Macon road tonight. McCook, in fact, still has not reached Fayetteville, about seven miles from Lovejoy's Station, having spent the evening tearing up track of the Atlanta and West Point Railroad around Palmetto and then burning a 500-wagon Confederate baggage train on the road to Fayetteville, taking hundreds of prisoners and killing (with sabers) more than 1,000 mules in the process. Stoneman, on the other hand, is at Monticello, forty road miles southeast of Lovejoy's and separated from it by the broad Ocmulgee River. Obviously McCook will not make it to the Macon railroad before morning, and Stoneman cannot get there until much later than that.

The explanation for McCook's being behind schedule is simple enough: in addition to being delayed by ripping up rails at Palmetto and destroying the baggage train, he had not managed to cross the Chattahoochee at Smith's Ferry, which had to be done on a pontoon bridge, until mid-afternoon. Stoneman's presence at Monticello, on the other hand, is a more complex matter. On the morning of July 28, after reaching Covington (where his Kentucky troopers got drunk on whiskey and brandy left unconsumed by Garrard's men during their visit to that town), he had headed, not southwest toward McDonough, but due south to Monticello, which he had reached in the evening. Monticello is on a road leading directly to Macon, thirty miles further south. Stoneman has no intention of meeting McCook at Lovejoy's Station. Back in the spring of 1863 Stoneman had held the command of the cavalry of the Army of the Potomac, only to lose it in disgrace because of his mishandling of his assignment during the Chancellorsville campaign. Ever since joining Sherman's army he has repeatedly sought to restore his reputation by a brilliant exploit and has repeatedly failed, with the latest setback being the aborted raid on the Atlanta and West Point prior to the advance on Atlanta. Now he believes he has a chance to carry out the most spectacular cavalry foray of the war, one that will make him a hero in the North, and he is not going to pass it up. McCook can take care of the Macon railroad and of himself.

If Stoneman knew what Wheeler is doing, he would be even more confident of getting to Macon and Andersonville. During the morning, Wheeler, upon learning that Garrard was at Flat Rock, had gone there (just as Stoneman hoped) and surrounded him, thereby forcing him to make a breakout and retreat northward to Lithonia. Next, late in the evening, having been notified by Shoup that McCook was heading for the Macon railroad, Wheeler had set out for Jonesboro with two brigades to intercept him after ordering three other brigades under Brigadier General Alfred Iverson to move toward McDonough for the purpose of doing the same to Stoneman. Wheeler supposes that Stoneman, whom he knows has turned south from Covington, intends to strike at the Macon line by way of McDonough and, despite what he later claims in his report, does not suspect that Stoneman's actual objective is Macon. Thus, as July 28 comes to an end, not only is Stoneman not being pursued by Wheeler, but the Confederate cavalry is far to his rear and marching away from him.

Early on the morning of July 29, McCook's column reaches Lovejoy's Station. Here it rips up two and a half miles of track and tears down five miles of telegraph wire. Then, there being no sign of Stoneman and having learned that Wheeler is approaching from the northeast, at 2 P.M. it starts back to the Chattahoochee by way of Fayetteville. Two miles from the railroad some of Jackson's troopers attack it in front. Beating them off, it then swerves toward Newnan, only to be assailed from the rear by Wheeler, now in hot pursuit. Throughout the night and on into the next day a running battle takes place. Finally, in the afternoon, Wheeler, Jackson, and a brigade of dismounted Alabama cavalry, which was on the way to Atlanta by train to serve as infantry, corner the raiders at Brown's Mill southwest of Newnan. The Federals attempt to break through and for a moment appear to succeed, scattering Ross's Texans and even capturing Ross himself. But then more Confederates come up, drive them back, and rescue Ross and the other prisoners. McCook, realizing that he is trapped, thereupon orders his men to escape any way they can. Most of them, including McCook, manage to slip through the enemy lines, then in small groups cross the Chattahoochee at various points. Even so, McCook's loss totals about 600, virtually all of them captives, and his division has been wrecked.

This very same afternoon, Stoneman gazes across the Ocmulgee River at Macon. Although, unbeknownst to him, the Confederates have sent off the prisoners at Camp Oglethorpe to forestall their liberation, the town contains an arsenal, a cannon foundry, warehouses, and the termini of three railroads, the destruction of which would make it difficult if not impossible for Hood to hold on at Atlanta. To get at these things and to find the glory he is seeking, he has to get to the other side of the river. He had hoped to pass over it much farther to the north at Planter's Factory, but the bridge that he had thought was there proved not to be, as also was the case at two alternative crossing points. Hence he now has no choice but to try to make it over by way of the railroad bridge and a nearby pontoon bridge that span the river east of Macon.

To prevent him from doing this, portly, pork-eating Major General Howell Cobb, the Confederate commandant at Macon, has assembled a motley force of 2,500 regular troops, home guards, and convalescents from the military hospitals, whom he has placed behind a line of breastworks covering the bridges. In addition, he has two artillery batteries, one of them next to Fort Hawkins, a log blockhouse originally built to guard against Indian raids, which is located on a hill immediately in front of the bridges. With him are Governor Joe Brown and, acting as an unofficial military advisor, General Joe Johnston.

Had Stoneman showed up at Macon yesterday afternoon—something he easily could have done, for the town is only thirty-some miles from Monticello, where he halted on the night of July 28—he would have faced virtually no opposition. The reason he did not is that he tarried on the march while detachments struck at the railroads around Milledgeville and while his troopers filled their saddlebags with loot and themselves with liquor taken from houses along the way. Assuming that Wheeler had gone after Garrard and McCook, Stoneman believed that there was little or no danger of pursuit, and he still believes this.

Perceiving that the Fort Hawkins hill is the key to the Rebel defense of Macon, Stoneman has his two Rodman guns bombard it, then orders Colonel Silas Adams's Kentucky brigade to charge on foot and seize it. This is a mistake. Throughout the campaign the Kentuckians (whose enlistments soon will expire) have distinguished themselves by their abhorrence of discipline, their fondness for whiskey, their propensity for plundering, and their chronic reluctance to engage in serious fighting, particularly when dismounted. Today they remain true to form as their "attack" on the hill consists of running toward it and then running back as soon as they come under fire. For another hour Stoneman's cannons endeavor to silence the battery on the hill—maybe then Adams's men will be able to carry it—but to no avail, and the shells they occasionally lob into Macon prove equally ineffective. At the end of that hour, Stoneman accepts the harsh fact that as much as he wants Macon and the glory that will come with it, they are not to be had, and that he also will have to forget about the even-greater glory to be gained from freeing the Andersonville prisoners.

Hence, ordering his men back into their saddles, Stoneman marches southward, evidently with the intention of passing through Georgia to Union-held Pensacola. But before he has gone far, a scout brings word—false, as it turns out—that a large number of enemy cavalry are entering Macon. Fearful that this force might intercept him before he can reach the ferry south of the town, where he plans to cross the Ocmulgee, he reverses course and heads north on the same road by which he came. At nightfall he reaches Clinton, twelve miles above Macon. From here a road branches east to Milledgeville, where it joins a road that leads to the rear of Sherman's army. Earlier he had said that he planned to take this route. Now, despite the protests of his brigade commanders, he insists on continuing north. The enemy, he argues, expect him to go by way of Milledgeville, whereas once he gets to Hillsboro, a mere eight miles farther, he will have the "choice of three roads at daylight."

A short distance beyond Clinton the advance guard encounters Rebel skirmishers. Their opposition becomes so strong that Stoneman calls a halt two miles from Hillsboro. As soon as it is daylight he resumes his march. After about a mile and a half, near Sunshine Church, he comes upon a log barricade that straddles the road and is shaped in the form of an inverted V. Behind the barricade, dismounted for battle, are Iverson's three brigades of Confederate cavalry.

Iverson, a thirty-five-year-old Georgian who once commanded an infantry brigade in the Army of Northern Virginia, learned on the night of July 29 that Stoneman, instead of going toward McDonough as Wheeler assumed he would, was moving south from Covington. Unsure as to Stoneman's objective—it might be Milledgeville or Macon or some point on the Macon and Western Railroad—Iverson wisely sent out scouts to ascertain what it was before pursuing. On the morning of July 30 they reported that the raiders had passed through Monticello. Iverson, who as a native of Clinton knows central Georgia intimately, concluded that Stoneman was heading for Macon and set out after him. It was one of his brigades that delayed and then stopped Stoneman's march during the night, thereby gaining time for the other two brigades to construct the V-shaped barricade.

Stoneman orders his men to make a breakthrough attack. It fails, with the Kentuckians again showing no inclination to close with the enemy. All morning and into the afternoon both sides take turns charging each other. Then on instructions from Iverson, the 1st and 3rd Georgia cavalry regiments circle around behind the Federals, causing them to think that the Confederate force at Macon has come up in their rear. Next, one of Iverson's batteries opens up an enfilading fire against their left. Most of Stoneman's troopers run back to their horses, mount, and then gallop off to the northeast, easily penetrating a thin line of Rebel skirmishers. Only Stoneman himself and about 700 remaining men continue the struggle. For awhile, with the aid of the two Rodmans, they hold out atop a hill. Then the big guns fire their last shells. Members of Stoneman's staff urge him to surrender. He agrees. A few minutes later he hands his sword to a Georgia colonel after vainly demanding that Iverson come for it in person. He then sits down on a log and buries his tear-streaked face in his hands.[102]

Stoneman should weep. He is responsible for the destruction of both his own and McCooks' divisions, close to two-thirds of Sherman's available cavalry. Furthermore, what he had endeavored to do was utterly unrealistic. As early as July 20 the Confederates had begun to build fortifications at Andersonville to protect against a cavalry raid, and it is doubtful that Stoneman's troopers, given their poor performance at Macon, would have broken through them even had they reached the place. But suppose Stoneman had freed the prisoners at Macon

George Stoneman: instead of glory, tears (William A. Crafts, *The Southern Rebellion* [Boston: S. Walker, 1870], 223)

and Andersonville: What then? Conceivably he could have mounted and armed most of the officers at Macon's Camp Oglethorpe and taken them with him, but the vast majority of the 30,000-plus prisoners at Andersonville's Camp Sumter (the official name of the place where they were confined) would have been on foot, unarmed, half-starved, and sick with dysentery and other diseases. They could not possibly have made it through a hundred miles of enemy territory to Sherman's army or, the sole alternative, to Pensacola, where presumably Stoneman would have headed. The prisoners would have had to try to escape on their own, and while so trying, Confederate cavalry, militia, home guards, and citizens would have recaptured practically all of those whom they did not kill. Finally, there is some indication that the guards at Andersonville had been prepared, should Union cavalry raiders approach or should the inmates attempt to break out, to sweep the prison compound with cannon fire. Thus, for example, on July 28, according to the diary of a Michigan prisoner, "In order to terrify the prisoners, the rebels throwed a solid shot over camp this afternoon."[103]

Sherman should have perceived, as in fact he belatedly will after its failure, that Stoneman's scheme to liberate the captives at Macon and Andersonville was inherently impracticable and therefore should have refused to give him permission to attempt it. Sherman should have, instead, explicitly directed Stoneman to link up with McCook as quickly as possible for the sole purpose of wreaking maximum havoc on the Macon railroad. This, in all likelihood, would have avoided the debacles that have befallen McCook and Stoneman, for their combined divisions could have held Wheeler's pursuit in check until they reached Union lines. As it is, the Confederates have gained one of the biggest cavalry victories of the war, thanks to Wheeler's vigor, Iverson's enterprise, Stoneman's glory-hunting and blunders, his men's lack of fighting spirit, and Sherman's chronic mishandling of mounted forces (see appendix B). Furthermore the Confederates already are rapidly relaying the rails that McCook's troopers ripped up at Lovejoy's and repairing the damage done by detachments from Stoneman's column to the track and bridges around Macon and Milledgeville. Far from compelling Hood to "do something desperate," the raid merely has made it easier for him to do something he had been planning to do anyway.[104]

"Truly this morning," captain Key writes in his diary for July 31, "appears like the Sabbath, for there is almost a perfect calm along the lines around the city." This unnatural quiet—so it seems to the soldiers—ends at noon when the opposing skirmishers and batteries resume their normal activities. The only new thing is that the Confederates begin firing "huge shells" that throw up geysers of dirt and rock when they explode and, when they don't, are found by curious Federals to weigh sixty-four pounds. (They come from long-range 3-inch rifles that Johnston had arranged to be brought to Atlanta from the fortifications at Mobile.) Toward 4 P.M. the heavy clouds that have darkened the sky all day open up, "pouring their watery substance upon the dirty and wearied soldiers in the entrenchments." For several hours, thunder and lightning mingle with the roar and flashes of the big guns. Then in the evening the rain subsides, and so, too, does the shower of shells and bullets. After a while, from behind the Union works north of Atlanta, the band of the 79th Pennsylvania plays a Sunday concert, sending forth "on the cool, calm night air sweet strains of music to cheer and comfort friend and foe alike."[105]

And so, hot and bloody July ends. The Confederate flag still flies, defiantly, over Atlanta. But for how much longer? That is the question being asked by Sherman's and Hood's troops, as well as by all Northerners and Southerners. Perhaps August will bring the answer.

CHAPTER EIGHT

AUGUST

Part One: North and South

GEN. GRANT'S ARMY

THE GREAT BATTLE BEFORE PETERSBURG

DISASTROUS RESULTS

THE ARMY DEFEATED AND FORCED TO RETIRE

CAUSE OF REPULSE

THE NEGRO TROOPS BECOME

PANIC-STRICKEN AND DEMORALIZED

FEARFUL SLAUGHTER

THESE HEADLINES in the *New York World* of August 2 report what soon becomes known as the Battle of the Crater. On July 30, Grant attempted literally to blast a way into Petersburg by setting off a giant powder mine beneath a Rebel fort. The explosion ripped a four-hundred-yard-wide hole in Lee's defenses. Union assault forces could have and should have poured through unopposed. Instead, cowardly and drunken commanders allowed them to mill about in the crater until a savage Confederate counterattack drove them back and inflicted 4,000 casualties, many of them on black troops who were massacred in a scene reminiscent of Fort Pillow. Adding disgrace to disaster, on that same day, Southern cavalry, having galloped unopposed into Pennsylvania, burned the town of Chambersburg when its citizens refused to pay $500,000 in greenbacks or $100,000 in gold as compensation for Yankee depredations in Virginia.

Employing their best "we told you so" style, the Democrats proclaim the Crater fiasco to be further proof that Grant, despite his geographical proximity, is no closer to taking Richmond than he had been three months ago, and they point to Chambersburg as demonstrating that the North itself "is almost defenseless." A large Rebel army, warns the *Chicago Times*, is already in Maryland, marching on Pittsburgh and Wheeling, and "if successful" it will head for Cincinnati: "The South stands upon the verge of victory," all because of the "blundering, incompetent, and fanatical" Lincoln administration "which has continually stood between the people and an honorable peace."

In public the Republicans do their best to minimize the Petersburg and Chambersburg debacles. The former, asserts the *Cincinnati Commercial,* merely is a "simple repulse at a single point of assault." The second, argues the *New York Times,* does not mean that Lee is about to invade the North again; but if he does, the Army of the Potomac will be delighted to engage him "out of his earthworks" in "equal combat." Privately, however, Republicans are stricken with gloom over what has happened and its inevitable impact on public opinion. Thus George Templeton Strong, head of the Sanitary Commission in New York, feels "most seriously perturbed by what I hear from independent trustworthy sources about the increasing prevalence of discouragement, and of aspirations for peace 'at any price.'" "Could we," he goes on in desperate tones, "but inspire our people with one-hundredth of the earnestness and resolution the rebel leaders show, all would be well." As it is, he feels "like going south in disguise as the modern Charlotte Corday and shooting Jefferson Davis."[1]

The sole ray of hope for the Republicans comes from Georgia. There, unlike in Virginia, victory seems possible. Indeed, late in July the newspapers, Democratic ones among them, had reported that Atlanta had been occupied, at least in part, and although these stories had proved to be false, there can be no doubting that the Confederates had suffered bloody repulses on July 20, 22, and 28 and that Sherman's cannons are bombarding the Gate City. Surely, therefore, it is only a question of time before it will fall. But how much time? At the end of August the Democrats will hold their long-postponed convention in Chicago. After that the presidential campaign will get under way, with the first crucial voting to take place in Indiana in October. It could be a calamity if the rebel flag is still flying over Atlanta then. If it does, the Democrats almost surely will carry the Hoosier state and, after that, the Midwest and thus the election.

This is why Senator John Sherman has written as follows to his brother the general in a July 24 letter which, if it takes the normal time to travel from Ohio to Georgia, reaches him at the beginning of August:

> We all feel that upon Grant and you, and the armies under your command, the fate of this country depends. If you are successful, it is ardently hoped that peace may follow with a restored union. If you fail, the wisest can hope for nothing but a long train of disasters and the strife of factions. . . . Every one feels that you have done your part nobly. Grant has not had such success. No doubt he has done as well as any one could with his resources and such adversaries. Still he has not taken Richmond, and I fear will not this campaign.

In other words, it now is all up to "Cump": the outcome of the election, the winning of the war, the fate of the nation—everything.[2]

Jefferson Davis understood full well the risk he ran when he replaced Johnston with Hood. Johnston is more than a high-ranking general; he also is the chief rallying point of all of those Southerners who, for whatever reason, dislike the Confederate president and his policies and who blame Davis for all the lost battles, cities, and territory. They were bound to denounce his removal of Johnston, and this they have done most vehemently, declaring that Davis had acted out of a "deliberate and long-abiding personal malignity," that he had denied Johnston the necessary means to defeat Sherman and then blamed him for not doing so, and that he had put the Army of Tennessee, at this time of crisis, under the command of a "young, inexperienced and not very remarkable officer." Only if Hood drives back Sherman or at least forces him into the same sort of stalemate at Atlanta that Lee has achieved against Grant at Richmond can the dismissal of Johnston be vindicated. Should Hood fail and should Atlanta fall, then Davis's critics will appear justified in their denunciations, and his credibility will be badly, perhaps fatally, impaired.[3]

So far, Davis has cause to believe that he is winning his gamble on Hood and with it much more besides. To be sure, Hood's attacks have not achieved all that might be hoped for; evidently they have incurred heavy losses, and Sherman's cannons are pounding Atlanta. Yet Hood has fought, and fought hard; according to his reports, he has dealt the Yankees some punishing blows; and above all he has held Atlanta and shows every sign of continuing to do so. This is more than Johnston would have done. He merely would have found another excuse to retreat, leaving Atlanta to fall into Sherman's hands like a ripe apple dropping from a tree.

That would have been a disaster, the very thing Davis had sought to forestall by removing Johnston. It would have enabled the Yankees to claim that in Georgia they were winning the war. Instead, thanks to Hood's steadfast stand, they cannot point to a significant success anywhere, and in Virginia they themselves are admitting to failure. Consequently their will to persist in their vicious, bloody, but futile effort to conquer the South is dissolving. Proof of this, already great, increases daily. Early's raid to Washington and Grant's latest repulse at Petersburg have sent the gold value of the greenback (that monetary index of Northern morale) plummeting. Lincoln has had to call for 500,000 more troops—that is twice the size of the entire Confederate army—and threatens to conscript them if enough volunteers fail to come forth. In the Midwest, violent anti-draft outbreaks have occurred, and the Federal authorities themselves report the existence of a giant Copperhead conspiracy to break away from the rule of Washington and establish a "Northwestern Confederacy" that would make peace with the Southern Confederacy. In Kentucky and Missouri, guerrilla war runs rampant, and Lincoln's minions hold tenuous sway solely by means of martial law, ruthlessly applied. Throughout the North the Democrats openly exult in Federal defeats and confidently predict victory in the forthcoming elections. Better still, the Republicans manifestly fear that this will happen and so have fallen into disarray, with some of them supporting Frémont, others refusing to back Lincoln, and a growing number urging that Lincoln be replaced with another candidate.

But best of all, Lincoln himself obviously is desperate. First there was the Jacquess-Gilmore mission to Richmond, which had been made with his knowledge and sanction. Then, immediately after that, no less a Republican leader than Horace Greeley and Lincoln's own private secretary, John Hay, had relayed to Confederate agents in Canada a letter from Lincoln offering them safe conduct to and from Washington for the purpose of discussing peace terms. That this offer was conditional on having them first accept the unacceptable—namely, the return of the South to the Union—does not alter the fact that it had been made and that thus twice within a matter of weeks Lincoln had approached the Confederate government in quest of peace. This is not the conduct of a victor or of one who expects victory; it is how someone acts who is losing and knows it.

So the South, in spite of the vast odds against it, in spite of the deep enemy penetrations of its territory, and in spite of the terrible suffering of its people, is outlasting the North; this year of 1864, which had begun in the gloom of impending defeat, can end in the brightness of assured victory. All that needs to be done is to continue to fend off and bleed dry the Yankee invaders for a few more months—just two, at most three, months will do—and the North will abandon out of despair and disunity its foolish attempt to restore a Union that can never be restored and its wicked effort to make slaves out of free white men under the hypocritical guise of freeing black slaves. In Virginia, thanks to Lee and his army, this goal already has been achieved; Grant can only lengthen the list of his defeats and casualties. Forrest stands guard over Mississippi and Alabama, so all will be well there; and in the Trans-Mississippi the Federals dare not emerge from the fortified towns where they seek refuge. Only in Georgia is there still a serious danger that things might turn out badly. Although Sherman has been checked at the gates of Atlanta, he must be driven away from them, and his army must be rendered impotent to return, before the city and all that it represents will be safe. That done, the war will be as good as won. Pray God, give Hood the ability to do it.[4]

Part Two: Utoy Creek

"Today," General Shoup writes in his "Memoranda of daily movements and events in Army of Tennessee" under the heading of August 1, "deserves to be marked with a white stone; good news has flowed in from all distant points." He then proceeds to record a dispatch from Wheeler stating that "we have just completed the killing, capturing, and breaking up of the entire raiding party under General McCook" and a report from Iverson: "General Stoneman, after having his force routed, yesterday surrendered with 500 men. The rest of his command are scattered and flying toward Eatonton. Many have been already killed and captured."[5]

The defeat of McCook's and Stoneman's forays makes more feasible what Hood had decided to do even as they were taking place—namely, to send Wheeler with a large force on a raid against Sherman's railroad supply line. Three times Hood has attempted to crush Sherman's army while it was divided and exposed, and each time he has failed (through no fault of his own he believes). Now that army is united, entrenched, and—barring a bad blunder on its part—no longer vulnerable to attack. Also Sherman obviously is trying to reach the railroad to Macon; if he does, then Atlanta becomes untenable. The best, perhaps the only and certainly the easiest, way to prevent this from happening is to cut his logistical artery first.

On August 2, Hood telegraphs Davis: "Since our late success over the enemy's cavalry I hope now to be able, by interrupting Sherman's communications, either to force him to fight me in position or to retreat. Please give me your advice freely at all times."

Davis welcomes Hood's proposal. Have not both Bragg and he repeatedly urged Johnston to strike Sherman's supply line with Wheeler's abundant cavalry instead of calling for Forrest to do it? Moreover he has received fuller, more accurate information about the losses in the July battles than was contained in Hood's ambiguous bulletins and Bragg's deceptive reports and so now knows the high price that has been paid in irreplaceable manpower for keeping the Yankees out of Atlanta. Hence on August 5, Davis telegraphs Hood:

> I concur in your plan, and hope you[r] cavalry will be able to destroy the railroad bridges and depots of the enemy on the line to Bridgeport, so as to compel the enemy to attack you in position or retreat. The loss consequent upon attacking him in his entrenchments requires you to avoid that if practicable. . . . If he can be forced to retreat for want of supplies he will be in the worst condition to escape or resist your pursuing army.

This gives Hood, as he no doubt expected, the president's sanction for the Wheeler raid. Does he and does Davis realize that in effect they have adopted

"Little Joe" Wheeler (*Photographic History,* 10:249)

Johnston's premise that the Army of Tennessee cannot realistically hope, except under the most favorable circumstances, to defeat Sherman's forces in offensive battle and that therefore the best if not the only way it can drive them out of Georgia is to make it impossible for them to live there by breaking their iron link to Chattanooga and Nashville? Probably not; certainly they never admit to it. As they see it, they merely are doing what Johnston could and should have done long ago.

The great danger is that now it might be too late. It will take time for Wheeler, whose troopers still are chasing McCook's and Stoneman's remnants, to get under way, and it will take longer yet for the raid to achieve its desired effect. Meanwhile Hood must continue to cling to Atlanta and the railroad that feeds his army. For this purpose he has approximately 56,000 men "present for duty." Although this is only 4,000 fewer than he had had on assuming command, about 5,000 of this number are militia, and more than 12,000 are cavalry, the greater portion of whom will be going off with Wheeler. Moreover, despite his efforts to fatten their thin ranks with clerks, teamsters, and the like, the front-line infantry and artillery total just 33,000—a drop of 6,000 since July 10. Finally, most of the infantry brigades are little larger and often are much smaller than regiments are supposed to be, and owing to the extremely heavy casualties among officers in the July battles, they sometimes are headed by men of dubious competency. For example, the alcoholic Deas again commands his brigade (all three of his successors having fallen in action), and the highly intellectual but rather ineffectual Colonel Charles Olmstead has taken over from the ailing Mercer, even though Cleburne, to whose division Mercer's Brigade has been assigned, deems Olmstead "not efficient."[6] (Ironically, in his memoirs, Olmstead praises Cleburne and proudly asserts that the Irishman had requested that Mercer's Brigade be added to his division. It is to be hoped that Olmstead, who lived until 1926, never saw Cleburne's critical comment about him.)

Accompanying the Army of Tennessee's decline in fighting strength is an ominous decline in fighting spirit. Its rank and file do not realize, nor would it make much difference to them if they did, that in all of his attacks Hood has sought to hit the Federals in the flank or rear or before they could fully fortify and that he has not been altogether unsuccessful in doing these things. What they do know is that sooner or later they have ended up making frontal assaults on dug-in foes and that, in the words of Captain Chambers, they have paid "a fearful sacrifice of men." Their total loss since July 18 comes to approximately 12,000 killed, wounded, and missing—more than Johnston had lost, at least in battle, throughout May, June, and early July. This is precisely what many of them feared would happen when Hood, "the fighter," had replaced "Old Joe." Now a dread of more such "killing times" permeates the army. "There seems to be," notes quartermaster clerk Patrick in his diary with reference to Stewart's Corps after Peachtree Creek, "a general dissatisfaction among the men on account of the headlong way in which they were put in yesterday, & they think that it 'costs more than it comes to.' They say that Hood cares no more for the lives of his men, than Grant does." In Hardee's Corps, reports Hosea Garrett of the 10th Texas to his uncle, "all I hear say anything about Genl. Hood say that he is too fond of charging the enemy's works," an observation echoed by Lieutenant Rennolds in his diary: "few if any relish the idea of again charging the enemy's works." In Lee's badly mauled corps, Lieutenant Gill believes that "the Federals with their style of fighting are almost invincible," and one of Clayton's officers considers "our death or permanent disability . . . merely a question of time."

Evidently other Confederates share this officer's dark view of their prospects. Thus toward the end of July the skirmishers of Tyler's Brigade had surrendered when a Federal force had advanced against them, and at about the same time in a different sector, Knipe's brigade had captured 117 Rebel pickets at the cost of only two wounded: it had met virtually no resistance. Also, with the stabilization of the lines around Atlanta, sizable numbers of Confederates again are deserting. Among them is Private Van Buren Oldham of the 9th Tennessee, Maney's Brigade. Although he has fought bravely in every major battle of the Army of Tennessee starting with Shiloh, he has decided to go home and swear allegiance to the Union. One of his reasons, and no doubt a reason of many other deserters, is revealed by a recent entry in his diary: "The plan Genl Hood has adopted of charging breastworks . . . will soon leave him without an army if continued as hitherto."[7]

These manifestations of demoralization and defeatism, however, do not mean that most of the men of the Army of Tennessee are ready to quit. Far from it. They draw hope from Lee's victories in Virginia and from reports of Northern war-weariness, they find encouragement in rumors that reinforcements are on the way from the Trans-Mississippi and Virginia, and they derive solace and inspiration from religion: surely God will not allow the South to go down before a foe so wicked and cruel as the Yankees! Many of them believe, too, surprising as it may seem, that the recent battles have been victories, albeit at excessive cost, in that they have (to quote Captain Hampton of the 53rd Virginia) "succeeded in stopping the [enemy's] flanking" and that consequently Sherman will be forced to try to take Atlanta by assault, in which case, like A. M. Walls of Reynold's Arkansas Brigade, they are "confident of success, let the issue come when it will." Finally, even if they share Lieutenant Gill's pessimism about the military situation, many of them, including Gill himself, will fight on out of a sense of duty or simply because they feel, along with Angus McDermid, that "I cant do nothing hear but fight and take care of myself."

The crucial truth is that the majority of Hood's troops resent what they perceive he has done to them and fear that he will continue doing it, that they rightly consider Sherman's army (again to quote Patrick) "too heavy for us" to defeat in open battle, and that although they will, as a deserter from the 36th Alabama tells Federal interrogators, "fight desperately if attacked in their works, they would refuse to make a general charge" against an entrenched

Union position or one that seemed to be such. In sum, the offensive potential of the Army of Tennessee, not strong to begin with, now lies buried with the dead of Resaca, Kolb's farm, Peachtree Creek, Bald Hill, and Ezra Church. Hence Hood's plan, approved by Davis—namely, of staying on the defensive while Wheeler attempts to close off Sherman's supplies—is the sole realistic strategy available to him. If Atlanta can be held and if Wheeler succeeds, Sherman indeed will be obliged to attempt to storm the city or else retreat. Either way the result will be Confederate victory, not only in Georgia but, potentially, in the war itself.[8]

Sherman receives the first definite word of McCook's debacle at Brown's Mill on the evening of August 1. It comes in the form of a telegram from Colonel James P. Brownlow of the 1st Tennessee (Union) Cavalry who has just arrived in Marietta "with a very few straggling cavalry, entirely demoralized"; he himself is barefoot. According to Brownlow, who is the son of "Parson" Brownlow, the East Tennessee Unionist leader, McCook destroyed twelve miles of the Macon railroad so thoroughly that it will take fifteen days to repair it, but while returning to Union lines, was overtaken by an overwhelming force of Rebel cavalry and infantry with the result that he and nearly all of his command were captured; only a few, like Brownlow and his followers, managed to cut their way out.

At once Sherman telegraphs Webster in Nashville to have all of the cavalry in Kentucky and Tennessee that "can possibly be spared" rushed to Georgia, "as the enemy surely will be on our railroad very soon." He also wires a similar warning to Brigadier General John Smith, who is commanding the District of the Etowah at Cartersville, and instructs Thomas to order Kilpatrick, who has just resumed command of his cavalry division after recuperating from the wound he had suffered back in May, to hasten to Marietta for the purpose of guarding the army's right flank along the Chattahoochee. Sherman is shocked by the McCook catastrophe—"I can hardly believe it," he informs Halleck in his nightly report—and his apprehension concerning Stoneman mounts.[9]

Yet his main concern continues to be reaching the railroad between Atlanta and East Point. Since July 28 no progress whatsoever has been made toward this goal. On the contrary, Howard actually has moved away from the railroad by extending his line westward instead of pushing southward, despite being reinforced by Davis's and Ward's divisions. McPherson himself could not be more cautious and less aggressive than Howard continues to be. Or could it be that, like their fellow veterans in gray, the men of the Army of the Tennessee prefer to receive rather than to deliver charges?

In any case, if the railroad between Atlanta and East Point is going to be blocked, it will have to be done by some force other than Howard's. Consequently, per orders issued by Sherman yesterday, during the night of August 1 Schofield's XXIII Corps withdraws from its trenches east of Atlanta and sets out for the right wing of the army. Garrard's troopers, again relegated to the role of infantry, take its place, and Stanley pulls back the left of the IV Corps to Pea Vine Creek so as to cover Buck Head and Pace's Ferry road.

Sherman believes, and Thomas agrees, that Schofield, who is to be supported by Davis's and Ward's divisions, can get to the railroad somewhere near East Point by swinging around Howard's right. Once Schofield is there, it will be impossible for the enemy to dislodge him as he will have a force "equal to Hood's mobile column." This in turn will leave Hood with no choice other than to evacuate Atlanta unless he wants to stay there and starve until he has to surrender. If all goes well—surely Hood's defense line is stretched to the breaking point—by the end of the week the campaign will be at an end.[10]

Already it has lasted far longer than Sherman had anticipated when it began. It also has been very costly. The XVII Corps, which bore the brunt of Bald Hill, is down to 6,400 "effective men," and Blair is attempting to replenish it by rounding up detailed soldiers and convalescents from as far north as St. Louis. In the XV Corps the five regiments of Walcutt's brigade have only 830 troops present for duty, and the 30th Ohio of Lightburn's brigade musters a mere 60 men after losing 32 at Ezra Church (this, however, leaves it "stronger" than the 30th Illinois, which was reduced at Bald Hill to a pathetically absurd 17 soldiers!). As a whole the Army of the Tennessee, with its three corps, numbers no more than 21,000 battle-ready troops, the same as it possessed early in May when it consisted of two corps. The Army of the Cumberland, which had begun with about 65,000 infantry and artillerists, now has 45,000 effectives, nearly half of whom are in the XIV Corps. Only the lone corps of the "Army of the Ohio" contains, thanks to a large excess of reinforcements over casualties, more men than it had had at the outset of the campaign—12,000. Counting cavalry (which at present is hard to do) and miscellaneous unattached units, Sherman altogether has at most 85,000 troops available for field operations. This, to be sure, gives him his customary 30,000 numerical margin over the Confederates, but even so it represents a 15,000-man drop in his strength since July 1. Moreover, although most of this decrease has come from battle losses (c. 9,000), sickness, and some desertions, a substantial portion is the result of troops who are not veteranized being discharged from service.[11]

This last worries him most. The enlistments of thousands of his soldiers, in some cases whole regiments, are expiring. Who will replace them and when? Writing to brother John on August 2 (probably in response to the latter's July 24 communication telling Sherman in effect that the outcome of the election and of the war depends on him), his mood, which is bad anyway because for the first and only time during the campaign he is feeling ill, is a mixture of pessimism, anger, and disgust:

> This army is much reduced in strength by deaths, sickness, and expiration of service. It looks hard to see regiments march away when their time is up. On the other [Confederate] side they have everybody, old and young, and for indefinite periods. I have to leave also along the railroad a large force to guard supplies; so that I doubt if our army much exceeds that of Hood. No recruits are coming, for the draft is not till September, and then I suppose it will consist mostly of niggers and bought recruits that must be kept well to the rear. I sometimes think our people do not deserve to succeed in war; they are so apathetic.[12]

For Sherman time is becoming an enemy, the most dangerous one he faces. If too much of it passes without his taking Atlanta, he might end up with an army too weak to take it at all.

During the afternoon of August 2 the XXIII Corps passes around the Union right and advances south beyond the Lick Skillet road until it reaches the north fork of Utoy Creek, another of the narrow, shallow, but steep-banked streams that lace the countryside west of Atlanta, an area so thickly wooded and sparsely populated that the Northern troops find it strange that a city should be close-by. Outflanked, the Confederate left falls back, and Howard finally is able to extend southward by swinging the XV Corps around to the east. On the following day, Hascall's division crosses the north fork of the creek at Herringer's Mill and establishes a bridgehead. Schofield wants to push on with his full force, but Sherman, who has recovered from yesterday's illness and is personally overseeing the operation, tells him to stay put until reinforced by Baird's division of the XIV Corps, which does not occur until evening. Instead of supporting Schofield with Davis's and Ward's divisions, as originally planned, Sherman has decided to bolster him with the entire XIV Corps. This will give Schofield, together with his own corps, 30,000 troops, more than enough, surely, to overpower anything Hood can bring against him without leaving Atlanta virtually defenseless. Besides, the XIV Corps—"Thomas's pets"—has suffered "fewer hard knocks than any other corps in the army," and Sherman is "anxious to give it a chance."

Early on the morning of August 4, Sherman issues his orders for the day: "Major General Schofield with his own command and General Palmer's corps will move directly on the railroad" between Atlanta and East Point "and will not stop until he has absolute control" of it. While this movement is taking place, Thomas and Howard "will press close on the enemy at all points" and be prepared to withstand a counterattack. Schofield, on the other hand, "must assume the offensive," the troops under him "are to be prepared to fight, leaving knapsacks, &c., in the present trenches," and "ordinary parapets will be charged and carried," for "every hour's delay enables the enemy to strengthen" his defenses. "Therefore let it [seizing the railroad] be done today."[13]

These orders, which resemble those promulgated by Hood prior to Peachtree Creek, obviously envision a bold, hard-hitting offensive. Instead they lead to what in some respects is one of the most muddled and absurd episodes of the Civil War.

It begins when Schofield, acting on Sherman's orders, directs Palmer to have Baird's division advance to the Sandtown road. (This should not be confused with the Sandtown road that figured so prominently in the operations around Kennesaw; it runs from the village on the lower bank of the Chattahoochee to the area between Atlanta and East Point.) Palmer refuses to obey. After studying Schofield's copy of Sherman's orders, Palmer, who has received no orders himself, sends a note to Thomas, stating: "The orders seem to be intended to give General Schofield control over my troops. Shall I turn them over to him?" Thomas answers: "No. Inform General Schofield that you are ready to co-operate with him. General Sherman does not intend to place you under General Schofield's orders." Palmer thereupon tells Schofield that he will execute Sherman's orders but expects to receive them through Thomas. Schofield at once telegraphs Sherman (who again is trying to control the movements of his entire army by means of wires) to inform him of Palmer's recalcitrance. In turn, Sherman telegraphs Palmer: "You will during the movement against the railroad report to and receive orders from General Schofield. . . . Obey his orders and instructions."

This, Sherman assumes, will settle the matter. It merely makes it worse. Repeatedly throughout the campaign Sherman has detached divisions from the XIV Corps to serve with other commands, and each time Palmer has taken it as a personal affront and on one occasion had offered to resign. Now Sherman in effect is depriving Palmer of his whole corps and turning it over to Schofield, whom Palmer considers junior to himself in rank as well as in years and experience. Hence Palmer's reply to Sherman is one of defiance, not compliance: "I am General Schofield's senior. We may co-operate but I respectfully decline to report to or take orders from him." At the same time he writes Schofield that "I will not obey either General Sherman's orders or yours, as they violate my self-respect."

Sherman, realizing that he has a very angry general on his hands, seeks to placate Palmer, first by telegraphing him that "I have no disposition to qualify [disregard] your true rank," then by going to talk to him. As a result, at 4 P.M., an hour later than the movement toward the Sandtown road was scheduled to get under way, Palmer instructs Baird to send one of his brigades on a "reconnaissance." The brigade (Colonel Newell Gleason's) moves out, captures twenty-five Confederate pickets, but then returns to its starting point when it encounters heavy fire from the enemy's main line. The all-out offensive by the XIV and XXIII that was to reach the railroad ends, at least for this day, even before it begins.[14]

Sherman, understandably, feels exasperated. Moreover, Colonel Silas Adams has shown up in Marietta along with his Kentucky brigade and other fragments from Stoneman's division, bringing confirmation of Rebel newspaper reports that Stoneman and a large number of his troopers had been captured on July 31. As late as yesterday, Sherman still was hoping that Stoneman might at least have liberated the officer prisoners at Macon. Now he knows that the raid has been an utter disaster and that an enemy cavalry thrust against his own rail communications is a virtual certainty.

In the evening, after telling Schofield and Palmer that the offensive will be resumed (or rather, attempted again) come morning, Sherman returns to his headquarters near the Turner's Ferry road, about three miles northwest of Atlanta. Here he ponders the issue of seniority between the two generals. At 10:45 P.M. he transmits his conclusion to Palmer: Schofield "ranks you as major general" because of "previous rank as brigadier general." Therefore "General Schofield's orders for movement tomorrow must be regarded as military orders and not in the nature of co-operation. . . . The Sandtown road and the railroad, if possible, must be gained tomorrow if it costs half your command. I regard the loss of time this afternoon as equal to the loss of 2,000 men."

No general in Sherman's army is less likely to be impressed by an exhortation to take an objective even if it costs one-half of his men than is John M. Palmer of Illinois. He believes, to quote a July 24 letter to his wife, in "suffering no man to be endangered while proper results can be accomplished without it," and so he is quite willing to let other generals win "glory" with "long lists of killed and wounded" while he saves his soldiers from useless "sacrifice" and their wives and children "from widowhood and orphanage." Besides, he is suffering from rheumatism and bilious attacks, he is so worn out from three months of campaigning that "nothing but the imminence of battle keeps me on my horse," and above all he longs to return to his family for a "good, quiet rest," something he plans to do, he wrote his wife two days ago, "as soon as Atlanta falls." Now this latest bit of West Point snobbery and bullying by Sherman provides a legitimate opportunity to do this much sooner than that, and he is quite happy to take advantage of it. "I am unable," he notifies Sherman shortly before midnight, "to acquiesce in the decision that Major General Schofield legally ranks me. . . . I respectfully ask, therefore, that some officer be designated to whom I may turn over the command of the Fourteenth Army Corps."

Under ordinary circumstances Sherman would be delighted to grant at once Palmer's request to be relieved: Sherman did not want him to command the XIV Corps in the first place, deems him unqualified for the post, and despises officers who put personal considerations ahead of military duty. Palmer, however, has powerful political connections extending to the White House, heads Thomas's favorite corps and possesses his confidence, and would have to be replaced, owing to seniority, by Brigadier Richard Johnson, who is no more aggressive than Palmer is. Consequently, early on the morning of August 5, Sherman sends Palmer a letter in which he refuses to relieve him and advises him "to wait a few days" to resign, then "allege some other reason—one that will stand the test of time. Your future [in politics] is too valuable to be staked on a mistake."

Palmer, on receiving this communication, informs Sherman that "as you have declined to remove me, I go, of course, to the field and will do what I can to give success to the operations of the day," but he adds that he wants permission "at the close of the day to turn the command over to Brigadier General Johnson." He then goes to Schofield's headquarters where, at 7 A.M., he tells him that he will relay his orders to the division commanders of the XIV Corps. Schofield, who at dawn has directed Baird to advance against the enemy only to meet with a flat refusal from that general, agrees to this arrangement. What else can he do?

Around midmorning, Baird, having received "authentic orders," advances and carries the same line of enemy skirmish pits that Gleason's brigade had seized yesterday, capturing 140 prisoners. He then wheels his division eastward, whereupon a torrent of shells cascades down upon it, indicating that the Confederates have massed their artillery on his front. Deciding, in the words of one of his staff officers, "that to advance against their main works would probably result in a repulse, and in the loss of hundreds of men without accomplishing any good," he orders his troops to halt and lie down. Soon afterward Davis's division moves up on his right and does the same, but facing southward. Schofield, seeing what is supposed to be an all-out assault bog down without so much as coming under rifle fire, instructs Johnson, via Palmer, to "make a rapid detour to the right, and try to strike the enemy in flank." Johnson instead takes position behind Davis's division and waits until evening before he conducts (to quote his report) "a reconnaissance to the right to find the flank of the rebel line." Before going far, however, he returns to Davis's rear because it is "too late to accomplish much." One gets the impression that the XIV Corps's division commanders have no desire, indeed no intention, of making an attack today.

At 7:15 P.M., Schofield disgustedly notifies Sherman, who throughout the day has sent him a series of telegrams asking, with mounting impatience, "How are you progressing?": "I am compelled to acknowledge that I have totally failed to make any aggressive movement with the Fourteenth Corps, and have very little hope of being able to do better. The efforts of yesterday and today on this flank have been much more than failures. I . . . propose tomorrow to take my own corps on to the right and try to recover what has been lost by two days of delay."

Sherman likewise is disgusted with the XIV Corps's "manifest determination not to move toward the enemy." It needs, he informs Thomas, "a head that will give it life and impulse," for "if an enemy can be seen by a spy-glass the whole corps is halted and intrenched for a siege." Accordingly Sherman telegraphs Palmer: "If you think of resigning it is probably better it should be now, as I fear the intention lessens your interests in our operations. . . . To be honest, I must say that the operations [of the XIV Corps] . . . yesterday and today have not been satisfactory."

Stung by Sherman's "inference of a want of interest in our operations" on Palmer's part, even though "I exerted myself more, I think, than any officer on the field to carry out General Schofield's orders," Palmer answers that "I will call upon you tomorrow morning and present a formal application to be relieved." This he does, and later in the day he takes a train for Chattanooga. He is on his way to where he had long and longingly wanted to go—home. Sherman, on the other hand, is free of a general whom he never wanted and who he believes has made the strongest corps in his army worthless for offensive purposes. In a telegram to Halleck, Sherman asks that Jeff C. Davis be promoted to major general so that he can be placed in command of the XIV Corps instead of Johnson, who lacks "the ability or vigor" needed for the post.[15]

All through the night the troops of Cox's division, now on the Union right in place of Johnson's division, have heard the "constant chopping and falling of trees" along the hillsides south of the Sandtown road. They believe that the Confederates are strengthening their fortifications in this area. They are correct. Hood is aware that Sherman is still seeking to get at the railroad between Atlanta and East Point. To stop him, Hood has reinforced Lee's Corps with Bate's Division and has directed that it be posted south of the Sandtown road. Despite being bolstered by Stevens's former brigade, now under the command of Brigadier General Henry R. Jackson, this division still numbers no more than 2,500 effectives and is deployed in a line of rifle pits that are ten yards apart, with a single file of eight men in each trench. Tyler's Tennessee Brigade and Lewis's Kentuckians hold the extreme left; they have covered their front with a hundred-yard-wide belt of trees cut so as to fall with their branches facing outward. It was the construction of these entanglements, which also mask the Confederate works, that Cox's troops have heard during the night.

Early on the morning of August 6, Schofield orders Cox to advance, attack, and if possible turn the Confederate left. Schofield believes that he has "reached about the end of Hood's rope" and that if he can take what he conceives to be the Rebel "outer line" south of the Sandtown road by a quick assault, he can then "gain the enemy's main line before his troops" can withdraw to it, thus opening the way to the railroad.

Moving southward across a valley, Cox's skirmishers easily drive back the Confederate pickets. So weak is the opposition that Cox concludes that the enemy in front cannot be "very formidable." Hence at 10 A.M. he directs Reilly to assault the west end of a ridge along which the Rebels appear to have entrenched. Cox believes, so he informs Reilly, that by taking advantage of the cover provided by a strip of timber just below the ridge "the movement . . . may be made with very strong prospect of success."

Troops of Reilly's brigade—approximately 1,500 Ohioans, Illinoisans, Kentuckians, and Tennesseans—reach and pass through the timber without difficulty. Then they encounter the belt of trees cut down by the Confederates during the night. The outcome is predictable. While they try desperately to work their way through these obstacles, a torrent of lead from Tyler's troops and two of Lewis's Kentucky regiments rips their ranks. The Union men drop by the scores, and their advance comes to a halt twenty-five to thirty yards from the enemy trenches, which are topped by head logs. Reilly, who recently has been promoted to brigadier general, brings up reserve regiments and renews the attack. This gains only a few more yards before suffering the same fate. Reilly thereupon orders his men to take cover, which they do, holding on despite a deadly enfilade fire from a battery posted to their right on the Sandtown road. Finally, covering volleys from Casement's brigade enable the survivors to crawl back out of the entanglements. Reilly's casualties come to 306 killed, wounded, and missing, 95 of them from the 160 troops the 8th Tennessee took into the charge. Little wonder that he sobs with grief and vows this is the last time his brigade "should go into such a place as that." Losses in Bate's Division come to a mere 15 or 20. In an effort to strengthen what he deems his own corps's inadequate martial spirit, Stephen Lee proclaims that he sees in its one-sided victory proof that "soldiers who fight with the coolness and determination" of

Tyler's Tennesseans "will always be victorious over any reasonable number."[16]

Schofield, correctly assuming that there must be an end somewhere to the Confederate line paralleling the Sandtown road, next orders Hascall to "find and turn the enemy left." Hascall sends out two brigades on a wide sweep to the south and west. Late in the afternoon, near Utoy Post Office, they drive back some cavalry and a battery guarding Bate's flank, but the approach of darkness and a rainstorm prevent them from following up this advantage. Nevertheless Bate's position now is untenable, and realizing this, Hood has Lee withdraw him to a line facing west and covering the railroad. Before leaving, Tyler's troops strip the shoes, uniforms, and other useful items from the Union dead who are lying in front of their trenches.

During the evening, Schofield telegraphs several reports to Sherman. Initially he is pessimistic, putting Cox's and Hascall's losses at a thousand and expressing doubt as to "my ability to either reach the enemy's left or break his lines." Not until he hears from Hascall and studies his maps does Schofield conclude that it is possible that "I have struck the flank of the defenses of East Point." Sherman, on receiving this message, orders Schofield to "continue to work tomorrow in such a manner as to best threaten the railroad." Despite Palmer's obstinacy, the recalcitrance of the XIV Corps, and the bloody repulse of Reilly's brigade, perhaps the attempt to force Hood out of Atlanta still can succeed.

On the morning of August 7 the XXIII Corps passes over the trenches evacuated by Bate, then cautiously advances down the Sandtown road until, three hundred yards distant, it beholds a line of Confederate fortifications extending southward as far as the eye can see. Well aware of what had happened to Reilly's brigade yesterday, it immediately entrenches, without so much as threatening an attack. So, too, does the XIV Corps, after carrying some of the enemy's outer works in an attack that nets 200 prisoners but costs it twice that number of casualties, 179 of them in Major John Edie's brigade of regular troops. By evening it is obvious that there is neither a weak spot nor a flankable flank in the Rebel defenses covering the railroad between Atlanta and East Point, and although Schofield notifies Sherman that he thinks Cox's division is "within a mile of the railroad," actually it is more than two miles from it.[17]

Thus ends, a week after it had begun, what can be best described as the Union fizzle at Utoy Creek. As might be expected, Sherman blames it on Palmer's quibbling about rank and the lack of aggressiveness on the part of the XIV Corps, an assertion that is echoed by virtually all historians.[18] Yet even if Palmer had welcomed serving under Schofield and even if his corps had rushed into battle with reckless abandon, the outcome almost surely would have been no different. Alert as they were to Sherman's intent and the danger it posed, the Confederates would have reacted to a faster and more vigorous movement against their left by themselves moving with greater speed and strength to counter it. Indeed, this is precisely what they did when the Federals finally mounted, in the form of Reilly's assault, a serious threat to the railroad: Hood at once reinforced Lee's Corps with Cleburne's Division, which had manned the works that Schofield's troops found running south from the Sandtown road. Had the XXIII and/or the XIV corps endangered the railroad on August 3, 4, or 5, Hood could and no doubt would have done the same thing with a like result. Hood has, contrary to Sherman's assumption when he launched the Utoy Creek operation, sufficient strength both to deter an assault on Atlanta and to fend off attempts to break through or outflank his defenses between that city and East Point.

Sherman now realizes this. The "enemy faces us," he telegraphed Halleck last night, "in force at all points" and "behind superior works." As a consequence, Sherman finds himself at the end of Sunday August 7 with four options: not counting one that is too impracticable, given the attitude of his troops, even to consider—namely, another Kennesaw Mountain-type attack: (1) to continue to extend his right, because maybe Hood has reached, or soon will reach, the limit of his ability to stretch his left; (2) to send the Army of Tennessee or its equivalent on a wide flanking march southward to cut the Macon railroad in what would be a repetition of the Snake Creek Gap maneuver; (3) to shift his whole army or the bulk of it, beyond the Confederate left, as he had done at Dalton, Allatoona, and Marietta, thereby leaving Hood, like Johnston before him, with a choice between attacking or retreating; (4) while maintaining relentless pressure on the Rebel army, to inflict a devastating artillery bombardment on Atlanta in hopes of making it untenable for Hood.

Sherman rejects the first option because he believes that his own army, with its eleven-mile front, already is overextended, whereas Hood (whom, as we have seen, he credits with having a strength nearly equal to his own) can hold Atlanta's increasingly formidable fortifications with militia (whose numbers Sherman also greatly overestimates), freeing his regular troops for field operations. For much the same reasons Sherman dismisses the second alternative: "I . . . despair," he replies when Schofield proposes it, "of making a quick move. It takes two days to do what ought to be done in one." Besides, south of East Point the Macon railroad swerves sharply eastward, which means that any Union column endeavoring to reach it in that area would be exposed to attack in flank and rear by superior enemy forces who, having less distance to travel, could easily get there first. If the Snake Creek Gap maneuver, which had the advantage of surprise, had failed to achieve success, why expect a similar move that would lack that advantage to be any less of a failure? Chances are it would be a disaster, both in itself and for the campaign as a whole.

As for the third choice—the oft-tried and always successful strategy of flanking the Confederates out of their otherwise impregnable positions by moving against their supply line with overwhelming force—it of course offers the best prospect of gaining Atlanta and possibly more. But not immediately. After nearly three weeks of incessant marching, skirmishing, fighting, trench digging, and sometimes grave digging, the Union troops need a respite before they will be capable of undertaking again with necessary spirit another large-scale offensive operation that could very well lead to a major, perhaps desperate, battle. Also Sherman hesitates, as he has throughout the campaign, to cut loose from his rail line, which now runs to the immediate rear of his army with the completion on August 5, in a mere four and a half days, of a new railroad bridge across the Chattahoochee. Increasing his reluctance to do this is an awareness that he is deep into a "country devoid of all necessary supplies" and "that a powerful cavalry raid against his communications is both likely and imminent."

Hence he elects, at least for the present, the fourth alternative: bombardment. If cannons can blast Hood out of Atlanta, fine; that will be a cheap way to secure victory. But if not, then his army will be ready to put into effect the third option, and that will settle the matter.

At 8 P.M., Sherman telegraphs Halleck his customary nightly report. After relating the day's events around Utoy Creek, "a noisy but not bloody battle," he announces that he intends to "make the inside of Atlanta too hot to be endured. . . . I am too impatient for a siege, but I do not know but here is as good a place to fight it out as farther inland. One thing is certain, whether we get inside of Atlanta or not, it will be a used-up community by the time we are done with it."[19]

Part Three: Rodmans, Railroads, and Raids

Since the afternoon when DeGress's Parrotts spat forth their heralds of death and destruction, Atlanta has been under sporadic bombardment, sometimes heavy, but usually light and rarely for more than a few hours at a time. In an August 4 letter to his sister Ella, Lieutenant Andrew Neal, whose battery is stationed in a fort north of the city near the railroad, writes:

> Almost all the shells they [the Federals] throw into the city come screaming just above our heads. Generally they commence on this fort and . . . then elevate their guns and send the balance into the city. For

Confederate fortifications north of Atlanta along the Marietta Road: near here Lieutenant Andrew Neal was killed and Mayor Calhoun surrendered Atlanta (*Photographic History,* 3:126)

awhile we exchanged shots with them but where Batteries are as well protected as ours and the Yankee Batteries before us [then] about as much is made of artillery duels as the sledge hammer makes out of the anvil. Atlanta is considerably marked by the enemy shots. In some parts of the town every house has been struck a dozen times. The houses about the foot of Alabama Street are much battered.

About a hundred yards from the fort that is being defended by Neal's cannons the once beautiful Ephraim Ponder house, a two-story white stucco structure, is being transformed into a shambles by Yankee shells. Neal's own family home in Atlanta has been hit twice: one projectile passed through the parlor and the other into the room of "Bud James," his older brother who is colonel of the 19th Georgia, Army of Northern Virginia. So far, however, not a single building has been completely destroyed or burned, and what is most important, trains continue to enter and leave the city freely, by day as well as night.

Sherman assumes that Atlanta's "inhabitants have, of course, got out." He is wrong. At least 2,000, perhaps as many as 5,000, remain. Most of them are refugees who either have no other place to go or lack the means to leave. Each day the army, on Hood's orders, issues 1,500 rations to these people, many of whom dwell in a camp on the southwest edge of the city. Only one grocery store remains open; all the other stores and the hotels are closed. Initially the Yankee shells produced consternation, even panic; now, after half a month, most residents regard them more as nuisances than anything else. To be sure they are dangerous, deadly ones. During the first week, in addition to the little girl who was slain on July 20, an old woman and a teamster have been killed, another child had a leg shattered, and on the night of August 3 a missile ripped through the house of J. F. Warner, superintendent of the gasworks, and exploded on the bed where he was lying with his six-year-old daughter Lizzie, "mangling them horribly and producing instant death." But experience has shown that the chances of suffering similar fates can be reduced considerably by exercising certain precautions. If at all possible, stay away from the Five Points and the Car Shed: that is where the shelling tends to be worst. Avoid the vicinity of church spires and tall chimneys: the Yankees sight their cannons on them. Above all, as soon as a bombardment begins, head for your cellar, if you have one, or, better still, for a dugout. By August there are scores of the latter—called "gopher holes," a phrase borrowed from the soldiers—in Atlanta's back-yards. Typically they are eight to ten feet deep and are covered with logs or heavy beams, then a layer of boards or tin sheeting, and finally a pile of dirt three to five feet thick. They vary in size according to the number of persons they are intended to accommodate, and they are entered via an L-shaped ditch leading to a small doorway. In addition, many people, particularly refugees, shelter themselves in caves that have been burrowed into the sides of ridges or railroad embankments.

On August 9 everybody in Atlanta who has access to a good cellar, cave, or "gopher hole" has reason to be thankful. Starting in the morning and continuing until evening, Yankee projectiles fall "every few minutes," sometimes "at the rate of sixty per minute." This bombardment surpasses by far all previous ones. When it ceases, Sherman's cannons (he telegraphs Halleck) have fired "about 3,000 solid shot and shells" into the city. Yet the sole observable effect, reports a Union signal officer from an observation post in the XX Corps's sector, has been the knocking off of the "top of a brick smoke-stack." Moreover, although a "great many" shells have exploded "immediately around Hood's headquarters at the corner of Whitehall Street and Faith Alley (thanks to spies and deserters the Federals know its location), they have caused neither casualties nor damage. In fact, not a single person in all of Atlanta has been injured, and before going

An Atlanta "Bombproof" *(Leslie's Weekly)*

to bed, Carrie Berry, a ten year old whose family resides in a house on Fairlie Street on the northwest side, matter-of-factly records in her diary: "We have had to stay in the cellar all day. . . . Cousin Beatty came in and wanted us to move, he thought we were in danger, but we will try it a little longer."

Most of August 10, during which there is a "hard, steady rain," passes with "but few shells," notes Carrie, and most of these few come after 5 P.M. from three 4½" Rodman rifles that have been brought from Chattanooga and placed in a fort atop a hill near the Howells' Mill road north of Atlanta. At a range of 2,100 yards, they are able to drop their 33-pound projectiles into the heart of the city. This they do, first at the rate of one shot every five minutes, then, on Sherman's orders, as fast as they can be reloaded. After watching them in action, Thomas informs Sherman that their shells "burst beautifully," and Sherman in turn notifies Howard that he intends to "destroy Atlanta and make it a desolation."[20]

The bombardment inflicts a few casualties, one of whom is Lieutenant Neal, who is killed while literally fighting for his home, but otherwise does little harm. Furthermore, although several missiles whiz by Hood's headquarters, they do not prevent Bishop Henry C. Lay of the Episcopal Diocese of Georgia and Father John T. Quintard from going there at sunset to confirm the church membership of Hood and three young officers. Normally this rite would be held at Quintard's church, St. Luke's, but late last month a Yankee shell had smashed through the side of that small wooden structure and wrecked the prayer desk. Despite the fact that a Bible had fallen on the shell, snuffing out its fuse and preventing it from exploding, Quintard has decided to hold no more services in the church; perhaps he feels it would be tempting providence.

Forty men, mainly generals and staff officers, have gathered for the ceremony. Hood stands, as he had when baptized by Polk, supported by his crutches, head bent. Outside, shells continue to explode nearby. The service, Bishop Lay later records, is "animated, the praying good." At the end he blesses Hood and the other confirmants, then, assisted by Quintard, administers communion to all present. "The reverence was so marked that one could not fail to thank God that he has put such a spirit into the hearts of our leaders."[21]

Among Hood's private prayers surely one is for the success of the great cavalry raid that has gotten under way today with the crossing of the Chattahoochee at Roswell by Wheeler at the head of 5,000 to 6,000 troopers from Humes's, Kelly's, and Major General Will Martin's divisions—the cream of his cavalry—supported by six light artillery pieces. According to Hood's instructions, Wheeler is to destroy the railroad at various points between Marietta and Chattanooga, cross the Tennessee, and break both of the rail lines from Nashville; then, after leaving 1,200 men to continue operation in Middle Tennessee, Wheeler is to return to Atlanta, again striking the Western and Atlantic as he does so. Hood, who expects Wheeler to be gone only a "few days," has requested Maury to send some of his Alabama cavalry into northern Georgia ("Small parties could do great service") and has asked President Davis to order Forrest into Tennessee. Hood's hopes, indeed his expectations, as to the outcome of the raid are revealed in the order he has given to his new chief of engineers, Major General M. L. Smith, this very day: "take immediate steps to prepare bridge timbers to reconstruct the bridges on the railroads leading from this place to Tennessee."[22]

Sherman has told Halleck that "I am too impatient for a siege." On August 11, Sherman begins to show that impatience. Receiving what later proves to be an erroneous report that the chief of artillery for the Army of the Cumberland has refused to turn over to the Army of the Tennessee a fourth Rodman gun that has just arrived, Sherman angrily accuses him of disobeying orders. Misreading some dispatches from Schofield, Sherman commands him to send a division to cut the West Point railroad, and when Schofield points out that this will be extremely hazardous, Sherman accuses him of lack of enterprise: "We must act. We cannot sit down and do nothing because it involves risk." What Sherman wants, he tells Schofield, is "to fight Hood the earliest possible moment he will come out of his trenches, and would risk a good deal to draw him out." As it is, "I feel mortified that he holds us in check by the aid of his militia . . . it seems we are more besieged" than he is.

Sherman's mood does not improve on the following day, even though he receives a telegram from Stanton notifying Sherman that he has been appointed a major general in the regular army. An attempt by Schofield, at Sherman's prodding, to make a "sort of raid" on the West Point railroad merely results in the enemy's extending his earthworks beyond East Point. A demonstration by Stanley's IV Corps to ascertain whether the Rebels have weakened their right so as to bolster their left proves inconclusive: "We can see them stand to arms in their works," Stanley reports, "but cannot determine their strength." At 5:10 P.M. a signal officer who is observing rail traffic into and out of Atlanta from a hill-top in the XV Corps's sector sends the discouraging message that "three trains of cars loaded with troops just arrived in Atlanta." Finally, to complete this list of disappointments and frustrations in appropriate fashion, soon after nightfall two 20-pounder Parrotts burst, and the Rodmans run out of ammunition.[23]

By then Sherman already has decided that the time has come to make another grand flanking move in an attempt to force Hood either to retreat or again to attack. Obviously bombardment is not achieving the hoped-for results, nor does it appear likely to do so. Each day, as more enlistments expire, his army is becoming weaker, whereas Hood's evidently is growing stronger. Potentially far worse, although his army at present has ample supplies, the once mammoth stockpiles at Nashville have been badly depleted, and unless they are replenished, Sherman will have to start drawing on his reserves at Chattanooga, Allatoona, and Marietta, in which case, chief commissary Colonel Amos Beckwith has warned the War Department in Washington, "Our supplies will soon be exhausted." To be specific, at the current rate of consumption, his troops will eat up all available food by September 15, and grain for animals will barely last until September 1.[24]

These are reasons enough for Sherman to seek a speedy decision at Atlanta.

Yet there is another reason for him to do this that is more compelling than all the others. It is to be found, succinctly stated, in a telegram recently sent him by Grant: "We [the North] must win, if not defeated at home." Sherman knows what everybody else knows: Grant's hideous losses in Virginia, unredeemed by victory, have depressed Northern morale. "The people of the North," he has written to Ellen, "already have slackened their efforts." As a consequence he fears that all that has been gained since 1861 at such great cost will be lost, making it necessary for the Union armies to start all over again, de novo. Also he does not need brother John to tell him—all he has to do is to read the newspapers, both Northern and Southern, which he does—to realize that the Republicans are looking to him to do what Grant so obviously has failed to achieve: namely, gain a victory that will enable them to proclaim that the war is being won and will be won. That is why, in conversations with Howard and his staff, he is speaking of the "influence the capture of Atlanta would have upon the fall election" and of his determination to exercise that influence. Even generals who despise politics and reject its being interjected into military operations sometimes must take into account political considerations.

At 8 A.M. on August 13, in a rare morning telegram, Sherman informs Halleck: "I have ordered army commanders to prepare for the following plan: Leave one corps strongly entrenched at the Chattahoochee bridge in charge of our surplus wagon trains and artillery; with 60,000 men, reduced to fighting trim, to make a circuit of devastation around the town, with a radius of fifteen or twenty miles." In doing this, he continues, "I go on the faith that the militia in Atlanta are only good for the defense of its parapets and will not come out." Moreover he wants the "utmost activity to be kept up in Mobile Bay," where eight days ago Farragut broke through the Confederate harbor fortifications in a daring "Damn the torpedoes!" attack, and also "to be assured that no material re-enforcements have come here from Virginia." "If," he concludes, "I should ever be cut-off from my base, look out for me about St. Mark's, Fla., or Savannah, Ga."25

Having thus decided on his plan (which, let it be noted, remains exactly what he had told Grant back in April he would do upon reaching Atlanta), he discusses it with Thomas, Howard, and Schofield and asks them to provide him with detailed proposals for implementing it. Then, about midmorning, a telegram arrives from Marietta: "Train No. 2, first section, engine 25, was fired upon one mile south of Acworth; the road entirely torn up for 8 rods; engine 25 badly off; ties all burnt and iron bent."

Has the anticipated Confederate cavalry raid begun? Two days ago Garrard had reported that a "large body of their cavalry is now in the neighborhood of Covington, and it is generally believed that they will soon make a grand raid to

Tennessee or Kentucky." Sherman promptly orders Brigadier General John McArthur, commanding at Marietta, to "see at once as to who and what force broke the road at or near Acworth." Shortly before 1 P.M., McArthur answers: "Damage to railroad repaired. Enemy's force, about seventy-five, came on the Alabama road." This information is inconclusive. Perhaps the raiders were merely guerrillas or one of the small bands of regular Rebel cavalry that have long been operating, with negligible success, north of the Chattahoochee. Nonetheless, suspecting that the attack at Acworth has "a bearing on something beyond," Sherman directs McArthur to "keep a good picket out" in the direction of Roswell and to post a regiment on Kennesaw along with a signal station. "The Macon papers," he explains, "announce the capture of Marietta by their cavalry. This indicates a purpose."[26]

During the next two days there is a spate of telegrams from the commanders at Cartersville, Resaca, and Dalton. From them Sherman learns that Wheeler's troopers, estimated to be 6,000 strong, indeed are on the loose in northern Georgia, that they have seized a large drove of cattle near Adairsville, captured a stockade and its garrison at Tilton, attacked unsuccessfully the fort at Dalton, and torn up some track between Dalton and Tilton. Sherman reacts by exhorting those commanders to pursue and crush the raiders; otherwise he expresses little concern. His wagon train carries "stores brought for two weeks," and he is confident that his construction crews "can in ten days repair any break that can be made in my rear." Besides, he sees in the raid a potential opportunity. Since the bulk of Hood's cavalry evidently is with Wheeler, that presumably means that only a small portion of it remains around Atlanta. Should that be the case, then it might be possible to do to Hood what Hood is trying to do to Sherman: slice his supply artery with a cavalry raid.

To find out if this can be done, Sherman on August 15 instructs Garrard to scout the Decatur area and Kilpatrick to "make a bold reconnaissance" toward Fairburn on the West Point railroad. On the following morning, Garrard reports that he encountered only Ferguson's Brigade, which he drove into Atlanta's fortifications, and Kilpatrick sends word via Thomas that he has reached Fairburn, where he has destroyed the station and three miles of track, and that Jackson's Division "has thus far refused to give me battle." The news from Kilpatrick elates Sherman. "I do believe," he wires Thomas, that Kilpatrick, "with his own and Garrard's cavalry, could ride right round Atlanta and smash the Macon road all to pieces." Through Schofield, Sherman directs Kilpatrick to inform him "if he does not think that with two of General Garrard's brigades in addition to his own he could break the Macon road effectually." While waiting for Kilpatrick's answer, telegrams arrive from the various commanders in North Georgia to the effect that Wheeler has headed for

East Tennessee, that there is no truth to earlier reports that a large force of Rebel cavalry was menacing the Etowah bridge and Allatoona, and that the damage done to the railroad between Dalton and Tilton will be repaired by tomorrow (which it is). This news confirms Sherman in the opinion that, as he puts it to Thomas, "Wheeler is out of the way, and when shall we use cavalry, if not now?"

Early on the morning of August 17, Sherman receives Kilpatrick's reply. After reading it, Sherman decides to suspend the orders he issued yesterday for a "movement of the army against the Macon railroad" to begin on the night of August 18; instead he will send Kilpatrick to do the job. Kilpatrick, he explains in a message to Thomas notifying him of the change of plan, "thinks it not only possible but comparatively easy to break the railroad to Macon effectually. I do not want to move this vast army and its paraphernalia around Atlanta unless forced to do so, and it does seem that the enemy has offered us the very opportunity we seek."

Later in the day, Sherman and Kilpatrick confer at the former's headquarters, a tent fly that shelters a crudely made table and a number of rickety camp stools and cracker barrels that serve as chairs. A twenty-eight-year-old native of New Jersey who is a West Point graduate (class of 1861), Kilpatrick has been well described by a staff officer in the Army of the Potomac as "a frothy braggart without brains"; but he is energetic and aggressive, qualities that appeal to Sherman. Kilpatrick assures Sherman that if supported by Schofield in such a way as to forestall enemy infantry opposing him, he can wreck the Macon railroad so badly that "it cannot be used in two weeks," and this without risking the destruction of his own force. Sherman, who has just received word that Wheeler definitely has gone into Tennessee, thereupon issues orders for what he terms "a deliberate attack" on the railroad to Macon "for the purpose of so disabling that road that the enemy will be unable to supply his army in Atlanta." Colonel Eli Long and two brigades from Garrard's division will join Kilpatrick's three brigades at Sandtown. Come tomorrow night, Kilpatrick will lead all five brigades, which constitute the bulk of Sherman's remaining cavalry, across the West Point railroad between Red Oak and Fairburn; he will strike the Macon railroad near Jonesboro. There he is to destroy as much of the track as possible, "working steadily until forced to take to his arms and horses for battle." During the raid, Schofield will "move to his right as far as prudent," and Stanley and Garrard will conduct a demonstration on the army's left with the object of preventing Hood from detaching infantry against Kilpatrick. Once Kilpatrick has completed his mission, he is to "advise us at the earliest possible moment of his success."

In the evening, Sherman, obviously in good spirits, telegraphs Halleck:

I have a tight grip on Atlanta, and was on the point of swinging around to the southeast when Wheeler went to my rear with 6,000 cavalry; he has passed into East Tennessee, having damaged us but little. I will avail myself of his absence to reciprocate the compliment, and to-morrow night the Macon road must be broken good. General Kilpatrick will undertake it. Wheeler cannot disturb Knoxville or Loudon. He may hurt some of the minor points, but, on the whole, East Tennessee is a good place for him to break down his horses, and a poor place to steal new ones. All well.[27]

Just after sundown on August 18, Kilpatrick sets out from Sandtown with 4,700 men, many of whom are armed with Spencers, and two batteries of horse artillery. The sole Confederate force blocking his way is Ross's Texas Brigade, a mere 400 troopers and a couple of light cannons. Nevertheless by destroying bridges, erecting barricades, sniping from the forests, and setting ambushes, the Texans slow the raiders's march literally to a walk. It is daylight on August 19 before Kilpatrick's main column (he has sent Lieutenant Colonel Robert Klein's small brigade of 309 sabers off toward Griffin as a decoy) enters Fairburn, and not until late afternoon does it cross the Flint River, one and a half miles west of Jonesboro, which Kilpatrick has promised Sherman he would reach by noon. Moreover Ross, via Red Jackson, has kept Hood well posted on the movements and strength of the raiding column, with the result that Hood, not in the least deterred by Schofield's and Stanley's demonstrations on his flanks, has ordered Ferguson's cavalry from the Decatur area to Rough and Ready, has shipped Reynolds's Arkansas infantry by train to Jonesboro, and has sent telegrams to all the post commanders along the Macon railroad alerting them to the danger. He has every reason, therefore, to feel confident that he can parry Kilpatrick's thrust and perhaps smash him in the process.

Unfortunately for Hood but most fortunately for Kilpatrick, somehow Brigadier General Frank Armstrong, whose cavalry brigade is stationed at Jonesboro, has received no word about Kilpatrick's approach either from Hood's headquarters or from Jackson's. Consequently, having learned from his scouts early in the afternoon that an enemy mounted force was heading "in direction of Griffin" (it is Klein's decoy detachment), he has gone off to Lovejoy's Station, and Reynolds, equally ignorant of the actual situation, has followed him there with his infantry. Their departure leaves only Ross's hopelessly outnumbered Texans to defend Jonesboro. They do their best. When, around 5 P.M., Kilpatrick nears the village, having taken close to twenty-four hours to cover less than that number of miles, they open fire from the shelter of a brick church and several other buildings. The Federals answer with artillery salvos and a fusillade of Spencer bullets; then they rush into Jonesboro, which is described by an Illinois trooper as "a row of stores, dwellings and shops on each side of the railroad, with a road or street on each side between the railroad and the buildings." The Texans, having no other rational choice, "skedaddle."

At once Kilpatrick puts his men to work tearing up track. But as they get under way, a heavy rain begins, making it impossible to heat and bend the rails over bonfires of piled-up ties. All they can do is pry the rails loose and toss them off to the side of the roadbed where, one of them later comments, they can be "relaid and repaired about as quickly as we had torn [them] up." The raiders do, however, succeed in burning the station, a train, warehouses, several houses and stores, and the Clayton County courthouse. Also they discover large quantities of "whisky and other necessary munitions of war," whereupon many of them get drunk. Appropriately, Kilpatrick's band—something that no well-conducted cavalry expedition should be without, even though Forrest somehow manages to get along without one—performs "Come Johnny, Fill up the Bowl," along with such rollicking tunes as "Yankee Doodle" and "Hail Columbia."

Meanwhile Armstrong, having driven away Klein's detachment, is marching back toward Jonesboro with orders from Jackson to join Ross and Ferguson in an attack on Kilpatrick. As Jackson plans it, Armstrong will strike from the west, Ferguson from the east, and Ross, who has withdrawn toward Lovejoy's, from the south. If all goes as it should, the Yankee raiders either will be trapped or else will be obliged to flee northward with Jackson's troopers hard on their heels and the Confederate infantry around Atlanta in position to block their escape. But luck, which does not necessarily favor the deserving, remains with Kilpatrick: he has intercepted a telegram that seems to indicate that Cleburne's Division and a cavalry brigade are en route to Jonesboro. Hence, at 10 P.M., deciding that he has done all the damage he prudently can at that town, he heads his column toward Lovejoy's. When scouts report that the direct route south is blocked by an enemy force of unknown size (it is Ross's Texans), he turns east so as to take the McDonough road. This should cause him to run into Ferguson. But Ferguson is not there; he has taken the wrong road. Is it because of the rain, or because of some other liquid? Whoever knows never tells.

Ross and Armstrong do not discover Kilpatrick's departure from Jonesboro until daylight on August 20, when they advance to attack him in accordance with Jackson's plan. They immediately give chase, Ross going by way of the McDonough road and Armstrong moving directly down the railroad in hopes of getting to Lovejoy's before the raiders. He does so and joins Reynolds's infantry, in the shelter of a deep railroad cut near the station.

Around 11 A.M., Kilpatrick's vanguard, consisting of Colonel Robert H. G.

Minty's brigade of Michiganians, Pennsylvanians, and regulars, approaches Lovejoy's from the northeast. Seeing no Rebels other than a few vedettes, Minty's troopers dismount and advance on foot, shouting "Forward to the railroad!" Reynolds's Arkansans and Armstrong's Mississippians hold their fire until they are within fifty yards; then they stand up and squeeze their triggers. Scores of Minty's troopers go down; the rest scurry back to their horses. Several minutes later, Ross's indefatigable Texans assail the federal rear. Quite literally Kilpatrick is caught between fires.

He quickly decides to abort the raid and return to Union lines. How to escape is the problem. His solution is the only sane one open to him: break through the Rebels in his rear and head northeast toward Decatur and the left wing of the Union army. Leaving a force to check Reynolds and Armstrong, he forms his command in a compact column spearheaded by Minty's brigade. Minty, a flamboyant former British cavalry officer, deploys his three regiments in as many lines, the men stirrup to stirrup. He then advances due north against Ross's Texans, who are behind a rail fence at the opposite end of an intervening field. On reaching the field, Minty's troopers draw their sabers and with a yell gallop forward full tilt. The charge sweeps over the Texans. A few are cut down, some surrender, but most escape, leaving behind a howitzer and, in an ambulance, the flag of the Third Texas Cavalry. It is the first, and will prove to be the last, successful mounted attack of the entire campaign. It also is the only time that one Union cavalryman "witnessed the use of the saber in a fight" during his three years of active service.

Kilpatrick regroups his forces, repulses an attack by Armstrong's Brigade, then sets out for McDonough. Marching in a heavy rain, he passes through that village around midnight, then turns north toward Lithonia. Armstrong conducts a perfunctory pursuit that ends on reaching a rain-swollen creek, and Ross, for obvious reasons, makes no attempt to pursue at all. On the afternoon of August 22, Kilpatrick's mud-splattered, bone-tired, and hollow-eyed horsemen reach Decatur, having traveled around both armies, lost 237 killed, wounded, and missing (most of them from Minty's brigade), and inflicted approximately the same number of casualties on their Confederate opponents.[28]

But what else have they done? That is what Sherman needs to know. As soon as he learns that Kilpatrick has returned, Sherman telegraphs Thomas that he wants to see him "soon as possible." In the evening, Kilpatrick, who entered Decatur riding in a carriage that had been laden with looted silver until it had tipped over while crossing a creek, arrives at Sherman's headquarters. He tells him that he has destroyed a three-mile stretch of the railroad at Jonesboro and another ten miles in sections—"enough to disable the road for ten days." Sherman listens to this, hopes it is true, but feels skeptical. Even if Kilpatrick

Sherman informs his generals of his intention to swing south round Atlanta *(Harper's Weekly)*

has wrecked as much track as he claims, will it take the Confederates a week and a half to repair it? Already they have had two days in which to do so, and during the day the signal station in the XV Corps's sector has reported that an eleven-car train has come into Atlanta. No, as much as he desired, indeed expected, Kilpatrick's raid to spare him the need of making "a long, hazardous flank march" around Atlanta, Sherman will have to undertake it after all. "I expect," he telegraphs Halleck at 10 P.M., "I will have to swing across" the Macon railroad "in force to make the matter certain."

His expectation is fully justified. In fact, Kilpatrick's troopers have torn up a mere one-half mile of track at Jonesboro, and the only other damage done to the railroad was by Klein's detachment, which removed a few rails "at intervals" south of Lovejoy's. By August 21 the Confederates had repaired both breaks, and Shoup was able to record in his journal that "a train came through on the Macon road at midnight." All that Kilpatrick has accomplished is to demonstrate in central Georgia what Wheeler has been demonstrating in northern Georgia: that cavalry are incapable of destroying a railroad so long as they have to worry about being destroyed themselves.

Early on the morning of August 23 the signal officer atop the XV Corps's lookout station spots a train pulled by three engines chugging into Atlanta. Sherman now knows for certain that Kilpatrick's raid has failed to achieve its objective. Accordingly he notifies Thomas, Howard, and Schofield that the "rebels have repaired the Macon road" and asks them when they can be ready to execute "our former plan." Thomas answers: "I would like to commence the movement without being hurried, and can do so by Thursday night," August 25. Sherman concurs and issues the necessary orders. The time has come to bring matters to a conclusion, one way or another, at Atlanta.[29]

Part Four: Washington and Richmond

At the beginning of August the Republicans had been despondent. As the month approaches its end they are close to despair. Grant remains bogged down outside Richmond and Petersburg; his only recent success, if such it can be called, has been the partial cutting of one of the three railroads serving Lee's army. The cost was 4,500 more casualties, 2,700 of them in a division that surrendered en masse when counterattacked in an ill-located defense line. In the Shenandoah the recently installed new Federal commander, Major General Phil Sheridan, has (like all of his predecessors) advanced and then retreated even though he outnumbers Jubal Early's Confederates more than two to one; this is scarcely encouraging. And down in Georgia, Sherman appears to be no closer to taking Atlanta than he had been a month ago, and what with Wheeler's cavalry slashing at his long supply line, it would not be the least bit surprising to learn that he is retreating back to Chattanooga, his campaign a disaster just as General Hooker, who is telling people that Sherman is crazy, predicts it will be. To be sure, that tough old sea dog Farragut has captured the forts and ships guarding Mobile Bay, thus closing that port and giving the North at long last something to cheer about. But it is a feeble cheer. Mobile itself still has not fallen, nor does it seem likely to anytime soon; and one can only groan over the latest news from Tennessee: Forrest, having slipped around A. J. Smith's army as it again invaded Mississippi, rode unopposed into Memphis on the night of August 21 with 2,000 of his troopers, occupied the city for several hours, almost captured generals Washburn and Hurlbut, and then returned virtually unscathed to whence he came. In a way this is more embarrassing even than Chambersburg, for Memphis supposedly was protected by a garrison and a fort. Furthermore, Smith has been obliged to abort his expedition, leaving Forrest free to go elsewhere, perhaps to Middle Tennessee.

"I see no bright spot anywhere," laments diarist George Templeton Strong in New York. "I fear the blood and treasure spent on this summer campaign has done little for this country." The Democrats say the same and more besides. The war is an "utter failure," pronounces arch-Copperhead Samuel Medary's *Columbus* (Ohio) *Crisis*. According to the *New York World,* the capture of Richmond is "further off now than ever before," and Grant's army soon will abandon the attempt. A correspondent for the same paper, who calls himself Druid and claims to have talked with high Confederate officials, reports that, thanks to reinforcements, many of whom are from Virginia, Hood now outnumbers Sherman, whose position is "critical." Waxing sarcastic, the *Chicago Times* celebrates the passing of "two whole weeks" without a "single Federal defeat!" and the achievement of "Three More Brilliant Failures by Ulysses S. Grant." And in an editorial widely quoted by other Democratic journals, the *Jefferson County* (N.Y.) *Union* presents the "Statistics of Carnage for the Northern Army":

> There has been enough already slain to encircle our State, if their dead bodies were laid in a continuous line.
> If they were placed in coffins and corded, they would count thirty-nine thousand cords.
> If piled upon a ten-acre lot, they would be nearly two hundred feet high.
> Seventy-five thousand tons of human blood have been spilled in Dixie's soil—enough to turn every spindle in Lowell, and if tears were added to the flood it would turn the machinery of the continent.
> And the end is not yet.

The carnage will not end, the Democrats declare, until the war ends, and that can only be achieved with peace. What is needed, therefore, is an armistice, an immediate suspension of hostilities. A convention of all the states then will be held, at which the Union will be restored on the basis of the North's granting the South all of its rights under the Constitution, in particular the right of slavery. The South will accept these terms. If Jefferson Davis balks, the Southern people, who are also weary of the hideous, useless carnage, will override him. The sole reason they battle on so desperately, yet invincibly, is because Lincoln and the Republicans have, to quote the August 16 *Chicago Times,* "changed this war from one in which a nation fought to preserve its existence to one in which a fanatical minority is attempting to subserve its own unrighteous ends"—the freeing of a race that is undeserving of freedom. Until this ceases to be the case, the stacks of corpses will grow higher, freedom and liberty will sink lower, and the government, already on the brink of bankruptcy, will be engulfed in total financial collapse, dragging down everything and everybody with it. "This," asserts the *New York World,* also on August 16, "is what mad fanatics and thoughtless demagogues have brought us to! One more year under the present administration would ruin us hopelessly. Can the republic yet be saved? Let the answer come next November."[30]

On August 29 the Democratic Convention, twice postponed, finally will gather in Chicago. Almost surely it will adopt a platform branding the war a failure and calling for a negotiated peace. Almost surely, too, it will nominate General George B. McClellan, former commander of the Army of the Potomac and still beloved by many of its soldiers, for president. And just as surely, unless the war takes a decisive turn for the better, McClellan will be elected. Such, at any rate, is the hope and even the expectation of the Democrats and the fear and apprehension of the Republicans. Among the latter is Thurlow Weed of New York, reputedly the canniest politician in the country. He believes that "the people are wild for peace," and he has told Lincoln, to whom he is an unofficial advisor, that his reelection is "an impossibility." Another is Horace Greeley, whose *New York Tribune* still refuses to endorse Lincoln's nomination. Declaring that "Mr. Lincoln is already beaten," Greeley has joined with some likeminded Republicans, including the mayor of New York and the national treasurer of the party, to bring about a new convention that will choose a new candidate: Grant, Ben Butler, and even Sherman are being considered. Butler, Senator Charles Sumner, and Governor John Andrew, all of Massachusetts, support this movement. So, too, does the *Cincinnati Gazette,* which has called for Lincoln to withdraw from the race, a plea that is echoed by other major Republican newspapers.

In fact, so widespread and intense is Republican defeatism that even Henry Raymond, editor of the *New York Times* and national chairman of the Union (Republican) party, believes that "unless some prompt and bold step be now taken all is lost." Hence he has sent Lincoln a letter, written August 22, designed to persuade him to take such a step:

> I feel compelled to drop you a line concerning the political condition
> of the country as it strikes me. I am in active correspondence with your
> staunchest friends in every State and from them all I hear but one report.
> The tide is setting strongly against us. Hon. E. B. Washburne writes that
> "were an election to be held now in Illinois we should be beaten." Mr.
> Cameron writes that Pennsylvania is against us. Gov. Morton writes that
> nothing but the most strenuous efforts can carry Indiana. This State
> [New York], according to the best information I can get, would go 50,000
> against us to-morrow. And so the rest.

There are, the letter continues, "Two special causes . . . for this great reaction in public sentiment—the want of military success, and the impression in some minds, the fear and suspicion in others, that we are not to have peace *in any event* under this administration until Slavery is abandoned" and that consequently Lincoln is "fighting not for the Union but for the abolition of Slavery." Little can be done, of course, about the military situation other than to hope for the best; but with respect to the second cause of disaffection, something can and must be done. Specifically, Lincoln should appoint a commission *"to make [a] distinct proffer of peace to Davis, as head of the rebel armies, on the sole condition of acknowledging the supremacy of the Constitution,* all other questions [including the status of slavery] to be settled by a convention of the people of all the States." This proposal would involve no armistice and would place Davis in a dilemma. Should Davis accept this proposal, which he won't, "the country would never consent to place the practical execution of its details in any but loyal hands"—that is, with Lincoln and the Republicans. On the other hand, should Davis reject it, which he will, "it would plant seeds of disaffection in the South, dispel all delusions about peace that prevail in the North, silence the clamors and damaging falsehoods of the opposition . . . and unite the North as nothing since the firing on Fort Sumter has."

Raymond wants Lincoln to seek to transform an impending Republican defeat into victory by pretending to adopt the essence of the Democratic nostrum of Union through peace. In effect, Raymond is stating that the only hope of warding off the calamitous political consequences of military frustration is through political means.

Raymond's letter still is on its way from New York City to Washington when, on the morning of August 23, the same morning that Sherman tells his generals to make ready for a move south around Atlanta, Lincoln meets with his cabinet. But he does not need to read it. He already realizes all too well, as he had admitted to a visitor two weeks ago, that he is going to be *"badly beaten"* unless "some great change" occurs in the way the war is going. Many besides Weed have told him this, and in any case he is second to none in his ability to discern the current of public sentiment. Hence he has decided to do what he now proceeds to do: he asks each cabinet member to sign a piece of paper that is folded and pasted in such a manner that what is written on it cannot be seen. None object, all sign. He then places the paper in a desk drawer, and they leave. Not until many years afterward will the few of them who are still living learn that they had affixed their signatures below these words, penned by Lincoln himself:

Executive Mansion, Washington, August 23, 1864
This morning, as for some days past, it seems exceedingly probable
that this Administration will not be reelected. Then it will be my duty to

so cooperate with the President-elect, as to save the Union between the election and the inauguration; as he will have secured his election on such ground that he cannot possibly save it afterwards.[31]

"We have arrived," begins an editorial in the *Richmond Sentinel* for August 20, "at a very critical stage of the war, and calm circumspection, caution and patient endurance are needed to carry successfully through it." This is not, it explains, because of the South's situation; rather it because of the North's. "To weather the next six weeks will be a most difficult task for the North." By the end of that time "it is not at all improbable that the armies of Grant, Sherman, and Sheridan . . . will have been almost annihilated." Within that time, too, the Democratic Convention in all likelihood "will have thrown its apple of discord and destruction into the already distracted and discordant ranks of the North." Furthermore, should the new Union draft fail, as it appears destined to do, "the North will be almost without an army," it "may give rise to mobs, riots, revolutionary outbursts, and civil war in that section," and will "certainly increase and exacerbate the hatred of New York, Pennsylvania, New Jersey, and the Northwest toward New England," which grows rich from the war while the rest of the North fights it. But even if the draft should succeed, "it will only put in raw, undisciplined, reluctant recruits and mercenary substitutes to supply the places of veteran volunteers" whose terms of service will be expiring, "continually weakening them and relatively strengthening us." And finally, but perhaps most decisively of all, the Northern currency "is sure to grow continually worse, and without money—money that is readily current—they cannot long prosecute the war."

Thus, predicts the *Richmond Sentinel:*

Six weeks hence we are almost sure to be in a much better condition to treat for peace than we are now, and our enemy in a much worse condition. Within that time it may be we shall have defeated and gotten rid of the armies of Grant, Sherman, and Sheridan, capturing part of them and expelling the balance from our territory. Six weeks hence, instead of waging defensive warfare, we may be invading the enemy's soil, and carrying out offensive warfare. We have little to apprehend and much to hope for within that period. Time is victory to us and death to our enemies.

The *Richmond Sentinel,* as all informed people know, speaks for Davis. If it does not necessarily mirror his thoughts, it definitely reflects what he desires others to think. In either case it is clear from this editorial that unlike Lincoln, who fears or even expects defeat, Davis late in August hopes for, even expects, victory. All that the South need do to achieve it is to hold fast a while longer— just six more weeks—until the Northern elections get under way (Maine and Vermont vote in September; crucial Indiana and several other key states vote in October). "We rely," writes Confederate War Department clerk Jones in his diary for August 21, "some little upon the success of the peace party." Moreover the vast majority of articulate Southerners share their president's optimism—or at least so they say in public. Even those newspapers that are hostile to him declare that the war is going well and express confidence as to the future; indeed, some assert that it would make no difference should Lincoln and the Republicans perchance retain their hold on power: the Confederacy still will prevail in the end. None predicts defeat, and when defeat is mentioned at all, it is always in the context of warning against the calamities that would ensue if it should happen. As August draws to a close, the chances of its happening seem far less than they had at the beginning of May.[32]

Part Five: Flint River

Word that Sherman is about to make another flanking move does not surprise his troops. They wonder only why he has waited so long. They also are pleased. Most of them have spent the past month engaged in the same sort of tedious, vicious, and essentially useless type of warfare that was rehearsed at Dalton and Resaca and perfected at New Hope Church and Kennesaw: digging, skirmishing ("woodchopping," they call it), sniping, and more digging—all punctuated with bombardments and counterbombardments, sporadic firefights, and occasional local assaults, delivered or resisted. Although parapets with dirt embankments twelve-feet thick, "bombproof" dugouts, and covered communication trenches have become standard, "We can get no place," Colonel Cavins has informed his wife, "but that balls will whiz in close proximity and no time during the day is there one minute during which a musket shot will not come near you." Sergeant Phinehas Hager of the 23rd Michigan, who wrote his wife on July 23 that "many brave boys must yet fall before this cruel war is over," was mortally wounded less than two weeks later by a "chance shot" while standing behind a breastwork distributing rations. In one week the 70th Ohio lost 31 men killed and wounded, even though it had never been engaged in anything remotely resembling a battle. Nor does rank necessarily provide immunity, as was demonstrated on August 19 when both Dodge and Lightburn went down with head wounds. Even a dog, pet of the captain of Battery I, 2nd Illinois Light Artillery, was shot deliberately by a Rebel sniper.

Bad as the bullets and shells are, as always far more men have succumbed to sickness, exhaustion, and the emotional strain of constant exposure to death or maiming. In Cavin's 69th Indiana, "there are but few of my men but that are worn out. We have 145 men bearing muskets; of this number about fifty are excused from fatigue and skirmish duty" and fight "only in case of attack." His officers consist of three captains, "none of whom are able for duty, and four lieutenants who have average health." Other than himself and his adjutant, every officer in the regiment "has been excused from duty on account of sickness at some time during the campaign." The need to stand for hours at a time, often under a broiling sun, sometimes knee-deep in water, and always "surrounded by offal, and all kinds of decaying matter," has helped fill to overflowing the hospitals at Marietta, where Othniel Gooding, a Michigan soldier who is suffering from "lung inflammation," shares a "little room" with "six besides myself," two of whom "are very sick while the rest are getting along with a prospect that looks as though they might soon be able to be shot at again." No doubt Captain James Theaker of the 50th Ohio tells the truth in the letter he writes his brother on August 11: "The energies & physical endurance of the men is taxed to the utmost and nothing but self-preservation could induce the men to do what they do"—that is, fight on.[33]

This desire for self-preservation, however, has had just the opposite effect on some Union soldiers. They are the nonveterans who, for understandable reasons, recoil at the prospect of being shot or captured just before their enlistments expire or, in some instances, after they have expired, at least according to their calculations. In Major Taylor's 47th Ohio, which fought so well on July 28, a near mutiny occurred in one company on August 1. And three days later, Taylor at first could not get the regiment to leave its trenches; then he had to take men "by the shoulders & lead them, drive them and shame them forward" in a vain attempt to recapture a line of rifle pits. Likewise the 11th Michigan, when ordered to perform picket duty on the third anniversary of its mustering in, had "bolted and wouldn't go," to quote the diary of Private Daniel Rose. Under military law such conduct makes the troops who engage in it liable to harsh punishment, even mass executions; in practice, in this quintessentially American army, it merely speeds up the process of sending them home to be mustered out. As a consequence Taylor finds himself reduced to the "farce of comndg. 59 pri, 6 Corps & 14 Sergts as a regiment." Ironically, his own enlistment has elapsed, and he is so incensed at being held in "servitude" that he seriously considers seeking a writ of habeas corpus to secure his release![34]

Becoming a "mackerel," as discharged soldiers are called, means escape from the trenches and the ever-present shadow of death. For the troops who remain, the best way out, if only for a brief while, is a cease-fire agreement with the enemy. A shakily literate Illinois private reports to his parents on August 25: "We maid a bargain with the rebs not to shoot at one annother here in the scourmish line unless one side or the other went to advance, so it makes it mutch pleasanter. We will stand and look at one annother not more than 25 rods apart, look at one annother like some wild beasts." In some sectors, fraternization again has occurred, with Federals and Confederates "chatting together quite freely, exchanging papers, tobaco [*sic*], coffee and other small articles. One of the 'Johnnies' remained in our camp last night and returned to his own in the morning." When obliged by orders to resume hostilities, Yanks and Rebs often express regret and always give each other plenty of time to get back in their respective "holes."

Enjoyable as they are, such interludes of peace and safety provide little relief from the miserable monotony of trench war and in some ways actually make it worse. Moreover many of the Union troops are beginning to feel "fidgety." Like Private Henry Orendorf of the 103rd Illinois, they realize that the Confederates are "holding us about level here," that they "have been within 3 miles of Atlanta for a month now," and that they are not "getting any closer." That is why they welcome the prospect of another flanking move. That is the best way, in fact the only way, to make the Rebels come out of their fortifications, either to retreat or to fight. Whichever it is, they hope it will bring about the fall of Atlanta and the end of the campaign. Surgeon Clairborne Walter of the XIV Corps expresses their sentiments vehemently but exactly when he declares: "I am sick, yes sick and tired of bloodshed. Weary and worn out with it. This campaign has been almost one continued scene of carnage from day to day." It is time it stop, and the sooner the better.[35]

On August 25, Private Samuel King Vann, 19th Alabama, Deas's Brigade, writes his sweetheart:

> Well Lizzie, if you could have seen me night before last when I came off *picket,* you would have thought that I was—well I don't know what you would have thought for I was a sight sure, for we had to lie in the ditches in the mud, over knee-deep for 24 hours, and you know that was awful sure, but we took it all fair and easy for we were obliged to do it. I have never seen the like before and I hope that I never will again. . . . We get somebody hurt every day in our Regt. and we lose one from our "Co." every time we go on picket, which is every three days, and tonight is our time again and who will get wounded this time or killed.

This same day another letter writer, William B. Honnell, a Mississippi soldier, informs his sisters that "it is a picket fight all the time we loose some men every day in our brigade eather killed or wounded . . . our pickets and the yankees pickets is in a bout fifty yards of each other and both party is digging yet. I reckon they will get together after while[.] It is work work every day and there is verry little rest here or sleap eather but we must put up with it."

Along with other brigadiers, Manigault has had to move his headquarters to a "bombproof" 150 yards behind the breastworks of his troops after "at least fifteen hundred shot and shell either struck or exploded within twenty paces" of where it was first located on the front line. In the trench held by Lieutenant Gill's company, a shell tore a man to "shreds," and being buried under avalanches of dirt has become a common experience. Also, as on the Union side, high rank does not necessarily bring immunity. The already crippled Bate received a leg wound on August 10, with the result that Brown has assumed command of his division, and shortly thereafter Stephen Lee and Patton Anderson narrowly escaped a similar or worse fate when a shell exploded six or eight feet away from them while they were observing the Yankees from a hill that Manigault had warned them was exposed to enemy fire. Because of the need to conserve ammunition, the Confederate artillery, in the words of an Alabama soldier, fires "in fits and starts," whereas the Union cannons "throw a shell every few minutes," and infantrymen have orders to shoot only when sure of their target or in the event of attack. Food, too, is in short supply, and despite a Tennessean's assurance to his family on August 23 that "we are living tolerably well at this time and get plenty of bacon and corn bread and sometimes [a] mess of peas," there have been periods when rations have been reduced to one-half or even one-fourth, and a lack of vegetables and fruit has produced widespread night blindness. Their inadequate diet, combined with the physical and psychological ordeal of defending day after day and night after night a fifteen-mile front against a numerically superior foe, is taking many Confederates to the limits of their endurance if not beyond. "There is much sickness among us," Lieutenant Gill reports to his wife in an August 11 letter. By modern standards, probably at least half of Hood's army is medically unfit for combat.

In the same letter quoted above, Gill also states: "There is much demoralization in the army—desertions are numerous, some of the best soldiers are leaving. The duties are very heavy indeed and the troops are getting tired of it. I never complain but endeavor to build up spirits. I meet with such little success that I am much disheartened." The situation is especially bad in Lee's Corps. There, early in August, Lee had considered it necessary to reprimand Baker's Brigade for having "lost its picket-line oftener than any other brigade in the corps" after one-hundred of its skirmishers had surrendered with no more than a semblance of resistance. About the same time, Stovall's Georgians had reached an "understanding" with the XIV Corps troops opposite them for both sides to fire high, and on August 13 nearly thirty of Clayton's pickets had thrown down their rifles and run over to the Union lines. This last incident, plus numerous desertions by men fraternizing with the Yankees, had impelled Hood on August 15 to issue an order stating that soldiers "who shall in any way communicate or attempt to communicate with the enemy without authority" were to be "fired upon by all parties in reach" and that officers "permitting such offense" were to be sent to the rear under guard for immediate trial. In other words, the troops would stand guard over each other.[36]

Although Hood's order has by no means stopped informal truces, fraternization, and desertion, it has reduced them considerably. In addition, since its promulgation, morale has been reviving. There are several reasons for this. One is the news of continued Union setbacks in Virginia, of increased war-weariness in the North, and the accordingly bright prospect of a Democratic victory there. Another is the fact that Sherman has been held in check for a month now, and that since Utoy Creek he has not so much as attempted a major offensive movement. But the main reason is Wheeler's raid. On August 14, Hood had announced to the army that Wheeler was in the enemy's rear and that "this week will decide the fate of Atlanta." During the ensuing days, rumors had circulated both by word of mouth and newspapers that Wheeler had torn up thirty miles of track, captured 4,000 prisoners, burned the bridges over the Etowah and the Oostanaula, and destroyed the tunnel through Tunnel Hill and that "the Yankees are starving, that they are living on green corn, that they are deserting by squads of ten and twenty." By August 19, Colonel Ellison Capers was predicting to his wife that Sherman would have to retreat by September; and on that same day, Colonel Beatty commented in his diary that if Wheeler "succeeds as well as reports say I think it will cause Sherman to fall back." Likewise on August 24, Patton Anderson told his troops (Hindman's former division) that "if we could hold our ground a few days longer at this place that the victory was assuredly ours, for General Wheeler has gone around in their [the Yankees'] rear and torn up the railroad, and if they can not flank us and cause us to retreat, that they will necessarily be compelled to charge us, or retreat toward Chattanooga, or be compelled to starve to death." Obviously enthused by Anderson's speech, Private Vann of the 19th Alabama on the following day describes it to "Dear Lizzie," then resolutely declares: "There are not many of us dirty Rebs here but what few of us are here are in fine spirits and can whip many a Yank yet."

Such is the hope inspired by Wheeler's foray. Accompanying it, though, is another and much stronger hope, one that the "dirty Rebs" share with the equally dirty Yanks—namely, that this campaign soon will end and, with it, perhaps the war itself. Indeed, it is more than a hope; it is a desire, a longing so intense as to be almost an expectation. "The most of the people," states Angus McDermid in an August 21 letter to his parents, "thinks that the war is very near ended. I do myself for things are about plaid out on both sides. I dont care mutch how it ends myself so it will end."[37]

Sherman's plan for swinging south around Atlanta, the details of which are based on a memorandum prepared by Thomas, calls for first sending "all surplus wagons, horses, men and materials" across the Chattahoochee and loading the remaining wagons with one hundred rounds of ammunition per man, a fifteen-day supply of food, and enough half-rations of forage to last for the same length of time, the rest to come from the ripening corn of central Georgia. By August 25 these preparations have been made, and in addition, the siege guns have been withdrawn and their embrasures filled with brush. Accordingly, at 8 P.M. the XX Corps falls back one-half mile toward the Chattahoochee, leaving behind only a picket line. As it does so the IV Corps in like manner pulls out of its trenches and passes behind the XX Corps, which then takes up position along the south bank of the Chattahoochee so as to cover the railroad bridge and adjoining crossings. On the morning of August 26, after a halt to rest and reform, the IV Corps proceeds to the Utoy Post Office area, where it deploys a line of battle facing north, ready to repel a Confederate attack upon what now is the rear of Sherman's army.[38]

None occurs. Despite having noticed yesterday the brush piles in front of the Union gun embrasures and despite having heard the sound of an "unusual train" of wagons moving to the north, the Confederates do not discover the withdrawal of the IV and XX corps until daylight, when they send forward scouts and skirmishers; even then they do not pursue. Instead, after making sure that the Federals indeed are gone from north and east of Atlanta and are not concentrating for an assault, they content themselves with occupying the abandoned fortifications. In them, to their delight, they find large quantities of blankets, clothing, hardtack, bacon, and even sutler's stores. Courier Trask records the result in his diary: "To-day our troops are feasting on sardines and lobsters, canned fruit of every kind, candies, cakes and raisins, besides many other good things their stomachs had long been strangers to."

Hood would like to believe that Sherman is retreating, retreating across the Chattahoochee, retreating toward Chattanooga. It would mean victory and vindication. Moreover there were reasons for so believing. Reports have been received by Shoup that the railroad in the enemy's rear has been "badly torn up." Prisoners state that Wheeler has blown up the tunnel at Tunnel Hill and burned the Etowah bridge. A woman spy, who had gone into the Union lines on

August 18, had been told by General Cox, when she had applied to him for rations, that he had none to give her and that he himself had been "living on short rations for seven days, and now that your people have torn up our railroad and stolen our beef-cattle, we must live a damn sight shorter." Yankee cavalrymen, complaining of hunger, have been taking hogs, corn, and other provisions from the farms around Atlanta. Two days ago, scouts brought word that "the enemy has not had a through train in six or seven days." And just today a detachment from Wheeler escorted into Atlanta one thousand head of captured cattle—dramatic (and edible) evidence of success. At Hood's headquarters, Shoup records in his journal for August 26, "the prevailing impression" is that the Federals "are falling back across the Chattahoochee River."

Yet, as Shoup also notes, "no reliable information has been received in regard to the intention of the enemy." All that is known definitely is that Sherman has pulled back the left wing of his army from the north and east of Atlanta; the other wing, so far at least, remains west of the city. This might well mean that he plans to make another attempt to reach the Macon railroad by extending southward. Hence, to guard against this very likely eventuality, during the day Hood instructs Maney, whose division has been opposing the IV Corps, to be ready to "move at a moment's notice"; sends an identical order to Walthall; alerts Jackson's cavalry to be on the lookout on the left; and directs Smith's militia to occupy, when it becomes dark, the fortifications between the Peachtree road and the railroad held by Stevenson's Division, which in turn is to retire to a "convenient point in the rear." In the evening, Hood telegraphs Seddon that "last night the enemy abandoned the Augusta railroad and all the country between that road and the Dalton railroad," but he makes no comment other than to state that Sherman "has not extended his right at all."[39]

During the night the second phase of Sherman's southward maneuver gets under way. The XIV Corps and the Army of the Tennessee, employing the same tactics used by the IV and XX corps, evacuate their trenches. Once clear of them, the XIV Corps, which since August 22 has been under the command of Davis, now a major general, marches in "excessive rain" to the south side of Utoy Creek, where at daylight it bivouacs. At the same time Howard's three corps proceed via Lick Skillet and Owl Creek Church to Camp Creek, a minor stream about four miles south of Utoy Creek. They arrive there around 8 A.M. on August 27, whereupon the IV Corps likewise sets out for Camp Creek, its destination being Mt. Gilead Church. All the while the XXIII Corps, strongly fortified, remains opposite East Point, screening these movements.

The Confederates, having been put on the qui vive by the Yankees' previous nocturnal withdrawal, shell Howard's and Davis's troops as they march away but make no attempt to attack or pursue them. During the morning, Stewart's

Corps (Stewart himself is again in command) occupies most of the lines hitherto held by the Army of the Tennessee, and Lee's Corps takes over the XIV Corps's trenches. Lieutenant Gill is among the first to climb into the enemy's works, where he sees "many of the boys pick up from 1 lb. to 12 lbs. bacon." He obtains a "a fine lot" of roasting ears and "a big mess of beans," the first he has eaten all year. They taste so good that he feels that "if I ever get home to live in peace, I am going to have plenty to eat and nice."

Equally pleasant, as far as Gill is concerned, is the absence of gunfire. He suspects, however, that Sherman may be playing a "Yankee trick." So, too, do other Confederate soldiers. Although they hope that the Federals in truth are retreating, like Captain James Douglas they consider it just as likely that "they have some grand move on foot"; or else, along with McDermid, they think that "the Yankies are a going to attack us." Even Captain Key, who believes that "the scales have turned in favor of the South, and the Abolitionists are moving to the rear toward their own homes," admits that the enemy "may be massing his forces to attack Hood's left."

Hood himself continues to be concerned about this danger. Not only are the Yankees still near East Point, but Ross reports that they are moving in strength toward Camp Creek, and a reconnaissance by French has ascertained that the XX Corps is entrenched along the south bank of the Chattahoochee around the railroad bridge. Hence he has sent Strahl's Brigade to reinforce Hardee, most of whose corps now is in the East Point area, and has instructed Jackson to have Armstrong's Brigade "oppose stoutly the enemy should he attempt to cross" Camp Creek in the direction of Rough and Ready, a village on the Macon railroad three miles southeast of East Point (it derives its name from Zachary Taylor's famous sobriquet). Furthermore, when in the evening he telegraphs Seddon, he states that Sherman's "right is unchanged" and that the Federals "appear to be moving troops in that direction." Far from being deluded by the Union withdrawals into thinking that Sherman is retreating, as contemporary critics and critical historians will subsequently charge, Hood realizes that Sherman most likely is launching, or is about to launch, another large-scale flanking movement to the south. What Hood does not know and, under the circumstances, cannot know is exactly what Sherman intends to do, where, when, and how. Try to strike the railroad at Rough and Ready? Or at Jonesboro? Or at some other point? Or, conceivably, does Sherman seek to draw the Confederates out of Atlanta, then have the XX Corps swoop down to seize it? Until Hood can, with reasonable confidence, answer these questions, all he will be able to do is what Shoup, in his journal entry for August 27 states he had done: dispose "his troops so as to be prepared for any emergency." Indeed, at this juncture it would be foolish for Hood to do anything other than this.[40]

On Sunday morning August 28, hundreds of civilians and soldiers crowd Atlanta's battle-scarred churches to thank God the bombardment has ceased. Since August 24 not a shell has fallen on the city. Until then, hardly a day or night passed without storms of missiles that seemed to keep growing in fury, as if the Yankees had a quota to be reached by a certain time. Carrie Berry's family had to leave the cellar of their house, because it no longer was safe, and move into a larger, deeper one below a Five Points store—a change that pleased Carrie because she and the other children could "run as much as we pleased and enjoy it." During the final twenty-four hours the shelling attained a crescendo, setting fires that leveled nine buildings, among them a warehouse, which was filled with cotton bales, and the "Lard Oil" factory and causing a reporter for the *Augusta Constitutionalist* to write about "shells all night, shells all day, shells for breakfast, dinner and tea, shells for all hours and sorts of weather." Most of the damage is centered along Marietta Street in the northwest part of the city and around Whitehall Street in the center. There virtually all buildings have been hit at least once and some repeatedly. Moreover, during the night of August 11, Confederate cavalrymen took advantage of the shelling to ransack again the business district, impelling Hood to issue an order denouncing "worthless men, especially from the mounted command," and calling for their arrest and execution so that "examples may be immediately made."

According to "Shadow," the Atlanta correspondent for the *Mobile Daily Advertiser and Register,* 497 people have been killed and 651 wounded. But these figures, with their extraordinarily high ratio of dead to injured, border on the incredible. If they are at all accurate, it would mean that as many as half and no fewer than one-fifth of the city's inhabitants, including military personnel stationed there, have fallen victim to Sherman's shells. Such a mass slaughter almost surely would have touched off a mass panic and exodus. Probably Sam Richards comes much closer to the truth in his diary entry for August 21, where he states that "it is said that about twenty lives have been destroyed by these terrible missiles, since the enemy began to throw them into the city."

Whatever the number of casualties, for more than a month, Death has stalked the streets of Atlanta, striking at random. Solomon Luckie, a black barber, died when hit by a shell fragment that ricocheted off a lamppost at the corner of Whitehall and Alabama Streets. Another man had his arm blown off while seeking refuge in the basement of the Presbyterian Church. Another shell killed a woman as she stood ironing clothes in a house on Pryor Street. On Forsyth Street a Confederate officer and a little boy bled to death in a front yard after an explosion ripped their bodies. No wonder Richards, whose house has been struck three times, has come to feel that "it is like living in the midst of a pestilence, no one can feel but he may be the next victim."

Under the rules and practices of war, Atlanta (since it was the headquarters of an army, was a railroad and supply center, and was fortified and garrisoned) was a legitimate target of bombardment. Furthermore, although Sherman deserves to be criticized for not having offered to allow the city's civilians an opportunity to leave once he knew, as he assuredly did, that many of them remained, Hood is equally at fault for not having requested such permission. Yet, if legal, militarily the bombardment, in the words of Captain Poe, "did no good at all"; and General Stanley is correct in calling it "a waste of ammunition." The only thing it achieved, other than to kill and maim a number of (again to quote Poe) "unoffending people," was to take a stride toward turning Atlanta into a "used up community." Writing in his diary on August 24, the last day of shelling, Captain Key had observed that "as a matter of fact, Sherman is gradually destroying the city." But even along this line there still is much more that can be done.[41]

While Atlantans rejoice in the disappearance of the Yankee army from the gates of the Gate City and hope it never returns, the bulk of that army continues advancing southward. Around noon on August 28 the XV and XVII corps reach the West Point railroad at Fairburn and, a few hours later, the IV and XIV corps do the same near Red Oak. Plenty of daylight remains, and the only opposition encountered so far has taken the negligible form of a few Rebel cavalry bands. By pushing on until nightfall, Sherman can put his forces in position to strike the Macon railroad between Rough and Ready and Jonesboro early tomorrow morning.

He does nothing of the kind. Instead he orders Thomas and Howard to set all of their troops to work destroying the West Point railroad and to keep them at it throughout August 29. "Let the destruction," he urges Thomas, "be so thorough that not a rail or tie can be used again," and he instructs Howard to "fill up some cuts in the railroad with logs and trees covered with dirt, so we may rest perfectly satisfied as regards the use of this railroad during the remainder of the campaign." Either he does not know or does not care that the West Point railroad, although the damage done by Rousseau in July now is fully repaired, has been carrying little traffic between Atlanta and Montgomery, because of its vulnerability to Union cavalry raids, and that Hood continues to receive practically all of his supplies via Macon. Evidently, too, it does not occur to Sherman that he could just as effectively wreck the West Point line by leaving behind a strong detachment for that purpose—the XVII Corps would be ideal—while pressing on with his main force toward the Macon railroad. Experience has demonstrated that 1,000 troops, with the know-how and proper equipment, can demolish five miles of track in a day.[42]

In the evening, Hood telegraphs Seddon: "The enemy have changed their entire position, the left of their line resting near the Chattahoochee about Sandtown, and their right extending to a point opposite and near the West Point railroad between East Point and Fairburn." Thus Hood has a reasonably accurate idea of where Sherman's main force is. What Hood still does not know is where that force is headed. Nor does the dispatch that has arrived during the day from Wheeler (the first since he set out on his raid) provide any help in figuring out Sherman's intentions. In fact, it does just the reverse. In it Wheeler, under the date of August 19, asserts that he has captured Dalton and a large quantity of supplies; that he has destroyed twenty-five miles of railroad, including a section of the line to Cleveland, Tennessee; that no train has passed between Chattanooga and the Chattahoochee for a week and that none would pass for another week; and that he has lost only thirty men and that his command is in fine condition.

All of this is arrant, lying nonsense. As we have seen, Wheeler damaged a mere two miles of track around Dalton and Tilton before scurrying off into Tennessee. Since August 16, trains have been passing freely along the Western and Atlantic. The force (Kelly's Division) that captured Dalton was routed by Steedman and barely escaped capture itself. Wheeler has placed one of his division commanders, Martin, under arrest for allegedly disobeying orders, and another, Humes, for a while lost contact with him. Hundreds of Wheeler's troopers, especially the Tennesseans, have left him to visit their homes or have simply deserted. Wheeler himself now is moving toward Middle Tennessee, having (as Sherman predicted) accomplished little in the eastern part of the state other than to lose more men and horses. Once again Wheeler's inability to control forces that are not under his personal supervision has been demonstrated, as well as his chronic inability to tell the truth about what has been done or, in this case, what has not been done.

Hood, of course, does not realize that Wheeler has sent him false, misleading intelligence. Probably he agrees with Shoup, who after recording the gist of Wheeler's dispatch in his journal, comments: "On the whole the reports of his operations are very encouraging." Perhaps, though, Hood is asking himself some questions; certainly he should be. If Wheeler has wrecked so much of the Western and Atlantic, why do scouts report that trains are still arriving at and leaving Vining's Station? Why, in the same connection, does a captured Federal officer (a member, furthermore, of the staff of the same General Cox who allegedly is going hungry) state that although Wheeler has torn up a considerable portion of the railroad, he doubts that his raid will "seriously inconvenience" Sherman's army? Why, too, have the Yankees left behind so much food in their fortifications? This hardly is a sign of imminent starvation! Above all, why is Sherman, if his supply line has been cut or disrupted, advancing southward instead of retreating northward?

That Sherman is doing this, that he has reached the West Point railroad around Fairburn, and that he maintains a bridgehead on the Chattahoochee are the only definite facts that Hood possesses. They leave him, he concludes, with no practical choice except to continue guarding against what obviously is the greatest threat to his army, namely, having the enemy break the rail link between Atlanta and Macon. At present it seems to him that most likely that threat will take the form of a cavalry raid (in the style of McCook's and Kilpatrick's attempts) against the railroad with the object of forcing him out of Atlanta without a battle. Should this be the case (the slowness of the Union shift southward, plus a report that the Federal wagon trains are passing down the Chattahoochee on its right bank, indicate that it is), then Sherman will find it no easier to succeed than he has before. Reynolds's Arkansas Brigade already has been sent to Jonesboro by train, and Lewis's Kentuckians will follow as soon as the train returns; both will cooperate with Armstrong in "repelling raids." Likewise Brown, with the remainder of Bate's Division, has gone to Rough and Ready bearing orders to fortify the place and be on the lookout for raiders coming from the direction of the West Point railroad. As Shoup notes in his journal on the evening of August 28, "every precaution has been taken by the commanding general to keep our line of communication from being cut by the enemy."43

Sherman has given detailed directions on how he wants the West Point railroad wrecked. On August 29 his troops put them into effect. While two-thirds of them, entrenched, stand guard against enemy attack, the other third line up along the track, two men to a tie, stick their bayoneted rifles into the ground so that they will be handy, and then at a "Yo heave!" grab the ties and lift, ripping up the track and tipping it over. Then they take sledge hammers, hand spikes, or anything else that serves the purpose, and knock the ties loose from the rails. That done, they pile up the ties, set them on fire, and lay the iron rails on top. When the rails are red hot in the middle, they pick them up at both ends and twist them around telegraph poles or trees. "That fixes them"; they can never be relaid. The wreckers, per Sherman's instructions, also fill the deeper cuts through which the rail bed passes with brush, logs, and rocks, to which they add shells fixed so that they will explode if the Confederates—for example, gangs of slaves—try to remove them. Altogether twelve and a half miles of the West Point railroad between the Red Oak and Fairburn areas receive this treatment.[44]

Not all Federals, however, spend the day working on the railroad or protecting those who are doing so. Swarms of them, mostly from the Army of the Tennessee, enter houses, steal knives, forks, and spoons, take food and ransack trunks, and smash furniture just for the sheer fun of it. Captain Poe finds it "perfectly pitiable to witness the distress of the people through here," and he prays to God "it may never be my duty to see the like again." Whenever he comes upon soldiers "robbing and plundering I lose my temper . . . and make pretty free use of the physical strength with which Providence has blessed me, as more than one 'bunged up' face in our army can testify." Yet his "attempts to stop these things are but a small & feeble effort, when we regard the great number of those [officers] who either wink at it or openly encourage it." Howard, on learning of the depredations from "a most reliable source," issues an order directing his corps commanders to "take measures and prevent conduct so shameful and so disgraceful to our army," adding that they "will be sustained in the infliction of punishment immediate and adequate to stop such offenses." He issues this order; and that is that. Among the hundreds of diaries, letters, and memoirs left behind by the officers and men of the Army of the Tennessee, there is not a single reference to the order, much less to its enforcement. It is as if it never was.[45]

In the evening, Sherman, having spent the day making sure that the Confederates cannot use an unusable railroad, gives his orders for tomorrow: Howard is to march toward Jonesboro but is to halt four miles west of it at Renfroe Place, where the road from Fairburn intersects the one to Fayetteville; Thomas will move the IV and XVI corps via Shoal Creek Church to Couch's house, three miles north of Renfroe Place on the Fayetteville road; and Schofield, following Thomas, will proceed to Morrow's Mill and entrench facing East Point and Rough and Ready so as to protect the army's left flank. Then, on August 31, Howard will occupy Jonesboro and start doing to the Macon railroad what has been done to the West Point railroad, thereby cutting Atlanta's main and last logistical link to the rest of the Confederacy.

After that, what next? It depends on Hood. Should he come out and fight, he will be fought. But Sherman, while taking the utmost precaution against this eventuality, does not expect an attack. According to Federal estimates, as many as 30,000 of Hood's troops are militia, who are incapable of effective offensive action, and his regular troops are so reduced in strength and morale by the July battles that it is unlikely he will risk them in another sally. That leaves two other possibilities. One is that Hood will try to hold out in Atlanta. If he does, Sherman intends to return to his Chattahoochee bridgehead by swinging east around Atlanta, pausing on the way to wreak further destruction on the Georgia Railroad, then wait for impending starvation to force Hood either to give battle or to retreat. The only other course of action open to Hood will be for him, realizing that his position in Atlanta now is untenable, to evacuate it at once. Sherman believes that this is the one Hood probably will take. Indeed, perhaps he already has done so. With a view to finding out, Sherman has had Thomas send a message to Slocum, who has assumed command of the XX Corps, directing him to reconnoiter toward Atlanta and, should he find the Confederates gone, occupy it.[46]

Hood, as Slocum's patrols will see tomorrow, still is there. Moreover he still is wrestling with the problem of how to stay. According to the reports received during the day from Jackson's cavalry, five or possibly six enemy corps are moving to the left in the general direction of Jonesboro and Rough and Ready. But where, when, and with what does Sherman intend to strike, if strike at all? Those questions remain unanswered and, so far, unanswerable. Consequently Hood has issued only two orders of significance. One is to Hardee, whom he visited at East Point in the morning, authorizing him (to quote Shoup's journal) to "use his own discretion" in deploying troops around East Point. The other is to Lee, directing him to "ascertain, if possible, the position of the enemy" in the same region. As he did yesterday, and for the same reason, Hood believes that with these measures he has (again to quote Shoup) "taken all necessary precautions, and made such disposition of his forces as to prevent" the seizure of Jonesboro and Rough and Ready while at the same time continuing to safeguard East Point.[47]

One of Captain Key's first thoughts after awakening at sunrise on August 30 is "that this day the Chicago Democratic peace convention assembles." He hopes that it will "lay down a Democratic platform recognizing the rights of States and proclaiming the fact that the South, on thousands of battlefields that now stain the soil of this young continent, has nobly defended herself and the great Democratic principles of States' Rights and States' Sovereignty."

Approximately ten miles to the southwest, near Fairburn, Captain Wills also has hopes concerning the Democratic Convention, but they are of a different order from Key's. Wills has heard that the Democrats might nominate Sherman and wishes that they would. Sherman, of course, "would hardly accept the nomination from such a party, but I [Wills] would cheerfully live under Copperhead rule if they would give us such as Sherman. Sherman believes with Logan, 'that if we can't subdue these Rebels and the rebellion, the next best thing we can do is to all go to hell together.'"[48]

At 7 A.M., Wills and the other troops of the XV Corps set out for Jonesboro, as does the XVI Corps on a parallel road to their right. The XVII Corps follows the latter, and Kilpatrick's troopers lead the way. Initially enemy resistance, still just cavalry, is slight. Then, after several miles, it stiffens, necessitating the reinforcement of Kilpatrick by Wells Jones's brigade of what is now Hazen's division, since Hazen has been brought over from the IV Corps to replace Morgan Smith, who is on sick leave. Every half-mile or so a Rebel barricade is encountered, and at Shoal Creek the Confederates—Armstrong's and Ross's brigades backed by artillery—make such a strong stand that not until they are outflanked do they perform what Major Taylor calls "the Southern quick-step." It is midafternoon when the advance of the XV Corps reaches Renfroe Place.

Here, per Sherman's instructions, Howard calls a halt. Hot and thirsty, his troops look for water. They find little is to be had in this sandy-soiled locale. The closest streams are Shoal Creek, one mile back, and the Flint River, three miles ahead. Learning of the water situation and having been authorized by Sherman in a conversation yesterday to go on to Jonesboro today if he thought he could make it, Howard decides to advance. The only alternative is to retreat, and Sherman would not like that.

The XV Corps, preceded by a detachment of cavalry under Captain Lewellyn Estes of Kilpatrick's staff, resumes its march along the main road to Jonesboro. Armstrong and Ross, who evidently have assumed that the Yankee column was going to bivouac at Renfroe Place, offer no opposition until it approaches the Flint, a narrow, shallow, but high-banked river whose reddish water flows on a southward course little more than a mile from Jonesboro. The Mississippians and Texans set fire to the bridge; then they deploy behind a log barricade on the west bank. At once Estes's troopers spread out along the east bank and unleash a hurricane of Spencer bullets. Under this cover some of them dash onto the bridge, put out the flames, then cross to the other side. Wells Jones's infantry, literally on the run, follows them. Again Armstrong and Ross give way, falling back toward Jonesboro. Logan, after getting his entire corps across, cautiously but steadily pursues. As the sun starts to set, his skirmishers approach to within one-fourth of a mile of the town and the railroad that runs through its narrow, straggling row of buildings.

Howard orders Logan to halt and entrench along a line of hills and ridges about a half-mile to the west. Night is coming on. There are trenches just outside of Jonesboro with Confederates in them. Howard does not know their strength: they could be most or even all of Hood's army. The XVI Corps, which had had to cut a road through the woods after crossing Shoal Creek, has not yet come up, and the XVII Corps is still farther to the rear. Besides, he already in effect has accomplished his mission. He is so near the railroad that he can interdict traffic on it with artillery. Hence, rather than recklessly risk a bloody repulse, perhaps even disaster, by attacking Jonesboro, it will be better to stay put and get ready for an enemy attack. Almost surely there will be one tomorrow. Unless the Confederates can drive him back, they will have to leave Atlanta.

Howard does not realize that, like McPherson at Resaca on May 9, he has drawn back from assailing an enemy force that is far inferior to his own. The Confederate force defending Jonesboro comprises no more than 2,500 men, most of them cavalry.[49]

All along, Hood has considered the Macon railroad in the Jonesboro area to be what it obviously is: a likely Union target. What he has failed to anticipate is that the Federals would get there so soon, so close, and so strong. Thus, at 1 P.M., shortly after Hardee had telegraphed from East Point that the enemy was moving on him in force and Jackson had sent word that Union infantry were advancing toward Jonesboro, Hood had had Shoup notify the former that "General Hood does not think the necessity would arise to send any troops to Jonesboro today" and inform the latter that "General Hood does not think there can be a large force advancing upon Jonesboro." Likewise, on receiving word from Jackson around 3 P.M. that the Federal column approaching Jonesboro was at Renfroe Place, Hood's response was limited to ordering Lewis and Armstrong to cooperate "in preventing the enemy crossing Flint River tonight," directing Hardee and Lee to have their corps "under arms" and ready to march, and dispatching a locomotive to East Point for the purpose of bringing both Hardee and Lee to Atlanta in the evening to discuss future operations. Not until about 6 P.M., after Armstrong had telegraphed that "there is a probability of the enemy striking the railroad tonight between Jonesborough and the left of the army" and Lewis had wired that the Yankees had crossed the Flint and attacked him, does Hood realize that the danger at Jonesboro is immediate and serious.

Were Johnston still in command, the news that Federal infantry had almost reached the sole railroad supplying his army would have resulted in the immediate evacuation of Atlanta and a rapid retreat south, supposing these had not occurred long before. Not so with Hood. His temperament, his pride, and all the reasons why he heads the Army of Tennessee prohibit such a reaction.

Instead he telegraphs Hardee to march his corps to Jonesboro tonight, orders Lee's Corps to follow it there, and urges Lewis to "hold your position at all hazards." Hood then waits for Hardee and Lee to come to Atlanta.

They arrive at his headquarters around 9 P.M. Hood tells them that their corps, under Hardee's command, are to attack the Federals at Jonesboro as early as they can in the morning and drive them into and across the Flint River. Once this has been accomplished, which should not be too difficult, for according to Jackson's cavalry the enemy column that is threatening Jonesboro consists of only two corps and Lewis states that it was "easily repulsed" when it tried to take the place, Lee's Corps will withdraw to Rough and Ready while Stewart's Corps and Smith's militia will march to East Point. Then on the morning of September 1 this whole force will fall upon Sherman's left flank and, in conjunction with an advance by Hardee, sweep the Yankees down the Flint River and the West Point railroad while the cavalry holds the XX Corps in check north of Atlanta. In the event, however, that tomorrow's attack should fail, Hardee is to send Lee's Corps back at night to or near Rough and Ready so that it can protect a retreat to Lovejoy's Station, as it then will be necessary to abandon Atlanta in order to save the army. Already Shoup has instructed the chief quartermaster, commissary, and ordnance officers to be ready by daylight to ship out of the city all locomotives, cars, food stores, ammunition, and heavy artillery.[50]

Lee and Hardee reboard the locomotive that brought them and proceed respectively to East Point and Jonesboro. Hardee's Corps, with Cleburne commanding, already is on its way to Jonesboro, accompanied by the army's provision and ordnance trains. At 11:30 P.M., Lee's Corps begins to follow it. Meanwhile Hood and Shoup pass a sleepless night, anxiously awaiting news from Hardee. Shortly before 3 A.M., Hardee telegraphs that he has arrived at Jonesboro but that his troops still are en route. About the same time, Colonel W. D. Pickett, Hardee's assistant adjutant, wires from Rough and Ready that Cleburne's and Brown's divisions are within three miles of Jonesboro. Immediately Shoup informs Hardee of Pickett's message, then adds: "As soon as you can get your troops in position the general says you must attack and drive the enemy across the river." Ten minutes later, Hood himself repeats this injunction, and after another ten-minute interval, Shoup repeats it yet again. Obviously Hood and Shoup, remembering what had happened on July 20 and 22, want to make sure that this time Hardee attacks promptly and vigorously.[51]

Their badgering, if it accomplishes anything at all, merely annoys Hardee, who during August has renewed his pleas to be transferred to a different command, only to have Davis urge him to put patriotism ahead of personal pride. Moreover, while warning his wife to avoid associating with Mrs. Johnston because "she is devoured by a bitter feeling of hatred [for the president] which is inconsistent with her Christian character," he himself has entered into correspondence with General Mackall for the purpose of supplying him, and through him General Johnston, with information for use against Hood. Thus, as Hood probably realizes, he has entrusted the salvation of Atlanta and, with it, his own military reputation to a man who loathes him. Such is the price that sometimes must be paid for realizing one's ambitions.[52]

Howard's success in getting to within easy cannon range of Jonesboro fills Sherman with anticipation and apprehension. He hopes that come morning, Howard will be able to reach and cut the railroad. He fears that Hood's whole army will fall upon Howard and overwhelm him. The second emotion is uppermost. As a consequence Sherman, who is with Thomas's column near the Couch house on the Fayetteville road, also stays awake through the night. During it he orders Thomas to have Davis send Carlin's (formerly Johnson's) division to Renfroe Place to cover Howard's rear, and he directs Schofield to push toward the railroad south of Rough and Ready while guarding against an attack by Hardee, whom he believes to be in that vicinity.

A little before 6 A.M. a message arrives from Howard. Marked 3 A.M., it states that Logan's center is a mere eight hundred yards from the Jonesboro depot; that the Confederates, who had four infantry brigades at Jonesboro yesterday, are receiving reinforcements; and that "I understand your anxiety to get the [rail] road; no exertion will be spared as soon as we can see."

At once Sherman replies: "I am satisfied you have as many men as can operate at that point now. Let Kilpatrick reach well to the right, break the telegraph, and take up a few rails, but I want you to get possession and fortify some one point of the road itself. . . . We must have that road, and it is worth to us a heavy battle."

It takes three hours for this message to reach Howard, who after reading it, sends Sherman another report. Kilpatrick has gone to the right and "secured a bridge over the Flint River about a mile from the railroad." The Confederates are "shoving troops down here with great rapidity" and "preparing, I think, to attack Logan's position." He has bolstered Logan by placing a division from the XVI Corps on his right and a brigade from the XVII Corps on his left. Also he has one battery posted so that it can fire directly at the depot at a range of only six hundred yards and another "where the trains can be seen passing." More than this, however, he cannot do, for the Rebel force at Jonesboro now is too strong to be assaulted successfully. "If," Howard adds hopefully, "the enemy will attack, as I think he will, that will simplify the matter."[53]

In Jonesboro, Hardee once more is experiencing frustration in mounting an attack. His own corps under Cleburne did not start arriving until dawn, having been delayed by a false report that Union forces were occupying the direct road from East Point, which caused it to take nearly twelve hours to traverse what should have been a mere twelve miles, and it was 9 A.M. before all of it got into position.[54] Furthermore, although it now is midmorning, most of Lee's Corps still is on the way and cannot be expected before noon, if then. It will, therefore, be impossible to attack until early afternoon. Meanwhile the Yankees outside of Jonesboro, identified as the three corps of Howard's command, are strengthening and extending their fortifications, constructing abatis, and receiving reinforcements. In addition, Ross's cavalrymen report that two or possibly three other enemy corps are moving toward Jonesboro from the north. If that is true (it would be folly to assume that it isn't), then he faces practically all of Sherman's army, or he soon will. Yet when, earlier in the morning, he had telegraphed Hood this information and urged him to come to Jonesboro and assume personal command, Hood had merely repeated his order to drive the Federals across the Flint, and Shoup again had notified him that "General Hood desires the men to go at the enemy with bayonets fixed, determined to drive everything they may come against." Obviously Hood does not trust him to execute the attack order. Well, he will execute it, but once this campaign has ended, no matter how it turns out, he will cease to serve Hood. It is demeaning.[55]

Howard's dispatch stating that he cannot reach the railroad at Jonesboro more than disappoints Sherman; it leaves him disgusted and depressed. All of these feelings are manifest in the reply he sends to Howard at 12:30 P.M.:

> Of course, now an attack by you on Jonesborough is out of the question. . . . The enemy is too smart for us, and we may have to maneuver thus down to Macon. It may happen that some accident will happen, of which we can take advantage. Get your guns in position and damage trains passing. . . . I cannot move the troops 100 yards without their stopping to intrench, though I have not seen an enemy. . . . Thomas is at Renfroe's, and will come to your aid if you need him . . . and so soon as I can hear from Schofield further I will commence to move to Griffin, the next accessible point. I have no idea that Hardee will attack you, if you have any cover whatever.

In sum, Sherman believes that his attempt to cut the Macon railroad between Rough and Ready and Jonesboro has been blocked, and so he is thinking in terms of another flanking move to the south. He neither intends nor expects a battle, not even a defensive one.[56]

At 1:30 P.M. the last of Lee's units reach Jonesboro. His troops have had little sleep for two nights, they have marched from twelve to fifteen miles over rough roads and sometimes no roads, many are shoeless and footsore, all are half-exhausted and hungry, and hundreds have dropped out along the way, unable or unwilling to keep going. Never has Major General Patton Anderson, veteran of most of the Army of Tennessee's campaigns starting with Shiloh, seen so much straggling. Moreover, and most ominously, Manigault's Brigade, bringing up the rear as guard of the ammunition train, has found the direct road to Jonesboro blocked by Federals about three miles south of Rough and Ready and thus has had to circle around them. If the Yankees were not on that road earlier when Cleburne passed down it, evidently they are now.57

About 2 P.M., Hardee telegraphs Hood that Lee's Corps is forming for the attack. Hood wires back to go ahead, and Shoup transmits word that a "considerable force" of the enemy has driven a cavalry regiment out of Mt. Gilead near Rough and Ready: "This sent to show that enemy have not all his troops in your front." Hood then goes to a tent in the backyard of his headquarters that is being used by Bishop Lay for religious services. During a visit there several hours ago he told the bishop that he "contemplated no surrender" of Atlanta, that he was "convinced the Almighty would prosper him." Now he asks Lay to pray for the success of his forces at Jonesboro.58

Hardee's front extends from just below Jonesboro to a little above it—in all, about one and a half miles. Its southern wing consists of his own corps, Cleburne still commanding, with Cleburne's Division under Lowrey on the left, Bate's Division under Brown on the right, and Cheatham's Division under Maney behind Lowrey (Cheatham, after serving as commander of Stewart's Corps, is on sick leave). Lee's Corps composes the north wing, with Stevenson's Division on the left, Anderson's on the right, and Clayton's behind Anderson's. One of Maney's five brigades, Strahl's, bolsters Brown's undersized division; Stovall's shaky Georgians have been posted in Stevenson's second line; and Manigault's Brigade augments Clayton's strength, which has been reduced by the sending of Baker's Alabamans to help defend beleaguered Mobile. In addition a small battalion of engineer troops and unmounted cavalry under Colonel John McGuirk is deployed in Cleburne's left rear, Lewis's Brigade has been assigned to Stevenson's Division to give it greater punch, Reynolds's Arkansas Brigade is in reserve, and Jackson's troopers picket the flanks and patrol the railroad north and south of Jonesboro. According to the Army of Tennessee's official returns for August 31, Hardee's and Lee's corps total close to 26,000 men "present for duty"; but because of straggling, as well as the usual causes, no more than 20,000 of them are in line of battle this afternoon.

Hood's headquarters in Atlanta (photo taken after Union occupation) (Atlanta Historical Society)

As he had done on July 20 and 22, Hardee plans to attack *en echelon*—apparently this expert on tactics knows no other tactic—but this time from left to right rather than from right to left. Lowrey is to lead off, swinging Cleburne's Division northward so as to strike the Federal right flank. Brown will go in next, and Maney is to advance with him, seeking to add weight both to his and to Lowrey's thrusts. Lee, when he hears the sound of battle on the left, will join in the assault with the object of shattering the other Union flank with the combined power of Anderson's and Clayton's divisions while Stevenson's weak-hitting division engages the enemy center. Hardee has informed Cleburne and Lee of Hood's injunction, so often repeated, "to go at the enemy with fixed bayonets," and they have passed it down to their troops. They receive it, as a rule, with marked apathy, and Manigault can see that there is "not much fight in them."[59]

Yesterday, upon encountering some Rebel cavalry while moving toward Morrow's Mill, General Cox ordered his troops to entrench in expectation of "an

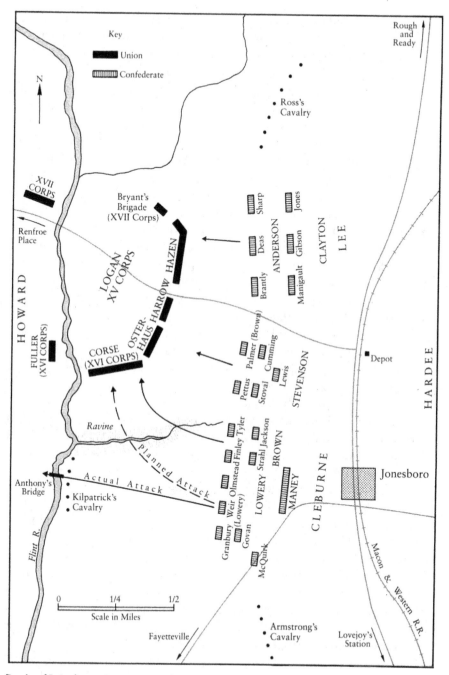

Battle of Jonesboro, August 31

attack by Hood in force." As they did so, he timed them to see how long it would take to dig a rifle pit so as to provide "sufficient cover to repel an infantry attack, if it came." It required fifteen minutes. West of Jonesboro the XV Corps has been in position for fifteen hours, Corse's division of the XVI Corps has been on its right nearly as long, and Bryant's brigade (formerly Force's) of the XVII Corps has been on its left since 11:15 A.M. In some sectors the Union front is protected by abatis or palisades or both, and everywhere batteries are posted so that they can deliver cross fire as well as direct fire. In addition a brigade of Kilpatrick's calvary is deployed on the right behind a rail barricade along the east bank of the Flint where, supported by a 4-gun battery on the other bank, it guards a crossing known as Anthony's Bridge. Altogether Howard has approximately 12,000 men in line and 7,500 more in reserve, half of them (Fuller's division) on his right and the other half (the rest of Blair's corps) on the left. Finally, if need be, he can call on the 1st Missouri Engineers, over 1,000 strong, which has just come from the Army of the Cumberland to reinforce him, and Carlin's division at Renfroe Place. He has available, in sum, a force that is at least equal in size to Hardee's and, moreover, that is strongly fortified, well fed and rested, and highly confident.[60]

The course of the ensuing battle simply is what could be expected. At 3 P.M., Hardee's artillery goes into action, and after ten minutes or so, Cleburne's skirmishers start forward. Lee, displaying the same aggressive spirit and talent for blundering that he revealed at Tupelo and Ezra Church, mistakes their fire for the beginning of Cleburne's assault. At once he commands his corps to charge. The first line advances briskly and in good order, driving the Federal pickets from their rail barricades. Then thousands of .58-caliber lead daggers, hurled by the rifles of Logan's veteran killers, rip it. It lurches to a stop. Some of the survivors take refuge behind the captured barricades, others huddle behind the palisades fronting the main Union works, and not a few—notably in Deas's Brigade—flee in utter rout. The second line repeats the experience of the first and reacts in the same way. To Major Taylor the Confederates seem like an "infuriated mob" and "wholly disorganized," their "colors advancing . . . with hardly a guard and the remainder of the line straggling after." Generals and officers desperately endeavor to rally their men for another charge, but more often than not the latter refuse to budge or even fire back. It is the "least determined" assault Taylor has ever seen Southern soldiers make. Sensing that there is little to fear, Logan's troops begin firing slowly but with terrible accuracy. It is less a battle than an execution.[61]

Meanwhile Cleburne's attack gets under way and almost immediately degenerates into farcical chaos. As Granbury's Brigade, with Granbury himself again commanding, starts swinging to the north in an attempt to strike the right flank of the Union salient, it comes under fire from Kilpatrick's troopers at Anthony's Bridge. Instead of ignoring this fusilade, which does little harm, it detours to the west and heads for the Yankee cavalry. Kilpatrick's men at once flee to the other side of the river, which can be easily waded, and the Texans chase after them. "Too full of impetuosity," to quote Lowrey's report, most of the rest of the division follows them, as does McGuirk's battalion. "Nothing," Howard subsequently comments, "even if I had planned it, could have been better done to head an entire Confederate division away from the battlefield." On the right, Brown's assault, which is from the south against the left of Corse's division, lacks support on either flank and quickly collapses beneath what Lieutenant Rennolds calls a "murderous fire of grape shrapnel and musketry." Large numbers of graybacks, in particular members of Finley's and Tyler's brigades, cower in a deep gully, and when Brigadier General Henry Jackson, commanding Stevens's old brigade, urges them to go forward with his men, they declare that they have been ordered to stay where they are. In the center, Maney's troops, which were to join in Lowrey's and Brown's attack, find themselves facing the Federal works all alone. Unsure as to what to do, Maney orders a halt and sends a messenger to Cleburne asking for additional instructions. While waiting for them, he regroups his forces, which have become badly dispersed, in the expectation of receiving an order to assault. Lowrey, having recalled his errant men, does likewise with the same expectation, even though he has concluded, after making a personal reconnaissance, that the Union position is impregnable.

No new attack takes place. Hardee, on being informed by a staff officer that Lee's Corps is demoralized and in danger of being driven from the field by an enemy counterattack, orders Cleburne to withdraw, then sends Lowrey to reinforce Lee. The battle is over. Hardee's attempt to hurl Howard back across the Flint has failed miserably.

Casualty figures reveal the terrible one-sidedness of the encounter. Howard's killed, wounded, and missing come to a mere 172, all but 18 in the XV Corps. Hardee's total at least 2,200, of whom about 1,400 belong to Lee's Corps.[62] Among the Confederate wounded are Brigadier General Alfred Cumming of Stevenson's Division and Patton Anderson, who was shot through the mouth and received a broken jaw while attempting, in Manigault's words, "to push forward 7 or 800 men against I don't know how many thousands." The dead include Lieutenant Gill, who was pierced by a bullet through the chest while "gallantly leading his men." He will not be returning to his Mississippi home "to live in peace" and "have plenty to eat and nice."

Hood in his memoirs and Lee in his report characterize the Confederate attack as "feeble." So it was, especially on the part of Hardee's own corps, most of which, apart from Brown's troops, scarcely came under fire. Colonel Ellison

Capers of Gist's Brigade attributes its weakness to the men being "physically unfit for the heroic exertion demanded of them." Although this no doubt was an important factor, Colonel Bushrod Jones comes closer to the truth in stating that "the men seemed possessed of some great horror of charging breast-works, which no power, persuasion, or example could dispel." To this explanation it needs only be added that even had the Confederates attacked with, in Lee's words, "the spirit and implacable determination that insures success," in all probability all they would have accomplished was an increase in their casualties. Thus Jackson's Brigade, which according to him made a determined assault, lost one-third of its strength while gaining nothing; and Gibson's Louisianans, who suffered 50 percent casualties on the afternoon of July 28, did so again on the afternoon of August 31, with the result that a colorbearer could not find a single member of his regiment who was willing to go forward with him in another charge. As Manigault comments, "The fire was too heavy."[63]

On the Union side Logan, one of his soldiers notes, is "in the best of spirits (some alcoholic, too), damning the rebels, etc." This makes the third time running that the XV corps has shot down hundreds of Confederates, and as at Ezra Church, its own losses are trifling. Moreover, close to half of Howard's available troops have not been engaged at all. Even so, Howard, judging it imprudent, attempts no counterattack. Instead he sends a note, marked 3:45 P.M., to Sherman: "The enemy attacked us in three distinct points, and were each time handsomely repulsed."

Howard's message reaches Sherman near Renfroe Place about an hour later. Almost simultaneously he receives a dispatch from Schofield containing more good news, indeed, much better news: "I struck the railroad a mile below Rough and Ready at 3 o'clock. Have Cox's division in position fortifying and breaking track. Stanley is now coming in on my right, and we soon will be abundantly strong." On reading these words, Sherman jumps to his feet and throws up his right arm as if cheering. Finally he has achieved what he has been trying to do for the past month and longer: he has cut Atlanta off from Macon! More than that, he now is between the two widely separated halves of Hood's army. He is in position not only to take Atlanta—it is as good as taken already—but also to overpower and capture the Confederate forces defending it.

But if the latter potentiality occurs to him, there is no sign of it in his reply to Schofield. "Break road down toward Jonesborough," he instructs him. "Put Garrard's cavalry at your back: work down the road, burning and breaking the road good." Garrard is to "push the enemy up to Rough and Ready, breaking the road as he goes, and you with Stanley move out doing the same." If Hardee should turn north, "I will give you timely notice." Meanwhile "Don't get off the track; hold it fast; we will get our whole army on the railroad as near Jones-borough as possible and push Hardee and Lee first, and then for Atlanta." Finally, "break the road good as you move south."[64]

After reading these orders, Schofield and Stanley, who receives a copy, have every reason to think that Sherman wants them to devote themselves to destroy-ing the railroad while moving toward Jonesboro. They would have to be extraordinarily obtuse or exceedingly imaginative to think anything else.

Hood has had no word from Hardee since midafternoon. All Hood knows for certain about the situation to the south is that late in the afternoon an enemy force reached the railroad below Rough and Ready, forcing two freight trains to return to Atlanta and evidently cutting the telegraph line to Jonesboro. Further-more, according to reports from the cavalry, this force is a strong one and shows indications of advancing northward. Could it be aiming for Atlanta? Hood thinks it could. All along he has considered it possible, even likely, that Sherman merely has been making a raid or a feint toward Jonesboro, that his main thrust will come elsewhere. In any event, Lee's Corps must return to or near Atlanta. If Hardee has, as he should have, driven back the Yankee column menacing Jonesboro, Lee will be needed either to help defend the city or to join in an attack on the Union left. On the other hand if Hardee has failed—rumors that Lee's Corps is "cut up" and the absence of any recent communication from Hardee make this seem only too possible—then Lee can be used, as already planned in the case of such a failure, to cover the retreat of Stewart's Corps and Smith's militia from Atlanta to Lovejoy's Station.

Shortly after 6 P.M., staff officers and couriers ride off from Hood's head-quarters carrying duplicate copies of an order to Hardee drafted by Shoup:

> General Hood directs that you return Lee's corps to this place. Let it march by 2 o'clock tomorrow morning. Remain with your corps and the cavalry, and so dispose your force as best to protect Macon and commu-nications in rear. Retain provision and ordnance trains. Please return Reynolds' brigade, and, if you think you can do so and still accomplish your object, send back a brigade or so of your corps also. There are some indications that the enemy may make an attempt upon Atlanta tomorrow.[65]

Around 7 P.M., Sherman receives a more detailed report from Howard on his battle at Jonesboro. Accompanying it is a 6:10 P.M. dispatch from a signal officer who is observing the Confederates from atop a tree in Logan's sector:

A very strong column of the enemy is now moving to their right. Has been moving about three-quarters of an hour. They pass directly through town toward Atlanta. [Probably this column was Lowrey's troops going to reinforce Lee; however, when it became apparent that the Federals were not going to attack Lee, Hardee recalled Lowrey.]

Howard believes that this indicates that "the enemy contemplates making connection again with his forces at East Point or Atlanta." Sherman is inclined to agree. Also he has just realized that there is another danger that must be guarded against. By ordering Schofield and Stanley both to move down the railroad toward Jonesboro, he will bring them together. Although Schofield commands an "army" and Stanley a corps, Stanley definitely is senior in rank to Schofield. The same sort of quarrel that had occurred between Schofield and Palmer might occur again. That could be disastrous. Accordingly Sherman writes Thomas:

I have reports from Generals Howard and Schofield, and from a signal dispatch of the former I infer Hardee will attempt tonight to move back to Atlanta to form a junction with Hood. It also appears that Stanley ranks Schofield, raising that old question of who commands. Of course my decision is that the senior commission, which is Stanley's; but as my instructions have been made to Schofield, I wish you would make them to Stanley to move very early in the morning down on Jonesborough (or the enemy wherever he may be), breaking railroad as he moves south. I don't believe anybody recognizes how important it is now to destroy this railroad.

Soon after Sherman has sent his message to Thomas, he receives a letter from Thomas marked 7 P.M. In it Thomas reports that Baird's division of the XIV Corps also has reached the railroad north of Jonesboro and "set 400 men at work immediately" destroying it and that prisoners state that "there are but two corps" in Jonesboro and that "the militia and probably one corps have been left in Atlanta." Therefore:

What do you think of this: Let Stanley and Schofield, covered by Garrard, destroy the railroad tomorrow to their rear until they come down to Baird; then for me to draw off the Army of the Cumberland and throw it on the railroad east of Fayetteville, say at Lovejoy's, or some point below, Howard confronting and holding the enemy at Jonesborough. . . . I think Hood has gone up or ordered to Macon.

In essence Thomas, who at 2 P.M. had reported to Sherman that he had learned from captured Confederates that "Hardee and Lee (S. D.) have passed on to Jonesborough," is proposing to Sherman that the IV and XIV corps be used to block Hood's retreat southward (the only direction he can retreat without abandoning both his supply line and Georgia) and thus put him in a position where he will have to attack the Union forces in a desperate attempt to break through to Macon. As he had done in his plan for the Snake Creek Gap maneuver, Thomas envisions trapping and wrecking the Confederate army in Georgia with one decisive stroke.

Sherman rejects the proposal. Writing Thomas at 9 P.M., Sherman declares: "Inasmuch as I have already given orders to Schofield, based on the idea that he and Stanley move down the railroad, breaking it, till they come to Baird and Davis, near Jonesborough, I think we had better adhere to that plan till we develop the first step in the enemy's game, after he knows we are between him and Atlanta." Furthermore, contrary to Thomas's opinion, "My own impression is that Hardee will try to join Hood in Atlanta." Hence, "I propose to go as far as Griffin, utterly destroying the road, and then act according to circumstances."[66]

Clearly Sherman's prime objective remains what it has been since he crossed the Chattahoochee: isolate and then take Atlanta by destroying the railroads that tie it to the rest of the Confederacy. Only a change in what he calls circumstances can cause him to change this objective.

Around midnight Hardee receives one, then a second, copy of Shoup's dispatch directing him to send Lee's Corps back to Atlanta. He considers the order absurd. Howard's three corps face him at Jonesboro, and although Hood obviously thinks that a large Federal force is heading for Atlanta, there can be no doubt that in fact all of Sherman's army, less the corps posted on the Chattahoochee, is moving toward Jonesboro. Nevertheless Hardee passes on the order to Lee. In addition he does what he had started to do earlier: he shifts Lowrey's troops to the right. Tomorrow six Yankee corps will attack his single corps. Despite the odds, he will do his best to obey Hood's injunction to "protect Macon and communications in rear." If he fails, it will not be his fault. The blame will rest squarely on a young upstart general who does not know the difference between the possible and the impossible.[67]

Far to the north in Chicago, those delegates to the Democratic National Convention who are so inclined—the vast majority—celebrate the nomination by unanimous vote on the first ballot of Major General George Brinton McClellan, former commander of the Army of the Potomac, for president. He will, they anticipate, lead their party back to power and the nation back to peace and union (in that order). To be sure, a small but not insignificant minority of the delegates distrust McClellan's military background and fear that he puts union ahead of peace and might try to go on with the war to obtain it. But they take comfort in the fact that although they were unable to get the kind of candidate they would have preferred, they do have the platform they wanted. Adopted yesterday, it is one of the briefest ever, consisting of just six planks. The key one, based on a draft written by Vallandigham himself, reads:

> *Resolved,* That this convention does explicitly declare, as the sense of the American people, that after four years of failure to restore the Union by the experiment of war, during which, under the pretence of military necessity, or war powers higher than the Constitution, the Constitution itself has been disregarded in every part, and public liberty and private right alike trodden down, and the material prosperity of the country essentially impaired, justice, humanity, liberty, and the public welfare demand that immediate efforts be made for a cessation of hostilities, with a view to an ultimate convention of the States or other peaceable means, to the end that at the earliest practicable moment peace may be restored on the basis of the Federal Union of the States.

Whatever McClellan might personally think, once he is in the White House, he will know he is there because the Northern people, just as Vallandigham predicted they would if the war still was going on come September of 1864, want peace and so will have to act accordingly. Tomorrow it will be September.[68]

CHAPTER NINE

SEPTEMBER

Part One: Jonesboro

SHORTLY AFTER MIDNIGHT on September 1, a courier arrives at Hood's head-quarters bearing, at long last, a dispatch from Hardee. Hood reads it, throws up his hands, and cries "My God!" What he has increasingly feared, as the evening has passed without any reliable word from Jonesboro, has happened: Hardee has failed to drive the Yankees back across the Flint, failed despite having been told repeatedly that he must not fail, failed even though he possessed close to three-fourth's of the army's infantry with which to succeed. Why?

The answer to that question will have to wait. Much more pressing matters have to be dealt with first. Hardee's repulse at Jonesboro ends any possibility of striking the Union left flank and restoring rail communications with Macon. Atlanta will have to be evacuated. If he could, Hood would head north from the city, reassembling his army as he marched, cross the Chattahoochee above the XX Corps's bridgehead by means of pontoons, destroy Sherman's supply depot at Marietta, and then proceed to Blue Mountain (Montevallo) in Alabama and establish a new supply line to Montgomery, leaving the Federals with no choice except to fall back toward Chattanooga. But Hood cannot do this; it would expose Andersonville to a cavalry raid that would turn loose its thousands of prisoners, armed and seeking vengeance, to ravage the heart of Georgia. Therefore he will retreat toward Macon. (Although, as previously pointed out, the prisoners at Andersonville probably would have suffered terribly both in getting out and after they were loose, this does not gainsay the fact that the Confederates greatly feared that this would happen.)

After making this decision, Hood notifies Stewart and Smith to have their troops ready to march out of Atlanta via the McDonough road come evening, and he instructs General M. L. Smith, his chief engineer, to find Lee and have him place his corps in position both to cover the retreat and to fend off an enemy attempt to enter the city from the south. As for Hardee, he already has been ordered to "protect Macon and communications in rear," and presumably he at least can do this: Jonesboro, which is located on a ridge between the Flint and Ogeechee rivers, provides an excellent defensive position.[1]

Since 1 A.M., Logan's pickets have been hearing wagons moving to the Confederate left, "apparently in great confusion." Howard, on being informed of this at 4 A.M., assumes that Hardee is withdrawing to the south and so notifies Sherman, adding that "preparations are made to follow."[2]

Howard's assumption is mistaken. The Confederate wagons merely are carrying wounded to Lovejoy's, from where they will be shipped by trains to the hospitals in Macon.* Hardee, as we have seen, intends to carry out Hood's order to stand and fight at Jonesboro, even though he believes his corps faces six Union corps. By so doing he will enable Hood to evacuate Atlanta, something (so he telegraphs President Davis) he has recommended that Hood do "while it was practicable." In the same telegram, Hardee also notifies Davis: "Last night Lee's corps was ordered back to Atlanta by General Hood" and that "my instructions are to protect Macon." Maybe this information, which reveals that the Army of Tennessee is divided into three widely separated parts, will open the president's eyes to the truth about Hood's competency as a commander.

During the predawn darkness, Hardee's Corps deploys for the upcoming battle. Cleburne's Division, still headed by Lowrey, moves to the right and occupies the works that Lee's Corps vacated when, between 1 and 2 A.M., it sets out for Atlanta. Cheatham's Division, which now is under the command of Brigadier General John C. Carter (Maney has been relieved because of his failure to engage the enemy yesterday), slides to the left so as to cover the sector hitherto held by Lowrey's troops. Brown's small division, remaining where it was, defends the center. Since Hardee has no more than 12,000 troops, inevitably his two-mile-long line is thin. This is especially so in Lowrey's case, replacing as he does an entire corps with a single division. His men are spread out in a single rank, six feet apart. Worse, the "fortifications" left by Lee's Corps consist mainly of "a few fence rails," there are no obstructions of any kind in front of them, and the Union skirmishers are so close that when Colonel Olmstead sends out a regiment to establish a picket line, 33 of its members are captured. At once Lowrey's troops set to work with spade, pick, and axe. Soon they have

---

*The description in *Gone with the Wind* and the famous scene in the movie version of hundreds of Confederate wounded from the August 31 battle at Jonesboro lying in and around Atlanta's Car Shed is historically false although dramatically magnificent. For a critical but sympathetic examination of the historical accuracy of the novel see Albert Castel, "'I Didn't Want to Get Caught Out,' or *Gone with The Wind* as History," *Blue & Gray Magazine,* July 1986: 36–40.

what Lowrey calls a "tolerably good line of works." Situated twenty to fifty yards from the edge of a dense forest, it runs from south to north, then bends slightly to the east toward the railroad, which makes a westward jog about a mile north of Jonesboro. Olmstead's brigade is on the left, connecting with the right of Brown's division; then comes Lowrey's Brigade (commanded by Colonel John Weir) followed in succession by Granbury's and Govan's. Six batteries support them, with two, Key's and Swett's, being on the right with Govan's Arkansans who, obviously, occupy the most vulnerable part of the line. Lowrey's men, however, make no attempt to construct an abatis or erect other obstacles. Why, no one ever explains. Possibly they lack tools, are too tired, or assume that the woods and undergrowth will break the momentum and formation of an advancing foe. But perhaps they simply consider it unnecessary. Off to the west, beyond the forest, lies a broad cornfield over which the Union attack will have to come. It is a perfect killing ground.

"We are expecting," scrawls Captain Foster in his diary, "a big fight here—all the forenoon we can see the Yankees passing to our right—Regt after Regt of blue coats going to the right. The report by noon is that they are massing their troops in our front.

"If that is so, just let them mass."[3]

Since dawn, Stanley's troops have been, per Sherman's oft-reiterated orders, ripping up track north of Jonesboro. That is, a small portion of them, mostly pioneers, have been; the remainder, the vast majority, merely have been standing guard and only occasionally moving forward as the work of destruction progresses slowly. As a result the head of Stanley's column does not reach Morrow's Station, four miles from Jonesboro, until 10 A.M., and at noontime it is still a couple of miles away. Following it at an equally slow pace and a goodly distance is Hascall's division, and Cox's division is near Rough and Ready, ruining rails in that area.

Sherman's objective, apart from destroying the railroad between Rough and Ready and Jonesboro, is to get the XIV Corps into line on Howard's left. Then, when the IV and XXIII corps come up, which he assumes will be soon, he will have all three corps assail Hardee's right flank while Howard demonstrates against his left. Sherman believes, in spite of Thomas's report to the contrary, that Lee's Corps remains with Hardee. Also, having learned of the movement of Confederate wagons southward from Jonesboro, he thinks that Hardee is preparing to retreat toward Macon rather than, as he predicted last night, attempting to rejoin Hood in Atlanta. Should Hardee manage to get away from Jonesboro before being attacked, Sherman plans to pursue him with his entire

Sherman's troops destroying the railroad between Rough and Ready and Jonesboro *(Harper's Weekly)*

force. He has no intention whatsoever of doing what Hood fears so much: namely, to make a thrust against Atlanta from the south, for which Stanley's and Schofield's corps provide ample strength. Nor has it occurred to Sherman that by sending Schofield a few miles east he could block the McDonough road, the only direct route between Atlanta and Jonesboro that is still open to Confederates. His only order so far today to Schofield (who has acquiesced "for the time being" to coming under Stanley's command) is a repetition of yesterday's injunction to move down the railroad, wrecking it as he goes. Since Schofield is following Stanley, who has been directed to do the same, it would seem that Sherman wants that line of track destroyed not merely once but twice.[4]

The Yankees that Captain Foster has observed passing to the Confederate right belong to Davis's XIV Corps. Hardee reacts to this obvious threat to his northern flank by sending Lewis's and Gist's brigades, the latter now under Colonel James McCullough, to reinforce Lowrey. While waiting for them to come, Lowrey orders the 6th/7th Arkansas Regiment on Govan's right to fall back about fifty yards (he considers it too close to the edge of the woods) and construct new entrenchments facing more to the south. Then, as soon as Lewis's Kentuckians arrive, he places them next to Govan's Arkansans along a line that bends back to the railroad, and he deploys McCullough's South

Jefferson C. Davis (*Photographic History*, 10:189)

Carolinians and Georgians on the other side of the tracks so that they are facing almost due east. Both brigades quickly erect rail-and-log barricades and create a "first rate" abatis in front of them by slashing small trees with pocket knives, then bending them down and interlacing their branches. In addition, McCullough's troops, on being told by Hardee in person that he is relying on them to hold his right, construct traverses at twenty- to thirty-foot intervals so as to protect their flanks. Deadly cross fire from the Yankee batteries to the north and west, however, prevents the 6th/7th Arkansas from completing its new works and leveling its old ones.[5]

All the while the three divisions of the XIV Corps continue moving toward the Confederate right. One of them, Morgan's, approaches from the west. The other two, Brigadier General William P. Carlin's (formerly Johnson's) followed by Baird's, advance from the north. In addition, Thomas, presumably at Sherman's behest, sends a 2:30 P.M. order to Stanley to "push forward down the railroad for Jonesborough at once"; and Howard instructs Blair, whose corps

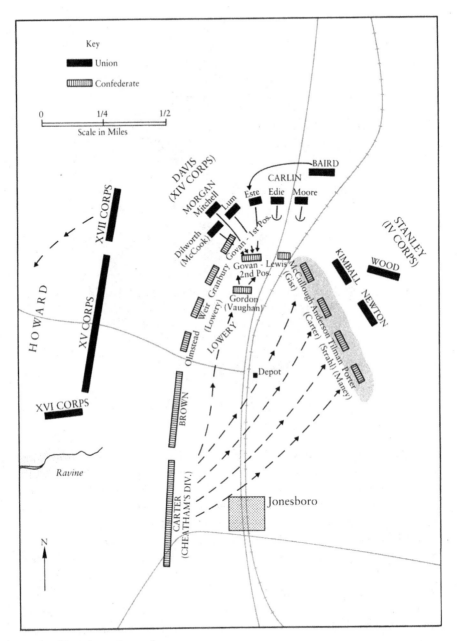

Battle of Jonesboro, September 1

has retired to the rear to make room for Morgan's division, to cross to the west side of the Flint, march south, recross the river at Anthony's Bridge, and then threaten the Confederate left flank.[6]

Sherman, who is with Howard in the XV Corp's sector, waits with mounting impatience for the XIV Corps to attack. It should have done so by now. Why hasn't it? What is it doing? He can barely see anything more than a few yards away. Smoke from cannons and burning railroad ties, as well as dust from marching troops, artillery, and wagons, fill the air, obscuring the sun itself. Finally he decides to go and find out for himself what is causing the XIV Corps to be, as always, so damnably slow. Major Holmes, recognizing Sherman as he passes by Dilworth's (McCook's) brigade, accompanied only by an orderly, salutes. He returns the salute, says "Major," and rides on.

Sherman still is riding when, shortly before 4 P.M., Davis, having been notified that Stanley had come up on the left of the XIV Corps and being satisfied (to quote his report) that "the enemy's works had not been extended to the railroad" and that consequently "a well directed attack would rout this part of his lines and turn his position completely," orders the assault. A few minutes later it begins. On the right, Morgan's division advances on a northeastward slant in double lines of battle, with Colonel Charles M. Lum's brigade on the left, Mitchell's in the center, and Dilworth's on the right. Swampy ground, cut by ditches, slows its progress and disrupts its formations. After about a third of a mile it reaches the shelter of a ravine three to four hundred yards from the woods wherein lie the Confederates, invisible except for the flashes of their cannons. Here it halts, and while skirmishers go forward to provide protection, details dig rifle pits in both front and rear. As soon as these are completed, a charge will be made, for the position is, in the estimation of a member of the 113th Ohio, Mitchell's brigade, "a good one, being hidden from our foes by an intervening hill, covered with corn."

Brigadier General William P. Carlins's division has only two of its three brigades on the field; the third is at Renfroe's, guarding wagons. Furthermore, when these two brigades advance, they encounter an obstacle far worse than swampy ground: brush so thick that it is difficult to move at all, and it is impossible to maintain contact with each other. Before long, one of them, Major John R. Edie's brigade, is floundering forward entirely on its own.

In a sense this is appropriate, for there is no other brigade like it in Sherman's army. It consists solely of regulars, 500 of them, not counting 92 recently arrived recruits who have been left in the rear because of inadequate training. Earlier in the afternoon it had occupied a hill that provided an excellent position for one of the batteries that so bothered the 6th/7th Arkansas. Now it is heading straight toward those same Arkansans. Emerging, finally, from the brush in a single ragged line, it passes through a morass covered with brambles, then climbs to the top of a low ridge. Here, for the first time since setting out, it beholds the enemy, and the enemy beholds it. A storm of bullets and canister sweeps over it. Some of the men falter, but their officers quickly rally them. On the right the 18th and 19th U.S. Infantry regiments overrun the breastworks abandoned earlier by the 6th/7th Arkansas and capture some pickets who are occupying them. On the left the 15th and 16th U.S. pushes on until within pistol range of the main Confederate line. Neither wing, however, can go further, and soon Edie order his troops to fall back behind the ridge. There simply are too few of them to reach, much less break through, the Arkansans, who are backed by Key's Battery.

Carlins's other brigade is the same one that, when headed by Colonel Benjamin Scribner, had displayed more prudence than determination on being belatedly sent against what was hoped would be the Confederate right flank at Pickett's Mill. This afternoon, now under the command of Colonel Marshall Moore (Scribner has been on sick leave since July 5), it experiences equally rough going and performs in much the same fashion as it assails another Rebel right flank, this one held by Lewis's Brigade. Not only does it encounter an abatis, but, to quote Moore's report, it is "exposed to an enfilading fire from the right, a cross fire from the left, and a very hot fire of musketry and artillery in front." In addition, a brigade from the IV Corps, which Stanley had assured Moore would support him, has failed to come up, thereby leaving Moore's left open to the abovementioned cross fire. Unable to advance and with several regiments giving way—they "claimed to be out of ammunition," he later comments—Moore orders a withdrawal.

As so often during the past four months, troops struggling blindly through junglelike timber and underbrush in uncoordinated piecemeal assaults against an entrenched and virtually invisible foe have been repulsed. Even so, in their failure, Edie's and Moore's brigades have succeeded in accomplishing one crucially important thing: Davis now realizes that the Confederate right, instead of being in the air, extends to and beyond the railroad, thereby constituting a potentially vulnerable salient. Hence he decides to renew the attack from the north, this time with Colonel George P. Este's brigade of Baird's division. At his order, relayed through Baird, Este moves forward to relieve Edie's battered regulars. As he does so, Morgan's troops, having completed their rifle pits, begin forming for a charge across the cornfield.

Baird and several of his staff accompany Este. Baird fears that Este does not fully understand Davis's purpose and that he will become confused, with the result that his attack will fail, or, worse, he will fail to attack at all. That must not be allowed to happen; too often already Sherman has subjected him and his division to insulting criticism for its alleged lack of offensive spirit, particularly during the Utoy Creek operations. Today he will make sure that his troops show what they can do if given a fair chance.

Halting fifty yards behind Edie's brigade, Baird deploys Este's 1,139 troops in a double line of battle, with the 10th Kentucky, backed by the 74th Indiana, on the right and with the 38th Ohio, supported by the 14th Ohio, on the left. He then orders them to unsling their knapsacks and fix their bayonets "so as to be ready for heavy work." At about 5 P.M., on receipt of an order from Davis to attack, they move forward, pass through the regulars, and ascend to the top of the ridge. Here, on prior instructions from Este, they flop down on their stomachs just in time to escape an enemy volley. They then jump up and charge. On the right the Kentuckians and Hoosiers reach the vacated works of the 6th/7th Arkansas, halt, fire a volley, and with a shout rush on and into the enemy entrenchments, followed closely by Baird on horseback. Using their bayonets "freely," they overwhelm the 6th/7th Arkansas, which at most numbers 150 men. They have punched a hole in Lowrey's line.

But they cannot yet exploit it. The reason is that the two Ohio regiments have been stopped by abatis in front and enfilade fire from the left. The Buckeyes need help. Seeing the 17th New York of Lum's brigade of Morgan's division approaching from the west, Este runs over to its commander, Colonel William Grower, and asks him to join in the assault. Grower agrees, and his regiment, which had joined Sherman's army only ten days ago, moves to the left of the Ohio regiments. Thus supported, the Ohioans rush forward, break through the abatis, and drive a portion of Lewis's Brigade from its works.

Now the 10th Kentucky and the 74th Indiana can sweep in behind Govan's Brigade. They do so. At the same time, Lum's, Mitchell's, and Dilworth's brigades, all converging in a huge mass, strike from the front. "Glory or a wooden leg!" shouts the commander of the 10th Michigan, Lum's brigade, as his regiment rushes the Rebel ramparts. The Arkansans, who, like all of Cleburne's men, have vowed "to die or be captured in the ditches before they will leave them," fight on until literally swamped by the blue tidal wave. Some are bayoneted or clubbed down; others have their rifles snatched from their hands; practically all, including Govan himself, are forced to surrender, often weeping from humiliation and swearing that never before have they been whipped in a fight. Este's Kentuckians and Indianans, along with Lum's brigade, also capture Key's Battery (but not Key himself: as acting divisional artillery commander, he is elsewhere), and Mitchell's and Dilworth's brigades combine to take Swett's Battery, bayoneting to death one of its officers when he refuses to surrender. Altogether the Federals take eight cannons, six of them pieces seized by Cleburne's Division on July 22. Major Holmes, although painfully wounded by a shell fragment in the left knee, feels "exultant": the bloody repulse at Cheatham's Hill has been avenged.

Over by the railroad a similar scene takes place as Este's Ohio regiments, the 17th New York, and Moore's brigade, which has advanced again, roll up Lewis's Brigade, then the left of McCullough's brigade, in the process taking hundreds of prisoners. Granbury, seeing hordes of Yankees swarming toward his rear, promptly pulls back his right and forms it along a line facing northeast. Hardee, who at this moment rides up to Granbury along with Lowrey, expresses alarm at what he mistakes for a retreat by the Texans. "General," Granbury assures him, "my men never fall back unless ordered back." They are, he explains, merely protecting against an attack from the rear. Lowrey tells Granbury to return his troops to their original position, because Vaughan's Tennessee Brigade is on the way. Several minutes later it arrives, Cleburne riding at its head. It hastily deploys, then launches, along with remnants of Govan's and Lewis's brigades, a counterattack which, even though many of the Tennesseans swerve off in the wrong direction, stops the Union onrush west of the railroad. East of the tracks, McCullough's brigade, utilizing its traverses, first stems the advance of Moore's brigade, which still is without the promised support of the IV Corps, then hurls it back.

Despite the availability of two unengaged brigades in Baird's division, Davis attempts no further offensive action. He and his troops are content to enjoy, in the words of one of his aides, Major James Connolly, "the rapture one feels in the moment of victory." They have made what until now no one has made during the entire campaign: a successful large-scale frontal assault. That is enough. If more is to be done, let someone else do it.[7]

This is Sherman's opinion too. Elated by the XIV Corps's breakthrough, he believes that all that is needed to smash the entire Confederate force at Jonesboro is for Stanley to hit it in the rear from the east. Yet, in spite of a report just before Davis's final attack that the IV Corps was coming into line with the XIV Corps, there has been no sign of any action whatsoever by Stanley's troops, and Davis is complaining about their nonappearance on his left. Soon it will be too dark, hence too late, to finish off the Rebels at Jonesboro. Where, then, is Stanley?

Stanley is exactly where Sherman wants him to be: well beyond the right of the Confederates who are confronting the XIV Corps west of the railroad. But instead of surging forward to strike Hardee's rear, his troops—specifically Kimball's and Newton's divisions—are digging trenches and erecting breastworks as a precaution against being attacked. Both of these divisions, with Wood's in reserve, in fact had started forward in conjunction with the XIV

David S. Stanley (*Photographic History*, 10:93)

Corps as it delivered its final assault. Immediately, however, they had encountered enemy skirmishers, artillery fire, and underbrush so thick that, in Fullerton's words, it was "almost impossible to move through it." As a consequence
Colonel Isaac Kirby's brigade of Kimball's division, which is on Stanley's right,
has failed to support Moore's attack, thereby making it easier for McCullough's
brigade to repel it. (Colonel Capers in his report states that "it is to be noted
that the [Union] assault did not reach the two regiments to the right of mine,
and that the heaviest attack was on my left and at the railroad." Thus even if
Kirby had joined in Moore's attack McCullough's brigade probably could have
held its position, given the terrain and the strength of its defenses.)

Now Kimball's division has come upon a line of log barricades protected by
"a perfect entanglement" of slashed trees and a deep, steep ravine (presumably
this is McCullough's line). Satisfied, after making what Fullerton calls a "feeble" attempt to penetrate this barrier, that an assault cannot succeed, Kimball
orders his men (who concur in his appraisal of the situation) to construct
fortifications. Newton tells his division, which is on Kimball's left, to do the
same. While trying to swing east toward the railroad, it captures a Confederate
field hospital but then comes under fire from both flank and rear. In addition,
Newton notifies Stanley that his skirmishers report that there are breastworks
ahead.

Stanley, who is feeling ill from a slight but painful bullet wound in his groin,
doubts the truth of this report about breastworks, especially since he has just
received a dispatch from Davis informing him that the IV Corps is beyond the
enemy's flank. Yet, with night fast approaching, he concludes that he has no
choice but to approve Kimball's and Newton's decisions to entrench. Subsequently in his report he will assert that with just one more hour of sunshine,
Newton would have been able not only to get across the railroad in the Confederate rear but also to bag most if not all of Hardee's forces.[8]

Possibly; but extremely unlikely. The breastworks are there, and Rebel troops
are behind them. Hardee, having received word that a strong enemy column
was approaching Jonesboro east of the railroad, has sent three brigades (Carter's, Strahl's, and Maney's) from Cheatham's Division to extend the Confederate right further to the east and south. These three brigades, along with
McCullough's, face Kimball's and Newton's divisions and are fully capable of
holding them in check. Far from having turned Hardee's flank, the IV Corps
has not even found it.

Of course, by transferring all of Cheatham's Division to the right, Hardee
has left only Brown's small division to oppose the entire Army of the Tennessee.
But this was a safe enough gamble. Other than to engage in some "demonstrations" that obviously failed in their purpose of keeping the Confederates pinned

down on their front, the XV and XVI corps have remained in their trenches all day, spectators of, rather than actors in, the fighting. Furthermore, at nightfall the XVII Corps is fortifying itself on the east bank of the Flint at Anthony's Bridge. Allegedly because of an incompetent guide, it has taken nearly five hours to march less than two miles, and according to a dispatch that Blair has sent Howard, the Confederates who are facing it occupy a "strong position." One has to conclude that Howard and the Army of the Tennessee are quite content with yesterday's easy victory and nothing short of a peremptory order from Sherman could compel them to take serious offensive action. It is doubtful that Sherman has so much as contemplated issuing such an order.[9]

The coming of night leaves Sherman frustrated and angry. He believes that a great opportunity to crush the Confederates at Jonesboro has been squandered and that Stanley is responsible. The basis for this belief is Sherman's utter ignorance of the actual military situation, an ignorance that is compounded by his having returned to Howard's headquarters, which is on the Flint River, two miles northwest of Jonesboro. Then, too, despite what now should be overwhelming evidence to the contrary, he continues to think that both Hardee's and Lee's corps are at Jonesboro and, to quote from his response to a 7:15 P.M. dispatch from Schofield, that "these corps are not entrenched farther than a straight barricade this side of and parallel to the railroad"! Almost as incredible, Audenried and Poe have informed Sherman, or so he understands them to have reported, that Stanley "remained today for hours on the railroad awaiting orders, when he heard firing to his front and right," and that in spite of this and orders from Thomas to support Davis's attack, Stanley had not so much as tried to advance until it was too late. At least this is what Sherman tells Thomas in a nighttime message, adding: "I don't know why Stanley could not have pushed along the railroad while General Davis was heavily engaged, and absolutely enveloped the enemy at Jonesborough. Now he [the enemy] has time to fortify [!], and we may be compelled to modify all our plans. If General Stanley lost a minute of time when he should have been in action, I beg you not to overlook it" (see Appendix C).

Regarding tomorrow's operations, Sherman intends, so he notifies all three of his army commanders, to endeavor to cut off and destroy the Confederates at Jonesboro should they remain there. If they retreat, as seems more likely, he will pursue them to Griffin, tearing up the railroad (!) as he proceeds. In either case, Schofield is to advance east of the railroad, Thomas is to push directly down it, and Howard is to move along its west side and try to intercept or at least harass Hardee with Blair's corps and Kilpatrick's cavalry. Hardee, Sherman advises Schofield, "cannot move south now without our seeing him, and if all of our army is concentrated on him we should make quick work." Sherman also believes that Stewart's Corps already has or soon will join Hardee and Lee at Jonesboro, leaving Atlanta defended, if defended at all, only by the militia. Hence Sherman directs Thomas to "renew your orders to General Slocum to make a dash at Atlanta before the enemy has time to haul off the artillery and stores." Thomas, who shares Sherman's opinion concerning Stewart's Corps and who has abandoned his earlier (and correct) view that Lee's Corps had gone back toward Atlanta, in turn sends a courier with a message informing Slocum that "there is but little doubt that the three corps of the rebel army are now at Jonesborough," that "it is undoubtedly Hood's intention to evacuate" Atlanta, and that the XX Corps is to make an effort to seize the city "but without exposing the tete-de-pont" on the Chattahoochee to capture.[10]

Part Two: Atlanta

Smith's militia, followed by Walthall's and Featherston's divisions, march out of Atlanta via the Decatur and McDonough roads. As they trudge through the warm, humid night, some of the troops sing the melancholy song *Lorena:*

> We loved each other then, Lorena,
> More than we ever dared to tell;
> And what we might have been, Lorena,
> Had but our dreams but prospered well.

Hood rides with them. His destination is Lovejoy's Station, where he hopes to reconcentrate his army. Lee's Corps, which is six miles south of Atlanta on the McDonough road, covers the retreat. The only forces remaining north of the city are French's Division, which has been designated the rear guard, and units of Ferguson's cavalry, which are picketing the roads.

For Atlantans it has been, records Sam Richards in his diary, "a day of terror." Early in the morning, deserters from Hardee's and Lee's Corps appeared, seeking refuge in the houses of friends and giving the lie by their very presence to reports that yesterday's battle at Jonesboro had been a victory. Next, garrison troops began, in the words of another resident, "moving in every direction," provost guards stopped asking civilians "to show their papers," and groups of "strange negroes" gathered in cellars and abandoned houses. Obviously "something was up, but the citizens could not tell what was coming. They could not believe that the city was to be given up. Their idea was that the Confederate forces were being massed for battle."

Not until nearly noon did Atlantans learn that the army was preparing to leave. At once hundreds of them filled the streets, some seeking a way to escape, others merely milling about in bewilderment. Most of the inhabitants, however, stayed in their homes, awaiting the Yankees and hoping for the best. What else could they do?

Toward evening, columns of troops, wagons, and artillery started filing through the city. Whenever they passed a garden, "several men would rush through it, stripping it in a minute of every stalk of corn, and every green thing that could be eaten by man or beast." On reaching the rail yards beside Decatur Street, the hungry soldiers joined with civilians in helping themselves to food from commissary warehouses that had been opened up to all comers. They were astonished, also resentful, to find in them huge quantities of "sugar, bacon, coffee, whiskey, shoes, and clothing of every description," for they had been "under the impression that no such stores existed in the army." Meanwhile, not content with this authorized looting, bands of stragglers, camp followers, and "licentious citizens," many of them drunk, ransacked and sometime set fire to empty houses.[11]

Now it is 11 P.M. French, in accordance with his instructions from Stewart, begins withdrawing his divisions from the fortifications astride the Marietta road. He is disgusted with the way the evacuation is being conducted: "Common sense is wanted." Thus at 5 P.M., two 64-pounders, which he was planning to spike because they are too heavy to be moved, had had their wooden carriages burned "by order of the chief of ordnance . . . a proclamation to the enemy in my front that we were evacuating the place." This act of folly, though, is nothing, so thinks French, compared to what happens next.

Lined up along a double row of Georgia Railroad tracks on the eastern edge of the city and next to the Schofield and Markham Rolling Mill are five locomotives and eighty-one boxcars, twenty-eight of which are packed with gunpowder, shells, and (according to a newspaper report) five thousand "entirely new" rifles and three million cartridges. Although during the night of August 31, Shoup ordered and reordered Lieutenant Colonel M. B. McMicken, the chief quartermaster, to send these trains out of Atlanta by daylight on September 1, for some reason ("gross negligence" resulting from his being "too much addicted to drink," according to Hood), McMicken failed to execute the order, and Shoup, whose experience with the Army of the Tennessee should have taught him to take nothing for granted, neglected to check on him. Hence, instead of being safely on the way to Griffin or Macon, as they would have been had they departed when stipulated, these engines and cars are trapped in Atlanta and must be destroyed if they are not to fall into Yankee hands.

After first telling all civilians living in the vicinity of the trains to clear out, some of Hood's staff officers set the ammunition cars ablaze. Sixteen-year-old Mary Rawson, asleep in her father's mansion, The Terraces, on Pryor Street, is awakened by "rapid and loud explosions." She and other family members rush to the windows. Off to the northeast they behold "a most beautiful spectacle" as "flaming rockets" and "innumerable spangles" of sparks fill the sky. Sam Richards, on his way to the Macon depot to get more sacks of cornmeal, feels the ground rock under him and hears the sound of breaking glass amidst the recurrent thunder of explosions. Shell fragments, canister pellets, and splinters of wood and iron rip through nearby buildings, wrecking some of them. At first many people think the Yankees are storming the city. When they realize the truth, they flock by the hundreds to hilltops and watch "with breathless excitement the volcanic scene on the Georgia Railroad." It is a scene none of them will ever forget; a few will live to see it recreated seventy-five years later on a movie screen.

The destruction of the trains intensifies the disgust of the already-much-disgusted French. He believes that "this should have been done the last of all, when the rear guard or pickets were withdrawn" to the south of the city. Once the demolitions had begun, there was no danger of the enemy's stopping them: "Who would extinguish an ordnance train of bursting shells?" As it is, if the Yankees have not guessed already that Atlanta is being evacuated, surely they know it now. So thinking, French marches with his division through Atlanta, the way "lighted by the glare of fires, flashes of powder, and bursting shells." Except for roving bands of Ferguson's troopers and deserted fortifications, nothing now stands between the city and the XX Corps.[12]

At his headquarters two miles northwest of Jonesboro, Sherman hears the "sounds of shells exploding" and noises "like that of musketry" coming from the direction of Atlanta, fifteen miles distant. Are the Confederates blowing up their magazines while evacuating the city? Or has Slocum become engaged in battle? Sherman walks over to the house of a farmer, calls him out, and asks his opinion. The farmer, who says he has lived here a long time, replies that the sounds are "just like those of a battle." Sherman, although still unsure, is inclined to agree. Besides, whether it is a battle or an evacuation, there is nothing he can do about it. The important thing is to finish off Hardee's forces at Jonesboro. He passes a sleepless night, impatiently awaiting the arrival of daylight.[13]

Hardee's weary troops, having silently stolen from their fishhook-shaped line, trudge toward Lovejoy's Station. Their retreat, contrary to Sherman's assurance to Schofield that "Hardee cannot move south now without our seeing him," goes undetected. They leave behind only stragglers and about two hundred unmovable wounded. Their casualties in yesterday's fighting total approximately 1,400, nearly 900 of them prisoners, most of whom are from Govan's

Where Hood blew up his munition train: The Georgia Railroad on the east side of Atlanta (*Photographic History*, 3:135)

and Lewis's brigades (the little that is left of the latter soon will be converted to cavalry). Nevertheless, in spite of the humiliation of a broken line and two captured batteries, they have held their position and prevented the Federals from cutting them and the rest of Hood's army off from Macon and consequently have enabled Stewart's Corps and the militia to march out of Atlanta with little danger of being intercepted. Thus, they have achieved a tactical and strategical victory: they have done it, furthermore, against ten and ultimately twelve enemy divisions in position to assail their three divisions from all four directions. Perhaps only Beauregard's stand at Petersburg against the bulk of Grant's army back in June provides a better example of the dominance that defense has gained over offense on the battlefield during the fourth year of the war.[14]

By 4 A.M. it seems to Sherman that the din of rifle and cannon fire to the north is coming closer. Could it be that the Confederates are attacking Garrard's cavalry, which he has stationed near Rough and Ready? He sends a dispatch to Schofield instructing him that "if the firing at the north be not explained, prepare to meet any interruption of our operations from that quarter," but otherwise "to attack Jonesborough from the east." At the same time he instructs Thomas to move his and Schofield's wagon trains nearer to the rear of the Army of the Tennessee. Although it is doubtful, he explains to Thomas, that the enemy approaching from the north can be "very formidable . . . we must be prepared."

Before either of these communications can reach their destinations, Union skirmishers discover that the Rebels are gone from around Jonesboro and are retreating toward Lovejoy's. News of this development reaches Sherman at about 6 A.M.. With it comes also the realization that he has failed to bag what he still believes to be Hardee's and Lee's corps and possibly Stewart's as well.[15] Then and later he blames the failure on Stanley for allegedly having moved too tardily, slowly, and timidly against Hardee's supposedly exposed right flank and rear. In reality, as we have seen, Sherman has only himself to blame by having the IV Corps spend all morning and half the afternoon of September 1 tearing up track instead of marching early and rapidly to Jonesboro, by not having ordered Howard to attack instead of merely demonstrating, and by not having sent Blair south of Jonesboro with definite and peremptory instructions to block the railroad and all wagon roads to Lovejoy's. As a consequence of Sherman's ineptitude, the XIV Corps has lost 1,272 killed, wounded, and missing, 330 of them in Este's brigade of 1,100, to accomplish nothing of strategic value, because as soon as Schofield's and Stanley's troops reached the Macon railroad south of Rough and Ready on the afternoon of August 31, Atlanta became untenable for Hood regardless of what happened at Jonesboro. Indeed, even the tactical success of the XIV Corps in breaking (or, to be more accurate, denting) the Confederate line—a victory about which its officers and men will brag and bicker for the rest of their lives—was more the product of fortune than fortitude, although the latter was in ample supply. Had not four brigades managed almost simultaneously to strike both sides of a weakly held and poorly fortified salient that was unprotected (this was the decisive factor) by abatis or equivalent obstructions, the Union assault would have ended in yet another bloody repulse. As it is, "headless trunks and mangled remains lay in profusion" among the woods and ravines north of Jonesboro, most of them in blue uniforms.

Sherman responds to Hardee's retreat by ordering a pursuit in accordance with the instructions he issued last night: Howard to advance down the west side of the railroad; Thomas, with the IV Corps, to go down the east side; and Schofield to come in on Thomas's left. The XIV Corps will remain in Jonesboro and, except for troops detailed to bury the dead and to guard prisoners, form a line facing north to defend against a possible attack from that direction. Sherman, still unsure that the Confederates have evacuated Atlanta, intends to act on the assumption that they remain there until he receives what he considers to be reliable information stating otherwise. So far there is none.[16]

Men, women, and children, blacks and whites, civilians and soldiers, roam Atlanta's Five Points, breaking into stores, then carrying off sacks of meal, salt, tobacco, and whatever else strikes their fancy. All are intent on getting all they can before the Yankees come.

They expect that to be soon. But then what will Sherman's men do? Loot? Burn? Murder? Rape? Mayor Calhoun holds an impromptu conference on the corner of Peachtree and Marietta streets with members of the city council and other leading citizens. They decide to make a formal surrender of the city in hopes of preventing such things. Carrying a white flag, they ride out on Marietta Street, picking their way through debris from shell-shattered houses. Just beyond the Confederate fort adjoining the Ponder home they see a party of Federal horsemen rapidly approaching. Led by Captain Henry M. Scott, inspector general of Ward's division, it consists of several other staff officers and a 25-man cavalry escort. Following it are 900 of Ward's infantry under the command of Colonel John Coburn, one of three columns that Slocum has sent out from each of his divisions to reconnoiter Atlanta with a view to ascertaining if it has been evacuated.

Captain Scott rides up to the civilians who are carrying the white flag and asks them who they are and what they want. Calhoun answers that he is the mayor of Atlanta and that he has come to see General Sherman about surrendering the city. Scott states that Sherman is down around Jonesboro and that Slocum commands the forces that will occupy Atlanta. At this point, Coburn joins the discussion. What about the Confederate troops? he inquires. Are they gone? Yes, replies Calhoun, except for Ferguson's cavalry; but Ferguson has assured him that he would leave without offering any resistance. Scott thereupon tells Calhoun to address a note to General Ward formally surrendering the city. (Obviously Scott knows the first duty of a staff officer, which is to secure all possible credit for his commander!) Taking a memorandum book from his pocket, Calhoun tears out a page and writes on it:

Atlanta, Ga., September 2, 1864

Brigadier General Ward,
    Comdg. Third Division, Twentieth Corps
Sir: The fortune of war has placed Atlanta in your hands. As mayor of the
city I ask protection to non-combatants and private property.
                                        James M. Calhoun,
                                        Mayor of Atlanta

Scott and two fellow staff officers sign the note attesting to its validity. Then
Scott and his cavalry escort start into the city. Some of Ferguson's troopers fire on
them from behind houses. Coburn warns Calhoun that his men will burn down the
houses unless the firing ceases. The mayor tries to stop it but nearly gets shot himself. Coburn thereupon orders his skirmishers forward. Ferguson's recalcitrants
beat a hasty retreat by way of the McDonough road. Coburn's main column then
marches into the city, as does a detachment from Geary's division by a different
route. The latter reaches the City Hall first and, around noon, hoists above it the
colors of the 111th Pennsylvania and the 60th New York. A loud cheer, followed
by two more, goes up from the Union troops. At long last Atlanta is theirs.

Among the Federals marching into Atlanta is Lieutenant John Wilkens of
Indianapolis, a quartermaster with Ward's division. He finds the Confederate
fortifications impressive, in fact awesome; even "to think of charging them
would be the idea of an idiot." The north side of the city, he notes, is "totally
devastated," and he cannot see a house "but what had a cannon ball hole
through it and the most of them more than one." Also, every yard "has a hole in
which the families would have to stay to keep clear of our shells and shot." He is
"somewhat disappointed" with the city itself, having expected it to be bigger
and to have finer buildings. Instead he judges it to be "only a little larger than
Jeffersonville, Ind.," and "there is not much taste displayed in there [sic] buildings," something he attributes to the inhabitants' desiring "to make money
[and] not caring much for the improvement of the place."

When they reach the Five Points, many of the soldiers, to quote the diary of
one of them, start "going for . . . tobacco *and everything else.*" Civilian pillagers, who had fled at the soldiers' approach, quickly join them. Sam Richards,
nearing his store, beholds "armful and baskets full of books and wall-paper
going up the street" from it, and on going inside, he finds it crowded with
"Yankees, men, women, children and niggers . . . each one scrambling to get
something to carry away, regardless, apparently, whether it was any thing they
needed, and still more heedless of the fact that they were stealing!" At first he is
so dismayed that he almost decides to "let them finish it," but indignation
prevails, and he manages to drive the looters away, then stands guard on what is
left of his wares until it is dark.

Union wagons on Peachtree Street, Atlanta *(Atlanta Historical Society)*

Other than to gulp down grapes in backyard arbors or to request, and sometime even pay for, home-cooked meals, the conquerors stay away from houses, many of which are bedecked with white flags. Carrie Berry, who is favorably impressed by their "orderly" behavior, thinks "I shall like the Yankees very much." Most Atlantans, though, view the Yankees with sullen resentment, and here and there small boys defiantly whistle "Dixie" and "The Bonnie Blue Flag." Only Unionists, of which there are a large but hitherto prudently silent number, openly welcome them.

Around 2 P.M., Slocum, a slender, quietly competent West Pointer from New York, enters the city and establishes headquarters at the Trout House. He then sends a telegram to the secretary of war in Washington. Its first sentence reads: "General Sherman has taken Atlanta."[17]

Part Three: Lovejoy's Station

This is something that Sherman himself does not know. Although prisoners assert that Atlanta has been abandoned, that the explosions heard during the night were caused by Hood's blowing up his ammunition trains, that Stewart's

Corps is retreating toward McDonough, and that the militia is retreating toward Covington, how can he be sure they are telling the truth? Likewise he is skeptical about messages from Schofield and Garrard that the Confederates have pulled out of Atlanta: the former cites as his highly dubious authority "a negro just in from Atlanta," and the latter simply cannot be trusted. Not until he hears from Slocum or some other thoroughly reliable source will he accept it as fact that Atlanta is his. Meanwhile he will continue after Hardee in the hope of overtaking and crushing him before he has time to entrench. There is no evidence that he so much as considers sending a force eastward—the XXIII Corps and units of the IV and XIV corps are available—to block the McDonough road in case the reports that the Confederates are retreating from Atlanta by that route prove true.

Sherman once again is destined to frustration in an attempt to catch a fleeing foe on the run or in the open. One mile north of Lovejoy's, Hardee's troops (10,000 at most; quite possibly no more than 8,000) are in line of battle along a low ridge called Cedar Bluffs that runs from east to west. It is a strong position, being covered on both flanks and front by little streams, swamps, ravines, and the ever-present tangle of timber and underbrush. Moreover it is rapidly becoming stronger with the construction of full-fledged entrenchments complete with head logs and abatises of tree limbs and saplings. During a pause in their labors, some survivors of Govan's Brigade ask Granbury's Texans if they have lost confidence in them because of what had happened yesterday at Jonesboro. The answer is "satisfactory."[18]

Around 2 P.M. the Federals approach within cannon range of Hardee's line. Eager to see what lies ahead, Sherman climbs up on the railroad embankment and studies the enemy fortifications through his field glass. Although they appear formidable, the fact that work still is under way on them might mean that they are vulnerable. Besides, the large numbers of prisoners, stragglers, and deserters rounded up during the morning is a sign that the Confederates are becoming demoralized. Hence he decides to attack, and he so informs Thomas and Howard.

At 2:35 P.M., Thomas directs Stanley to move forward on the east side of the railroad as soon as Howard notifies him that he is ready to advance on the other side. Stanley in turn orders Wood and Kimball, whose divisions form respectively the center and the left of his battle line, to make the assault. Stanley believes, after reconnoitering the front, that an attack by Newton's division on the right and next to the railroad would be "inadvisable" because the ground over which it would have to pass is too exposed to artillery fire, whereas he is "under the impression that if the Army of the Tennessee attracted the attention of the enemy I should be able to reach the rebel right flank" with Kimball's division.

By 3:20, Howard is ready, and he so notifies Stanley. A few minutes later the XV and XVI corps begin advancing, as do Wood's and Kimball's divisions. Leading Howard's thrust, Walcutt's brigade quickly overruns a line of Confederate skirmish pits, in the process capturing some South Carolina troops and a tactically advantageous hill. But before Howard can attempt to follow up this success, he receives, at 4 P.M., an order from Sherman to suspend the attack and "stand on the defensive for the present." According to Major Thomas Osborn, Howard's chief of artillery, a "close inspection" of the Confederate defenses (by whom, he does not say) had "found that an attack would be attended with difficulties not worth our while to encounter" and that "the loss would be too great for the benefits gained."

No similar order reaches Thomas or Stanley; neither do they learn that Howard's attack has been called off. Since Sherman is nearby, in position to observe Stanley's operations and to communicate quickly with him and Thomas, there can be only two possible explanations of why this is so. One, highly unlikely, is that Sherman has left it up to Howard to notify Stanley that his attack has been called off but Howard has neglected to do so. The other, much more probable, is that Sherman, bitter over what he deems to be the inexcusable failure of the IV Corps to attack yesterday, deliberately is making it attack today. (Sherman's proximity to Thomas and Stanley is established by Eben D. Sturges, an officer on Thomas's staff, who states in his diary for September 2 that at midafternoon Sherman and Thomas "rode forward about a half mile to a home on the left of the railroad and staid [*sic*] there until dark.")

Moving through what Fullerton describes as "an almost impenetrable swamp" and across "deep ravines and high ridges," Wood's and Kimball's divisions do not come in sight of the Confederate works until nearly 6 P.M. Wood, after studying them, concludes that "the most favorable point of attack" in his sector is in front of Colonel Frederick Knefler's brigade of Ohio, Indiana, and Kentucky troops. Since it is posted on the left of his line, Wood goes over to Kimball's division and, without informing Kimball, orders the commanders of its two lead brigades, Brigadier General William Grose and Colonel Jacob Taylor, to assault in concert with Knefler. Wood then heads back to his own division. On the way, while passing over an open space, a bullet strikes his left foot. While aides are carrying him from the field, he sends a staff officer to Knefler with an order to proceed with the attack.

Several minutes later, Knefler's brigade, formed in two lines of battle, starts forward. On its left, Grose's and Taylor's brigades do likewise. After clawing their way through a "dense thicket of wild plums," all three units come upon a line of Rebel rifle pits. They charge and carry the pits, taking several dozen prisoners, then push on until they find themselves facing a "deep ravine full of thick brush and fallen timber" and, beyond that, the enemy's main works. Wisely, Grose and Taylor order their men to halt and dig in. Not so wisely (perhaps he is drunk), Knefler orders his men to charge. They at once meet such a "perfect hail" of bullets and canister that they run back and take cover in the captured rifle pits, thereby keeping their loss down to a mere 38 killed and wounded. No doubt they know from the prisoners that they are up against the same Confederates that Wood's division had encountered with such bloody consequences at Pickett's Mill: Cleburne's.

After the repulse of Wood's assault, if thus it can be called, Stanley asks Hascall, whose division of the XXIII Corps is coming up on the left, to try to strike the Rebel right flank, which extends, he thinks, only to the center of Kimball's division. Hascall refuses. Stanley, he declares, has troops of his own that he can use for this purpose. (Hascall in his report makes no mention of Stanley's request and merely states that he took position on Kimball's left "too late to take part in the advance, which had already ended.") Since it now is almost dark, Stanley decides to cease his offensive efforts, and he orders all of the IV Corps to entrench. Then, at 7:30 P.M., he addresses a report to Thomas describing the day's operations and their outcome. "I have never," he states, "seen the enemy take a stronger position."

Sherman would agree. Moreover there still is no definite word about the situation in Atlanta, and this "bothers me." Hence at 8 P.M. he informs Thomas, Howard, and Schofield that for the time being there are to be no more attacks on Hardee. "Until we hear from Atlanta the exact truth," he explains to Thomas, "I do not care about you pushing your men against breast-works. Destroy the railroad well up to your lines; keep skirmishers well up, and hold your troops in hand for anything that may turn up. As soon as we know positively that our troops are in Atlanta I will determine what to do." Meanwhile, Sherman adds, Schofield will "feel for the McDonough road, to prevent re-enforcement coming to the enemy from that direction." Finally, but rather belatedly, it has occurred to Sherman that it might be worthwhile to try to block that road.[19]

At 9 P.M., two brigades of Alpheus Williams's division march into Atlanta "with bands playing," the last of the XX Corps to enter the city. Riding at the head of the column "through the dark streets, made intensely so by the heavy shade trees," Williams hears a window slide up and a woman's voice cry out "Welcome!" Many women bring buckets of water for his men, who are sweating from a four-mile march "as fast as we could walk" on an evening made "very warm by thunder showers brewing all around." While they drink, the women speak bitterly about Hood's army, declaring that it had "robbed them of everything that could be carried off, with the excuse that the Yankees would steal it anyway."

Around midnight, one of Williams's soldiers, Private William Wallace of the 3rd Wisconsin, having pitched his tent in a camp on the east side of the city, decides to take a tour. Wrapping his rubber groundsheet around him because it now is raining, he strolls out along the tracks of the Georgia Railroad. Such a sight he has never seen before: "4 large trains of cars and 5 locomotives all in ashes, except for the iron." Amidst the debris are cannon barrels, huge chunks of lead created by melted bullets, and "no end" of canister lying around the track "like wheat about a threshing machine." A "little piece further" he comes to the rolling mill. Nothing remains of it "but the chimneys" and "steam boilers, fly wheels, [and] great piles of iron in various states of manufacture."

After some more explorations in the vicinity of the Georgia Railroad, during which he notes "7 large siege guns that they could not get away in their hurry," he visits the center of the city. Here he finds the freight depot "nearly filled with rebel deserters" and on the streets "large groups of Georgia Milittia [*sic*] who have deserted." The latter are "mostly old men" who do not "care much about fighting." In the Five Points all the stores are vacant: "nothing that could be used by a soldier" remains in them. The owner of one of the stores is "about half crazy" over the loss of fifty-six boxes of tobacco taken by Federals during the day. Wallace then goes "down to a cellar where some folks had taken refuge from the shell." It contains cornmeal piled up in sacks, and soldiers are helping themselves to "a little bit of it." He does the same, taking "about a peck." To the victor belong the spoils.[20]

Just before breakfast on September 3, the word about Atlanta that he anxiously has been awaiting finally reaches Sherman. It comes in the form of a dispatch by Slocum and is brought by a courier who traveled in a locomotive from Atlanta to Rough and Ready, which was as far as he could go in that fashion because of the destruction of the track south of there, and then proceeded on foot until picked up by some of Garrard's troopers. Sherman reads the dispatch, notes that it is dated inside Atlanta, and concludes that indeed Hood is out of the city and that Slocum is in it. Even so he sends a staff officer to fetch Thomas, whose bivouac is close by. Thomas soon arrives, examines the message, and agrees that it is genuine and that Atlanta has been taken.

Sherman decides to end the campaign. It would be pointless, perhaps risky, to go on with it. By now Hood probably has reunited his army or soon will. The only way he can be dislodged from Lovejoy's would be to make another flanking move. But this merely would cause him to fall back to another strong defensive position. Besides, short of Macon, nearly a hundred miles further south, there is nothing of strategic value to be gained by plunging deeper into Georgia; and to do so, Sherman would have to supply his army, portions of which are beginning to run low on food, by means of wagons traveling all the way from Rough and Ready, for by destroying the railroad between that point and Lovejoy's, he has in effect cut himself off from his own base! No, the sensible thing to do is to withdraw to the conquered city of Atlanta, then to rebuild and recuperate his forces in preparation for the next phase of the war. Concerning that, he already has some ideas.

Hence he dictates to Dayton a special order announcing to the army that Slocum "occupied Atlanta yesterday at 11 A.M., the enemy having evacuated the night before," and declaring that "our present task is, therefore, well done, and all the work of destruction on the railroad will cease." Then, while this order is being read along the lines, where it is greeted with cheers and band music, he pens a dispatch to Halleck, which, after being carried there by courier, is telegraphed from Atlanta. In it he tells about the movement to Jonesboro, the battles of August 31 and September 1, and the evacuation of Atlanta by Hood and its occupation by Slocum. "So," he concludes, in words soon to be famous, "Atlanta is ours, and fairly won. I shall not push much farther on this raid, but in a day or so will march to Atlanta and give my men some rest. Since May 5 we have been in one constant battle or skirmish, and need rest."[21]

While the Union troops celebrate and their bands play, skirmishing and cannonading continue in the woods and thickets north of Lovejoy's. Yankee sharpshooters kill several men in Captain Foster's regiment. Across the way a young soldier, "almost a boy," in the 101st Ohio is shot through the shoulder. "I have been all through the campaign," he comments bitterly, "without being hit and now they had to shoot me." During the afternoon Stewart's Corps joins Hardee, followed in the evening by Lee's. They come by way of the road from McDonough that Sherman last night had ordered Schofield to "feel for" in the morning. Instead, evidently because he believed statements from prisoners that Stewart and Lee already had reached Hardee, Schofield merely sent out some patrols and made no attempt to block the road. Had he done so, the consequences might have been disastrous for the Confederates. Toward noon, quartermaster clerk Patrick, barely able to walk and straggling, found the road littered with "broken wagons and caisons [sic], artillery ammunition of all kinds, and boxes of ammunition for small arms"—signs of exhaustion if not demoralization.

Confederate prisoners taken at Jonesboro being marched to Atlanta *(Harper's Weekly)*

For the next two days the Union artillery pound the Rebel lines, forcing them back in some sectors and inflicting severe losses, notably on French's Division, which is hit by a "reverse fire" from the hill captured by Walcutt's brigade. Hood, who has warned Richmond that "to prevent this country from being overrun reenforcements are absolutely necessary," believes that Sherman "will not content himself with Atlanta, but will continue offensive movements," most likely by using the Flint River to screen a thrust around the Confederate left. If he does, Hood intends to "strike him with my entire force in his flank and rear," even though "for the offensive, my troops at present are not more than equal to their own numbers." Patrick, writing in his diary on the evening of September 5, wonders "what delays the enemy. If they would only come on, they can capture the whole concern."

Not long after Patrick inscribes these words, Sherman's troops, under the double cover of darkness and heavy rain, pull out of their entrenchments and head north. Despite the downpour and ankle-deep mud, they are in a joyful, even jubilant, mood. The campaign is over, they have survived it, and Atlanta has been taken. That is enough. If more needs to be done, it can wait until later. Right now they want a vacation from marching, fighting, and digging, from living and dying like wild beasts. They believe they have earned it.

Those cold, lifeless indices of agony and death—the casualty and medical statistics—confirm their belief. Close to 4,500 comrades lie rotting in graves and pits and in woods, fields, and obscure ravines between Tunnel Hill and Macon; an equal number are in Andersonville and other Rebel prison pens, where many of them will die also; 23,000 more have been wounded, some two or three times; and 55,000 of them at one time or another have had to go to a hospital suffering from sickness or exhaustion, and large numbers of them remain there. Thus their combat strength, which at the beginning of the campaign totaled nearly 100,000, has dwindled to barely 80,000, in spite of the accession of Blair's corps, recruits, and convalescents. Several divisions—Geary's, Fuller's, Newton's, Giles Smith's— have been reduced to half their original size; most brigades cannot put a thousand men into battle; and numerous regiments are mere remnants: for example, the 68th Ohio, which had mustered 900 rank and file in May, now stacks just 245 muskets; and yet, according to one of its members, it is "amongst the largest in the Army of the Tennessee"! No wonder Sherman's soldiers, as they march for Atlanta, not only desire but also, as one of them puts it, "expect to reap and derive a great benefit from a rest of thirty or forty days." Then, he adds, "we will be ready for another campaign."[22]

In the morning, Hood telegraphs a laconic message to Bragg: "The enemy withdrew from my front in the direction of Jonesborough." For the Confederates, as for the Federals, the campaign has ended. The difference, of course, is that for them it has ended in defeat. Atlanta, for which they have fought, suffered, and poured out their blood through four long, hideous months, has been lost.

Hood thinks it should not have been. "According to all human calculations," he bitterly writes President Davis later in the day, "we should have saved Atlanta had the officers and men of this army done what was expected of them." The officer he blames most, of course, is Hardee. In his report, Hood states that had Hardee attacked early in the morning, as ordered, "the enemy would have been found but partially protected by works," which could have been overcome because "the number of men on our side considerably exceeded that of the enemy"; and in his memoirs, Hood implies that Hardee was guilty of willful disobedience. As for the men, in a September 4 letter to Bragg, Hood attributes their lack of offensive spirit to their having been "so long confined to trenches" and to their having been "taught to believe that entrenchments cannot be taken," with the result that "I am officially informed that there is a tacit if not expressed determination among the men of this army, extending to officers as high in some instances as colonel, that they will not attack breastworks."[23]

Hood is unjust to both Hardee and his troops. As we have seen, Hardee had attacked on August 31 as soon as he possibly could have unless he was to attack with just his own corps; Howard was well entrenched by morning and had roughly the same strength as Hardee; and although many of the Confederates indeed had charged forward halfheartedly or even failed to engage the Federals, the only thing they would have gained by assaulting with greater determination was greater casualties, which is why they had conducted themselves as they had. They knew from experience—Ezra Church, Bald Hill, Peachtree Creek, Kolb's farm, Resaca, Chickamauga—what was likely to happen when a charge is made against a strong, tough foe who has had time to make himself even "partially protected by works."

The root of the defeat at Jonesboro on August 31 lies, not in Hardee and his half-exhausted men, but in Hood himself. Misled by or misinterpreting the reports of his cavalry, he had misconceived the strength and intent of the Union column approaching Jonesboro and so attempted, as he had done on July 22, to do too much in too little time with too few men (although he had employed all that could be spared from defending Atlanta itself). Furthermore, even if by some near miracle, Hardee's attack had succeeded in driving Howard back across the Flint, it would have made no strategic difference. Schofield's and Stanley's corps already were astride the Macon railroad, and the XIV Corps was close-by. Nothing that the Confederates could have done short of a full-fledged miracle could have forced the Federals off of it, and thus Hood still would have had to evacuate Atlanta. The Army of the Tennessee simply lacked the offensive punch to dislodge any strong Union force from a position it had time to fortify.

In Captain Poe's opinion, which probably reflects Sherman's view of the matter, Hood's best chance of parrying the Federal thrust toward the Macon railroad would have been to give battle at Morrow's Mill, two and a half miles southwest of Rough and Ready and near the terminus of the Confederate fortifications running down from Atlanta. His failure to do so, Poe states in a September 12 letter to his wife, had given the Union commanders "a great deal of assurance, for it indicated that the enemy did not comprehend the movement."[24] But, it will be recalled, Hood did "comprehend," at least in a general way, what Sherman was up to and hence had contemplated falling on his flank and rear, only to decide that this was impracticable because of the numerous creeks and ravines that would have obstructed the swift execution of such a maneuver. Moreover, even if Hood had carried out this move and overcome the terrain obstacles, it is extremely doubtful that he could have achieved decisive results. Sherman, fearful that Hood indeed would try to strike his rear, took care at all times to protect it, using the XXIII Corps for this purpose, and it alone could have held the Confederates in check until reinforced by the IV and XIV corps. Hood, to be sure, would have stopped the advance of Thomas and

Schofield toward the railroad, but meanwhile Howard—unless Sherman had panicked and ordered him to halt—would have gone on to Jonesboro. Then not only would Atlanta have become untenable for Hood but his army would also have been put in a worse predicament than it was on September 1-2, with Thomas and Schofield in its immediate front and Howard in position to block its retreat south.

In sum, given the disparity of forces between Sherman and himself, there probably was no way that Hood by offensive operations could have prevented the Federals from cutting the Macon railroad. Could he, however, have achieved this by defensive means? One of his critics, the most prominent of all, answers yes. This is Johnston, who in his postwar writings claims that he could have held Atlanta "forever" (or at least "indefinitely") by constructing a chain of strong points south from the city to protect the Macon railroad. Many have believed him. There is no reason why they should. Sherman was prepared, as demonstrated by his reaction on the evening of August 30 to word that the Confederates had blocked access to Jonesboro, to go as far as Griffin to reach the railroad. A defense line stretching that far south from Atlanta would have been at least fifty miles long. Not even Lee was able to hold Richmond when, at the end of March 1865, he had to extend his line more than thirty miles in an attempt to protect his communications.[25]

Some of his other critics argue that had Hood retained Wheeler instead of sending him off on a futile raid, this would have enabled him to detect Sherman's thrust against the Macon railroad sooner and so to act faster to counter it.[26] Perhaps; but this is not likely. Given Wheeler's performance during the Snake Creek Gap maneuver and along the Chattahoochee early in July, there is no reason to believe that he necessarily would have provided Hood with more timely intelligence about Sherman's movements than Jackson in fact did. Furthermore, although Wheeler's and Jackson's cavalry combined presumably could have delayed longer the Federal advance toward the railroad than Jackson's alone, they could not have stopped it, and the ultimate outcome would have been the same. Finally, the above critics premise their criticism on the assumption that Hood was totally fooled by Sherman's maneuver toward Jonesboro, whereas, to state the truth again, Hood soon realized, along with everybody else, including privates and even newspaper editors, that Sherman was aiming for the Macon railroad. What Hood did not know (also in common with all other Confederates, among them Hardee) was exactly where, when, and in what strength Sherman would strike it. Wheeler's cavalry, had it been present, might have sent Hood better information on these matters. If so, Hood in turn might have made a more realistic assessment of his strategic situation and, as a consequence, evacuated Atlanta without making a foredoomed and nearly disastrous attempt to hold onto it. Otherwise, however, it is difficult to conceive of any significant benefit that could have derived from Wheeler's retention with the Army of Tennessee.

Once Hood had failed to defeat or drive back Sherman with his July sorties, Atlanta became extremely vulnerable because of its logistical dependence on a single exposed railroad line. Well aware of this, Hood played his sole remaining strategic card by sending Wheeler to cut Sherman's communications before his own were cut, but the card turned out to be a joker. Hood held Atlanta as long as he did mainly because Sherman took so long to do what was necessary to make it impossible for Hood to hold it. When Sherman finally did do what had to be done, Hood had no choice except to abandon the city in order to save his army from destruction. This he succeeded in achieving, thanks to two men he never would think of thanking. One was Hardee, through his skillfully conducted stands at Jonesboro on September 1 and at Lovejoy's on the following day. The other was Sherman.

Victorious Sherman, like defeated Hood, is dissatisfied with the outcome of the just-completed operations south of Atlanta. "I ought," he complains in a September 4 letter to Halleck, "to have reaped larger fruits of victory." He blames this inadequate military harvest on the Army of the Cumberland in general—like its commander, it is "too slow"—and on Stanley in particular for dallying on the road to Jonesboro rather than hastening to the sound of the guns. On the other hand he considers his own performance to have been "skillful and well-executed," and although he regrets not having "taken 10,000 of Hardee's men, and all of his artillery," that is of little consequence in comparison with the capture of "the town of Atlanta, which, after all, was the prize I fought for."[27]

Sherman is right in believing he should have "reaped larger fruits of victory." Where he is wrong is in assigning the responsibility to others: it belongs to him and to him alone. Six times from August 27 through September 3 he had an opportunity to destroy or to mangle or, at the very least, to drive Hood's army to the eastern edge of Georgia, thus leaving that state and Alabama at Sherman's mercy. Each time he muffed the opportunity, even when, as happened on one occasion, it was pointed out to him.

The first and worst muff occurred at the outset, when he halted, in effect for two days, to engage in the utterly unnecessary wrecking of a strategically meaningless stretch of track. As noted, had he pushed on without delay and with even moderate speed, he would have reached the Macon railroad somewhere between Rough and Ready before Hood could have reacted. This in itself would have forced Hood to evacuate Atlanta, assuming (as it seems safe to do) that he would not have been so foolhardy as to try to drive Sherman from the railroad by means of an attack. It also would have put Sherman in a position (whether he would have taken advantage of it is another matter) to strike toward Atlanta from the south, a move that Hood obviously feared greatly and with great cause: it would have compelled him to attempt either to cut through or to slip by Sherman in an effort to restore his communications with Macon or else to retreat eastward to Augusta, thereby removing his army from the military chessboard in the West.

Sherman committed his next two mistakes on the evening of August 31. One—minor and, under the circumstances, perhaps forgivable—was not to order Schofield to head, as soon as it was daylight, for the McDonough road. Such a move, supposing Schofield had executed it with sufficient vigor, would have blocked Hood's retreat from Atlanta, with possible consequences ranging from Hood's having to take a longer route to reach Hardee all the way to mass panic, surrender, and flight on the part of Stewart's and especially Lee's corps. Sherman's other mistake—this one major and definitely unforgivable—was his rejection of Thomas's proposal to have the IV and XIV corps move around to Lovejoy's while Howard pinned down Hardee at Jonesboro. Had this been done, assuming a modicum of competent management on the Union side, all of the Confederate army, Hardee's Corps included, would have been cut off from Macon, leaving Hood with no rational choice except to withdraw in the direction of Augusta, in effect abandoning Alabama and Georgia. Twice, first at the beginning of the campaign and then at the end of it, Thomas presented Sherman with plans that offered a splendid chance of making it impossible for the South to continue the war in the West and, as a result, in the East as well. On the first occasion, Sherman implemented the plan in an inadequate fashion; on the second, he did not implement it at all.

Sherman's fourth, and in some ways his most incredible, blunder was to have Stanley and Schofield spend the morning and early afternoon of September 1 breaking the already broken Macon railroad while advancing, of necessity slowly, toward Jonesboro. Had he ordered it to march rapidly south at dawn, the IV Corps certainly would have arrived in ample time and in full strength to participate with the XIV Corps in the attack on Hardee while there still was plenty of daylight. Because he did not do this and because he also failed to require Howard to make at least a convincing semblance of an attack on the Confederates west of Jonesboro—his fifth major mistake—Sherman enabled Hardee to escape from being overwhelmed and crushed, an outcome that would have reduced the Army of Tennessee so badly in manpower, morale, and matériel that it would have been rendered strategically impotent.

Sherman passed up his sixth and last chance to inflict serious, perhaps fatal, damage to the Confederates at Lovejoy's. There, with twelve divisions at his disposal, he did little more than skirmish with Hardee's three divisions; then he ceased offensive operations on learning that Slocum indeed had occupied Atlanta. Although neither he nor his troops, obviously, were in a mood for a full-fledged battle, a vigorous demonstration against Hardee's front, accompanied by moves around his flanks, could have, if nothing else, obliged him to make another retreat and might have led to the interception of Stewart's and Lee's highly vulnerable columns. As it was, Hood's army had no trouble regrouping at Lovejoy's, and apart from a galling artillery bombardment, it escaped further punishment at a time when large portions of it were on the verge of collapse. Sherman, standing before the tottering wall of Confederate resistance in Georgia, gave it a slight tap but then pulled back his hand.[28]

How can one explain this curious performance on the part of a commander who, whatever else he may lack, is not deficient in intelligence, diligence, and experience? Why did Sherman neglect and reject so many opportunities to achieve a victory comparable to what Thomas will gain over the same enemy at Nashville in December and to what Grant will score against Lee in April? No doubt some of the answer can be found in defective maps, deficient information about the enemy (the "fog of war"), difficult terrain, and inadequate cavalry (although it is doubtful that Sherman was capable of making effective use of mounted forces however strong). But the basic reason why Sherman did less than he might have done between August 27 and September 6 is that he had never intended to do more than he did. His sole purpose during what turned out to be the end of the campaign was what it had been from the start of the campaign—namely, to take Atlanta; and his strategy for accomplishing this was the same one that he had laid down in April and had followed persistently upon reaching the environs of the city in July—namely, to cut its rail lines to the rest of the South. Hence, both in conception and in execution, the Jonesboro operation indeed had been as Sherman termed it in his September 3 telegram to Halleck, a "raid" (to be sure, a mammoth one) during which he would destroy those communications, including even the already-destroyed Georgia Railroad, and then either return to his base on the Chattahoochee and wait for Hood to retreat or, in desperation, attack him. Sherman expected the former.

Behind this plan were two assumptions: one, that Hood had lost so heavily in the July fighting and so many of his troops consisted of militia that he lacked major offensive potential; and two, as a consequence he would remain inside his fortifications throughout the raid, although the possibility that he might sally forth again must be guarded against, given his boldness and unpredictability. Accordingly, Sherman saw no need for haste in marching around Atlanta or for blocking likely enemy escape routes from the city or—except when he had belatedly realized Hardee's precarious situation at Jonesboro—for assaulting Confederate forces in an attempt to smash them. By the same token, when convinced that Hood, sooner than anticipated, had evacuated Atlanta, Sherman had been quite content to call it quits and bring the campaign to a close. To him, as to his army, Atlanta truly was "the prize we fight for," and as Major Osborn, Howard's artillery chief observes in a September 10 letter to a brother in St. Louis, "General Sherman did not desire to do any more fighting than was strictly necessary to gain possession of the city."[29]

Such is the explanation of why Sherman, with Hood's army in his grasp, did not close his fist. It is not, because it should not be, an excuse. It merely provides another demonstration of Sherman's preference for raiding over fighting, of his penchant for conducting operations on the basis of optimistic preconceptions of what the enemy will do, and of his unwillingness to engage his full force in battle. Thanks to these quirks in his military personality, Hood's army has been able to escape destruction. To be sure it has suffered a severe physical and psychological battering. Its effective strength, not counting the militia, which Governor Brown soon will order home, probably totals less than 30,000, as a result of the casualties at Jonesboro, straggling, and hundreds if not thousands of desertions. It has lost enormous quantities of valuable and to a large extent irreplaceable stores, ammunition, and equipment of every kind. And not only has it again been defeated and forced to retreat, which would be bad enough in itself, but it also must now bear the far-worse burden of knowing that all of the hardships and sacrifices of the past four months have been in vain: the Yankees have Atlanta. Yet Hood's army has survived, and as it proved at Lovejoy's, it still is battleworthy; it retains a large core of veterans who, if they no longer have much hope of Confederate victory, nevertheless are prepared to fight out of pride, a sense of duty and honor, and sheer hatred of the Yankee invaders who are laying waste their Southland; and while obviously it is too weak to defeat Sherman in offensive battle, it can defend, march, and maneuver. For these reasons it remains a factor in the calculus of the war. Already Hood, who (whatever else he may or may not be) is indomitable, has a plan in mind which, he is confident, will force Sherman to make such a reckoning—that, and much more besides.[30]

But if Sherman has failed to achieve the military triumph he could and should have achieved, he has succeeded in fulfilling what has been, ever since Grant's campaign in Virginia has bogged down in siege and stalemate, his strategic-political mission of taking Atlanta before Northern voters go to the polls in October and November. This is enough: it will suffice. How true this is can be seen in the reaction of the North and the South to what he has done.

Part Four: North and South

Throughout the North the capture of Atlanta, first word of which arrived on September 3 via Slocum's telegram from the city and then was confirmed beyond all doubt two days later by Sherman's message to Halleck declaring "So Atlanta is ours, and fairly won," produces jubilation and celebration. From Maine to California, in towns large and small, crowds march, cheer, and sing with joy while bells ring, fireworks crackle, cannons roar, and speakers orate. Thousands, too, respond to a proclamation from Lincoln urging that "in all places of worship in the United States, thanksgiving be offered to God," and thousands more do the same in their homes, in fields and on streets, everywhere and wherever. To the vast majority of Northerners, the fall of Atlanta means that the war can be won—indeed, that it *is* being won. "Let the Loyal North take heart," proclaims the *New York Tribune* and so it has.

Republicans, of course, take heart most of all. "The political skies," exults the *New York Times,* "begin to brighten. The clouds that lowered over the Union [Republican] cause a month ago are breaking away." In similar language the *Chicago Tribune* declares: "The dark days are over. We see our way out." It urges "Union men" to "close up the ranks! Forward march!" And close ranks they do. On September 6, Horace Greeley, who only four days ago had joined with two other influential Republican editors in making yet-another attempt to have Lincoln replaced as the candidate, announces: "Henceforth, we fly the banner of ABRAHAM LINCOLN for our next President." Likewise the disgruntled politicians who have rallied around Frémont soon return to the party fold. Facing what seemed like almost certain defeat come November, overnight the Republicans find themselves gazing at almost certain victory, all because of what George Templeton Strong hails in his diary for September 3 as the "Glorious news this morning—*Atlanta taken at last!!!*"[31]

An Albany, New York, newspaper advises its readers, "If you want to know who is for McClellan, mention Atlanta to them. The long face and the growl is sufficient." For the Democrats the fall of Atlanta could not have come at a worse time. Just three days before it occurred, they had adopted at their national convention in Chicago—a convention that had deliberately been postponed to the last possible moment in order to be sure about the military situation—a platform branding the war a failure. Now this assertion has become manifest nonsense; or as the *Hillsdale* (Mich.) *Standard* puts it, "Sherman's capture of Atlanta makes the slivers fall from the Chicago platform."

Declaring that McClellan's nomination on such a platform is an "absolutely worthless one now," the *New York Herald* predicts on September 5 that he will reject it. Instead he endeavors to salvage his candidacy by means of the letter in which he accepts it. The final version of numerous drafts, which is not published until September 9, the letter states that "the Union is the one condition of peace" and that there can be "no peace . . . without Union." In other words, if elected president, McClellan will go on with the war until the South submits to United States authority. "I could not look in the face," he explains, "my gallant comrades of the army and navy who have survived so many bloody battles, and tell them that their labors and the sacrifice of so many of our slain and wounded brethren had been in vain, that we had abandoned that Union for which we have so often periled our lives." So, "believing that the views here expressed are those of the Convention and the people it represents I accept the nomination."

McClellan's letter, as George Templeton Strong notes, is "artfully framed." Yet, despite its effort to do so, it cannot conceal the fact that it in effect repudiates the Vallandigham plank of the Democratic platform. This puts peace before Union, whereas it affirms that Union must come first. Extreme Peace Democrats—the real Copperheads, those who have deluded themselves into believing that the South will come back into the Union if the war only will cease—promptly denounce McClellan as no better than Lincoln and even try to summon a new convention to nominate a new candidate. Vallandigham himself does not go that far. He pretends, in public at least, that the platform, not the candidate, sets party policy; but it is clear that he views the impending election with scant enthusiasm and less hope. His prediction, made fifteen months ago—namely, that if the war should last until now, the North would repudiate it—has not, all too obviously, come true. The Republicans, on the other hand, gleefully pounce on the contradiction between the Democratic platform and the Democratic nominee. Which, they ask, is a voter to believe? If the first, then that would be to abandon the Union even as it is being saved, or at best restore it by permitting the survival of the very thing that nearly destroyed it: slavery. But if the second, then what reason is there to trust McClellan to do a better job of winning the war as president than he had done as a general? Besides, under Lincoln the war is being won anyway; Atlanta proves it. So why change? Northerners listen, and most of them agree. When they go to the polls in October and November, they will give Lincoln 212 electoral votes and McClellan 21—from Delaware, Kentucky, and New Jersey.[32]

All that McClellan's acceptance letter accomplishes is to save his honor. Whatever chance he had had of winning the election—it had seemed a very good one—had disappeared on the very day he had been nominated when some troops from Cox's division had reached the Macon railroad near Rough and Ready (see Appendix D).

"The only news of importance we have to announce this morning," sarcastically states the *Richmond Examiner* on September 5, "is

THE FALL OF ATLANTA."

To Confederate War Department clerk Jones the news, which first reached Richmond on September 3 in the form of an "ugly rumor" and then was confirmed that night by a telegram from Hood, "is a stunning blow." It is the same to most other people in Richmond, where, according to a correspondent for the *Mobile Advertiser*, not even the loss of Vicksburg and the defeat at Gettysburg produced so "painful an impression." For a while the government, concerned about the effect on morale, tries to keep the full story from the troops in the trenches around the city, but in one way or another they learn about it: a mammoth celebration bombardment by Grant's cannons provides a strong hint; and once they learn the news, a question that they fear to answer begins to gnaw at them: Have all their efforts, sacrifices, and victories been brought to naught by the failure, yet again, of the western army? Gloomily, a Georgia soldier who is serving in Virginia writes his mother that "ill boding spirits seem to hover a round us and over us."

In Georgia itself, Ella Thomas of Augusta notes that as a result of the fall of Atlanta, "many persons are very desponding with regard to the future"; and in Macon, presumed by its inhabitants to be Sherman's next target, the *Telegraph* reports that "our good people have been thrown into consternation," adding that the town is "overflowing with negroes" who—ominously—"are conducting themselves generally like they were free." In Montgomery, also considered a likely future objective of Sherman's army, a reporter for a Mobile paper finds that "a sudden paralysis" has fallen over the city where, back in February 1861, a cheering crowd had hailed Jefferson Davis as he had taken his oath of office as president of the Confederate States of America. In South Carolina, Mary Chesnut, who early in August had written in her diary that "our all now depends on that army at Atlanta" and that if it should fail, "the game is up," comments laconically on learning that it has failed: "No hope." In North Carolina, planter David Schenck is equally pessimistic as he confides to his diary: "Never until now did I feel hopeless but since God seems to have forsaken us I despair." In Mississippi the Reverend William Agnew thinks that "if we could not hold Atlanta I do not see what hope there is of being able to hold another point." Even Mary Mallard, who finally has made her way to the safety of Liberty County south of Savannah, wonders "What will go next?" Could the Yankees get that far?[33]

Intensifying the shock of the loss of Atlanta is that it has happened just as it seemed (to quote editor Edwin Pollard in the *Richmond Examiner* for August 30) that "the prospects of the Confederacy were never brighter and better." On the military front, Lee continued to bid invincible defiance to Grant at Richmond, Early still held Sheridan in check in the Shenandoah, Forrest had the Yankees cowed in Mississippi, and—most encouraging of all, given the crisis that had existed there in July—not only had Hood stopped the enemy at the gates of Atlanta but by all accounts Sherman, his supply line slashed by Wheeler, either was retreating or else was making a last desperate attempt to take the city before his army starved. Politically, thanks to the army's success in foiling the Yankee invaders, the situation seemed equally promising. Faced by an increasingly war-weary public and with his own party rent by dissension, Lincoln obviously feared defeat in November. How else explain the Gilmore-Jacquess mission, Greeley's dealings with the Confederate commissioners in Canada, and the recurrent rumors of other peace feelers and offers of an armistice? By the same token, all signs were pointing to a Democratic victory on a platform calling for an end to the war. Should this occur, peace and recognition of Southern independence soon would follow. All that had to be done to make sure it did occur was to do for the next two months what had been done for the past four: deny the North a major military triumph. "The scales of decision," declared the *Richmond Sentinel* on September 1, "are hanging in uncertain balance at the North—let us, by brilliant exertions in war, throw what we can on the side of peace."

Now the scales have tipped in favor of the Republicans and against the Democrats. Southerners realize this and what it means. "I am afraid," a North Carolina soldier in Lee's army writes his father, "that the fall of Atlanta will secure Lincoln's re-election," and Colonel Gorgas comments dourly in his diary that as a result of the loss of Atlanta, "there will be little left for the peace party [in the north] to stand on."[34] If the war can be won at all, it will have to be by the South on its own. The North, having tasted victory, will only want more of it, not peace.

Is there still a chance the war can be won, even so? The Southern press, striving to prop up tottering morale, answers yes. It has been foolish to place much hope in the Northern Democrats; never have they matched their words with deeds. It would make no difference if McClellan were elected; his acceptance letter shows he is just as keen on subduing the South as Lincoln is. In fact, he would be more dangerous than Lincoln, for his opposition to abolition might seduce Southerners into sacrificing their own freedom in order to keep slavery. As for the loss of Atlanta, to be sure that is unfortunate, but it is not a calamity. Without its factories and shops, long since transferred to safety elsewhere, the city is just an "empty shell," and in capturing it, Sherman merely has acquired another place that he must fortify and hold at the end of his tenuous supply line. Besides, the Confederacy, which has survived the loss of such cities as New Orleans, Nashville, and Memphis, can stand the loss of an overgrown town that was not even on the map twenty years ago. More important by far is the escape of Hood's army. So long as it remains in the field, "invincible and unconquerable," Sherman really has gained nothing. Southerners therefore should not despair. Instead let them redouble their efforts to defeat, drive back, and annihilate the Yankee invaders. Once that has been done, the Northern government, whether it be headed by Lincoln or McClellan, will have to make peace on the basis of Southern independence. "The prospects of the Confederacy," asserts Pollard in the September 7 *Richmond Examiner,* echoing what he had written on the eve of Atlanta's fall, "were never brighter than at this moment, if she deserves success and is resolved to win it."[35]

These assertions and exhortations ring hollow. Like Pollard's, they have been heard before and too often have proved false. They also contradict too many words about the vital necessity of holding Atlanta and the dire consequences, both military and political, of not holding it. Worse, they soon are contradicted by events as well. Out of Virginia, hitherto the source solely of good news, comes the terrible tidings of another disaster to Confederate arms. On September 19, near Winchester in the Shenandoah Valley, Sheridan uses a four-to-one superiority in numbers to overwhelm Early, inflicting heavy losses. Then, three days later, Sheridan strikes a second time; at Fisher's Hill he utterly routs the army that once had menaced Washington. Slowly but relentlessly he pursues, devastating the valley, the prime source of supplies for Lee's beleaguered paladins. What Sherman has done in Georgia, Sheridan has done in Virginia: penetrated the very vitals of the Confederacy. While again in the North bells ring, bands play, and crowds cheer, in the South there is, admits the *Richmond Enquirer,* "great dejection"; and Mary Chesnut, reflecting that mood, writes in her diary: "these stories of our defeats in the Valley fall like blows upon a dead body. Since Atlanta I have felt as if all were dead within me, forever."[36]

CHAPTER TEN

FALL

ON WEDNESDAY, September 7, Sherman and his staff ride into Atlanta. No bands play, no soldiers cheer, and civilians merely stare. The sole voice of jubilation arises from an elderly black man, now no longer a slave. "Lord, massa, is dat General Sherman? . . . I'se glad I'se seen him. . . . I just wanted to see de man what made old massa run."[1]

Sherman establishes his headquarters in the vacant home of Lieutenant Neal's family, a Corinthian-columned mansion on the southwest corner of Washington and Mitchell streets across from the courthouse.[2] Once ensconced, he summons Mayor Calhoun and hands him a letter for Hood. It states that all of Atlanta's remaining inhabitants are to be expelled. Those who wish to may go north; all who wish to go south will be transported to Rough and Ready, for which purpose he proposes a ten-day truce in that area.

Sherman wants, as he has explained in a September 4 telegram to Halleck announcing his intention to remove all of Atlanta's civilian population, to have the "entire use of the railroad" for his army and to turn the city into a "pure Gibralter" that can be, if necessary, defended by a small force. He expects the Southern people to "raise a howl against my barbarity and cruelty," in which case "I will answer that war is war, and not popularity seeking. If they want peace they and their relatives must stop the war."

On the following day, Hood accepts Sherman's proposition for a truce: "I do not consider I have any alternative in the matter." But he protests Sherman's expulsion order: it "transcends, in studied and ingenious cruelty, all acts ever before brought to my attention in the dark history of this war." Hood's protest avails naught. "Talk thus to the marines," Sherman answers, "but not to me." Likewise he rejects a plea from Calhoun and three city-council members to revoke or at least modify the order, the consequences of which would be "appalling and heart-rending." "You might as well," he tells them, "appeal against the thunderstorm as against these terrible hardships of war."[3]

From September 12 through 21 a total of 709 adults (mostly women), 867 children, and 79 "servants," along with 1,651 parcels of furniture and household goods, travel in railroad cars, wagons, and ambulances to Rough and Ready. There they and their possessions are transferred to Confederate wagons, which

548

haul them to Lovejoy's Station, whence they proceed by trains to Macon and other points south, with the largest portion going to a hastily erected camp of log cabins at Dawson, Georgia, called Fosterville, after Colonel Ira Foster, the state's quartermaster general.[4] Simultaneously many other Atlantans, perhaps more, head north by rail; among them is Sam Richards, who takes his family to New York where he has relatives. The only civilians who remain in Atlanta are blacks, the vast majority of whom chose not to accompany their erstwhile masters, and about fifty white families who, like Carrie Berry's, have been allowed to stay.[5]

Other than the expulsion of the inhabitants of three guerrilla-infested Missouri counties along the Kansas border after the Lawrence, Kansas, Massacre of 1863, the depopulation of Atlanta is the harshest measure taken against civilians by Union authorities during the entire Civil War. Lincoln and Grant silently sanction it, and Halleck commends Sherman, declaring: "Your mode of conducting war is just the thing we want now. We have tried the kid glove policy long enough."[6] What had begun as the spontaneous action of ordinary Union soldiers—terrorism of the Southern populace—now is the deliberate policy of their generals and government. Sherman, owing to circumstances and thanks to his knack for pithy phraseology, merely is its most conspicuous practitioner.

So Atlanta becomes a "pure Gibralter," one soon ringed with a new and much more compact line of fortifications constructed under the direction of Poe. But what next? Sherman knows what he would like to do once his army has had a chance to rest, refit, and be reinforced: move on to take Macon and/or Augusta, thereby isolating Mississippi, Alabama, and Georgia from the rest of the eastern Confederacy. The problem is getting to these places. He believes, with good cause, that he dare not proceed deeper into Georgia dependent on his railroad supply line, which now stretches nearly 300 miles to Nashville. Moreover, it is 103 and 175 miles respectively to Macon and Augusta from Atlanta, and although (as he observes in a message to Grant) the countryside "will afford forage and many supplies," there is "not enough in any one place to admit of delay." Hood's army, while too weak to stop Sherman from advancing, remains strong enough to slow him down considerably.[7]

Sherman's initial solution to the problem is to propose to Grant that Canby's forces at Mobile move up the Alabama River to Montgomery, then over to Columbus, Georgia, so as to provide him with a new supply line. But this, he quickly learns, is impracticable. Canby has only 15,000 men, and A. J. Smith's two divisions at Memphis, which could provide Sherman with adequate strength, are on the way to St. Louis to help repel a raid out of Arkansas into Missouri by 12,000 Rebel cavalry under Major General Sterling Price. Furthermore, to make matters worse, with Smith gone from Memphis, the way now is open for Forrest to strike the railroads in Middle Tennessee.[8]

Next Sherman calls on Grant to send a navy-army expedition to seize Savannah by a *"coup de main."* Once Sherman knows that supplies will be waiting for him there, he will have no hesitation about marching across Georgia to the sea. "Where a million of people live my army won't starve," and by threatening Macon and Augusta simultaneously, he can foil any attempt by Hood to check his advance. Grant replies that he thinks that this is an excellent plan and that he will implement it as soon as he can—that is, after he has sealed off the main Confederate blockade-running port at Wilmington, North Carolina, to which end all available Union amphibious forces on the Atlantic Coast have been committed. When this will be done, however, he does not say; as it turns out, it won't happen until January 15, 1865.[9]

Thus, as summer passes into fall, Sherman finds himself a victor who cannot exploit his victory, a conqueror who is unable to continue conquering. All he can do is remain in Atlanta—he spends much of the time sitting on the porch of his mansion headquarters, wearing slippers, smoking cigars, and reading newspapers—and hope that something will occur that will enable him to resume his march into Georgia. Such is the consequence of his having failed to smash Hood's army or, at the very least, to drive it out of the state, when he had had the opportunity.

While Sherman ponders futilely how to advance beyond Atlanta without undue risk of having to return in order to escape starvation and surrender, three Confederate leaders are on the move. One is Forrest: at the head of 4,500 cavalry he is riding toward the Tennessee River with orders from Lieutenant General Richard Taylor, the new commander of Mississippi and Alabama, to wreck the railroads between Nashville and Chattanooga. Another is Hood: having evacuated most of the prisoners at Andersonville so that he no longer has to protect that place from a Yankee raid, he is shifting his army from Lovejoy's to Palmetto, a village on the Montgomery and West Point Railroad twenty-four miles southwest of Atlanta and close to the Chattahoochee, with the intention (he has informed Davis) of cutting Sherman's communications and compelling him to abandon Atlanta, whereupon he will pounce upon the Federals as they flee through northern Georgia and then go on into Tennessee, even Kentucky. And the third is Jefferson Davis himself: he is aboard a train traveling to Georgia, where he will visit the Army of Tennessee, about whose condition he has received alarming reports, and confer with Hood and his generals about future operations. All three have the same objective, namely, to reverse the course of the war in the West and hence as a whole. Hood and Davis truly believe that this can be done, for by dedication and temperament they are incapable of believing otherwise. Forrest, on the other hand, being more realistic, is less optimistic. Although resolved to fight on—he deems it his duty, and perhaps he is loath to cease doing what he does so well—privately he considers the war lost and has told the slaves who serve him as teamsters that they are free.[10]

Davis reaches Macon on the morning of September 23, and at 11 he delivers a speech at the First Baptist Church to an overflow audience. He justifies removing Johnston ("If I knew that a General did not possess the right qualities to command, would I not be wrong if he were not removed?") and defends replacing him with Hood: "I thus put a man in command who I knew would strike an honest and manly blow" for Atlanta, "and many a Yankee's blood was made to nourish the soil before the prize was won." But that is the past. What is important now is the future. Regarding that,

> though misfortune has befallen our arms from Decatur to Jonesboro, our cause is not lost. Sherman cannot keep up his long line of communications, and retreat, sooner or later, he must. And when that day comes, the fate that befell the Army of the French Empire in its retreat from Moscow will be reacted. Our cavalry and people will harass and destroy his army as did the Cossacks of Napoleon, and the Yankee General, like him, will escape with only a bodyguard.

From Macon, Davis proceeds to Palmetto, arriving on September 25. On the following morning he reviews the troops in company with Hood, the corps commanders, and a cavalcade of staff officers and politicians. There are no cheers, only sullen silence, punctuated by occasional shouts from the ranks of "Give us Johnston! Give us our old commander!" Davis, notes General Manigault, looks "thin, care-worn, and angry," with a "scornful" expression on his face. Then, after a speech to the Tennesseans of Cheatham's Division in which he promises them that "within a short time your faces will be turned homeward and your feet pressing Tennessee soil," he spends the rest of that day and the next in private conversations with Hood, Stewart and Lee, Hardee, and some of the division commanders.

Davis has visited the Army of Tennessee twice before, first in December 1862 and again in the wake of Chickamauga. Each time he came under great pressure to relieve its commander (Bragg); both times he refused. This third visit produces no departure from that pattern. On September 28, while on the way to Montgomery to meet Taylor, Davis telegraphs Hood that Hood has Davis's permission to lead the Army of Tennessee in a strike at Sherman's supply line. To replace Hood with someone else, most of all Johnston, would be the same as admitting that it had been a mistake to put him in command in the first place, and Davis is no more prepared to do that than he is to concede that the Confederacy cannot still win the war and its independence. His sole concession to those who are denouncing Hood as incompetent is a meaningless one: Beauregard will be brought from Virginia to head a new "Military Division of the West," combining both Hood's and Taylor's forces, but with authority merely to advise, not order. In addition, Davis finally allows Hardee to escape from the humiliation of serving under Hood by appointing him to command the coastal defenses of South Carolina, Georgia, and Florida. Cheatham, on Hood's recommendation, takes over Hardee's Corps, an appointment that presumably is designed to placate its troops.[11]

On September 29–30 the Army of Tennessee crosses the Chattahoochee via pontoons near Campbellton and by the evening of October 1 has advanced eight miles beyond it toward Marietta. It numbers approximately 40,000 troops of all arms, its morale has been revived by rest and by being on the offensive, and it senses that its mission is nothing less than transforming defeat into victory for the Confederacy. The odds against doing this, it knows, are long; yet it is willing to try. The only alternative would be to quit, and it is not ready to do that so long as there is any hope of whipping the Yankees, something it believes it can do if given a fair chance. Maybe this time around it will get such a chance.[12]

Hood's northward march comes as no surprise to Sherman. He has anticipated it for a week, and both to guard against it and to fend off Forrest's raid, he has sent two divisions to Chattanooga and another one to Rome. When, on October 2, he learns that Hood's whole army is across the Chattahoochee and moving toward Marietta, he sets out in pursuit with all of his forces save the XX Corps, which garrisons Atlanta. For the next two weeks, Sherman endeavors to overtake, trap, and smash Hood. In turn, Hood strikes repeatedly at the Western and Atlantic Railroad, tearing up all the track from Big Shanty to Acworth and between Tunnel Hill and Dalton, in the process capturing the latter and thus returning the Army of Tennessee to the place where, so to speak, it all began. On the other hand a desperate attack by French's Division on the great Union depot at Allatoona fails at the cost of 1,000 casualties, Lee makes no attempt at all to seize Resaca when its garrison commander scoffs at a threat that "no prisoners will be taken" unless he surrenders, and Sherman warily avoids being lured into any of the ambushes that Hood sets for him. Worse, the damage done to the railroad, extensive as it is, soon can be and soon will be repaired, and although Forrest renders a large portion of the Nashville and Decatur inoperable, he finds it impossible to so much as reach the far-more-important Nashville and Chattanooga before having to make a hairbreadth escape back across the Tennessee River. Thus the Federals parry the Confederate thrust against their communications, and instead of Sherman's starving army fleeing through the wilderness of northern Georgia, it is Hood who has to withdraw toward Alabama in quest of supplies for his hungry and footsore troops.[13]

Yet Sherman derives little satisfaction from this outcome. On the contrary he feels like he had felt when bogged down at Kennesaw or stymied outside of Atlanta: frustrated and fretful. Not only has Hood drawn him northward to the Tennessee, he is preventing him from marching toward the sea. This, he remains convinced, is the only move that makes strategic sense. He also believes that it now has become both necessary and feasible. It is necessary because, if he continues futilely chasing Hood's nimble army, the moral and political effect of capturing Atlanta will be reduced, perhaps lost. It is feasible because Hood no longer is in a position to impede a march to Savannah, which Sherman himself can then capture, thus eliminating the need for that to be done first by an amphibious expedition.

Hence again and again Sherman urges Grant to let him turn his back on Hood and march to the sea. "I can make this march," he declares, "and make Georgia howl!" Grant agrees with this plan in principle but hesitates to approve it in practice out of fear that while Sherman is heading for the Atlantic, Hood will sweep through Tennessee and Kentucky. "Do you not think it advisable," he telegraphs Sherman on November 1, "now that Hood has gone so far north, to entirely ruin him before starting on your proposed campaign?" "No single army," Sherman replies, "can catch Hood, and I am convinced the best results will follow from our defeating Jeff. Davis's cherished plan of making me leave Georgia by maneuvering." Should Hood advance northward, he will be met by Thomas, who will be left in Tennessee with "a force strong enough to prevent his reaching any country in which we have an interest." Or "if Hood turns to follow me," then Thomas will "push for Selma," the capture of which would deprive Hood of his supply base.

These arguments persuade Grant. "I do not see," he telegraphs Sherman on November 2, "that you can withdraw from where you are to follow Hood, without giving up all we have gained in territory. I say, then, go on as you propose." His sole condition is that Thomas be furnished with sufficient strength to "take care of Hood and destroy him." Sherman promises that this will be done.

Ten days of furious activity ensue. All of Sherman's field forces return to Atlanta except the IV and XXIII corps: they go to Thomas in Tennessee. From Atlanta, trains carry sick and unfit soldiers, surplus stores and equipment, and all else that might impair mobility. To Atlanta, trains bring recruits, veterans back from furlough, convalescents, and huge quantities of provisions and ammunition. In Atlanta, engineer troops, directed by Poe, demolish the Car Shed, the roundhouse, and all other buildings and facilities that conceivably could be of use to the Confederates when they reoccupy the city. And outside of Atlanta, between the Chattahoochee and Chattanooga, all garrisons depart, leaving behind detachments with instructions to destroy every bridge and trestle along the Western and Atlantic. Just as stout Cortéz had cut off his conquistadores from the sea by burning their ships prior to setting out for the Halls of Montezuma, Sherman intends to detach his army from its land communications before marching to the sea. What Wheeler, Forrest, and Hood have failed to do, Sherman himself will do.[14]

His march, Sherman has notified Grant, will start as soon as possible after the presidential election. That will occur, or to be precise will be concluded, on November 8. The result, already presaged by October ballotings in Indiana, Ohio, and Pennsylvania, is an overwhelming victory for Lincoln, who carries every Union state except New Jersey, Delaware, and Kentucky. Or so it seems at first glance. Examined closely, the election figures reveal that McClellan lost in the key states of New York, Pennsylvania, and Indiana by very narrow margins and that Lincoln's popular majority is a mere 400,000 votes out of 4,000,000 cast. Had Atlanta still been in Confederate hands, where would those 400,000 votes have gone? Certainly not all to Lincoln, and perhaps McClellan would have gotten enough of them and in the right states to have won. The election would have been, at the very least, a lot closer.[15]

On November 12, most preparations for the march having been completed, Sherman leaves Kingston, where he has been making his headquarters, for Atlanta. At noon he reaches Cartersville, where he sits down on the edge of a porch to rest. After a while he goes over to where a telegraph wire has been attached to a small instrument and listens as the operator taps out "Chattanooga." Soon a reply comes in the form of message relayed from Thomas in Nashville: "I have no fears that Beauregard [Hood] can do us any harm now . . . your success will fully equal your expectations." Sherman has the operator tap back: "Dispatch received—all right." The line then goes dead as the demolition squads set to work along the railroad. All rail and wire connection to the North ceases to exist.

That night Sherman arrives in Atlanta. Four days later, on November 16, he marches out on the Decatur road with his army. It consists of 62,000 men, most of them hardened veterans of the XIV, XV, XVII, and XX corps (the two divisions of the XVI Corps have been assigned to the XV and XVII corps in order to bring them up to requisite strength). Kilpatrick's cavalry precedes it, and wagons crammed with twenty days' provisions and two hundred cartridges for each rifle accompany it. Behind it, to quote what this time is a quite accurate description in Sherman's *Memoirs*, lies Atlanta, "smouldering and in ruins, the black smoke rising high in the air, and hanging like a pall over the ruined city." Ahead of it lies Savannah and the sea. When, by chance, a band strikes up the stirring music of the "Battle Hymn of the Republic," the Union soldiers begin singing it. Never before and never again does Sherman hear "the chorus of 'Glory, glory Halleuah!' done with more spirit, or in better harmony of time and place."[16]

As Sherman heads east, Hood moves north across the Tennessee to Florence, Alabama. He intends to take Nashville, then to invade Kentucky. There, should Sherman pursue him, he will give battle with an army augmented by recruits from that state and Tennessee. If victorious, he will send troops to Lee while at the same time advancing on Cincinnati. If defeated or unable to fight Sherman, he will join Lee at Richmond to crush Grant with their combined forces, after which they can take Washington and/or dispose of Sherman.

This is more a dream than a plan. Yet Hood can see no better alternative. Turning back in pursuit of Sherman would be regarded as a retreat by his troops, and it would have a disastrous effect on their morale. He probably could not catch up with Sherman in any case, given the latter's long head start, and the way would be left open for Thomas to seize Selma, Montgomery, and Mobile. Going forward at least offers hope—perhaps the last hope the Confederacy has.[17]

On November 21 the Army of Tennessee begins marching, and on the following day it enters the state whose name it bears. Forrest leads the advance with his and Jackson's cavalry. Wheeler, with the survivors of his disastrous foray behind Union lines, has been sent to try to slow down Sherman in Georgia. Despite the accession of Forrest's command, Hood still has no more than 40,000 men, 30,000 of whom are infantry. To oppose him, Thomas can muster 55,000 troops; but only half of them—the IV and XXIII corps under Schofield—presently are in front of the Confederates, whereas the rest either are at Nashville or, like A. J. Smith's far-roaming divisions, still en route there. Should Hood be able to get in between Schofield and Thomas and then hit them separately, he stands an excellent chance of realizing his dream.[18]

This is exactly what he tries to do. He almost succeeds. On November 28–29 he uses Lee's Corps to feint against Schofield's front at Columbia while sending Forrest, Cheatham, and Stewart swinging around to his rear at Spring Hill. Barely in time, Stanley, with elements of the IV Corps, manages both to reach there first and to keep open the direct road to Nashville. Even so, Hood is in position, if not to cut off the Federals from that city, at least to strike them as they retreat; he gives orders accordingly. They are to no avail. Either they are not delivered or, if delivered, they are not executed. During the night of November 29, Schofield's troops march right by the Confederates, their way lighted by the campfires of Cheatham's Corps.

The bitter fury of one final frustration too many grips Hood. Can't this Army of Tennessee ever do anything right? Is it still afraid to attack? On the morning of November 30 he sets out after Schofield, resolved to overtake and smash him before he can get to Nashville. He finds him at Franklin, with his army deployed behind a line of breastworks, its back to the Harpeth River. Forrest advises Hood to flank the Yankees from their position by sending a force across the narrow, shallow Harpeth southwest of Franklin. Hood ignores Forrest and orders a frontal assault. Nothing fancy; nothing that requires perfect coordination and exact timing is called for here. Simply go at the enemy and drive him into the river. Surely the Army of Tennessee ought to be able to do that. Let it prove that it can do that.

Hitherto the weather has been miserable: cloudy, cold, rain, sleet. But today, this last one of November, the sun shines brightly, the air is warm, and it seems almost like summer as the Confederates, their bands playing, form for the charge. "Boys," declares one of their generals, "this will be short but desperate." They know this already, yet they do not care. Like Hood, they feel that it is time to settle matters once and for all. Writing about it years later, Sam Watkins of the 1st Tennessee will recall that "I had made up my mind to die—felt glorious."

Around 4 P.M. the Confederates begin moving forward in dense masses, bands still playing, flags fluttering in the breeze. Numbering 18,000, they advance astride the Columbia Pike, which runs due north into Franklin. This is a larger assault force concentrated on a narrower front than the one that Lee had hurled against Cemetery Ridge at Gettysburg on July 3, 1863. If it cannot break through, nothing can.

Sitting on a blanket, Hood watches from the side of Winstead Hill, just west of the pike and two miles south of Franklin, as his troops advance in magnificent order across the level, open fields. Union artillery and rifle fire begins tearing holes in their ranks, but they close them quickly and keep going, keening the "Rebel yell." Along the pike, Cleburne's and Cheatham's divisions, charging side by side, pour over and around two IV Corps brigades that, for some foolish reason, have remained a half-mile in front of the main Union line. Those Federals who are not captured break and run. "Let's go into the works with them!" Cheatham's exultant Tennesseans shout. And into them they go— into them and over. They have broken through!

But no. Opdycke's "Tigers," waiting in reserve, counterattack. On the left flank, Reilly's and Casement's XXIII Corps brigades deliver a murderous enfilade fire with their breechloading rifles. The Confederates, some of whom have penetrated to the edge of Franklin, reel backward to and then out of the works. Here, though, they remain, clinging to the front of the parapet while the Federals hold on to the other side. East of the pike, Stewart's troops, equally determined, charge again and again after their initial surge is repulsed by a hurricane of bullets and canister. Thick clouds of powder smoke cover the field. Soon, too, it grows dark. Yet the fighting rages on, the sound a great, unabated roar.

On Winstead Hill, Hood can see nothing. At 7 P.M., in response to a plea from Cheatham for reinforcements, Hood sends in Major General Edward Johnson's division (formerly Anderson's) of Lee's Corps, which is beginning to arrive. It, too, is swallowed up in the smoke and darkness. Finally, after five hours, the battle subsides, then it ceases save for occasional flareups. The Confederates, those who can, stagger and crawl to the rear. The Federals also withdraw, then resume their retreat to Nashville. They would have done this much earlier had Hood not attacked.

Dawn on December 1 reveals a ghastly sight. Gray-clad, blood-splattered corpses litter the brown fields south of Franklin. In the ditches fronting the Union works, bodies lie in heaps, some seven deep. Here and there, dead men remain erect, unable to fall because they are surrounded by so many other dead men. Altogether, 6,000 Confederates have been killed and wounded, another 700 have been captured. These casualties equal, perhaps exceed, those of Pickett's Charge.

Among the slain is Cleburne, who lies fifty-some yards from the enemy rampart, riddled by no less than forty-nine bullets. Dead, too, are Granbury, Gist, Strahl, and Brigadier General John Adams of Stewart's Corps, whose horse, "Old Charlie," is found with its front hooves across the parapet. Wounded generals include Brown (who commanded Cheatham's Division), Manigault, Quarles, Cockrell, Scott, and John C. Carter, who soon will die. Cleburne's and Cheatham's divisions no longer exist other than in name. Majors and captains now head brigades; captains and lieutenants replace the fifty-five regimental commanders who have been put out of action. They might as well, for most brigades are the size of regiments, and many regiments are little larger than companies. Lieutenant Rennolds and two others are the sole survivors of the hundred-plus men who had formed his company back in 1861.

The Union loss totals 2,300, 1,000 of whom are prisoners, mostly from the two brigades overrun by Cheatham's and Cleburne's men. All that Hood has accomplished in his attempt to annihilate Schofield's army is to wreck his own.

Even so, he lurches on to the outskirts of Nashville. Here he entrenches and waits for Thomas to come out from the fortifications of Nashville and attack him. His sole hope now is to repulse that attack and then "enter the city on the heels of the enemy," after which, with his army resupplied, reinspirited, and reinforced (he expects troops to arrive from the Trans-Mississippi), he will go on to link up with Lee in Virginia. Hood realizes that his chances of doing this are slim, but he believes "it more judicious the men should face a decisive issue rather than retreat," that "rather than renounce the honor of their cause," they should make "a last and manful effort to lift up the sinking fortunes of the Confederacy."

Two weeks pass. Then on December 15, Thomas, having resisted badgering from Grant to attack before he was ready and able to do so with maximum effectiveness, comes forth. In a two-day battle waged in cold, drizzling rain, he routs Hood's half-starved, half-frozen, and totally outmatched Confederates, sending them in headlong flight toward the Tennessee River. When on Christmas Day they start crossing it, they number less than 20,000; all the others who had set out with Hood for the Ohio River a month ago are dead, wounded, prisoners, or deserters. What Thomas, had he had his way, would have done in Georgia in May and again in August has been accomplished by him in December in Tennessee: the elimination of the Army of Tennessee from the war. In essence the Confederacy is reduced to Lee's ragged men, shivering in their trenches around Richmond and Petersburg.[19]

While Hood marches up the map to Nashville and then down again, Sherman's 62,000 tramp steadily, irresistibly through Georgia. Nothing opposes them except Wheeler's ragtag cavalry and bands of graybeards and boys called militia. Marching in snakelike columns, they obey instructions from Sherman to "forage liberally," delighted to have official permission to do what they would do anyway. With them they take thousands of former slaves; in their wake they leave a sixty-mile-wide trail of devastation. They reach and then occupy Savannah in time for Sherman to present it to Lincoln as a Christmas gift. They have demonstrated that they can go anywhere they want to, that no place in the South is safe from the Yankees.

Not even Liberty County. On Sunday, January 1, 1865, Mary Mallard watches helplessly while some of Kilpatrick's merry men kill sheep, hogs, and cattle on her plantation.[20] A year ago in Atlanta she had put a custard on her porch to be transformed into ice cream by the cold northern wind. When she had done so, the South had possessed a vision of victory, a victory to be won by denying the

North victory. Throughout the winter, spring, and summer of 1864 the South had sustained itself with this vision. For a while it even seemed that the vision would be realized. Now it is gone, gone forever despite the desperate efforts of desperate men to revive it, gone amidst the red clay and green forests of Georgia.

AFTERWORD

The foregoing pages, it is hoped, provide the reasons why the South's vision of a victory to be won by not losing failed in 1864. They may be summed up as follows:

1. Jefferson Davis badly overestimated the military potential, especially for offensive warfare, of the Army of Tennessee with respect to that of the Union forces arrayed against it, whose power he greatly underestimated. As a result he asked and expected too much of it, particularly in view of its past failures. Indeed, as it turned out, he probably should not even have insisted on its holding Atlanta. Important as that city was both in substance and as a symbol of the South's ability to defend itself, the Army of Tennessee was more important still, for in the final analysis the Confederacy was incarnated in its armies, especially the major ones; as long as they remained formidable, the South would have remained unconquered and—equally crucial—been increasingly perceived by the North as unconquerable. Davis, however, was by the very nature of his temperament and concept of warfare incapable of realizing this and therefore of implementing the appropriate strategy, which would have called for delaying the Union advance toward Atlanta as long as possible but then abandoning the city in order to preserve the fighting power of the Army of Tennessee. Furthermore, it was an incapability that he shared with the Southern people, of whom he was, if not the best conceivable leader, surely a most valid representative both in his strengths and in his weaknesses. To them, as to him, the Confederacy was its land and its cities, which had to be defended to the utmost. When it became manifestly impossible to defend them any longer, the Southern will to go on with the war collapsed.[1]

2. To the extent that there was any chance at all, Johnston had the best, perhaps the sole, chance of saving Atlanta. While he commanded it, the Army of Tennessee was as strong in manpower relative to the Union forces as it possibly could be, its morale on the whole was high, it possessed ample means and choices for strategic maneuver, and the terrain offered it great tactical advantages. With leadership that combined a proper proportion of boldness and prudence and that compensated for inferior numbers with superior skill, it could have, if not defeated or stopped Sherman, delayed and worn him down so long and so much

that he would have reached the gates of Atlanta a lot later and so weakened that he could have been held outside of the city in the same way that Lee stymied Grant at Richmond—or at least until after the North's presidential election. But Johnston did not, because he could not, provide that sort of leadership, with the result that Sherman's army, contrary to Johnston's subsequent assertions, was comparatively stronger in numbers and morale by July than it had been at the beginning of May.

With Johnston, prudence far outweighed boldness on the scale of military values, and although a technically able commander up to a point, he suffered from serious defects of mind and character that made him a foreordained loser against any opponent who heavily outnumbered him and who refrained from committing egregious blunders. What the Army of Tennessee required in the spring and summer of 1864 was a Robert E. Lee (and also probably the Army of Northern Virginia's generally better generals and its tradition of victory). Unfortunately for it and the Confederacy, the only Robert E. Lee available was needed in Virginia.

3. Hood, of course, was an inadequate substitute for a Lee, despite (or perhaps because of) his earnest efforts to emulate him. Yet, in justice to this one-legged warrior, he inherited (as a consequence of his own and Bragg's machinations) a virtually impossible situation which it is doubtful Lee himself could have salvaged. Moreover, there can be no denying that with what he had, Hood did his best to fulfill the mission that his government gave him, which is more than Johnston did. The trouble is, Hood's best merely made worse what already was bad, as he constantly endeavored to do too much with too little and without sufficient allowance for the factors of time and distance, physical and emotional endurance, and chance. In sum, while possessing many of the attributes of a fine commander—notably, indomitable determination—he was lacking in realism about his own army, the enemy's army, and above all the nature of war itself as it had evolved in America by 1864.

4. Equally unrealistic is the contention of some historians, in particular biographers of Forrest, that if Davis had sent "The Wizard of the Saddle" against Sherman's supply line before instead of after the fall of Atlanta, that fall would not have occurred. First of all, Davis was justified in believing that the defense of Atlanta and of Georgia as a whole depended on preserving Confederate control over the agricultural and industrial resources of Mississippi and Alabama and that this in turn required Forrest to stand guard against the Federal forces operating out of Memphis. Second, as noted on pages 345–46, even had Forrest made such a raid during the campaign, Sherman's great fear of him would have resulted in his encountering enormous and dangerous resistance, and while Forrest probably would have done more damage than Wheeler did (which is not saying much), it is unlikely he could have done enough, given the capabilities of

the Union repair crews, to have stopped Sherman, much less caused him to turn back. Third, and perhaps most persuasive of all, not once during the entire Civil War did cavalry succeed in halting, other than briefly, traffic on a railroad that an enemy army considered crucial to its operations. There is no convincing reason for believing that Forrest, notwithstanding his brilliance and enterprise, would have provided the sole exception to this historical fact.[2]

5. The Federals possessed great numerical and material superiority. Indeed, this was the main ingredient of their success. Without it they could not have undertaken the campaign, much less made their way across northern Georgia against a stalwart and stubborn foe to take Atlanta. Yet, while essential, this superiority did not guarantee victory. It had to be put to effective use, which, of course, brings us to Sherman.

6. Concerning Sherman's performance, the first thing that must be remembered is that at the outset of the campaign neither the Army of Tennessee nor Atlanta was his primary objective, Grant's instructions notwithstanding. To Sherman the most important task was to forestall Johnston from reinforcing Lee, thereby assuring Grant's expected war-ending victory in Virginia. Hence during May and most of June, Sherman concentrated on maintaining pressure on Johnston while taking minimum risks himself so as to avoid a serious setback in Georgia. Should he in the process take Atlanta and/or defeat Johnston, so much the better, but he operated on the premise that Grant first would take Richmond and defeat Lee.

Not until late June, when Grant in effect declared that the war could not be won in Virginia in the foreseeable future and that if it was to be won at all before the presidential election, it would have to be done in Georgia, did Sherman make the capture of Atlanta his chief (one might even say sole) goal. Even then, however, he did not depart from his methodical, low-risk style of warfare, a style well described (allowing for obvious bias) in the *Macon Intelligencer* shortly after the campaign ended:

> Sherman prosecutes war deliberately, like a business or laboring man works. He marches his men into position all the day long, usually by long stages, and in the evening for an hour or two, delivers battle, or at least invites it. Thus it occurs that if our troops gain any advantages, nightfall prevents any advance or continuation of it, but if the Yankees gain the advantage, or advance, they render their position very strong during the night, and it is thus that Sherman has forwarded his army by impregnable and perfect parallels, over almost every mile of ground that he has traveled from the Tennessee River to Lovejoy's in Georgia. Such a network of fortifications has never been seen or made on earth, before the present campaign.[3]

Such tactics and the immense dominance of defense over offense on the Civil War battlefield made it virtually impossible for the Confederates, with their smaller army, to attack the Federals successfully. In turn, Sherman took advantage of this fact and his greater numerical strength to conduct a series of flanking moves that forced first Johnston and then Hood to relinquish otherwise impregnable positions, including eventually Atlanta itself. Yet, despite the effectiveness of this modus operandi, it scarcely deserves to be hailed as an example of (to quote Liddell Hart) "strategic artistry." With the exceptions of the bypassing of Allatoona and the crossing of the Chattahooche, Sherman ordered every one of his flanking moves with reluctance and out of sheer necessity, and he executed them without sufficient speed and force to attain maximum results. What Joseph Miller, correspondent of the *Cincinnati Commercial,* said about Sherman's conduct of operations in mid June applies to the whole campaign and comes much closer to the truth than such superficial eulogies as Liddell Hart's: "Sherman has not made a single [successful] move but what common sense would have dictated under the circumstances."[4]

7. Closely allied to the flanking maneuvers was Sherman's avoidance of the tactical offensive. Just six times during the campaign did *portions* of his army deliver major attacks. The first three—those of May 14 and 15 at Resaca and Hooker's at New Hope Church on May 25—took place because Sherman mistakenly assumed that the Confederates were retreating; the fourth, Howard's at Pickett's Mill, was the unintentional outcome of a flanking attempt that failed and that Sherman, too late, canceled; and the last, that of the XIV Corps at Jonesboro on September 1, likewise derived from an erroneous belief on Sherman's part that the enemy's flank was exposed, whereas it merely was vulnerable. Only the fifth and by far the largest attack, that of June 27 at Kennesaw, represented a deliberate effort to break the Confederate line by frontal assault, and it occurred only because Sherman gave way to impatience and his concern over Johnston's reinforcing Lee. By thus sparing his army excessive losses, he enabled it to reach Atlanta still strong in manpower and stronger still in morale. In contrast, Grant, by seeking to defeat Lee quickly and totally by bold moves and brute force, ended up outside of Richmond with his army so badly depleted and demoralized that it remained there for ten months.

This does not mean that Sherman was a better general than Grant. He was not. As he himself acknowledged, he lacked Grant's supreme self-confidence and self-control and his instinctive talent for war. Had Sherman been the one to have gone against Lee and his Army of Northern Virginia in the spring of 1864 (Meade, when Grant visited him in March of that year, assumed that Sherman would be given command of the Army of the Potomac), in all likelihood he would have cracked beneath their terrible hammer blows. But as it was, he and

the forces under his command were more than a match for the overrated Johnston, the overaggressive Hood, and the gallant but ill-starred Army of Tennessee.

8. Although Sherman's campaign achieved a decisive strategic-political result, from a strictly military standpoint it was inconclusive; as he himself later
admitted, it was after the capture of Atlanta that the "real trouble" began.[5]
Again and again, from Dalton to Lovejoy's Station, he overlooked, ignored, and
even rejected opportunities to crush or fatally cripple the Confederate forces in
Georgia or at the very least drive them from the state. Never once, moreover,
did he engage or even try to engage the enemy with his full available strength;
frequently he assumed that the Rebels were retreating when they were not, or he
wishfully thought they would do other than what they did; and too often he
wasted time in operations that either were obviously futile or patently unnecessary. One must conclude that while Sherman by 1864 had learned to control his
fear of what the enemy might be up to, he had not mastered it, and that his
preference for a war of maneuvering and raiding derived, not from a considered
military philosophy, but rather from a deep-seated fear of the consequences of
trusting to what he rightly called "the fickle fortunes of battle." He was, in
short, a general who did not like to fight. Had Thomas's personal relationship
with Grant permitted him to command in Georgia in 1864, almost surely the
Union victory would have been easier, quicker, and more complete.[6]

Still, Sherman did take Atlanta, and in so doing, to quote from a letter of
congratulation sent him by Grant, "accomplished the most gigantic undertaking given to any general in the war."[7] This in itself gave, and always will give,
Sherman a distinguished place in the history of the Civil War and of his nation.
Whether he deserves more than that lies beyond the purview of this book.

Sherman, Thomas, and the Snake Creek Gap Maneuver

THE FAMOUS British military historian and theoretician B. H. Liddell Hart argues in his *Sherman: Soldier, Realist, American* (New York: Frederick A. Praeger, 1958), 239–40, that Thomas's plan was impractical and too risky: (1) It would have meant "a crossing of routes and a probable entanglement of the lines of supply" because Thomas would have had to swing out to the right while McPherson moved to the center; (2) "in this spy-ridden country the sudden disappearance of Thomas's army which had been so long facing the Confederates" would have been "likely to put them on their guard"; and (3) the "turning movement had to be made by an uncertainly known route, and with still greater uncertainty as to whether Snake Creek Gap would be blockaded," in which case two-thirds of Sherman's army would have "found itself locked out in front of this narrow defile, with Johnston free to strike swiftly at the remaining third and at Sherman's precious base" of Chattanooga.

The counterargument to the above is as follows: (1) It would seem reasonable to assume that a commander of Thomas's experience and competence would not have proposed a logistically impractical plan. (2) In fact he did not, for McPherson's army, contrary to what Liddell Hart implies, moved into Georgia via the "center" at Chattanooga anyway, and it easily could have taken over the position of the Army of the Cumberland north of Ringgold without any "crossing of routes" or "entangling of lines of supply" while Thomas set out for Snake Creek Gap, a movement he thus could have begun sooner and made faster than did McPherson. (3) If the region was "spy-ridden," then obviously the Confederate spies failed Johnston most miserably when he needed them, for throughout the first week of the campaign he lacked precise and reliable information about the movements and location of the Army of the Tennessee until after it attacked Cantey at Resaca. (4) Thanks to his February demonstration and subsequent reconnaissances, the way to Snake Creek Gap was not an "uncertainly known route" to Thomas, and certainly Thomas's knowledge of it was superior to that of McPherson, who never had seen that area and had to rely on inadequate maps. (5) Since Thomas would have had cavalry with him, he could easily have made sure of his passage through Snake Creek Gap before committing his main column to it. (6) Even if Thomas had been "locked out in front of this narrow defile," he presumably would not have remained there stationary but would have turned back in ample time to help defend Chattanooga in the extremely unlikely event of Johnston's launching an offensive to take it.

Liddell Hart in effect abandons his own argument by admitting that Sherman might have "augmented McPherson's army from Thomas's." However, he then tries to salvage it by asserting that Sherman dared not do this because of "Thomas's sensitiveness" and the danger of offending the Army of the Cumberland's "jealous esprit de corps" by detaching units from it to reinforce McPherson. Liddell Hart ignores or overlooks the fact that Thomas himself suggested sending the XX Corps to McPherson when the latter failed to take Resaca or cut the railroad. Sherman, not Thomas, was the one afflicted by "sensitiveness" and a "jealous esprit de corps": After suffering the humiliation, which rankled him the rest of his life, of having his beloved Army of the Tennessee stopped cold at Missionary Ridge while the Army of the Cumberland broke the Confederate line, he was resolved that the former would play the star role in the next encounter with the enemy.

Sherman and Stoneman

THIS ACCOUNT and analysis of the Stoneman fiasco is based on the assumption that Sherman in fact did order Stoneman to join McCook in destroying the Macon railroad at Lovejoy's Station before attempting to liberate the prisoners at Macon and Andersonville, and he was to do this only if he deemed it feasible. It is, however, possible that Sherman gave Stoneman unofficial verbal authorization to go straight for Macon and Andersonville. The reasons for suggesting that this might have been the case are: (1) As has been noted, Stoneman's troopers from the beginning believed that their objective was Macon and Andersonville. (2) Sherman, on learning that Stoneman had not met McCook but had headed directly for Macon, expressed neither surprise nor displeasure; instead, in telegrams to Halleck, Sherman strongly implied that this is what he expected Stoneman to do (see 38 OR 5:308, 320) and declared that although it was a "bold and rash adventure . . . I sanctioned it, and hoped for its success from its very rashness" (ibid., 340). (3) Not until after he had learned about Stoneman's failure and capture did Sherman stress in dispatches to Halleck and Grant that his authorization to Stoneman to attempt the rescue of the prisoners at Macon and Andersonville was conditional, and even then he did not criticize him for disobeying orders. Instead, in a note to Thomas on August 16, Sherman implied that Garrard was responsible for what happened to both McCook and Stoneman (ibid., 350, 409, 526). (4) Sherman also indicated in letters to his wife on August 5 and 9, 1864, that Stoneman's primary mission was the liberation of prisoners; thus, in the second letter, he states that "I have . . . lost Stoneman & 2000 cavalry in attempting to rescue the prisoners at Macon" (Sherman Letters, Notre Dame). (5) Late in September 1864, Sherman arranged for Stoneman's exchange, but instead of court-martialing or at least reprimanding him, he gave him a new cavalry command, and Stoneman was promoted at the end of the war to the rank of brevet major general in the regular army—strange treatment for an officer whose alleged disobedience of orders resulted in the destruction of two divisions! If there is somewhere a frank and full account by Stoneman of his foray to Macon, it perhaps makes for interesting reading.

Sherman, Stanley, Thomas, and
the Second Battle of Jonesboro

IN HIS MEMOIRS (*Memoirs of Gen. W. T. Sherman,* 4th ed. [New York: Charles L. Webster & Co., 1891]), 2: 107–8, Sherman asserts that while Davis was preparing to make his attack on September 1, "I . . . dispatched orders after orders to hurry forward Stanley, so as to lap around Jonesboro on the east, hoping thus to capture the whole of Hardee's corps. I sent first Captain Audenried (aide-de-camp), then Colonel Poe, of the Engineers, and lastly General Thomas himself (and that is the only time during the campaign I can recall seeing General Thomas urge his horse into a gallop)." Neither Thomas nor Stanley in their reports mention that Thomas personally delivered an order to Stanley, and although Stanley, in a 7:45 P.M. dispatch to Thomas's headquarters, states that "at 3:30 P.M. I received orders from Major General Thomas to push forward for Jonesborough" (38 OR 5: 746), it is clear from Fullerton's journal (ibid., 1: 932) that Thomas sent this order verbally via Fullerton and did not deliver it personally. Furthermore, Fullerton's journal contains no reference to any orders coming to IV Corps headquarters from Sherman or to visits there by Audenried, Poe, and Thomas, occurrences that certainly would have been recorded had they occurred. To be sure, in his memoirs (*Personal Memoirs of Major General D. S. Stanley, U.S.A.* [Cambridge, Mass.: Harvard University Press, 1917]), 182, Stanley states: "About 4 P.M. General Thomas came to me and said that the division on my right was about to assault the enemy's works and I was to form my corps and move on the right flank of the 14th Corps and protect their flank." Almost surely Stanley's memory betrayed him, as it does frequently in his *Memoirs,* which he wrote late in life with little research and much bitterness, with the result that he misremembered the verbal order from Thomas that Fullerton passed on to him at 3:30 as having been given in person by Thomas. Finally, although Audenried and Poe did go over to the IV Corps's sector, Sherman's own nighttime letter to Thomas indicates that they did not do so until after the fighting had ended. Also, the lack of any mention of them in Fullerton's journal and the erroneous nature of the report that they gave Sherman would seem to demonstrate that they did not talk to Stanley, Fullerton, or anyone qualified to provide an accurate account of the IV Corps's operations during the day. (Frustratingly for the historian, Poe's extant letters to his wife say nothing about this matter.) In all probability, therefore, Sherman's statements in his *Memoirs* about what he and Thomas did and what Stanley did not do on the afternoon of September 1, 1864, are just another example of his defective (one might say selective) memory. As for his parenthetical description of Thomas riding off at a gallop for "the only time during the campaign I can recall," a description that has been quoted countless times, it deserves no credence except as another example of his persistent disparaging of Thomas as being chronically slow and plodding.

McClellan and the War

SOME HISTORIANS argue that in view of McClellan's commitment to restoring the Union, it would have made no difference if he had replaced Lincoln as president because McClellan also would have continued the war until the South submitted. There are, however, three weaknesses in this argument. First, McClellan would have been elected mainly because the North, discouraged by the lack of any decisive victories, had succumbed to defeatism and so had lost the will to go on with the war. Second, as Lincoln pointed out in his "blind memorandum" of August 23, 1864, McClellan would have "secured his election on such ground" that it would have been difficult for him to resist pressure from his own party to suspend military operations after taking office for the purpose of entering into negotiations with the South, and once that had been done, it would have been even more difficult to resume hostilities. Third, and perhaps most conclusive, as Arthur Simms, a Confederate soldier serving in Virginia pointed out in a September 14, 1864, letter to his sister in Georgia, "if McClellan is elected, the Republican Party who are fighting for the abolishment of slavery will not fight any longer, for they believe that there can be no Union with Slavery" (Simms, "Letters," 121). Civil War historian James M. McPherson, in his *Struggle for Equality: Abolitionists and the Negro in the Civil War and Reconstruction* (Princeton, N.J.: Princeton University Press, 1964), 283, affirms Simm's observation: "Since all abolitionists and most Republicans by this time [autumn 1864] linked Union with emancipation as inseparable war aims, McClellan's position [in favor of restoring the Union with slavery] was as abhorrent to them as Vallandigham's." Thus it is at least possible that McClellan's victory would have led to Confederate victory, for it would have occurred only if the North had lost the will to win, and its occurrence in turn would have made it next to impossible for the North to regain that will because too many Democrats would have wanted to stop the war and too many Republicans would have felt that the war was no longer worth winning. Indeed, it is conceivable that McClellan's election would have resulted, as Colonel Charles Russell Lowell of Massachusetts predicted in early September 1864, in a further breakup of the Union (see Edward Waldo Emerson, *Life and Letters of Charles Russell Lowell*, 333–34).

NOTES

CHAPTER ONE: JANUARY

1. *Cincinnati Daily Commercial,* Jan. 2, 1864; Charles F. Hubert, *History of the Fiftieth Regiment Illinois Volunteer Infantry in the War of the Union* (Kansas City, Mo.: Western Veteran Publishing, 1894), 49–50 (freezing of 39th Ohio soldiers); George H. Puntenney, *History of the Thirty-seventh Regiment of Indiana Infantry Volunteers* (Rushville, Ind.: Jacksonian Book & Job Department, 1896), 67; Robert Patrick, *Reluctant Rebel: The Secret Diary of Robert Patrick (1861–1865),* ed. F. Jay Taylor (Baton Rouge: Louisiana State University Press, 1959), 137; Robert Manson Myers, ed., *The Children of Pride* (New York: Popular Library, 1972), 1133; Milledgeville (Ga.) *Southern Recorder,* Jan. 5, 1864, and accompanying analytical material about weather in Savannah provided in personal communication from Rayther L. Plummer, state climatologist, Athens, Ga.

2. *New York Herald,* Jan. 3, 1864; George Augustus Sala, *My Diary in America in the Midst of War* (London, 1865), 2:145–46.

3. George Templeton Strong, *The Diary of George Templeton Strong, 1835–1875,* ed. Allan Nevins and Milton H. Thomas (New York: Macmillan, 1952), 3:379; *New York Times,* Jan. 1, 1864; *Indianapolis Daily Journal,* Jan. 1, 1864.

4. M. A. Rogers, "An Iowa Woman in Wartime. Part Two," *Annals of Iowa* 35 (1961): 30–31.

5. Allan Nevins, *The War for the Union* (New York: Charles Scribner's Sons, 1959–71), 3:212–70; *New York Times,* Jan. 1, 1864; *Indianapolis Daily Journal,* Feb. 9, 1864; William Fuller, "Thesis on Malingering" (University of Michigan Medical School Records, Ann Arbor, 1864), 1; D. D. Woodruff to Eli Griffin, March 6, 1864, Eli Augustus Griffin Diary and Letters.

6. *New York World,* Jan. 1, 1864; Frank L. Klement, *The Copperheads of the Middle West* (Chicago: University of Chicago Press, 1960), 107–16; Richard Curry, "The Union as It Was: A Critique of Recent Interpretations of the Copperheads," *Civil War History* 13 (1969): 25–39.

7. Nevins, *War for the Union,* 2:318–22; Klement, *Copperheads,* 113, 121–33.

8. Frank L. Klement, *The Limits of Dissent: Clement L. Vallandigham and the Civil War* (Lexington: University Press of Kentucky, 1970), 61–256 *passim.*

9. Kenneth M. Stampp, *Indiana Politics during the Civil War* (Bloomington: Indiana University Press, 1978), 59, 158–85; U.S. War Department, *The War of the Rebellion: A Compilation of the Official Records of the Union and Confederate Armies* (Washington, D.C.: Government Printing Office, 1880–1901), ser. 1, vol. 4:38–39. Hereafter this source will be cited as *OR,* with all references being to Series 1 unless otherwise indicated, and whenever a volume consists of two or more parts, the volume number will precede the *OR* and the part number will follow.

10. Bruce Catton, *This Hallowed Ground: The Story of the Union Side of the Civil War* (Garden City, N.Y.: Doubleday & Co., 1956), 317–18.

11. Franc B. Wilkie, *Pen and Powder* (Boston: Ticknor & Co., 1888), 15; William Bircher, *A Drummer Boy's Diary: Comprising Four Years of Service with the Second Regiment Minnesota Veteran Volunteers, 1861–1865* (St. Paul, Minn.: Acme Press; 1889), 106–7;

Thomas W. Connelly, *History of the Seventieth Ohio Regiment* (Cincinnati: Peak Bohrs, 1902), 70–73; T. F. Dornblasser, *Sabre Strokes of the Pennsylvania Dragoons in the War of 1861–1865* (Philadephia: Lutheran Publication Society, 1884), 38–43; Day Elmore to Parents, Feb. 3, 1864, Day Elmore Letters; Hubert, *Fiftieth Illinois*, 244–64; Ephraim A. Wilson, *Memoirs of the War* (Cleveland: W. M. Bayne, 1893), 286–97.

12. Manning F. Force Letter Book, 1:393, Manning F. Force Papers.

13. 32 OR 2:100–101, 142–43.

14. Ibid., 23–24, 45–46; James F. Rusling, *Men and Things I Saw in Civil War Days* (New York: Eaton Mains, 1899), 318; Darwin Cody, "Letters of Darwin Cody," *Ohio History* 68 (1959): 394–95; W. W. Calkins, *The History of the 104th Regt. of Ill. Volunteer Infantry* (Chicago: Donohue & Henneberry Printers, 1895), 192; John Wesley Marshall, Civil War Journal of John Wesley Marshall, Jan. 10–13, 1864; Puntenney, *Thirty-seventh Indiana*, 67–69; Levi W. Wagner, Recollections of an Enlistee, 1861–1864, 113; James A. Barnes, et al., *The Eighty-sixth Regiment Indiana Volunteer Infantry: A Narrative of Its Services in the Civil War of 1861–1865* (Crawfordsville, Ind.: Journal Co. Printers, 1895), 308–9.

15. OR ser. 3, vol. 4:948–53, 957–58, 962–65; Duncan K. Major and Roger S. Fitch, *Supply of Sherman's Army during the Atlanta Campaign* (Fort Leavenworth, Kans.: Army Service Schools Press, 1911), 28–32, 39, 88–89, 143–45; 32 OR 2:237–38, 454–55; Francis F. McKinney, *Education in Violence: The Life of George H. Thomas and the History of the Army of the Cumberland* (Detroit: Wayne State University Press, 1961), 307–8, 311–12.

16. 32 OR 2:99–101, 105, 143, 183–84, 192–93, 208, 229–30.

17. Ibid., 201–2, 278–81.

18. Hudson Strode, *Jefferson Davis: Confederate President* (New York: Harcourt, Brace & Co., 1959), 515–16; Bell I. Wiley, *Confederate Women* (Westport, Conn.: Greenwood, 1975), 93; J. Cutler Andrews, *The South Reports the Civil War* (Princeton, N.J.: Princeton University Press, 1970), 255. That herpes was the primary cause of Davis's losing the sight of his left eye comes from William C. Davis, *Jefferson Davis: The Man and His Hour* (New York: HarperCollins, 1991), 261–64.

19. OR, ser. 4, vol. 3:95–103; Paul D. Escott, *After Secession: Jefferson Davis and the Failure of Confederate Nationalism* (Baton Rouge: Louisiana State University Press, 1978), 107–9; Albert Burton Moore, *Conscription and Conflict in the Confederacy* (New York: Hillary House Publishers, 1963), 305.

20. Myrtie Long Candler, "Reminiscences of Life in Georgia during the 1850s and 1860s: Part IV," *Georgia Historical Quarterly* 33 (1949): 303–4; Margaret Ketcham Ward, "Testimony of Margaret Ketcham Ward on Civil War Times in Georgia," ed. Aaron M. Boom, *Georgia Historical Quarterly* 39 (1955): 383–85; Nevins, *War for the Union*, 4:240–50; Lawrence M. Keitt to Wife, Feb. 11, 1864, Lawrence M. Keitt Papers; Josiah Gorgas, *The Civil War Diary of General Josiah Gorgas*, ed. Frank E. Vandiver (University: University of Alabama Press, 1947), 87–88; Henry Wilson Ravenel, *The Private Journal of Henry Wilson Ravenel, 1859–1897*, ed. Arney Robinson Childs (Columbia: University of South Carolina Press, 1947), 191.

21. Nevins, *War for the Union*, 2:504–10.

22. Moore, *Conscription and Conflict*, 219–27; Clement Eaton, *Jefferson Davis* (New York: Macmillan, 1977), 238–39; Escott, *After Secession*, 113–19, 155–56, 190–215; Edgar E. Folk and Bynum Shaw, *W. W. Holden: A Political Biography* (Winston-Salem, N.C.: John F. Blair, Publisher, 1982), 138–41, 166–80; Mary Boykin Chesnut, *Mary Chesnut's Civil War* ed. C. Vann Woodward (New Haven, Conn., and London: Yale University Press, 1981), 527.

23. Emory M. Thomas, *The Confederate Nation, 1861–1865* (New York: Harper & Row, 1979), 210–12; Nevins, *War for the Union*, 3:16–19.

24. William L. Nugent, *My Dear Nellie. The Civil War Letters of William L. Nugent to Eleanor Smith Nugent*, ed. William M. Cash and Lucy Somerville Howorth (Jackson: University Press of Mississippi, 1977), 129.

25. Fay quotation from Larry Earl Nelson, "The Confederacy and the United States Presidential Election of 1864" (Ph.D. diss., Duke University, 1975), 35.

26. *OR* ser. 4, vol. 3:136.

27. Ibid., 67–70, 114–15, 140–52, 159–61, 178–84, 203–4; Moore, *Conscription and Conflict*, 80–83, 223; John B. Jones, *A Rebel War Clerk's Diary at the Confederate States Capital*, ed. Howard Swiggett (New York: Old Hickory Bookshop, 1935), 2:115.

28. C. G. Chamberlayne, ed., *Ham Chamberlayne, Virginian: Letters and Papers of an Artillery Officer in the War for Southern Independence, 1861–1865* (Richmond, Va.: Press of the Dietz Publishing Co., 1932), 253.

29. 31 *OR* 3:765.

30. Alfred P. James, "General Joseph Eggleston Johnston, Storm Center of the Confederate Army," *Mississippi Valley Historical Review* 14 (1927): 342–53; Richard M. McMurry, "'The Enemy in Richmond': Joseph E. Johnston and the Confederate Government," *Civil War History* 27 (1981): 5–28; Strode, *Davis*, 502–3, 509–511; Gilbert E. Govan and James W. Livingood, *A Different Valor: The Story of Joseph E. Johnston, C.S.A.* (Indianapolis and New York: Bobbs-Merrill, 1956), 27–28, 66–71, 226–27, 235–39. See ibid., 66, 170 for Johnston's jealousy of Lee.

31. 31 *OR* 3:856–57.

32. Ibid., 2:10–11, 510–11, 559, 839–40, 860, 869–70, 873–74; Benjamin Robert Glover to "Dear Betty," Jan. 6, 1864, Benjamin Robert Glover Letters; Edwin H. Rennolds, Jan. 6, 8, 1864, Diary; John W. Cotton, *Yours til' Death: Civil War Letters of John W. Cotton,* ed. Lucille Griffith (University: University of Alabama Press, 1951), 98; John W. DuBose, *General Joseph Wheeler and the Army of Tennessee* (New York: Neale Publishing Co., 1912), 265; Richard Manning to Mother, Jan. 17, 1864, Letters, Williams-Chesnut-Manning Papers; Patrick, *Reluctant Rebel*, 138; Johnny Green, *Johnny Green of the Orphan Brigade: The Journal of a Confederate Soldier,* ed. A. D. Kirwan (Lexington: University of Kentucky Press, 1956), 118–20; Thomas L. Connelly, *Autumn of Glory: The Army of Tennessee, 1862–1865* (Baton Rouge: Louisiana State University Press, 1971), 290–91.

33. Louis T. Wigfall to Johnston, Dec. 18, 1863, Joseph E. Johnston Papers, Huntington Library; 32 *OR* 2:510–11; Govan and Livingood, *Different Valor*, 240–43.

34. Richard Manning to Mother, Jan. 17, 1864, Letters, Williams-Chesnut-Manning Papers; Sam R. Watkins, *"Co. Aytch": A Sideshow of the Big Show* (New York: Collier Books, 1962), 125–26; Charles T. Jones, ed., "Five Confederates: The Sons of Bolling Hall in the Civil War," *Alabama Historical Quarterly* 24 (1962): 190–91; Govan and Livingood, *Different Valor*, 243.

35. 32 *OR* 2:530–35, 548–49, 591–92, 603–4. For a detailed discussion of Johnston's problems in feeding his army via the Western & Atlantic, see Jeffrey N. Lash, *Destroyer of the Iron Horse: General Joseph E. Johnston and Confederate Rail Transport, 1861–1865* (Kent, Ohio: Kent State University Press, 1991), 104–30.

36. Elbert D. Willett, *History of Company B (Originally Pickens' Planters)* (Anniston, Ala.: Nerwood, 1902), 53; Thomas J. Key, *Two Soldiers: The Campaign Diaries of Thos. J. Key, C.S.A., and Robt. J. Campbell, U.S.A.,* ed. Armistead Cate (Chapel Hill: University of North Carolina Press, 1938), 21–63 (hereafter cited as *Key Diary*); Edwin H. Rennolds, Jan. 15–Feb. 7, 1864, Diary; John Davidson and Julia Davidson, "A Wartime Story: The Davidson Letters, 1862–1865," ed. Jane Bonner Peacock, *Atlanta Historical Bulletin* 29 (1975): 80–81.

37. Charles Edward Nash, *Biographical Sketches of Gen. Pat Cleburne and Gen. T. C. Hindman* (Dayton: Press of the Morningside Bookshop, 1977), 7–11; Irving A. Buck, ed., *Cleburne and His Command* (Jackson, Tenn.: McCowat-Mercer Press, 1959), 72–80, 82–185, 187–200; Thomas R. Hay, "Pat Cleburne—Stonewall Jackson of the West," ibid., 41–50; Wilbur G. Kurtz to Thomas R. Hay, June 23, 1953, Wilbur G. Kurtz Collection; *Key Diary*, 16–18. See Escott, *After Secession*, 242–43, for Davis's attitude toward freeing slaves.

38. 32 *OR* 2:559–60, 603–4, 644–45.

CHAPTER TWO: FEBRUARY

1. Walt Whitman, *Walt Whitman's Civil War,* ed. Walter Lowenfels (New York: Alfred A. Knopf, 1961) 247.

2. Albert Castel, "W. T. Sherman, Part One: The Failure," *Civil War Times Illustrated,* July 1979: 4–7, 42–46, and "W. T. Sherman, Part Two: The Subordinate," ibid., 12–22. Lloyd Lewis, *Sherman: Fighting Prophet* (New York: Harcourt, Brace & Co., 1932), contains the best account of Sherman's pre-1861 career, but its account of his Civil War military activities is superficial, although magnificently written. B. H. Liddell Hart's *Sherman: Soldier, Realist, American* (New York: Frederick A. Praeger, 1958), provides a more detailed description and deeper analysis of Sherman's military operations but relies on inadequate sources and endeavors to demonstrate that Sherman incarnated the author's pet theory about the proper way to conduct warfare. John Marszalek's forthcoming biography of Sherman will supersede Lewis's work as the prime source of information on Sherman's personal life.

3. Castel, "Sherman: The Subordinate," 19.

4. William Pitt Chambers, "My Journal," *Publications of the Mississippi Historical Society* 5 (1925): 299.

5. 32 OR 1:174–75; 2:259–61; W. T. Sherman, *Memoirs of Gen. W. T. Sherman,* 4th ed. (New York: Charles L. Webster & Co., 1891), 1:417–19, 422.

6. Ibid., 364–69; Lewis, *Sherman,* 330.

7. Seymour Dwight Thompson, *Recollections of the Third Iowa Regiment* (Cincinnati: 1864), 335–36, 366–69.

8. 32 OR 2:278–81; W. T. Sherman, *Home Letters of General Sherman,* ed. M. A. DeWolfe Howe (New York: Charles Scribner's Sons, 1909), 268. See also Lt. Col. Aden Cavins, 57th Indiana, to his wife, Dec. 30, 1863, stating "most men are subdued when the ties of early life are sundered and all the bygone memories of 'home, sweet home' are trampled underfoot," and that "When, therefore, the rebels are driven from their homes and their places become occupied by our soldiers . . . they will give up the conflict" (*War Letters of Aden G. Cavins Written to His Wife* [Evansville, Ind.: N.p., n.d.], 75).

9. The best critiques of Polk's military career and character appear in Thomas L. Connelly's *Army of the Heartland: The Army of Tennessee, 1861–1862* (Baton Rouge: Louisiana State University Press, 1967), and *Autumn of Glory: The Army of Tennessee, 1862–1865* (Baton Rouge: Louisiana State University Press, 1971).

10. 32 OR 1:174–75, 332–35; 2:114, 146–47, 201–2, 616–17.

11. John Bennett Walters, *Merchant of Terror: General Sherman and Total War* (New York: Bobbs-Merrill, 1973), 120–22.

12. 32 OR 1:216, 222; Chambers, "Journal," 300–301.

13. 32 OR 1:175–76; 2:718, 721, 737, 768; Walters, *Merchant of Terror,* 116.

14. 32 OR 1:174, 181–82, 262–68; 2:315–17, 326–27, 340, 346, 363, 370.

15. 32 OR 2:662, 700, 716–17, 727, 729–30, 751–52, 755; John W. DuBose, *General Joseph Wheeler and the Army of Tennessee* (New York: Neale Publishing Co., 1912), 267.

16. Thomas A. Head, *Campaigns and Battles of the Sixteenth Regiment, Tennessee Volunteers* (McMinnville, Tenn.: Womack Printing Co., 1961), 313–15; Charles H. Olmstead, *The Memoirs of Charles H. Olmstead,* ed. Lilla Mills Howe (Savannah: Georgia Historical Society, 1964), 177; Bragg to Davis, Dec. 8, 1863, quoted in Clement Eaton, *Jefferson Davis* (New York: Macmillan, 1977), 86. Christopher Losson, *Tennessee's Forgotten Warriors: Frank Cheatham and His Confederate Division* (Knoxville: University of Tennessee Press, 1990), is an excellent study of its subject that fills a gap long empty in Civil War historiography.

17. W. J. Worsham, *The Old Nineteenth Tennessee Regiment, C.S.A.* (Blountsville, Tenn.: Tony Marion, 1973), 107.

18. Edwin H. Rennolds Diary, Feb. 19–22, 1864.

19. 32 *OR* 2:337, 352–53, 373–75, 421, 435.

20. 32 *OR* 1:176–77, 217; 2:427, 432, 471; Walters, *Merchant of Terror*, 124.

21. Charles W. Wills, *Army Life of an Illinois Soldier* (Washington, D.C.: Globe Printing Co., 1906), 127; Sylvester Fairfield to his wife, June 28, 1864, Sylvester Wellington Fairfield Letters; Fenwick Y. Hedley, *Marching Through Georgia* (Chicago: R. R. Donnelley & Sons, 1887), 192–93.

22. 32 *OR* 1:176; 2:448.

23. 32 *OR* 1:256–59, 265–70; 2:370, 431; George E. Waring, Jr., "The Sooy Smith Expedition," in *Battles and Leaders of the Civil War,* ed. Robert U. Johnson and Clarence C. Buel (New York: Century Co., 1887), 416–18; Robert Selph Henry, *"First with the Most" Forrest* (Indianapolis: Bobbs-Merrill Co., 1944), 22–23; John Meriless Diary, Feb. 26, 27, 1864; Stephen D. Lee, "Sherman's Meridian Expedition," *Southern Historical Society Papers* 8 (1880): 50–58.

24. 32 *OR* 1:423–26, 449–53, 456–61, 476–77; 2:458–59, 461, 475, 480–82, 798–99, 808; Corydon Edward Foote, *With Sherman to the Sea: A Drummer Boy's Story of the Civil War,* ed. Olive Deane Hormel (New York: John Day Co., 1960), 163–65; Irving A. Buck, ed., *Cleburne and His Command* (Jackson, Tenn.: McCowat-Mercer Press, 1959), 203; DuBose, *Wheeler,* 270; Thomas B. Van Horne, *History of the Army of the Cumberland* (Cincinnati: Robert Clarke & Co., 1875), 2:21–22, 24–25, 43.

25. 32 *OR* 1:273; 2:498.

26. Lee, "Meridian Expedition," 59–60; 32 *OR* 1:339, 344–45; 3:622; Chambers, "Journal," 302–3.

27. *Atlanta Daily Appeal,* Feb. 17, 27, 29, 1864; *Atlanta Southern Confederacy,* Mar. 16, 1864; *Richmond Daily Examiner,* Feb. 24, 25; Mar. 15, 1864; *New York Times,* Mar. 1–5, 1864; *New York World,* Mar. 1–5, 1864; 32 *OR* 1:338, 345–46; George Templeton Strong, *The Diary of George Templeton Strong, 1835–1875,* ed. Allan Nevins and Milton H. Thomas (New York: Macmillan, 1952), 3:407; Josiah Gorgas, *The Civil War Diary of General Josiah Gorgas,* ed. Frank E. Vandiver (University: University of Alabama Press, 1947), 86; John B. Jones, *A Rebel War Clerk's Diary at the Confederate States Capital,* ed. Howard Swiggert (New York: Old Hickory Bookshop, 1935), 2:156–57.

28. Ibid., 157–58; Shelby Foote, *The Civil War, A Narrative: Fredericksburg to Meridian* (New York: Random House, 1963), 957–58.

29. 38 *OR* 2:805; Gilbert E. Govan and James W. Livingood, *A Different Valor: The Story of General Joseph E. Johnston, C.S.A.* (Indianapolis and New York: Bobbs-Merrill, 1956), 249.

30. *The American Annual Cyclopaedia and Register of Important Events of the Year 1864* (New York: D. Appleton & Co., 1871), 67.

CHAPTER THREE: MARCH

1. Binford to "Cousin Bob," George C. Binford Letters.

2. By all criteria the best biography of Hood is Richard M. McMurry, *John Bell Hood and the War for Southern Independence* (Lexington: University of Kentucky Press, 1982).

3. 32 *OR* 2:763.

4. Douglas Southall Freeman, *R. E. Lee* (New York: Charles Scribner's Sons, 1935), 2:466–70; 3:98.

5. *Atlanta Southern Confederacy,* Mar. 18, 1864; McMurry, *Hood,* 81–92, 99; Mary Boykin Chesnut, *Mary Chesnut's Civil War,* ed. C. Vann Woodward (New Haven, Conn., and London: Yale University Press, 1981), 588.

6. 32 *OR* 3:13.

7. Ibid., 18–19.

8. *Cincinnati Daily Commercial,* March 24, 1864, quoting *Columbus, Ohio, State Journal,* n.d.

9. Ulysses S. Grant, *Personal Memoirs of U. S. Grant* (New York: Charles Scribner's Sons, 1885), 2:144–23; Shelby Foote, *The Civil War, A Narrative: Red River to Appomattox* (New York: Random House, 1974), 3–11.

10. 32 *OR* 3:34–35, 40–41, 50; Sherman, *Memoirs,* 1:424–31.

11. Ibid., 427–28.

12. 32 *OR* 3:58, 67, 83, 87.

13. Grant, *Memoirs,* 2:118–19; William T. Sherman, *Memoirs of Gen. W. T. Sherman,* 4th ed. (New York: Charles L. Webster & Co., 1891), 2:5–7; Julia Dent Grant, *The Personal Memoirs of Julia Dent Grant,* ed. John Y. Simon (New York: G. P. Putnam's Sons, 1975), 128–29; *Cincinnati Daily Commercial,* Mar. 24, 1864; Lloyd Lewis, *Sherman: Fighting Prophet* (New York: Harcourt, Brace & Co., 1932), 344–45.

14. Robert Gibbons, "Life at the Crossroads of the Confederacy: Atlanta, 1864–1865," *Atlanta Historical Bulletin* 23 (1979): 11–15; Paul D. Lack, "Law and Disorder in Confederate Atlanta," *Georgia Historical Quarterly* 56 (1982): 171–89; Franklin M. Garrett, *Atlanta and Environs: A Chronicle of Its People and Events* (New York: Lewis Historical Publishing Co., 1954), 1:562, 567–69 (hereafter all citations of this work will refer to volume one); *Atlanta Daily Intelligencer,* July 2, 1864; Robert Manson Myers, ed., *The Children of Pride* (New York: Popular Library, 1972), 1152–53.

15. Urban G. Owen, "Letters of a Confederate Surgeon in the Army of Tennessee to his Wife," ed. Enoch L. Mitchell, *Tennessee Historical Quarterly* 5 (1946): 165, 171; Sneed to his wife, June 7, 1864, Sebron G. Sneed Family Papers. Before the war Sneed studied for the priesthood in Rome, Italy, but was not ordained.

16. 32 *OR* 2:808; 3:584–85, 613–15, 653–54.

17. 32 *OR* 3:606–7. Hood, it should be noted, is not the only general in the Army of Tennessee to write such a letter in violation of military protocol. Not only did Walker write to Davis in January regarding Cleburne's proposal to enlist blacks, but both he and Wheeler are engaged in direct correspondence with Bragg, and on March 19 Major General Alexander P. Stewart, a division commander in Hood's Corps, will also write Bragg to voice the same complaint as Hood: "Are we to hold still, remaining on the defensive in this position until . . . Grant comes down with his combined armies to drive us out?" (Walker to Bragg, March 8, 1864, and Stewart to Bragg, March 19, 1864, Bragg Papers; Wheeler to Bragg, February 14, 1864, Wheeler Papers.)

18. Chesnut, *Mary Chesnut's Civil War,* 565.

19. 32 *OR* 3:666, 674.

20. Quoted in J. Cutler Andrews, *The South Reports the Civil War* (Princeton, N.J.: Princeton University Press, 1970), 443–44, n. 10.

21. Richard M. McMurry, "The Atlanta Campaign: Dec. 23, 1863 to July 18, 1864," Ph.D. diss., Emory University, 1967, 52–62.

22. McMurry, *Hood,* 95; Thomas L. Connelly, *Autumn of Glory: The Army of Tennessee, 1862–1865* (Baton Rouge: Louisiana State University Press, 1971), 313–18.

23. Oliver Otis Howard, *Autobiography of Oliver Otis Howard* (New York: Baker & Taylor Co., 1907), 1:495; 32 *OR* 3:5, 17–18, 202.

24. 32 *OR* 3:207–10, 657–58, 685, 720–21; Connelly, *Autumn of Glory,* 299–301; Lewis, *Sherman,* 327.

25. Connelly, *Autumn of Glory,* 297–306, gives the best critique of the various proposed Confederate plans during this period.

26. 32 *OR* 3:67–68; Thompson, *Third Iowa,* 335; Sherman, *Memoirs,* 2:7–8; Lewis, *Sherman,* 346–47.

27. 32 *OR* 3:163–65.

28. Albert Castel, "Black Jack Logan," *Civil War Times Illustrated,* Nov. 1976: 4–10, 41.

29. 32 *OR* 3:165, 171, 178, 187–88, 199–200.

30. John W. Bates Diary, Aug. 25, 1864; Eben P. Sturges to "Dear Folks," June 9, 1864, Eben P. Sturges Diary and Letters; Oliver O. Howard to his wife, Sept. 29, 1864, Oliver Otis Howard Letters; William F. G. Shanks, *Personal Recollections of Distinguished Generals* (New York: Harper & Brothers, 1866), 262; Thomas B. Van Horne, *The Life of Major General George H. Thomas* (New York: Charles Scribner's Sons, 1882), 19–20. A thorough, scholarly study of Thomas's military career does not yet exist and is much needed. The most recent and detailed biography, Francis P. McKinney, *Education in Violence: The Life of George H. Thomas and the History of the Army of the Cumberland* (Detroit: Wayne State University Press, 1961), is badly impaired by an excessive bias in favor of Thomas and against Grant and Sherman.

31. Lewis, *Sherman*, 346; Shanks, *Recollections*, 71–72.

32. McKinney, *Education in Violence*, 313–14; Freeman Cleaves, *Rock of Chickamauga: The Life of General George H. Thomas* (Norman: University of Oklahoma Press, 1948), 208–9.

33. Van Horne, *Thomas*, 197–200; McKinney, *Education in Violence*, 274.

34. John M. Schofield, *Forty-six Years in the Army* (New York: Century Co., 1897), 106–19; Jacob D. Cox, *Military Reminiscences of the Civil War* (New York: Charles E. Scribner, 1900), 2:140.

35. 32 *OR* 3:178, 181; Schofield, *Forty-six Years*, 119–20; Sherman to John Sherman, Apr. 14, 1864, William Tecumseh Sherman Papers, Library of Congress.

36. 32 *OR* 3:199–200.

37. *Key Diary*, 66.

CHAPTER FOUR: APRIL

1. 32 *OR* 3:220–21, 247–49, 311–13; Richard M. McMurry, "The Opening Phase of the 1864 Campaign in the West," *Atlanta Historical Journal* 27 (1983): 12–15.

2. 32 *OR* 3:246.

3. Sherman to McPherson, Apr. 24, 1864, ibid., 479: "Of course the movement in Virginia is principal and ours is secondary, and must conform."

4. Grant to Sherman, Apr. 19, 1864, ibid., 409.

5. Ibid., 220, 236–37, 247–49, 270, 279–81, 301–2, 311, 330, 420, 434, 466, 548; William T. Sherman, *Memoirs of Gen. W. T. Sherman*, 4th ed. (New York: Charles L. Webster & Co., 1891), 2:8–11; Lloyd Lewis, *Sherman: Fighting Prophet* (New York: Harcourt, Brace & Co., 1932), 350–52; Alfred Lacy Hough, *Soldier in the West: The Civil War Letters of Alfred Lacy Hough*, ed. Robert G. Athearn (Philadelphia: University of Pennsylvania Press, 1956), 184, 186; James F. Rusling, *Men and Things I Saw in Civil War Days* (New York: Eaton Mains, 1899), 322; Charles A. Dana, *Recollections of the Civil War* (New York: D. Appleton & Co., 1902), 154–55; Lyman S. Widney Diary, Apr. 20, 22, 1864; David Power Conyngham, *Sherman's March Through the South* (New York: Sheldon & Co., 1865), 29–30; Duncan K. Major and Roger S. Fitch, *Supply of Sherman's Army during the Atlanta Campaign* (Fort Leavenworth, Kans.: Army Service Schools Press, 1911), 11–12, 18–19, 24–28; *Cincinnati Daily Commercial*, Mar. 19, May 25, 1864. In his *Memoirs* 2:11–12, Sherman states that he authorized the president of the Louisville and Nashville, James Guthrie, to compensate his line for the loss of its rolling stock by, in collaboration with the Quartermaster Department, taking control of trains arriving at Jeffersonville, Indiana, across the Ohio River from Louisville, with the result that "in a short time we had cars and locomotives from almost every road at the North; months afterward I was amused to see, way down in Georgia, cars marked 'Pittsburg & Fort Wayne,' 'Delaware & Lackawanna,' 'Baltimore & Ohio,' and indeed with the names of almost every railroad north of the Ohio River." However, McCallum in his report on railroads in the campaign (*OR*, ser. 3, 5:985–86) makes no

mention of utilizing trains from Northern lines; and it would have been difficult, if not impossible, to have done so, given that the standard track gauge in the North was 4'8", whereas in Kentucky, Tennessee, Alabama, and Georgia it was 5'. But it makes a good story.

6. Albert Castel, "The Fort Pillow Massacre: A Fresh Examination of the Evidence," *Civil War History* 4 (1958): 37–51; Clark to his sisters, Achilles V. Clark Letter.

7. 32 *OR* 3:366–67, 402, 410–11, 441, 497, 527; Forrest to Johnston, 52 *OR* 2:653.

8. 32 *OR* 3:221–22.

9. Shelby Foote, *The Civil War, A Narrative: Fredericksburg to Meridian* (New York: Random House, 1963), 261–316, 848–49; Walter H. Hebert, *Fighting Joe Hooker* (Indianapolis: Bobbs-Merrill Co., 1944), 192–203; Ulysses S. Grant, *Personal Memoirs of U. S. Grant* (New York: Charles Scribner's Sons, 1885), 2:539; Hooker to Stanton, Feb. 25, 1864, and on Grant being "simple minded," 32 *OR* 2:313–15, 467–69; Alpheus S. Williams, *From the Cannon's Mouth: The Civil War Letters of General Alpheus S. Williams,* ed. Milo M. Quaife (Detroit: Wayne State University Press, 1959), 264–65; William G. LeDuc, *Recollections of a Civil War Quartermaster* (St. Paul, Minn.: North Central Publishing Co., 1963), 119. There is no good study of Hooker, but then none is possible, owing to the absence of necessary sources.

10. Howard to Wife, Apr. 25, Oliver Otis Howard Letters; Lewis, *Sherman,* 349–50; Kenneth P. Williams, *Lincoln Finds a General* (New York: Macmillan, 1949–59), 2:584–89.

11. 32 *OR* 3:221, 292, 313; John Love to his parents, Mar. 4, 1864, John C. Love Letters; Eben P. Sturges to "Dear Folks," Eben P. Sturges Diary and Letters; George T. Palmer, *A Conscientious Turncoat: The Story of John M. Palmer, 1817–1900* (New Haven, Conn.: Yale University Press, 1941), 106–7, 118–20, 125–26, 135.

12. 32 *OR* 3:422, 437, 443. Banks never figured in a major way in Grant's and Sherman's plans for the West in 1864. Grant, as we have noted, did not believe that Banks would be able to carry out the Red River expedition on schedule, and although Sherman was more optimistic about that, his April 10 letter to Grant demonstrates that he was not counting on Banks's taking Mobile and Montgomery but merely hoping that he might. Moreover, even if the Red River expedition had been successful, it is highly doubtful that Banks could have gotten back to New Orleans in time or would have had the strength, without Smith's divisions, to have launched an attack on Mobile in conjunction with Sherman's invasion of Georgia. The day Banks started up the Red River he ceased, exactly as Grant expected, to be an important factor in the war east of the Mississippi.

13. Ibid., 465–70.

14. Ibid., 756; 52 *OR* 2:655.

15. 32 *OR* 3:781, 839–42; 38 *OR* 3:626; 52 *OR* 2:657–58; Richard M. McMurry, "The Atlanta Campaign: December 23, 1863 to July 18, 1864," Ph.D. diss., Emory University, 1967, 55–56; Thomas L. Connelly, *Autumn of Glory: The Army of Tennessee, 1862–1865* (Baton Rouge: Louisiana State University Press, 1971), 311–12.

16. 32 *OR* 3:684–86.

17. Ibid., 772–74.

18. 38 *OR* 3:622–25; Wheeler to Bragg, Apr. 16, 1864, Braxton Bragg Papers.

19. 32 *OR* 3:781.

20. Gilbert E. Govan and James W. Livingood, *A Different Valor: The Story of General Joseph E. Johnston, C.S.A.* (Indianapolis and New York: Bobbs-Merrill, 1956), 257.

21. *OR*, ser. 4, vol. 3:327–43; *New York Tribune,* Mar. 17, 1864; Shelby Foote, *The Civil War, A Narrative: Red River to Appomattox* (New York: Random House, 1974), 129.

22. Benjamin quotation, Larry Earl Nelson, "The Confederacy and the United States Presidential Election of 1864," Ph.D. diss., Duke University, 1975, 156; T. B. Kelly to Miss L. A. Honnell, Honnell Family Papers; *Indianapolis Daily Sentinel,* May 6, 1864, quoting *New York World,* n.d.; *Chicago Daily Times,* Apr. 26, 1864.

23. Bliss to his father, Apr. 24, 1864, Robert Lewis Bliss Letters; J. Cutler Andrews, *The*

South Reports the Civil War (Princeton, N.J.: Princeton University Press, 1970), 260–63; 31 OR 3:779; 32 OR 3:595, 737.

24. *Key Diary,* 72.

25. 32 OR 3:865–66. In a letter of May 4, 1864, H. C. Day, a Confederate ordnance officer, informs Capt. George Little, an ordnance officer in Bate's Division, that "I learn from pretty good sources" that Johnston's army at the end of April had "present for duty" a total of "45,000 muskets" (letter in W. T. Sherman Papers, Library of Congress). See also James Cooper Nisbet, *Four Years on the Firing Line,* ed. Bell I. Wiley (Jackson, Tenn.: McCowat-Mercer Press, 1963), 141.

26. Arthur M. Manigault, *A Carolinian Goes to War: The Civil War Narrative of Arthur Middleton Manigault, Brigadier General, C.S.A.,* ed. R. Lockwood Tower (Columbia: University of South Carolina Press, 1983), 188.

27. Nisbet, *Four Years,* 208; *Key Diary,* 110; Andrew J. Neal to "Dear Pa," Apr. 14, 1864, Neal Letters; Robert L. Thompson, "From Missionary Ridge to Dalton," *Confederate Veteran* 14 (1906): 406–7 (for clanging sound of Confederate artillery); Larry J. Daniel, *Cannoneers in Gray: The Field Artillery of the Army of Tennessee, 1861–1865* (University: University of Alabama Press, 1984) 102–3.

28. Irving A. Buck, *Cleburne and His Command* (Jackson, Tenn.: McCowat-Mercer Press, 1959), 201–2; Isaac N. Shannon, "Sharpshooters in Hood's Army," *Confederate Veteran* 15 (1907): 123–26; James Taylor Holmes, *Fifty-second Ohio Volunteer Infantry: Then and Now,* vol. 1 (Columbus, Ohio: Berlin Printing Co., 1898), 251.

29. Andrew J. Neal to "Dear Ella," Apr. 8, 1864, Neal Letters; Robert Lewis Bliss to his mother, Mar. 5, 1864, Bliss Letters; Newton Cannon, *The Reminiscences of Sergeant Newton Cannon,* ed. Campbell H. Brown (Franklin, Tenn.: Carter House Association, 1963), 54; John Johnston, "The Civil War Reminiscences of John Johnston: Part III," ed. William T. Alderson, *Tennessee Historical Quarterly* 14 (1955): 338; Francis W. Dunn Diary, Sept. 9, 1864, Francis Wayland Dunn Diaries and Correspondence; *Atlanta Southern Confederacy,* June 29, 1864; John W. Dyer, *Reminiscences; or, Four Years in the Confederate Army* (Evansville, Ind.: 1898), 157–58, 165; W. C. Dodson, ed., *Campaigns of Wheeler and His Cavalry, 1862–1865* (Atlanta: Hudgins Publishing Co., 1899), 160–61, 409–11. On the strength of the Army of Tennessee's cavalry at end of April 1864, see 38 OR 3:866, 870–71, and Connelly, *Autumn of Glory,* 330–31. Reliably accurate figures on Confederate cavalry strength measured in terms of men actually available for combat are difficult to obtain due to scanty and poor records and the high rate of absenteeism on the part of Southern troopers. On this last subject, see Jacob D. Cox, *Military Reminiscences of the Civil War,* (New York: Charles E. Scribner, 1900), 1:266. For Sherman's description of the Southern cavalry, see Sherman, *Memoirs,* 1:365.

30. The description and characterization of Wheeler given here derives mainly from John P. Dyer, *"Fighting Joe" Wheeler* (Baton Rouge: Louisiana State University Press, 1941), and Thomas L. Connelly's *Army of the Heartland: The Army of Tennessee, 1861–1862* (Baton Rouge: Louisiana State University Press, 1967), and *Autumn of Glory,* passim.

31. 38 OR 3:676; William Honnell to his sister, Apr. 24, 1864, Honnell Family Papers.

32. 32 OR 3:550–72.

33. Charles W. Wills, *Army Life of an Illinois Soldier* (Washington, D.C.: Globe Printing Co., 1906), 218.

34. John J. Hight, *History of the Fifty-eighth Regiment of Indiana Volunteer Infantry* (Princeton, Ind.: Press of the Clarion, 1895), 283–84; Day Elmore to his parents, Apr. 3, 1864, Day Elmore Letters; Bernard F. Mullen to Hugh D. Gallagher, Apr. 30, 1864, Hugh D. Gallagher Correspondence and Papers; Henry S. Dunn to "My Dear Friend," May 2, 1864, Warden Family Papers; Michael H. Fitch, *Echoes of the Civil War as I Hear Them* (New York: William S. Porter Press, 1905), 196; Thaddeus H. Capron, "War Diary of Thaddeus H. Capron, 1861–1865," *Journal of the Illinois Historical Society* 12 (1919): 380,

382; Chesley A. Mosman, *The Rough Side of War: The Civil War Journal of Chesley A. Mosman, 1st Lieutenant, Company D, 59th Illinois Volunteer Infantry Regiment*, ed. Arnold Gates (Garden City, N.Y.: Basin Publishing Co., 1987), 251; Newlin, W. H., comp., *A History of the Seventy-third Regiment of Illinois Volunteer Infantry* (Springfield, Ill.: 1890), 301; Manning F. Force Letter Book, vol. 1:407 (June 1862), Force Papers.

35. 38 OR 1:120–23; Cox, *Reminiscences*, 1:182–83.

36. 38 OR 1:115; 2:745–46.

37. Benjamin F. McGee, *History of the 72d Indiana Volunteer Infantry of the Mounted Lightning Brigade* (Lafayette, Ind.: S. Vater & Co., 1882), 499; George H. Puntenney, *History of the Thirty-seventh Regiment of Indiana Infantry Volunteers* (Rushville, Ind.: Jacksonian Book & Job Department, 1896), 77–78; David Nichol to his father and mother, Apr. 24, 1864, David Nichol Diary and Letters; Joseph F. Culver, *"Your Affectionate Husband, J. F. Culver." Letters Written during the Civil War*, ed. Leslie W. Dunlap (Iowa City: Friends of the University of Iowa Libraries, 1978), 272–73; F. M. McAdams, *Every-Day Soldier Life, or a History of the One Hundred and Thirteenth Ohio Volunteer Inf.* (Columbus: Charles M. Gott, Printers, 1884), 74–75; Charles Laforest Dunham, *Through the South with a Union Soldier*, ed. Arthur H. DeRosier (Johnson City: Publications of the East Tennessee State University Research Advisory Committee, 1969), 116; Joseph Whitney, *Kiss Clara for Me: The Story of Joseph Whitney*, ed. Robert J. Snetsinger (State College, Pa.: Carnation Press, 1969), 137; Lyman S. Widney to Parents, May 1, 1864, Lyman S. Widney Diary and Letters.

38. 32 OR 3:496–97, 630–31; 52 OR 1:697; Edward Hagerman, *The American Civil War and the Origins of Modern Warfare* (Bloomington and Indianapolis: University of Indiana Press, 1988), 279.

39. Lyman S. Widney Diary, Apr. 30, 1864, Lyman S. Widney Diary and Letters.

40. 32 OR 3:343, 353; J. Cutler Andrews, *The North Reports the Civil War* (Pittsburgh: University of Pittsburgh Press, 1955), 552–53.

41. 32 OR 3:488–89, 491–93, 510, 521, 531; 52 OR 1:622.

42. *Key Diary*, 76–77; Angus McDermid, "Letters from a Confederate Soldier," ed. Benjamin Rountree, *Georgia Review* 18 (1964): 285; Julius M. Macon to Miss Clifford, May 4, 1864, Julius Montgomery Macon Letters; Lyman S. Widney to his parents, May 1, 1864, Lyman S. Widney Diary and Letters.

43. Quoted in Foote, *Red River to Appomattox*, 138.

44. Orlando M. Poe to his wife, Apr. 30, 1865, Orlando M. Poe Letters to Wife; William Honnell to his sisters, Apr. 30, 1864, Honnell Family Papers.

CHAPTER FIVE: MAY

1. 32 OR 3:282; Thomas B. Van Horne, *The Life of Major General George H. Thomas* (New York: Charles Scribner's Sons, 1882), 210–11, 220–21.

2. 38 OR 1:63; 4:3, 9, 27, 35, 38–40.

3. Charles Laforest Dunham, *Through the South with a Union Soldier*, ed. Arthur H. DeRosier (Johnson City: Publications of the East Tennessee State University Research Advisory Committee, 1969), 116, 120; Daniel Devine Rose, Letter of May 4, 1864, Daniel Devine Rose Diary and Letters.

4. John B. Brobst, *Well Mary: Civil War Letters of a Wisconsin Volunteer*, ed. Lydia M. Post (Madison: University of Wisconsin Press, 1960), 53–54; Phinehas A. Hager to his wife, May 5, 1864, Phinehas A. Hager Letters; Stephen Pierson, "From Chattanooga to Atlanta in 1864—A Personal Reminiscence," in *The Atlanta Papers*, comp. Sydney C. Kerkis (Dayton: Press of the Morningside Bookshop, 1980), 269–70; Chauncey H. Cooke, "A Badger Boy in Blue: The Letters of Chauncey M. Cooke," *Wisconsin Magazine of History* 4 (1934): 65.

5. John D. Billings, *Hardtack and Coffee,* ed. Richard Harwell (Chicago: Lakeside Press, 1960), 381-89; James A. Barnes, et al., *The Eighty-sixth Regiment Indiana Volunteer Infantry: A Narrative of Its Services in the Civil War of 1861-1865* (Crawfordsville, Ind.: Journal Co. Printers, 1895), 300; C. C. Carpenter, "A Commissary in the Union Army: Letters of C. C. Carpenter," ed. Mildred Throne, *Iowa Journal of History* 53 (1955): 73; Cooke, "Letters," 65.

6. Benjamin T. Smith Recollections of the Late War, 113-15.

7. Judson L. Austin to his wife, May 3, 1864, Judson L. Austin Letters; Theodore F. Upson, *With Sherman to the Sea: The Civil War Letters, Diaries and Reminiscences of Theodore F. Upson,* ed. Oscar G. Winther (Bloomington: University of Indiana Press, 1958), 167; William Sumner Dodge, *A Waif of the War; or, The History of the Seventy-fifth Illinois Infantry* (Chicago: Church & Goodman, 1866), 119-20.

8. 38 OR 4:25.

9. Ibid., 19, 33; 52 OR 1:622.

10. 38 OR 4:34-35, 37-40, 53; Benjamin F. McGee, *History of the 72d Indiana Volunteer Infantry of the Mounted Lightning Brigade* (Lafayette, Ind.: S. Vater & Co., 1882), 291-93.

11. James Taylor Holmes, *Fifty-second Ohio Volunteer Infantry: Then and Now,* vol. 1 (Columbus: Berlin Printing Co., 1898), 168.

12. George H. Puntenney, *History of the Thirty-seventh Regiment of Indiana Infantry Volunteers* (Rushville, Ind.: Jacksonian Book & Job Department, 1896), 79-80; W. W. Calkins, *The History of the 104th Regt. of Ill. Volunteer Infantry* (Chicago: Donohue & Henneberry Printers, 1895), 200; Daniel Devine Rose Diary, May 6, 1864.

13. 38 OR 4:659-63, 669-70; Speech made by Jefferson Davis at Montgomery, Alabama, September 1864, printed in Montgomery *Mail,* n.d., and quoted in *New York Weekly Tribune,* Oct. 15, 1864; Thomas L. Connelly, *Autumn of Glory: The Army of Tennessee, 1862-1865* (Baton Rouge: Louisiana State University Press, 1971), 331-32.

14. 38 OR 4:654, 657-60, 663-65; The Thomas B. Mackall Journal and Its Antecedents: The Five Versions of the Journal, 3-10 (hereafter cited as Thomas B. Mackall Journal). This unpublished manuscript (highly deserving of publication), edited by Richard M. McMurry and deposited with the Joseph E. Johnston Papers, College of William and Mary, contains four unpublished versions of Lieutenant Mackall's journal plus the version that is published in 38 OR 3:978-91. This is an extraordinarily valuable source, for it provides Mackall's original and authentic journal, whereas the journal as published contains material inserted many years later, almost surely at the behest of Johnston, and designed to discredit Hood. See Richard M. McMurry, "The Mackall Journal and Its Antecedents," *Civil War History* 20 (1974): 311-28.

Johnston's order to Wheeler, as written by Mackall, called for him to have the "east" side of Taylor's Ridge scouted (38 OR 4:664). This is such an obvious error that almost surely Wheeler noticed it and hence was not misled by it—a supposition that would seem to be confirmed by the fact that some of Wheeler's scouts did operate west of the ridge.

15. Samuel T. Foster, *One of Cleburne's Command: The Civil War Reminiscences and Diary of Capt. Samuel T. Foster, Granbury's Texas Brigade, C.S.A.,* ed. Norman D. Brown (Austin: University of Texas Press, 1980), 71. This, along with Captain Key's Diary, is one of the most valuable sources on the Confederate side of the Atlanta Campaign.

16. *Key Diary,* 82; Holmes, *Then and Now,* 168, 245; Puntenney, *Thirty-seventh Indiana,* 86; Nixon B. Stewart, *Dan McCook's Regiment. 52nd O.V.I. A History of the Regiment, Its Campaigns and Battles* (Alliance, Ohio: Review Print, 1900), 98; William E. Sloan Diary, May 7, 1864; Lyman S. Widney Diary, May 7, 1864; Lot D. Young, *Reminiscences of a Soldier of the Orphan Brigade* (Louisville: Louisville Courier Job Print, 1912), 76.

17. 38 OR 4:56-58, 64-67; McGee, *72nd Indiana,* 293-94.

18. 38 OR 4:673-76.

19. Chesley A. Mosman, *The Rough Side of War: The Civil War Journal of Chesley A.*

Mosman, 1st Lieutenant, Company D, 59th Illinois Volunteer Infantry Regiment, ed. Arnold Gates (Garden City, N.Y.: Basin Publishing Co., 1987), 193; Lyman S. Widney Diary, May 8, 1864; John W. Tuttle Diary, 8–10; Charles T. Clark, *Opdycke's Tigers* (Columbus: Spahr & Glenn, 1895), 225–26; 38 OR 1:189, 291–92, 367–68.

20. Oliver Otis Howard, *Autobiography of Oliver Otis Howard* (New York: Baker & Taylor Co., 1907), 1:504; Lyman S. Widney Diary, May 8, 1864; Puntenney, *Thirty-seventh Indiana,* 81–83. See 38 OR 4:91, for damming of Mill Creek.

21. William F. G. Shanks, *Personal Recollections of Distinguished Generals* (New York: Harper & Brothers, 1866), 317–18; George W. Nichols, *The Story of the Great March from the Diary of a Staff Officer* (New York: Harper & Brothers, 1865), 98–99; Albert R. Greene, *From Bridgeport to Ringgold by Way of Lookout Mountain* (Providence, R.I.: 1870), 21, 29–30; Alpheus S. Williams, *From the Cannon's Mouth: The Civil War Letters of General Alpheus S. Williams,* ed. Milo M. Quaife (Detroit: Wayne State University Press, 1959), 330–31. For Geary's incompetent performance at Gettysburg, see Edwin B. Coddington, *The Gettysburg Campaign: A Study in Command* (Dayton: Press of the Morningside Bookshop, 1979), 433–34.

22. 38 OR 2:114–17; 3:615, 720–21; 4:70, 76, 79, 116; Wilbur G. Kurtz, Snake Creek Gap, 2, Wilbur G. Kurtz Collection; William E. Sloan Diary, Feb. 25, 1864 (description of Dug Gap); Stephen Pierson, "From Chattanooga to Atlanta in 1864—A Personal Reminiscence," in *The Atlanta Papers,* comp. Sydney C. Kerksis (Dayton: Press of the Morningside Bookshop, 1980), 271–72; Geary to Wife, May 11, 1864, John W. Geary Letters; Irving A. Buck, ed., *Cleburne and His Command* (Jackson, Tenn.: McCowat-Mercer Press, 1959), 207; Foster, *Diary,* 72; Sebron G. Sneed to his wife, June 7–8, 1864, Sebron G. Sneed Family Papers; W. C. P. Breckinridge, "The Opening of the Atlanta Campaign," in *Battles and Leaders of the Civil War,* ed. Robert U. Johnson and Clarence C. Buel (New York: Century Co., 1887), 4:279. Captain Irving Buck, who probably was present but may not have been, asserts in *Cleburne,* 207, that Granbury's men mounted the horses of Grigsby's Kentuckians and rode them to the top of Dug Gap. However, neither Captain Sneed nor Captain Samuel Foster of Granbury's Brigade, both of whom definitely were present, makes any mention of this in his account of the fight at Dug Gap, nor does Breckinridge in his article. Moreover, owing to the terrain, it would be virtually impossible to ride horses to the top of Dug Gap except by way of the road.

23. 38 OR 3:30, 90, 375, 397; 4:85–88; Wilbur G. Kurtz, Snake Creek Gap, 3, Wilbur G. Kurtz Collection; Henry W. Wright, *A History of the Sixth Iowa Infantry* (Iowa City: Iowa State Historical Society, 1923), 264–65.

24. 38 OR 4:82–84.

25. Ibid., 677–80; Thomas B. Mackall Journal, sec. 1:13–14.

26. 38 OR 3:30–31, 375, 452, 457; 4:105, 681–84; Sebron G. Sneed to his wife, June 7–8, 1864, Sebron G. Sneed Family Papers; John W. Dyer, *Reminiscences; or Four Years in the Confederate Army* (Evansville, Ind.: 1898), 180–81; W. C. P. Breckinridge, "The Opening of the Atlanta Campaign," in *Battles and Leaders of the Civil War,* ed. Robert U. Johnson and Clarence C. Buel (New York: Century Co., 1887), 4:279–80; Charles Wright, *A Corporal's Story* (Philadelphia: James Beal, 1887), 94–96.

27. 38 OR 3:18, 31, 90–91, 375–77, 483; 4:105–6; Rowland Cox, "Snake Creek Gap and Atlanta," in *The Atlanta Papers,* comp. Sydney C. Kerksis (Dayton: Press of the Morningside Bookshop, 1980), 331–39; Leslie Anders, *The Eighteenth Missouri* (Indianapolis and New York: Bobbs-Merrill, 1968), 205–9; Charles F. Hubert, *History of the Fiftieth Regiment Illinois Volunteer Infantry in the War of the Union* (Kansas City, Mo.: Western Veteran Publishing, 1894), 271–72; Wright, *Corporal's Story,* 94–95; Charles W. Wills, *Army Life of an Illinois Soldier* (Washington, D.C.: Globe Printing Co., 1906), 236–37; Joseph A. Saunier, ed., *A History of the Forty-seventh Regiment Ohio Veteran Volunteer Infantry* (Hillsboro, Ohio: Lyle Printing Co., 1903), 226; William Henry Chamberlin,

History of the Eighty-first Regiment Ohio Volunteers during the War of the Rebellion (Cincinnati: Gazette Steam-Print House, 1865), 62; Grenville M. Dodge, *Personal Recollections of President Abraham Lincoln, General Ulysses S. Grant and General William T. Sherman* (Council Bluffs, Iowa: Monarch Printing Co., 1914), 210–21; Robert Patrick, *Reluctant Rebel: The Secret Diary of Robert Patrick, 1861–1865,* ed. F. Jay Taylor (Baton Rouge: Louisiana State University Press, 1959), 159–63; James Cooper Nisbet, *Four Years on the Firing Line,* ed. Bell J. Wiley (Jackson, Tenn.: McCowat-Mercer Press, 1963), 177–85; Breckinridge, "Opening of Atlanta Campaign," 280–81; Robert W. Banks, "Civil War Letters of Robert W. Banks: Atlanta Campaign," ed. George C. Osborn, *Georgia Historical Quarterly* 27 (1943): 211.

28. 38 OR 1:292, 368, 845–47; 4:89–91, 100–102; Lyman S. Widney Diary, May 8, 1864; James I. Hall, Memoir, 19–20, James I. Hall Papers.

29. 38 OR 2:510; 4:97–103; Theodore C. Tracie, *Annals of the Nineteenth Ohio Battery; or, Lights and Shadows of Army Life* (Cleveland: J. B. Savage, 1878), 294–95; Oliver Lyman Spaulding, Military Memoirs of Brig. Gen. Oliver L. Spaulding, 38–39; L. G. Bennett and Wm. M. Haigh, *History of the 36th Illinois Volunteers* (Aurora, Ill.: Knickerbocker & Hodder Printers, 1876), 577–78.

30. 38 OR 3:614; Joseph E. Johnston, *Narrative of Military Operations* (New York: D. Appleton & Co., 1874), 317; Thomas B. Mackall Journal, sec. 1:16; Richard M. McMurry, *John Bell Hood and the War for Southern Independence* (Lexington: University of Kentucky Press, 1982), 102. Johnston, *Narrative,* 307, asserts that "at night on the 9th General Cantey reported that he had been engaged with those troops [McPherson's] until dark." No such dispatch from Cantey appears in the *Official Records,* Mackall's Journal does not mention it, it is inconsistent with other Confederate dispatches printed in the *Official Records* or referred to by Mackall, and Johnston's official report is silent about it. It therefore is extremely unlikely that Johnston received on the night of May 9 a report from Cantey that he had been attacked at Resaca by McPherson, especially since Union cavalry by then had cut the telegraph line between Resaca and Dalton.

31. 38 OR 4:88–89, 99, 105, 110–12; Lloyd Lewis, *Sherman: Fighting Prophet* (New York: Harcourt, Brace & Co., 1932), 357.

32. 38 OR 3:16–17; 4:106, 125.

33. 38 OR 4:112–14, 116, 121–23, 126–27.

34. Ibid., 111.

35. 38 OR 3:17; 4:125–29, 132–33; Lorenzo Barker Diary, May 9, 1864.

36. 38 OR 4:686–89; Thomas B. Mackall Journal, sec. 1:16–18; Buck, *Cleburne,* 208–10.

37. Cooke, "Letters," 69; Saunier, *Forty-seventh Ohio,* 224–25.

38. 38 OR 4:692–97; Thomas B. Mackall Journal, sec. 1:18–20.

39. 38 OR 4:135–36, 138–39.

40. Ibid., 139, 144–45; Ira B. Read, "The Campaign from Chattanooga to Atlanta as Seen by a Federal Soldier," ed. Richard B. Harwell, *Georgia Historical Quarterly* 25 (1941): 264; L. W. Day, *Story of the One Hundred and First Ohio Infantry* (Cleveland: W. M. Bayne Printing Co., 1894), 200–201.

41. 38 OR 4:139.

42. Hubert, *Fiftieth Illinois,* 272; Patrick, *Reluctant Rebel,* 164–65.

43. Arthur H. Noll, ed., *Doctor Quintard, Chaplain C.S.A.* (Sewanee, Tenn.: University of the South, 1905), 96–97; McMurry, *Hood,* 103.

44. 38 OR 4:151; Stewart, *McCook's Regiment,* 101; Widney Diary, May 12, 1864; Ross Diary, May 12, 1864.

45. 38 OR 4:698–703.

46. Cox, "Snake Creek Gap," 341.

47. 38 OR 4:147, 158; Widney Diary, May 12, 1864.

48. Smith, "Recollections," 147–48; Bennett and Haigh, *36th Illinois,* 580; Wilbur F.

Hinman, *The Story of the Sherman Brigade* (Alliance, Ohio: Press of the Daily Review, 1897), 525–26; Charles A. Partridge, *History of the Ninety-sixth Regiment Ill. Vol. Inf.* (Chicago: Brown, Pettibone Co., 1887), 331–34; W. H. Newlin, comp., *A History of the Seventy-third Regiment of Illinois Volunteer Infantry* (Springfield, Ill.: 1890), 293.

49. 38 OR 4:163–64.

50. Ibid., 1:64; 3:91; 4:160–61, 163; Saunier, *Forty-seventh Ohio*, 227; David Power Conyngham, *Sherman's March Through the South* (New York: Sheldon & Co., 1865), 47–49; Smith D. Atkins, "With Sherman's Cavalry," in *The Atlanta Papers*, comp. Sydney C. Kerksis (Dayton: Press of the Morningside Bookshop, 1980), 625.

51. 38 OR 3:615; 4:705–8; Joseph E. Johnston, "Opposing Sherman's Advance to Atlanta," in *Battles and Leaders of the Civil War*, ed. Robert U. Johnson and Clarence C. Buel (New York: Century Co., 1887), 4:265; Connelly, *Autumn of Glory*, 342.

52. 38 OR 1:64, 520–21, 627; 3:91–92, 377; 4:160–62, 168; Oliver Otis Howard to his wife, May 26, 1864, Oliver Otis Howard Letters; James I. Hall, Memoir, 20–21, James I. Hall Papers.

53. 38 OR 3:722, 761, 874–75; Connelly, *Autumn of Glory*, 342.

54. 38 OR 4:160–62, 168–70.

55. John J. Hight, *History of the Fifty-eighth Regiment of Indiana Volunteer Infantry* (Princeton, Ind.: Press of the Clarion, 1895), 290, 293–96.

56. 38 OR 4:184, 187; Stewart, *McCook's Regiment*, 102.

57. Robert Hale Strong, *A Yankee Private's Civil War*, ed. Ashley Halsey, Jr. (Chicago: Henry Regnery Co., 1964), 13–14; Thomas V. Moseley, "Evolution of the American Civil War Infantry Tactics," Ph.D. diss., University of North Carolina, 1967, 354, plate 4. For the tactical problems faced by Civil War commanders and how they sought to solve them, see Albert Castel, "Mars and the Reverend Longstreet: Or, Attacking and Dying in the Civil War," *Civil War History* 33 (1987): 103–14.

58. See Baird's and Judah's attacks in 38 OR 1:734–36; 2:511, 581–82, 610–11; Oliver Lyman Spaulding, Military Memoirs, 39–40; Tracie, *Lights and Shadows*, 304–6; Buck, *Cleburne*, 211. See Cox's attack in 38 OR 2:511, 675–78; Jacob D. Cox, *Military Reminiscences of the Civil War* (New York: Charles E. Scribner, 1900), 1:432–36; 2:189–91, 219–20.

59. Arthur M. Manigault, *A Carolinian Goes to War: The Civil War Narrative of Arthur Middleton Manigault, Brigadier General, C.S.A.*, ed. R. Lockwood Tower (Columbia: University of South Carolina Press, 1983), 181; R. A. Jarman, The History of Company K, 27th Mississippi Infantry, 24; Ephraim A. Wilson, *Memoirs of the War* (Cleveland: W. M. Bayne, 1893), 323; Ed Porter Thompson, *History of the Orphan Brigade* (Louisville: Lewis N. Thompson, 1898), 128–29; W. J. McMurray, *History of the Twentieth Tennessee Regiment Volunteer Infantry, C.S.A.* (Nashville: 1904), 310; Philip L. Secrist, "Resaca: For Sherman a Moment of Truth," *Atlanta Historical Bulletin* 22 (1978): 19–20.

60. 38 OR 3:399–400, 420–24, 435, 447–48, 457, 461; James Compton, "The Second Division of the 16th Army Corps in the Atlanta Campaign," in *The Atlanta Papers*, comp. Sydney C. Kerksis (Dayton: Press of the Morningside Bookshop, 1980), 241–44, 246; W. H. Chamberlin, "The Skirmish Line in the Atlanta Campaign," ibid., 315–16; Hight, *Fifty-eighth Indiana*, 296–97; Conyngham, *Sherman's March*, 104.

61. See Hood's attack and repulse in 38 OR 1:189–90, 220–21, 241, 488–89; 2:27–28, 85–86; 3:615, 812, 816–17; Nichols, *Story of the Great March*, 288 (Williams's appearance); Williams, *Cannon's Mouth*, 308; Partridge, *Ninety-sixth Illinois*, 319–23; James S. Robinson to "Friend Hunt," May 21, 1864, James S. Robinson Letters; Charles E. Benton, *As Seen from the Ranks* (New York: G. P. Putnam's Sons, 1902), 135–38; Samuel Toombs, *Reminiscences of the War* (Orange, N.J.: Journal Office, 1878), 131–32; Howard, *Autobiography*, 1:514–16; Joseph Kimmel, Reminiscences; Read, "Campaign from Chattanooga to Atlanta," 265; J. H. Curry, "A History of Company B, 40th Alabama Infantry, C.S.A., from the Diary of J. H. Curry," *Alabama Historical Quarterly* 17 (1955): 195 (Baker being drunk);

John N. Beach, *History of the Fortieth Ohio Volunteer Infantry* (London, Ohio: Shepherd & Craig Printers, 1884), 68; *New York Weekly Tribune,* June 4, 1864 (Hooker quote).

62. See Logan's attack and Polk's counterattack in 38 OR 3:32, 92–93, 142–43, 190–91, 219–220; 4:185; Thomas B. Mackall Journal, sec. 1:22–25; Saunier, *Forty-seventh Ohio,* 228–30; John T. Buegel, "The Civil War Diary of John T. Buegel, Union Soldier. Part Two," trans. and ed. William G. Bek, *Missouri Historical Review* 40 (1946): 517–18; Secrist, "Resaca," 24–29.

63. 38 OR 4:709–10; Thomas B. Mackall Journal, sec. 1:22–26.

64. Samuel H. Hurst, *Journal-History of the Seventy-third Ohio Volunteer Infantry* (Chillicothe, Ohio: 1866), 117; Lyman S. Widney Diary, May 14, 1864; James I. Hall Memoir, 19–21.

65. 38 OR 4:173, 175, 186, 188–90, 199.

66. James I. Hall Memoir, 21–23.

67. 38 OR 4:705, 712.

68. 38 OR 3:945; *Atlanta Daily Appeal,* May 18, 1864; William E. Sloan Diary, May 15, 1864; W. L. Trask Diary, The Georgia Campaign of 1864, May 15, 1864.

69. 38 OR 4:196–97; Compton, "The Second Division," 245–46.

70. 38 OR 1:190–91, 422; William B. Hazen, *A Narrative of Military Service* (Boston: Ticknor & Co., 1885), 252.

71. See Hooker's assault in 38 OR 2:112–317 passim, 321–24, 340–464 passim; 3:812–13; 4:191, 194; *Atlanta Daily Intelligencer,* May 17, 1864; Robert L. Kilpatrick, "The Fifth Ohio Infantry at Resaca," in *The Atlanta Papers,* comp. Sydney C. Kerksis (Dayton: Press of the Morningside Bookshop, 1980), 355–60; E. B. Fenton, "From the Rapidan to Atlanta," ibid., 224–25; David Nichol to his father, May 17, 1864, David Nichol Diary and Letters; Eli Augustus Griffin Diary, May 15, 16, 1864; Eli S. Richer, From Atlanta to the Sea: The Civil War Letters of Corporal Eli S. Richer, 1862–1865, 83–85; Harvey Reid, *The View from Headquarters: Civil War Letters of Harvey Reid,* ed. Frank L. Byrne (Madison: State Historical Society of Wisconsin, 1965), 145–50; Harry Siever, *Benjamin Harrison: Hoosier Warrior, 1833–1865* (Chicago: Henry Regnery Co., 1952), 237–42; Strong, *Yankee Private's Civil War,* 14–18; Henry G. Noble Diary, May 15, 16, 1864, and Noble to "Dear Ruth" (?), May 21, 1864, Harry G. Noble Diary and Letters; Charles H. Dickinson Diary, May 15, 1864; Secrist, "Resaca," 33–38; Richard M. McMurry, "The Atlanta Campaign: December 23, 1863 to July 18, 1864," Ph.D. diss., Emory University, 1967, 106–7.

72. See Stewart's assault in 38 OR 2:28–29, 40–41, 59–60, 86–87, 511; 3:615, 813, 817–18, 825, 832, 842, 845, 848, 851; Williams, *Cannon's Mouth,* 308–9; James S. Robinson to "Friend Hunt," June 7, July 16, 1864, James S. Robinson Letters; William Wallace, "William Wallace's Civil War Letters: The Atlanta Campaign," *Wisconsin Magazine of History* 57 (1973–74): 96; Edwin E. Bryant, *History of the Third Regiment of Wisconsin Veteran Volunteer Infantry, 1861–1865* (Madison: Democrat Print Co., 1891), 117–21; John Wesley Marshall, Journal, 26, 28–29; Curry, "40th Alabama," 196; Bromfield L. Ridley, *Battles and Sketches of the Army of Tennessee* (Mexico, Mo.: Missouri Printing & Publishing Co., 1906), 295–301; *Atlanta Daily Intelligencer,* May 18, 1864; *Atlanta Daily Appeal,* May 19, 1864; Alpheus Baker to Joseph E. Johnston, July 4, 1874, Johnston Papers, College of William and Mary; Secrist, "Resaca," 32–33. Secrist's article contains much useful information about the battle and battlefield of Resaca, but its analyses are impaired by an extreme pro-Confederate bias.

73. 38 OR 3:401, 422; 4:189, 194, 197, 713; Compton, "Second Division," 245–46.

74. 38 OR 3:704, 813; 4:713, 716; Thomas B. Mackall Journal, sec. 2:3; John Bell Hood, *Advance and Retreat* (New York: Krauss Reprint Co., 1969), 96.

75. 38 OR 2:120, 164–65, 169, 323, 372; Kilpatrick, "Fifth Ohio at Resaca," 361–62; Fenton, "From the Rapidan," 225–26; Charles H. Dickinson Diary, May 15, 1864; Pierson, "Reminiscence," 274. Interestingly, Lieutenant Charles Harding Cox, acting adjutant of the

70th Indiana, states in a letter of June 20, 1864, to his sister that the regiment halted its charge two hundred yards from the "rebel works," which he describes as containing *two* four-gun batteries, and "sought such shelter as trees and the nature of the ground afforded and fought them [the Confederates] behind their breastworks until 9 p.m. before we were relieved" (Charles Harding Cox, "Gone for a Soldier: The Civil War Letters of Charles Harding Cox," ed. Lorna Lutes Sylvester, *Indiana Magazine of History* 68 [1972]: 182–224). Unless Harrison and a large number of others carried out a lifelong successful conspiracy to lie about this matter, one must conclude that Cox was with a portion of the 70th Indiana that did not participate in the charge on the battery, a conclusion supported by his assertion that there were two batteries.

76. Thomas B. Mackall Journal, sec. 2:3–4; Manigault, *Narrative,* 183; Foster, *Diary,* 69–70; Albert Quincy Porter, Civil War Diary, 12.

77. 38 *OR* 3:94; Bennett and Haigh, *36th Illinois,* 584; Levi W. Wagner, Recollections of an Enlistee, 1861–1864, 120–21; *New York Weekly Tribune,* June 4, 1864.

78. William T. Sherman, *The Sherman Letters: Correspondence between General and Senator Sherman from 1837 to 1891,* ed. Rachel Sherman Thorndike (New York: Charles Scribner's Sons, 1894), 236; William T. Sherman, *Home Letters of General Sherman,* ed. M. A. De Wolfe Howe (New York: Charles Scribner's Sons, 1909), 296; William T. Sherman, *Memoirs of Gen. W. T. Sherman,* 4th ed. (Charles L. Webster & Co., 1891), 2:34.

79. Henry Stone, "Part I: Opening of the Campaign," in *The Atlanta Papers,* comp. Sydney C. Kerksis (Dayton: Press of the Morningside Bookshop, 1980), 62–64; Alfred H. Burne, *Lee, Grant and Sherman: A Study in Leadership in the 1864–65 Campaign* (Wellington Works, Aldershot, England: Gale & Polden, 1938), 62–64; and John M. Schofield, *Forty-six Years in the Army* (New York: Century Co., 1897), 125–27, all express criticism of Sherman's performance during the first phase of the Atlanta Campaign similar to that in the text. When it comes to Civil War controversies, originality is next to impossible.

80. Joseph E. Johnston, *Narrative of Military Operations* (New York: D. Appleton & Co., 1874), 315–17.

81. 38 *OR* 3:721 (Cleburne quotation). Wilbur G. Kurtz, in his unpublished paper on the Snake Creek Gap operation (Wilbur G. Kurtz Collection), also holds Johnston responsible for the failure to guard against a Federal move through the gap and states that Johnston has "little or no knowledge" of its existence or of its "strategic implications," a judgment sustained by Richard M. McMurry, "The Opening Phase of the 1864 Campaign in the West," *Atlanta Historical Journal* 27 (1983): 20–22, 24. Making Johnston's ignorance of the danger represented by Snake Creek Gap all the more puzzling is Wilbur F. Foster, a Confederate cartographic officer, in a postwar article entitled "Battle Field Maps in Georgia," *Confederate Veteran* 20 (1912): 369, stating that the Confederates possessed excellent maps of the area between Dalton and Resaca.

82. 38 *OR* 4:201–2, 211, 215–17, 219–20.

83. Benton, *As Seen from the Ranks,* 144–45; Bennett and Haigh, *36th Illinois,* 584; Partridge, *Ninety-sixth Illinois,* 331–32; S. F. Fleharty, *Our Regiment: A History of the 102d Ill. Inf. Vols.* (Chicago: Brewster & Hanscom Printers, 1865), 60–62, 64; Orlando M. Poe to his wife, May 16, 1864.

84. 38 *OR* 2:523–24, 526–38.

85. James F. Overholser, *Three Years with the Union Army: Personal Experiences of a Private Soldier* (n.p., n.d.), 133–35.

86. Lorenzo Barker Diary, May 17–22, 1864; Washington Gardner, "Civil War Letters of Washington Gardner," *Michigan History* 1 (1917): 14.

87. 38 *OR* 1:65, 191; 4:205–6, 210; *New York Weekly Tribune,* June 4, 1864; Orlando M. Poe to his wife, May 16, 1864; Hight, *Fifty-eighth Indiana,* 298–300; Schofield, *Forty-six Years,* 140–41; Cox, *Reminiscences,* 2:225–27.

88. 38 *OR* 3:33, 94, 378–79; 4:213; Compton, "Second Division," 248; Wright, *Corporal's Story,* 102–5.

89. 38 *OR* 1:627–28; 4:197–98, 202–4; Lyman S. Widney Diary, May 16, 1864; Magee, *Seventy-second Indiana*, 297–98.

90. William Henry Stiles to his wife, May 15, 1864, McKay-Stiles Papers; W. L. Trask Diary, May 16, 1864; Albert Quincy Porter Diary, May 16, 1864; 38 *OR* 3:615; Johnston, "Opposing Sherman's Advance," 267.

91. 38 *OR* 4:219.

92. Ibid., 1:191, 857; 4:219–20, 222–24, 227; *New York Weekly Tribune*, June 4, 1864; Beach, *Fortieth Ohio*, 69; Bennett and Haigh, *36th Illinois*, 587–88; Howard, *Autobiography*, 1:521–23.

93. 38 *OR* 3:615, 704; 4:719; Thomas B. Mackall Journal, sec. 2:4–6; Johnston, *Narrative*, 319–20; Johnston, "Opposing Sherman's Advance," 267–68.

94. Gilbert E. Govan and James W. Livingood, *A Different Valor: The Story of General Joseph E. Johnston, C.S.A.* (Indianapolis and New York: Bobbs-Merrill, 1956), 272; William Mackall to his wife, May 21, 1864, William W. Mackall Papers.

95. 38 *OR* 1:628–29; 4:220, 236; Samuel G. French, *Two Wars: An Autobiography* (Nashville: Confederate Veteran, 1901), 193–94; Frank A. Montgomery, *Reminiscences of a Mississippian in Peace and War* (Cincinnati: Robert Clarke Co., 1901), 161–62; Margaret Ketcham Ward, "Testimony of Margaret Ketcham Ward on Civil War Times in Georgia," ed. Aaron M. Boom, *Georgia Historical Quarterly* 39 (1955): 385–86.

96. *New York Weekly Tribune*, June 4, 1864; Partridge, *Ninety-sixth Illinois*, 335.

97. 38 *OR* 4:233, 238–39, 241–43, 245, 247.

98. Ibid., 1:629–30; 4:235–37, 244–45; George F. Drake, *The Mail Goes Through, or The Civil War Letters of George F. Drake*, ed. Julia A. Drake (San Angelo, Tex.: Privately published, 1964), 79; Stewart, *McCook's Regiment*, 103–4; F. M. McAdams, *Every-Day Soldier Life, or a History of the One Hundred and Thirteenth Ohio Volunteer Inf.* (Columbus: Charles M. Gott, Printers, 1884), 80; Levi Ross Diary, 222–23; Leroy S. Mayfield, "A Hoosier Invades the Confederacy: Letters and Diaries of Leroy S. Mayfield," ed. John D. Barnhart, *Indiana Magazine of History* 39 (1943): 184.

99. Columbus Sykes to his wife, June 13, 1864, Columbus Sykes, Letters to Wife. Sykes was a lieutenant colonel in command of the 43rd Mississippi, Adams's Brigade, Loring's Division, Polk's Corps.

100. 38 *OR* 3:634–35; Thomas B. Mackall Journal, sec. 2:7–8. The above description of Johnston's conference with his generals on the evening of May 18 basically follows, as does the entire ensuing account of the Cassville Affair, Hood's version as presented in his official report and memoirs, and it rejects for the most part Johnston's version as given in his report and postwar writings. Hood is not necessarily more reliable than Johnston, but when it comes to what happened at Cassville, Hood's testimony is explicitly and implicitly supported by others, whereas the only backing for Johnston's assertions comes from the "journal" of Lieutenant Mackall as published in the *Official Records*. Richard M. McMurry, in "The Mackall Journal and Its Antecedents," *Civil War History* 20 (1974): 311–28, demonstrates that this document is spurious, having been concocted long after the war at the behest of Johnston for the purpose of discrediting Hood.

101. 38 *OR* 3:634–35, 983–84; 4:728; Thomas B. Mackall Journal, sec. 2:8–10, 15; Hood, *Advance and Retreat*, 99–104; William Mackall, "Memoranda of the operation at Cassville on May 19, 1864," a manuscript dated Sept. 22, 1864, in William Mackall Papers; Johnston, *Narrative*, 322–24; Johnston, "Opposing Sherman's Advance," 268; Taylor Beatty Diary, May 19, 1864; McMurry, *Hood*, 109, 218 n. 40. Connelly, *Autumn of Glory*, 347–48, although criticizing Johnston, judges Hood's version of the affair to be false. When he wrote, however, he did not realize that the Mackall Journal as published was spurious, and evidently he did not have access to Beatty's diary. It is also worth noting that General Mackall in a May 21, 1864, letter to his wife (William Mackall Papers) merely states that "we could not strike" the Federals on May 19, and makes no allegations against Hood.

102. 38 OR 2:751–52, 801; 4:224–25, 241–43, 245, 255–56. Wilbur G. Kurtz in an unpublished paper, "General Joseph E. Johnston's Review of Sherman's Memoirs, published in Drake's Annals of the Army of Tennessee, Nashville, April, 1878" (Wilbur G. Kurtz collection), identifies McCook's and Stoneman's cavalry divisions as the Federal units on Hood's flank and concludes that Johnston lied about what happened on May 19 in order to preserve his own reputation.

103. 38 OR 3:704–5; 4:250; Partridge, *Ninety-sixth Illinois;* John W. Tuttle Diary, May 19, 1864; Sam R. Watkins, *"Co. Aytch": A Sideshow of the Big Show* (New York: Collier Books, 1962), 168–69.

104. 38 OR 3:616, 635; Hood, *Advance and Retreat,* 104–7; French, *Two Wars,* 196–97 and map following page 111; Johnston, "Opposing Sherman's Advance," 268.

105. 38 OR 1:192, 489; 2:437, 468, 680; Cox, *Reminiscences,* 2:230.

106. Albert Quincy Porter Diary, May 19, 1864; William Pitt Chambers, "My Journal," *Publications of the Mississippi Historical Society* 5 (1925): 321; French, *Two Wars,* 196.

107. 38 OR 3:616, 635; 4:723–26; Thomas B. Mackall Journal, sec. 2:11; Hood, *Advance and Retreat,* 105–16; Johnston, "Opposing Sherman's Advance," 268–69; French, *Two Wars,* 196–98; Samuel G. French, "Letter to the Editor of *New Orleans Picayune,* Dec. 12, 1893," *Southern Historical Society Papers* 22 (1894): 1–9; Manigault, *Narrative,* 186–87. Connelly, *Autumn of Glory,* 348–52, casts doubt on Hood's version of events on May 19 but McMurry, *Hood,* 108–9, using sources unavailable to Connelly, concludes that the evidence supports Hood, as does Colonel Burne, *Lee, Grant and Sherman,* 89–90, who states that "I as an artilleryman have no doubt that the centre portion of the position [occupied by Polk's Corps] would have been rendered untenable by the Federal artillery." In his memoirs, *Two Wars,* French states that he felt that he could have held his position. But he does not explain why, except to assert that the Confederate line was not enfiladed, an assertion that is contradicted by the Federal reports and the topography, not to mention the testimony of Captain Morris and a number of other Confederates. Although a West Point-trained artillerist, French had never been in a major battle prior to May 1864 and had not experienced the potency of Northern cannons at Resaca. Also, when he wrote his memoirs, he harbored a strong personal grudge against Hood.

108. 38 OR 3:705; Thomas B. Mackall Journal, sec. 2:11–13; Manigault, *Narrative,* 187.

109. Eli Augustus Griffin Diary, May 20, 1864; Oliver C. Haskell Diary, May 20, 1864; Tracie, *Lights and Shadows,* 313–15; Williams, *Cannon's Mouth,* 310–311.

110. 38 OR 4:267, 271–72, 730–31; Thomas B. Mackall Journal, sec. 2:12–13; W. L. Trask Diary, May 20, 1864; Albert Quincy Porter Diary, May 20, 1864; Jacob D. Cox Diary.

111. Sherman, *Home Letters,* 293.

112. Thomas T. Taylor Diary, May 20, 1864, Thomas T. Taylor Diary and Letters.

113. 38 OR 4:725.

114. Ibid., 736.

115. Govan and Livingood, *A Different Valor,* 277; Mary Boykin Chesnut, *Mary Chesnut's Civil War,* ed. C. Vann Woodward (New Haven, Conn., and London: Yale University Press, 1981), 616; 51 OR 2:952.

116. *Atlanta Daily Intelligencer,* May 18, 19, June 30, 1864; *Atlanta Daily Appeal,* May 18, 19, 1864; *New York Herald,* June 7, 1864, quoting the *Atlanta Southern Confederacy,* May 22, 1864; Robert Manson Myers, ed., *The Children of Pride* (New York: Popular Library, 1972), 1171; J. Cutler Andrews, *The South Reports the Civil War* (Princeton, N.J.: Princeton University Press, 1970), 440; Patrick, *Reluctant Rebel,* 168.

117. Howard, *Autobiography,* 1:535, 539; Sherman, *Home Letters,* 290–93.

118. 38 OR 4:249, 260–61, 265, 269, 274–75, 277–79, 287, 289, 294–95.

119. Ibid., 271–73, 291; Cooke, "Letters," 274.

120. 38 OR 4:272; *New York Times,* June 5, 1864; J. Cutler Andrews, *The North Reports the Civil War* (Pittsburgh: University of Pittsburgh Press, 1955), 558.

121. Strong, *Yankee Private's Civil War*, 24.

122. 38 OR 2:680 (destruction of Etowah Iron Works); Buck, *Cleburne*, 243 (Sweeny's proposal to Cleburne).

123. Howard, *Autobiography*, 1:535–36.

124. Israel Atkins to "Pa and Ma," May 20, 1864, Israel Atkins Letters to Parents; William C. Robinson to "Friend Hunt," May 21, 1864; Wills, *Army Life*, 244.

125. Saunier, *Forty-seventh Ohio*, 286; Andrew J. Neal Letters; Banks, "Letters," 211.

126. 38 OR 4:288–89, 296, 299; Reid, *View from Headquarters*, 152–54; Wills, *Army Life*, 246; Aden G. Cavins, *War Letters of Aden G. Cavins Written to His Wife* (Evansville, Ind.: N.p., n.d.), 75; Newlin, *Seventy-third Illinois*, 300; Oliver Otis Howard to his wife, May 26, 1864, Howard Letters.

127. 38 OR 3:946–47; 4:734, 737–39; Foster, *Diary*, 80; Thomas B. Mackall Journal, sec. 2:15–19.

128. 38 OR 1:65; 2:806; *Cincinnati Daily Commercial*, June 7, 1864; Oliver Lyman Spaulding Memoirs, 42; Wills, *Army Life*, 245; Henry Stone, "Part II: From the Oostenaula to the Chattahoochee," in *The Atlanta Papers*, comp. Sydney C. Kerksis (Dayton: Press of the Morningside Bookshop, 1980), 405–6.

129. 38 OR 3:616, 625, 705, 818, 947–48; 4:303–4, 739, 742; Mackall Journal, sec. 2: 19–21.

130. 38 OR 1:66, 143, 192–93, 861–63; 2:14, 29–30, 122–25; 3:616, 761, 813, 818, 843; 4:312; Stone, "Oostenaula to Chattahoochee," 407–9; Williams, *Cannon's Mouth*, 311–13, 319; Julian W. Hinkley, *A Narrative of Service with the Third Wisconsin Infantry* (Madison: Wisconsin Historical Commission, 1912), 122–24; Reid, *View from Headquarters*, 154–57; David Noble to "Dear Ruth" (?), May 29, 1864; Eli Augustus Griffin Diary, May 25, 1864; John W. Tuttle Diary, May 25, 1864; James H. Kelly Journal, 80–81; Pierson, "Reminiscence," 338–39; Rufus Mead, "With Sherman through Georgia and the Carolinas: Letters of a Federal Soldier. Part One," ed. James A. Padgett, *Georgia Historical Quarterly* 32 (1948): 293; Manigault, *Narrative*, 187–89; Curry, "40th Alabama," 197–98; Albert Quincy Porter Diary, May 25, 1864; John W. DuBose, *General Joseph Wheeler and the Army of Tennessee* (New York: Neale Publishing Co., 1912), 306–7; Ridley, *Army of Tennessee*, 303–5; Wilbur G. Kurtz to Thomas R. Hay, June 23, 1953, Wilbur G. Kurtz Collection; McMurry, "Atlanta Campaign," 152–59.

131. *Atlanta Daily Appeal*, May 27, 1864; *Atlanta Daily Intelligencer*, May 28, 1864; Myers, *Children of Pride*, 1173–75.

132. Jacob D. Cox, *Atlanta* (New York: Charles Scribner's Sons, 1882), 80–83; C. C. Carpenter, "A Commissary in the Union Army: Letters of C. C. Carpenter," ed. Mildred Throne, *Iowa Journal of History* 53 (1955): 84–85.

133. Foster, *Diary*, 81–82.

134. 38 OR 4:323.

135. 38 OR 1:193–95, 377–479 passim, 864–67; 2:523–681 passim; 3:616, 724–26, 948; 4:324–26; Howard, *Autobiography*, 1:550–56; Oliver Otis Howard to his wife, May 29, 1864; Ambrose Bierce, "The Crime at Pickett's Mill," in *The Collected Works of Ambrose Bierce* (New York: Gordian Press, 1966), 279–96; Hazen, *Narrative of Military Service*, 254–59; Alexis Cope, *The Fifteenth Ohio Volunteers and Its Campaigns* (Columbus: Press of the Edward T. Miller Co., 1918), 450–73; Richard W. Johnson, *A Soldier's Reminiscences in Peace and War* (Philadelphia: J. B. Lippincott & Co., 1886), 279; George W. Lewis, *The Campaigns of the 124th Ohio Volunteer Infantry* (Akron: Werner Co., 1894), 148–56; Puntenney, *Thirty-seventh Indiana*, 89–92 (Scribner's condition); Barnes, *Eighty-sixth Indiana*, 304–6; William Huntsinger, *History of the 79th Regt. Indiana Volunteer Infantry* (Indianapolis: 1891), 140–42; McGee, *72nd Indiana*, 302–3 (for McPherson's initial belief that Confederates were not in force on his front); Johnston, "Opposing Sherman's Advance," 279; Buck, *Cleburne*, 218–19; Sebron G. Sneed to his wife, June 7–8, 1864; Mark P.

Lowrey Autobiography, 5-6; William Mackall to his wife, May 28, 1864; Manigault, *Narrative*, 190; William E. Sloan Diary, May 27, 1864; Foster, *Diary*, 82-88; *Atlanta Daily Appeal*, June 21, 1864; *Atlanta Southern Confederacy*, June 29, 1864; McMurry, "Atlanta Campaign," 161-69. Jack Dean, "The Battle of Pickett's Mill," *Blue & Gray Magazine*, April 1989: 4-9, 45-48, presents a detailed account of the battle, reflecting an intimate knowledge of the terrain.

136. 38 OR 4:331.

137. For food and forage shortage in Sherman's army, see ibid., 317, 387; 52 OR 1:697; Reid, *View from Headquarters*, 155; Eli S. Richer Letters, 92; Brobst, *Well Mary*, 66; Magee, *72nd Indiana*, 305-6; Fleharty, *Our Regiment*, 73; Mead, "Letters. Part One," 293; Byron D. Paddock Diary, June 6, 1864; Orson Brainard, "Orson Brainard: A Soldier in the Ranks," ed. Wilfred W. Black, *Ohio History* 76 (1967): 67; Joseph Kimmel Reminiscences (unpaged); Eli Augustus Griffin Diary, June 1, 1864; Huntsinger, *79th Indiana*, 143; Hinman, *Sherman Brigade*, 534; T. F. Dornblasser, *Sabre Strokes of the Pennsylvania Dragoons in the War of 1861-1865* (Philadelphia: Lutheran Publication Society, 1884), 160.

138. 38 OR 4:333-34, 341-42.

139. See Hood's attempted flank attack in ibid., 3:616, 635-36, 706; Johnston, *Narrative*, 333-34; Johnston, "Opposing Sherman's Advance," 270; Hood, *Advance and Retreat*, 120-23; Manigault, *Narrative*, 190; Edmund W. Pettus to Joseph E. Johnston, June 25, 1874, Johnston Papers, College of William and Mary; Thomas B. Mackall Journal, sec. 2:23-24. Both Johnston and Hood misdate this event in their wartime and postwar accounts as occurring on May 29, an error that has misled some historians. The only Federal commander who seems to have had an inkling of Hood's march is McCook, whose cavalry was posted to the north of Howard's position. Thus, at 8:45 A.M. McCook reported to Thomas's headquarters that he was being hard pressed by dismounted Confederate cavalry, and expressed fear that this was the prelude to an infantry assault. However, at 11 A.M. he reported that the enemy had "desisted," and by 6 P.M. he concluded that there never had been a threat! (38 OR 4:335-37).

140. See Bate's attack and repulse in 38 OR 3:95-96, 130-31, 279, 380, 687, 706; Johnston, *Narrative*, 334; William B. Bate, Report on Atlanta Campaign, 6-13; Thompson, *Orphan Brigade*, 254-57; Montgomery, *Reminiscences of a Mississippian*, 170-73; Johnny Green, *Johnny Green of the Orphan Brigade: The Journal of a Confederate Soldier*, ed. A. D. Kirwan (Lexington: University of Kentucky Press, 1956), 132-33; Lot D. Young, *Reminiscences of a Soldier of the Orphan Brigade* (Louisville: Louisville Courier Job Print, 1912), 86-88; Thomas T. Taylor to Wife, May 29, 1864, Taylor Diary and Letters; Wills, *Army Life*, 250-51; Cavins, *Letters*, 81; Buegel, "Diary," 519; Wright, *Corporal's Story*, 107; Brobst, *Well Mary*, 66-68; William C. Davis, *The Orphan Brigade: The Kentucky Confederates Who Couldn't Go Home* (Baton Rouge: Louisiana State University Press, 1980), 221-23; McMurry, "Atlanta Campaign," 171-73. Bate in his unpublished report puts his loss at a little more than three hundred and claims to have inflicted a thousand casualties on the Federals—figures that obviously are preposterous. The *Augusta Daily Chronicle and Sentinel*, June 16, 1864, contains a letter from a correspondent, who signs himself "Kentuckian" and who probably is a member of Lewis's Brigade, declaring that Bate's attack was "one of the most wicked and stupid blunders of the war" and stating that Bate was unfit to command a division. It is difficult to disagree.

141. 38 OR 4:339-40; Brobst, *Well Mary*, 68; Saunier, *Forty-seventh Ohio*, 242.

142. William Mackall to his wife, May 29, 1864, Mackall Papers.

143. 38 OR 3:849; William O. Norrell Diary, May 30, 1864; Albert Quincy Porter Diary, May 28, 1864; Cavins, *Letters*, 82; Newlin, *Seventy-third Illinois*, 301; Daniel Devine Rose to his mother, June 2, 1864, Rose Letters; Fleharty, *Our Regiment*, 70-71; Charles H. Dickinson Diary, 117; David Noble Diary, May 26-29, 1864; Eli Augustus Griffin Diary, May 26-29, 1864; Wills, *Army Life*, 252-53; Partridge, *Ninety-sixth Illinois*, 349-50; Hin-

man, *Sherman Brigade*, 532–33; French, *Two Wars*, 199; Thomas B. Mackall Journal, sec. 2:28.

144. 38 OR 3:221, 706–7; Wright, *Corporal's Story*, 108–9; Wills, *Army Life*, 251–52; Brobst, *Well Mary*, 69; Saunier, *Forty-seventh Ohio*, 242; Thomas B. Mackall Journal, sec. 2:25–26; Foster, *Diary*, 89–90.

145. McGee, *72nd Indiana*, 305–6.

146. 38 OR 3:96–97, 380; 4:343–44, 346–47, 349–50, 352, 357, 362–63, 366–67, 380–82.

147. *New York Times*, June 2, 1864; *Indianapolis Daily Sentinel*, May 13, June 6, 1864.

148. *The American Annual Cyclopedia and Register of Important Events of the Year 1864* (New York: D. Appleton & Co., 1871), 389–90, 393–94, 789; *Cincinnati Daily Commercial*, June 3, 1864; *Indianapolis Daily Sentinel*, June 11, 1864; Louis M. Starr, *Bohemian Brigade: Civil War Newsmen in Action* (New York: Alfred A. Knopf, 1954), 315–20; R. G. Dun, "Letters of R. G. Dun," ed. James D. Norris, *Ohio History* 71 (1962): 147.

CHAPTER SIX: JUNE

1. Phinehas A. Hager Letters.

2. Stephen Pierson, "From Chattanooga to Atlanta in 1864—A Personal Reminiscence," in *The Atlanta Papers*, comp. Sydney C. Kerksis (Dayton: Press of the Morningside Bookshop, 1980), 278; 38 OR 4:379.

3. Thomas B. Mackall Journal, sec. 2:30–31.

4. *Atlanta Daily Appeal*, June 3, 1864; Joseph A. Saunier, ed., *A History of the Forty-seventh Regiment Ohio Veteran Volunteer Infantry* (Hillsboro, Ohio: Lyle Printing Co., 1903) 243.

5. 38 OR 2:512, 681; 4:386–89; Jacob D. Cox Diary, June 1–3, 1864; John M. Schofield, *Forty-six Years in the Army* (New York: Century Co., 1897), 130–31; Jacob D. Cox, *Military Reminiscences of the Civil War* (New York: Charles E. Scribner, 1900), 2:244–47; John M. Schofield, "Notes on Sherman's Memoirs," 7–8, John M. Schofield Papers; Thomas B. Mackall Journal, sec. 2:30–31.

6. Joseph E. Johnston, *Narrative of Military Operations* (New York: D. Appleton & Co., 1874), 334–35; Thomas B. Mackall Journal, sec. 2:32–35; 38 OR 4:752–53, 755–56.

7. Ibid., 400; Shelby Foote, *The Civil War, A Narrative: Red River to Appomattox* (New York: Random House, 1974), 288–99.

8. 38 OR 4:401, 403–4, 407.

9. Samuel T. Foster, *One of Cleburne's Command. The Civil War Reminiscences and Diary of Capt. Samuel T. Foster, Granbury's Texas Brigade, C.S.A.*, ed. Norman D. Brown (Austin, University of Texas Press, 1980), 91; John Davidson and Julia Davidson, "A Wartime Story: The Davidson Letters, 1862–1865," ed. Jane Bonner Peacock, *Atlanta Historical Bulletin* 29 (1975): 90; Walter A. Roher to "Cousin Susan," June 8, 1864, Roher Letters; William Joseph Hardee to his wife, June 5, 1864, Hardee Letters; Edward Young McMorries, *History of the First Regiment, Alabama Volunteer Infantry, C.S.A.* (Montgomery: Brown Printing Co., 1904), 73–74; J. H. Curry, "A History of Company B, 40th Alabama Infantry, C.S.A., from the Diary of J. H. Curry," *Alabama Historical Quarterly* 17 (1955): 200.

10. Charles W. Wills, *Army Life of an Illinois Soldier* (Washington, D.C.: Globe Printing Co., 1906), 254–55; Taylor to his wife, June 7, 1864, Thomas T. Taylor Diary and Letters; Charles H. Dickinson Diary, 170. Union diaries and letters for early June are almost unanimous in expressing belief that the Confederates were on the run and that Atlanta soon would be taken, probably by July 4.

11. 38 OR 4:408–9, 414, 418.

12. Ibid., 418; William T. Sherman, *Home Letters of General Sherman*, ed. M. A. DeWolfe Howe (New York: Charles Scribner's Sons, 1909), 294.

13. Columbus Sykes to his wife, June 6, 1864, Columbus Sykes Letters. On Confederate morale early in June, see also John Offield, Joseph Offield, and William Offield, "Letters from the Offield Brothers, Confederate Soldiers from Upper East Tennessee," ed. Leona Taylor Aiken, *East Tennessee Historical Society Publications* 46 (1974): 127; Urban G. Owen, "Letters of a Confederate Surgeon in the Army of Tennessee to His Wife," ed. Enoch L. Mitchell, *Tennessee Historical Quarterly* 5 (1946): 167; John W. Hagan, "The Confederate Letters of John W. Hagan," ed. Bell I. Wiley, *Georgia Historical Quarterly* 38 (1954): 272–73; William Milner Kelly, "A History of the Thirtieth Alabama Volunteers (Infantry) Confederate States Army," *Alabama Historical Quarterly* 9 (1947): 155; James G. Terry, "Record of the Alabama State Artillery from Its Organization in May, 1861 to the Surrender in April, 1865," *Alabama Historical Quarterly* 20 (1958): 355. Henry Stone of Thomas's staff ("From the Oostenaula to the Chattahoochee," 84, and "The Strategy of the Campaign," 148–49, in *The Atlanta Papers,* comp. Sydney C. Kerksis [Dayton: Press of the Morningside Bookshop, 1980]) and Lieutenant Colonel Alfred H. Burne, a British historian (*Lee, Grant, and Sherman: A Study in Leadership in the 1864–65 Campaign* [Wellington Works, Aldershot, Eng.: Gale & Polden, 1938], 93–95) argue that Sherman should have adhered to his original intention of sweeping around the Confederate left to the Chattahoochee in spite of Johnston's unanticipated stand at New Hope Church. In Burne's words, if Sherman "was able, as he was, to sideslip 15 miles to his left, to the railway, why should it have been impossible for him to sideslip equally to his right, and reach the river?" Stone and Burne, however, credit Sherman with having two weeks' supply of food available when he abandoned the movement to the Chattahoochee, whereas actually, as we have seen, his troops were hungry, and his animals were starving. Also, they overlook the difference between moving toward and moving away from a supply line. B. H. Liddell Hart (*Sherman: Soldier, Realist, American* [New York: Frederick A. Praeger, 1958], 260–61), despite making the same mistake concerning Sherman's supply situation, comes closer to the truth when he states that "it is almost inconceivable that Sherman would have been able to give his opponent the slip and get around his flank in time to reach the Chattahoochee before he was again blocked" and that it is "far more probable that the two [armies] would have remained in a locked embrace" until a shortage of food forced Sherman "to make a precipitate and difficult retreat to his starting point." By backtracking to Acworth, Sherman not only did the prudent thing but also the only realistic thing he could have done under the circumstances.

14. Byron D. Paddock to his brother, June 3, 1864, Byron D. Paddock Diary and Letters; Angus McDermid, "Letters from a Confederate Soldier," ed. Benjamin Rountree, *Georgia Review* 18 (1964): 287–88; Chauncey H. Cooke, "A Badger Boy in Blue: The Letters of Chauncey H. Cooke," *Wisconsin Magazine of History* 4 (1934): 82; William E. Sloan Diary, June 4, 5, 7, 12, 1864; Charles A. Partridge, *History of the Ninety-sixth Regiment Ill. Vol. Inf.* (Chicago: Brown, Pettibone Co., 1887), 352; Thomas B. Hampton to his wife, June 7, 1864, Hampton Correspondence. Sherman puts his total loss by early June at only 9,299 (William T. Sherman, *Memoirs of Gen. W. T. Sherman,* 4th ed. [New York: Charles L. Webster & Co., 1891], 2:47); but the *Official Records* (38 OR 1:115–17, 119) indicate about 12,000. The estimate of Confederate casualties derives from ibid., 3:676–77, 686–87, and from Johnston, *Narrative,* 334–35. It also takes into account, as do all calculations of Confederate losses in this book, the Confederate practice of not counting as casualties men so lightly wounded that they still are capable of duty.

15. 38 OR 4:405–6.

16. Orlando M. Poe Letters; Ira Van Deusen, "Ira Van Deusen: A Federal Volunteer in North Alabama," ed. Ron Bennett, *Alabama Historical Quarterly* 5 (1943): 207. Confirming Poe's and Van Deusen's descriptions, General Geary writes in a June 8 letter to his wife: "As we pass through the country, we leave it as though all the locusts of Egypt had been upon it" (John W. Geary Letters).

17. Joseph Kimmel Reminiscences (no pagination); Partridge, *Ninety-sixth Illinois,* 352.

18. 38 OR 4:751–52, 754–55; Sidney Champion to his wife, June 9, 1864, Sidney Champion Letters; Columbus Sykes to his wife, June 10, 1864, Sykes Letters. For additional accounts of plundering by Confederate soldiers, see W. L. Trask Diary, May 31, 1864, and Celathiel Helms to his wife, May 26, June 6, 1864, Celathiel Helms Letters.

19. 38 OR 4:408.

20. Ibid., 433; Manning Force to Mrs. Kilber, June 8, 1864, Manning F. Force Papers; John D. Travis to "Dear Brother and Sister," June 7, 1864, John D. Travis Letters; Alonzo Miller to his sister, May 27, 1864, Alonzo Miller Letters; John J. Hight, *History of the Fifty-eighth Regiment of Indiana Volunteer Infantry* (Princeton, Ind.: Press of the Clarion, 1895), 317.

21. David Power Conyngham, *Sherman's March Through the South* (New York: Sheldon & Co., 1865), 106; George W. Nichols, *The Story of the Great March from the Diary of a Staff Officer* (New York: Harper & Brothers, 1865), 97–98; Franc B. Wilkie, *Pen and Powder* (Boston: Ticknor & Co., 1888), 242–43; Manning Force to Mrs. Kilber, May 28, 1864, Force Papers.

22. 38 OR 2:522, 540–41; 4:438–39, 443–44, 448.

23. Ibid., 388, 399, 401, 408, 428; OR, ser. 3, vol. 5:984, 1002; Fenwick Y. Hedley, *Marching through Georgia* (Chicago: R. R. Donnelley & Sons, 1887), 73–74; Hight, *Fifty-eighth Indiana*, 316.

24. 38 OR 4:445; Sherman, *Home Letters*, 294.

25. 39 OR 3:616–17; Thomas B. Mackall Journal, sec. 3:23; Walter A. Roher to Susan, June 9, 1864, Roher Letters.

26. 38 OR 4:762 (Bragg's letter); Thomas B. Mackall Journal, sec. 3:6; Richard Manning Letters.

27. *New York Times*, June 9, 1864; *New York Daily Tribune*, June 9, 1864; *New York World*, June 9, 1864; *Richmond Daily Examiner*, June 13, 1864; *Atlanta Daily Intelligencer*, June 14, 1864.

28. 38 OR 1:67, 148; 2:512; 3:35; 4:445, 448–52; Benjamin F. McGee, *History of the 72nd Indiana Volunteer Infantry of the Mounted Lightning Brigade* (Lafayette, Ind.: S. Vater & Co., 1882), 308–11; Hight, *Fifty-eighth Indiana*, 325–26; William B. Hazen, *A Narrative of Military Service* (Boston: Ticknor & Co., 1885), 262; Orlando M. Poe to his wife, June 12, 1864, Poe Letters; Charles Wright, *A Corporal's Story* (Philadelphia: James Beal, 1887), 109–110; William R. Plum, *The Military Telegraph during the Civil War in the United States* (Chicago: Jansen, McClurg & Co., 1955), 2:179; Wills, *Army Life*, 257.

29. *Atlanta Daily Appeal*, June 2, 9, 14, 16, 1864; *Atlanta Daily Intelligencer*, June 1, 10, 1864; *Atlanta Southern Confederacy*, June 18, 1864; Samuel P. Richards Diary, June 10, 1864; Robert Manson Myers, ed., *The Children of Pride* (New York: Popular Library, 1972), 1176, 1181–82; Mrs. Richard B. Jett to "Dear Husband," June 12, 1864, Richard B. Jett Correspondence; Robert Gibbons, "Life at the Crossroads of the Confederacy: Atlanta, 1861–1865," *Atlanta Historical Bulletin* 23 (1979): 43–44.

30. 38 OR 4:758; *Atlanta Daily Intelligencer*, June 4, 1864; William James Dickey to "My Dear Anna," May 27, May 29, June 9, 1864, and to "Dear Shack," May 29, 1864, William James Dickey Letters. Robert W. Banks, an Alabama soldier, also describes "Joe Brown's Pets" as being "the finest-looking men I ever saw" (Robert W. Banks, "Civil War Letters of Robert W. Banks: Atlanta Campaign," ed. George C. Osborn, *Georgia Historical Quarterly* 27 [1943]: 213).

31. 38 OR 2:807; 3:707; 4:454–55; Alpheus S. Williams, *From the Cannon's Mouth: The Civil War Letters of General Alpheus S. Williams*, ed. Milo M. Quaife (Detroit: Wayne State University Press, 1959), 320; Hazen, *Narrative of Military Experience*, 262; Samuel Merrill, *The Seventieth Indiana Volunteer Infantry* (Indianapolis: Bowen-Merrill Co., 1900), 127; Thomas L. Thoburn Diary, June 14, 1864 (eating of sheep sorrel); Thomas T. Taylor Letters, June 12, 1864; Sherman, *Memoirs*, 2:51.

32. 38 OR 4:767, 769; Thomas B. Mackall Journal, sec. 3:7; William Joseph Hardee to his wife, June 12, 1864, Hardee Letters.

33. 38 OR 4:772, 774; Thomas B. Mackall Journal, sec. 3:8–9.

34. 38 OR 4:466; Albert Quincy Porter Diary, June 13, 17, 1864.

35. Sherman, *Memoirs*, 2:52–53; Oliver Otis Howard, *Autobiography of Oliver Otis Howard* (New York: Baker & Taylor Co., 1907), 1:563–64; Johnston, *Narrative*, 337; Irving A. Buck, ed., *Cleburne and His Command* (Jackson, Tenn.: McCowat-Mercer Press, 1959), 222–24; *Atlanta Daily Appeal*, June 16, 29, 1864; *Atlanta Southern Confederacy*, June 16, 1864; Arthur H. Noll, ed., *Doctor Quintard, Chaplain C.S.A.* (Sewanee, Tenn.: University of the South, 1905), 97–98.

36. 38 OR 4:474.

37. Ibid., 3:708; 4:775–78; Ed Porter Thompson, *History of the Orphan Brigade* (Louisville: Lewis N. Thompson, 1898), 259; Johnny Green, *Johnny Green of the Orphan Brigade: The Journal of a Confederate Soldier*, ed. A. D. Kirwan (Lexington: University of Kentucky Press, 1956), 136.

38. Foote, *Red River to Appomattox*, 312–16.

39. Frank L. Klement, *Dark Lanterns: Secret Political Societies, Conspiracies, and Treason Trials in the Civil War* (Baton Rouge: Louisiana State University Press, 1984), 111–12; James L. Vallandigham, *A Life of Clement L. Vallandigham* (Baltimore: 1872), 351–53.

40. Conyngham, *Sherman's March*, 112; Ira B. Read, "The Campaign from Chattanooga to Atlanta as Seen by a Federal Soldier," ed. Richard B. Harwell, *Georgia Historical Quarterly* 25 (1941): 268.

41. 38 OR 1:149, 196; 2:513; 4:480–84, 486–88; Pierson, "Reminiscence," 280–82; Harry Sievers, *Benjamin Harrison: Hoosier Warrior, 1833–1865* (Chicago: Henry Regnery Co., 1952), 255–56; William M. Anderson, *They Died to Make Men Free: A History of the 19th Michigan Infantry in the Civil War* (Berrien Springs, Mich.: Hardscrabble Books, 1980), 211–13; Foster, *Diary*, 95–96; McDermid, "Letters," 289; "Letters from Soldiers," *Cincinnati Daily Commercial*, June 28, 1864.

42. 38 OR 3:97–98, 279, 317; 4:481, 488–89; Wills, *Army Life*, 261–62; Henry Orendorff, *We Are Sherman's Men: The Civil War Letters of Henry Orendorff*, ed. William M. Anderson (Macomb: Western Illinois University, 1986), 91–92; Aden G. Cavins, *War Letters of Aden G. Cavins Written to His Wife* (Evansville, Ind.: N.p., n.d.), 84; Curry, "40th Alabama," 201–3; Elbert D. Willett, *History of Company B (Originally Pickens' Planters)* (Anniston, Ala.: Nerwood, 1902), 68–69; *Atlanta Daily Appeal*, June 17, 20, 1864; Alpheus Baker to Joseph E. Johnston, July 4, 1874, Johnston Papers, College of William and Mary.

43. 38 OR 1:149, 197; 2:475, 480, 513, 682; 4:481, 492–96, 499; John N. Beach, *History of the Fortieth Ohio Volunteer Infantry* (London, Ohio: Shepherd & Craig Printers, 1884), 74 (Simonson's death); Eli S. Richer Letters, 99–100; Johnston, *Narrative*, 338; Buck, *Cleburne*, 224; William Mackall to his wife, June 18, 1864, Mackall Letters; "Letters from Soldiers," *Cincinnati Daily Commercial*, June 28, 1864.

44. 38 OR 1:149, 197, 879–80; 2:513; 4:499–501, 503, 507–8; Hazen, *Narrative of Military Experience*, 263.

45. Thomas B. Mackall Journal, sec. 3:12–14; 38 OR 3:617; Johnston, *Narrative*, 337–38.

46. 38 OR 4:507–8.

47. Samuel G. French, *Two Wars: An Autobiography* (Nashville: Confederate Veteran, 1901), 203; Wilbur G. Kurtz, "Kennesaw: The Mountain and the Battlefield," Kurtz Collection.

48. 38 OR 4:519.

49. William Pitt Chambers, "My Journal," *Publications of the Mississippi Historical Society* 5 (1925): 325–26; French, *Two Wars*, 203; Larry J. Daniel, *Cannoneers in Gray: The Field Artillery of the Army of Tennessee, 1861–1865* (University: University of Alabama Press, 1984), 151.

50. Wills, *Army Life*, 264; 38 OR 1:197–98; 2:682; 4:519.

51. Foote, *Red River to Appomattox*, 427–46.

52. 38 OR 1:243–45, 247, 883–84; 4:544–46; Dennis Kelly, "Mountains to Pass, A River to Cross: The Battle of Kennesaw Mountain and Related Actions from June 10 to July 9, 1864," *Blue & Gray Magazine*, June 1989: 22. On Whitaker, see Albert R. Greene, *From Bridgeport to Ringgold by Way of Lookout Mountain* (Providence, R.I.: 1870), 37–38. Heavy drinking by Kentuckians seems to have been common; see John W. Tuttle Diary, June 15, 20, 1864.

53. 38 OR 4:551–52, 783–84; Thomas B. Mackall Journal, sec. 3:15–16; Curry, "40th Alabama," 203.

54. Byron D. Paddock Diary, June 22, 1864; Albert Quincy Porter Diary, June 20, 21, 1864.

55. 38 OR 4:557–58, 566.

56. *Cincinnati Daily Gazette*, June 13, 1864 (casualties of XX Corps); 38 OR 4:537–38; Robinson to "Friend Hunt," June 3, 7, 8, 24, 1864, James S. Robinson Letters; William F. G. Shanks, *Personal Recollections of Distinguished Generals* (New York: Harper & Brothers, 1866), 185; Williams, *Cannon's Mouth*, 334–35; *New York Times*, July 11, 1864; Butterfield to Hooker, June 12, 1864, in Julia L. Butterfield, ed., *A Biographical Memorial of General Daniel Butterfield* (New York: Grafton Press, 1903), 146–48.

57. See Battle of Kolb's Farm in 38 OR 1:151; 2:14–15, 31–318 passim, 513–14, 569, 655, 683; 3:617, 760, 762, 814–15; 4:558–65; Schofield, *Forty-six Years*, 132–33; Cox, *Reminiscences*, 2:258; Williams, *Cannon's Mouth*, 327–29, 333–34; Robinson to "Friend Hunt," June 24, 1864, Robinson Letters; Charles H. Dickinson Diary, 119–20; Byron D. Paddock Diary, June 22, 1864; Rufus Mead, "With Sherman through Georgia and the Carolinas: Letters of a Federal Soldier. Part One," ed. James A. Padgett, *Georgia Historical Quarterly* 32 (1948): 296–97; Eli S. Richer Letters, 102; Edwin E. Bryant, *History of the Third Regiment of Wisconsin Veteran Volunteer Infantry, 1861–1865* (Madison: Democrat Print Co., 1891), 247–48; Thomas L. Thoburn Diary, June 22, 1864; Harvey Reid, *The View from Headquarters: Civil War Letters of Harvey Reid*, ed. Frank L. Byrne (Madison: State Historical Society of Wisconsin, 1965), 163–64; Samuel Toombs, *Reminiscences of the War* (Orange, N.J.: Journal Office, 1878), 140–41; Charles Laforest Dunham, *Through the South with a Union Soldier*, ed. Arthur H. DeRosier (Johnson City: Publications of the East Tennessee State University Research Advisory Committee, 1969), 126; Theodore C. Tracie, *Annals of the Nineteenth Ohio Battery; or Lights and Shadows of Army Life* (Cleveland: J. B. Savage, 1878), 335–43; Arthur M. Manigault, *A Carolinian Goes to War: The Civil War Narrative of Arthur Middleton Manigault, Brigadier General, C.S.A.*, ed. R. Lockwood Tower (Columbia: University of South Carolina Press, 1983), 192–94; French, *Two Wars*, 205; Thomas B. Hampton to his wife, June 26, 1864, Hampton Correspondence; Bell I. Wiley, "A Story of Three Southern Officers [with Abstracts from the Letters of Lieutenant Robert M. Gill]," *Civil War Times Illustrated*, April 1964: 32; Thomas Jefferson Newberry, "The Civil War Letters of Thomas Jefferson Newberry," ed. Enoch C. Mitchell, *Journal of Mississippi History* 10 (1948): 77; Terry, "Alabama State Artillery," 336; James P. Douglas, *Douglas's Texas Battery C.S.A.*, ed. Lucia Rutherford Douglas (Tyler, Tex.: Smith County Historical Society, 1966), 102; Kelly, "30th Alabama," 155–56; Thomas B. Mackall Journal, sec. 3:16; *Atlanta Daily Intelligencer*, June 30, 1864; Conyngham, *Sherman's March*, 129–31; Richard M. McMurry, "The Affair at Kolb's Farm," *Civil War Times Illustrated*, December 1968: 20–27; Richard M. McMurry, *John Bell Hood and the War for Southern Independence* (Lexington: University of Kentucky Press, 1982), 112–13.

58. 38 OR 4:558–61, 566, 569.

59. Sherman, *Memoirs*, 2:57–59.

60. 38 OR 2:326; 4:560–64, 574 (on Butterfield's division).

61. Schofield, *Forty-six Years*, 133–36, 38 OR 4:562–63.

62. Ibid., 573.

63. Sherman, *Memoirs*, 2:57–58.

64. For evidence of presence of elements of Hardee's and Loring's corps on Hooker's front see 38 OR 2:133, 326; 4:561, 785–87; Thomas B. Mackall Journal, sec. 3:16. Sherman himself in his report (38 OR 1:68) states that at Kolb's Farm Hooker was attacked by "Hood's corps with detachments from the others [Hardee's and Loring's]." As early as 1893 Henry Stone of Thomas's staff exposed Sherman's slanders of Hooker with regard to Kolb's Farm in his paper "Part II: From the Oostenaula to the Chattahoochee," in *The Atlanta Papers,* comp. Sydney C. Kerksis (Dayton: Press of the Morningside Bookshop, 1980), 90. For Robinson's praise of Hooker, see Robinson to "Friend Hunt," June 24, 1864, James S. Robinson Letters. Williams, *Cannon's Mouth,* 327, 333, also indicates a belief that the XX Corps faced more than just Hood's Corps, and in a July 17 letter to a Detroit friend he, too, praises Hooker highly as a corps commander (334–35). Hooker's failure to file a report on the Atlanta Campaign or to write a memoir is a great handicap to the historian. Although any account by him would no doubt contain many lies, it could also present some revealing truths.

65. 38 OR 4:572–73, 575–76, 580–81; Sherman, *Memoirs,* 2:66; Philip Sidney Post to his mother, June 24, 1864, Philip Sidney Post Correspondence and Diary.

66. See Blair's report in 38 OR 3:552; 4:585–86. See also 4:565 for reports of McPherson and Logan.

67. 38 OR 4:582.

68. 38 OR 4:784, 787; Francis A. Shoup, "Dalton Campaign—Works at Chattahoochee River," *Confederate Veteran* 3 (1895): 262–63; William Joseph Hardee to his wife, June 19, 20, 21, 1864, Hardee Letters; William Joseph Hardee to Jefferson Davis, June 22, 1864, Jefferson Davis Papers.

69. Gilbert E. Govan and James W. Livingood, *A Different Valor: The Story of General Joseph E. Johnston, C.S.A.* (Indianapolis and New York: Bobbs-Merrill, 1956), 296–98; Thomas B. Mackall Journal, sec. 3:18; William Joseph Hardee to his wife, June 25, 1864, Hardee Letters; 39 OR 2:657–58 (for Lee's telegraph to Davis and Davis's memorandum). The only account of the meeting between Johnston and Wigfall is an undated memorandum written after the war by Wigfall and sent to Johnston for his use in an on-going controversy with Davis (Govan and Livingood, *A Different Valor,* 430 n. 18). Given its origin and purpose, the reliability of this document would be highly suspect, but since most of what Wigfall states that Johnston told him parallels what Johnston subsequently wrote to Bragg (see 38 OR 4:795–96), it is probably accurate on the whole. It also seems reasonable, and hence likely, that Johnston would have shown Wigfall the communications from S. D. Lee and Davis that had been sent him by Bragg.

70. 38 OR 4:588, 590; Howard, *Autobiography,* 1:582.

71. Henry Stone, "Part IV: Strategy of the Campaign," in *The Atlanta Papers,* comp. Sydney C. Kerksis (Dayton: Press of the Morningside Bookshop, 1980), 150; Thomas B. Van Horne, *The Life of Major General George H. Thomas* (Charles Scribner's Sons, 1882), 233–34; Mrs. John A. Logan, *Reminiscences of a Soldier's Wife: An Autobiography* (New York: Charles Scribner's Sons, 1913), 155–56; Edward R. Hutchins, comp., *The War of the Sixties* (New York: Neale Publishing Co., 1912), 140; Schofield, *Forty-six Years,* 144. Sherman, *Memoirs,* 2:60, asserts that Thomas, McPherson, and Schofield "all agreed" that "there was no alternative but to attack 'fortified lines,' a thing carefully avoided up to that time" [note the quotation marks around fortified lines, an obvious attempt to imply that the Confederates were not strongly fortified]. When Sherman published this statement, Thomas and McPherson were dead and Schofield was in no position to challenge it in public, for Sherman was then-commanding general of the U.S. Army and could block Schofield's rise to the same post—something he eventually achieved. In his memoirs, published after Sherman's death, Schofield explicitly repudiates Sherman's assertion.

72. 38 OR 4:589, 591–92; Schofield, *Forty-six Years,* 144.

73. 38 OR 1:151; 3:36, 98–99; 4:590, 602–3, 605–6; Stone, "Strategy of the Campaign," 150.

74. 38 OR 4:596–600, 604; Cox, *Reminiscences,* 2:263–65.

75. French, *Two Wars,* 206; Orlando M. Poe to his wife, June 25, 1864, Poe Letters; Sherman, *Home Letters,* 298; William Joseph Hardee to his wife, June 26, 1864, Hardee Letters; Nixon B. Stewart, *Dan McCook's Regiment. 52nd O.V.I. A History of the Regiment, Its Campaigns and Battles* (Alliance, Ohio: Review Print, 1900), 113.

76. 38 OR 1:632; 3:99; Logan to Wife, June 26, 1864, John A. Logan Letters; Howard, *Autobiography,* 1:582–83; Atlanta Campaign Diary, 20 (this diary shows internal evidence of having been kept by a staff officer of the IV Corps); J. R. Kinnear, *History of the Eighty-sixth Regiment Illinois Vol. Inf.* (Chicago: Tribune Co., 1866), 56; Cavins, *Letters,* 85; Wright, *Sixth Iowa,* 288–89; George H. Puntenney, *History of the Thirty-seventh Regiment of Indiana Infantry Volunteers* (Rushville, Ind.: Jacksonian Book & Job Department, 1896), 103; Wills, *Army Life,* 268; James Taylor Holmes, *Fifty-second Ohio Volunteer Infantry: Then and Now* (Columbus: Berlin Printing Co., 1898), 1:176–77, 182; Thomas V. Mosely, "Evolution of the American Civil War Infantry Tactics," Ph.D. diss., University of North Carolina, 1967, 354, 361.

77. See Battle of Kennesaw Mountain and Logan's assault in 38 OR 3:98–99, 178–79, 187–88, 193–95, 216, 221–22, 317–18; Theodore F. Upson, *With Sherman to the Sea: The Civil War Letters, Diaries and Reminiscences of Theodore F. Upson,* ed. Oscar G. Winther (Bloomington: University of Indiana Press, 1958), 115–16; Wills, *Army Life,* 268–71; Wright, *Sixth Iowa,* 288–93; Saunier, *Fortieth Ohio,* 259–60; Thomas T. Taylor Diary, June 27, 1864; Thaddeus H. Capron, "War Diary of Thaddeus H. Capron, 1861–1865," *Journal of the Illinois Historical Society* 12 (1919): 383–84; Cavins, *Letters,* 86–87.

See Davis's assault in 38 OR 1:632–33, 638–39; 648, 680, 685–86, 697–98, 703–5, 710–11, 724, 731; Holmes, *Then and Now,* 176–88; Kinnear, *Eighty-sixth Illinois,* 56–58; Leroy S. Mayfield, "A Hoosier Invades the Confederacy: Letters and Diaries of Leroy S. Mayfield," ed. John D. Barnhart, *Indiana Magazine of History* 39 (1943): 190; Allen L. Fahnestock Diary, June 27, 1864; F. M. McAdams, *Every-Day Soldier Life, or a History of the One Hundred and Thirteenth Ohio Volunteer Inf.* (Columbus: Charles M. Gott, Printers, 1884), 87–89; F. B. James, "McCook's Brigade at the Assault upon Kennesaw Mountain, Georgia, June 27, 1864," in *The Atlanta Papers,* comp. Sydney C. Kerksis (Dayton: Press of the Morningside Bookshop, 1980), 255–70.

See Newton's assault in 38 OR 1:199, 295–96, 304, 314, 319–20, 335–36, 355, 359, 370–71, 887–88; W. H. Newlin, comp., *A History of the Seventy-third Regiment of Illinois Volunteer Infantry* (Springfield, Ill.: 1890), 311–13; L. G. Bennett and Wm. M. Haigh, *History of the 36th Illinois Volunteers* (Aurora, Ill.: Knickerbocker & Hodder Printers, 1876), 608–11; Read, "Chattanooga to Atlanta," 270; John Wesley Marshall Journal, June 27, 1864; Partridge, *Ninety-sixth Illinois,* 370; Benjamin T. Smith Recollections, 151–59; William Sumner Dodge, *A Waif of the War; or, The History of the Seventy-fifth Illinois Infantry* (Chicago: Church & Goodman, 1866), 156; George W. Lewis, *The Campaigns of the 124th Ohio Volunteer Infantry* (Akron: Werner Co., 1894), 158–60; Philip Sidney Post to his mother, June 28, 1864, Sidney Correspondence; Orson Brainard, "Orson Brainard: A Soldier in the Ranks," ed. Wilfred W. Black, *Ohio History* 76 (1967): 72.

See Confederate defense in 38 OR 3:900–901, 913–15; Johnston, *Narrative,* 341–44; French, *Two Wars,* 206–11; James I. Hall Memoir, 27–29; Sam R. Watkins, "Co. Aytch": A Sideshow of the Big Show (New York: Collier Books, 1962), 156–61; James Cooper Nisbet, *Four Years on the Firing Line,* ed. Bell I. Wiley (Jackson, Tenn.: McCowat-Mercer Press, 1963), 198–99; Foster, *Diary,* 97–98; Robert Davis Smith Diary, June 27, 1864; John W. Tuttle Diary, June 27, 1864; W. D. Pickett, "The Dead Angle," *Confederate Veteran* 14 (1906): 458–59; George W. Hargis, "Dead Angle—Georgia Campaign," *Confederate Veteran* 11(1903):

560; T. G. Dabney, "Campaigning in North Georgia," *Confederate Veteran* 14 (1906): 75–76; H. K. Nelson, "Dead Angle, or Devil's Elbow, Ga.," *Confederate Veteran* 11 (1903): 321; T. H. Maney, "Battle of Dead Angle on Kennesaw Line," *Confederate Veteran* 11 (1903): 159; *Atlanta Southern Confederacy*, June 29, 1864; *Atlanta Daily Intelligencer*, June 30, 1864; Buck, *Cleburne*, 224–25; Daniel, *Cannoneers in Gray*, 152–54.

See general accounts in *New York World*, July 8, 1864; *Chicago Daily Tribune*, July 3, 1864; Conyngham, *Sherman's March*, 135–36; Richard M. McMurry, "The Atlanta Campaign: December 23, 1863 to July 18, 1864," Ph.D. diss., Emory University, 1967, 213–21; Richard M. McMurry, "Kennesaw Mountain," *Civil War Times Illustrated*, January 1970: 25, 28–30; Kelly, "Mountains to Pass," 25–30, 46–51.

78. 38 OR 4:609–10.

79. Ibid., 2:514, 682; 4:607, 616–21; Cox, *Reminiscences*, 2:265–68.

80. 38 OR 4:607.

81. George F. Drake, *The Mail Goes Through, or The Civil War Letters of George F. Drake*, ed. Julia A. Drake (San Angelo, Tex.: Privately published, 1964), 89; 38 OR 1:69, 205, 637, 711, 721, 724, 726, 731; 3:99; Holmes, *Then and Now*, 189; *Atlanta Daily Appeal*, July 3, 1864; James I. Hall Memoirs, 29; Daniel, *Cannoneers in Gray*, 154; Cavins, *Letters*, 86. A Union surgeon estimated in a letter to his wife on June 25 that the Federal casualties in the assault per se came to 2,000 (Claiborne J. Walton, "'One Continued Scene of Carnage': A Union Surgeon's View of the War," *Civil War Times Illustrated*, August 1976: 35–36).

82. Johnston, *Narrative*, 343; *Atlanta Daily Appeal*, July 3, 1864 (list of casualties for 1st and 27th Tennessee); James I. Hall to his children, July 8, 1864, James I. Hall Papers; McMurry, "Atlanta Campaign," 226. McMurry, "Kennesaw Mountain," 32, estimates the total Confederate loss at 750 but includes probable casualties in Hood's Corps, which did not participate in the repulse of the assault as such, and in Wheeler's cavalry, which did little if any fighting on June 27.

83. 38 OR 1:69; 5:91; Sherman, *Home Letters*, 301; Manning F. Force to Mrs. Kilber, July 6, 1864; Force Papers. Captain Poe, most likely reflecting Sherman's opinion, wrote his wife on June 28 that the battle was "a very feeble attempt to carry the rebel entrenchments by assault" (Poe Letters).

84. David S. Stanley, *Personal Memoirs of Major General D. S. Stanley, U.S.A.* (Cambridge, Mass.: Harvard University Press, 1917), 174. Although Stanley passionately disliked Sherman and was afflicted with a faulty memory when he wrote his memoirs, there is little reason to doubt the essential accuracy of the statement he here attributes to Newton, for it is both likely and justified under the circumstances. As Sergeant Puntenney comments (*Thirty-seventh Indiana*, 103), "Every private in that great army knew that that assault would prove a disastrous failure." Liddell Hart's attempt to justify the assault as a psychological use of the "indirect approach," his professed secret for military success, is laughable (B. H. Liddell Hart, *Sherman: Soldier Realist, American* [New York: Frederick A. Praeger, 1958], 264).

85. 38 OR 4:795–97, 800–801; Johnston, *Narrative*, 344; Govan and Livingood, *A Different Valor*, 295.

86. 38 OR 4:517, 531–32, 546, 557, 579–81, 631; 52 OR 1:697.

87. 38 OR 4:629.

88. Ibid., 1:181, 304; Wesley T. Leeper, *Rebels Valiant: Second Arkansas Mounted Rifles (Dismounted)* (Little Rock, Ark.: Pioneer Press, 1964), 233–34; Upson, *With Sherman to the Sea*, 117; Wilbur F. Hinman, *The Story of the Sherman Brigade* (Alliance, Ohio: Press of the Daily Review), 551–52; Robert L. Bliss to his mother, June 29, 1864, Bliss Letters; Partridge, *Ninety-sixth Illinois*, 371; McAdams, *Every-Day Soldier Life*, 92; Read, "Chattanooga to Atlanta," 270–71; Levi Ross Diary, June 29, 1864; Lyman S. Widney Diary, June 30, 1864; John W. Tuttle Diary, June 28, 29, 1864; *Atlanta Daily Appeal*, July 1, 1864; "From Sherman's Army," *Cincinnati Daily Commercial*, July 11, 1864; Conyngham, *Sherman's March*, 136; Daniel, *Cannoneers in Gray*, 154.

89. Oliver Otis Howard to his wife, June 30, 1864, Howard Letters; James I. Hall Memoirs, 29–31; Maney, "Dead Angle," 159–60; Allen L. Fahnestock Diary, June 29, 1864; Kinnear, *Eighty-sixth Illinois,* 59; Holmes, *Then and Now,* 183, 186–91; Stewart, *McCook's Regiment,* 127; James Nourse to his father, July 8, 1864, James Nourse Diary and Letters.

90. 38 OR 4:631, 639, 643–47, 649–50; 52 OR 1:697.

91. 38 OR 4:649; Sherman, *Home Letters,* 299.

92. Atlanta Campaign Diary, June 30, 1864.

CHAPTER SEVEN: JULY

1. Robert Manson Myers, ed., *The Children of Pride* (New York: Popular Library, 1972), 1188.

2. 38 OR 2:570–71, 683; 3:7–11.

3. 52 OR 2:704–6; Jefferson Davis, *The Rise and Fall of the Confederate Government* (New York: D. Appleton & Co., 1881), 2:557–61. Hill is the sole source for this conversation with Johnston and Hood. Johnston, "Opposing Sherman's Advance to Atlanta," in *Battles and Leaders of the Civil War,* ed. Robert U. Johnson and Clarence C. Buel (New York: Century Co., 1887), 277, asserts that "no such conversation" occurred and that "no soldier above idiocy could express the opinions" Hill ascribes to him. The opinions ascribed by Hill to Johnston are precisely those opinions Johnston expressed during his meeting with Wigfall and which he reiterated in telegrams to Bragg.

4. 38 OR 2:514–15; 5:3, 14–25, 860; James Taylor Holmes, *Fifty-second Ohio Volunteer Infantry: Then and Now* (Columbus: Berlin Printing Co., 1898), 187; Nixon B. Stewart, *Dan McCook's Regiment. 52nd O.V.I. A History of the Regiment; Its Campaigns and Battles* (Alliance, Ohio: Review Print, 1900), 129; Allen L. Fahnestock Diary, July 2, 3, 1864; Aden G. Cavins, *War Letters of Aden G. Cavins Written to His Wife* (Evansville, Ind.: N.p., n.d.), 87–88; Daniel Devine Rose to his mother, July 6, 1864, Rose Letters.

5. W. L. Trask Diary, July 2, 1864; Samuel G. French, *Two Wars: An Autobiography* (Nashville: Confederate Veteran, 1901), 214–15; *Atlanta Daily Intelligencer,* Aug. 3, 1864; Arthur M. Manigault, *A Carolinian Goes to War: The Civil War Narrative of Arthur Middleton Manigault, Brigadier General, C.S.A.,* ed. R. Lockwood Tower (Columbia: University of South Carolina Press, 1983), 194; 38 OR 5:29–30, 33–34.

6. John D. Boardman to his father, July 5, 1864, John D. Boardman Letters; Chesley A. Mosman, *The Rough Side of War: The Civil War Journal of Chesley A. Mosman, 1st Lieutenant, Company D, 59th Illinois Volunteer Infantry Regiment,* ed. Arnold Gates (Garden City, N.Y.: Basin Publishing Co., 1987), 233; Charles W. Wills, *Army Life of an Illinois Soldier* (Washington, D.C.: Globe Printing Co., 1906), 272; Alpheus S. Williams, *From the Cannon's Mouth: The Civil War Letters of General Alpheus S. Williams,* ed. Milo M. Quaife (Detroit: Wayne State University Press, 1959), 322, 331; Henry Stewart Dean Diary, July 2 [3], 1864; F. M. McAdams, *Every-Day Soldier Life, or a History of the One Hundred and Thirteenth Ohio Volunteer Inf.* (Columbus: Charles M. Gott, Printers, 1884), 93; Alfred H. Trego Diary, July 3, 1864. On Ward's drunkeness, see Charles H. Dickinson Diary, 125–27; John A. Wilkens Correspondence, July 9, 1864; Harvey Reid, *The View from Headquarters: Civil War Letters of Harvey Reid,* ed. Frank L. Byrne (Madison: State Historical Society of Wisconsin, 1865), 165–67. On Whitaker, see 38 OR 1:245, and on Deas, William Joseph Hardee to his wife, June 13, 1864, Hardee Letters.

7. Benjamin F. McGee, *History of the 72nd Indiana Volunteer Infantry of the Mounted Lightning Brigade* (Lafayette, Ind.: S. Vater and Co., 1882), 327; 38 OR 5:30–31.

8. Henry W. Wright, *A History of the Sixth Iowa Infantry* (Iowa City: Iowa State Historical Society, 1923), 298; Theodore C. Tracie, *Annals of the Nineteenth Ohio Battery; or, Lights and Shadows of Army Life* (Cleveland: J. B. Savage, 1878), 354; Oliver Otis Howard, *Autobiography of Oliver Otis Howard* (New York: Baker & Taylor Co., 1907),

1:596-97; Philip Sidney Post to his mother, July 5, 1864, Post Letters; Edward Young McMorries, *History of the First Regiment, Alabama Volunteer Infantry, C.S.A.* (Nashville: 1904), 74-75; Thomas T. Taylor Diary, July 4, 1864.

9. Charles H. Smith, *The History of Fuller's Ohio Brigade, 1861-1865* (Cleveland: Press of A. J. Watt, 1909), 157-58; Charles Wright, *A Corporal's Story* (Philadelphia: James Beal, 1887), 116; Watkins to Wife, July 4, 17, 1864, James W. Watkins Letters; 38 *OR* 3:617; 5:42, 46-47, 60-61; Thomas B. Mackall Journal, sec. 3:23-24; Gustavus W. Smith, "The Georgia Militia About Atlanta," in *Battles and Leaders of the Civil War*, ed. Robert U. Johnson and Clarence C. Buel (New York: Century Co., 1887), 332-33.

10. Francis A. Shoup, "Dalton Campaign—Works at Chattahoochee River," *Confederate Veteran* 3 (1895): 262-63.

11. Robert Patrick, *Reluctant Rebel: The Secret Diary of Robert Patrick, 1861-1865*, ed. F. Jay Taylor (Baton Rouge: Louisiana State University Press, 1959), 192; William O. Norrell Diary, July 5, 1864; Samuel T. Foster, *One of Cleburne's Command. The Civil War Reminiscences and Diary of Capt. Samuel T. Foster, Granbury's Texas Brigade, C.S.A.*, ed. Norman D. Brown (Austin: University of Texas Press, 1980), 102; French, *Two Wars*, 215-16; Shoup, "Dalton Campaign," 63-64.

12. William T. Sherman, *Memoirs of Gen. W. T. Sherman*, 4th ed. (New York: Charles L. Webster & Co., 1891), 2:66-67; 38 *OR* 5:52; William B. Hazen, *A Narrative of Military Service* (Boston: Ticknor & Co., 1885), 267; James Austin Connolly, "Major Connolly's Letters to His Wife, 1862-1865," *Transactions of the Illinois Historical Society* 35 (1928): 345.

13. Sherman, *Memoirs*, 2:67-68; Connolly, "Letters to Wife," 346; Thomas Taylor to his wife, July 9, 1864, Thomas T. Taylor Letters; John Wesley Marshall Journal, July 5, 1864; *New York Weekly Tribune*, July 23, 1864; George W. Lewis, *The Campaigns of the 124th Ohio Volunteer Infantry* (Akron: Werner Co., 1894), 163.

14. Samuel P. Richards Diary, July 3, 1864; William James Dickey to his wife, July 5, 1864, Dickey Letters; Taylor Beatty Diary, July 7, 1864.

15. 38 *OR* 2:515; 5:68-69, 75-76, 78-79; Wills, *Army Life*, 280; Theodore F. Upson, *With Sherman to the Sea: The Civil War Letters, Diaries and Reminiscences of Theodore F. Upson*, ed. Oscar G. Winther (Bloomington: University of Indiana Press, 1958), 119; McGee, *72nd Indiana*, 332-38. For good accounts of the occupation of Roswell and what happened to the factory women, see David Evans, "Wool, Women, and War," *Civil War Times Illustrated*, September 1978: 38-42, and Dennis Kelly, "Mountains to Pass, A River to Cross: The Battle of Kennesaw Mountain and Related Actions from June 10 to July 9, 1864," *Blue & Gray Magazine*, June 1989: 57. According to Hartwell T. Bynum, "Sherman's Expulsion of the Roswell Women in 1864," *Georgia Historical Quarterly* 54 (1970): 176-80, most of the Roswell women, plus a large number of female laborers from Sweetwater Factory, were sent to Indiana and few of them ever returned to Georgia.

16. 38 *OR* 5:868; 52 *OR* 2:646-47; Gilbert E. Govan and James W. Livingood, *A Different Valor: The Story of General Joseph E. Johnston, C.S.A.* (Indianapolis and New York: Bobbs-Merrill, 1956), 293; Stewart to Bragg, March 19, 1864, Braxton Bragg Papers; Sykes to his wife, July 8, 1864, Columbus Sykes Letters to Wife; B. B. Blue to Miss Karen, June 3, 1864, B. B. Blue Letters.

17. Shoup, "Dalton Campaign," 264; 38 *OR* 5:865.

18. Ibid., 2:515-16, 571, 684-85; 5:75-77, 89-90.

19. 38 *OR* 5:869-71.

20. Ibid., 92-93, 99-100; Henry Albert Potter to his father, July 10, 1864, Henry Albert Potter Diary and Letters; John M. Barnard to his wife, July 11, 1864, John M. Barnard Letters; Alva C. Griest Diary, July 9, 1864; Magee, *72nd Indiana*, 332-38.

21. 38 *OR* 5:871-73; Thomas B. Mackall Journal, sec. 3:27; Manigault, *Narrative*, 198; William O. Norrell Diary, July 9, 1864; French, *Two Wars*, 216; Shoup, "Dalton Campaign," 264; Mrs. D. Giraud Wright, *A Southern Girl in '61: The War-Time Memories of a*

Confederate Senator's Daughter (New York: Doubleday, Page & Co., 1905), 178–79; Sarah Huff, *My Eighty Years in Atlanta* (Atlanta: Privately printed, 1937), 11; William Mackall to his wife, July 10, 1864.

22. *New York Times*, Aug. 7, 1864, quoting "Atlanta Correspondent of Mobile News"; Myers, *Children of Pride*, 1191–92; *Atlanta Daily Intelligencer*, January 28, 1861 (quoted in Donald F. Reynolds, *Editors Make War: Southern Newspapers in the Secession Crisis* [Nashville: Vanderbilt University Press, 1966], 174), June 30, 1864; *Atlanta Southern Confederacy*, July 4, 5, 1864; *Cincinnati Daily Commercial*, July 22, 1864, quoting *Atlanta Southern Confederacy*, n.d.; *Atlanta Daily Appeal*, July 12, 1864, quoted in *New York Times*, August 5, 1864; *Cincinnati Daily Commercial*, Aug. 10, 1864, quoting (via the *Richmond Dispatch*) the *Atlanta Southern Confederacy*, n.d.; Samuel P. Richards Diary, July 10, 1864; W. L. Trask Diary, July 12, 1864; John Davidson and Julia Davidson, "A War Time Story: The Davidson Letters, 1862–1865," ed. Jane Bonner Peacock, *Atlanta Historical Bulletin* 29 (1975): 90–93; Huff, *Eighty Years*, 19–20; Mrs. Henry Huntington, "Escape from Atlanta: The Huntington Memoir," ed. Ben Kremenak, *Civil War History* 11 (1965): 166; Robert Gibbons, "Life at the Crossroads of the Confederacy: Atlanta, 1861–1865," *Atlanta Historical Bulletin* 23 (1979): 48–49; Franklin M. Garrett, *Atlanta and Environs: A Chronicle of Its People and Events* (New York: Lewis Historical Publishing Co., 1954), 600; Bell I. Wiley, *The Life of Johnny Reb: The Common Soldier of the Confederacy* (Indianapolis and New York: Bobbs-Merrill, 1951), 47 (for Georgia soldier quote).

23. On weakness of Confederate forces east of Marietta and criticisms of Sherman's conduct of operations, see 38 OR 3:592; 4:787; 5:123–24; 52 OR 1:565–66; Thomas Taylor to his wife, June 29, 1864, Taylor Letters; David S. Stanley, *Personal Memoirs of Major General D. S. Stanley, U.S.A.* (Cambridge, Mass.: Harvard University Press, 1917), 174; Williams, *Cannon's Mouth*, 324; John M. Schofield, "Notes on Sherman's Memoirs," 23–24, John M. Schofield Papers. Although extreme in some of its statements, the critique of Sherman's operations from Kennesaw to the Chattahoochee by Henry Stone, "Part II: From Oostenaula to Chattahoochee," in *The Atlanta Papers,* comp. Sydney C. Kerksis (Dayton: Press of the Morningside Bookshop, 1980), 421–27, is basically correct.

24. The best examination of Johnston's conduct of operations from June 10 to July 9 and of the condition of the Army of Tennessee at the end of them is Richard M. McMurry, "The Atlanta Campaign of 1864: A New Look," *Civil War History* 22 (1976): 12–14. See also Thomas L. Connelly, *Autumn of Glory: The Army of Tennessee, 1862–1865* (Baton Rouge: Louisiana State University Press, 1971), 392–97.

25. Davis, *Rise and Fall*, 2:557–61; 39 OR 2:694, 696–98; 38 OR 5:873; Hudson Strode, *Jefferson Davis: Tragic Hero* (New York: Harcourt, Brace & Co., 1954), 69–71. Hill, in a letter of October 12, 1878, to Davis's private secretary, Major E. C. Walthall (quoted in Davis, *Rise and Fall*, 2:557), states that he arrived in Richmond on July 9 and went almost "immediately" to see Davis, but since he also says that this was on a Sunday and July 9 was a Saturday, most likely the meeting took place on July 10, a conclusion supported by other evidence (see 38 OR 3:874–76).

26. Connelly, *Autumn of Glory,* 389–90; 38 OR 3:678.

27. Hardee to Davis, June 22, 1864, Jefferson Davis Papers; Wheeler to Bragg, July 1, 1864, Braxton Bragg Papers; 38 OR 3:677; Connelly, *Autumn of Glory,* 407–11.

28. Davis, in a letter of July 11, 1864, to Johnston, pointed out these consequences of abandoning Mississippi and Alabama. According to a notation on the letter by Johnston, the letter was sent to him by a courier who did not leave Richmond until July 20, and it did not reach him until July 24—by which time he no longer commanded the Army of Tennessee (see 38 OR 5:875–76). Presumably, however, this letter, like the doctored version of the Thomas B. Mackall Journal, was furnished to the compilers of the *Official Records* by Johnston, and hence this notation must be viewed with suspicion.

29. *New York Weekly Tribune*, July 13, 1864; *Hillsdale* (Michigan) *Democrat*, July 7,

1864; *New York World,* July 12, 1864; *Chicago Daily Times,* June 23, 30, 1864; Frank L. Klement, *The Copperheads of the Middle West* (Chicago: University of Chicago Press, 1960), 232–34; James M. McPherson, *Battle Cry of Freedom: The Civil War Era* (New York: Oxford University Press, 1988), 756–60.

30. Dunbar Rowland, ed., *Jefferson Davis, Constitutionalist: His Letters, Papers, and Speeches* (Jackson: Mississippi Department of Archives and History, 1923), 7:319–20, 336, 339; 8:77–79, 215–16, 337–38, 349, 355–57; French, *Two Wars,* 218; 39 OR 2:695–96; Larry Earl Nelson, "The Confederacy and the United States Presidential Election of 1864," Ph.D. diss., Duke University, 1975, 24.

31. Richard M. McMurry, "Rousseau's Raid: Riding through Alabama. Part I," *Civil War Times Illustrated,* August 1981: 12.

32. 38 OR 5:103–5, 107–8, 112–14, 120–21, 123–24, 140–41.

33. 34 OR 4:212; 38 OR 5:84–85; 39 OR 2:79, 121–24, 126, 142–43, 150–52; Robert Selph Henry, *"First with the Most" Forrest* (Indianapolis: Bobbs-Merrill Co., 1944), 302–3.

34. 38 OR 1:127–28; 5:105, 110, 112–13, 120–23, 141–43; William T. Sherman, *Home Letters of General Sherman,* ed. M. A. DeWolfe Howe (New York: Charles Scribner's Sons, 1909), 301.

35. James Zearing to his wife, July 11, 1864, James Robert Zearing Papers; Walt Whitman, *Walt Whitman's Civil War,* ed. Walter Lowenfels (New York: Alfred A. Knopf, 1961) 99; Wills, *Army Life,* 274–78; Charles A. Partridge, *History of the Ninety-sixth Regiment Ill. Vol. Inf.* (Chicago: Brown, Pettibone Co., 1887), 373; John M. Barnard to his wife, July 13, 1864, Barnard Letters; John Richards Boyle, *Soldiers True: The Story of the One Hundredth and Eleventh Pennsylvania Veteran Volunteers* (New York: Eaton & Mains, 1903), 228; *Indianapolis Daily Sentinel,* July 25, 1864; Phinehas A. Hager to his wife, July 11, 1864, Hager Letters; D. Morris to "Friend Olds," June 30, 1864, William C. Olds Letters; 38 OR 1:115–16. See also William Huntsinger, *History of the 79th Reg. Indiana Volunteer Infantry* (Indianapolis: 1891), 153; Oliver Otis Howard to his wife, June 30, 1864, Howard Letters; and Day Elmore to his parents, July 2, 1864, Elmore Letters, in which he states that the IV Corps has lost "nearly 6,000" in killed, wounded, and missing "since we began work out from Dalton."

36. For condition and morale of Confederates, see Manigault, *Narrative,* 198; Leonidas Mackey, Letter of July 5, 1864; Urban G. Owen, "Letters of a Confederate Surgeon in the Army of Tennessee to His Wife," ed. Enoch L. Mitchell, *Tennessee Historical Quarterly* 5 (1946): 171; Robert L. Bliss to his mother, July 14, 1864, Bliss Letters; Patrick, *Reluctant Rebel,* 195; John Offield, Joseph Offield, and William Offield, "Letters from the Offield Brothers, Confederate Soldiers from Upper East Tennessee," ed. Leona Taylor Aiken, *East Tennessee Historical Society Publications* 46 (1974): 122; John R. Crittenden to his wife, July 7, 1864, Crittenden Papers; and Charles Henry Thiott to his wife, June 24, 1864, Thiott Family Papers, in which he states that his regiment, the 1st Georgia Volunteers of Mercer's Brigade, Walker's Division, which did not join the Army of Tennessee until late May and which was much larger than the average Confederate regiment, had been reduced to "a little over 300 effective men . . . without a regular battle" as a consequence of "severe skirmishing" and a "great many" cases of diarrhea. Richard M. McMurry, "Confederate Morale in the Atlanta Campaign of 1864," *Georgia Historical Quarterly* 54 (1970): 231–35, and William J. McNeil, "A Survey of Confederate Soldier Morale during Sherman's Campaign through Georgia and the Carolinas," *Georgia Historical Quarterly* 45 (1971): 9–14, present contrasting but not necessarily conflicting views of the state of morale in the Army of Tennessee at this stage of the campaign.

On the strength of the Army of Tennessee as of July 10, see 38 OR 3:679; 5:178–79; McMurry, "Atlanta Campaign: A New Look," 12–14; Connelly, *Autumn of Glory,* 392–97; and Joseph Gorgas to Joseph Johnston, June 27, 1874, Johnston Papers, College of William and Mary; citing an article by Colonel Hypolite Oladowski, former chief ordnance officer of the Army of Tennessee, in the June 7, 1874, *New Orleans Times* stating that Johnston lost "about 19,000 muskets" (meaning men) from Dalton to Atlanta.

37. Edwin E. Bryant, *History of the Third Regiment of Wisconsin Veteran Volunteer Infantry, 1861–1865* (Madison: Democrat Print Co., 1891), 253; Corydon Edward Foote, *With Sherman to the Sea: A Drummer Boy's Story of the Civil War,* ed. Olive Deane Hormel (New York: John Day Co., 1960), 189–90; John W. DuBose, *General Joseph Wheeler and the Army of Tennessee* (New York: Neale Publishing Co., 1912), 352; Williams, *Cannon's Mouth,* 330; W. L. Trask Diary, July 17, 1864; Phinehas A. Hager to his wife, July 11, 1864, Hager Letters; John R. Crittenden to his wife, July 11, 1864, Crittenden Papers.

38. 38 OR 5:876; 52 OR 2:692; McMurry, "Atlanta Campaign," 349–50.

39. Eliza Frances Andrews, *The War-Time Journal of a Georgia Girl, 1864–1865* (New York: D. Appleton & Co., 1908), 206; 38 OR 5:878; 52 OR 2:692, 704; Thomas B. Mackall Journal, sec. 3:29.

40. 38 OR 5:879–81; 52 OR 2:707; 39 OR 2:712–14; Thomas B. Mackall Journal, sec. 3:29–30; McMurry, "Atlanta Campaign," 351–59; Richard M. McMurry, *John Bell Hood and the War for Southern Independence* (Lexington: University of Kentucky Press, 1982), 118–21; Connelly, *Autumn of Glory,* 411–21.

41. 38 OR 5:879, 882–83. For Hardee's statement of his reasons for refusing to accept the permanent command of the Army of Tennessee, see 31 OR 3:765.

42. 38 OR 5:143–46, 149–51; John J. Hight, *History of the Fifty-eighth Regiment of Indiana Volunteer Infantry* (Princeton, Ind.: Press of the Clarion, 1895), 346.

43. 38 OR 5:885; Larry E. Nelson, "Independence or Fight," *Civil War Times Illustrated,* June 1976: 11–14.

44. 38 OR 5:887–89 John Bell Hood, *Advance and Retreat* (New York: Krauss Reprint, 1969), 126–28; Johnston, *Narrative,* 348–50, 369; Thomas B. Mackall Journal, sec. 3:30–32; Hasley Wigfall to his sisters, July 31, 1864, in Wright, *A Southern Girl,* 181; *New York Times,* Aug. 5, quoting a Southern press report that Johnston arrived in Macon on July 19; McMurry, *Hood,* 121–24.

45. William Joseph Hardee to his wife, June 20, 1864, Hardee Letters; Alpheus Baker to Joseph Johnston, July 4, 1874, Johnston Papers, College of William and Mary; French, *Two Wars,* 217; W. L. Trask Diary, July 18, 1864; Van Buren Oldham Diary, July 18, 1864; 38 OR 5:890–91; W.H.T. Walker to his wife, July 16–18, 1864, Walker Papers; James I. Hall to his daughter, July 8, 1864, Hall Papers.

46. For reaction of the rank and file of Army of Tennessee to Johnston's removal see 38 OR 3:717 (Walker's Division salutes Johnston); Wiley, "Three Southern Officers," 33 (Gill quote); Foster, *Diary,* 105–7; Benjamin M. Seaton, *The Bugle Softly Blows: The Confederate Diary of Benjamin M. Seaton,* ed. Harold B. Simpson (Waco: Texian Press, 1965) July 9, 1864; Sykes to his wife, July 8, 1864, Sykes Letters; Joel Murphee, "Autobiography and Civil War Letters of Joel Murphee of Troy, Alabama, 1864–1865," ed. H. E. Sterrkx, *Alabama Historical Quarterly* 19(1957): 184; John W. Hagan, "The Confederate Letters of John W. Hagan," ed. Bell I. Wiley, *Georgia Historical Quarterly* 38 (1954): 282; James I. Hall to his daughter, July 8, 1864, Hall Papers. McMurry, "Confederate Morale," 233–35, demonstrates that the morale of many Confederate soldiers had declined by mid-July because of Johnston's retreats, and not all of them were displeased by his removal. Nevertheless, the overwhelming weight of the evidence from diaries, letters, and memoirs makes it manifest that the vast majority were unhappy and worried by the change from Johnston to Hood. Citations of all of the sources so indicating would be an exercise in pedantic overkill, but they will be supplied gladly to any seriously interested qualified scholar.

47. "D. B.," *Cincinnati Daily Commercial,* July 26, 1864; *New York Weekly Tribune,* September 24, 1864; 38 OR 5:169–70, 172, 175.

48. 38 OR 3:630; 5:892–94; Hood, *Advance and Retreat,* 162–66. In his postwar writings

(*Narrative*, 347–48; "Opposing Sherman's Advance to Atlanta," 4: 275–76) Johnston claims that Hood derived his plan for attacking the Federals at Peachtree Creek from him, that he told Hood of it on July 18. Hood, *Advance and Retreat*, 141, states that Johnston "may have said somewhat to me in regard to his plans" but that he "had no recollection thereof." It is impossible to know which one is telling the truth, but it makes no difference from a historical standpoint, as Hood's plan differs markedly from the one Johnston states he intended to implement. That was to attack the Federals *while* they were crossing Peachtree, whereas Hood's calls for attacking them *after* they had crossed it.

49. 38 OR 3:383–84, 891–94; 5:182–86, 189–90, 193; Holmes, *Then and Now*, 204–8; J. R. Kinnear, *History of the Eighty-sixth Regiment Illinois Vol. Inf.* (Chicago: Tribune Co., 1866), 61–62; McGee, *72nd Indiana*, 342; Wills, *Army Life*, 282; Sherman, *Memoirs*, 2:72 (here Sherman misdates his learning that Hood had replaced Johnston).

50. Hood, *Advance and Retreat*, 167–68; 38 OR 3:871, 876, 880–81; Thomas B. Mackall Journal, sec. 3:32; McMurry, *Hood*, 127–28.

51. The following account of the Battle of Peachtree Creek is based on the relevant Union and Confederate reports and correspondence as found in 38 OR 1, 2, 3, and 5. In addition, the following nonofficial primary sources were consulted: for the Union side in general: Sherman, *Memoirs*, 2:72–73; Thomas B. Van Horne, *The Life of Major General George H. Thomas* (New York: Charles Scribner's Sons, 1882), 241–45; Hight, *Fifty-eighth Indiana*, 242; Richard W. Johnson, *A Soldier's Reminiscences In Peace and War* (Philadelphia: J. B. Lippincott & Co., 1886), 280; Chester Whitman to his brother, July 30, 1864, Whitman Letters; Charles Harding Cox, "Gone for a Soldier: The Civil War Letters of Charles Harding Cox," ed. Lorna Lutes Sylvester, *Indiana Magazine of History* 68 (1972): 211. For the IV Corps (Newton's division): Boyle, *Soldiers True*, 230–37; L. G. Bennett and Wm. M. Haigh, *History of the 36th Illinois Volunteers* (Aurora, Ill.: Knickerbocker & Hodder Printers, 1876), 613–15; Benjamin T. Smith, Recollections of the Late War, 156–58; W. H. Newlin, comp., *A History of the 73rd Regiment of Illinois Volunteer Infantry* (Springfield, Ill.: 1890), 324–25; William Sumner Dodge, *A Waif of the War; or, The History of the Seventy-fifth Illinois Infantry* (Chicago: Church & Goodman, 1866), 162–63; William D. Hynes, Letter of July 29, 1864, Hynes Letters (particularly valuable for map of Newton's sector drawn by Hynes immediately after battle). For the XX Corps: Williams, *Cannon's Mouth*, 335–36, 339; John W. Geary to his wife, July 24, 1864, Geary Letters; William Wallace, "William Wallace's Civil War Letters: The Atlanta Campaign," *Wisconsin Magazine of History* 57 (1973–74): 102; Fergus Elliott to Secretary of War Elihu Root, c. 1900, Elliott Papers (particularly valuable for role of Candy's brigade of Geary's division and for the sketch maps that accompany it); G. S. Bradley, *The Star Corps; or, Notes of an Army Chaplain during Sherman's Famous "March to the Sea"* (Milwaukee: Jermain & Brightman, 1865), 132–34; S. F. Fleharty, *Our Regiment: A History of the 102d Ill. Inf. Vols.* (Chicago: Brewster & Hanscom Printers, 1865), 89–94; L. R. Coy Diary, July 20, 1864; Samuel Merrill, *The Seventieth Indiana Volunteer Infantry* (Indianapolis: Bowen-Merrill Co., 1900), 139–47; Rufus Mead, "With Sherman through Georgia and the Carolinas: Letters of a Federal Soldier. Part One," ed. James A. Padgett, *Georgia Historical Quarterly* 32 (1948): 301–302; David Nichol to his father, July 23, 1864, Nichol Letters; James Theodore Reeve Diary, July 20, 1864; Eli S. Richer, Atlanta to the Sea, Richer Letters, 116–19; Harry Sievers, *Benjamin Harrison: Hoosier Warrior, 1833–1865* (Chicago: Henry Regnery Co., 1952), 259–62; Reid, *View from Headquarters*, 170–73; James H. Kelly Journal, July 20, 1864; Charles H. Dickinson Diary, July 20, 1864; Stephen Pierson, "From Chattanooga to Atlanta in 1864—A Personal Reminiscence," in *The Atlanta Papers*, comp. Sydney C. Kerksis (Dayton: Press of the Morningside Bookshop, 1980), 289–92. For the XIV Corps: W. W. Calkins, *The History of the 104th Regt. of Ill. Volunteer Infantry* (Chicago: Donohue & Henneberry Printers, 1895), 220–25; Allen L. Fahnestock Diary, July 19–20, 1864; William Strawn Narrative of Atlanta Campaign, 13–27.

For general Confederate sources see Hood, *Advance and Retreat,* 230–31; T. B. Roy, "General Hardee and Military Operations about Atlanta," *Southern Historical Society Papers* 8 (1880): 346–53, 378–87; Thomas B. Mackall Journal, sec. 3:32–33; "Personne," *Savannah Daily Republican,* July 25, 1864. For Hardee's Corps see Irving A. Buck, ed., *Cleburne and His Command* (Jackson, Tenn.: McCowat-Mercer Press, 1959), 230–31; J.L.P. Campbell, ed., *John Angus Campbell, PFC, C.S.A.* (Atlanta: N.p., n.d.), 3; Joseph B. Cumming War Recollections, 60; James Cooper Nisbet, *Four Years on the Firing Line,* ed. Bell I. Wiley (Jackson, Tenn.: McCowat-Mercer Press, 1963), 209–10; W. J. Worsham, *The Old Nineteenth Tennessee Regiment, C.S.A.* (Blountsville, Tenn.: Tony Marion, 1973), 128; W. L. Trask Diary, July 20, 1864; James I. Hall Memoir, 34, Hall Papers; Alfred Tyler Fielder Diary, July 19, 20, 1864; *Key Diary,* 92; Van Buren Oldham Diary, July 20, 1864; Charles H. Olmstead, *The Memoirs of Charles H. Olmstead,* ed. Lilla Mills Hawes (Savannah: Georgia Historical Society, 1964), 148–49; Edwin H. Rennolds Diary, July 20, 1864; Carroll Henderson Clark Memoir, Article 23; Ed Porter Thompson, *History of the Orphan Brigade* (Louisville: Lewis N. Thompson, 1898), 261; *New York Times,* Aug. 5, 1864, quoting Southern newspapers on the wounding of Stevens. For Stewart's Corps see Murphee, "Autobiography and Letters," 186; French, *Two Wars,* 218–19; Wesley T. Leeper, *Rebels Valiant: Second Arkansas Mounted Rifles (Dismounted)* (Little Rock: Pioneer Press, 1964), 239.

For newspapers see *Cincinnati Daily Commercial,* July 26, 1864; *Atlanta* (Macon) *Daily Appeal,* July 24, quoted in ibid., Aug. 3, 1864; *Chattanooga* (Griffin, Ga.) *Daily Rebel,* n.d., quoted in ibid., Aug. 10, September 17, 1864; *New York Herald,* July 27, 29, 1864; *Chicago Daily Tribune,* July 29, 1864; *New York Times,* July 29, 1864, quoting *Atlanta Daily Appeal,* July 20, 1864; *Indianapolis Daily Journal,* July 28, 1864.

For analytical sources see Henry Stone, "Part III: The Siege and Capture of Atlanta, July 9 to Sept. 8, 1864," in *The Atlanta Papers,* comp. Sydney C. Kerksis (Press of the Morningside Bookshop, 1980), 110–14; Henry Stone, "Part IV: Strategy of the Campaign," ibid., 154–56; McMurry, *Hood,* 128–30; Larry J. Daniel, *Cannoneers in Gray: The Field Artillery of the Army of Tennessee, 1861–1865* (University: University of Alabama Press, 1984), 157–60; Connelly, *Autumn of Glory,* 439–44; Jacob D. Cox, *Atlanta* (New York: Charles Scribner's Sons, 1882), 154–62; Errol McGregor Clauss, "The Atlanta Campaign, 18 July–2 September 1864," Ph.D. diss., Emory University, 1965, 67–103; Stephen Davis, "The Battles of Atlanta: Events from July 10 to September 2, 1864," *Blue & Gray Magazine,* August 1989: 12–17; Steven J. Adolphson, "An Incident of Valor in the Battle of Peachtree Creek, 1864," *Georgia Historical Quarterly* 57 (1973): 406–20.

52. 38 OR 3:101–2, 265, 384, 543, 579–80; 5:208; 52 OR 1:569; Thomas T. Taylor Diary, July 20, 1864; Stone, "Strategy of the Campaign," 155–56; Garrett, *Atlanta,* 626.

53. 38 OR 3:871; 5:893 (the dispatch from Hood's headquarters to Wheeler printed here is misdated July 19); Hood, *Advance and Retreat,* 169–73; Thomas B. Mackall Journal, sec. 3:32–33.

54. 38 OR 5:196–98, 208. Sherman's account of operations on July 20 in his *Memoirs,* 2:72–73, is so filled with absurd mistakes (he states that the Confederates attacked "Thomas's right"!) and self-serving lies (he claims to have heard the assault on Thomas early in the afternoon) that it is worse than worthless.

55. Mead, "With Sherman through Georgia," 302; Boyle, *Soldiers True,* 236–38 (111th Pennsylvania); Williams, *Cannon's Mouth,* 336; William Strawn Narrative of Atlanta Campaign, 15 (for 104th Illinois); 38 OR 1:298, 538; 2:34, 39, 92, 141, 329, 347, 391; *Chattanooga* (Griffin, Ga.) *Daily Rebel,* n.d., as quoted in *Cincinnati Daily Commercial,* September 17, 1864 ("Our steps marked with blood"); Report of F. Rice, Chief Surgeon, Cheatham's Division, in Benjamin F. Cheatham Papers; *Atlanta* (Macon) *Daily Intelligencer,* Aug. 6, 1864, re: casualties of 1st Georgia; Nisbet, *Firing Line,* 210; 38 OR 3:877, 882–84, 895, 897, 908–9, 931, 938, 942.

56. 38 OR 3:543–44, 564, 730, 733–34, 746, 748–52, 952; Foster, *Diary,* 108–9; *Key Diary,*

92–94; Buck, *Cleburne*, 232–34; *Atlanta Daily Appeal*, July 20, 1864, as quoted in *New York Times*, July 29, 1864; James P. Snell, Diary and Memorandum Book, 1864, 20; William S. Morris, *History of the 31st Regiment Illinois Volunteers, Organized by John A. Logan* (Evansville, Ind.: Keller Printing & Publishing Co., 1902), 104; Gilbert D. Munson, "Battle of Atlanta," in *The Atlanta Papers*, comp. Sydney C. Kerksis (Dayton: Press of the Morningside Bookshop, 1980) 213–19.

57. Samuel P. Richards Diary, July 22, 1864; A. A. Hoehling, *Last Train from Atlanta* (New York and London: Thomas Yoseloff, 1958), 117.

58. 38 OR 2:337; 5:212–13, 218; John Wesley Marshall Journal, July 21, 1864; L. R. Coy Diary, July 21, 1864; Calkins, *104th Illinois*, 226–27; John W. Tuttle Diary, July 21, 1864; Judson L. Austin to his wife, July 21, 1864, Austin Letters; S. F. Fleharty, *Our Regiment: A History of the 102d Ill. Inf. Vols.* (Chicago: Brewster & Hanscom Printers, 1865), 94; Phinehas A. Hager to his wife, July 23, 1864, Hager Letters; Henry Stewart Dean Diary, July 21, 1864.

59. Hood, *Advance and Retreat*, 173–78; 38 OR 3:544, 631; 5:219–20, 898–99; Buck, *Cleburne*, 233.

60. 38 OR 1:203, 906–7; 3:384, 407; 5:211–15, 218, 222; Edwin Brown Diary, July 21, 1864.

61. 38 OR 3:631, 699, 737; 5:899–900; Taylor Beatty Diary, July 21, 1864; Sykes to his wife, July 22, 1864, Sykes Letters; Roy, "Hardee Around Atlanta," 354–59; William B. Bate's Unpublished Report, 15; Joseph B. Cumming Recollections, 60–61; Alfred Tyler Fielder Diary, July 21–22, 1864; James I. Hall Memoir, Hall Papers 35; Foster, *Diary*, 110–11; Garrett, *Atlanta*, 615.

62. W. L. Trask Diary, July 23, 1864; Samuel P. Richards Diary, July 22, 1864; Andrew J. Neal to his mother, July 23, 1864, Neal Letters; Patrick, *Reluctant Rebel*, 200; Wilbur G. Kurtz, "What James Bell Told Me about the Siege of Atlanta," Kurtz Collection.

63. 38 OR 5:222, 224–25, 229, 231.

64. Hood, *Advance and Retreat*, 179; Garrett, *Atlanta*, 621; 38 OR 3:737; W. L. Trask Diary, July 24, 1864; William B. Bate's Unpublished Report, 15–16; Van Buren Oldham Diary, July 21, 1864; T. B. Roy to Wheeler, February 27, 1880, Joseph A. Wheeler Papers; Roy, "Hardee around Atlanta," 365.

65. William B. Bate's Unpublished Report, 16; Roy, "Hardee around Atlanta," 359–60; Wilbur G. Kurtz, "Memo of Data from J. M. McWilliams, June 30, 1930," Kurtz Collection; Wilbur G. Kurtz, "The Death of Major General W. H. T. Walker, July 22, 1864," 175–78, Kurtz Collection; Joseph B. Cumming Recollections, 61–62; Garrett, *Atlanta*, 615.

66. 38 OR 1:72–73; 5:223, 225; Sherman, *Memoirs*, 2:74–76; Cox, "Snake Creek Gap," 342–45; William E. Strong, "The Death of General James B. McPherson," in *The Atlanta Papers*, comp. Sydney C. Kerksis (Dayton: Press of the Morningside Bookshop, 1980), 512–18; Garrett, *Atlanta*, 618.

67. William B. Bate's Unpublished Report, 15–19; Wilbur G. Kurtz, "Memo of Data from McWilliams," "Death of Walker," 177–79, Kurtz Collection; Garrett, *Atlanta*, 615, 617.

68. 38 OR 3:731–32, 737–38, 747; 5:900–901; I. V. Moore Diary, July 22, 1864; Buck, *Cleburne*, 239–40; Roy, "Hardee around Atlanta," 360. Buck (*Cleburne*, 235) and Roy ("Hardee around Atlanta," 359–60) state that during the conference at the Cobb house, Hardee, Walker, and Wheeler ascertained from a civilian (presumably Cobb himself) that a large millpond lay athwart Walker's route of advance. If this be so—and both Buck and Roy were in a position to know and Roy also cites Wheeler as a source—then Hardee, in his haste to get the attack under way, disregarded this information, and Walker, filled with anger at Hardee's insult (and possibly with peach brandy) forgot about it. The full truth of this matter probably is beyond recovery, but it does seem that Walker was not in full control of himself on July 22.

69. Thomas B. Mackall Journal, sec. 3, part 2:n.176; Garrett, *Atlanta*, 621; Gibbons, "Crossroads of the Confederacy," 48; Hoehling, *Last Train*, 130–31; *Atlanta Daily Appeal*

quotation in *New York Times,* July 29, 1864. In his report (38 OR 3:699) Hardee asserts that Hood, on receiving this message, "exclaimed to Brigadier General Mackall, his chief of staff, with his finger on the map, 'Hardee is just where I wanted him.'" The obvious source for this statement is Mackall, whose hatred of Hood makes him a highly suspect witness. Furthermore, since Hardee himself did not know "just where" he was in relation to the Union lines, it is unlikely that he would have reported this to Hood. He might, however, have informed Hood that he was in the enemy's rear, in which case Hood naturally would have been pleased, thus providing a basis for Mackall's story.

70. Kurtz, "Death of Walker," 177–179, Kurtz Collection; Strong, "Death of McPherson," 322.

71. See Attack by Bate and Walker and its repulse in 38 OR 3:369–70, 384–85, 393–96, 407–8, 418–19, 450–51, 474–82, 758–59; William B. Bate's Unpublished Report, 17–19; Nisbet, *Firing Line,* 211–12; Lot D. Young, *Reminiscences of a Soldier of the Orphan Brigade* (Louisville: Louisville Courier Job Print, 1912), 91–92; Thompson, *Orphan Brigade,* 263–64; Grenville M. Dodge, "The Battle of Atlanta," in *The Atlanta Papers,* comp. Sydney C. Kerksis (Dayton: Press of the Morningside Bookshop, 1980), 491–93; John J. McKee Diary, July 22, 1864; W. H. Chamberlin, "Recollections of the Battle of Atlanta," in *The Atlanta Papers,* comp. Sydney C. Kerksis (Dayton: Press of the Morningside Bookshop, 1980), 456–58; Robert N. Adams, "The Battle and Capture of Atlanta," in Kerksis, comp., *Atlanta Papers,* 472–74.

72. 38 OR 3:506–7, 952–53; William H. Records Diary, July 22, 1864; James Nourse Diary, July 22, 1864; Edward R. Hutchins, comp., *The War of the Sixties* (New York: Neale Publishing Co., 1912), 236–38.

73. Strong, "Death of McPherson," 520–24; *New York Times,* Aug. 1, 1864. There are numerous other candidates for the distinction of shooting McPherson; see Foster, *One of Cleburne's Command,* 11–12 nn.48, 49. However, Beard's account (which appears in Strong, "Death of McPherson," 531–34) seems to be the most reliable because the most circumstantial.

74. David C. Bradley, "Recollections of the Autumn and Winter of 1864," 3–4, Bradley Letters and Papers; Sherman, *Memoirs,* 2:77–78; 38 OR 3:24.

75. See Hardee's first attack and repulse in 38 OR 3:318–19, 545–46, 564–68, 581–82, 588, 594, 605–6, 608–10, 731–32, 738–39, 747–54; Manning F. Force, Letter of July 23, 1864, and Report, Force Papers; William W. Belknap, *History of the Fifteenth Regiment, Iowa Veteran Volunteer Infantry* (Keokule, Iowa: R. B. Ogden & Son, 1887), 349–71; Carroll Henderson Clark Memoir, Article 24.

76. See Cheatham's attack and repulse in Thomas B. Mackall Journal, sec. 3:33–34; Taylor Beatty Diary, July 22, 1864; Hood, *Advance and Retreat,* 179–81; Alfred Tyler Fielder Diary, July 22, 1864; 38 OR 3:25–26, 139–40, 174, 179–80, 217–18, 223–24, 235, 245–47, 280–81, 819, 970–71; Cavins, *War Letters,* 88–89; Thomas T. Taylor Diary, July 22, 1864; Taylor to his wife, July 26, 1864; Taylor Letters; Joseph A. Saunier, ed., *A History of the Forty-seventh Regiment Ohio Veteran Volunteer Infantry* (Hillsboro; Ohio: Lyle Printing Co., 1903), 277–95; Wills, *Army Life,* 283–84; Thaddeus H. Capron, "War Diary of Thaddeus H. Capron, 1861–1865," *Journal of the Illinois Historical Society* 12 (1919): 387–88; Edward F. Schweitzer Diary, July 22, 1864; Hugh Moore, "A Reminiscence of Confederate Prison Life," *Journal of the Illinois Historical Society* 65 (1972): 452–57; John M. Schofield, *Forty-six Years in the Army* (New York: Century Co., 1897), 146–48; Isaac Sherwood, *Memoirs of the War* (Toledo: H. J. Chittenden Co., 1923), 118–20; Wiley, "Three Southern Officers," 33; James P. Douglas, *Douglas's Texas Battery, C.S.A.,* ed. Lucia Rutherford Douglas (Tyler, Tex.: Smith County Historical Society, 1966), 115–16; Manigault, *Narrative,* 225–29, 289–94; James W. Watkins to "Franky," July 24, 1864, Watkins Letters; Unpublished Reports of Bushrod Jones, Thomas Herndon, John Dumas, Ada Johnson, John Higley, R. K. Wells, J. C. Hendrick, J. H. Minton, and E. S. Gurley in Benjamin F. Cheatham Papers; "Personne," *Savannah Republican,* July 27, 1864.

77. See Hardee's final attack and repulse in 38 OR 3:26–27, 547, 565, 573, 582–83, 588, 594–95, 732, 739–40, 754, 759; Henry O. Dwight, "The Battle of July 22, 1864," *New York Times,* Aug. 12, 1864; Henry O. Dwight, "How We Fight at Atlanta," *Harper's New Monthly Magazine,* November 1864: 665; D. W. Wood, comp., *History of the 20th O.V.I. Regiment* (Columbus: Paul & Thrall Printers, 1876), 24–25; Munson, "Battle of Atlanta," 421–27; Richard S. Tuthill, "An Artilleryman's Recollections of the Battle of Atlanta," in *The Atlanta Papers,* comp. Sydney C. Kerksis (Dayton: Press of the Morningside Bookshop, 1980), 442–48; Peter Hitchcock to Sarah J. Wilcox, July 24, 1864, Hitchcock Papers; William F. Graham Diary, July 22, 1864; Alfred Tyler Fielder Diary, July 23, 1864; Hosea Garrett to his uncle, Aug. 1, 1864, Garrett Letter; *Key Diary,* 96–97; James I. Hall Memoir, 36–38, Hall Papers; Worsham, *Nineteenth Tennessee,* 129; W. J. McMurray, *History of the Twentieth Tennessee Regiment Volunteer Infantry, C.S.A.* (Nashville: 1904), 321; John W. Bates Diary, July 22, 1864.

78. Hood to Seddon, July 22, 1864, *Richmond Enquirer,* July 25, 1864, as quoted in *New York Herald,* July 29, 1864 (a somewhat shorter version of the telegram appears in 38 OR 5:900); R. E. Lee to Davis, 1864, 38 OR 5:903; Josiah Gorgas, *The Civil War Diary of General Josiah Gorgas,* ed. Frank E. Vandiver (University: University of Alabama Press, 1947), 128; John B. Jones, *A Rebel War Clerk's Diary at the Confederate States Capital,* ed. Howard Swiggett (New York: Old Hickory Bookshop, 1935), 2:253; Sykes to his wife, July 23, 1864, Sykes Letters; Catherine Ann Devereux Edmonston, *"Journal of a Secesh Lady": The Diary of Catherine Ann Devereux Edmonston,* ed. Beth G. Crabtree and James W. Patton (Raleigh, N.C.: Division of Archives and History, Department of Cultural Resources, 1979), 596; Ella Gertrude Thomas Diary, July 24, 1864; McMurry, "Confederate Morale," 235–36.

79. 38 OR 3:27–28.

80. Ibid., 1:74; Roy, "Hardee Around Atlanta," 367; Surgeon Rice's Report, Cheatham Papers; 38 OR 3:679–80, 756, 971; *Key Diary,* 98–99; Manigault, *Narrative,* 229; Jones's and Johnson's Unpublished Reports, Cheatham Papers; Thompson, *Orphan Brigade,* 263. Davis, "Atlanta Campaign," 25, comes to basically the same conclusions about Confederate losses in his excellent analysis of the July 22 battle.

81. 38 OR 3:631; Hood, *Advance and Retreat,* 179–80.

82. Sherman, *Memoirs,* 2:80–82; Schofield, *Forty-six Years,* 147–49; Stanley, *Memoirs,* 177–78; Howard, *Autobiography,* 2:12–13. Regarding the time Wheeler approached Decatur, see James Nourse Diary, July 22, 1864. On the defensive-minded attitude of the Army of the Cumberland as it approached Atlanta on July 22, see L. R. Coy Diary, July 22, 1864; Allen L. Fahnestock Diary, July 22, 1864; David Noble Diary, July 22, 1864; General John M. Palmer to his wife, July 24, 1864, Palmer Papers; McAdams, *Every-Day Soldier Life,* 94–95; Calkins, *104th Illinois,* 227; William Strawn Narrative, 27–28; George H. Puntenney, *History of the Thirty-seventh Regiment of Indiana Infantry Volunteers* (Rushville, Ind.: Jacksonian Book & Job Department, 1896), 118–19; Daniel Devine Rose to "Dear Friends at Home," July 23, 1864, Rose Letters; 38 OR 1:157, 908. For Sherman on fighting of battles, see Fenwick Y. Hedley, *Marching through Georgia* (Chicago: R. R. Donnelley & Sons, 1887), 64. Neither the *Official Records* nor any other source contains or even mentions an order by Sherman to Thomas directing him to "make a lodgement" in Atlanta; and Captain Stone, "Siege and Capture of Atlanta," 447, states that "such order never came." Significantly, Sherman does not refer to this alleged order in his report.

83. 38 OR 5:248; Morris, *31st Illinois,* 114; Cavins, *War Letters,* 90–91; Hugh D. Gallagher to his brother, Sept. 12, 1864, Gallagher Correspondence and Papers; Huff, *Eighty Years,* 22–24; Frank A. Montgomery, *Reminiscences of a Mississippian in Peace and War* (Cincinnati: Robert Clarke Co., 1901), 190; Edwin H. Rennolds Diary, July 23, 1864; Henry O. Dwight Album (unpaged); John W. Bates Diary, July 23, 1864; Huntington, "Escape from Atlanta," 171; *Chattanooga* (Griffin, Ga.) *Daily Rebel,* n.d., quoted in *Cincinnati Daily Commercial,* Aug. 10, 1864.

84. 39 *OR* 1:250–53, 256, 320–24; 2:182–84, 204; John Meriless Diary, July 12–15, 1864; *Atlanta Daily Appeal,* July 21, 1864, quoted in *Chicago Tribune,* July 29, 1864; John Allen Wyeth, *Life of Lieutenant-General Nathan Bedford Forrest* (Dayton: Press of the Morningside Bookshop, 1975), 439–42, 456–59; Henry, *Forrest,* 316–18; Herman Hattaway, *General Stephen D. Lee* (Jackson: University Press of Mississippi, 1976), 120–23.

85. 38 *OR* 1:75; 5:235–38, 240, 245, 251; Richard M. McMurry, "Rousseau's Raid: Riding through Alabama. Part II," *Civil War Times Illustrated,* Oct. 1981: 40–41.

86. 38 *OR* 5:242.

87. Ibid., 2:809; 5:240; Bell I. Wiley, *The Life of Billy Yank: The Common Soldier of the Union* (Indianapolis and New York: Bobbs-Merrill, 1943), 255 (Union cavalryman quotation).

88. 38 *OR* 3:240–41; Sherman, *Memoirs,* 2:85–86; William T. Sherman, *The Sherman Letters: Correspondence between General and Senator Sherman from 1837 to 1891,* ed. Rachel Sherman Thorndike (New York: Charles Scribner's Sons, 1894), 218; Albert Castel, "Black Jack Logan," *Civil War Times Illustrated,* November 1976:4–10, 41–45. In his *Memoirs,* Sherman merely states that Thomas "remonstrated warmly against my recommending that General Logan should be regularly assigned to the command of the Army of the Tennessee by reason of his accidental seniority." However, according to Dodge, at some unspecified time after the war, Sherman told him, and Dodge recorded it in his diary, that he intended to leave Logan in command, that Thomas on his own initiative came to him to oppose this and threatened to resign if Logan was appointed, and that this was the decisive reason he did not give Logan the command (Mrs. John A. Logan, *Reminiscences of a Soldier's Wife: An Autobiography* [New York: Charles Scribner's Sons, 1913], 171–72). In addition, in an 1886 newspaper interview, Sherman allegedly declared that Thomas told him that he opposed Logan's assignment because if Logan "had an army I am afraid he would edge over on both sides and annoy Schofield and me. Even as a corps commander he is given to edging out beyond his jurisdiction"—presumably a reference to the friction between Logan and Thomas during the winter over the use of the railroad to Chattanooga (George F. Dawson, *Life and Services of Gen. John A. Logan* [Chicago: and New York: Belford, Clarke & Co., 1899], 517–18). In view of the numerous false and malicious statements made by Sherman about Thomas both during and after the war, neither of these accounts can be credited unless supported by reliable independent testimony, which they are not. It is impossible to believe that Thomas would have given such a silly reason as being afraid that Logan "would edge over on both sides" for opposing him for command of the Army of the Tennessee, and it would have been totally out of character for Thomas, he who had trained himself not to feel, to threaten to resign at a crucial point in a crucial campaign because someone with whom he had had a minor quarrel months ago was left at the head of an army half the size of his own. One suspects that Sherman, who was subjected to much postwar criticism by Logan and others for not keeping Logan in command, sought to deflect this criticism by putting the blame on Thomas, who was not alive to contradict him. Van Horne does not mention the Logan case in his biography of Thomas, which would seem to indicate that Thomas indeed objected to Logan, but on the other hand, Stone, "Siege and Capture of Atlanta," 118, criticizes Sherman for not retaining Logan, which would imply that Thomas had no strong feelings on the matter.

89. 38 *OR* 5:252–53; James P. Snell Diary, 30; Leslie Anders, "Fisticuffs at Headquarters: Sweeny vs. Dodge," *Civil War Times Illustrated,* Aug. 1977:8–15.

90. 38 *OR* 3:40; 5:260, 276–77; Mrs. John A. Logan, *Reminiscences of a Soldier's Wife: An Autobiography* (New York: Charles Scribner's Sons, 1913), 170–71; John A. Logan to his wife, July 29, 1864, Logan Letters.

91. 38 *OR* 5:272–74; Sherman, *Memoirs,* 2:86–87; Williams, *Cannon's Mouth,* 338; Sherman, *Sherman Letters,* 303; Daniel Butterfield to Hooker, June 12, 1864, in Julia L. Butterfield, ed., *A Biographical Memorial of General Daniel Butterfield* (New York: Grafton Press, 1903), 146–47.

92. John M. Schofield, "McPherson's Successor," Notes on Sherman's Memoirs, Schofield Papers.

93. Thomas B. Mackall Journal, sec. 3:34–35; Taylor Beatty Diary, July 25, 1864; 38 OR 3:688.

94. Ibid., 5:898, 904, 906–12, 917; 52 OR 2:712–14; William Decatur Howell, undated and unaddressed letter, Howell Journal and Letters; Andrew J. Neal to his mother, July 23, 1864, Neal Letters; Foster, *Diary*, 114.

95. 38 OR 1:77; 3:40; Howard, *Autobiography*, 2:17–19. Howard gives basically the same account of events on July 27 in his *Autobiography*, which was published after Sherman's death, as he does in his "The Battles about Atlanta," *Atlantic Monthly* 37 (1876): 396, which appeared while Sherman not only was alive but also commanding general of the army in which Howard was serving. Hence it can be deemed reliable.

96. 38 OR 1:75–76; 5:255, 260–61, 264–65.

97. Ibid., 3:631–32, 688, 762, 872, 953; 5:909, 912–17; Garrett, *Atlanta*, 625 (Hood's new headquarters).

98. See Battle of Ezra Church in 38 OR 1:77–78, 633, 650; 3:40–41, 104, 148, 167–68, 222–23, 228–29, 247–48, 281–82, 762–63, 767–68, 775–94, 799–800, 802–3, 807, 821, 872, 926–28, 931–32, 939–40, 942–43; 5:279–80, 918–21; Sherman, *Memoirs*, 2:88–89; Howard, *Autobiography*, 2:19–33; Howard, "Battles about Atlanta," 396–98; Thomas T. Taylor Diary, July 28, 1864; Taylor to his wife, July 30, 1864, Taylor Letters; Saunier, *Forty-seventh Ohio*, 257–301; Edward F. Schweitzer Diary, July 28, 1864; Matthew H. Jamison, *Recollections of Pioneer and Army Life* (Kansas City, Mo.: 1911), 353; Thomas W. Connelly, *History of the Seventieth Ohio Regiment* (Cincinnati: Peak Bohrs, 1902), 92–93; Connolly, "Letters to Wife," 253–54 (Sherman "beat their brains out"); Henry J. Aten, *History of the Eighty-fifth Regiment, Illinois Volunteer Infantry* (Hiawatha, Kans.: 1901), 211–13 (on Davis's condition and the march of his division); Manigault, *Narrative*, 231–35; Richard F. Eddins to his sister, July 29, 1864, Eddins Correspondence (attack of Gibson's Brigade); McMorries, *First Alabama*, 76–80; *New York Times*, Aug. 9, 1864. Stewart's July 24 address to his troops in *Richmond Dispatch*, n.d., as quoted in *New York Times*, Aug. 21, 1864.

99. Howard, "Battles About Atlanta," 398; 38 OR 1:650; 5:280–81, 283–84; Levi Ross Diary, July 27, 1864 (for self-inflicted wound). In his *Memoirs*, 2:91, Sherman states that he "sent repeated orders to Schofield and Thomas to make an attempt to break it." According to the *Official Records*, however, he merely sent them one order during the afternoon and that was to probe the Confederate fortifications for a weak spot, which they did, with the result described above. Thomas, because both the XIV and XX corps were being held in readiness to go to the assistance of Howard if necessary, gave the assignment of probing the fortifications to the IV Corps. Hence only that corps and the XXIII Corps actually were available for an assault, and they would have gone against Hardee's Corps, less Bate's Division.

100. 38 OR 3:42, 105, 196, 229, 768, 821, 927, 932, 940, 943; 5:917; Saunier, *Forty-seventh Ohio*, 301; Cavins, *War Letters*, 91; Montgomery, *Reminiscences*, 193; Davis, "Atlanta Campaign," 33; McMorries, *First Alabama*, 77 (on absence of Federal artillery fire).

101. Hood, *Advance and Retreat*, 194–95; 38 OR 5:920, 936; William Joseph Hardee to his wife, July 30, 1864, in Roy, "Hardee Around Atlanta," 370 (indicates that Hardee went to the scene of the Ezra Church battle on the evening of July 28); Thomas T. Taylor to his wife, July 30, 1864, Taylor Letters; Wills, *Army Life*, 287.

102. See McCook-Stoneman Raid in 38 OR 1:76–77; 2:761–64, 769–73, 780–84, 914–21, 925–29; 3:953–57; 5:280, 314, 320–21, 921–24, 927–30, 932, 935–40; William H. Records Diary, July 24–30, 1864; Daniel Devine Rose to his mother, July 29, 1864, Rose Letters; McGee, *72nd Indiana*, 344–50; Oliver C. Haskell Diary, July 28–31, 1864; Eastham Tarrant, *The Wild Riders of the First Kentucky Cavalry* (Lexington, Ky.: Henry Clay Press, 1969), 359–73; Granville C. West, "McCook's Raid in the Rear of Atlanta and Hood's Army,

August, 1864," in Kerksis, comp., *Atlanta Papers,* 546-66; Horace Capron, "Stoneman's Raid to the South of Atlanta," ibid., 673-83; Albert Banfield Capron, "Stoneman Raid to Macon, Georgia, in 1864," ibid., 709-17; Alva C. Griest Diary, July 29, 1864; William E. Sloan Diary, July 29-31, 1864; Samuel Barron, *Lone Star Defenders: A Chronicle of the 3rd Texas Cavalry* (New York: Neale Publishing Co., 1908), 199-203; D. M. Guthrey, "Wheeler's Cavalry Around Atlanta," *Confederate Veteran* 13 (1905): 267; "Harvey," in *Atlanta* (Macon) *Daily Intelligencer,* Aug. 4, 1864 (the best Confederate account of the pursuit and capture of Stoneman); *New York Times,* Aug. 14, 17, 1864 (removal of prisoners from Camp Oglethorpe); *Indianapolis Daily Journal,* August 16, 18, 1864; *Cincinnati Daily Commercial,* Aug. 25, 1864, quoting Macon *Intelligencer,* n.d. (Stoneman crying after surrendering); William Harris Bragg, "The Union General Lost in Georgia," *Civil War Times Illustrated,* June 1985: 16-23. For plundering of civilians by Stoneman's cavalry, see Dolly Sumner Lunt, *A Woman's Wartime Journal* (Macon, Ga.: 1927), 21-25; Louise Reese Cornwell, "Stoneman's and Sherman's Visit to Jasper County," 1-4, Bessie Reese Cornwell Diary.

103. Edward S. Lathrop, "Gossipy Letter from Georgia," *Confederate Veteran* 20 (1912): 520; Hutchins, *War in the '60's,* 296; Henry Wilson Ravenel, *The Private Journal of Henry Wilson Ravenel, 1859-1897,* ed. Arney Robinson Childs (Columbia: University of South Carolina Press, 1947), 199; Edward Ellington Boate, "The True Story of Andersonville Told by a Federal Prisoner," *Southern Historical Society Papers* 10 (1882): 25-32; Michael H. Fitch, *Echoes of the Civil War, as I Hear Them* (New York: William S. Porter Press, 1905), 128-29; George W. Bailey, *The Civil War Diary and Biography of George W. Bailey,* ed. Gerald R. Post (Colleyville, Tex.: Privately printed, 1990), 76-77 (firing of cannon shot over heads of Andersonville prisoners); *Atlanta* (Macon) *Daily Intelligencer,* Aug. 5, 1864, quoting the Macon *Confederate,* n.d.; Byron H. Matthews, Sr., *The McCook-Stoneman Raid* (Philadelphia: Dorrance & Co., 1976), 191.

104. 38 OR 5:339-40; *Atlanta* (Macon) *Daily Intelligencer,* Aug. 5, 1864.

105. *Key Diary,* 106; Levi Ross Diary, July 31, 1864; Alfred Tyler Fielder Diary, July 31, 1864; Atlanta Campaign Diary, July 31, 1864; *New York Herald,* Aug. 10, 1864; Partridge, *Ninety-sixth Illinois,* 385; Puntenney, *Thirty-seventh Indiana,* 121-22; Johnston, *Narrative,* 363 (for bringing "heavy rifled cannon from Mobile").

CHAPTER EIGHT: AUGUST

1. *New York World,* Aug. 2, 1864; *Chicago Daily Times,* Aug. 8, 1864; *Cincinnati Daily Commercial,* Aug. 6, 1864; *National Intelligencer,* Aug. 6, as quoted in *New York Times,* Aug. 8, 1864; George Templeton Strong, *The Diary of George Templeton Strong, 1835-1875,* ed. Allan Nevins and Milton H. Thomas (New York: Macmillan, 1952), 3:470-71; William Wilkins Glenn, *Between North and South: A Maryland Journalist Views the Civil War,* ed. Boyly Ellen Marks and Mark Norton Schatz (London: Associated University Presses, 1976), 139.

2. *New York Herald,* July 24, Aug. 5, 1864; *New York World,* July 25, 1864; William T. Sherman, *The Sherman Letters: Correspondence between General and Senator Sherman from 1837 to 1891,* ed. Rachel Sherman Thorndike (New York: Charles Scribner's Sons, 1894), 236-37.

3. *Richmond Whig,* July 20, 1864, quoted in *New York World,* July 25, 1864; *Richmond Daily Examiner,* July 25, 28, 1864; *Richmond Sentinel,* July 21, 1864, quoted in *Atlanta* (Macon) *Daily Intelligencer,* Aug. 12, 1864; *Chattanooga* (Griffin, Ga.) *Daily Rebel,* n.d., quoted in *Cincinnati Daily Commercial,* Aug. 5, 1864; *Augusta Daily Chronicle and Sentinel,* July 21, 1864; Thomas R. Hay, "The Davis-Hood-Johnston Controversy of 1864," *Mississippi Valley Historical Review* 11 (1924): 71-74.

4. Larry Earl Nelson, "The Confederacy and the United States Presidential Election of

1864," Ph.D. diss., Duke University, 1975, 179-98, 222-25; Paul D. Escott, *After Secession: Jefferson Davis and the Failure of Confederate Nationalism* (Baton Rouge: Louisiana State University Press, 1978), 217-18; *Chicago Tribune,* Aug. 14, 1864; *Indianapolis Daily Journal,* Aug. 3, 1864.

5. 38 OR 3:689.

6. Ibid., 661-68, 679-80, 970-71; 5:927, 930, 940, 949, 951; William Joseph Hardee to his wife, Aug. 5, 1864, Hardee Letters; Ellison Capers to his wife, Aug. 11, 1864, Capers Letters; Albert Milton Walls to his parents, Aug. 3, 1864, Walls Letters; Hosea Garrett to his uncle, Aug. 1, 1864, Garrett Letter; John B. Jones, *A Rebel War Clerk's Diary at the Confederate States Capital,* ed. Howard Swiggett (New York: Old Hickory Bookshop, 1935), 2:256; John Bell Hood, *Advance and Retreat* (New York: Krauss Reprint Co., 1969), 218, 226; Charles H. Olmstead, *The Memoirs of Charles H. Olmstead,* ed. Lilla Mills Hawes (Savannah: Georgia Historical Society, 1964), 151; 38 OR 5:949.

7. Hosea Garrett to Uncle, Aug. 1, 1864, Garrett Letter; Edwin H. Rennolds Diary, July 31, 1864; Van Buren Oldham Diary, July 29, 1864; Bell I. Wiley, "A Story of Three Southern Officers," *Civil War Times Illustrated,* Apr. 1964: 34; William Pitt Chambers, "My Journal," *Publications of the Mississippi Historical Society* 5 (1925): 330; Robert Patrick, *Reluctant Rebel: The Secret Diary of Robert Patrick, 1861-1865,* ed. F. Jay Taylor (Baton Rouge: Louisiana State University Press, 1959), 199-200, 202; Julius Montgomery Macon to Miss Clifford, Aug. 4, 1864, Macon Letters; Thomas Ward Osborn, *The Fiery Trail: A Union Officer's Account of Sherman's Last Campaigns,* ed. Richard Harwell and Philip N. Racine (Knoxville: University of Tennessee Press, 1986), 5; 38 OR 2:44 (Knipe's brigade); 5:494-95; Henry Jackson to Benjamin F. Cheatham, Dec. 10, 1864, Cheatham Papers; Christopher Losson, *Tennessee's Forgotten Warriors: Frank Cheatham and His Confederate Division* (Knoxville: University of Tennessee Press, 1990), 186-87, 317 n.62.

8. Thomas B. Hampton to his wife, July 27, Aug. 7, 1864, Hampton Correspondence; Albert Milton Walls to his parents, August 3, 1864, Walls Letters; Angus McDermid, "Letters from a Confederate Soldier," ed. Benjamin Rountree, *Georgia Review* 18 (1964): 292; 38 OR 5:495; Errol McGregor Clauss, "The Atlanta Campaign, 18 July-2 September 1864," Ph.D. diss., Emory University, 1965, 235-36; Richard M. McMurry, "Confederate Morale in the Atlanta Campaign of 1864," *Georgia Historical Quarterly* 54 (1970): 235-39.

9. 38 OR 5:320-23, 326.

10. Ibid., 308-9, 311-15, 327.

11. Ibid., 1:115-17; 4:594; 5:305, 316-19; Aden G. Cavins, *War Letters of Aden G. Cavins Written to His Wife* (Evansville, Ind.: N.p., n.d.), 91; Edward F. Schweitzer Diary, July 28, 1864; Daniel O'Leary, "The Civil War Letters of Captain Daniel O'Leary, U.S.A.," ed. Jenny O'Leary and Harvey H. Jackson, *Register of the Kentucky Historical Society* 77 (1979): 174-75; William B. Hazen, *A Narrative of Military Service* (Boston: Ticknor & Co., 1885), 279; Osborn, *Fiery Trail,* 6.

12. William T. Sherman, *Home Letters of General Sherman,* ed. M. A. DeWolfe Howe (New York: Charles Scribner's Sons, 1909), 305; 38 OR 5:330 (Sherman ill).

13. *New York Times,* Aug. 14, 1864; 38 OR 5:341-42, 364.

14. Ibid., 1:745-46; 2:517; 5:311, 352-54, 361, 364-65; John M. Palmer to his wife, July 24, 1864, Palmer Papers; George T. Palmer, *A Conscientious Turncoat: The Story of John M. Palmer, 1817-1900* (New Haven, Conn.: Yale University Press, 1941), 154. Schofield's and Palmer's major general commissions bear the same date—November 29, 1862; but Schofield's is a retroactive one, as his promotion to that rank was not confirmed by the Senate until early 1864. Moreover, although technically Schofield is Palmer's superior by virtue of being an army and department commander, Palmer has served as a major general longer than Schofield. Perhaps most fundamental of all, Palmer despises West Pointers because he senses, not without cause, that they despise him as a "political general." As regards

Schofield specifically, it is also worth noting that throughout the campaign Palmer has always addressed him in dispatches as commander of the XXIII Corps, never as commander of the Army of the Ohio (see Palmer, *Conscientious Turncoat*, 157–58; and John M. Schofield, *Forty-six Years in the Army* (New York: Century Co., 1897), 150–51.

15. 38 OR 1:510, 525, 746; 2:517–18; 5:365–66, 368–72, 378–85, 391–94, 438; John M. Palmer to his Wife, July 24, 1864, Palmer Papers; Jacob D. Cox Diary, Aug. 5, 1864; Palmer, *Conscientious Turncoat*, 154; James Austin Connolly, "Major Connolly's Letters to His Wife, 1862–1865," *Transactions of the Illinois Historical Society* 35 (1928): 356.

16. 38 OR 2:518, 573, 689–90, 705–7; 3:763; 5:397–401, 403, 933–34, 941, 943–44, 947, 950; Jacob D. Cox Diary, Aug. 6, 1864; Henry Clay Weaver, "Georgia through Kentucky Eyes: Letters Written on Sherman's March to Atlanta," ed. James M. Merrill and James F. Marshall, *Filson Club Historical Quarterly* 30 (1956): 332 (Reilly sobbing); Jacob D. Cox, *Atlanta* (New York: Charles Scribner's Sons, 1882), 192; Ed Porter Thompson, *History of the Orphan Brigade* (Louisville: Lewis N. Thompson, 1898), 264–68; James L. Cooper Memoirs, 164; Letter of an Officer in Tyler's Brigade, *Richmond Dispatch*, Aug. 18, 1864, quoted in *New York Times*, Aug. 28, 1864.

17. 38 OR 1:746–47; 2:518, 690; 5:415–16, 438, 462–63; Jacob D. Cox Diary, Aug. 7, 1864; Cox, *Atlanta*, 192–93; Atlanta Campaign Diary, Aug. 7, 1864; *New York Times*, Aug. 21, 1864.

18. William T. Sherman, *Memoirs of Gen. W. T. Sherman*, 4th ed. (New York: Charles L. Webster & Co., 1891), 2:99–101; B. H. Liddell Hart, *Sherman: Soldier, Realist, American* (New York: Frederick A. Praeger, 1958), 292–93; Clauss, "Atlanta Campaign," 227–28.

19. 38 OR 1:79; 5:408–9, 412, 417, 422–23, 434–35; William T. Sherman to Ellen, Aug. 6, 9, 1864, Sherman Papers, Notre Dame; Sherman, *Memoirs*, 2:101–2; Cox, *Atlanta*, 194.

20. 38 OR 2:489; 3:690, 993; 5:434–37, 439–40, 448–49; Andrew J. Neal to Ella, Aug. 4, 1864, Neal Letters; Alfred Lacy Hough, *Soldier in the West: The Civil War Letters of Alfred Lacy Hough*, ed. Robert G. Athearn (Philadelphia: University of Pennsylvania Press, 1956), 213; Noble C. Williams, *Echoes from the Battlefields; or, Southern Life during the War* (Atlanta: 1902), 33; John Davidson and Julia Davidson, "A Wartime Story: The Davidson Letters, 1862–1865," ed. Jane Bonner Peacock, *Atlanta Historical Bulletin* 29 (1975): 99; *Chattanooga* (Griffin, Ga.) *Daily Rebel*, n.d., and *Macon Daily Telegraph*, n.d., quoted in *Cincinnati Daily Commercial*, Aug. 10, 1864; *Columbia Carolinian*, Aug. 5, 1864, quoted in *New York Times*, Aug. 28, 1864; *Richmond Daily Examiner*, Sept. 1, 1864; Carrie Berry Diary, Aug. 9, 10, 1864; Franklin M. Garrett, *Atlanta and Environs: A Chronicle of Its People and Events* (New York: Lewis Historical Publishing Co., 1954), 626–27, 638–39; A. A. Hoehling, *Last Train from Atlanta* (New York and London: Thomas Yoseloff, 1958), 285–86 (Hood and Bishop Lay).

21. Charles T. Quintard Diary, Aug. 9, 10, 1864; Hoehling, *Last Train*, 285–86, quoting Aug. 11, 1864 letter by Bishop Lay; Arthur H. Noll, ed., *Doctor Quintard, Chaplain C.S.A.* (Sewanee, Tenn.: University of the South, 1905), 100–101; Garrett, *Atlanta*, 639.

22. 38 OR 3:632, 957; 5:941, 951, 953–54; William E. Sloan Diary, Aug. 9, 10, 11, 1864.

23. 38 OR 5:328–29, 350, 367–68, 410–11, 433–34, 447, 461.

24. 52 OR 1:621, 698–99; Sherman to Ellen, Aug. 6, 1864; Sherman to Thomas Ewing Sr., Aug. 11, 1864, in Sherman, *Home Letters*, 307.

25. 38 OR 5:434, 482, 609; William T. Sherman to Ellen, Aug. 6, 1864; Schuyler Colfax to Sherman, Aug. 2, 1864; John Sherman to Sherman, Aug. 6, 1864; and Sherman to Colfax, Aug. 12, 1864, all in Sherman Papers, Notre Dame; Osborn, *Fiery Trail*, 18 (for Sherman's comments to Howard and his staff).

26. 38 OR 5:457, 459, 486–87.

27. Ibid., 523–33, 538–43, 546–51, 555–63; Edwin B. Coddington, *The Gettysburg Cam-*

paign: A Study in Command (Dayton: Press of the Morningside Bookshop, 1979), 548–49, 820 (for Kilpatrick's character); James F. Rusling, *Men and Things I Saw in Civil War Days* (New York: Eaton Mains, 1899), 133 (Sherman's headquarters).

28. James Hibbard and Albert Castel, "Kilpatrick's Jonesboro Raid, August 18–22, 1864," *Atlanta Historical Journal* 29 (1985): 32–42, which also presents all pertinent sources. For Kilpatrick's expectation that he would reach Jonesboro by noon, August 19, see Sherman to Howard, August 18, 1864, 38 OR 5:603–4. An account of Minty's charge, far different from that given by Union participants, will be found in a letter by one of Ross's officers in the *Chattanooga* (Griffin, Ga.) *Daily Rebel*, Aug. 29, 1864, as quoted in the *New York Herald*, Sept. 16, 1864. Minty's men will claim, for they sincerely believe it, that they broke through Cleburne's Division. Presumably this mistake arises from the telegram intercepted at Jonesboro stating that that division was coming out of Atlanta and from the presence at Lovejoy's of both Arkansas (Reynolds's Brigade) and Texas (Ross's Brigade) troops. Had Minty's troopers indeed charged Cleburne's Division or any considerable portion of it, few of them would have survived to tell the tale. In his report (38 OR 3:825–26) Minty asserts that "hundreds" of Confederates "fell beneath our keen blades." This sort of bombast typifies his reports on the campaign throughout, causing General Garrard to endorse one of them with the sarcastic comment: "This report is forwarded; but lest there should be some misunderstanding in the matter, I would respectfully state that I was in command of the Second Cavalry Division [in which Minty's brigade served] during the past campaign" (ibid., 815).

29. 38 OR 3:692; 5:628–29, 631, 639, 642, 649; David S. Stanley, *Personal Memoirs of Major General D. S. Stanley, U.S.A.* (Cambridge, Mass.: Harvard University Press, 1917), 179 (for Kilpatrick riding in a carriage).

30. *New York World*, Aug. 16, 17, 18, 22, 1864; *Chicago Daily Times*, Aug. 12, 16, 23, 24, 1864; *Jefferson County* (New York) *Union*, n.d., quoted in *Hillsdale* (Michigan) *Democrat*, Sept. 8, 1864; Strong, *Diary*, 3:474; Shelby Foote, *The Civil War, A Narrative: Red River to Appomattox* (New York: Random House, 1974), 544–47.

31. James G. Randall and David Donald, *The Civil War and Reconstruction*, 2d ed. (New York: D.C. Heath & Co., 1969), 473–74; Roy P. Basler, et al., eds., *The Collected Works of Abraham Lincoln* (New Brunswick, N.J.: Rutgers University Press, 1953–55), 7:514; James G. Randall and Richard N. Current, *Last Full Measure: Lincoln the President* (New York: Dodd, Mead & Co., 1955), 210–13; Carl Sandburg, *Abraham Lincoln: The War Years* (New York: Harcourt, Brace & Co., 1939), 3:202–12.

32. *Richmond Sentinel*, Aug. 20, 1864, quoted in *Cincinnati Daily Commercial*, Aug. 25, 1864; Jones, *Rebel War Clerk's Diary*, 2:269; Nelson, "Election of 1864," 260–64.

33. Samuel L. Cleveland to Mrs. Hagar (*sic*), Aug. 8, 1864, Phinehas A. Hager Letters; Henry Orendorff, *We Are Sherman's Men: The Civil War Letters of Henry Orendorff*, ed. William M. Anderson (Macomb: Western Illinois University, 1986), 100; Cavins, *War Letters*, 92–93; 38 OR 3:716; 5:595, 604–5; Clyde C. Walton, ed., *Behind the Guns: A History of Battery I, 2nd Regiment, Illinois Light Artillery* (Carbondale: Southern Illinois Press, 1965), 98–99; Othniel Gooding to Lucy Dexter, Aug. 18, 1864, Gooding Letters; James P. Snell Diary, Aug. 26, 1864; James G. Theaker, *Through One Man's Eyes. Letters of James G. Theaker*, ed. Paul E. Rieger (Mount Vernon, Ohio: Printing Arts Press, 1974), 121.

34. Thomas T. Taylor Diary, Aug. 1, 4, 20–22, 1864; Taylor to his wife, Aug. 22, 1864; Taylor Letters; Daniel Devine Rose Diary, Aug. 25, 1864.

35. Israel Atkins to his parents, Aug. 16, 1864, Atkins Letters; O'Leary, "Letters," 174–75; David Noble to his mother, Aug. 22, 1864, Noble Diaries and Letters; William Strawn Narrative, 34–36; Orendorff, *We Are Sherman's Men*, 101; John A. Barnard, *Portrait of a Hero: The Story of Absalom Baird, His Family and the American Military Tradition* (Philadelphia: Dorrance & Co., 1972), 155 (Walter quote). See also Michael H. Fitch, *Echoes of the Civil War as I Hear Them* (New York: William S. Porter Press, 1905), 217, and Cavins, *War Letters*, 92.

36. Samuel King Vann to Lizzie, Aug. 25, 1864, Vann Letters; Honnell to his sisters, Aug. 25, 1864, Honnell Family Papers; Arthur M. Manigault, *A Carolinian Goes to War: The Civil War Narrative of Arthur Middleton Manigault, Brigadier General, C.S.A.*, ed. R. Lockwood Tower (Columbia: University of South Carolina Press, 1983), 241–42; Elbert D. Willett, *History of Company B* (Anniston, Ala.: Nerwood, 1902), 78; B. P. Weaver to his father and mother, Aug. 18, 1864, Weaver Letters; Wiley, "Three Southern Officers," 34; McDermid, "Letters," 293; 38 OR 1:533, 538, 543, 551; 3:706; 5:962–63, 965.

37. Ervin Godfrey to his wife, Aug. 14, 1864, Godfrey Letters; Sykes to his wife, Aug. 14, 1864, Sykes Letters; Ellison Capers to his wife, Aug. 19, 1864, Capers Letters; Taylor Beatty Diary, Aug. 19, 1864; Edwin H. Rennolds Diary, Aug. 19, 1864; *Key Diary*, Aug. 23, 1864; Charles Henry Thiott to his wife, Aug. 24, 1864, Thiott Family Papers; James P. Douglas, *Douglas's Texas Battery, C.S.A.*, ed. Lucia Rutherford Douglas (Tyler, Tex.: Smith County Historical Society, 1966), 123; Douglas Cater to his cousin, Aug. 18, 1864, quoted in William James McNeil, "The Stress of War: The Confederacy and William Tecumseh Sherman during the Last Year of the Civil War," Ph.D. diss., Rice University, 1973, 66; Samuel King Vann to Lizzie, Aug. 25, 1864, Vann Letters; undated issues of *Augusta Daily Constitutionalist* and *Mobile Daily Advertiser and Register*, quoted in *New York Times*, Sept. 6, 1864; *Macon Daily Telegraph*, Aug. 24, 1864, quoted in *Cincinnati Daily Commercial*, Sept. 8, 1864, expressing optimism based on belief that Wheeler was destroying Sherman's supply line; *Macon Confederate*, n.d., quoted in *New York Times*, Aug. 23, 1864; W. C. Dodson, ed., *Campaigns of Wheeler and His Cavalry, 1862–1865* (Atlanta: Hudgins Publishing Co., 1899), 262–64; Eliza Walker, "Other Days," *Alabama Historical Quarterly* 5 (1943): 56.

38. 38 OR 1:79–80, 164, 212–13; 2:18–19; W. H. Newlin, comp., *A History of the Seventy-third Regiment of Illinois Volunteer Infantry* (Springfield, Ill.:1890), 341.

39. W. L. Trask Diary, Aug. 26, 1864; Samuel G. French, *Two Wars: An Autobiography* (Nashville: Confederate Veteran, 1901), 221; *Key Diary*, 116, 121; Edwin H. Rennolds Diary, Aug. 19, 26, 1864; Taylor Beatty Diary, Aug. 19, 23, 26, 1864; Douglas, *Douglas's Texas Battery*, 123; Ellison Capers to his wife, Aug. 19, 1864, Capers Letters; *Macon Daily Telegraph*, Aug. 15, 1864, quoted in *New York Times*, Aug. 26, 1864; *Atlanta* (Macon) *Daily Intelligencer*, Aug. 19, 1864; 38 OR 3:692–93; 5:990–92.

40. 38 OR 1:164, 213, 512, 927; 2:518; 3:42–43, 632–33, 693; 5:993–96; Wiley, "Three Southern Officers," 34; Douglas, *Douglas's Texas Battery*, 126; McDermid, "Letters," 293.

41. Carrie Berry Diary, Aug. 11–28, 1864; Samuel P. Richards Diary, Aug. 14, 18, 21, 27, 28, 1864; *Key Diary*, 119–23; Joseph F. Culver, *"Your Affectionate Husband, J. F. Culver."* Letters Written during the Civil War, ed. Leslie W. Dunlop (Iowa City: Friends of the University of Iowa Libraries, 1978), 359; *Mobile Daily Advertiser and Register*, Sept. 3, 1864 ("Shadow" report); *Augusta Daily Constitutionalist*, n.d., quoted in *New York Times*, Aug. 28, Sept. 6, 1864; *Atlanta* (Macon) *Daily Intelligencer*, Aug. 18, 27, 1864; *New York Times*, Aug. 23, 1864, quoting telegrams from Atlanta, source not given; 38 OR 1:123; Stanley, *Memoirs*, 176; Orlando M. Poe to his wife, Sept. 7, 1864, Poe Letters; Garrett, *Atlanta*, 626–29; Hoehling, *Last Train*, 346–67. On August 25, 1864, Joseph Semmes, a commissary officer stationed in Atlanta, wrote his wife that "the surgeon of the Post Hospital informed me that he has performed 107 amputations on men, women, and children since the enemy commenced shelling the city, all citizens" (quoted in Hoehling, *Last Train*, 365). Assuming, as is probable, that Semmes reported the surgeon's statement accurately, this on the surface would seem to support "Shadow's" figures as to casualties. But Semmes's letter still leaves unexplained, and hence close to incredible, the almost 5:6 ratio of killed to wounded, whereas Richards's statement that 20 people had been killed is compatible with 107 amputations. Furthermore in an earlier letter to his wife (quoted in ibid., 348) Semmes wrote that although 2,000 shells fell in the city on the night of August 13, "but one soldier was killed and several women and children killed and wounded,"

adding that the shells "are only dangerous when they burst before reaching us or when striking a building."

42. 38 OR 5:688, 695.

43. Ibid., 3:693–94, 957–59; 5:905–6, 971, 997–99; Taylor Beatty Diary, Aug. 28, 1864; French, *Two Wars,* 221–22; O. P. Hargis, Thrilling Experiences of a First Georgia Cavalryman in the Civil War, 12–13; William E. Sloan Diary, Aug. 15–20, 1864 (on Wheeler's operations).

44. 38 OR 1:80. Description of railroad destruction based mainly on Theodore F. Upson, *With Sherman to the Sea: The Civil War Letters, Diaries and Reminiscences of Theodore F. Upson,* ed. Oscar G. Winther (Bloomington: University of Indiana Press, 1958), 123–24.

45. Orlando M. Poe to his wife, Aug. 30, 1864, Poe Letters; 38 OR 5:709; James P. Snell Diary, Aug. 29, 1864. On September 5, 1864, General Corse was "very much grieved to find in the Twelfth Illinois Infantry, lying shamelessly exposed to the whole command, a lot of male and female clothing and wearing apparel, shirts, bed-quilts, &c., evidently recently pillaged from some of the neighboring helpless citizens" (38 OR 5:803). This indicates how effective Howard's order against plundering was.

46. 38 OR 5:697–709. For Federal estimate of militia strength in Atlanta, see ibid., 498–99, 579.

47. 38 OR 3:694; 5:999; William Joseph Hardee to his wife, Aug. 30, 1864, Hardee Letters.

48. *Key Diary,* 123; Charles W. Wills, *Army Life of an Illinois Soldier* (Washington, D.C.: Globe Printing Co., 1906), 291–92.

49. 38 OR 2:860; 3:43–44; Oliver Otis Howard *Autobiography of Oliver Otis Howard* (New York: Baker & Taylor Co., 1907), 2:34–37; Oliver Otis Howard to his wife, Sept. 11, 1864, Howard Letters. Confederate strength at Jonesboro on August 30: Reynolds's Brigade, on the basis of its strength and losses at Ezra Church (38 OR 3:940) probably numbers at most 500; and Lewis's Brigade, if an August 31 telegram from Shoup to Hardee with regard to mounting it is a valid indication, totals around 600. Likewise it is unlikely that either Ross's or Armstrong's brigades are any larger than they were during Kilpatrick's raid on Jonesboro.

50. This description of Hood's conference with Hardee and Lee on the night of August 30 and of his plans for August 31 and September 1 is based mainly on Hood, *Advance and Retreat,* 205. Although Hood's account cannot, of course, be considered absolutely trustworthy, there is no reason to doubt its essential truth. Not only is the plan that Hood says he sought to implement in character; it is the only one he could have adopted, unrealistic as it might be, consistent with holding onto Atlanta. Moreover Hood's testimony is supported in part by Lee's report (38 OR 3:764) and by Captain Benjamin Lane Posey, commander of the 38th Alabama, Lee's Corps, in a letter to be found in the *Mobile Daily Advertiser and Register,* Sept. 20, 1864.

51. 38 OR 3:694, 700, 764; 5:1000–1006; William Joseph Hardee to his wife, Aug. 30, 1864, Hardee Letters; Hood, *Advance and Retreat,* 204–5; Thomas L. Connelly, *Autumn of Glory: The Army of Tennessee, 1862–1865.* (Baton Rouge: Louisiana State University Press, 1971), 458–62.

52. William Joseph Hardee to his wife, Aug. 4, 5, 17, 29, 1864; Hardee to Davis, Aug. 3, 6, 1864; Davis to Hardee, Aug. 4, 7, 1864, all in Hardee Letters. See also 38 OR 5:987–88.

53. Ibid., 721, 725–26, 730–31.

54. Colonel Phillip Sidney Post, now commanding Hazen's former brigade, reports (38 OR 1:428) that during the night of August 30 "a large force of the enemy, with artillery and trains, moved past our position in a southerly direction." Thus the IV Corps could have blocked or at least attempted to block the march of Hardee's Corps to Jonesboro. No known source reveals why it did not do so. Captain Posey, in his aforementioned letter in

the *Mobile Daily Advertiser and Register,* Sept. 20, 1864, criticizes Hood for not sending Hardee's and Lee's corps to Jonesboro by rail. The Confederates, however, did not have sufficient rolling stock available to transport these corps, which were accompanied by the Army of Tennessee's provision and ordnance trains, to Jonesboro quickly. Also it would have been extremely hazardous to have attempted it, for a single squad of Union cavalry could have halted the movement by burning a bridge or tearing up a section of track, and the troops aboard the trains would have been virtually defenseless if intercepted by a large Federal force. Posey was a knowledgable and intelligent officer, but he seems to have been curiously ill informed concerning railroad matters. Thus, in his letter he states that Atlanta still had a rail connection with Augusta, Georgia!

55. 38 OR 3:700, 764; 5:1007; Irving A. Buck, ed., *Cleburne and His Command* (Jackson, Tenn.: McCowat-Mercer Press, 1959), 250.

56. 38 OR 5:726–27.

57. 38 OR 3:700, 764, 772–73; Manigault, *Narrative,* 244; Francis P. Fleming, "Francis P. Fleming in the War for Southern Independence: Letters from the Front," ed. Edward C. Williamson, *Florida Historical Quarterly* 28 (1949): 153–54; *Mobile Daily Advertiser and Register,* Sept. 20, 1864, containing letter from Captain Benjamin Lane Posey, commander of the 38th Alabama, Bushrod Jones's Brigade, who states that one third of Lee's men dropped from the ranks during the march to Jonesboro.

58. 38 OR 3:694; 5:1007; Wilbur G. Kurtz, "Unofficial Glimpses of Hood," 2 (cites Bishop Lay's journal as source), Kurtz Collection.

59. 38 OR 3:682–83, 700, 708, 727, 735, 741, 743–44, 755, 764, 773, 821–22, 824, 857; Edwin H. Rennolds Diary, Aug. 31, 1864; Captain Posey in *Mobile Daily Advertiser and Register,* Sept. 20, 1864; Manigault, *Narrative,* 245–46. That Stevenson's Division was on the right of Cleburne's (Hardee's) corps is established by Henry W. Wright, *A History of the Sixth Iowa Infantry* (Iowa City: Iowa State Historical Society, 1923), 323–24, and Granbury's report, 38 OR 3:743–44. For Cheatham's illness, see Losson, *Tennessee's Forgotten Warriors,* 189.

60. Jacob D. Cox, *Military Reminiscences of the Civil War* (New York: Charles E. Scribner, 1900), 2:282; Jacob D. Cox Diary, Aug. 30, 1864; 38 OR 3:44–45, 108–9; 5:728, 743–44; Oliver Otis Howard, "The Battles about Atlanta," *Atlantic Monthly* 37 (1876): 563–64.

61. 38 OR 3:764–65, 773–74, 822, 824, 835, 857–58; Thomas T. Taylor Diary, August 31, 1864; Manigault, *Narrative,* 246–47; Posey in *Mobile Daily Advertiser and Register,* Sept. 20, 1864; Taylor Beatty Diary, Aug. 31, 1864 (on Deas's Brigade).

62. 38 OR 3:412–13, 700, 708–11, 727, 735, 742, 744, 755–56; Edwin H. Rennolds Diary, August 31, 1864; Jackson to Benjamin F. Cheatham, Dec. 10, 1864, Cheatham Papers (on refusal of Finley's and Tyler's brigades to advance); Fleming, "Letters from the Front," 154; Samuel T. Foster, *One of Cleburne's Command. The Civil War Reminiscences and Diary of Capt. Samuel T. Foster, Granbury's Texas Brigade, C.S.A.,* ed. Norman D. Brown (Austin: University of Texas Press, 1980), 125–26; James L. Cooper Memoirs, 47–48; Howard, *Autobiography,* 2:37.

For Confederate casualties see Lee's report, 38 OR 3:764; Hood to Bragg, September 5, 1864, ibid., 5:1021; Jackson to Cheatham, December 10, 1864, Cheatham Papers; W. J. McMurray, *History of the Twentieth Tennessee Regiment Volunteer Infantry, C.S.A.* (Nashville: 1904), 325; Fleming, "Letters from the Front," 154; and Hazen, *Narrative of Military Service,* 250. Again illustrating the unreliability of estimates by either side of enemy casualties, Howard in his report (38 OR 3:45) asserts that the Rebels lost 6,000. This would be well over one-half of the Confederate troops that were seriously engaged. Manigault, *Narrative,* 246, citing Lee as his source, accuses Hardee of endeavoring "to throw the brunt of the fight" on Lee's Corps and therefore making no real effort to attack the Federals. The curious performance of Lowrey's and Maney's divisions seems to support this allegation, but most likely this was the result of an unwillingness of the troops to charge breastworks, rather than military malfeasance on the part of Hardee, although it is worth noting that General French (*Two Wars*, 222) claims in his published diary that Hardee once deliberately put his division into an exposed position where it suffered heavy casualties.

63. 38 OR 3:109–10, 633, 727, 764–65, 835; Wiley, "Three Southern Officers," 34; Julius Montgomery Macon to Miss Clifford, Sept. 6, 1864, Macon Letters; Manigault, *Narrative*, 247.

64. 38 OR 5:727, 732–33; William C. Titze Diary, Aug. 31, 1864 (Logan "in best of spirits"); Eben P. Sturges to "Dear Folks," Sept. 6, 1864, Sturges Diary and Letters (Sherman's reaction to Schofield's message); Howard, *Autobiography*, 2:39.

65. 38 OR 3:694, 701; 5:1007–9; Wilbur G. Kurtz, "What James Bell Told Me About the Siege of Atlanta," Kurtz Collection (for return of freight trains).

66. 38 OR 5:718–19; 52 OR 1:612. Both Sherman's report (38 OR 1:81) and his *Memoirs*, 2:107, give brief and misleading accounts of the operations of August 31. Henry Stone, "Part III. The Siege and Capture of Atlanta," in *The Atlanta Papers*, comp. Sydney C. Kerksis (Dayton: Press of the Morningside Bookshop, 1980), 452–57, was the first to point out Sherman's obsession with destroying the railroads around Atlanta and its consequences. Despite some erroneous dates, Alfred H. Burne, *Lee, Grant and Sherman: A Study in Leadership in the 1864–65 Campaign* (Wellington Works, Aldershot, Eng.: Gale & Polden, 1938), 120–22, makes the same point, but Liddell Hart, *Sherman*, 297–300, either ignores it or, when that is impossible, endeavors to conceal it in a smokescreen of verbiage.

67. 38 OR 3:701, 727, 765.

68. *American Annual Cyclopaedia and Register of Important Events of the Year 1864* (New York: D. Appleton & Co., 1871), 793; *New York Herald*, Sept. 1, 1864; Frank L. Klement, *The Copperheads of the Middle West* (Chicago: University of Chicago Press, 1960), 235.

CHAPTER NINE: SEPTEMBER

1. 38 OR 3:633, 694, 765, 906; 5:1011–13; John Bell Hood, *Advance and Retreat* (New York: Krauss Reprint Co., 1969), 206–8; W. L. Trask Diary, Aug. 31, 1864; *Atlanta* (Macon) *Daily Intelligencer*, Sept. 8, 1864; *Cincinnati Daily Commercial*, Sept. 29, 1864. Hood's reaction to news of Hardee's repulse in Posey's "Letter from the Army of Tennessee," *Mobile Daily Advertiser and Register*, Sept. 20, 1864.

2. 38 OR 5:752–53.

3. Ibid., 3:701, 718–19, 728, 742, 744, 756; 5:1011; Samuel T. Foster, *One of Cleburne's Command. The Civil War Reminiscences and Diary of Capt. Samuel T. Foster, Granbury's Brigade, C.S.A.*, ed. Norman D. Brown (Austin: University of Texas Press, 1980), 126.

4. 38 OR 1:213, 932; 2:519; 5:746, 753.

5. 38 OR 3:719, 729, 742.

6. On the basis of the available evidence it is impossible to determine exactly what Blair's orders were or who originated them. In his *Memoirs*, 2:107, Sherman asserts that he "ordered General Howard to send the two divisions of the Seventeenth Corps (Blair's) round by his [Howard's] right rear, to get below Jonesboro, and to reach the railroad, so as to cut off retreat in that direction." However, in his report (38 OR 1:82) Sherman states that Blair's corps was "sent well to the right below Jonesborough to act against that flank, along with General Kilpatrick's cavalry." Probably Blair's movement was, as Howard's report (ibid., 3:46) indicates, simply a part of the demonstration being carried out by the Army of the Tennessee with the intention of pinning Hardee down at Jonesboro and preventing him from reinforcing his right. One also gets the impression that the XVII Corps, as a consequence of its ordeal on July 22, has such an intense fear of being attacked in the open that it is incapable of offensive action.

7. Battle of Jonesboro, Sept. 1, 1864; Union sources: 38 OR 1:514–15, 558–600, 641–42, 644–45, 655–56, 681–82, 714–15, 749–53, 756; James Taylor Holmes, *Fifty-second Ohio Volunteer Infantry: Then and Now* (Columbus: Berlin Printing Co., 1898), 1:214–23, 256; C. C. Carpenter, "A Commissary in the Union Army: Letters of C. C. Carpenter," ed. Mildred Throne, *Iowa Journal of History* 53 (1955): 79; Albert L. Slack to his parents, Aug. [Sept.] 10, 1864, Slack Letters; Corydon Edward Foote, *With Sherman to the Sea: A Drummer Boy's Story of the Civil War*, ed. Olive Deane Hormel (New York: John Day Co., 1960), 194–95; James Austin Connolly, "Major Connolly's Letters to His Wife, 1862–1865" *Transactions of the Illinois Historical Society* 35 (1928): 360–61; *New York Weekly Tribune*, Sept. 21, 1864; *New York Times*, Sept. 13, 1864; *New York Herald*, Sept. 8, 1864; *Cincinnati Daily Commercial*, Sept. 13, 1864; Clyde C. Walton, ed., *Behind the Guns: A History of Battery I, 2nd Regiment, Illinois Light Artillery* (Carbondale: Southern Illinois Press, 1965), 110–11. Confederate sources: 38 OR 3:719–20, 729, 742–45; Foster, *Diary*, 125; Ed Porter Thompson, *History of the Orphan Brigade* (Louisville: Lewis N. Thompson, 1898), 266–68; *Key Diary*, 126–27; Charles H. Olmstead, *The Memoirs of Charles H. Olmstead*, ed. Lilla Mills Hawes (Savannah: Georgia Historical Society, 1964), 154–56; Robert Lewis Bliss to his father, June 15, 1864 (on determination of Cleburne's troops to hold position), Bliss Letters; Larry J. Daniel, *Cannoneers in Gray: The Field Artillery of the Army of Tennessee, 1861–1865* (University: University of Alabama Press, 1984), 164, Edward R. Hutchins, comp., *The War of the Sixties* (New York: Neale Publishing Co., 1912), 398–99; Joseph Erwin, "Swett's Battery at Jonesboro," *Confederate Veteran* 12 (1904): 112.

After the battle, Morgan angrily challenged the claim of Baird and Este in their reports that Este's brigade had made the breakthrough that led to victory, even going so far as to assert that his division had rescued Este's men from capture (38 OR 1:644–46)! Confederate accounts support the Baird-Este version in all essentials, and that version has on the whole been followed above, with the main departure from it being to credit Lum's brigade with sharing in the capture of Key's Battery, something that Baird and Este denied. It is worth noting too that whereas Morgan's division as a whole lost 540 killed, wounded, and missing, Este's brigade alone lost in all those categories 341 (nearly one-third of its strength), that nearly half of Morgan's casualties occurred in Lum's brigade (263), and that slightly more than one-third of Lum's casualties were suffered by the 17th New York (97), which participated in Este's assault. These figures provide further evidence of the key role played by Este's brigade and also demonstrate that its success was not easy; it came at a high price (ibid., 517–18, 678).

8. 38 OR 1:214–15, 299, 932–33; 3:719 (Capers's report); 5:746–47; David S. Stanley, *Personal Memoirs of Major General D. S. Stanley, U.S.A.* (Cambridge, Mass.: Harvard University Press, 1917), 183. For confirmation of Stanley's wound, which made him ill, see Chesley A. Mosman, *The Rough Side of War: The Civil War Journal of Chesley A. Mosman, 1st Lieutenant, Company D, 59th Illinois Volunteer Infantry Regiment*, ed. Arnold Gates (Garden City, N.Y.: Basin Publishing Co., 1987), 270.

9. 38 OR 3:46, 110, 391, 596, 696; Mark P. Lowrey Autobiography, 6; Edwin H. Rennolds Diary, September 1, 1864; Ellison Capers, *South Carolina. Confederate Military History: A Library of Confederate States History, in Twelve Volumes, Written by Distinguished Men of the South and Edited by Gen. Clement A. Evans of Georgia* (Atlanta: Confederate Publishing Company, 1899), 339; James P. Snell Diary, Sept. 1, 1864.

Oliver Otis Howard, "The Battles about Atlanta," *Atlantic Monthly* 37 (1876): 565, states that on being informed by Sherman on the night of August 31 that Schofield's and Thomas's forces were astride the railroad between Jonesboro and Atlanta, he concluded that "I could then wait for Thomas to push Jeff. C. Davis's and Stanley's corps upon Hardee's exposed right flank" and so "decided to run no risk by a hasty advance." It would be more accurate to say that Howard had decided to run no risk at all.

10. 38 OR 5:746, 749, 751, 755.

11. 38 OR 3:695, 765, 906; 5:1014; Carrie Berry Diary, Sept. 1, 1864; Samuel P. Richards Diary, Sept. 1, 1864; G. W. Smith to Governor Brown, Sept. 5, 1864, *Macon Southern Confederacy,* Sept. 14, as quoted in *Cincinnati Daily Commercial,* Sept. 29, 1864; "Rover," in *Atlanta* (Macon) *Daily Intelligencer,* September 8, 1864; Samuel G. French, *Two Wars: An Autobiography* (Nashville: Confederate Veteran, 1901), 222; Noble C. Williams, *Echoes from the Battlefields; or, Southern Life during the War* (Atlanta: 1902), 34; Arthur M. Manigault, *A Carolinian Goes to War: The Civil War Narrative of Arthur Middleton Manigault, Brigadier General, C.S.A.,* ed. R. Lockwood Tower (Columbia: University of South Carolina Press, 1983), 249 (on reaction of soldiers to finding supposedly nonexistent supplies in Atlanta's warehouses); Wilbur G. Kurtz, "The Jonesboro Campaign," Kurtz Collection; Franklin M. Garrett, *Atlanta and Environs: A Chronicle of Its People and Events* (New York: Lewis Historical Publishing Co., 1954), 633.

12. 38 OR 3:633, 906, 991–92; Mary Rawson Diary, 1; French, *Two Wars,* 222; Columbus, Georgia, *Sun,* Sept. 6, 1864, quoted in *New York Herald,* Sept. 16, 1864.

13. William T. Sherman, *Memoirs of Gen. W. T. Sherman,* 4th ed. (New York: Charles L. Webster & Co., 1891), 2:108. In his *Forty-six Years in the Army,* 158, Schofield sarcastically comments that "an untutored farmer may well have thought 'these sounds were just like those of a battle,' but a practiced ear could not have failed to note the difference." In fact many Union officers and troops, including some with more experience of war than Schofield, shared Sherman's uncertainty as to the nature of the noise coming from Atlanta; see Harvey Reid, *The View from Headquarters: Civil War Letters of Harvey Reid,* ed. Frank L. Byrne (Madison: State Historical Society of Wisconsin, 1965), 182; Taylor Diary, Sept. 1, 1864; Hazen, *Narrative of Military Service,* 295; Alpheus S. Williams, *From the Cannon's Mouth: The Civil War Letters of General Alpheus S. Williams,* ed. Milo M. Quaife (Detroit: Wayne State University Press, 1959), 339–40; Alexis Cope, *The Fifteenth Ohio Volunteers and Its Campaigns* (Columbus: Press of the Edward T. Miller Co., 1918), 556–58. What is puzzling is that Sherman would ask the farmer's opinion on the matter. Although the farmer presumably had heard the sounds of the battles of July 20, 22, and 28, he had no basis for comparing them with the sound of magazines being blown up and thus was almost sure to give the answer he did. One is tempted to dismiss this story as just another of Sherman's yarns, but since it does him no credit and is in keeping with his eccentric ways, let us accept it as probably true.

14. 38 OR 3:729, 743, 745; "Hardee's Fight Near Jonesboro," *Atlanta* (Macon) *Daily Intelligencer,* Sept. 10, 1864; *New York Herald,* Sept. 8, 1864, reporting capture of 200 Confederate wounded at Jonesboro; Stephen Davis, "The Battles of Atlanta: Events from July 10 to September 2, 1864," *Blue & Gray Magazine,* Aug. 1989: 60.

15. 38 OR 5:764, 767; *Cincinnati Daily Commercial,* Sept. 13, 1864; *New York Weekly Tribune,* Sept. 21, 1864.

16. 38 OR 1:527, 563, 642, 752, 764, 766, 772–73, 812, 933; Thompson, *Orphan Brigade,* 267–68; Hugh D. Gallagher to his brother, Sept. 12, 1864, Gallagher Correspondence and Papers.

17. 38 OR 1:20–21, 145–46, 319–20, 330–33, 392–93; 5:763; Mary Rawson Diary, 1; John W. Bates Diary, Sept. 2, 1864; Samuel P. Richards Diary, Sept. 2, 1864; Carrie Berry Diary, Sept. 2, 1864; John A. Wilkens to his sister, Sept. 5, 1864, Wilkens Correspondence; Williams, *Echoes from the Battlefield,* 40–43; Julian M. Hinkley, *A Narrative of Service with the Third Wisconsin Infantry* (Madison: Wisconsin History Commission, 1912), 140–44; Samuel Merrill, *The Seventieth Indiana Volunteer Infantry* (Indianapolis: Bowen-Merrill Co., 1900), 166–67; *New York Herald,* Sept. 8, 1864; *Cincinnati Daily Commercial,* Sept. 13, 1864; *New York Times,* Sept. 15, 1864; Garrett, *Atlanta,* 634–36.

18. 38 OR 1:82, 933; 3:696; 5:772, 776, 784, 1016; Eben P. Sturges Diary, Sept. 2, 1864; Edwin H. Rennolds Diary, Sept. 2, 1864; Foster, *Diary,* 129–30; Irving A. Buck, ed., *Cleburne and His Command* (Jackson, Tenn.: McCowat-Mercer Press, 1959), 258; Man-

igault, *Narrative,* 250; T. B. Roy, "General Hardee and Military Operations around Atlanta," *Southern Historical Society Papers* 8 (1880):375 (for incident regarding Govan's men); *Cincinnati Daily Commercial,* Sept. 13, 1864.

19. 38 OR 1:216, 251–52, 261–62, 299, 384, 451–52, 455, 465, 470; 2:574 (Hassall's report); 3:46; 5:764–65, 771, 774–75; Oliver Otis Howard, *Autobiography of Oliver Otis Howard* (New York: Baker & Taylor Co., 1907), 2:43; Thomas Ward Osborn, *The Fiery Trail: A Union Officer's Account of Sherman's Last Campaigns,* ed. Richard Harwell and Philip N. Racine (Knoxville: University of Tennessee Press, 1986), 37; Philip Sidney Post to his mother, September 4, 1864, Post Correspondence; *Key Diary,* 128; Buck, *Cleburne,* 258; Alexis Cope, *The Fifteenth Ohio Volunteers and Its Campaigns* (Columbus: Press of the Edward T. Miller Co., 1918), 557.

20. Alpheus S. Williams, *From the Cannon's Mouth: The Civil War Letters of General Alpheus S. Williams,* ed. Milo M. Quaife (Detroit: Wayne State University Press, 1959), 341; Hinkley, *Narrative of Service,* 141–42; William Wallace, "William Wallace's Civil War Letters: The Atlanta Campaign," *Wisconsin Magazine of History* 57 (1973–74): 108–10.

21. 38 OR 1:82; 5:777, 789.

In his *Memoirs,* 2:109, Sherman asserts that "the news [from Slocum] seemed [to Thomas] too good to be true" and that Thomas "snapped his fingers, whistled, and almost danced." In view of the fact that Thomas early on the afternoon of September 2 notified Stanley that "we have Atlanta" (Fullerton's Journal, 38 OR 1:933), it is unlikely that he considered the information conveyed in Slocum's dispatch "too good to be true" or that he reacted to it in the manner described by Sherman. Also, in his report (ibid., 82) Sherman states that he received Slocum's message on the night of Sept. 4 (an obvious error), and in his *Memoirs,* 2:108, he says it arrived "Later in the day" on Sept. 2 (another obvious error). The time of arrival given above is based on the Eben Sturges Diary, Sept. 3, 1864, and Henry Stone ("The Siege and Capture of Atlanta," in *The Atlanta Papers,* comp. Sydney C. Kerksis [Dayton: Press of the Morningside Bookshop, 1980], 128); both Sturges and Stone, being with Thomas's headquarters staff, were in a position to know. The account of the means by which Slocum's courier traveled from Atlanta to Sherman's headquarters derives from Colonel Post to Mollie, Sept. 4, 1864, Post Letters, and from McGee, 378.

22. 38 OR 1:115–19, 753–54, 803–4; 2:153, 446; 3:555; 5:785–86; Robert Patrick, *Reluctant Rebel: The Secret Diary of Robert Patrick, 1861–1865,* ed. F. Jay Taylor (Baton Rouge: Louisiana State University Press, 1959), 223; Ira B. Read, "The Campaign from Chattanooga to Atlanta as Seen by a Federal Soldier," ed. Richard B. Harwell, *Georgia Historical Quarterly* 25 (1941): 276; Eben P. Sturges Diary, Sept. 5, 1864; Charles E. Benton, *As Seen from the Ranks: A Boy in the Civil War* (New York: G. P. Putnam's Sons, 1902), 153; Mosman, *Rough Side of War,* 273. Cope, *Fifteenth Ohio,* 561, states that "there were those [in Sherman's army] who remembered that the Confederate Army was the main objective and who felt a secret humiliation in turning our backs to it." No doubt this was true, and it was a justified feeling. Nonetheless, the overwhelming majority of the Union troops, as manifested in their diaries, letters, and memoirs, considered Atlanta to be the objective and hence, like Sherman, were content with having achieved it. Indeed, so strong and pervasive was this attitude that it would have been difficult, perhaps impossible, for Sherman to have gone on with the campaign even had he so desired.

23. 38 OR 3:633; 5:1016, 1021, 1023; 52 OR 2:729–30; Hood, *Advance and Retreat,* 204–6.

24. Orlando M. Poe to his wife, Sept. 12, 1864, Poe Letters.

25. In his *Narrative of Military Operations* (New York: D. Appleton & Co., 1874), 350, Johnston uses the word *forever* to describe how long he could have held Atlanta had he remained in command, but then in his article "Opposing Sherman's Advance to Atlanta," in *Battles and Leaders of the Civil War,* ed. Robert U. Johnson and Clarence C. Buel (New York: Century Co., 1887), 76, which was published thirteen years later, he modifies that

word to *indefinitely*—a highly indefinite term. Both Stanley F. Horn, *The Army of Tennessee: A Military History* (Indianapolis: Bobbs-Merrill Co., 1941), 348–49, and Thomas Connelly, *Autumn of Glory: The Army of Tennessee, 1862–1865* (Baton Rouge: Louisiana State University Press, 1971), 398–405, demonstrate the flimsiness of Johnston's claim—the latter devastatingly so.

Another option open to Hood would have been to do what the *New York Herald* sometime in August had predicted he would do: namely, pull his forces out of Atlanta and shift them to the East Point area, thereby continuing to protect his rail connections while putting himself in position to extend his lines further southward (*New York Herald*, n.d., quoted in *Macon Intelligencer*, Sept. 7, 1864). But since Hood's mission was to hold Atlanta, doing this would have been the strategic equivalent of Lee's abandoning Richmond in order to safeguard better his communications to Petersburg!

26. For examples, see Jacob D. Cox, *Atlanta* (New York: Charles Scribner's Sons, 1882), 218; B. H. Liddell Hart, *Sherman: Soldier, Realist, American* (New York: Frederick A. Praeger, 1958), 298–300; Errol McGregor Clauss, "The Atlanta Campaign, 18 July–2 September 1864," Ph.D. diss., Emory University, 1965, 379.

27. 38 OR 5:791–92.

28. Liddell Hart, *Sherman*, 307, contends that had Sherman "opened out his net [advanced on a broad front] after discovering Hardee's retreat [from Jonesboro] it is unlikely he could have intercepted any of the Confederate columns [Stewart and Lee], for they had only to continue eastward from McDonough to be out of reach." Since Stewart and Lee were desperately endeavoring to join Hardee at Lovejoy's and since this meant that they had to do what in fact they did do—march *westward* from McDonough—this assertion, like many of Liddell Hart's speculations and ruminations concerning the Atlanta Campaign, is meaningless except as an indication of his superficial knowledge of the subject.

29. Osborn, *Fiery Trail*, 15, 18–23. Liddell Hart, *Sherman*, 300, excuses Sherman's failure to achieve greater results on September 1–2 on the grounds that Hood's ordering Lee's Corps from Jonesboro back to Atlanta was "incalculably irrational," a view he evidently derives from Cox, *Atlanta*, 208, where it is stated that Lee's "eccentric march back toward Atlanta, in obedience to Hood's order, could not have been imagined by any military man." As has been demonstrated in the text, Hood planned to have Lee return to Atlanta regardless of the outcome of Hardee's August 31 attack, for that was in accordance with his quite rational plan (given his assumptions and concerns about Sherman's intentions) to repel the Union thrust south of Atlanta. The word *eccentric* can be better applied to Sherman's conduct during the Jonesboro operation than to Hood's.

For criticisms of Sherman's performance during the Jonesboro operation similar to those presented in the text, see Henry Stone, "Part III. Siege and Capture of Atlanta," 122–32, and "Part IV. Strategy of the Campaign," 160–62, in *The Atlanta Papers*, comp. Sydney C. Kerksis (Press of the Morningside Bookshop, 1980); Stanley, *Memoirs*, 180–83; Cope, *Fifteenth Ohio*, 561; William B. Hazen, *A Narrative of Military Service* (Boston: Ticknor & Co., 1885), 297–98; John M. Schofield, *Forty-six Years in the Army* (New York: Century Co., 1897), 160; Manigault, *Narrative*, 250; Alfred H. Burne, *Lee, Grant and Sherman: A Study in Leadership in the 1864–65 Campaign* (Wellington Works, Aldershot, England: Gale & Polden, 1938), 114–24.

30. On morale, strength, and general condition of the Army of Tennessee at the end of the campaign, see Major General Samuel G. French to Jefferson Davis, September 14, 1864, 39 OR 2:836; French, *Two Wars*, 223; Patrick, *Reluctant Rebel*, 224–25; *Macon Southern Confederacy*, Sept. 14, 1864, quoted in *Cincinnati Daily Commercial*, Sept. 29, 1864; John V. Richards, *From Wisconsin to the Sea: The Civil War Letters of Sergeant John V. Richards, Thirty-first Regiment Wisconsin Infantry, 1862–1865*, ed. Richard Rattenbury (Houston: D. Armstrong & Co., 1986), 63; E. C. Dawes, "Confederate Strength in the Atlanta Campaign," in *Battles and Leaders of the Civil War*, ed. Robert U. Johnson and Clarence C.

Buel (New York: Century Co., 1887), 292 (which puts Confederate losses from all causes in the campaign at ca. 40,000). The September 20, 1864, returns for the Army of Tennessee (39 *OR* 2:850-51) show nearly 43,000 troops "present for duty," but this figure includes 8,000 men in Wheeler's cavalry who still had not rejoined the main army and who, according to a dispatch from Forrest (ibid., 859) numbered at most 1,000 and "in all probability not over 500."

31. 38 *OR* 5:763; *New York Times,* Sept. 3-10, 1864; *New York Herald,* Sept. 3, 5, 8, 1864; *New York Tribune,* Sept. 3, 6, 7, 1864; James M. McPherson, *The Struggle for Equality: Abolitionists and the Negro in the Civil War and Reconstruction* (Princeton, N.J.: Princeton University Press, 1964), 282-83; James G. Randall and David Donald, *The Civil War and Reconstruction,* 2d ed. (New York: D. C. Heath & Co., 1969), 475; George Templeton Strong, *The Diary of George Templeton Strong, 1835-1875,* ed. Allan Nevins and Milton H. Thomas (New York: Macmillan, 1952), 3:480-81.

32. *New York World,* Sept. 3, 5, 1864; *Chicago Times,* Sept. 3, 5-7, 1864; Columbus *Crisis,* n.d., quoted in *Cincinnati Daily Commercial,* Sept. 14, 1864; *Chicago Daily Tribune,* Sept. 17, 1864; *Hillsdale* (Michigan) *Standard,* Sept. 20, 1864; Strong, *Diary,* 3:479-84; *American Annual Cyclopedia and Register of Important Events of the Year 1864* (New York: D. Appleton & Co., 1871), 794; McPherson, *Struggle for Equality,* 282-83; James M. McPherson, *Battle Cry of Freedom: The Civil War Era* (New York: Oxford University Press, 1988), 773-76; Frank L. Klement, *The Copperheads of the Middle West* (Chicago: University of Chicago Press, 1960), 235; Clauss, "Atlanta Campaign," 367-68. Stephen W. Sears, "McClellan, and the Peace Plank of 1864," *Civil War History* 36 (Mar. 1990):57-64, demonstrates that contrary to a longstanding historical misconception, McClellan did not initially draft a letter accepting the peace plank and that his slowness in responding to the Democratic nomination was occasioned by his desire to put "the best possible face on his split with the peace wing of the party."

33. *Richmond Daily Examiner,* Sept. 5, 1864; John B. Jones, *A Rebel War Clerk's Diary at the Confederate States Capital,* ed. Howard Swiggett (New York: Old Hickory Bookshop, 1935), 2:276-77; Josiah Gorgas, *The Civil War Diary of General Josiah Gorgas,* ed. Frank E. Vandiver (University: University of Alabama Press, 1947), 139; James Conner, *Letters of General James Conner, C.S.A.,* ed. Mary Conner Moffett (Columbia, S.C.: R. L. Bryan Company, 1950), 121; J. Cutler Andrews, *The South Reports the Civil War* (Princeton, N.J.: Princeton University Press, 1970), 463; Ella Gertrude Thomas Diary, 191; *Macon Daily Telegraph,* September 6, 1864; Mary Boykin Chesnut, *Mary Chesnut's Civil War,* ed. C. Vann Woodward (New Haven, Conn., and London: Yale University Press, 1981), 628, 642; Schenck quote in Larry Earl Nelson, "The Confederacy and the United States Presidential Election of 1864," Ph.D. diss., Duke University, 1975, 278; Agnew quote in William James McNeil, "The Stress of War: The Confederacy and William Tecumseh Sherman during the Last Year of the Civil War," Ph.D. diss., Rice University, 1973, 195; Arthur Benjamin Simms, "A Georgian's View of War in Virginia," ed. June Bonner Peacock, *Atlanta Historical Journal* 23 (1975): 119-20; Robert Manson Myers, ed., *The Children of Pride* (New York: Popular Library, 1972), 1201.

34. Paul D. Escott, *After Secession: Jefferson Davis and the Failure of Confederate Nationalism* (Baton Rouge: Louisiana State University Press, 1978), 216-17 (North Carolina soldier quote); Gorgas, *Diary,* 141-42.

35. *Richmond Daily Examiner,* Sept. 5-7, 1864; *Richmond Sentinel,* September 16, 1864, quoted in *Cincinnati Daily Commercial,* Sept. 27, 1864; *Richmond Enquirer,* n.d., *Richmond Dispatch,* n.d., and *Richmond Whig,* n.d., all quoted in *Atlanta* (Macon) *Daily Intelligencer,* Sept. 15, 1864; *Atlanta* (Macon) *Daily Intelligencer,* Sept. 10, 1864; Nelson, "Election of 1864," 281-82; Escott, *After Secession,* 218; Andrews, *South Reports,* 463; Clauss, "Atlanta Campaign," 372-73.

36. Chesnut, *Mary Chesnut's Civil War,* 648. For impact of Early's defeats on North, see

New York Times, Sept. 20-25, 1864, and on South, see *Richmond Enquirer,* Sept. 27, 1864, quoted in *Cincinnati Daily Commercial,* Oct. 3, 1864.

CHAPTER TEN: FALL

1. Franklin M. Garrett, *Atlanta and Environs: A Chronicle of Its People and Events* (New York: Lewis Historical Publishing Co., 1954), 638-39; David Power Conyngham, *Sherman's March Through the South* (New York: Sheldon & Co., 1865), 216; George W. Pepper, *Personal Recollections of Sherman's Campaigns in Georgia and the Carolinas* (Zanesville, Ohio: Hugh Dunne Co., 1866), 171. William T. Sherman, *Memoirs of Gen. W. T. Sherman,* 4th ed. (New York: Charles L. Webster & Co., 1891), 2:111, states that he rode into Atlanta on September 8, but his correspondence in 38 OR 5:821-22 indicates that he entered the city on September 7, the date also used by Garrett.

2. Garrett, *Atlanta,* 639. Sherman, *Memoirs,* 2:111, refers to his headquarters being in "the house of Judge Lyons," but as Garrett demonstrates, Lyons, who only recently had purchased the house from John Neal, Lieutenant Neal's father, never lived in it and was unable to pay for it, with the result that it reverted to John Neal.

3. 38 OR 5:794, 822, 839; 39 OR 2:414-22.

4. For number and composition of Atlantans who were sent south, see Sherman to Tyler, 39 OR 2:481. However, Major William Clare, the Confederate officer in charge of receiving the refugees, states in his report (38 OR 3:993) that they totaled 1,168, nearly 500 fewer than Sherman reports. Perhaps most if not all of this discrepancy derives from refugees going off on their own on reaching Rough and Ready rather than reporting to the Confederates. For the "Fosterville" camp, see photonegative of unnamed and undated South Carolina newspaper in the Civil War Collection of the Atlanta Historical Society.

5. Garrett, *Atlanta,* 642-43; Charles E. Benton, *As Seen From the Ranks: A Boy in the Civil War* (New York: G. P. Putnam's Sons, 1902), 209; Carrie Berry Diary, September 10, 13, 1864.

6. 39 OR 2:480, 503.

7. Ibid., 355-56.

8. Ibid., 354-55, 358, 362-65, 367.

9. Ibid., 364, 411-13, 432.

10. 38 OR 5:1023-24; 39 OR 2:818-19, 836; Robert Selph Henry, *"First with the Most" Forrest* (Indianapolis: Bobbs-Merrill, 1944), 345-50.

11. *Atlanta* (Macon) *Daily Intelligencer,* Sept. 24, 1864; Dunbar Rowland, ed., *Jefferson Davis, Constitutionalist, His Letters, Papers, and Speeches* (Jackson: Mississippi Department of Archives and History, 1923), 6:341-61; John Bell Hood, *Advance and Retreat* (New York: Krauss Reprint Co., 1969), 253-54; Arthur M. Manigault, *A Carolinian Goes to War: The Civil War Narrative of Arthur Middleton Manigault, Brigadier General, C.S.A.,* ed. R. Lockwood Tower (Columbia: University of South Carolina Press, 1983), 276-77; Thomas Robson Hay, *Hood's Tennessee Campaign* (Dayton: Press of the Morningside Bookshop, 1976), 221-22; Sam R. Watkins, *"Co. Aytch": A Sideshow of the Big Show* (New York: Collier Books, 1962), 214; Richard M. McMurry, *John Bell Hood and the War for Southern Independence* (Lexington: University of Kentucky Press, 1982), 156-58.

12. 39 OR 2:850-51, 884; Manigault, *Narrative,* 277-79; Edwin H. Rennolds Diary, Sept. 28-30, 1864; Hood, *Advance and Retreat,* 255-56; Stanley F. Horn, *The Army of Tennessee: A Military History* (Indianapolis: Bobbs-Merrill Co., 1941), 374-75.

13. 39 OR 2:464, 517-18, 532, 540; Sherman, *Memoirs,* 2:140-58; Hood, *Advance and Retreat,* 256-63; Horn, *Army of Tennessee,* 375-78; John Allen Wyeth, *Life of Lieutenant-General Nathan Bedford Forrest* (Dayton: Press of the Morningside Bookship, 1975), 488-513; Henry, *Forrest,* 351-65. Both Wyeth and Henry contend that the damage done by Forrest to the Nashville & Decatur was extensive, whereas Sherman, *Memoirs,* 2:157-58,

and Jacob D. Cox, *Atlanta* (New York: Charles Scribners' Sons, 1882), 223, dismiss it as inconsequential. In fact, it was serious, but not so serious that it could not have been repaired in a few weeks if there had been a compelling need to do so (see McCallum's report, 39 *OR* 1:507, and Anderson to McCallum, October 3, 1864, 52 *OR* 1:642). Wyeth, incidentally, quotes McCallum's report (*Forrest*, 512), but in so doing he omits a key passage in order to make it seem that his hero did more damage than he did.

14. Sherman, *Memoirs*, 2:152–67.

15. *American Annual Cyclopaedia and Register of Important Events of the Year 1864* (New York: D. Appleton & Co., 1871), 798.

16. Sherman, *Memoirs*, 2:169–79.

17. Hood, *Advance and Retreat*, 266–69.

18. Ibid., 278, 281–82; Edwin H. Rennolds Diary, Nov. 21, 22, 1864; Horn, *Army of Tennessee*, 383–84. On the situation of Union forces in Tennessee, see Thomas to Grant, Dec. 2, 1864, 45 *OR* 2:17–18. This indicates that if Hood had knocked out Schofield's army and/or gotten to Nashville before it did, he would have had a reasonable chance of taking the place. Schofield commanded both his and Stanley's corps because his view that his being an "army" commander superseded Stanley's seniority in rank had been upheld by the War Department.

19. Source materials on Hood's Tennessee Campaign, both primary and secondary, are enormous in quantity and horrendous in controversy. The above account is based mainly on Watkins, "*Co. Aytch*," 234; Shelby Foote, *The Civil War, A Narrative: Red River to Appomattox* (New York: Random House, 1974), 654–710; Horn, *Army of Tennessee*, 383–423; Thomas L. Connelly, *Autumn of Glory: The Army of Tennessee, 1862–1865* (Baton Rouge: Louisiana State University Press, 1971), 490–514; McMurry, *Hood*, 170–82. The best book so far published on Hood's Tennessee Campaign, although weak on the background to it, is Wiley Sword, *Embrace an Angry Wind: The Confederacy's Last Hurrah: Spring Hill, Franklin, and Nashville* (New York: Harper Collins, 1991).

20. Robert Manson Myers, ed., *The Children of Pride* (New York: Popular Library, 1972), 1238. Much, and in some ways too much, has been written about the March to the Sea. The best recent study, supporting the view that Sherman's troops would have ransacked Georgia even if he had tried to prevent them, is Joseph T. Glatthaar, *The March to the Sea and Beyond: Sherman's Troops in the Georgia and Carolina Campaigns* (New York and London: New York University Press, 1985).

AFTERWORD

1. Of course it could be—and has been—argued that Johnston was pursuing such a Fabian strategy as suggested above prior to his being removed from command. To a degree this is true; certainly he was in practice trading space for time, and many of his troops expected him to abandon Atlanta. At no time before or during the campaign, however, did Johnston state that this was his strategy or advocate its adoption. Instead he at first said he would defeat Sherman in a defensive battle, then go over to the offensive; and then when it became apparent that his army was incapable of doing that, the sole solution he offered for turning back the Union invasion was to have Forrest's cavalry cut Sherman's supply line. Furthermore, in his postwar writings he declared that not only had he intended to hold Atlanta but also that he would have held it—"forever" or "indefinitely"—had he been left in command. Consequently it is difficult, in fact impossible, to give him credit for something he himself did not claim. Craig L. Symonds, *Joseph E. Johnston: A Civil War Biography* (New York: W. W. Norton, 1992), 386, also concludes that Johnston "changed his mind" about how to deal with Sherman after the campaign got under way.

2. Richard M. McMurry, "The Atlanta Campaign of 1864: A New Look," *Civil War History* 22 (1976): 13, comes to the same conclusion regarding the probability of Forrest

being able to stop or turn back Sherman. Ulysses S. Grant, *Personal Memoirs of U.S. Grant* (New York: Charles Scribner's Sons, 1885), 2:174, states that although Civil War cavalry raids "annoyed," the damage they did was "soon repaired" and that they "contributed but very little to the grand result" of the war.

3. *Atlanta* (Macon) *Daily Intelligencer,* Sept. 8, 1864.

4. B. H. Liddell Hart, *Sherman: Soldier, Realist, American* (New York: Frederick A. Praeger, 1958), 306; *Cincinnati Daily Commercial,* June 28, 1864, containing dispatch by Miller dated June 14, 1864.

5. William T. Sherman, "The Grand Strategy of the Last Year of the War," in *Battles and Leaders of the Civil War,* ed. Robert U. Johnson and Clarence C. Buel (New York: Century Co., 1887), 254.

6. Sherman himself in effect admitted his distaste for battle in a January 19, 1864, letter to his daughter Minnie: "Of course I must fight when the times comes but wherever a result can be accomplished without Battle I prefer it," William Tecumseh Sherman Papers, Ohio Historical Society.

7. 39 OR 2:365.

BIBLIOGRAPHY

Abbreviations

ADA	Alabama Department of Archives and History, Montgomery
AHS	Atlanta Historical Society, Atlanta, Georgia
CHS	Chicago Historical Society, Chicago, Illinois
CL	Clements Library, University of Michigan, Ann Arbor
CMP	Chickamauga-Chattanooga National Military Park Library, Chattanooga, Tennessee
DU	Duke University, Durham, North Carolina
EU	Robert W. Woodruff Library, Special Collections Department, Emory University, Decatur, Georgia
GDA	Georgia Department of Archives, Atlanta
Ill HS	Illinois Historical Society, Springfield
Ind HS	Indiana Historical Society, Indianapolis
ISL	Indiana State Library, Indianapolis
KNBP	Kennesaw National Battlefield Park Library, Kennesaw, Georgia
LC	Library of Congress, Manuscripts Division, Washington, D.C.
MDA	Mississippi Department of Archives and History, Jackson
MHC	Michigan Historical Collections, Bentley Library, University of Michigan, Ann Arbor
MSU	Michigan State University Archives, Michigan State University Library, East Lansing
OHS	Ohio Historical Society, Columbus
SHC	Southern Historical Collection, University of North Carolina, Chapel Hill
TSLA	Tennessee State Library and Archives, Nashville
US-MHRC	U.S. Army Military History Research Collection, Carlisle Barracks, Pennsylvania
UT	University of Texas Library, Austin
WR	Western Reserve Historical Society, Cleveland, Ohio
WSHS	Wisconsin State Historical Society, Madison

Primary Sources

Official Records

U.S. War Department. *Atlas to Accompany the Official Records of the Union and Confederate Armies*. Washington, D.C.: Government Printing Office, 1891–95. (One-volume reprint edition published under the title *Official Military Atlas of the Civil War* [New York: Fairfax Press, 1983].)

————. *The War of the Rebellion: A Compilation of the Official Records of the Union and Confederate Armies.* 128 vols. Washington, D.C.: Government Printing Office, 1880–1901.

Manuscripts

Atkins, Israel. Letters to Parents. MSU.
Atlanta Campaign Diary (typed copy). CMP.
Austin, Judson L. Letters. Ness Collection, MHC.
Barker, Lorenzo. Diary. MHC.
Barnard, John M. Letters. Ind HS.
Bate, William B. Report on Atlanta Campaign. Photocopy, KNBP.
Bates, John W. Diary. US-MHRC.
Beatty, Taylor. Diary. SHC.
Berry, Carrie. Diary (typed copy). AHS.
Binford, George C. Letters. Virginia Historical Society, Richmond.
Bliss, Robert Lewis. Letters. ADA.
Blue, B. B. Letters. KNBP.
Boardman, John D. Letters. Ness Collection, MHC.
Bradley, David C. Letters and Papers. US-MHRC.
Bragg, Braxton. Papers. WR.
Brown, Edwin. Diary, 1864. US-MHRC.
Capers, Ellison. Letters. DU.
Champion, Sidney. Letters. EU.
Cheatham, Benjamin F. Papers. TSLA.
Clark, Achilles V. Letter. TSLA.
Clark, Carroll Henderson. Memoir. TSLA.
Cleveland, Albert C. Letters. Schoff Civil War Collection, CL.
Cooper, James L. Memoirs. TSLA.
Cornwell, Louise Reese. Stoneman's and Sherman's Visit to Jasper County, copied from diary of Bessie Reese Cornwell. KNBP.
Cox, Jacob D. Diary, Apr. 1864 to May 1865 (typed copy). KNBP.
Coy, L. R. Diary (typed copy). KNBP.
Crew, James R. Letters. AHS.
Crittenden, John R. Papers. UT.
Cumming, Joseph B. War Recollections. EU.
Davis, Jefferson. Papers. EU.
Dean, Henry Stewart. Diary, 1864. MHC.
Dickey, William James. Letters. GDA.
Dickinson, Charles H. Diary. WSHS.
Dunn, Francis Wayland. Diaries and Correspondence. MHC.
Dunn, Henry S. Diary and Letters. Warden Family Papers, MHC.
Dwight, Henry O. Album. OHS.
Eastman, Charles H. Letters. Eastman Family Papers, Small Collection, TSLA.
Eddins, Richard F. Correspondence. Civil War Times Illustrated Collection, US-MHRC.
Elliott, Fergus. Papers. Civil War Times Illustrated Collection, US-MHRC.
Elmore, Day. Letters. OHS.
Fahnestock, Allen L. Diary. Ill HS.

Fairfield, Sylvester Wellington. Letters. Ind HS.

Fielder, Alfred Tyler. Diary. TSLA.

Force, Manning F. Papers. University of Washington, Seattle.

Fuller, William. Thesis on Malingering, 1864. University of Michigan Medical School Records, Ann Arbor.

Gale-Polk Papers. SHC.

Gallagher, Hugh D. Correspondence and Papers. Ind HS.

Galpin, Alfred. Diary, 1864. WSHS.

Garrett, Hosea. Letter of 1 Aug. 1864. AHS.

Gaskill, J. W. Diary. WR.

Geary, John W. Letters. AHS.

Glover, Benjamin Robert. Letters. ADA.

Godfrey, Ervin. Letters. EU.

Gooding, Othniel. Letters. MSU.

Graham, William F. Diary. Ill HS.

Graves, Henry L. Letters. GDA.

Griest, Alva C. Diary (typed copy). CMP.

Griffin, Eli Augustus. Diary and Letters. MHC.

Hager, Phinehas A. Letters. MHC.

Hall, James I. Memoirs and Letters. James I. Hall Papers, SHC.

Hampton, Thomas B. Correspondence. UT.

Hardee, William Joseph. Letters. ADA.

Hargis, O. P. Thrilling Experiences of a First Georgia Cavalryman in the Civil War. EU.

Haskell, Oliver C. Diary. Ind HS.

Helms, Celathiel. Letters to Wife. GDA.

Higinbotham, H. G. Letters. Collection of the author.

Hitchcock, Peter. Papers. WR.

Honnell Family Papers. EU.

Howard, Oliver Otis. Letters to Wife. Bowdoin College, Brunswick, Maine.

Howell, William Decatur. Journal and Letters. EU.

Humphrey, John. Papers. EU.

Hynes, William D. Letters. ISL.

Jarman, R. A. The History of Company K, 27th Mississippi Infantry (typescript). CMP.

Jett, Richard B. Correspondence. Photocopies presented to author by Dr. Bell I. Wiley, 1976.

Johnston, Joseph E. Papers. College of William and Mary, Williamsburg, Va.

——. Papers. Huntington Library, Los Angeles, Calif.

Keitt, Lawrence M. Papers. DU.

Kelly, James H. Journal (transcript). Ind HS.

Kimmel, Joseph. Reminiscences. OHS.

King, James. Letter. Henry L. Talbott Letters. Ind HS.

Kurtz, Wilbur G. Collection. AHS.

Labouisse, John W. Letters. Tulane University, New Orleans, La.

Logan, John A. Letters to Wife, 1864. Ill HS.

Love, John C. Letters. MHC.

Lowrey, Mark P. An Autobiography (typescript). Civil War Times Illustrated Collection, US-MHRC.

Mackall, Thomas B. The Mackall Journal and Its Antecedents: The Five Versions of the Journal. Ed. Richard M. McMurry (typescript). Joseph E. Johnston Papers, College of William and Mary, Williamsburg, Va.

Mackall, William W. Papers. SHC.

McKay-Stiles Papers, SHC.

McKee, John J. Diary, 1864. Iowa Historical Society, Iowa City.

Mackey, Leonidas. Letter, July 5, 1864. AHS.

McKittrick, Samuel. Letters to Wife (typed copies). KNBP.

Macon, Julius Montgomery. Letters. Tulane University, New Orleans, La.

Manning, Richard. Letters. Williams-Chesnut-Manning Papers, South Carolinian Library, University of South Carolina, Columbia.

Marshall, John Wesley. Civil War Journal of John Wesley Marshall (typed copy). OHS.

Meriless, John. Diary (typed copy). CHS.

Miller, Alonzo. Letters. AHS.

Moore, I. V. Diary. GDA.

Neal, Andrew J. Letters (typed copies). KNBP.

Nichol, David. Diary and Letters. Civil War Times Illustrated Collection, US-MHRC.

Noble, David. Diary and Letters. Civil War Times Illustrated Collection, US-MHRC.

Noble, Henry G. Diary and Letters. MHC.

Norrell, William O. Diary (typed copy). KNBP.

Nourse, James. Diary and Letters. DU.

Oldham, Van Buren. Diary, 1864. TSLA. Photocopy courtesy of Christopher Losson.

Olds, William C. Letters. Ind HS.

Paddock, Byron D. Diary and Letters. Schoff Civil War Collection, CL.

Palmer, John M. Papers. Ill HS.

Pickett, W. D. Letter to B. F. Cheatham, 5 December 1863. Private Collection of Doug Schanz, Roanoke, Va. Photocopy courtesy of Larry Daniel and Richard M. McMurry.

Poe, Orlando M. Letters to Wife. LC.

Porter, Albert Quincy. Civil War Diary (typed copy). MDA.

Post, Philip Sidney. Correspondence and Diary. Knox College, Galesburg, Ill.

Potter, Henry Albert. Diary and Letters. MHC.

Quintard, Charles T. Diary. University of the South, Sewanee, Tenn.

Rawson, Mary. Diary (typed copy). AHS.

Records, William H. Diary. ISL.

Reeve, James Theodore. Diary, 1864. WSHS.

Rennolds, Edwin H. Diary, 1864. Special Collections, University of Tennessee Library, Knoxville.

Richards, Samuel P. Diary (typed copy). AHS.

Richer, Eli S. From Atlanta to the Sea: The Civil War Letters of Corporal Eli S. Richer, 1862–1865. Ed. Edward G. Longacre. Copy presented to author by Dr. Longacre.

Robinson, James S. Letters. OHS.

Robinson, William C. Letters. Ill HS.

Roher, Walter A. Letters. James M. Wilcox Papers, DU.

Rose, Daniel Devine. Diary and Letters. Collection of the author.

Ross, Levi. Diary. Ill HS.

Schofield, John M. Papers. LC.

Schweitzer, Edward F. Diary. Civil War Times Illustrated Collection, US-MHRC.

Sears, Claudius Wistar. Papers. MDA.

Seaton, Benjamin. Letters. EU.

Sherman, William Tecumseh. Papers. LC.

———. Papers. OHS.

———. Papers. University of Notre Dame, South Bend, Ind.

Slack, Albert L. Letters. OHS.

Sloan, William E. Diary (typed copy). TSLA.

Smith, Benjamin T. Recollections of the Late War. Ill HS.

Smith, Robert Davis. Diary. KNBP.

Sneed, Sebron G. Letter of 7–8 June 1864 to Wife. Sebron G. Sneed Family Papers, UT.

Snell, James P. Diary and Memorandum Book, 1864. Ill HS.

Spaulding, Oliver Lyman. Military Memoirs of Brig. Gen. Oliver L. Spaulding. MHC.

Strawn, William. Narrative of Atlanta Campaign (typescript). CHS.

Sturges, Eben P. Diary and Letters. Civil War Times Illustrated Collection, US-MHRC.

Suiter, James P. Letters and Diary. Ill HS.

Sykes, Columbus, Letters to Wife. KNBP.

Taylor, Thomas T. Diary and Letters. OHS.

Thiott, Charles Henry. Letters. Thiott Family Papers, EU.

Thoburn, Thomas L. My Experience in the Civil War (typed copy of diary). KNBP.

Thomas, Ella Gertrude. Diary, 1864 (typed copy). DU.

Titze, William C. Diary. Ill HS.

Trask, W. L. Diary: The Georgia Campaign of 1864 (typescript). KNBP.

Travis, John D. Letters. MHC.

Trego, Alfred H. Diary. CHS.

Tuttle, John W. Extracts from Diary of John W. Tuttle (typed copy). CMP.

Vann, Samuel King. Letters. ADA.

Wagner, Levi W. Recollections of an Enlistee, 1861–1864. Civil War Times Illustrated Collection, US-MHRC.

Walker, W. H. T. Papers. DU.

Walls, Albert Milton. Letters. Civil War Times Illustrated Collection, US-MHRC.

Watkins, James W. Letters. EU.

Weaver, B. P. Letters. EU.

Wheeler, Joseph A. Papers. ADA.

———. Papers. Harvard University, Cambridge, Mass.

Whitman, Chester. Letters. Regional History Collection, Western Michigan University, Kalamazoo.

Widney, Lyman S. Diary and Letters (typed copies). KNBP.

Wilkens, John A. Correspondence. Ind HS.

Zearing, James Robert. Papers (typed copies). CHS.

Newspapers

Atlanta (Macon) *Daily Appeal*

Atlanta (Macon) *Daily Intelligencer*

Atlanta (Macon) *Southern Confederacy*

Augusta Daily Chronicle and Sentinel

Augusta Daily Constitutionalist

Charleston Courier

Charleston Mercury
Chattanooga (Griffin, Ga.) *Daily Rebel*
Chicago Daily Times
Chicago Daily Tribune
Cincinnati Daily Commercial
Cincinnati Daily Enquirer
Cincinnati Daily Gazette
Columbia Carolinian
Indianapolis Daily Journal
Indianapolis Daily Sentinel
Hillsdale (Michigan) *Democrat*
Hillsdale (Michigan) *Standard*
Macon Daily Telegraph
Macon Southern Confederacy
Mobile Daily Advertiser and Register
Nashville Dispatch
New York Daily Tribune
New York Herald
New York Times
New York Weekly Tribune
New York World
Niles (Michigan) *Register*
Richmond Daily Examiner
Richmond Dispatch
Richmond Enquirer
Richmond Sentinel
Richmond Whig
Savannah Daily Republican
Southern Recorder (Milledgeville, Ga.)

Published Diaries, Letters, Memoirs, and Unit Histories That Are Primarily Personal Accounts

Books

Alexander, E. Porter. *Military Memoirs of a Confederate.* New York: Charles E. Scribner, 1907.

Andrews, Eliza Frances. *The War-Time Journal of a Georgia Girl, 1864–1865.* New York: D. Appleton & Co., 1908.

Bailey, George W. *The Civil War Diary and Biography of George W. Bailey.* Ed. Gerald R. Post. Colleyville, Tex.: Privately printed, 1990.

Basler, Roy P., et al., eds. *The Collected Works of Abraham Lincoln.* 9 vols. New Brunswick, N.J.: Rutgers University Press, 1953–55.

Beers, Fannie A. *Memories. A Record of Personal Experience and Adventure during Four Years of War.* Philadelphia: J. B. Lippincott, 1888.

Benton, Charles E. *As Seen from the Ranks: A Boy in the Civil War.* New York: G. P. Putnam's Sons, 1902.

Bircher, William. *A Drummer Boy's Diary: Comprising Four Years of Service with the*

Second Regiment Minnesota Veteran Volunteers, 1861–1865. St. Paul, Minn.: Acme Press, 1889.

Bradley, G. S. *The Star Corps; or, Notes of an Army Chaplain during Sherman's Famous "March to the Sea."* Milwaukee: Jermain & Brightman, 1865.

Brobst, John B. *Well Mary: Civil War Letters of a Wisconsin Volunteer.* Ed. Lydia M. Post. Madison: University of Wisconsin Press, 1960.

Buck, Irving A., ed. *Cleburne and His Command.* Jackson, Tenn.: McCowat-Mercer Press, 1959. (Originally published 1908.)

Bull, Rice C. *Soldiering: The Civil War Diary of Rice C. Bull, 123rd New York Infantry.* Ed. K. Jack Bauer. San Rafael, Calif.: Presidio Press, 1978.

Campbell, J. L. P., ed. *John Angus Campbell, PFC, C.S.A.* Atlanta: N.p., n.d.

Cannon, Newton. *The Reminiscences of Sergeant Newton Cannon.* Ed. Campbell H. Brown. Franklin, Tenn.: Carter House Association, 1963.

Capers, Ellison. *South Carolina.* Vol. 5 of *Confederate Military History: A Library of Confederate States History, in Twelve Volumes, Written by Distinguished Men of the South and Edited by Gen. Clement A. Evans of Georgia.* Atlanta: Confederate Publishing Company, 1899.

Cavins, Aden G. *War Letters of Aden G. Cavins Written to His Wife.* Evansville, Ind.: N.p., n.d.

Chamberlayne, C. G., ed. *Ham Chamberlayne, Virginian: Letters and Papers of an Artillery Officer in the War for Southern Independence, 1861–1865.* Richmond, Va.: Press of the Dietz Publishing Co., 1932.

Chesnut, Mary Boykin. *Mary Chesnut's Civil War.* Ed. C. Vann Woodward. New Haven, Conn., and London: Yale University Press, 1981.

Coe, Hamlin Alexander. *Mine Eyes Have Seen the Glory: Combat Diaries of Union Sergeant Hamlin Alexander Coe.* Ed. David Coe. Cranbury, N.J.: Fairleigh Dickinson University Press, 1975.

Conner, James. *Letters of General James Conner, C.S.A.* Ed. Mary Conner Moffett. Columbia, S.C.: R. L. Bryan Company, 1950.

Conyngham, David Power. *Sherman's March through the South.* New York: Sheldon & Co., 1865.

Cope, Alexis. *The Fifteenth Ohio Volunteers and Its Campaigns.* Columbus: Press of the Edward T. Miller Co., 1918.

Cotton, John W. *Yours til' Death: Civil War Letters of John W. Cotton.* Ed. Lucille Griffith. University: University of Alabama Press, 1951.

Cox, Jacob D. *Military Reminiscences of the Civil War.* 2 vols. New York: Charles E. Scribner, 1900.

Culver, Joseph F. *"Your Affectionate Husband, J. F. Culver." Letters Written during the Civil War.* Ed. Leslie W. Dunlap. Iowa City: Friends of the University of Iowa Libraries, 1978.

Cumming, Kate. *A Journal of Hospital Life in the Confederate Army of Tennessee from the Battle of Shiloh to the End of the War.* Louisville: 1866.

Dacus, Robert H. *Reminiscences of Company "H," First Arkansas Mounted Volunteers.* Dardanelle, Ark.: 1897.

Dana, Charles A. *Recollections of the Civil War.* New York: D. Appleton & Co., 1902.

Davis, Jefferson. *The Rise and Fall of the Confederate Government.* 2 vols. New York: D. Appleton & Co., 1881.

Dodge, Grenville M. *Personal Recollections of President Abraham Lincoln, General Ulysses S. Grant and General William T. Sherman.* Council Bluffs, Iowa: Monarch Printing Co., 1914.

Douglas, James P. *Douglas's Texas Battery, C.S.A.* Ed. Lucia Rutherford Douglas. Tyler, Tex.: Smith County Historical Society, 1966.

Drake, George F. *The Mail Goes Through, or The Civil War Letters of George F. Drake.* Ed. Julia A. Drake. San Angelo, Tex.: Privately published, 1964.

Dunham, Charles Laforest. *Through the South with a Union Soldier.* Ed. Arthur H. DeRosier. Johnson City: Publications of the East Tennessee State University Research Advisory Committee, 1969.

Dyer, John W. *Reminiscences; or, Four Years in the Confederate Army.* Evansville, Ind.: 1898.

Edmonston, Catharine Ann Devereux. *"Journal of a Secesh Lady": The Diary of Catharine Ann Devereux Edmonston.* Ed. Beth G. Crabtree and James W. Patton. Raleigh, N.C.: Division of Archives and History, Department of Cultural Resources, 1979.

Fitch, Michael H. *Echoes of the Civil War as I Hear Them.* New York: William S. Porter Press, 1905.

Foote, Corydon Edward. *With Sherman to the Sea: A Drummer Boy's Story of the Civil War.* Ed. Olive Deane Hormel. New York: John Day Co., 1960.

Foster, Samuel T. *One of Cleburne's Command. The Civil War Reminiscences and Diary of Capt. Samuel T. Foster, Granbury's Texas Brigade, C.S.A.* Ed. Norman D. Brown. Austin: University of Texas Press, 1980.

French, Samuel G. *Two Wars: An Autobiography.* Nashville: Confederate Veteran, 1901.

Glenn, William Wilkins. *Between North and South: A Maryland Journalist Views the Civil War.* Ed. Boyly Ellen Marks and Mark Norton Schatz. London: Associated University Presses, 1976.

Gorgas, Josiah. *The Civil War Diary of General Josiah Gorgas.* Ed. Frank E. Vandiver. University: University of Alabama Press, 1947.

Grainger, Gervis D. *Four Years with the Boys in Gray.* Dayton, Ohio: Morningside Bookshop, 1972. (Originally published 1902.)

Grant, Julia Dent. *The Personal Memoirs of Julia Dent Grant.* Ed. John Y. Simon. New York: G. P. Putnam's Sons, 1975.

Grant, Ulysses S. *Personal Memoirs of U. S. Grant.* 2 vols. New York: Charles Scribner's Sons, 1885.

Green, Johnny. *Johnny Green of the Orphan Brigade: The Journal of a Confederate Soldier.* Ed. A. D. Kirwan. Lexington: University of Kentucky Press, 1956.

Greene, Albert R. *From Bridgeport to Ringgold by Way of Lookout Mountain.* Providence, R.I.: 1870.

Griscom, George L. *Fighting with Ross's Texas Cavalry Brigade, C.S.A. The Diary of George L. Griscom, Adjutant, 9th Texas Cavalry Regiment.* Hillsboro, Tex.: Hill Junior College Press, 1976.

Hazen, William B. *A Narrative of Military Service.* Boston: Ticknor & Co., 1885.

Hedley, Fenwick Y. *Marching through Georgia.* Chicago: R. R. Donnelley & Sons, 1887.

Hight, John J. *History of the Fifty-eighth Regiment of Indiana Volunteer Infantry.* Princeton, Ind.: Press of the Clarion, 1895.

Hinkley, Julian W. *A Narrative of Service with the Third Wisconsin Infantry.* Madison: Wisconsin History Commission, 1912.

Hitchcock, Henry. *Marching with Sherman.* Ed. M. A. DeWolfe Howe. New Haven, Conn.: Yale University Press, 1927.

Holmes, James Taylor. *Fifty-second Ohio Volunteer Infantry: Then and Now.* Vol. 1. Columbus: Berlin Printing Co., 1898.

Hood, John Bell. *Advance and Retreat.* New York: Krauss Reprint Co., 1969. (Originally published 1880.)

Hough, Alfred Lacy. *Soldier in the West: The Civil War Letters of Alfred Lacy Hough.* Ed. Robert G. Athearn. Philadelphia: University of Pennsylvania Press, 1956.

Howard, Oliver Otis. *Autobiography of Oliver Otis Howard.* 2 vols. New York: Baker & Taylor Co., 1907.

Huff, Sarah. *My Eighty Years in Atlanta.* Atlanta: Privately printed, 1937.

Jamison, Matthew H. *Recollections of Pioneer and Army Life.* Kansas City, Mo.: 1911.

Johnson, Richard W. *A Soldier's Reminiscences in Peace and War.* Philadelphia: J. B. Lippincott & Co., 1886.

Johnston, Joseph E. *Narrative of Military Operations.* New York: Appleton, 1874.

Jones, John B. *A Rebel War Clerk's Diary at the Confederate States Capital.* Ed. Howard Swiggett. 2 vols. New York: Old Hickory Bookshop, 1935.

Key, Thomas J. *Two Soldiers: The Campaign Diaries of Thos. J. Key, C.S.A., and Robt. J. Campbell, U.S.A.* Ed. Wirt Armistead Cate. Chapel Hill: University of North Carolina Press, 1938.

LeDuc, William G. *Recollections of a Civil War Quartermaster.* St. Paul, Minn.: North Central Publishing Co., 1963.

Logan, Mrs. John A. *Reminiscences of a Soldier's Wife: An Autobiography.* New York: Charles Scribner's Sons, 1913.

Lowell, Charles Russell. *Life and Letters of Charles Russell Lowell.* Ed. Edward W. Emerson. New York: Kennikak Press, 1971. (Originally published 1907.)

Lunt, Dolly Summer. *A Woman's Wartime Journal.* Macon, Ga.: 1927.

McGee, Benjamin F. *History of the 72d Indiana Volunteer Infantry of the Mounted Lightning Brigade.* Lafayette, Ind.: S. Vater & Co., 1882.

Manigault, Arthur M. *A Carolinian Goes to War: The Civil War Narrative of Arthur Middleton Manigault, Brigadier General, C.S.A.* Ed. R. Lockwood Tower. Columbia: University of South Carolina Press, 1983.

Montgomery, Frank A. *Reminiscences of a Mississippian in Peace and War.* Cincinnati: Robert Clarke Co., 1901.

Mosman, Chesley A. *The Rough Side of War: The Civil War Journal of Chesley A. Mosman, 1st Lieutenant, Company D, 59th Illinois Volunteer Infantry Regiment.* Ed. Arnold Gates. Garden City, N.Y.: Basin Publishing Co., 1987.

Myers, Robert Manson, ed. *The Children of Pride.* New York: Popular Library, 1972.

Newlin, W. H., comp. *A History of the Seventy-third Regiment of Illinois Volunteer Infantry.* Springfield, Ill.: 1890.

Nichols, George W. *The Story of the Great March from the Diary of a Staff Officer.* New York: Harper & Brothers, 1865.

Nisbet, James Cooper. *Four Years on the Firing Line.* Ed. Bell I. Wiley. Jackson, Tenn.: McCowat-Mercer Press, 1963.

Nugent, William L. *My Dear Nellie. The Civil War Letters of William L. Nugent to Eleanor Smith Nugent.* Ed. William M. Cash and Lucy Somerville Howorth. Jackson: University Press of Mississippi, 1977.

Olmstead, Charles H. *The Memoirs of Charles H. Olmstead.* Ed. Lilla Mills Hawes. Savannah: Georgia Historical Society, 1964.

Orendorff, Henry. *We Are Sherman's Men: The Civil War Letters of Henry Orendorff.* Ed. William M. Anderson. Macomb: Western Illinois University, 1986.

Osborn, Thomas Ward. *The Fiery Trail: A Union Officer's Account of Sherman's Last Campaigns.* Ed. Richard Harwell and Philip N. Racine. Knoxville: University of Tennessee Press, 1986.

Overholser, James P. *Three Years with the Union Army: Personal Experiences of a Private Soldier.* N.p., n.d.

Patrick, Robert. *Reluctant Rebel: The Secret Diary of Robert Patrick, 1861-1865.* Ed. F. Jay Taylor. Baton Rouge: Louisiana State University Press, 1959.

Pepper, George W. *Personal Recollections of Sherman's Campaign in Georgia and the Carolinas.* Zanesville, Ohio: Hugh Dunne Co., 1866.

Ravenel, Henry Wilson. *The Private Journal of Henry Wilson Ravenel, 1859-1897.* Ed. Arney Robinson Childs. Columbia: University of South Carolina Press, 1947.

Reid, Harvey. *The View from Headquarters: Civil War Letters of Harvey Reid.* Ed. Frank L. Byrne. Madison: State Historical Society of Wisconsin, 1965.

Richards, John V. *From Wisconsin to the Sea: The Civil War Letters of Sergeant John V. Richards, Thirty-first Regiment Wisconsin Infantry, 1862-1865.* Ed. Richard Rattenbury. Houston: D. Armstrong & Co., 1986.

Rowland, Dunbar, ed. *Jefferson Davis, Constitutionalist, His Letters, Papers, and Speeches.* 10 vols. Jackson: Mississippi Department of Archives and History, 1923.

Rusling, James F. *Men and Things I Saw in Civil War Days.* New York: Eaton Mains, 1899.

Sala, George Augustus. *My Diary in America in the Midst of War.* London: 1865.

Schofield, John M. *Forty-six Years in the Army.* New York: Century Co., 1897.

Seaton, Benjamin M. *The Bugle Softly Blows: The Confederate Diary of Benjamin M. Seaton.* Ed. Harold B. Simpson. Waco: Texian Press, 1965.

Shanks, William F. G. *Personal Recollections of Distinguished Generals.* New York: Harper & Brothers, 1866.

Sherman, William T. *Home Letters of General Sherman.* Ed. M. A. DeWolfe Howe. New York: Charles Scribner's Sons, 1909.

———. *Memoirs of Gen. W. T. Sherman.* 4th ed. 2 vols. New York: Charles L. Webster & Co., 1891.

———. *The Sherman Letters: Correspondence between General and Senator Sherman from 1837 to 1891.* Ed. Rachel Sherman Thorndike. New York: Charles Scribner's Sons, 1894.

Sherwood, Isaac. *Memoirs of the War.* Toledo: H. J. Chittenden Co., 1923.

Stanley, David S. *Personal Memoirs of Major General D. S. Stanley, U.S.A.* Cambridge, Mass.: Harvard University Press, 1917.

Strong, George Templeton. *The Diary of George Templeton Strong, 1835-1875.* Ed. Allan Nevins and Milton H. Thomas. 4 vols. New York: Macmillan, 1952.

Strong, Robert Hale. *A Yankee Private's Civil War.* Ed. Ashley Halsey, Jr. Chicago: Henry Regnery Co., 1961.

Taylor, Richard. *Destruction and Reconstruction: Personal Experiences of the Late War.*

Ed. Charles P. Roland. Waltham, Mass.: Blaisdell Publishing Co., 1968. (Originally published 1879.)

Theaker, James G. *Through One Man's Eyes. Letters of James G. Theaker.* Ed. Paul E. Rieger. Mount Vernon, Ohio: Printing Arts Press, 1974.

Thoburn, Thomas L. *My Experiences during the Civil War.* Ed. Lyle Thoburn. Cleveland: 1963.

Toombs, Samuel. *Reminiscences of the War.* Orange, N.J.: Journal Office, 1878.

Upson, Theodore F. *With Sherman to the Sea: The Civil War Letters, Diaries and Reminiscences of Theodore F. Upson.* Ed. Oscar G. Winther. Bloomington: University of Indiana Press, 1958.

Watkins, Sam R. *"Co. Aytch": A Sideshow of the Big Show.* New York: Collier Books, 1962. (Originally published 1882.)

Westervelt, William B. *Lights and Shadows of Army Life as Seen by a Private Soldier.* Marlboro, N.Y.: C. H. Cochrane, 1886.

Whitman, Walt. *Walt Whitman's Civil War.* Ed. Walter Lowenfels. New York: Alfred A. Knopf, 1961.

Whitney, Joseph. *Kiss Clara for Me: The Story of Joseph Whitney.* Ed. Robert J. Snetsinger. State College, Pa.: Carnation Press, 1969.

Wilkie, Franc B. *Pen and Powder.* Boston: Ticknor & Co., 1888.

Willett, Elbert D. *History of Company B (Originally Pickens' Planters).* Anniston, Ala.: Nerwood, 1902.

Williams, Alpheus S. *From the Cannon's Mouth: The Civil War Letters of General Alpheus S. Williams.* Ed. Milo M. Quaife. Detroit: Wayne State University Press, 1959.

Williams, Noble C. *Echoes from the Battlefields; or, Southern Life during the War.* Atlanta: 1902.

Willison, Charles A. *Reminiscences of a Boy's Service with the 76th Ohio.* Menasha, Wis.: George Banta, 1902.

Wills, Charles W. *Army Life of an Illinois Soldier.* Washington, D.C.: Globe Printing Co., 1906.

Wilson, Ephraim A. *Memoirs of the War.* Cleveland: W. M. Bayne, 1893.

Wilson, Thomas B. *Reminiscences of Thomas B. Wilson.* N.p., 1939.

Wright, Charles. *A Corporal's Story.* Philadelphia: James Beal, 1887.

Wright, Mrs. D. Giraud. *A Southern Girl in '61: The War-Time Memories of a Confederate Senator's Daughter.* New York: Doubleday, Page & Co., 1905.

Young, Lot D. *Reminiscences of a Soldier of the Orphan Brigade.* Louisville: Louisville Courier Job Print, 1912.

Periodicals and Compilations

Atkins, Smith D. "With Sherman's Cavalry." In *The Atlanta Papers,* comp. Sydney C. Kerksis, 625–40. Dayton: Press of the Morningside Bookshop, 1980.

Banks, Robert W. "Civil War Letters of Robert W. Banks: Atlanta Campaign." Ed. George C. Osborn. *Georgia Historical Quarterly* 27(1943): 208–16.

Bierce, Ambrose. "The Crime at Pickett's Mill." In *The Collected Works of Ambrose Bierce,* 1:315–27. 12 vols. New York: Gordian Press, 1966.

Boate, Edward Ellington. "The True Story of Andersonville Told by a Federal Prisoner." *Southern Historical Society Papers* 10(1882): 25–32.

Brainard, Orson. "Orson Brainard: A Soldier in the Ranks." Ed. Wilfred W. Black. *Ohio History* 76(1967): 54–72.

Breckinridge, W. C. P. "The Opening of the Atlanta Campaign." In *Battles and Leaders of the Civil War,* ed. Robert U. Johnson and Clarence C. Buel, 4:277–81. 4 vols. New York: Century Co., 1887.

Buegel, John T. "The Civil War Diary of John T. Buegel, Union Soldier. Part Two." Trans. and ed. William G. Bek. *Missouri Historical Review* 40(1946): 503–40.

Candler, A. D. "Watch on the Chattahoochee: A Civil War Letter." *Georgia Historical Quarterly* 43(1959): 427–28.

Candler, Myrtie Long. "Reminiscences of Life in Georgia during the 1850s and 1860s. Part IV." *Georgia Historical Quarterly* 33(1949): 303–13.

———. "Reminiscences of Life in Georgia during the 1850s and 1860s. Part V." *Georgia Historical Quarterly* 34(1950): 10–18.

Capron, Albert B. "Stoneman's Raid to Macon." In *The Atlanta Papers,* comp. Sydney C. Kerksis, 709–20. Dayton: Press of the Morningside Bookshop, 1980.

Capron, Horace. "Stoneman's Raid to the South of Atlanta." In *The Atlanta Papers,* comp. Sydney C. Kerksis, 669–705. Dayton: Press of the Morningside Bookshop, 1980.

Capron, Thaddeus H. "War Diary of Thaddeus H. Capron, 1861–1865." *Journal of the Illinois Historical Society* 12(1919): 330–406.

Carpenter, C. C. "A Commissary in the Union Army: Letters of C. C. Carpenter." Ed. Mildred Throne. *Iowa Journal of History* 53(1955): 59–88.

Chamberlin, William H. "Hood's Second Sortie at Atlanta." In *Battles and Leaders of the Civil War,* ed. Robert U. Johnson and Clarence C. Buel, 4:326–31. 4 vols. New York: Century Co., 1887.

———. "Recollections of the Battle of Atlanta." In *The Atlanta Papers,* comp. Sydney C. Kerksis, 451–63. Dayton: Press of the Morningside Bookshop, 1980.

———. "The Skirmish Line in the Atlanta Campaign." In *The Atlanta Papers,* comp. Sydney C. Kerksis, 311–26. Dayton: Press of the Morningside Bookshop, 1980.

Chambers, William Pitt. "My Journal." *Publications of the Mississippi Historical Society* 5(1925): 221–335.

Cody, Darwin. "Letters of Darwin Cody." *Ohio History* 68(1959): 371–401.

Compton, James. "The Second Division of the 16th Army Corps in the Atlanta Campaign." In *The Atlanta Papers,* comp. Sydney C. Kerksis, 237–57. Dayton: Press of the Morningside Bookshop, 1980.

Connolly, James Austin. "Major Connolly's Letters to His Wife, 1862–1865." *Transactions of the Illinois Historical Society* 35(1928): 215–438.

Cooke, Chauncey H. "A Badger Boy in Blue: The Letters of Chauncey H. Cooke." *Wisconsin Magazine of History* 4(1934): 75–100; 5(1935): 63–98.

Cox, Charles Harding. "Gone for a Soldier: The Civil War Letters of Charles Harding Cox." Ed. Lorna Lutes Sylvester. *Indiana Magazine of History* 68(1972): 182–224.

Cox, Rowland. "Snake Creek Gap and Atlanta." In *The Atlanta Papers,* comp. Sydney C. Kerksis, 329–51. Dayton: Press of the Morningside Bookshop, 1980.

Curry, J. H. "A History of Company B, 40th Alabama Infantry, C.S.A., from the Diary of J. H. Curry." *Alabama Historical Quarterly* 17(1955): 159–222.

Curry, W. L. "Raid of the Union Cavalry, Commanded by General Judson Kilpatrick, Around the Confederate Army in Atlanta, August, 1864." In *The Atlanta Papers,* comp. Sydney C. Kerksis, 599–621. Dayton: Press of the Morningside Bookshop, 1980.

Dabney, T. G. "Campaigning in North Georgia." *Confederate Veteran* 14(1906): 75–76.

Davidson, John, and Julia Davidson. "A Wartime Story: The Davidson Letters, 1862–1865." Ed. Jane Bonner Peacock. *Atlanta Historical Bulletin* 29(1975): 8–121.

Dodge, Grenville M. "The Battle of Atlanta." In *The Atlanta Papers,* comp. Sydney C. Kerksis, 489–503. Dayton: Press of the Morningside Bookshop, 1980.

Dun, R. G. "Letters of R. G. Dun." Ed. James D. Norris. *Ohio History* 71(1962): 138–47.

Dwight, Henry O. "The Battle of July 22, 1864." *New York Times,* 12 August 1864.

———. "How We Fight at Atlanta." *Harper's New Monthly Magazine* November 1864: 663–66.

Erwin, Joseph. "Swett's Battery at Jonesboro." *Confederate Veteran* 12(1904): 112.

Fenton, E. B. "From the Rapidan to Atlanta." In *The Atlanta Papers,* comp. Sydney C. Kerksis, 215–34. Dayton: Press of the Morningside Bookshop, 1980.

Fleming, Francis P. "Francis P. Fleming in the War for Southern Independence: Letters from the Front." Ed. Edward C. Williamson. *Florida Historical Quarterly* 28(1949): 38–210.

Foster, Wilbur F. "Battle Field Maps in Georgia." *Confederate Veteran* 20(1912): 369–70.

French, Samuel G. "Letter to the Editor of *New Orleans Picayune,* December 12, 1893." *Southern Historical Society Papers* 22(1894): 1–9.

Gardner, Washington. "Civil War Letters of Washington Gardner." *Michigan History* 1(1917): 3–18.

Guthrey, D. M. "Wheeler's Cavalry around Atlanta." *Confederate Veteran* 13(1905): 267.

Hagan, John W. "The Confederate Letters of John W. Hagan." Ed. Bell I. Wiley. *Georgia Historical Quarterly* 38(1954): 170–200, 268–89.

Hargis, George W. "Dead Angle—Georgia Campaign." *Confederate Veteran* 11(1903): 560.

Howard, Oliver Otis. "The Battles about Atlanta." *Atlantic Monthly* 37(1876): 385–99, 559–67.

———. "The Struggle for Atlanta." In *Battles and Leaders of the Civil War,* ed. Robert U. Johnson and Clarence C. Buel, 4:293–325. 4 vols. New York: Century Co., 1887.

Huntington, Mrs. Henry. "Escape from Atlanta: The Huntington Memoir." Ed. Ben Kremenak. *Civil War History* 11(1965): 160–77.

James, F. B. "McCook's Brigade at the Assault upon Kennesaw Mountain, Georgia, June 27, 1864." In *The Atlanta Papers,* comp. Sydney C. Kerksis, 367–408. Dayton: Press of the Morningside Bookshop, 1980.

Johnston, John. "The Civil War Reminiscences of John Johnston: Part III." Ed. William T. Alderson. *Tennessee Historical Quarterly* 14(1955): 329–54.

Johnston, Joseph E. "Opposing Sherman's Advance to Atlanta." In *Battles and Leaders of the Civil War,* ed. Robert U. Johnson and Clarence C. Buel, 4:260–77. 4 vols. New York: Century Co., 1887.

Jones, Charles T., ed. "Five Confederates: The Sons of Bolling Hall in the Civil War." *Alabama Historical Quarterly* 24(1962): 133–221.

Kelly, William Milner. "A History of the Thirteenth Alabama Volunteers (Infantry) Confederate States Army." *Alabama Historical Quarterly* 9(1947): 115–89.

Kilpatrick, Robert L. "The Fifth Ohio Infantry at Resaca." In *The Atlanta Papers,* comp. Sydney C. Kerksis, 355–63. Dayton: Press of the Morningside Bookshop, 1980.

Lathrop, Edward S. "Gossipy Letter from Georgia." *Confederate Veteran* 20(1912): 520.

Lee, Stephen D. "Sherman's Meridian Expedition." *Southern Historical Society Papers* 8(1880): 49–61.

McDermid, Angus. "Letters from a Confederate Soldier." Ed. Benjamin Rountree. *Georgia Review* 18(1964): 267–97.

Maney, T. H. "Battle of Dead Angle on Kennesaw Line." *Confederate Veteran* 11(1903): 159–60.

Mayfield, Leroy S. "A Hoosier Invades the Confederacy: Letters and Diaries of Leroy S. Mayfield." Ed. John D. Barnhart. *Indiana Magazine of History* 39(1943): 144–91.

Mead, Rufus. "With Sherman through Georgia and the Carolinas: Letters of a Federal Soldier. Part One." Ed. James A. Padgett. *Georgia Historical Quarterly* 32(1948): 284–322.

Mims, W. J. "Letters of Major W. J. Mims, C.S.A." *Alabama Historical Quarterly* 3(1941): 203–31.

Moore, Hugh. "A Reminiscence of Confederate Prison Life." *Journal of the Illinois Historical Society* 65(1972): 451–61.

Munson, Gilbert D. "Battle of Atlanta." In *The Atlanta Papers,* comp. Sydney C. Kerksis, 411–29. Dayton: Press of the Morningside Bookshop, 1980.

Murphee, Joel. "Autobiography and Civil War Letters of Joel Murphee of Troy, Alabama, 1864–1865." Ed. H. E. Sterrkx. *Alabama Historical Quarterly* 19(1957): 170–208.

Nelson, H. K. "Dead Angle, or Devil's Elbow, Ga." *Confederate Veteran* 11(1903): 321–22.

Newberry, Thomas Jefferson. "The Civil War Letters of Thomas Jefferson Newberry." Ed. Enoch C. Mitchell. *Journal of Mississippi History* 10(1948): 44–80.

Newton, George. "Battle of Peachtree Creek." In *The Atlanta Papers,* comp. Sydney C. Kerksis, 393–408. Dayton: Press of the Morningside Bookshop, 1980.

Offield, John, Joseph Offield, and William Offield. "Letters from the Offield Brothers, Confederate Soldiers from Upper East Tennessee." Ed. Leona Taylor Aiken. *East Tennessee Historical Society Publications* 46(1974): 116–25.

O'Leary, Daniel. "The Civil War Letters of Captain Daniel O'Leary, U.S.A." Ed. Jenny O'Leary and Harvey H. Jackson. *Register of the Kentucky Historical Society* 77(1979): 157–85.

Owen, Urban G. "Letters of a Confederate Surgeon in the Army of Tennessee to His Wife." Ed. Enoch L. Mitchell. *Tennessee Historical Quarterly* 5(1946): 142–81.

Pickett, W. D. "The Dead Angle." *Confederate Veteran* 14(1906): 458–59.

Pierson, Stephen. "From Chattanooga to Atlanta in 1864—A Personal Reminiscence." In *The Atlanta Papers,* comp. Sydney C. Kerksis, 261–95. Dayton: Press of the Morningside Bookshop, 1980.

Read, Ira B. "The Campaign from Chattanooga to Atlanta as Seen by a Federal Soldier." Ed. Richard B. Harwell. *Georgia Historical Quarterly* 25(1941): 262–78.

Rogers, M. A. "An Iowa Woman in Wartime. Part Two." *Annals of Iowa* 35(1961): 16–44.

Roy, T. B. "General Hardee and Military Operations around Atlanta." *Southern Historical Society Papers* 8(1880): 335–87.

Shannon, Isaac N. "Sharpshooters in Hood's Army." *Confederate Veteran* 15(1907): 123–26.

Sherman, William T. "The Grand Strategy of the Last Year of the War." In *Battles and Leaders of the Civil War,* ed. Robert U. Johnson and Clarence C. Buel, 4:247-55. 4 vols. New York: Century Co., 1887.

Shoup, Francis A. "Dalton Campaign—Works at Chattahoochee River." *Confederate Veteran* 3(1895): 262-65.

Simms, Arthur Benjamin. "A Georgian's View of the War in Virginia." Ed. June Bonner Peacock. *Atlanta Historical Journal* 23(1975): 91-136.

Smith, Gustavus W. "The Georgia Militia about Atlanta." In *Battles and Leaders of the Civil War,* ed. Robert U. Johnson and Clarence C. Buel, 4:331-35. 4 vols. New York: Century Co., 1887.

Stone, Henry. "Part I: Opening of the Campaign"; "Part II: From the Oostenaula to the Chattahoochee"; "Part III: The Siege and Capture of Atlanta"; "Part IV: Strategy of the Campaign." In *The Atlanta Papers,* comp. Sydney C. Kerksis, 11-162. Dayton: Press of the Morningside Bookshop, 1980.

Strong, William E. "The Death of General James B. McPherson." In *The Atlanta Papers,* comp. Sydney C. Kerksis, 507-39. Dayton: Press of the Morningside Bookshop, 1980.

Terry, James G. "Record of the Alabama State Artillery from Its Organization in May, 1861 to the Surrender in April, 1865." *Alabama Historical Quarterly* 20(1958): 141-447.

Thompson, Robert L. "From Missionary Ridge to Dalton." *Confederate Veteran* 14(1906): 405-7.

Tuthill, Richard S. "An Artilleryman's Recollections of the Battle of Atlanta." In *The Atlanta Papers,* comp. Sydney C. Kerksis, 433-50. Dayton: Press of the Morningside Bookshop, 1980.

Van Deusen, Ira. "Ira Van Deusen: A Federal Volunteer in North Alabama." Ed. Ron Bennett. *Alabama Historical Quarterly* 27(1965): 159-211.

Walker, Eliza. "Other Days." *Alabama Historical Quarterly* 5(1943): 71-97, 209-33.

Wallace, William. "William Wallace's Civil War Letters: The Atlanta Campaign." *Wisconsin Magazine of History* 57(1973-74): 91-116.

Walton, Claiborne J. "'One Continued Scene of Carnage': A Union Surgeon's View of War." *Civil War Times Illustrated,* August 1976: 34-36.

Ward, Margaret Ketcham. "Testimony of Margaret Ketcham Ward on Civil War Times in Georgia." Ed. Aaron M. Boom. *Georgia Historical Quarterly* 39(1955): 268-93, 375-400.

Waring, George E., Jr. "The Sooy Smith Expedition." In *Battles and Leaders of the Civil War,* ed. Robert U. Johnson and Clarence C. Buel, 4:416-18. 4 vols. New York: Century Co., 1887.

Weaver, Henry Clay. "Georgia Through Kentucky Eyes: Letters Written on Sherman's March to Atlanta." Ed. James M. Merrill and James F. Marshall. *Filson Club Historical Quarterly* 30(1956): 324-59; 32(1958): 336-49.

West, Granville C. "McCook's Raid in the Rear of Atlanta and Hood's Army, August, 1864." In *The Atlanta Papers,* comp. Sydney C. Kerksis, 543-66. Dayton: Press of the Morningside Bookshop, 1980.

Williamson, John Coffee. "The Civil War Diary of John Coffee Williamson." Ed. J. C. Williamson. *Tennessee Historical Quarterly* 15(1956): 61-74.

Unit Histories By Participants

Union

Aten, Henry J. *History of the Eighty-fifth Regiment, Illinois Volunteer Infantry.* Hiawatha, Kans.: 1901.

Barnes, James A., et al. *The Eighty-sixth Regiment Indiana Volunteer Infantry: A Narrative of Its Services in the Civil War of 1861–1865.* Crawfordsville, Ind.: Journal Co. Printers, 1895.

Beach, John N. *History of the Fortieth Ohio Volunteer Infantry.* London, Ohio: Shepherd & Craig Printers, 1884.

Belknap, William W. *History of the Fifteenth Regiment, Iowa Veteran Volunteer Infantry.* Keokuk, Iowa: R. B. Ogden & Son, 1887.

Bennett, L. G., and Wm. M. Haigh. *History of the 36th Illinois Volunteers.* Aurora, Ill.: Knickerbocker & Hodder Printers, 1876.

Boyle, John Richards. *Soldiers True: The Story of the One Hundredth and Eleventh Pennsylvania Veteran Volunteers.* New York: Eaton & Mains, 1903.

Bryant, Edwin E. *History of the Third Regiment of Wisconsin Veteran Volunteer Infantry, 1861–1865.* Madison: Democrat Print Co., 1891.

Calkins, W. W. *The History of the 104th Regt. of Ill. Volunteer Infantry.* Chicago: Donohue & Henneberry Printers, 1895.

Chamberlin, William Henry. *History of the Eighty-first Regiment Ohio Volunteers during the War of the Rebellion.* Cincinnati: Gazette Steam-Print House, 1865.

Clark, Charles T. *Opdycke's Tigers* [125th Ohio Infantry Regiment]. Columbus: Spahr & Glenn, 1895.

Connelly, Thomas W. *History of the Seventieth Ohio Regiment.* Cincinnati: Peak Bohrs, 1902.

Day, L. W. *Story of the One Hundred and First Ohio Infantry.* Cleveland: W. M. Bayne Printing Co., 1894.

Dodge, William Sumner. *A Waif of the War; or, The History of the Seventy-fifth Illinois Infantry.* Chicago: Church & Goodman, 1866.

Dornblasser, T. F. *Sabre Strokes of the Pennsylvania Dragoons in the War of 1861–1865* [7th Pennsylvania Cavalry]. Philadelphia: Lutheran Publication Society, 1884.

Fleharty, S. F. *Our Regiment: A History of the 102d Ill. Inf. Vols.* Chicago: Brewster & Hanscom Printers, 1865.

Hinman, Wilbur F. *The Story of the Sherman Brigade.* Alliance, Ohio: Press of the Daily Review, 1897.

Hubert, Charles F. *History of the Fiftieth Regiment Illinois Volunteer Infantry in the War of the Union.* Kansas City, Mo.: Western Veteran Publishing, 1894.

Huntsinger, William. *History of the 79th Regt. Indiana Volunteer Infantry.* Indianapolis: 1891.

Hurst, Samuel H. *Journal-History of the Seventy-third Ohio Volunteer Infantry.* Chillicothe, Ohio: 1866.

Kinnear, J. R. *History of the Eighty-sixth Regiment Illinois Vol. Inf.* Chicago: Tribune Co., 1866.

Lewis, George W. *The Campaigns of the 124th Ohio Volunteer Infantry.* Akron: Werner Co., 1894.

McAdams, F. M. *Every-Day Soldier Life, or a History of the One Hundred and Thirteenth Ohio Volunteer Inf.* Columbus: Charles M. Gott, Printers, 1884.

Merrill, Samuel. *The Seventieth Indiana Volunteer Infantry.* Indianapolis: Bowen-Merrill Co., 1900.

Morris, William S. *History of the 31st Regiment Illinois Volunteers, Organized by John A. Logan.* Evansville, Ind.: Keller Printing & Publishing Co., 1902.

Partridge, Charles A. *History of the Ninety-sixth Regiment Ill. Vol. Inf.* Chicago: Brown, Pettibone Co., 1887.

Pierce, Lyman B. *History of the Second Iowa Cavalry.* Burlington, Iowa: Hawk-Eye Printing Establishment, 1865.

Puntenney, George H. *History of the Thirty-seventh Regiment of Indiana Infantry Volunteers.* Rushville, Ind.: Jacksonian Book & Job Department, 1896.

Saunier, Joseph A., ed. *A History of the Forty-seventh Regiment Ohio Veteran Volunteer Infantry.* Hillsboro, Ohio: Lyle Printing Co., 1903.

Smith, Charles H. *The History of Fuller's Ohio Brigade, 1861–1865.* Cleveland: Press of A. J. Watt, 1909.

Stewart, Nixon B. *Dan McCook's Regiment. 52nd O. V.I. A History of the Regiment, Its Campaigns and Battles.* Alliance, Ohio: Review Print, 1900.

Tarrant, Eastham. *The Wild Riders of the First Kentucky Cavalry.* Lexington, Ky.: Henry Clay Press, 1969. (Originally published 1894.)

Thompson, Seymour Dwight. *Recollections of the Third Iowa Regiment.* Cincinnati: 1864.

Tracie, Theodore C. *Annals of the Nineteenth Ohio Battery; or, Lights and Shadows of Army Life.* Cleveland: J. B. Savage, 1878.

Walton, Clyde C., ed. *Behind the Guns: A History of Battery I, 2nd Regiment, Illinois Light Artillery.* Carbondale: Southern Illinois Press, 1965. (Edited version of book originally published ca. 1897.)

Wood, D. W., comp. *History of the 20th O.V.I. Regiment.* Columbus: Paul & Thrall Printers, 1876.

Wright, Henry W. *A History of the Sixth Iowa Infantry.* Iowa City: Iowa State Historical Society, 1923.

Wuslin, Lucian. *The Story of the Fourth Regiment, Ohio Veteran Volunteer Cavalry, 1861–1865.* Cincinnati: 1912.

Confederate

Barron, Samuel. *Lone Star Defenders: A Chronicle of the 3rd Texas Cavalry.* New York: Neale Publishing Co., 1908.

Head, Thomas A. *Campaigns and Battles of the Sixteenth Regiment, Tennessee Volunteers.* Facsimile of 1885 edition. McMinnville, Tenn.: Womack Printing Co., 1961.

McMorries, Edward Young. *History of the First Regiment, Alabama Volunteer Infantry, C.S.A.* Montgomery: Brown Printing Co., 1904.

McMurray, W. J. *History of the Twentieth Tennessee Regiment Volunteer Infantry, C.S.A.* Nashville: 1904.

Ridley, Bromfield L. *Battles and Sketches of the Army of Tennessee.* Mexico, Mo.: Missouri Printing & Publishing Co., 1906.

Thompson, Ed Porter. *History of the Orphan Brigade.* Louisville: Lewis N. Thompson, 1898.

Worsham, W. J. *The Old Nineteenth Tennessee Regiment, C.S.A.* Blountsville, Tenn.: Tony Marion, 1973. (Originally published 1903.)

Secondary Sources

Books and Dissertations

Anders, Leslie. *The Eighteenth Missouri.* Indianapolis and New York: Bobbs-Merrill, 1968.

Anderson, William M. *They Died to Make Men Free: A History of the 19th Michigan Infantry in the Civil War.* Berrien Springs, Mich.: Hardscrabble Books, 1980.

Andrews, J. Cutler. *The North Reports the Civil War.* Pittsburgh: University of Pittsburgh Press, 1955.

———. *The South Reports the Civil War.* Princeton, N.J.: Princeton University Press, 1970.

Barnard, John A. *Portrait of a Hero: The Story of Absalom Baird, His Family and the American Military Tradition.* Philadelphia: Dorrance & Co., 1972.

Billings, John D. *Hardtack and Coffee.* Ed. Richard Harwell. Chicago: Lakeside Press, 1960. (Originally published 1887.)

Bryan, T. Conn. *Confederate Georgia.* Athens: University of Georgia Press, 1953.

Burne, Alfred H. *Lee, Grant and Sherman: A Study in Leadership in the 1864-65 Campaign.* Wellington Works, Aldershot, England: Gale & Polden, 1938.

Butterfield, Julia L., ed. *A Biographical Memorial of General Daniel Butterfield.* New York: Grafton Press, 1903.

Carter, Samuel, III. *The Siege of Atlanta.* New York: St. Martin's Press, 1973.

Catton, Bruce. *This Hallowed Ground: The Story of the Union Side of the Civil War.* Garden City, N.Y.: Doubleday & Co., 1956.

Clauss, Errol McGregor. "The Atlanta Campaign, 18 July-2 September 1864." Ph. D. diss., Emory University, 1965.

Cleaves, Freeman. *Rock of Chickamauga: The Life of General George H. Thomas.* Norman: University of Oklahoma Press, 1948.

Coddington, Edwin B. *The Gettysburg Campaign: A Study in Command.* Dayton: Press of the Morningside Bookshop, 1979. (Originally published 1968.)

Connelly, Thomas L. *Army of the Heartland: The Army of Tennessee, 1861-1862.* Baton Rouge: Louisiana State University Press, 1967.

———. *Autumn of Glory: The Army of Tennessee, 1862-1865.* Baton Rouge: Louisiana State University Press, 1971.

Cox, Jacob D. *Atlanta.* New York: Charles Scribner's Sons, 1882.

Daniel, Larry J. *Cannoneers in Gray: The Field Artillery of the Army of Tennessee, 1861-1865.* University: University of Alabama Press, 1984.

Davis, William C. *Jefferson Davis: The Man and His Hour.* New York: HarperCollins, 1991.

———. *The Orphan Brigade: The Kentucky Confederates Who Couldn't Go Home.* Baton Rouge: Louisiana State University Press, 1980.

Dawson, George F. *Life and Services of Gen. John A. Logan.* Chicago and New York: Belford, Clarke & Co., 1887.

Dodson, W. C., ed. *Campaigns of Wheeler and His Cavalry, 1862–1865.* Atlanta: Hudgins Publishing Co., 1899.

DuBose, John W. *General Joseph Wheeler and the Army of Tennessee.* New York: Neale Publishing Co., 1912.

Dyer, John P. *"Fighting Joe" Wheeler.* Baton Rouge: Louisiana State University Press, 1941.

Eaton, Clement. *Jefferson Davis.* New York: Macmillan, 1977.

Escott, Paul D. *After Secession: Jefferson Davis and the Failure of Confederate Nationalism.* Baton Rouge: Louisiana State University Press, 1978.

Folk, Edgar E., and Bynum Shaw. *W. W. Holden: A Political Biography* (Winston-Salem, N.C.: John F. Blair, 1982).

Foote, Shelby. *The Civil War, A Narrative: Fredericksburg to Meridian.* New York: Random House, 1963.

———. *The Civil War, A Narrative: Red River to Appomattox.* New York: Random House, 1974.

Freeman, Douglas Southall. *R. E. Lee.* 4 vols. New York: Charles Scribner's Sons, 1935.

Garrett, Franklin M. *Atlanta and Environs: A Chronicle of Its People and Events.* 2 vols. New York: Lewis Historical Publishing Co., 1954.

Glatthaar, Joseph T. *The March to the Sea and Beyond: Sherman's Troops in the Georgia and Carolina Campaigns.* New York and London: New York University Press, 1985.

Govan, Gilbert E., and James W. Livingood. *A Different Valor: The Story of General Joseph E. Johnston, C.S.A.* Indianapolis and New York: Bobbs-Merrill, 1956.

Hagerman, Edward. *The American Civil War and the Origins of Modern Warfare.* Bloomington and Indianapolis: University of Indiana Press, 1988.

Hattaway, Herman. *General Stephen D. Lee.* Jackson: University Press of Mississippi, 1976.

Hattaway, Herman, and Archer Jones. *How the North Won: A Military History of the Civil War.* Urbana: University of Illinois Press, 1983.

Hay, Thomas Robson. *Hood's Tennessee Campaign.* Dayton: Press of the Morningside Bookshop, 1976. (Originally published 1929.)

Hebert, Walter H. *Fighting Joe Hooker.* Indianapolis: Bobbs-Merrill Co., 1944.

Henry, Robert Selph. *"First with the Most" Forrest.* Indianapolis: Bobbs-Merrill Co., 1944.

Hoehling, A. A. *Last Train from Atlanta.* New York and London: Thomas Yoseloff, 1958.

Horn, Stanley F. *The Army of Tennessee: A Military History.* Indianapolis: Bobbs-Merrill Co., 1941.

Hutchins, Edward R., comp. *The War of the Sixties.* New York: Neale Publishing Co., 1912.

Klement, Frank L. *The Copperheads of the Middle West.* Chicago: University of Chicago Press, 1960.

———. *Dark Lanterns: Secret Political Societies, Conspiracies, and Treason Trials in the Civil War.* Baton Rouge: Louisiana State University Press, 1984.

———. *The Limits of Dissent: Clement L. Vallandigham and the Civil War.* Lexington: University Press of Kentucky, 1970.

Lash, Jeffrey N. *Destroyer of the Iron Horse: General Joseph E. Johnston and Confederate Rail Transport, 1861–1865.* Kent, Ohio: Kent State University Press, 1991.

Leeper, Wesley T. *Rebels Valiant: Second Arkansas Mounted Rifles (Dismounted)*. Little Rock, Ark.: Pioneer Press, 1964.

Lewis, Lloyd. *Sherman: Fighting Prophet*. New York: Harcourt, Brace & Co., 1932.

Liddell Hart, B. H. *Sherman: Soldier, Realist, American*. New York: Frederick A. Praeger, 1958. (Originally published in 1929.)

Losson, Christopher. *Tennessee's Forgotten Warriors: Frank Cheatham and His Confederate Division*. Knoxville: University of Tennessee Press, 1990.

McCallister, Anna. *Ellen Ewing: Wife of General Sherman*. New York: Benziger Brothers, 1936.

McKinney, Francis F. *Education in Violence: The Life of George H. Thomas and the History of the Army of the Cumberland*. Detroit: Wayne State University Press, 1961.

McMurry, Richard M. "The Atlanta Campaign: December 23, 1863 to July 18, 1864." Ph.D. diss., Emory University, 1967.

———. *John Bell Hood and the War for Southern Independence*. Lexington: University of Kentucky Press, 1982.

McNeil, William James. "The Stress of War: The Confederacy and William Tecumseh Sherman during the Last Year of the Civil War." Ph.D. diss., Rice University, 1973.

McPherson, James M. *Battle Cry of Freedom: The Civil War Era*. New York: Oxford University Press, 1988.

———. *The Struggle for Equality: Abolitionists and the Negro in the Civil War and Reconstruction*. Princeton, N.J.: Princeton University Press, 1964.

Major, Duncan K., and Roger S. Fitch. *Supply of Sherman's Army during the Atlanta Campaign*. Fort Leavenworth, Kans.: Army Service Schools Press, 1911.

Marszalek, John F. *Sherman's Other War: The General and the Civil War Press*. Memphis, Tenn.: Memphis State University Press, 1981.

Matthews, Byron H., Sr. *The McCook-Stoneman Raid*. Philadelphia: Dorrance & Co., 1976.

Moore, Albert Burton. *Conscription and Conflict in the Confederacy*. New York: Hillary House Publishers, 1963. (Originally published 1923.)

Moseley, Thomas V. "Evolution of the American Civil War Infantry Tactics." Ph.D. diss., University of North Carolina, 1967.

Nash, Charles Edward. *Biographical Sketches of Gen. Pat Cleburne and Gen. T. C. Hindman*. Dayton: Press of the Morningside Bookshop, 1977. (Originally published 1898.)

Nelson, Larry Earl. "The Confederacy and the United States Presidential Election of 1864." Ph.D. diss., Duke University, 1975.

Nevins, Allan. *The War for the Union*. 4 vols. New York: Charles Scribner's Sons, 1959–71.

Noll, Arthur H., ed. *Doctor Quintard, Chaplain C.S.A.* Sewanee, Tenn.: University of the South, 1905.

Palmer, George T. *A Conscientious Turncoat: The Story of John M. Palmer, 1817–1900*. New Haven, Conn.: Yale University Press, 1941.

Plum, William R. *The Military Telegraph during the Civil War in the United States*. 2 vols. Chicago: Jansen, McClurg & Co., 1882.

Randall, James G., and Richard N. Current. *Last Full Measure: Lincoln the President*. New York: Dodd, Mead & Co., 1955.

Randall, James G., and David Donald. *The Civil War and Reconstruction*. 2d ed. New York: D. C. Heath & Co., 1969.

Reed, Wallace P., ed. *History of Atlanta, Georgia, with Illustrations and Biographical Sketches of Some of Its Prominent Men and Pioneers.* Syracuse, N.Y.: D. Mason & Co., 1889.

Reynolds, Donald F. *Editors Make War: Southern Newspapers in the Secession Crisis.* Nashville: Vanderbilt University Press, 1966.

Sandburg, Carl. *Abraham Lincoln: The War Years.* 4 vols. New York: Harcourt, Brace & Co., 1939.

Sievers, Harry. *Benjamin Harrison: Hoosier Warrior, 1833-1865.* Chicago: Henry Regnery Co., 1952.

Stampp, Kenneth M. *Indiana Politics during the Civil War.* 2d ed. Bloomington: Indiana University Press, 1978.

Starr, Louis M. *Bohemian Brigade: Civil War Newsmen in Action.* New York: Alfred A. Knopf, 1954.

Strode, Hudson. *Jefferson Davis: Tragic Hero.* New York: Harcourt, Brace & Co., 1954.

———. *Jefferson Davis: Confederate President.* New York: Harcourt, Brace & Co., 1959.

Sword, Wiley. *Embrace an Angry Wind: The Confederacy's Last Hurrah: Spring Hill, Franklin, and Nashville.* New York: HarperCollins, 1991.

Symonds, Craig L. *Joseph E. Johnston: A Civil War Biography.* New York: W. W. Norton, 1992.

Tatum, Georgia Lee. *Disloyalty in the Confederacy.* Chapel Hill: University of North Carolina Press, 1934.

Thomas, Emory M. *The Confederate Nation, 1861-1865.* New York: Harper & Row, 1979.

Vallandigham, James L. *A Life of Clement L. Vallandigham.* Baltimore: 1872.

Van Horne, Thomas B. *History of the Army of the Cumberland.* 2 vols. Cincinnati: Robert Clarke & Co., 1875.

———. *The Life of Major General George H. Thomas.* New York: Charles Scribner's Sons, 1882.

Walters, John Bennett. *Merchant of Terror: General Sherman and Total War.* New York: Bobbs-Merrill, 1973.

Wiley, Bell I. *Confederate Women.* Westport, Conn.: Greenwood, 1975.

———. *The Life of Billy Yank: The Common Soldier of the Union.* Indianapolis and New York: Bobbs-Merrill, 1951.

———. *The Life of Johnny Reb: The Common Soldier of the Confederacy.* Indianapolis and New York: Bobbs-Merrill, 1943.

Williams, Kenneth P. *Lincoln Finds a General.* 5 vols. New York: Macmillan, 1949-59.

Wyeth, John Allen. *Life of Lieutenant-General Nathan Bedford Forrest.* Dayton: Press of the Morningside Bookshop, 1975. (Originally published 1899.)

Articles

Adolphson, Steven J. "An Incident of Valor in the Battle of Peachtree Creek, 1864." *Georgia Historical Quarterly* 57(1973): 406-20.

Anders, Leslie. "Fisticuffs at Headquarters." *Civil War Times Illustrated,* Aug. 1977: 8-15.

Bragg, William H. "The Union General Lost in Georgia." *Civil War Times Illustrated,* June 1985: 16-23.

Bynum, Hartwell T. "Sherman's Expulsion of the Roswell Women in 1864." *Georgia Historical Quarterly* 54(1970): 169-82.

Castel, Albert. "Black Jack Logan." *Civil War Times Illustrated,* Nov. 1976: 4-10, 41-45.

―――. "The Fort Pillow Massacre: A Fresh Examination of the Evidence." *Civil War History* 4(1958): 37-51.

―――. "'I Didn't Want to Get Caught Out,' or *Gone with the Wind* as History," *Blue & Gray Magazine,* July 1986: 3, 36-40.

―――. "Mars and the Reverend Longstreet: Or, Attacking and Dying in the Civil War." *Civil War History* 33(1987): 103-14.

―――. "W. T. Sherman, Part One: The Failure." *Civil War Times Illustrated,* July 1979: 4-7, 42-46.

―――. "W. T. Sherman, Part Two: The Subordinate." *Civil War Times Illustrated,* July 1979: 13-22.

Curry, Richard. "The Union as It Was: A Critique of Recent Interpretations of the Copperheads." *Civil War History* 13(1967): 25-39.

Davis, Stephen. "The Battles of Atlanta: Events from July 10 to September 2, 1864." *Blue & Gray Magazine,* Aug. 1989: 9-62.

Dawes, E. C. "Confederate Strength in the Atlanta Campaign." In *Battles and Leaders of the Civil War,* ed. Robert U. Johnston and Clarence C. Buel, 4:281-83. New York: Century Co., 1887.

Dean, Jeff. "The Battle of Pickett's Mill." *Blue & Gray Magazine,* Apr. 1989: 28-37.

Evans, David. "Wool, Women, and War." *Civil War Times Illustrated,* Sept. 1978: 38-42.

Gibbons, Robert. "Life at the Crossroads of the Confederacy: Atlanta, 1861-1865." *Atlanta Historical Bulletin* 23(1979): 11-64.

Hay, Thomas R. "The Davis-Hood-Johnston Controversy of 1864." *Mississippi Valley Historical Review* 11(1924): 54-84.

―――. "Pat Cleburne—Stonewall Jackson of the West." In *Cleburne and His Command,* ed. Irving A. Buck, 13-66. Dayton: Press of the Morningside Bookshop, 1982.

Hibbard, James, and Albert Castel. "Kilpatrick's Jonesboro Raid, August 18-22, 1864." *Atlanta Historical Journal* 29(1985): 31-46.

James, Alfred P. "General Joseph Eggleston Johnston, Storm Center of the Confederate Army." *Mississippi Valley Historical Review* 14(1927): 342-59.

Kelly, Dennis. "Mountains to Pass, A River to Cross: The Battle of Kennesaw Mountain and Related Actions from June 10 to July 9, 1864." *Blue & Gray Magazine,* June 1989: 8-60.

Kurtz, Wilbur G. "The Death of Major General W. H. T. Walker, July 22, 1864." *Civil War History* 6(1960): 174-79.

Lack, Paul D. "Law and Disorder in Confederate Atlanta." *Georgia Historical Quarterly* 56(1982): 171-95.

McMurry, Richard M. "The Affair at Kolb's Farm." *Civil War Times Illustrated,* Dec. 1968: 20-27.

―――. "Atlanta Campaign of 1864: A New Look." *Civil War History* 22(1976): 5-15.

―――. "Cassville." *Civil War Times Illustrated,* Dec. 1971: 4-9, 45-48.

―――. "Confederate Morale in the Atlanta Campaign of 1864." *Georgia Historical Quarterly* 54(1970): 226-43.

―――. "'The Enemy in Richmond': Joseph E. Johnston and the Confederate Government." *Civil War History* 27(1981): 5-31.

———. "Kennesaw Mountain." *Civil War Times Illustrated,* Jan. 1970: 19–33.

———. "The Mackall Journal and Its Antecedents." *Civil War History* 20(1974): 311–28.

———. "The Opening Phase of the 1864 Campaign in the West." *Atlanta Historical Journal* 27(1983): 5–24.

———. "Rousseau's Raid: Riding through Alabama. Part I." *Civil War Times Illustrated,* Aug. 1981: 12–17.

———. "Rousseau's Raid: Riding through Alabama. Part II." *Civil War Times Illustrated,* Oct. 1981: 36–41.

McNeill, William J. "A Survey of Confederate Soldier Morale during Sherman's Campaign through Georgia and the Carolinas." *Georgia Historical Quarterly* 45(1971): 1–25.

McWhiney, Grady. "Jefferson Davis and the Art of War." *Civil War History* 21(1975): 101–12.

Nelson, Larry E. "Independence or Fight." *Civil War Times Illustrated,* June 1976: 10–15.

Sears, Stephen W. "McClellan and the Peace Plank of 1864." *Civil War History* 36(1990): 57–64.

Secrist, Philip L. "Resaca: For Sherman a Moment of Truth." *Atlanta Historical Bulletin* 22(1978): 9–42.

Wiley, Bell I. "A Story of Three Southern Officers [with Abstracts from the Letters of Lieutenant Robert M. Gill]." *Civil War Times Illustrated,* Apr. 1964: 6–9, 28–34.

Miscellaneous Sources and Aids

American Annual Cyclopaedia and Register of Important Events of the Year 1864. New York: D. Appleton & Co., 1871.

Barnard, George N. *Photographic Views of Sherman's Campaign.* New York: Dover Publications, 1977.

Coggins, Jack. *Arms and Equipment of the Civil War.* Garden City, N.Y.: Doubleday & Co., 1962.

Dornbusch, C. E., comp. *Military Bibliography of the Civil War.* 3 vols. New York: New York Public Library, 1961–72.

Faust, Patricia L., ed. *Historical Times Illustrated Encyclopedia of the Civil War.* New York: Harper & Row, 1986.

Long, E. B. *The Civil War Day by Day.* Garden City, N.Y.: Doubleday & Co., 1971.

Warner, Ezra J. *Generals in Blue: Lives of the Union Commanders.* Baton Rouge: Louisiana State University Press, 1964.

———. *Generals in Gray: Lives of the Confederate Commanders.* Baton Rouge: Louisiana State University Press, 1959.

INDEX

/